ECONOMICS

BRONFENBRENNER · SICHEL · GARDNER · Second Edition

Study Guide

ROSE PFEFFERBAUM MESA COMMUNITY COLLEGE

HOUGHTON MIFFLIN COMPANY   BOSTON

DALLAS   GENEVA, ILLINOIS   LAWRENCEVILLE, NEW JERSEY   PALO ALTO

Dedicated to the memory of J. R. M.

Printed in the U.S.A.

Library of Congress Catalog Card Number: 85-80495

ISBN: 0-395-42515-8

ABCDEFGHIJ-H-89876

Contents

Preface   vii

Comparative Tables of Contents   xi

1   What Economics Is   1

2   The Actors on the Economic Stage   11

3   How Economists Approach Problems   33

4   Scarcity: The Economic Problem   54

5   Demand and Supply—or Supply and Demand   70

6   Unemployment and Inflation   98

7   National Income Accounting   131

8   The Circular Flow and Macroeconomic Equilibrium   148

9   The Keynesian Model   166

10 The Multiplier and Business Fluctuations   193

11 Fiscal Instruments   211

12 Money and Banks   230

13 The Federal Reserve System and Monetary Instruments   243

14 Monetary Economics and Monetarism   257

15 Aggregate Demand and Aggregate Supply   277

16 Macroeconomic Policy: Demand Side   296

17 Macroeconomic Policy: Supply Side   317

18 International Macroeconomics: Exchange Rates and
    the Balance of Payments   332

19 Economic Growth and Development   361

20   A New International Economic Order? North–South
      Confrontation   375

21   Consumer Choice   388

22   Market Demand and Elasticity   415

23   Business Firm Choice   432

24   Market Supply and Elasticity   457

25   Pure Competition   472

26   Monopoly   491

27   Monopolistic Competition and Oligopoly   512

28   Oligopoly: The Real World   530

29   Resource Supply and Demand   545

30   Labor, Wages, and Collective Bargaining   566

31   Capital, Interest, and Investment   591

32   Government and Taxation   605

33   Poverty and Income Distribution   631

34   Government Antitrust and Regulation Policy   650

35   International Microeconomics: Free Trade
      Versus Protection   666

36   Agriculture, Food, and Hunger   686

37   Natural Resources and the Environment   701

38   Comparative Economic Systems—More Planning or
      Less?   729

39   Radical Economics   746

Preface

To the Student   Several specific concerns have guided the preparation of this study guide. First, it has been my intention that the study guide be sufficiently thorough and rigorous to be of real value to you in learning to analyze economic phenomena and in identifying some of the subtleties of the discipline. Second, it should help you prepare for the tests that you will take in your principles of economics course(s). Finally, in doing all of this, the study guide should contribute to your appreciation of the discipline.

Organization   Each chapter of the study guide includes:

A summary of the corresponding text chapter. (Chapter numbers in the study guide are the same as those of the hardcover text; if you are using the paperback *Macroeconomics* or *Microeconomics*, please consult the chart following this preface for the appropriate study guide chapter.)

Major objectives

Review terms (from previous chapters)

New terms and concepts

Completion exercises

Problems and applications

True-false statements

Multiple choice questions

Discussion questions

Within each of these sections of a study guide chapter, the material is presented in the same order as in each chapter of your text.

Using the Study Guide Effectively

As you begin to use the study guide, read through the objectives but do not allow yourself to be deterred by those that initially seem complex to you. Instead, let the objectives represent a preview of what it is that you can learn in each chapter. When you have finished your study of the material, review the objectives again and test your accomplishment of them.

I have included some terms in your lists of important terms that are not defined in your textbook when I have considered these terms necessary for an understanding of the material.

The particular placement of the Problems and Applications, True-False, and Multiple Choice sections is not arbitrary. Though applications may carry you a step beyond a particular concept, the problems are often building blocks to help you recognize concepts and draw conclusions. You are often led through problems step by step so that you can learn to analyze material in the manner of an economist. Often true-false and multiple choice questions will require you to engage in problem solving similar to that which you may have undertaken in a previous problem. The true-false or multiple choice question differs, however, in that it requires you to proceed with this analysis independently. Hence the problems and applications precede the true-false and multiple choice questions. This also permits the true-false and multiple choice questions to form a test of your understanding of the material. This will be advantageous to many of you who will find that your tests are primarily of the true-false and/or multiple choice formats.

Within the True-False and Multiple Choice sections, sometimes a statement is false or a choice is incorrect simply because of one word. This is deliberate and designed to help you ascertain subtle differences in similar statements. You will notice that in the answers to the true-false questions corrected statements of false items are included. This is to further assist you in learning to distinguish seemingly unimportant differences and to help you learn the language of economics.

This study guide stresses graphical analysis. Graphing is an important tool in learning and analyzing the subject matter of economics. Even when you are not specifically directed to do so, drawing a graph may be the easiest way to approach a problem. For this reason, Chapter 3 in your text and in the study guide is designed to familiarize you with graphing. Plan now to take the time you need to become comfortable reading, constructing, and interpreting graphs. These skills will allow you to *analyze*, not just *memorize*, the many possible situations and outcomes you will confront in your study of economics.

Basically, there are two ways in which a study guide such as this may be useful. It may form an integral part of your study in process; that is, you would use it while you study a particular unit, perhaps between readings of any given chapter. Additionally, the study guide may be used as a test of your understanding of a chapter after you have completed your study of that chapter. These two uses are not mutually exclusive. In order to derive the maximum benefit from the study guide, I would urge you to use it in both capacities.

From the beginning, I have intended that this study guide be a friend to the conscientious student. As such, it should help you recognize your strengths. Even more, it should help you to identify your weaknesses and assist you in correcting them. Regardless of the success of my undertaking, I hope that you find your study of economics exciting as well as rewarding.

R. P.
Mesa, Arizona

Comparative Tables of Contents

	Chapter Number in		
	ECONOMICS	MACRO-ECONOMICS	MICRO-ECONOMICS
INTRODUCTION TO ECONOMICS			
What Economics Is	1	1	1
The Actors on the Economic Stage	2	2	2
How Economists Approach Problems	3	3	3
Scarcity: The Economic Problem	4	4	4
Demand and Supply—or Supply and Demand	5	5	5
Essay: Classical Economics: The Dismal Science?	√	√	√
THE MACROECONOMY			
Unemployment and Inflation	6	6	
National Income Accounting	7	7	
The Circular Flow and Macroeconomic Equilibrium	8	8	
Essay: Headaches in the Economics of Inflation	√	√	
KEYNESIAN ECONOMICS AND FISCAL POLICY			
The Keynesian Model	9	9	
The Multiplier and Business Fluctuations	10	10	
Fiscal Instruments	11	11	
Essay: John Maynard Keynes and the Great Depression	√	√	

	Chapter Number in		
	ECONOMICS	MACRO-ECONOMICS	MICRO-ECONOMICS
MONEY, BANKING, AND MONETARY POLICY			
Money and Banks	12	12	
The Federal Reserve System and Monetary Instruments	13	13	
Monetary Economics and Monetarism	14	14	
Essay: Friedman and Monetarism: Do Not Confuse Them!	✓	✓	
AGGREGATE DEMAND, AGGREGATE SUPPLY, AND MACROECONOMIC POLICY			
Aggregate Demand and Aggregate Supply	15	15	
Macroeconomic Policy: Demand Side	16	16	
Macroeconomic Policy: Supply Side	17	17	
Essay: Macroeconomic Policy: From the New Frontier to Supply Side	✓	✓	
INTERNATIONAL TRADE, ECONOMIC GROWTH, AND ECONOMIC DEVELOPMENT			
International Macroeconomics: Exchange Rates and the Balance of Payments	18	18	22
Economic Growth and Development	19	20	
A New International Economic Order? North–South Confrontation	20	21	
Essay: Japan's Economic Miracles and the International Economy	✓	✓	✓
THE BEHAVIOR OF CONSUMERS AND FIRMS			
Consumer Choice	21		6
Market Demand and Elasticity	22		7
Business Firm Choice	23		8
Market Supply and Elasticity	24		9
Essay: Neoclassical Economics: The Complacent Science	✓		✓

	Chapter Number in		
	ECONOMICS	*MACRO-ECONOMICS*	*MICRO-ECONOMICS*
MARKET STRUCTURES AND ECONOMIC PERFORMANCE			
Pure Competition	25		10
Monopoly	26		11
Monopolistic Competition and Oligopoly	27		12
Oligopoly: The Real World	28		13
Essay: Living with Oligopoly	√		√
RESOURCE MARKETS			
Resource Supply and Demand	29		14
Labor, Wages, and Collective Bargaining	30		15
Capital, Interest, and Investment	31		16
Essay: A Real Threat to the Labor Movement?	√		√
APPLIED MICROECONOMICS			
Government and Taxation	32		17
Poverty and Income Distribution	33		18
Government Antitrust and Regulation Policy	34		19
International Microeconomics: Free Trade Versus Protection	35	19	23
Agriculture, Food, and Hunger	36		20
Natural Resources and the Environment	37		21
Essay: The Deregulation Movement	√		√
COMPARATIVE ECONOMIC SYSTEMS			
Comparative Economic Systems—More Planning or Less?	38	22	24
Radical Economics	39	23	25
Essay: From Karl Marx to the New Left	√	√	√

1 What Economics Is

Summary

Economics may be defined in terms of the problems it addresses or the methods it employs. A problems-oriented definition would concentrate on the basic economic concern with scarcity, a situation of unlimited wants coupled with a limited ability to satisfy them. The existence of scarcity means that choices or decisions will have to be made. From a methods standpoint, economics is the study of this decision-making process.

Economics is often divided into microeconomics and macroeconomics. These two main branches of the discipline deal with the same basic topics; they simply address them from different perspectives. Microeconomics focuses on the individual decision-making units that comprise an economy; macroeconomics focuses on the economy at large. Microeconomic analysis centers around three basic questions that must be addressed by every economy: what to produce, how to produce it, and for whom to produce it. Macroeconomics concentrates on aggregate economic activity, with special emphasis on the two major economic problems of unemployment and inflation.

Another important area of concern to the economist is that of economic growth and development. Economic growth means more (per capita) output of the same goods and services. Development means growth coupled with "progress," though progress may be difficult to measure precisely.

Economic systems are generally classified on the basis of their mechanism or ownership. The mechanism classification distinguishes economic systems as market, planned, or traditional in terms of how they go about answering the three basic economic questions of what, how, and for whom to produce. The ownership classification distinguishes economies as capitalist or collectivist (including socialist), according to who owns the means of production and distribution. In reality, all economic systems are mixed rather than pure examples of any particular classification.

Any comparative evaluation of economic systems will involve value judgments. There is no general agreement as to the appropriate criteria for such an evaluation. Nonetheless, these criteria might reasonably include current standard of living, economic growth, equity of distribution, security of the living standard, compatibility with human rights, and compatibility with physical and mental health.

Because economic systems typically adopt numerous and often conflicting goals, policy tradeoffs are necessary. This inability to have everything and need to make choices is the very foundation of economics.

Major Objectives   After you have read this chapter, you will be able to do the following:

1. Define economics from both a problems and a methods approach.
2. Define scarcity and indicate its importance in economics.
3. Define and distinguish between micro- and macroeconomics.
4. Identify and explain the three basic economic questions.
5. Define *aggregate*.
6. Define *inflation* and *unemployment*.
7. Define, distinguish between, and recognize examples of microeconomic and macroeconomic unemployment.
8. Define and distinguish between economic growth and development.
9. Define *economic system* and indicate the types of systems associated with the mechanism and the ownership bases of classification.
10. Define and cite an example of each of the following types of economic systems: market, planned, traditional, capitalist, collectivist, socialist.
11. Distinguish between pure and mixed economies.
12. Cite an example of planning and of collective ownership in a basically market-capitalist economy.
13. Cite an example each of private ownership and of market incentives in a basically planned, collectivist economy.
14. Identify a major contribution made by Adam Smith.
15. Identify six criteria for evaluating economic systems.
16. Distinguish between *equity* and *equality*.
17. Explain "the big tradeoff."

**Important Terms
and Concepts**

economics
scarcity
microeconomics
macroeconomics
three basic economic questions
aggregate
inflation
unemployment
microeconomic unemployment
macroeconomic unemployment
economic growth
per capita
economic development
economic system
market economy

planned economy
traditional economy
capitalism
socialism
collectivism
mixed economy
pure economy
barter
communism
criteria for evaluating economic
  systems
standard of living
equity vs. equality
"the big tradeoff"
basic human needs

Completion

scarcity

The basic problem in economics is _____ , meaning that the amount of something would not be sufficient to satisfy the

free of charge

desire for it if it were made available _____ .

microeconomics

One of the major areas of economics, _____ , concentrates on the individual units that make up the economy. The other major area concentrates on the economy as a whole. This

macroeconomics

second area is called _____ .
    There are three basic questions that every economic system must

what to produce

address. These are _____ ,

how to produce it,
for whom to
produce it

_____ , and _____ .
  Economic systems can be classified in terms of the way they answer

market

these three questions. In a _____ economy, the questions are answered indirectly as a result of the interplay of demand

planned

and supply or the price system. In a _____ economy, the government answers the basic questions.
    As an alternative, economic systems are sometimes classified in terms of the ownership of the means of production and distribution.

capitalist

In a _____ economy, ownership is private; in a

collectivist

_____ economy, ownership is held by a collective

collectivist

body. Socialism is an example of a _____ economy in

the state

which _____ is the owner of the resources. A

communist

_____ is a socialist who believes that socialist economies will eventually reach a state where most important goods will be free and scarcity will have been eliminated.

No real-world economy fits any of the classifications perfectly. As

mixed

a result, real-world economies are said to be _____.
Nevertheless, the United States is usually referred to as a

market-capitalist

_____ economy and the Soviet

planned-socialist

Union is referred to as a _____
economy.

Problems and Applications

1. Identify each of the following concerns as basically either macro or micro in character.
   a. the total output of an economy
   b. the breakeven point for a firm
   c. the imposition of a cigarette tax to discourage smoking
   d. a decrease in the personal income tax to fight recession
   e. a 10% unemployment rate for the economy
   f. the hiring policy of a small firm

2. For each of the following examples, identify the unemployment as being microeconomic or macroeconomic in nature. In the case of microeconomic unemployment, indicate whether it is related to the question of what to produce or how to produce it.
   a. a factory worked replaced by a robot
   b. the manufacturer of whizzos, last year's hottest item, no longer in demand
   c. an advertising executive laid off because of generally lagging sales in the economy
   d. the secretary replaced by word-processing equipment
   e. the producer of a product currently being boycotted
   f. the auto workers who lose their jobs as a result of recession
   g. the butcher, the baker, and the candlestick maker who lose their jobs along with 10% of the work force

3. Consider an economy that produces only two products: theze and thoze. Firms X and Y are responsible for the production of theze, each firm producing $200 worth of output. Firms A, B, and C are the only producers of thoze, producing $55, $105, and $140 worth of output, respectively. There are fifty people living in the economy.
   a. Calculate the dollar value of aggregate output for the economy.
   b. Calculate the per-capita dollar value of output for the economy.

True-False   Indicate whether each of the following statements is basically true or false. If the statement is false, rewrite it so that it is true.

_____ 1. Economics is concerned with the way societies use their resources to produce goods and services that people want.

_____ 2. Economists typically assume that both resources and wants are unlimited.

_____ 3. Scarcity necessitates decision making.

_____ 4. Pure economic systems do not experience scarcity.

_____ 5. Microeconomics focuses on the economy at large rather than on the individual decision-making units that make up the economy.

_____ 6. Every economic system must address three basic questions: what to produce, how to produce it, and for whom to produce it.

_____ 7. The three basic questions of what, how, and for whom to produce arise because resources are scarce.

_____ 8. Microeconomics and macroeconomics can be distinguished in terms of the types of problems they address as well as the perspectives from which they address problems. For example, only macroeconomics is concerned with unemployment.

_____ 9. Aggregate economic activity, a concern of microeconomics, refers to the distribution of activity in an economy.

_____ 10. Inflation is a sustained increase in the general level of prices and may be measured by an index such as the consumer price index.

_____ 11. The reasons for microeconomic unemployment can be traced to the basic economic questions of what to produce and how to produce it, whereas macroeconomic unemployment is not related to particular decisions about production.

_____ 12. Microeconomic unemployment is the type of unemployment associated with a recession.

_____ 13. Individuals who lose their jobs because of the introduction of automated production processes at plants where they have worked are experiencing microeconomic unemployment.

_____ 14. Unemployment associated with product obsolescence is microeconomic.

_____ 15. *Economic growth* and *development* are two terms used interchangeably to mean more output, per capita, of essentially the same collection of goods and services.

_____ 16. An economic system is the combination of institutions that a society develops to deal with its economic problems.

_____ 17. Even though economic systems can be distinguished on the basis of either mechanism or ownership, all real-world economies are mixed.

_____ 18. A collectivist economy is the same as a planned economy; both refer to a system in which land and machinery are owned by collective bodies.

_____ 19. Capitalism is characterized by private ownership of the means of production.

_____ 20. In a market economy, people vote with their dollars, but since such voters are not typically organized into a collective body, the three basic economic questions are not answered.

_____ 21. A market economy must also be a capitalist economy.

_____ 22. Traditional economies never engage in barter.

_____ 23. The term *standard of living* refers specifically to the quality of life in a particular economy.

_____ 24. *Equitable* always implies *equal.*

_____ 25. Policy tradeoffs are likely to exist in all economic systems.

Multiple Choice Choose the *one best* answer in each of the following cases:

_____ 1. Which of the following statements best describes economics?
   a. Economics is basically concerned with long-range planning in a business environment.
   b. Economics is basically concerned with how a government formulates and implements economic policy.
   c. Economics is basically concerned with the day-to-day decision making associated with running a business.
   d. Economics is basically concerned with how a society uses its limited resources to produce goods and services.
   e. Economics is basically concerned with the budget decisions of households, businesses, and governments.

_____ 2. To the economist, scarcity means that
   a. poverty can never be eliminated.
   b. we have less than we would like to have.
   c. we are running out of an independent source of energy.
   d. there is not enough food to feed the population of the world.
   e. no economic system can meet the basic needs of all its people.

_____ 3. All real-world economies
   a. are mixed.
   b. experience scarcity.
   c. must answer the three basic economic questions.
   d. can be described by all of the above.
   e. can be described by none of the above.

_____ 4. Which of the following areas would most likely be subject matter for a course in macroeconomics?
  a. a comparison of advertising campaigns among rival firms
  b. a study of the effects of unionization in the auto industry
  c. an explanation of how a business firm determines the price to charge for its product
  d. a study of the importance of economic growth for the steel industry
  e. an analysis of the consequences of unemployment for the economy at large

_____ 5. Which of the following statements is true of unemployment?
  a. It may be either a microeconomic or a macroeconomic problem.
  b. It is microeconomic if it affects the entire economy.
  c. Microeconomic unemployment is sometimes called cyclical unemployment.
  d. Both a and c above are true.
  e. All of the above are true.

_____ 6. Microeconomic unemployment is
  a. associated with recessions and depressions.
  b. generally caused by a layoff of government workers.
  c. a minor problem and therefore of little concern to economists.
  d. characterized by both a and b above.
  e. characterized by none of the above.

_____ 7. Economic growth, as distinguished from economic development, is characterized by
  a. increased output.
  b. the elimination of poverty.
  c. an improved standard of living.
  d. the introduction of new products.
  e. all of the above.

_____ 8. Which of the following statements is true of economic development?
  a. It is equivalent to economic growth.
  b. It is economic growth in the absence of economic progress.
  c. It is economic progress in the absence of economic growth.
  d. It is economic growth accompanied by progress.
  e. It does not occur in the real world.

_____ 9. An economic system is said to be
   a. a market system if it is characterized by barter.
   b. capitalist if its resources are privately owned.
   c. planned if its resources are collectively owned.
   d. collectivist if the government makes the economic decisions.
   e. traditional if decision making basically relies on the market mechanism.

_____ 10. Capitalist and collectivist economic systems are distinguished by their different
   a. ownership of machinery and tools.
   b. emphases on micro- and macroeconomic concerns.
   c. degree of specialization and division of labor.
   d. amount of trade that occurs in organized markets.
   e. extent of government involvement in decision making.

_____ 11. Which of the following examples best illustrates the market mechanism?
   a. a military draft
   b. clearance sales
   c. licensing of medical doctors
   d. product testing by the Food and Drug Administration
   e. a government-imposed minimum wage

Discussion Questions

1. What do you suppose the authors of your text mean when they use the concept "free of charge" in defining scarcity? Does a zero price mean that a good is in fact free of charge?

2. Economics deals with decision making under scarcity. Your text suggests an approach you might use to determine whether or not to memorize a definition of economics. Would your decision be different if you knew for sure whether or not you would be tested on one of the definitions? Why?

3. Using economic reasoning, identify what factors might influence a decision regarding whether or not to
   a. take a math class.
   b. purchase a new pair of shoes.
   c. have your hair cut this weekend or put it off one more week.

4. Identify potential responses to the what, how, and for whom questions in respect to the production of robots.

5. Explain the interrelationships among the what, how, and for whom questions for a market economy and then for a planned economy. In particular, identify the roles of households, business, and government in each.

6. Identify some aspects of the United States economy that keep it from being
   a. a pure market system.
   b. a pure capitalist system.

7. Your text suggests six criteria for evaluating economic systems. Identify them and name two additional criteria.

8. Suggest some standard of living measures other than per capita income, wealth, and consumption. What do you consider the best measure of standard of living? Why?

9. Would a more equal distribution of income and wealth be more equitable?

Answers

Problems and Applications

1. a. macro   b. micro   c. micro
   d. macro   e. macro   f. micro

2. a. micro, how to produce   b. micro, what to produce
   c. macro   d. micro, how to produce
   e. micro, what to produce   f. macro   g. macro

3. a. $700   b. $14

True-False

1. T.
2. F. Economists typically assume that resources are limited or scarce and wants are unlimited.
3. T.
4. F. All economic systems experience scarcity.
5. F. Macroeconomics focuses on the economy at large rather than on the individual decision-making units that make up the economy.
6. T.
7. T.
8. F. Microeconomics and macroeconomics are concerned with the same problems but address these problems from different perspectives. Both, for example, are concerned with the problem of unemployment.
9. F. Aggregate economic activity, a concern of macroeconomics, refers to total economy activity.
10. T.
11. T.

12. F. Macroeconomic unemployment is the type of unemployment associated with a recession.
13. T.
14. T.
15. F. Economic growth means more output, per capita, of essentially the same collection of goods and services; development means progress.
16. T.
17. T.
18. F. A collectivist economy is one in which land and machinery are owned by collective bodies; a planned economy is one in which the basic economic decisions are made by some agency of the government.
19. T.
20. F. In a market economy, the three basic economic questions are answered via a system of dollar votes.
21. F. A market economy is likely to be a capitalist economy but may be a collectivist system, depending on who owns the means of production.
22. F. Traditional economies are often characterized by barter.
23. F. *Standard of living* is not equivalent to *quality of life*; the standard of living is typically measured in terms of income or consumption per capita.
24. F. Equitability implies being fair or just, but it need not require that conditions actually be equal.
25. T.

Multiple Choice

1. d	2. b	3. d	4. e	5. a
6. e	7. a	8. d	9. b	10. a
11. b				

2 The Actors on the Economic Stage

Summary

There are four major decision-making units in a nation's economy: households, business firms, government, and the rest of the world, with its foreign households, business firms, and governments. Households and business firms comprise the private sector, government is the public sector, and "the rest of the world" is the international sector.

A household may be defined as one person or more who live and operate as an economic unit. In a capitalist-market system, households are the owners of resources as well as a major consumer group responsible for buying goods and services. Money for consumption comes primarily from income earned as a result of supplying resources to business, government, and the international sector, and from accumulated wealth. Changes in the characteristics of the general population, households, and families may have pronounced effects on both the consumption of goods and services in the economy and the availability of resources for production. Consumption patterns may also be affected by the distribution of income and wealth in the economy.

Business firms hire resources to produce goods and services for households, business, government, and the international market. There are three basic forms of business organization: the proprietorship, the partnership, and the corporation. The easiest to form is the single-owner proprietorship, but it has the disadvantages of limited life and unlimited liability. The partnership combines the resources of two or more persons who share in the profits and losses of the business. Like the proprietorship, the partnership is characterized by limited life and unlimited liability. Only the corporate form of business organization has unlimited life and limited liability. The corporation is a legal entity that is entitled to many of the privileges of and assumes many of the responsibilities of individuals. For example, corporations may enter into contracts and must pay income taxes. Corporations are further distinguished from proprietorships and partnerships by the fact that ownership and management are separate in a corporation.

Companies have two basic financial statements: the balance sheet and the income statement. The balance sheet is a report on the condition of a business at a given point in time. It identifies the assets, liabilities, and net worth of the company. The income statement reports on the operations of a business over a certain period, indicating its revenues, costs, and profits during this time. The income statement explains the activities of the business between balance sheets.

The public sector, or government, generally plays an important role in any economic system, even one that is a basically capitalist-market system. Economists typically identify at least three important functions of government: allocation of resources, distribution of wealth, and stabilization of the economic environment. The allocation function centers around questions of resource utilization. It essentially attempts to correct for market failures in situations characterized by, for example, monopolization and external economic forces or externalities. The distribution function deals with the equitable distribution of income and wealth. The stabilization function involves government in an attempt to maintain a reasonable level of employment, price stability, and economic growth. There may be considerable disagreement over what constitutes a "reasonable level" and over the ability of government to perform this function adequately.

International economic activity includes exporting, importing, and financial transactions involving more than one economy. For the U.S. economy, "the rest of the world" has become increasingly important in recent decades.

Major Objectives   After you have read this chapter, you will be able to do the following:

1. Describe a household in its economic sense.
2. Recognize and discuss the importance of major trends in the size and age distribution of the U.S. population.
3. Define *income* and identify the various sources of it, how it is earned and distributed, and the major trends associated with these issues.
4. Distinguish between money income and nonmoney income.
5. Describe the importance of nonmoney income in measuring economic well-being.

6. Differentiate between income and wealth.
7. Assess the importance of wealth in measuring economic well being.
8. Define *labor force participation rate* and discuss the major trends associated with labor force participation.
9. Recognize the major trends in household spending and saving activity.
10. Identify and describe the three basic forms of business organization.
11. Compare and contrast the three basic forms of business organization.
12. Describe and explain the importance of the stock market.
13. Read a stock exchange report in a newspaper.
14. Name and describe the two basic types of financial statements of a company and describe how they relate to each other.
15. Define *assets*, *liabilities*, and *net worth*, and, given any two of the three, calculate the third.
16. Interpret simple balance sheets and income statements.
17. Name, describe, and provide examples of the three functions of government in a capitalist-market system.
18. Identify the types of market failure that lead to government involvement in allocating resources.
19. Define *externalities*, distinguish between its positive and negative forms, recognize examples of each, discuss how externalities can result in market failure, and explain how the government might take corrective action against them.
20. Define and recognize examples of collective goods.
21. Identify causes of inequality in income distribution in a capitalist-market system.
22. Give some examples of government programs aimed at income redistribution.
23. Recognize examples of the major instruments that government has to establish a stabilization policy.
24. Explain what is meant by "the rest of the world."
25. Explain why "the rest of the world" may be important to any particular economic system.
26. Distinguish between an open and a closed economy.

Review Terms	market economy	macroeconomics
	capitalism vs. socialism	microeconomics
	three basic economic questions	unemployment
	equitable	inflation
	economic growth	

Important Terms and Concepts

household
"dollar votes"
"baby boom"
"population ripple"
income
national income
money income
median
nonmoney income
wealth
labor force participation rate
proprietors' income
proprietorship
partnership
corporation
limited vs. unlimited liability
limited vs. unlimited life
stockholder
shares of stock
dividends
stock exchange
stockbroker
price/earnings ratio
block of stock
commission
balance sheet
assets

liabilities
net worth
current vs. fixed or long-term assets
current vs. long-term liabilities
income, or profit-and-loss, statement
allocation function
distribution function
stabilization function
market failure
positive externalities
negative externalities
collective good
subsidy
price stability
business cycles
deficit
surplus
exports
imports
"the rest of the world"
open economy
closed economy
financial or "capital account" transaction

Completion

The percentage of the noninstitutional population, age 16 or older, that is working or looking for work is measured by the

labor force partici-
pation rate

_____ . This

increasing

percentage has been _____ (increasing/decreasing) over the last few decades as a result of a dramatic increase in the

females

participation rate for _____ .

national income

    Earned income data, that is, _____ , during this period shows an increase in the proportion of labor in-

compensation of
employees

come. Labor income is referred to as _____ .
    There are three basic forms of business organization: the

proprietorship,
partnership

_____ , the _____ ,

corporation

and the _____ . The only form that requires a

corporate

government charter is the _____ form. A charter

shares of stock

authorizes the business to issue and sell _____ ,
which represent ownership in the business. The charter also estab-

legal person

lishes the corporation as a _____ .
    If someone has complete responsibility for all the debts of a

unlimited liability

business, he or she is said to have _____ .
When a business can continue to exist even though those owning it

unlimited life

may change, the business has _____ .
Limited liability and unlimited life generally would be considered

advantageous

_____ (advantageous/disadvantageous).
    In a capitalist-market economy, economists usually recognize

allocation

three economic functions of government: the _____

stabilization

function, the _____ function, and the

distribution

_____ function. A desire to eliminate business
cycles and the problems of unemployment and inflation gives rise to

stabilization

the _____ function. Sometimes the market
system fails to produce the optimal quantity of a good or service,
producing too much or too little. When the government addresses
this problem of resource utilization it is performing the

allocation, dis-
tribution

_____ function. The _____
function is concerned with providing an equitable distribution of
income and wealth. Programs that redistribute income and wealth
alter people's ability to buy goods and services and consequently

demand

may have pronounced effects on the _____ side of
markets.

importing

    International economic activity includes _____ ,

exporting, financial
transactions

_____ , and _____

"the rest of the
world"

between a particular economy and _____ .
    An economy that permits trade with other economies is

open

a(n) _____ economy; an economy that severely restricts

closed

international activity is a(n) _____ economy.

Problems and Applications

1. Distinguish each of the following as a form of either income or wealth:
   a. the $1 tip a waitress receives
   b. $1,000 worth of stock in General Motors
   c. 2 acres of land valued at $50,000
   d. $200 received each month from the occupant of an apartment you own
   e. $50 in interest on your savings account
   f. a savings account with a balance of $500
   g. a dividend check from ABC Corporation
   h. a wage payment of $4 per hour

2. Assume that the information below is from a newspaper report of yesterday's stock-market transactions.

Stock Exchange Composite Transactions

52 Weeks High	Low	Stock	Div.	Yld. %	PE Ratio	Sales 100s	High	Low	Last	Net Chg.
$26^1/4$	17	ABC	.60	2.5	15	104	$23^7/8$	$23^3/4$	$23^3/4$	$-^1/4$
21	$11^3/4$	XYZ	.40	2.0	17	366	$19^3/4$	$19^1/4$	$19^5/8$	$+^3/3$

   a. What was the highest price per share of ABC stock over the past year?
   b. What was the annual dividend paid per share of ABC stock?
   c. The current price of ABC stock is how many times the amount of the annual profits per share? What is this figure called?
   d. What is a *block* of stock?
   e. What did the lowest-priced block of ABC stock sell for yesterday?
   f. What did the last block of ABC stock sell for yesterday?
   g. How did yesterday's closing transaction for ABC stock compare with the closing transaction the previous day?
   h. What was the lowest price per share of XYZ stock over the past year?
   i. What was the yield on the current price of XYZ stock?
   j. What was the price/earnings ratio for XYZ stock?
   k. What did the highest-priced block of XYZ stock sell for yesterday?
   l. How did yesterday's closing transaction for XYZ stock compare with the closing transaction the previous day?

3. For each of the following, indicate where you would turn for the requested information—to a balance sheet, or an income statement?
    a. accounts payable at a point in time
    b. taxes paid in 1986
    c. cash on hand at the end of the year
    d. value of stock at a specific time
    e. dividends paid on stock during the year
    f. year-end inventory holdings
    g. value of plant and equipment at the end of a production period
    h. depreciation on plant and equipment during a production period
    i. labor costs during the year
    j. earnings retained during a given period
    k. retained earnings at a particular point in time

4. Early in 1984, the Pretend sisters combined their assets of $45,000, acquired a bank loan of $25,000, and started their own company, the Pretend Partnership. On December 31, 1984, the Partnership had plant and equipment valued at $55,000, raw materials and supplies totaling $7,000, work in process worth $2,000, a product inventory worth $4,000, and $10,000 in cash. As of that date, the sisters still owed $1,000 for supplies they had purchased.
    a. Construct a balance sheet for December 31, 1984. What was the owners' equity as of that date?
    b. In 1985, the sisters paid the bank $3,000 in interest on their loan. They also paid the $1,000 they owed on supplies and purchased an additional $40,000 worth of these supplies, paying for all but $5,000 worth by the end of the year. Yearly labor costs for the Partnership amounted to $25,000. Depreciation on plant and equipment was figured at 15%. The sisters paid themselves a total of $60,000 for the year. Yearly sales totaled $140,000. In addition, the Partnership found that at the end of the year it still had $7,000 worth of raw materials and supplies, work in process worth $2,000, and a product inventory worth $4,000. Construct an income statement for the company for 1985. Also, construct the company's balance sheet for December 31, 1985.

5. The following data describe Fictitious Firm on December 31, 1982.

Accounts payable	$ 10,000
Balances in checking and savings accounts	9,000
Buildings	70,000
Cash on hand	1,000
Common stock	90,000
Equipment	120,000
Inventory	80,000
Long-term liabilities	70,000
Notes payable	40,000
Preferred stock	10,000

a. Determine the retained earnings of the firm and construct a balance sheet for December 31, 1982.

b. In 1983, Fictitious Firm had net sales of $240,000, and a year-end inventory of $63,000. During 1983, Fictitious Firm bought raw materials valued at $40,000, hired labor services in the amount of $70,000, contracted for $3,000 in advertising and other selling activities, paid $7,000 in interest, and had administrative costs amounting to $30,000. Depreciation on plant and equipment was figured at 15%. State and local taxes amounted to $5,000, and corporate income taxes were $15,800. The firm paid dividends totaling $12,000, of which $11,000 were paid to holders of common stock. Construct an income statement for Fictitious Firm for 1983.

6. In each of the following cases, identify which function the government is performing.
   a. Imposition of a progressive tax to ensure greater equity in the distribution of income.
   b. Imposition of a sales tax on cigarettes to limit smoking.
   c. Government spending specifically designed to provide jobs.
   d. Provision of public funds for education.
   e. Tightening money and credit conditions to fight inflation.

True-False

Indicate whether each of the following statements is basically true or false. If the statement is false, rewrite it so that it is true.

_____ 1. A single person living alone and supporting herself constitutes a household.

_____ 2. An unmarried couple living together and sharing income and expenses constitute a household.

_____ 3. Although population is a major concern in economics because it influences production and spending, age distribution is of little concern.

_____ 4. Population statistics reveal that there was a "baby boom" in the 1950s and 1960s, followed by a sharp drop in the birth rate during the 1970s.

_____ 5. The labor force participation rate measures the percentage of the labor force that is working.

_____ 6. Income and wealth are equivalent.

_____ 7. Nonmoney income, which includes subsidized housing, for example, may be an important factor determining a family's economic well-being.

_____ 8. In recent years, U.S. households have spent an increasing portion of their income on taxes.

_____ 9. In a capitalist-market economy, households are suppliers in the market for resources.

_____ 10. A proprietorship is a business venture involving two or more persons who have filed a legal declaration of intent to do business.

_____ 11. Unlimited liability and limited life are characteristics of proprietorships and partnerships.

_____ 12. Limited liability and unlimited life are characteristics of the corporate form of business organization.

_____ 13. Corporations must be chartered by the federal government.

_____ 14. In terms of total business receipts, corporations are the most important form of business organization in the United States.

_____ 15. Dividends are distributions of money (or additional stock) from a corporation.

_____ 16. Anyone can trade on the floor of the New York Stock Exchange.

_____ 17. Stock-exchange memberships are limited in number and are bought and sold.

_____ 18. The two basic financial statements of a company are its assets and liabilities statements.

_____ 19. Net worth is the balancing feature of an income statement.

_____ 20. Because accounting statements are all dated, changing price levels create no serious accounting problems for a firm.

_____ 21. One of the advantages of the pure market system is that it always provides acceptable answers to the basic economic questions.

_____ 22. If in a capitalistic democracy the market system is deficient in some regard, the government will always be able to correct the problem adequately.

_____ 23. National defense is an example of a collective good.

_____ 24. The allocation function of government comes into play because the market system does not always produce optimal amounts of goods and services.

_____ 25. Externalities may be positive or negative and may be associated with production or consumption.

_____ 26. Markets tend to underproduce goods characterized by negative externalities because some of the costs of these goods are not recognized in the market.

_____ 27. Collective goods are those that, if produced, must be consumed by everyone in the area.

_____ 28. The theories of John Maynard Keynes and his followers provide a rationale for the stabilization function of government.

_____ 29. The Great Depression so successfully illustrated the importance of the stabilization function of government that today there is unanimous agreement as to the specifics of this government function.

_____ 30. Imports are important in the operation of the U.S. economy, but exports are not.

_____ 31. Economic interaction between a particular economy and the international sector may include exporting, importing, and financial transactions between households, business firms, and governments, as well.

_____ 32. An open economy is one that permits no trade across its borders.

Multiple Choice   Choose the *one best* answer in each of the following cases:

_____ 1. A household is best defined as
  a. a family.
  b. an adult.
  c. any individual.
  d. a person or persons living together.
  e. a person who owns and occupies a house.

_____ 2. Population statistics regarding size, age distribution, and family structure are important in economics because these factors may affect
  a. political decision making.
  b. the labor force participation rate.

    c. the total level of production and spending in the economy.

    d. the specific mix of goods and services that will be produced and consumed.

    e. all of the above.

_____ 3. U.S. population data suggest that

    a. the older working-age group will begin its growth spurt in the 1990s.

    b. the over-65 age group will experience a sizable decline between now and the end of the century.

    c. the younger working-age group will continue to increase throughout the remainder of the century.

    d. the percentage of the population under age nineteen will increase dramatically between now and the end of the century.

    e. all of the above are true.

_____ 4. Which of the following statements is true with respect to the labor force?

    a. The labor force includes everyone who is sixteen years of age or older.

    b. The labor force includes everyone between the ages of sixteen and sixty-five.

    c. The labor force includes only people who are actually working.

    d. The labor force includes institutionalized people if they are working.

    e. The labor force includes people who are unemployed if they are at least sixteen years old and looking for work.

_____ 5. Which of the following statements is true of income and wealth?

    a. They are essentially the same thing.

    b. They both measure what a household has accumulated in the way of assets.

    c. Income is measured before taxes, whereas wealth is income after taxes.

    d. Income is the return to productive resources, whereas wealth refers to accumulated assets.

    e. Both a and b are true.

_____ 6. In a capitalist-market economy, households typically

    a. are the suppliers of resources.

    b. are the consumers of goods and services.

    c. influence all three of the basic economic choices.

    d. are characterized by all of the above.

    e. are characterized by a and b.

_____   7. In recent years, U.S. households have
   a. ceased to save.
   b. spent over half their incomes on paying taxes.
   c. spent about half their incomes on food, clothing, and shelter.
   d. done a and b above.
   e. done none of the above.

_____   8. In the proprietorship form of business organization
   a. there is unlimited life.
   b. any profits must be paid to stockholders.
   c. a charter must be granted by the state government.
   d. the owner is responsible for all the debts of the business.
   e. none of the above is true.

_____   9. A partnership is typically characterized by
   a. limited life.
   b. limited liability of all partners.
   c. the issuance of stocks as a source of financing.
   d. all of the above
   e. none of the above

_____   10. A corporation differs from a partnership in that
   a. a corporation is considered a legal entity but a partnership is not.
   b. a state charter is required for a corporation but not for a partnership.
   c. the owners of a corporation are not liable for the debts of the business but partners are.
   d. a corporation has an unlimited life, but the life of a partnership is limited.
   e. all of the above are true.

_____   11. By comparison to the other forms of business organization, the chief disadvantage of the corporate form is its
   a. limited life.
   b. limited liability.
   c. difficulty in raising funds.
   d. responsibility for special income-tax payments.
   e. difficulty in separating ownership and management.

_____   12. Which of the following statements is correct with regard to a corporation?
   a. All profits must be distributed via dividend payments.
   b. Stockholders can buy shares at any time but can sell shares only during the first fifteen days of a quarter.
   c. Anyone can become a member of a stock exchange, simply by filing the appropriate registration documents.

    d. If the price/earnings ratio of a stock is 15, the current price of the stock is 15 times the annual profits per share of the corporation.

    e. A block of stock refers to a combination of stock from two or more corporations.

_____ 13. A firm's balance sheet would most likely show
    a. cash and inventories as fixed assets.
    b. retained earnings as part of net worth.
    c. buildings and equipment as fixed liabilities.
    d. all claims against the business as current liabilities.
    e. all of the above.

_____ 14. A balance sheet and an income statement
    a. both report a firm's financial activity at a point in time.
    b. both use net worth as the balancing item but differ in how they treat inventories and depreciation.
    c. are related in that any difference in data on two balance sheets is explained by the income statements that cover the time period between the balance sheets.
    d. are unrelated, since the balance sheet is used by proprietorships and partnerships and the income statement is used by corporations.
    e. differ in that the balance sheet details the net worth of the firm, whereas the income statement identifies the assets and liabilities of the firm.

_____ 15. Net worth is
    a. equal to liabilities minus assets.
    b. equal to assets minus liabilities.
    c. the sum of assets and liabilities.
    d. the balancing item in an income statement.
    e. both b and d.

_____ 16. Which of the following statements is correct?
    a. Current liabilities are obligations that normally are payable during the current quarter.
    b. Items on a balance sheet are typically listed according to how quickly they can be converted into cash.
    c. Inventories are considered to be part of the liabilities of a company.
    d. The balancing feature of an income statement is profit or loss.
    e. None of the above is correct.

_____ 17. Which of the following statements is true of the allocation function of government?
- a. It tends to create externalities.
- b. It arises because the government misallocates goods.
- c. It may come about because of the existence of monopolies.
- d. Its major purpose is to assure a more equitable distribution of income.
- e. All of the above are true.

_____ 18. Positive and negative externalities
- a. always cancel each other out.
- b. are the result of business cycles.
- c. do not exist in pure market systems.
- d. are said to exist whenever government engages in production.
- e. may be exemplified by education and pollution, respectively.

_____ 19. When there are external benefits associated with the consumption of a particular good,
- a. the government should tax the good.
- b. the market places too great a value on this good.
- c. the market system allocates too many resources to its production.
- d. government intervention may be required to assure production of the optimal amount of the good.
- e. the market fails to recognize all of the costs associated with the consumption of this good.

_____ 20. The existence of external costs in the production of a good suggests that
- a. taxes are too high.
- b. not enough resources will be used in its production.
- c. the government should subsidize production of the good.
- d. both b and c are true.
- e. none of the above is true.

_____ 21. Which of the following policies is most appropriate to correct a negative externality when one exists in the production of a good?
- a. a subsidy for the production of the good
- b. a policy to lower the price of the good
- c. a policy to cause a reduction in output of the good
- d. all of the above
- e. none of the above

_____ 22. The misallocation of resources associated with the existence of externalities
- a. requires a market solution.
- b. may be corrected by taxes or subsidies.
- c. is an example of government failure.

d. cannot be corrected by government intervention.

e. can be corrected only by government production of the good.

_____ 23. Collective goods
   a. exist whenever there are negative externalities associated with the consumption of a good.
   b. exist whenever there are positive externalities associated with the consumption of a good.
   c. are those that, if made available for one, are automatically available to all.
   d. are desirable because they result in budget surpluses.
   e. are undesirable consequences of budget deficits.

_____ 24. The distribution function of government
   a. relates to the "for whom" decision that all economic systems must answer.
   b. arises in the attempt to create a more equitable distribution of income and wealth.
   c. has led to a more equal distribution of income in the United States, as judged by most measures.
   d. may result in progressive income taxes, welfare programs, minimum wage laws, and farm subsidies.
   e. has all of these characteristics.

_____ 25. Which of the following statements is true of the stabilization function of government?
   a. It has always been recognized by economists.
   b. It arises because of fluctuations in economic activity that result in business cycles.
   c. Traditionally, it has been considered the most important of the three functions of government.
   d. All of the above are true.
   e. None of the above is true.

_____ 26. Which of the following statements is correct?
   a. The international sector is of virtually no importance in the U.S. economy.
   b. The Soviet Union is an example of a relatively open economy.
   c. The United States is an example of a relatively closed economy.
   d. "The rest of the world" is likely to be of greater importance to a relatively small economy than to a relatively large economy.
   e. International finance is restricted to governments.

_____ 27. An open economy is best described as one in which
    a. the government performs no economic function.
    b. business firms are the owners of the means of production.
    c. the government production of goods and services is encouraged.
    d. international trade is prohibited.
    e. none of the above is true.

Discussion Questions

1. Explain the role of households and business firms in terms of the three basic economic questions.

2. Have you noticed any recent advertisements that you imagine are attributable to the aging of the post-World War II baby-boom generation?

3. Identify at least three changes in consumption patterns over the last twenty to thirty years that might be attributable to the increased labor-force participation rate of women.

4. Do you think nonmoney income is of greater, or less, importance today as compared to twenty-five years ago? One hundred years ago? Why?

5. Compare the three basic forms of business organization by indicating the advantages and disadvantages of each.

6. What does it mean to say that a balance sheet must balance?

7. All three functions of government tend to redistribute income and wealth. Provide specific examples to show the redistributive effects of each.

8. How do you think demand for goods and services would change if there were more income redistribution in favor of low-income groups? Provide some specific suggestions.

9. It is generally assumed that there are considerable external benefits associated with a grade-school education. What are some of these external benefits? Do you think there are external benefits associated with your college education? If so, what might they be?

10. Collective goods are those that, if they are produced, must be consumed by everyone in the area. What are some examples? Should the public or the private sector produce collective goods? Explain.

11. Explain the importance of "the rest of the world" to the U.S. economy.

12. Why is the international sector likely to be of greater importance to a small economy than to a large one?

Answers   *Problems and Applications*

1. a. income   b. wealth   c. wealth   d. income
   e. income   f. wealth   g. income   h. income

2. a. $26.25   b. $.60
   c. 15; the price/earnings ratio (p/e ratio)
   d. 100 shares   e. $23.75 per share
   f. $23.75 per share
   g. It was lower, by 25 cents per share.
   h. $11.75   i. 2%
   j. 17   k. $19.75 per share
   l. It was up, by $0.375 per share.

3. a. balance sheet   b. income statement
   c. balance sheet   d. balance sheet
   e. income statement   f. balance sheet or income statement
   g. balance sheet   h. income statement
   i. income statement   j. income statement
   k. balance sheet

4. a.

Pretend Partnership
Balance Sheet
December 31, 1984

Assets		Liabilities	
Current Assets		Current Liabilities	
Cash	$10,000	Accounts Payable	$ 1,000
Inventory			
Materials	7,000	Long-Term Liabilities	
Work in Process	2,000	Bank Loan	25,000
Product	4,000	Total Liabilities	$26,000
Fixed Assets		Net Worth	
Plant and Equipment	55,000	Owners' Equity	$52,000
		Total Liabilities and Net Worth	$78,000
Total Assets	$78,000		

4. b.

Pretend Partnership
Income Statement
for the Year 1985

Sales		$140,000
Costs		
Materials	$40,000	
Labor	25,000	
Depreciation	8,250	
Administrative	60,000	
Interest	3,000	
Total Costs		136,250
Profit		$ 3,750

Pretend Partnership
Balance Sheet
December 31, 1985

Assets		Liabilities	
Current Assets		Current Liabilities	
Cash	$26,000	Accounts Payable	$ 5,000
Inventory			
Materials	7,000	Long-Term Liabilities	
Work in Process	2,000	Bank Loan	25,000
Product	4,000	Total Liabilities	$30,000
Fixed Assets			
Plant and		Net Worth	
Equipment	46,750	Owners' Equity	$55,750
		Total Liabilities	
Total Assets	$85,750	and Net Worth	$85,750

5. a. The retained earnings are $60,000.

Fictitious Firm
Balance Sheet
December 31, 1982

Assets			Liabilities	
Current Assets			Current Liabilities	
Cash	$	1,000	Accounts Payable	$ 10,000
Checking and			Notes Payable	40,000
Savings		9,000	Long-Term Liabilities	70,000
Inventory		80,000	Total Liabilities	$120,000
Fixed Assets			Net Worth	
Equipment		120,000		
Buildings		70,000	Preferred Stock	10,000
			Common Stock	90,000
			Retained Earnings	60,000
			Total Net Worth	$160,000
			Total Liabilities	
Total Assets		$280,000	and Net Worth	$280,000

5. b.   Fictitious Firm
                            Income Statement
                            for the Year 1983

Net Sales $240,000

Manufacturing Cost
  Materials $40,000
  Labor   70,000
  Depreciation   28,500
                              ————
  Subtotal $138,500
Plus Beginning Inventory $80,000
Less Closing Inventory   −63,000
                              ————
  Subtotal   17,000
    Total Manufacturing Cost   155,500
Gross Profit from Sales $ 84,500
  Selling Costs $ 3,000
  Administrative Costs   30,000
  Fixed Interest Charges   7,000
  State and Local Taxes   5,000
                              ————
  Subtotal   45,000
Net Income before Income Taxes $ 39,500
Corporate Income Taxes   15,800
Net Income after Taxes $ 23,700
Dividends Paid on Preferred Stock   1,000
Net Income after Preferred Stock Dividends $ 22,700
Dividends Paid on Common Stock   11,000
Addition to Retained Earnings $ 11,700

6. a. distribution   b. allocation   c. stabilization
   d. allocation   e. stabilization

True-False

1. T.
2. T.
3. F. Both the size and the age distribution of the population are
   important because they influence production and spending.
4. T.

5. F. The labor force participation rate measures the percentage of the noninstitutionalized population, age sixteen years and older, that is working or looking for work.

6. F. Income is money households earn by allowing someone to use their factors of production; wealth is accumulated assets that are capable of generating income.

7. T.

8. T.

9. T.

10. F. A proprietorship is a single-owner business venture and typically requires no legal declaration of intent to do business.

11. T.

12. T.

13. F. Corporate charters are issued by state governments.

14. T.

15. T.

16. F. Only members (those who own a seat) can trade on the floor of the New York Stock Exchange.

17. T.

18. F. The two basic financial statements of a company are the balance sheet and the income statement.

19. F. Net worth is the balancing feature of a balance sheet; there is no balancing feature in an income statement.

20. F. Accounting statements are dated; nonetheless, changing price levels can create some difficult accounting problems for a firm.

21. F. The pure market system does provide answers to the basic economic questions, but there is no guarantee that these answers will be generally acceptable.

22. F. If the market system is deficient in some regard, the government may be able to correct the problem, but there is no guarantee.

23. T.

24. T.

25. T.

26. F. Markets tend to overproduce goods with negative externalities because some of the costs of these goods are not recognized in the market.

27. T.

28. T.

29. F. The Great Depression did illustrate the importance of the stabilization function of government, but there is still considerable debate as to the specifics of this function.

30. F. Both imports and exports are important in the operation of the U.S. economy.

31. T.
32. F. An open economy permits trade across its borders; a closed economy severely restricts trade across its borders.

Multiple Choice

1. d	2. e	3. a	4. e	5. d
6. d	7. c	8. d	9. a	10. e
11. d	12. d	13. b	14. c	15. b
16. b	17. c	18. e	19. d	20. e
21. c	22. b	23. c	24. e	25. b
26. d	27. e			

3 *How Economists Approach Problems*

Summary   A theory or model is a body of knowledge that is organized to reveal principles or relationships that occur regularly. In order to simplify reality and concentrate on only the most important variables surrounding the phenomena they study, economists (like all theorists) must employ many assumptions. One of the most important assumptions is the *ceteris paribus*, or "other things equal," assumption. Another commonly used assumption in economics is that of economic rationality, the assumption that people are motivated by self-interest and will behave in a manner consistent with maximizing expected net gains.

Economic theory is positive, that is, it deals with what is, that which can be observed and tested. However, this does not mean that economists need limit themselves to only positive issues. In fact, economic theory would be of limited concern if it were never used to support conclusions about what ought to be. Normative economics is the application of economic theory to such concerns.

Relationships between variables are often expressed in terms of a function, a statement of how one variable depends on other variables. Relationships are said to be direct or positive when the dependent and independent variables change in the same direction; relationships are inverse or negative when the dependent and independent variables change in opposite directions.

One of the most important concepts in economics is that of a marginal unit. Marginal refers to either the last or the next unit to be considered. The total amount is always the sum of the marginal amounts. When the marginal amount is positive, the total will increase; when the marginal amount is negative, the total will decrease;

and when the marginal amount is zero, the total will not change. The average amount is the total amount divided by the number of units. If the marginal amount is greater than the average, the average will increase; if the marginal amount is less than the average, the average will decrease; consequently, the marginal and the average will be equal at the extreme point on the average.

Rational decision making often relies on a comparison of marginal benefits and marginal costs. When marginal benefits are decreasing and marginal costs are increasing, an individual will maximize his or her well-being by equating marginal benefits with marginal costs.

Another important concept in economics is that of equilibrium. Equilibrium is a state of balance between opposing forces. Economists typically deal with stable equilibrium situations, those that restore themselves after a temporary disturbance.

Major Objectives

After you have read this chapter, you will be able to do the following:

1. Define *theory*, *model*, and *variable*.
2. Discuss the role of experiments in economics.
3. Explain the role of assumptions in economic theory.
4. Define and use the term *ceteris paribus*.
5. Define *economic rationality*.
6. Describe what it means to be a rational consumer, a rational businessperson, a rational owner of resources, and a rational government.
7. Distinguish between self-interest and selfish behavior.
8. Define *entrepreneur*.
9. Differentiate between positive and normative statements.
10. Define *function*.
11. Distinguish between dependent and independent variables.
12. Contrast direct and inverse relationships.
13. Construct, read, and interpret graphs.
14. Calculate the slope of a line.
15. Distinguish between linear and nonlinear relationships.
16. Identify and explain the relation between variables on curves that are linear and those that are nonlinear.
17. Define, calculate, utilize, and interpret marginal concepts.
18. Explain why economists often use marginal analysis.
19. State, use, and explain the relationship between marginal and total amounts.
20. State, use, and explain the relationship between marginal and average amounts.
21. Determine an optimum position using marginal cost and marginal benefit.

22. Determine an optimum position using total cost and total benefit.
23. Determine an optimum position using average cost and average benefit.
24. Briefly describe the institutionalist and radical schools of economic theory.
25. Define and locate equilibrium positions.
26. Distinguish between stable and unstable equilibrium positions.
27. Explain the concept of equilibrium as being a moving target.
28. Distinguish between partial and general equilibrium analysis.
29. Define and cite examples of capital.
30. Define and give examples of investment.
31. Recognize and explain the problem of mistaken causation.
32. Recognize and explain the fallacy of composition.
33. Recognize and describe the importance of time lags, expectations, nonrational ways of knowing, and temporal limitations in economics.

Important Terms and Concepts

theory
model
variable
assumptions
ceteris paribus
economic rationality
self-interest
entrepreneur
positive vs. normative
function
dependent variable
independent variable
direct vs. inverse relationships
quadrants
origin
scaled
perpendicular
slope of a line
positive vs. negative slope

linear vs. nonlinear relationships
marginal
average
marginal cost
marginal benefit
institutionalist
radical political economist
equilibrium
stable vs. unstable equilibrium
partial vs. general equilibrium analysis
capital
investment
mistaken causation
fallacy of composition
time lags
expectations
nonrational ways of working
temporal limitations

Completion

function

A relationship between variables is called a _____ .

dependent

A variable is said to be _____ if its value depends on another variable; this other variable (the variable on which something

independent

depends) is the _____ variable. When equal changes in the independent variable bring about uniform changes in the depen-

linear

dent variable, the relationship is said to be _____ ; when equal changes in the independent variable bring about unequal changes in the dependent variable, the relationship is said to be

nonlinear

_____ .
When economists assume that all other variables are held constant

ceteris paribus

they are likely to use the phrase _____ . This assump-

"other things being equal"

tion might also be expressed as _____ .
Another common assumption in economics is that people will behave in a manner that makes them better off or keeps them from becoming

economic rationality

worse off. This is referred to as _____ .
When economists talk about an additional unit or the last unit

marginal

they are referring to the _____ unit. Maximizing one's

marginal cost

well-being typically requires equating _____ with

marginal benefit

_____ .
If the marginal amount of something is positive, the total amount

increase

will _____ ; if the marginal amount is positive and in-

increase, increasing

creasing, the total will _____ at a(n) _____ rate; if the marginal amount is positive and decreasing, the total will

increase, decreasing

_____ at a(n) _____ rate. If the marginal

decrease

amount of something is negative, the total amount will _____ ; if the marginal amount is negative and increasing, the total will

decrease, increasing

_____ at a(n) _____ rate; if the marginal

decrease

amount is negative and decreasing, the total will _____

decreasing

at a(n) _____ rate.
If the average amount of something is increasing, the marginal

greater than

amount must be _____ the average; if the average is

less than

decreasing, the marginal amount must be _____ the average; if the average is at an extreme point, the marginal amount

equal to it

must be _____ .

When the forces for change within a system offset each other so

equilibrium

that there is no tendency for change, the system is in _____ .

stable

The equilibrium is said to be _____ if the system automatically restores itself to equilibrium after a temporary disturbance. When economists study the effects of some disturbance on one set of economic variables, assuming that all other variables are unaffected,

partial

they are engaging in _____ equilibrium analysis. When economists take into account all the different effects of the distur-

general

bance, they are engaging in _____ equilibrium analysis.
In studying economics, one should be careful to note that a number of terms take on different meanings from their everyday usage.

capital

For example, a businessperson is likely to think of _____ as money, whereas an economist uses the term to refer to real goods that are used in the production of other goods and services. Similarly,

investment

a businessperson thinks of _____ as the purchase of financial securities, whereas an economist uses the term to refer to purchases of capital goods.

Problems and Applications

1. For each of the curves in the graph below, indicate whether the relationship is direct or inverse.

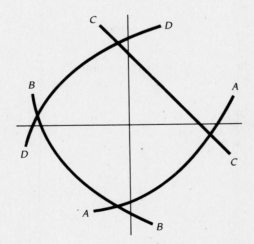

2. Refer to the graph in question 1.
   a. Identify the curves that are positively sloped. Do any of these curves have an increasing positive slope? If so, which one(s)? Do any of these curves have a decreasing positive slope? If so, which one(s)? Do any of these curves have a constant slope? If so, which one(s)?
   b. Identify the curves that are negatively sloped. Do any of these curves have a negative slope with increasing absolute value? If so, which one(s)? Do any of these curves have a negative slope with decreasing absolute value? If so, which one(s)? Do any of these curves have a constant slope? If so, which one(s)?

3. Consider the total curve in the graph below.

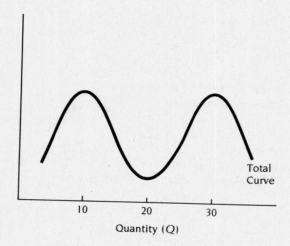

For each of the following examples, indicate whether the marginal curve would be positive, negative, or zero.
   a. $Q < 10$
   b. $Q = 10$
   c. $10 < Q < 20$
   d. $Q = 20$
   e. $20 < Q < 30$

4. Consider the average curve in the graph below.

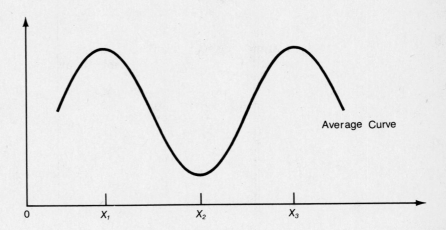

For each of the following cases, indicate whether the marginal curve would be greater than, less than, or equal to the average.
a. X < X1
b. X = X1
c. X1 < X < X2
d. X = X2
e. X2 < X < X3
f. X = X3

5. Consider the following decision-making situation in which you are attempting to maximize net benefits (total benefits minus total costs). Total benefits and total costs are indicated in the table below.

Quantity	Total Benefits	Marginal Benefits	Total Costs	Marginal Costs
0	0		0	
1	10		3	
2	18		7	
3	25		14	
4	30		30	
5	32		50	

a. Complete the columns for marginal benefits and marginal costs.
b. Identify the optimal (equilibrium) quantity. What is the net benefit associated with this quantity?

c. Identify the quantity associated with a net benefit of zero. Use marginal concepts to explain why this is not the optimal (equilibrium) quantity.

6. Consider the following decision-making situation in which you are attempting to maximize net benefits. Total benefits and total costs are indicated in the table below.

Quantity	Total Benefits	Marginal Benefits	Total Costs	Marginal Costs
0	0		0	
1	10		23	
2	18		27	
3	25		34	
4	30		50	
5	32		70	

a. Complete the columns for marginal benefits and marginal costs.
b. Identify the optimal (equilibrium) quantity if the quantity must be greater than zero. What is the net benefit associated with this quantity?
c. By computing the net benefit associated with each output level, verify that even though the net benefit is negative, it is maximized at a quantity of 3 units.

7. What must be true of your marginal test score in order for your average score to rise?

8. What will happen to your grade-point average if your grades this semester are below your current average?

True-False   Indicate whether each of the following statements is basically true or false. If the statement is false, rewrite it so that it is true.

_____ 1. Economic theory is normative.

_____ 2. Theories explain observed relationships and may enable us to predict the consequence of a specific disturbance.

_____ 3. *Ceteris paribus* is the assumption that all other variables are held constant.

_____ 4. Economically rational behavior is necessarily selfish behavior.

_____ 5. A rational entrepreneur is a businessperson who seeks to maximize profits.

_____ 6. A rational worker is one who always seeks the maximum money wage.

_____ 7. A rational worker is one who always seeks the maximum wage, *ceteris paribus.*

_____ 8. Rationality in government decision making may mean that elected officials always support causes associated with their re-election; it may also mean maximizing social welfare.

_____ 9. Economic theory deals with the positive; economists deal with both the positive and the normative.

_____ 10. With enough time and effort, people can presumably resolve differences in normative issues.

_____ 11. Linear relationships are characterized by having positive slopes.

_____ 12. The slope is calculated by dividing the variable measured on the vertical axis by the variable measured on the horizontal axis.

_____ 13. The slope is calculated as the change in the variable measured on the vertical axis divided by the change in the variable measured on the horizontal axis.

_____ 14. The total amount of something is the average amount multiplied by the number of units.

_____ 15. The total amount of something can be calculated by adding the marginal amounts.

_____ 16. *Marginal* refers to the last unit or the next unit.

_____ 17. If the price of good X is $2 per unit and you purchase 10 units, the marginal cost of the first unit cannot be determined from the information given.

_____ 18. If the price of good X is $2 per unit and you purchase 10 units, the marginal cost of the fifth unit cannot be determined from the information given.

_____ 19. If the price of good X is $2 per unit and you purchase 10 units, the marginal cost of the tenth unit is $2.

_____ 20. If the price of good X is $2 per unit and you purchase 10 units, the marginal cost of the eleventh unit cannot be determined from the information given.

_____ 21. When the marginal benefit exceeds the marginal cost, the net benefit is positive.

_____ 22. Institutionalists and radical political economists are critical of marginal analysis, arguing that it ignores the importance of both history and institutions in shaping economic choice.

_____ 23. Equilibrium is a state of balance wherein opposing forces for change exactly offset each other so that there is no net tendency for change.

_____ 24. All equilibrium positions are stable in the sense that there will be an automatic tendency to restore an equilibrium position that has been disturbed.

_____ 25. A study of the direct effects of a cigarette tax on cigarette consumption, *ceteris paribus*, is an example of partial equilibrium analysis.

_____ 26. Capital refers to money, and investment refers to any action that is aimed at acquiring more money.

_____ 27. When it is observed that one event typically follows another, one can assume a cause-and-effect relationship.

_____ 28. If you assume that just because something holds true at the micro level it will also necessarily hold true at the macro level, you may be committing the fallacy of composition.

_____ 29. Time is of considerable importance to an economist interested in prediction and policy.

_____ 30. Since people rarely act on the basis of expectations, economists assume that decisions are made in a world of perfect information.

Multiple Choice   Choose the *one best* answer in each of the following cases:

_____ 1. *Ceteris paribus* is a Latin term meaning
   a. "one by one."
   b. "equal under the law."
   c. "other things being equal."
   d. "in accordance with the law."
   e. "under conditions of scarcity."

_____ 2. Which of the following statements is a positive one?
   a. We ought to buy U.S. savings bonds.
   b. An increase in demand for a product causes an increase in the price of the product.
   c. The president should decrease government spending in order to balance the budget.
   d. An increase in taxes is undoubtedly the worst thing that could happen to the economy.
   e. Our economic situation would improve if people would only spend the money they have earned and stop buying on credit.

_____ 3. Which of the following is most descriptive of a theory?
   a. It is only as useful as its assumptions are realistic.
   b. It must be represented by a mathematical model.
   c. It has predictive power only in situations where the assumptions hold exactly.

    d. It is a description of particular relationships that occur by coincidence.

    e. It is a systematically organized body of knowledge that may be helpful in problem solving.

4. The concept of economic rationality refers to
   a. all financial decision making.
   b. behavior that is in one's own self-interest.
   c. the goals and objectives of an economic system.
   d. the decisions made by a professional economist.
   e. that which is in the public interest and which promotes the general welfare.

5. Which of the following statements is true?
   a. Economists are the only rational workers.
   b. There is no such thing as a rational government.
   c. Rational workers always have perfect information.
   d. A rational resource owner will attempt to maximize his net return.
   e. In order for economists to consider a government to be rational, the government would have to maximize the social welfare of its people.

6. Which of the following statements is a positive one?
   a. Inflation is our worst economic problem.
   b. Welfare programs should be discontinued, *ceteris paribus.*
   c. The United States should pass legislation to ensure a balanced budget.
   d. An increase in price will result in a decrease in quantity demanded, *ceteris paribus.*
   e. None of the above is a positive statement.

7. Which of the following comments about positive and normative statements is correct?
   a. Positive statements are always accurate.
   b. Because positive statements are always accurate, they need not be tested.
   c. Normative statements deal with what is.
   d. Normative statements cannot be verified.
   e. Both a and b are correct.

8. Partial equilibrium analysis
   a. considers only unstable equilibrium situations.
   b. is rarely appropriate in economics and so is seldom used.
   c. deals with the effects of an economic disturbance on one set of economic variables, *ceteris paribus.*
   d. takes into account all the possible consequences of an economic disturbance but disregards any policy implications.
   e. does none of the above.

_____ 9. The slope of a curve is
   a. constant in the case of a straight line.
   b. positive in the case of a direct relationship.
   c. negative in the case of an inverse relationship.
   d. equal to the change in vertical movement divided by the change in horizontal movement.
   e. all of the above.

Use the following graph to answer questions 10 and 11.

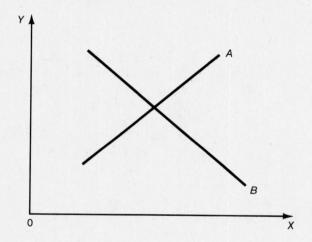

_____ 10. Which of the following statements is correct with respect to curve *A* in the preceding graph?
   a. The slope of curve *A* is X divided by Y.
   b. Curve *A* illustrates a normative issue.
   c. Curve *A* illustrates a direct relationship.
   d. The slope of curve *A* is increasing at an increasing rate.
   e. The slope of curve *A* cannot be determined, because curve *A* is linear.

_____ 11. Which of the following statements is correct with respect to curve *B* in the graph?
   a. Curve *B* illustrates a direct relationship.
   b. The slope of curve *B* is negative with increasing absolute value.
   c. The slope of curve *B* is variable X divided by variable Y.
   d. The slope of curve *B* is variable Y divided by variable X.
   e. The slope of curve *B* is the change in variable Y divided by the change in variable X.

Use the following graph to answer questions 12 and 13.

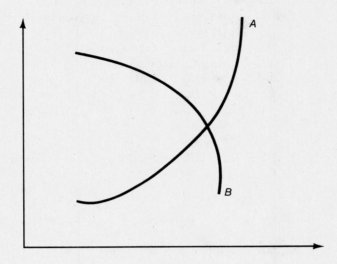

___   12. Which of the following statements is true with respect to curve
        A in the preceding graph?
        a. Curve A is nonlinear.
        b. The dependent variable is increasing at an increasing rate.
        c. Curve A has a positive slope with increasing absolute value.
        d. The slope is calculated as the change in the dependent vari-
           able divided by the change in the independent variable.
        e. All of the above are true.

___   13. Which of the following statements is true with respect to curve
        B in the graph?
        a. Curve B has a negative slope with increasing absolute value.
        b. The slope of curve B cannot be determined, because curve B
           is nonlinear.
        c. Curve B illustrates a direct relationship between the depen-
           dent and independent variables.
        d. The slope of curve B cannot be determined, because the rela-
           tionship described by curve B is inverse.
        e. None of the above is true.

_____ 14. Assume that the price of good X is $5 per unit. You have purchased 12 units of X before you notice that X sells for $4 per unit at a store next door. Assuming that you behave rationally, what will you most likely do if you cannot return your original purchase?
    a. Buy 12 more units of X at the lower price.
    b. Buy no additional units of X at this time.
    c. Never again buy units of X at a price of $5 per unit.
    d. Buy another unit of X at $4 if the marginal benefit of X exceeds $4.
    e. Do none of the above.

_____ 15. If the quantity of X increases whenever the price of X decreases, one can conclude that
    a. the relationship between the price and the quantity of X is direct.
    b. the relationship between the price and the quantity of X is inverse.
    c. the relationship between the price and the quantity of X is linear.
    d. the relationship between the price and the quantity of X is nonlinear.
    e. both b and c are true.

_____ 16. Assume that a firm finds that the total revenue associated with the sale of 10 units is $30 and the total revenue from the sale of 11 units is $32. One can accurately conclude that
    a. the marginal revenue associated with selling a total of 11 units is $2.
    b. the marginal revenue associated with selling the eleventh unit is $2.
    c. the firm should sell the eleventh unit.
    d. the firm should not sell the eleventh unit.
    e. none of the above apply.

_____ 17. Peggy has to decide whether to study economics for another hour tonight or go out with her friends. If she is rational, she will study the extra hour, *provided that*
    a. she has a test tomorrow.
    b. there are no marginal costs.
    c. the marginal benefits exceed the marginal costs.
    d. the marginal benefits from study are positive and increasing.
    e. none of the above are relevant.

_____ 18. Marginal analysis is
   a. rarely used by economists.
   b. concerned with all-or-nothing decisions.
   c. useful in normative—but not positive—economics.
   d. appropriate in micro- but not macroeconomic analysis.
   e. characterized by none of the above.

_____ 19. According to the graph below, the optimal value of Q is

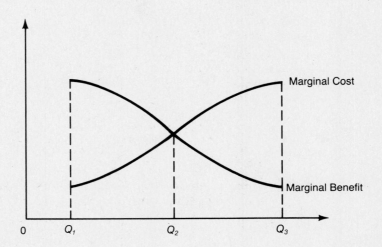

   a. Q_1.
   b. Q_2.
   c. Q_3.
   d. one unit short of Q_2.
   e. indeterminate.

Use the following graph to answer questions 20 and 21.

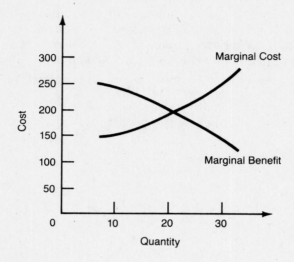

_____ 20. Which of the following statements is correct with respect to the preceding graph if the objective is to maximize net benefits?
a. The optimal quantity is 10.
b. The optimal quantity is 20.
c. The optimal quantity is 30.
d. The optimal quantity is slightly less than 20.
e. The optimal quantity cannot be determined from the information given.

_____ 21. Which of the following statements is correct with respect to the graph?
a. The maximum net benefit is 100.
b. The maximum net benefit is 200.
c. The maximum net benefit is 250.
d. The maximum net benefit is 400.
e. The maximum net benefit cannot be determined from the information given.

_____ 22. When the marginal benefit of studying exceeds the marginal cost of studying, we can correctly conclude that
a. it is not worth studying.
b. the net benefit is maximized.
c. the student will receive a passing grade.
d. the net benefit can be increased by studying more.
e. both c and d are true statements

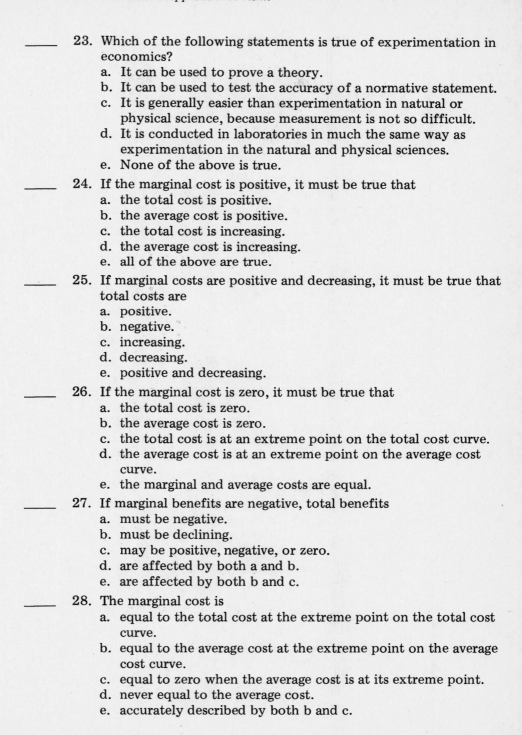

_____ 23. Which of the following statements is true of experimentation in
economics?
a. It can be used to prove a theory.
b. It can be used to test the accuracy of a normative statement.
c. It is generally easier than experimentation in natural or
physical science, because measurement is not so difficult.
d. It is conducted in laboratories in much the same way as
experimentation in the natural and physical sciences.
e. None of the above is true.

_____ 24. If the marginal cost is positive, it must be true that
a. the total cost is positive.
b. the average cost is positive.
c. the total cost is increasing.
d. the average cost is increasing.
e. all of the above are true.

_____ 25. If marginal costs are positive and decreasing, it must be true that
total costs are
a. positive.
b. negative.
c. increasing.
d. decreasing.
e. positive and decreasing.

_____ 26. If the marginal cost is zero, it must be true that
a. the total cost is zero.
b. the average cost is zero.
c. the total cost is at an extreme point on the total cost curve.
d. the average cost is at an extreme point on the average cost
curve.
e. the marginal and average costs are equal.

_____ 27. If marginal benefits are negative, total benefits
a. must be negative.
b. must be declining.
c. may be positive, negative, or zero.
d. are affected by both a and b.
e. are affected by both b and c.

_____ 28. The marginal cost is
a. equal to the total cost at the extreme point on the total cost
curve.
b. equal to the average cost at the extreme point on the average
cost curve.
c. equal to zero when the average cost is at its extreme point.
d. never equal to the average cost.
e. accurately described by both b and c.

_____ 29. If the average cost is decreasing, it must be true that
   a. the total cost is decreasing.
   b. the marginal cost is decreasing.
   c. the marginal cost is negative.
   d. the marginal cost is less than the average.
   e. the average cost is negative.

_____ 30. According to an economist, capital would include
   a. money.
   b. a tractor.
   c. a cement mixer.
   d. all of the above.
   e. both b and c.

_____ 31. Which of the following examples constitutes investment, in the sense used in economics?
   a. purchase of a municipal bond
   b. construction of a new factory
   c. purchase of stock in a major corporation
   d. acquisition of 100 acres of undeveloped land
   e. all of the above

_____ 32. Errors and problems in economic analysis may arise
   a. because of temporal limitations.
   b. when one commits the fallacy of composition.
   c. when one relies on nonrational ways of knowing.
   d. when one fails to recognize time lags and expectations.
   e. from all of these causes.

_____ 33. To conclude that all economic concepts are difficult because you have difficulty with one concept is most likely to be a case of
   a. mistaken causation.
   b. temporal limitations.
   c. the fallacy of composition.
   d. nonrational ways of knowing.
   e. all of the above.

_____ 34. If you assume that good grades are the result of good weather conditions you are illustrating
   a. time lags.
   b. mistaken causation.
   c. a temporal limitation.
   d. the fallacy of composition.
   e. a nonrational way of knowing.

Discussion Questions

1. Which would you consider more important in determining the usefulness of a model: the accuracy of the assumptions, or the accuracy of the predictions?

2. At what point would a theory cease to be useful?

3. If rational behavior does not require perfect information, how might you decide whether or not to acquire more information?

4. What would be rational behavior for the manager of a corporation?

5. Rational government may mean maximizing social welfare. How would you measure social welfare?

6. Some economists assume that there are certain goods, like national defense, that the private economy cannot be expected to provide adequately. Name others. What are the common characteristics of these goods?

7. Positive statements have to do with "what is." Does this mean that all positive statements must be accurate?

8. Can you think of any circumstances in which money might be capital?

Answers

Problems and Applications

1. *A*: direct   *B*: inverse   *C*: inverse   *D*: direct

2. a. *A, D*; yes, *A*; yes, *D*; no   b. *B, C*; no; yes, *B*; yes, *C*

3. a. positive   b. zero   c. negative   d. zero
   e. positive

4. a. greater than   b. equal to   c. less than
   d. equal to   e. greater than   f. equal to

5. a.

Quantity	Marginal Benefits	Marginal Costs
1	10	3
2	8	4
3	7	7
4	5	16
5	2	20

b. 3; 11

c. 4. At a quantity of 4, the marginal cost exceeds the marginal benefit, indicating that the last unit added more to costs than to benefits and should not have been taken.

6. a.

Quantity	Marginal Benefits	Marginal Costs
1	10	23
2	8	4
3	7	7
4	5	16
5	2	20

b. 3, -9

c.

Quantity	Net Benefits
1	-13
2	-9
3	-9
4	-20
5	-38

7. The marginal test score must be higher than the average test score.

8. The grade-point average will decrease

True-False

1. F. Economic theory is positive.
2. T.
3. T.
4. F. Economically rational behavior is motivated by self-interest, but it need not be selfish.
5. T.
6. F. A rational worker is one who seeks the maximum money wage, *ceteris paribus.*
7. T.
8. T.
9. T.
10. F. Because normative issues involve opinions and value judgments, it is possible that differences can never be resolved. However, positive issues deal with what is, and they may therefore be subject to being tested.
11. F. Linear relationships are characterized by constant slopes.
12. F. The slope is calculated by dividing the change in the variable measured on the vertical axis by the change in the variable measured on the horizontal axis.
13. T.
14. T.
15. T.

16. T.
17. F. If the price of good X is $2 per unit and you purchase 10 units, the marginal cost of the first unit is $2.
18. F. If the price of good X is $2 per unit and you purchase 10 units, the marginal cost of the fifth unit is $2.
19. T.
20. F. If you can continue to buy good X at a price of $2 per unit, the marginal cost of the eleventh unit of X would be $2.
21. F. When the marginal benefit exceeds the marginal cost, one can *not* correctly conclude that the net benefit is positive; one *can* correctly conclude that the net benefit can be increased by increasing the quantity.
22. T.
23. T.
24. F. Unstable equilibrium positions can be observed. When subjected to a disturbance, such equilibrium situations do not automatically restore themselves.
25. T.
26. F. Capital refers to goods that have been produced for the purpose of producing other goods; investment refers to the creation of capital.
27. F. That one event follows another does not necessarily mean that there is a cause-and-effect relationship between the two events.
28. T.
29. T.
30. F. Economists sometimes assume that decisions are made in a world of perfect information, but they also recognize that expectations may play an important role in many decision-making situations.

Multiple Choice

1. c	2. b	3. e	4. b	5. d
6. d	7. d	8. c	9. e	10. c
11. e	12. e	13. a	14. d	15. b
16. b	17. c	18. e	19. b	20. b
21. e	22. d	23. e	24. c	25. c
26. c	27. e	28. b	29. d	30. e
31. b	32. e	33. c	34. b	

4 Scarcity: The Economic Problem

Summary   Scarcity refers to a situation in which the amount of something that is available is not sufficient to meet people's requirements for it at a price of zero. Most goods and services command a positive price because the resources used to produce them are scarce.

Resources or factors of production may be classified as labor resources, natural resources, or capital resources. Labor includes all kinds of human work, natural resources are productive inputs made available by nature, and capital resources are those things that are produced so that they can be used to produce something else.

Because resources are scarce, any decision to use them in producing one good or service means that they can not be available for the production of something else. Similarly, if a person's ability to buy goods is limited, a decision to buy one good may interfere with the ability to buy another. The economic cost of choosing one alternative over another is measured by the opportunity cost. Specifically, the opportunity cost is the value of the best alternative foregone.

An economy's production possibilities boundary illustrates the concept of opportunity cost in production. The production possibilities boundary is a schedule or curve showing the various combinations of goods that an economy is capable of producing with a given supply of resources and technology. The construction of the boundary assumes that the economy's resources are fully and efficiently employed. Realistically, since resources are not equally well suited to the production of different goods and services, the production possibilities boundary is bowed out. This shape indicates increasing marginal opportunity costs. At any point in time, an economy might be operating on its production possibilities boundary, indicating the full and efficient employment of all resources. Alternatively, the economy might be operating inside its boundary, indicating an unemployment or underemployment of resources. It is impossible to ascertain the desirability of any particular production point without knowing something about the goals, objectives, and trade opportunities facing the economy. Over time, the production possibilities boundary may shift in response to a change in the supply of resources and/or technology. An outward shift in the boundary is conducive to economic growth. An inward shift is associated with economic decline.

Major Objectives

After you have read this chapter, you will be able to do the following:

1. Define *scarcity* and explain its significance in economics.
2. Explain what is meant by a zero price.
3. Identify and define the three classes of inputs and categorize inputs according to this classification scheme.
4. Define and explain the role of the entrepreneur in the production of goods and services.
5. Distinguish between an inventor and an innovator.
6. Explain what is meant by human capital.
7. Describe and explain the role of technological know-how in the production of goods and services.
8. Define *opportunity cost* and explain the concept in terms of both consumption and production.
9. Identify the opportunity cost associated with the consumption or production of a good, given adequate information.
10. Explain how the concept of opportunity costs relates to a production possibilities boundary.
11. State the assumptions that underlie the development of a production possibilities boundary.
12. Indicate the shape of a realistic production possibilities boundary for an economy and explain this shape in terms of marginal opportunity costs.
13. Explain why real-world economies tend to experience increasing marginal opportunity costs.
14. Interpret the meaning of given points on, inside, or outside a production possibilities boundary.
15. Discuss the concept of an optimal point in terms of an economy's production possibilities boundary.
16. Indicate the potential for economic growth and decline in terms of an economy's production possibilities boundary and cite explanations for the occurrence of growth and decline.

Review Terms	the three economic questions	income
	capital	wealth
	marginal	

Important Terms and Concepts	scarcity	enterprisers or entrepreneurs
	zero price	inventor
	input	innovator
	factor of production	human capital
	resource	technological know-how
	output	opportunity cost
	labor resources	production possibilities boundary
	natural resources	marginal opportunity cost
	capital resources	

Completion

When the amount of something available is not sufficient to meet

scarce

some requirement, the item is said to be _____ . In economics, scarcity exists where there is not a sufficient amount to

zero

satisfy people's desire for the item when the price is _____ .

need not

Price _____ (must/need not) be restricted to monetary terms.

The production of goods and services requires certain inputs, some-

resources, factors of production

times called _____ or _____ .
Though they are often difficult to distinguish and classify precisely,

Labor resources

there are three classes of inputs. _____ include

natural resources

all forms of human work; _____ are those
that are provided directly by nature, such as raw materials; and

capital resources

_____ refers to those things that are
produced in order to produce something else. The risk taker in a

enterpriser or entrepreneur

business enterprise is called a(n)_____

labor

and is an example of _____ input. Skills and technological

capital

know-how are considered to be a form of _____ input,
because they are produced through education and training. This
particular type of capital is sometimes referred to as

human capital

_____ .

scarcity

The existence of _____ means that people have to
make choices. When economists refer to the true or total cost of

choosing one alternative over another, they are concerned with the

opportunity cost

_____ . This cost can be measured by the

the best foregone
alternative

value of _____ . There are
opportunity costs associated with both production and consumption.

A curve that illustrates the concept of opportunity costs in production, that is, which shows potential productive tradeoffs among

production possibili-
ties boundary

goods, is called a _____ .
At the macro level, this boundary identifies those combinations of

capable

goods that an economy is _____ of producing with a given

negatively

supply of resources. The curve is _____ sloped, which
reflects the fact that at any point in time an economy cannot produce more of both goods. Furthermore, a realistic boundary has a

bowed out

_____ shape, indicating

increasing marginal

_____ opportunity costs.
Unemployment of resources or an inefficient use of resources would

a point inside the
boundary

be represented by _____ .

shift

When the supply of resources changes, the curve will _____ .
An outward shift represents the potential for

economic growth

_____ . An inward shift is asso-

economic decline

ciated with _____ .

**Problems and
Applications**

1. Consider the tradeoff between goods A and B described by the
   table below.

Good A	Good B
0	8
1	6
2	4
3	2
4	0

   a. What is the cost of the first unit of A?
   b. What is the cost of the second unit of A?
   c. What is the cost of the fourth unit of A?
   d. What is the cost of the first three units of A?
   e. Are the marginal opportunity costs increasing, decreasing, or
      constant?

f. Graph this schedule.
g. Why is the curve negatively sloped?
h. What does it mean that the curve is a straight line?

2. Consider the production possibilities schedule below.

Zigs	Zags
0	18
1	14
2	___
3	0

a. If the marginal opportunity cost of the second unit of zigs is 6 zags, how many units of zags can be produced if the economy is producing 2 zigs?
b. What would it cost the economy to produce 3 units of zigs?
c. What would it cost the economy to produce 4 units of zigs?

3. Consider the production possibilities boundary described in the graph below.

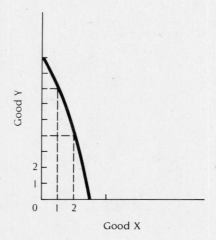

a. What is the cost of the first unit of good X?
b. What is the cost of nine units of good Y?
c. Are the marginal opportunity costs increasing, decreasing, or constant? What does this pattern suggest about the economy?

4. Consider the economy described by the production possibilities boundary in the graph below.

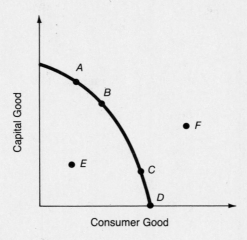

a. *Ceteris paribus*, will the economy be apt to experience the greatest growth if it produces bundle *A* or *C*? Explain.
b. Which is the best bundle?
c. What could you say about resource utilization if the economy is actually producing bundle *B*? bundle *D*? bundle *E*?

5. Classify each of the following inputs as labor, natural resource, and/or capital resource:
   a. a born singer
   b. an accountant
   c. a ditch digger
   d. a hammer
   e. a computer
   f. mineral deposits
   g. undeveloped land
   h. a factory

True-False   Indicate whether each of the following statements is basically true or false. If the statement is false, rewrite it so that it is true.

_____ 1. Scarcity means having less than we would like to have.

_____ 2. A zero price means that there is no monetary charge, though there may be nonmonetary sacrifices.

_____ 3. We have to pay a price for goods and services because resources are scarce.

_____ 4. Labor resources include only manual labor.

_____ 5. Enterprise is a labor input.

_____ 6. Money is the most important factor of production.

_____ 7. An innovator is one who discovers or devises a new product or production technique.

_____ 8. An entrepreneur is often an inventor but is rarely an innovator.

_____ 9. Worker attitudes toward their jobs contribute to the qualitative aspects of the labor input.

_____ 10. Capital includes tools, equipment, and technological know-how.

_____ 11. Technological know-how or skill is the ability to combine resources to produce goods and services.

_____ 12. Monetary price is a measure of the total cost associated with consuming or producing a good.

_____ 13. Opportunity cost is the value of all foregone alternatives.

_____ 14. An economy's production possibilities boundary illustrates the concept of opportunity costs in production.

_____ 15. To move from one point to another along a production possibilities boundary requires additional resources.

_____ 16. A bowed-out production possibilities curve indicates increasing marginal opportunity costs.

_____ 17. Realistic production possibilities curves are likely to be bowed out because resources are scarce.

_____ 18. In terms of production possibilities, unemployment and inefficiency are represented as points inside the boundary.

_____ 19. In terms of production possibilities, economic growth is represented as a point outside the boundary.

_____ 20. In terms of production possibilities, the best production point is at the top of the curve.

Multiple Choice   Choose the *one best* answer in each of the following cases:

_____ 1. Which of the following statements is true of scarcity?
a. It is the basic economic problem.
b. It does not affect a rich economy such as that of the United States.
c. It applies to resources, but not to goods and services.
d. Both a and b are true.
e. None of the above is true.

_____ 2. As defined in the text, labor resources include
   a. enterprise.
   b. workers' learned skills.
   c. everyone.
   d. all human inputs except that which is managerial.
   e. none of the above.

_____ 3. The entrepreneur is most closely defined as
   a. an inventor.
   b. an innovator.
   c. a risk taker.
   d. an inventor who is also an innovator.
   e. an inventor who is also a risk taker.

_____ 4. Capital resources include which of the following elements?
   a. money
   b. machinery and tools
   c. technological know-how
   d. both b and c
   e. all of the above

_____ 5. Which of the following statements is true of opportunity cost?
   a. It is the true economic cost.
   b. It may be expressed as a tradeoff.
   c. It applies in consumption as well as in production.
   d. It is important to decision making in the government as well
      as in the private sector.
   e. All of the above are true.

_____ 6. If you have a choice of consuming good X, good Y, or good Z,
   the opportunity cost of good X is
   a. good Y.
   b. good Z.
   c. both goods Y and Z.
   d. the monetary price of good X.
   e. good Y or good Z, depending on which yields the greater
      net benefit.

_____ 7. In constructing a production possibilities boundary, we must
   assume that
   a. resources are unspecialized.
   b. monetary prices are constant.
   c. all resources are fully and efficiently employed.
   d. the quality, but not the quantity, of resources may change.
   e. all of the above are true.

Use the table below to answer questions 8 through 11.

Good X	Good Y
0	20
1	18
2	15
3	11
4	6
5	0

_____ 8. Which of the following statements is true of the economy
described by the production possibilities schedule in the
preceding table?
a. The economy can produce a bundle containing 5 units of X
and 20 units of Y.
b. The optimal production bundle for the economy contains 3
units of X and 11 units of Y.
c. The economy can produce 5 units of X, but only when all
resources are fully and efficiently employed.
d. When all resources are fully and efficiently employed, the
economy will produce 2 units of X and 18 units of Y.
e. All of the above are true.

_____ 9. For the nation described by the production possibilities schedule
in the table, a combination containing 1 unit of good X and 15
units of good Y
a. would be unattainable.
b. represents a loss in resources.
c. could be produced with less than full employment.
d. could be produced only with full employment of resources.
e. could be produced only if its technological know-how
improves.

_____ 10. Which of the following statements is true of the economy
described by the production possibilities schedule in this table?
a. The cost of X is constant.
b. The cost of the second unit of X is 5 units of Y.
c. The cost of Y decreases as the production of Y increases.
d. The cost of X can be measured in terms of a sacrifice of Y.
e. All of the above are true.

_____ 11. Which of the following statements is true of the economy
described by the production possibilities schedule in the table?
a. The cost of the first unit of X is 18 units of Y.
b. The cost of the fifth unit of X is 20 units of Y.
c. If the economy produces 5 units of X, it will not be able to
produce Y.

    d. The economy should produce 2 units of X and 15 units of Y.

    e. The production of 2 units of X and 11 units of Y requires a full and efficient use of resources.

Use the graph below to answer questions 12 and 13.

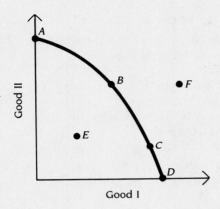

12. Which of the following statements is true of the economy described in the production possibilities curve in the preceding graph?
    a. Bundle *E* cannot be produced.
    b. Bundle *C* is the optimal bundle.
    c. If the economy is producing bundle *D*, its resources are not being used efficiently.
    d. Bundle *F* can be produced if there is a full and efficient use of all resources.
    e. The production of bundle *A* means that all resources are being used in the production of Good II.

13. Which of the following statements is true of the economy described in the production possibilities curve in the graph?
    a. The production of bundle *B* rather than bundle *C* requires additional resources.
    b. The production of bundle *D* rather than bundle *A* requires additional resources.
    c. Bundle *E* cannot be produced.
    d. Bundle *B* can be produced, if there is full and efficient employment of resources.
    e. Bundle *F* can be produced, if there is full and efficient employment of resources.

_____ 14. In terms of production possibilities, the potential for economic growth can be represented by
    a. a curve that is bowed inward.
    b. a point outside the boundary.
    c. an outward shift of the curve.
    d. a movement upward along the boundary.
    e. a movement downward along the boundary.

_____ 15. Which of the following factors will cause a shift in the production possibilities curve?
    a. unemployment
    b. economic growth
    c. economic decline
    d. a change in technological know-how
    e. all of the above except a

_____ 16. In an economy that produces only two goods, increasing marginal opportunity costs mean that
    a. an equal number of each good will be produced.
    b. in order to produce more of one good, production of the other good must cease.
    c. as the economy produces additional units of both goods, the cost of both goods increases.
    d. the monetary price of additional units of a good must increase as those additional units are produced.
    e. as the economy produces additional units of one of the goods, each additional unit requires a larger sacrifice of the other good.

_____ 17. If the production possibilities curve for goods A and B is a negatively sloped straight line,
    a. resources are highly specialized.
    b. the marginal opportunity cost is decreasing.
    c. technological know-how has been maximized.
    d. resources are equally able to produce either good.
    e. the economy will employ all its resources fully.

_____ 18. Increasing marginal opportunity costs suggest that the production possibilities curve will
    a. be bowed out.
    b. shift outward.
    c. be a vertical line.
    d. be a straight line.
    e. be positively sloped.

19. If an economy's production possibilities curve is negatively sloped with increasing absolute value, one can correctly conclude that
    a. the economy will operate on its production possibilities boundary.
    b. the economy will operate outside its production possibilities boundary.
    c. the economy is experiencing increasing marginal opportunity costs.
    d. the economy is experiencing decreasing marginal opportunity costs.
    e. none of the above is true.

20. Consider the economy described by the production possibilities curves in the graph below. Which of the following statements describes this economy accurately?

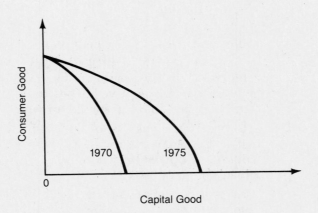

a. The economy produced more capital goods in 1975 than in 1970.
b. The economy was capable of producing more capital goods in 1975 than 1970.
c. The economy experienced a decrease in resources associated with the production of consumer goods.
d. The economy experienced unemployment in the consumer goods industries in 1970 and 1975.
e. Both a and b are true.

_____ 21. Which of the following sayings best illustrates the concept of
           opportunity cost?
           a. "Do as I say, not as I do."
           b. "All's fair in love and war."
           c. "Two wrongs don't make a right."
           d. "You can't have your cake and eat it too."
           e. "Early to bed, early to rise makes a man healthy, wealthy,
              and wise."

**Discussion
Questions**

1. Explain what an economist means by a zero price. Can you
   think of something with a zero price? Does your answer surprise
   you? Why? What is the price associated with breathing?

2. Traditionally, an entrepreneur was thought of as the owner-
   manager of a business. The corporate structure is characterized
   by a separation of ownership and management. In such a setting,
   does the entrepreneurial input refer to ownership, or to management? Explain.

3. Referring to managerial input, explain how the labor and human
   capital inputs may be difficult to distinguish.

4. The textbook suggests that crude oil did not have value as a
   natural resource until we learned to use it in production. Can
   you think of another resource for which this has been true?

5. The owner of a business often uses personally owned resources
   without actually making a monetary payment for them. Use the
   concept of opportunity cost to demonstrate that these inputs
   are not actually free.

6. Using the concept of opportunity cost, determine the costs of
   taking this course in economics, of reading your textbook, and
   of answering this question.

7. Chapter 1 refers to an incident in the 1960s when Nikita
   Khrushchev banged his shoe on a table at the United Nations
   and shouted, "We shall bury you!" Not long before this, Richard
   Nixon, then vice president, traveled to Russia and came home to
   report on the relatively low standard of living enjoyed by the
   Russian people. Can you explain this apparent inconsistency in
   terms of a production possibilities boundary? (*Hint:* Consider a
   tradeoff between consumer goods and capital goods and indicate
   how different actual production decisions could lead to different
   future boundaries.)

8. What factors would be important in determining the optimal
   production bundle for an economy?

9. Market and planned economies differ in terms of the way they go about answering the basic economic questions of what, how, and for whom. Would you expect these two types of economies to differ in terms of their current production possibilities boundaries? their actual production bundles? their preferred production bundles?

Use the following graph to answer questions 10 and 11.

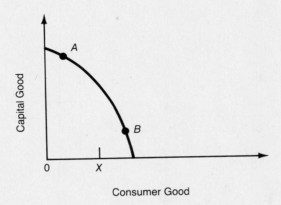

10. Consider the economy facing the production possibilities curve in the preceding graph. Assume that the economy plans to produce either bundle A or B. Which bundle is likely to lead to greater economic growth? Explain.

11. Consider the economy facing the production possibilities curve in the graph. What is the likely consequence of producing bundle A if the economy needs X units of a certain consumer good to sustain its population? How might the economy acquire these units of the consumer good if it does not produce them?

Answers   *Problems and Applications*

1. a. 2 units of B   b. 2 units of B   c. 2 units of B
   d. 6 units of B   e. constant
   f.

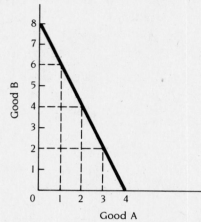

   g. To indicate that it is impossible to have more of both A and B;
       that is, more of either one requires a sacrifice of the other.
   h. As the amount of A increases, the tradeoff between A and B
       remains constant; that is, the marginal opportunity cost is
       constant.

2. a. 8 zags   b. 18 zags
   c. The economy is not able to produce 4 units of zigs.

3. a. 2 units of Y   b. 3 units of X
   c. Increasing; the economy's resources are not equally well suited
       to the production of X and Y.

4. a. Bundle *A*; the production of capital goods adds to the
       economy's resource base.
   b. Impossible to determine from the information given.
   c. Production of bundle *B* indicates a full and efficient use of all
       resources; production of bundle *D* indicates that all resources
       are being fully and efficiently employed in the production of
       consumer goods; bundle *E* indicates unemployment and/or
       inefficient employment of resources.

5. a. labor   b. labor, human capital
   c. labor   d. capital
   e. capital   f. natural resources
   g. natural resource   h. capital

True-False

1. T.
2. F. A zero price means that there are neither monetary nor nonmonetary sacrifices.
3. T.
4. F. Labor resources includes all forms of human work.
5. T.
6. F. Money is not typically a factor of production.
7. F. An inventor discovers or devises a new product or production technique; an innovator introduces the invention.
8. F. An entrepreneur is often an innovator but is rarely an inventor.
9. T.
10. T.
11. T.
12. F. Opportunity cost is a measure of the total cost associated with consuming or producing a good.
13. F. Opportunity cost is the value of the best foregone alternative.
14. T.
15. F. The construction of a production possibilities boundary assumes a fixed supply of resources.
16. T.
17. F. Realistic production possibilities curves are likely to be bowed out, because resources are specialized.
18. T.
19. F. In terms of production possibilities, economic growth is represented by a rightward shift of the curve.
20. F. In terms of production possibilities, the best production point depends on the goals, objectives, and trade opportunities of the economy involved.

Multiple Choice

1. a	2. c	3. c	4. d	5. e
6. e	7. c	8. c	9. c	10. d
11. c	12. e	13. d	14. c	15. e
16. e	17. d	18. a	19. c	20. b
21. d				

5 *Demand and Supply–or Supply and Demand*

Summary

Knowledge of the concepts of demand and supply and the functioning of the free market is essential for an understanding of economics and for the operation of a basically capitalistic, free-enterprise system.

Demand is a relationship between the potential prices of a good and the quantities that someone would buy at these alternative prices, *ceteris paribus*. Similarly, supply is a relationship between the potential prices of a good and the quantities that a firm or firms would make available for sale at these alternative prices, *ceteris paribus*. Both demand and supply have to do with a willingness and ability to engage in the exchange. Wanting or needing a good, for example, is not equivalent to demanding it. To suggest that an individual quantity is demanded or supplied at a given price indicates that that quantity would be demanded or supplied if the particular price were to prevail in the market.

According to the law of demand, price and the quantity demanded are inversely related, *ceteris paribus*. That is, a demand curve is negatively sloped. This negative relationship may be explained by considering the substitution and income effects of a price change. The substitution effect considers the effect of a price change on relative prices; the income effect considers the effect of a price change on real income and the subsequent effect of this change in real income on purchases.

According to the law of supply, price and the quantity supplied are directly related, *ceteris paribus*. That is, the supply curve is positively sloped. This relationship can be most easily understood by noting that higher prices indicate greater profits and, because business is typically motivated by profits, higher prices encourage an increase in quantity supplied.

It is important to distinguish between a change in the quantity demanded and a change in demand. A change in quantity demanded is associated with a change in the price of the good and is indicated graphically as movement along a demand curve. The direction of change in the quantity demanded is known from the law of demand. A change in demand is caused by a change in something other than the price of the good itself, that is, by a relaxation of the *ceteris paribus* assumption. For example, a change in demand may be caused by a change in tastes and preferences, income, or the price of a related good. A change in demand is graphically represented as a shift of the demand curve: a shift of the demand curve to the right represents an increase in demand; a shift of the demand curve to the left represents a decrease in demand.

It is equally important to distinguish between a change in the quantity supplied and a change in supply. A change in the quantity supplied is associated with a change in the price of the good and is graphically represented as a movement along the supply curve. It is possible to determine the direction of a change in the quantity supplied if the law of supply is upheld. A change in supply is caused by a change in something other than the price of the good, that is, by a relaxation of the *ceteris paribus* assumption. For example, a change in supply might be caused by a change in cost of production, technology, goals, or profit expectations in related markets. Supply is said to increase when the supply curve shifts to the right, since a shift to the right indicates that for any given price, more will be available for sale on the new curve than on the original curve. Similarly, a shift of the supply curve to the left indicates a decrease in supply.

A market exists when potential buyers and sellers come together to engage in trade. The market is said to be free if market outcomes are determined by the interplay of market demand and market supply relationships. Market demand and supply refer to the sum of the individual demand and supply relationships, respectively.

At any given price, the quantity traded in a free market is determined by the short side of the market. That is, the quantity traded is determined by the smaller of the two—quantity demanded or quantity supplied. An individual cannot buy a unit unless someone is willing to sell it, and a firm cannot sell a unit unless someone is willing to buy it, so the quantity that is actually traded (that is, purchased) is determined by the lesser of the two. Be very careful to note the quantity demanded is not equivalent to quantity bought; similarly, quantity supplied is not equivalent to quantity sold.

When, at a given price, the quantity demanded exceeds the quantity supplied, there is a shortage of the product at that particular price. The amount of the shortage is the difference between the quantities demanded and those supplied at that price. The existence of a shortage puts upward pressure on the price as consumers bid the product away from each other. This bidding process illustrates the role of price as a rationing device.

When, at a given price, the quantity supplied exceeds the quantity demanded, there is a surplus of the product at that particular price. The amount of the surplus is the difference between the quantities supplied and demanded at that price. The existence of a surplus puts downward pressure on the price as suppliers try to sell their surpluses.

In a free market, price will tend to fluctuate until any surpluses or shortages are eliminated. That is, the price will fluctuate until the quantity demanded and the quantity supplied are equal. When there is no further tendency for the price to change, the market is said to be in equilibrium. The equilibrium point occurs at the intersection of the demand and supply curves. The equilibrium price is the price that equates the quantity demanded and the quantity supplied.

Sometimes government interferes with the free operation of the market by altering the price and quantity traded. This change may be accomplished by the imposition of price controls. The controls may be in the form of price ceilings, which set upper limits on legal selling prices. Alternatively, the controls may be in the form of price floors, which set lower limits on legal selling prices. The imposition of price controls may be accomplished through equilibrium or disequilibrium approaches.

Market demand and supply are microeconomic relationships. Aggregate demand and supply are macroeconomic concepts. "To aggregate" means to add up or to total. Hence, aggregate demand and supply refer essentially to the sum of market demands and supplies across all markets. Because unlike units cannot be added, quantities are expressed in terms of their monetary values and then added. The average price of the goods and services produced, that is, the general price level, is used as the price variable. Economists define inflation (or deflation) as an increase (or decrease) in the general price level. The concepts of aggregate demand and aggregate supply can therefore provide insight into the problems and potential policies associated with the goal of price stability. Furthermore, because greater output has generally meant greater employment, the concepts of aggregate demand and aggregate supply might also be used to better understand the problems and potential policies associated with a full employment objective.

Major Objectives   After you have read this chapter, you will be able to do the following:

1. Define *demand* at three levels: individual demand, market demand, and aggregate demand.
2. Define *supply* at three levels: individual supply, market supply, and aggregate supply.
3. Distinguish between demand and the quantity demanded.
4. Distinguish between supply and the quantity supplied.
5. Construct, read, and interpret the curves associated with given demand and supply schedules.
6. Express the laws of supply and demand in terms of (a) whether the price and the quantity variables move in the same or opposite directions, (b) whether the relationship is direct or inverse, and (c) the slope of the curve.
7. Explain the law of demand using income and substitution effects.
8. Distinguish between a change (an increase and a decrease) in demand and a change in quantity demanded, represent these changes graphically, and identify the causes of each.
9. Differentiate normal and inferior goods.
10. Differentiate substitutes and complements.
11. Distinguish between a change (an increase and a decrease) in supply and a change in the quantity supplied, represent these changes graphically, and identify the causes of each.
12. Define *market* and *free market*.
13. Describe quantity demanded, quantity supplied, and quantity traded.
14. Given a market described by demand and supply schedules or curves, determine the quantity traded at alternatives prices.
15. Define *equilibrium*.
16. Given a free market, determine the equilibrium price and the quantity traded.
17. Define *excess demand*, *excess supply*, *shortage*, *surplus*, and *disequilibrium*.
18. Explain the process by which the interplay of demand and supply automatically move a free market to the equilibrium point.
19. Determine the effect on equilibrium price and quantity of changes in demand and/or supply.
20. Name and define the two basic types of price control.
21. Explain how price controls are imposed through both equilibrium and disequilibrium approaches and analyze the consequences of each approach.
22. Define *rationing* and distinguish between formal and informal rationing.

23. Given market characteristics and a specific price control, determine if a shortage or a surplus will result and specify the magnitude of the shortage or surplus.
24. Define, explain, and utilize the concepts of aggregate demand, aggregate supply, Gross National Product, real value, and macroeconomic equilibrium.
25. Explain the concepts of demand-side economics and supply-side economics.
26. Define *stagflation*.

Review Terms

aggregate
ceteris paribus
functional relationship
independent variable
dependent variable
direct relationship
inverse relationship
positive slope
negative slope

input
technological know-how
equilibrium
equitable
microeconomics
macroeconomics
inflation
unemployment

Important Terms and Concepts

individual demand
quantity demanded
law of demand
real income
income effect
substitution effect
change in demand (increase and decrease)
movement along a demand curve
shift of the demand curve
shift variable
normal good
inferior good
substitute
complement
individual supply
quantity supplied
law of supply
change in supply (increase and decrease)

movement along a supply curve
shift of the supply curve
market
free market
market demand
market supply
quantity traded
equilibrium price
equilibrium quantity
excess supply
excess demand
disequilibrium
collusion
equilibrium method of market manipulation
disequilibrium method of market manipulation
shortage
rationing
formal rationing vs. informal rationing

ceiling price   inflation
floor price   deflation
support price   Gross National Product
surplus   real value
farm price supports   macroeconomic equilibrium
OPEC   demand-side economics
aggregate demand   supply-side economics
aggregate supply   stagflation
Consumer Price Index

Completion

A relationship showing the amounts of a good that an individual

demand

would purchase at different prices is called _____ . Similarly, a relationship showing the amounts of a good that an individual

supply

would make available for sale at different prices is called _____ . In constructing the demand and supply relationships, one must impose the *ceteris paribus* assumption. This assumption essentially

all other variables
are held constant

means that _____ .

prices

In terms of demand and supply, only _____ and

quantities

_____ are allowed to change.

According to the law of demand, the relationship between price

inverse

and quantity demanded is _____ . There are two reasons why the law of demand can be expected to hold: the

substitution effect,
income effect

_____ and _____ .

Both the substitution and income effects measure the effect that a

income effect

price change has on purchases. The _____ does so by determining the effect of the price change on real income and the subsequent change in purchases that results from this change in

increase

real income. A price decrease causes a(n) _____ (increase/

more

decrease) in real income. Generally, people buy _____ (more/less) when real income increases. Thus, a price decrease normally

increase

causes a(n) _____ (increase/decrease) in quantity demanded.

substitution effect

The _____ measures the effect that a price change has on purchases by first determining the effect that the price change has on relative prices. When the price of a good de-

less

creases, that good becomes relatively _____ (more/less)

increase

expensive and consumers will tend to _____ (increase/ decrease) their purchases of it.

It is important to distinguish between demand and quantity de-

Demand

manded. _____ (Demand/Quantity demanded) refers to a relationship between prices and quantities; that is,

demand

_____ (demand/quantity demanded) is a whole set of prices and corresponding quantities. The term

quantity demanded

_____ (demand/quantity demanded) refers to a certain amount that would be purchased at a particular price. In

quantity demanded

terms of a schedule, _____ (demand/ quantity demanded) refers to one point in the schedule, whereas

demand

_____ (demand/quantity demanded) refers

quantity demanded

to the entire schedule. Similarly, _____ (demand/quantity demanded) would be represented graphically as a

demand

point on a curve, and _____ (demand/ quantity demanded) would be the curve itself.

quantity demanded

A change in _____ (demand/ quantity demanded) is associated with a change in the price of the

movement along

good. This is represented by a _____ (shift of/movement along) the demand curve. The law of demand indicates the specific nature of this change: when price increases,

quantity demanded decreases

_____ ; when price

quantity demanded increases

decreases, _____ .

demand

A change in _____ (demand/quantity demanded) occurs when the *ceteris paribus* assumption is relaxed. A change in tastes, income, or in the price of a related good might rea-

demand

sonably be expected to cause a change in _____ (demand/quantity demanded). Such a change is represented by a

shift of

_____ (shift of/movement along) the demand curve. Demand is said to increase when the demand curve

shifts to the right

_____ . Such a shift indicates that at any

more

price the consumer will buy _____ (more/less) now than previously. It also indicates that for any quantity, the consumer will

more

pay _____ (more/less) now than previously. This is the

increase

meaning of a(n) _____ (increase/decrease) in demand.

According to the law of supply, the relationship between price and

direct
the quantity supplied is _____ . Basically, the law of supply

profits
holds because higher prices mean higher _____ , which in turn provide incentive for increased production.

As with the demand side of the market, it is important to distin-

supply
guish between supply and quantity supplied. The term _____ (supply/quantity supplied) refers to a relationship between prices and

supply
quantities; that is, _____ (supply/quantity supplied) is a whole set of prices and corresponding quantities. The

quantity supplied
term _____ (supply/quantity supplied) refers to a certain amount that would be offered for sale at a particular

quantity supplied
price. In terms of a schedule, _____ (supply/quantity supplied) refers to one point in the schedule, whereas

supply
_____ (supply/quantity supplied) refers to

quantity supplied
the entire schedule. In terms of a graph, _____ (supply/quantity supplied) would be represented by a point on a

supply
curve and _____ (supply/quantity supplied) would be the entire curve.

quantity supplied
A change in _____ (supply/quantity supplied) is associated with a change in the price of a good. Such a change is

movement along
represented by a _____ (shift of/movement along) the supply curve. The law of supply indicates that as price

quantity supplied
increases
increases, _____ ; when price

quantity supplied
decreases
decreases, _____ .

supply
A change in _____ (supply/quantity supplied) occurs when the *ceteris paribus* assumption is relaxed. This

shift of
change is represented by a _____ (shift of/movement along) the supply curve. As with the demand side of the

right
market, a shift of the curve to the _____ (right/left)

left
represents an increase and a shift to the _____ (right/left) represents a decrease. When the supply curve shifts to the right, it

more
indicates that, at any price, _____ (more/less) of a good will be available for sale now than previously. It also indicates that

lower
any given quantity will be available now at a _____

(higher/lower) price than before. This condition is the meaning of

increase

a(n) _____ (increase/decrease) in supply.

quantity supplied

    A change in _____ (supply/quantity supplied) would be caused by a change in the price of the good. A

supply

change in _____ (supply/quantity supplied) could be caused by a change in input prices, technology, expectations, or goals.

market

    A _____ exists when potential buyers and sellers

market demand

come together to engage in trade. One can derive _____ by adding up all the individual demands for a particular good. Market

adding all individual supplies of the good

supply is derived by _____ .

demand

    At any given price, the _____ relationship identifies how much of a good consumers might buy at that price. It should not be assumed that consumers will necessarily buy the indicated quantity, however. Consumers cannot buy the indicated quantity

sell it

unless someone will _____ to them. Similarly, at any

supply

given price the _____ relationship identifies how much will be offered for sale. Again, one should not assume that the quantity supplied will necessarily be sold. In order for the quantity sup-

buy it

plied to be sold, someone has to be willing and able to _____ at the indicated price. Trade is a two-sided activity requiring both a buyer and a seller. If, at a given price, the quantity demanded and the quantity supplied are equal, then the quantity traded will

equal

_____ the quantities demanded and supplied. If, at a given price, the quantity demanded and the quantity supplied are not

smaller

equal, the quantity traded will be equal to the _____ (larger/smaller) of the two.
    If, at a given price, the quantity supplied exceeds the quantity

excess supply

demanded, there is an _____ or a

surplus

_____ (surplus/shortage) in the market. The existence

downward

of a surplus puts _____ (downward/upward) pressure on price as suppliers attempt to sell a product.
    If, at a given price, the quantity demanded exceeds the quantity

excess demand

supplied, there is an _____ or a

shortage

_____ (surplus/shortage) in the market. The existence

upward

of a shortage puts _____ (downward/upward) pressure on the price as consumers bid the product away from each other.

When there is excess supply or excess demand, the market is said

disequilibrium

to be in a state of _____ . In a free market, the

change

price can be expected to _____ until there is no longer excess supply or excess demand. When the price is such that the quantity demanded equals the quantity supplied, there is no longer a tendency for the price to change and the market is then said to be in

equilibrium

_____ . That is, the equilibrium price is the price

equates

that _____ the quantity demanded and the quantity supplied.

Sometimes government imposes price controls in particular markets. A price _____ sets an upper limit on the legal

ceiling

floor

selling price, whereas a price _____ sets a lower limit on the legal selling price. Price controls tend to result in disequilibrium

shortage

situations. A price ceiling typically results in a _____

surplus

(surplus/shortage); a price floor typically results in a _____ (surplus/shortage).

macro

Aggregate demand and aggregate supply are the _____ (micro/macro) economic counterparts of individual or market demand and supply. In the case of aggregate demand and aggregate

index number

supply, the price variable is an _____ reflecting the

average price

general price level or _____ of all individual goods and services in the economy. The quantity variable is a measure of

total output

ure of _____ in the economy. Adding the quantities of the many different goods and services in the economy requires that they be measured in the same units. This measurement

money or dollar values

is accomplished by using the _____ of the goods and services.

The concepts of aggregate demand and aggregate supply can be used to investigate the problems of inflation and unemployment.

increase

Inflation occurs when there is a(n) _____ (increase/decrease) in the general price level. This could result from a(n)

increase

_____ (increase/decrease) in aggregate demand and/or

decrease

a(n) _____ (increase/decrease) in aggregate supply. If one assumes that an increase in employment is associated with an increase in output, then unemployment can be decreased by increasing   _____ (increasing/decreasing) aggregate demand

increasing   and/or _____ (increasing/decreasing) aggregate supply.

Problems and Applications

1. Consider the following demand and supply schedules for commodity R.

Price/Unit	Quantity Demanded	Quantity Supplied
$10	1	5
8	2	4
6	3	3
4	4	2
2	5	1

   a. If the price of R were $2 per unit, how many units would be offered for sale? How much would people be willing to buy? How much would actually be traded if the price remained at $2 per unit? Does this constitute a surplus, or a shortage? Of how much? If the market process is allowed to work, what would you expect to see happen to the price?

   b. If the price of R rose to $8 per unit, how many units would be offered for sale? What quantity would be demanded? If the price remained at $8 per unit, how many units would actually be traded? Does this constitute a surplus, or a shortage? Of how much? What would you expect to happen to the price if the market process is allowed to work?

   c. Identify the equilibrium price and quantity.

2. a. Consumers' incomes decrease and demand for product X decreases. Is product X a normal, or an inferior good? How would you represent the decrease in demand for product X?

   b. The demand for product Y increases as a result of a decrease in consumers' incomes. Is product Y a normal, or an inferior good? How would you represent the increase in demand for product Y?

   c. Product Z is an inferior good and demand for it has recently decreased as a result of a change in consumers' incomes. Was there an increase, or a decrease in consumers' incomes?

3. a. Assume that the price of butter increases. What happens in the market for butter when the price of butter increases? How do you know? How would you represent this change?

   b. If people buy a smaller quantity of butter when the price of butter increases, what do you suppose happens in the market for margarine? How would you represent this change?

4. a. Assume that the price of nail polish increases. What happens in the market for nail polish? How do you know? How would you represent this change?

    b. If people buy a smaller quantity of nail polish when the price of nail polish increases, what do you suppose happens in the market for polish remover? How would you represent this change?

5. In the graph below, assume that the original demand and supply curves are given by D_1 and S_1, respectively. Locate the original equilibrium point, identifying both the original equilibrium price and quantity.

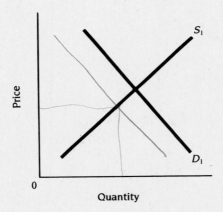

Now assume that demand decreases. How is a decrease in demand represented? Locate the new equilibrium point. What happens to the equilibrium price when demand decreases? What happens to the equilibrium quantity when demand decreases?

6. In the graph below, assume that the original demand and supply curves are given by D_1 and S_1, respectively. Locate the original equilibrium point, identifying both the original equilibrium price and the quantity.

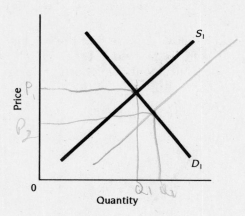

Now assume that supply increases. How is an increase in supply represented? Locate the new equilibrium point. What happens to the equilibrium price when supply increases. What happens to the equilibrium quantity when supply increases?

7. Consider the market described by the graph below, in which D_1 and S_1 represent the initial demand and supply curves and D_2 and S_2 represent the new demand and supply curves.

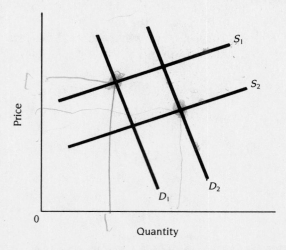

a. Locate the initial equilibrium point, identifying the equilibrium price and quantity.

b. Does the shift of the demand curve represent an increase, or a decrease in demand? *increase*
c. Does the shift of the supply curve represent an increase, or a decrease in supply? *Increase*
d. Locate the new equilibrium point, identifying the price and quantity.
e. What happens to the equilibrium price? *falls*
f. What happens to the equilibrium quantity? *increases*

8. Study the market described by the graph below.

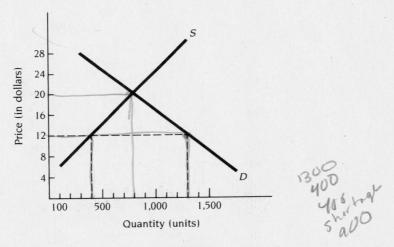

Assume that a price ceiling is imposed at a price of $12. What is the quantity demanded? What is the quantity supplied? What is the quantity traded? Is there a surplus or a shortage? Of how much?

True-False

Indicate whether each of the following statements is basically true or false. If the statement is false, rewrite it so that it is true.

T 1. A free market is one in which demand and supply determine the terms of trade.

F 2. According to the law of supply, price and the quantity sold are directly related.

T 3. A change in a shift variable for demand is likely to result in a new demand curve.

T 4. An increase in price will typically result in a decrease in demand.

T 5. An increase in demand will typically result in an increase in price.

_____ 6. An increase in supply is represented by a movement along the supply curve.

_____ 7. According to the income effect, people tend to buy fewer units of a good that has become relatively more expensive.

_____ 8. According to the substitution effect, an increase in the price of X will typically result in a decrease in the quantity demanded of it, because X has become relatively more expensive.

_____ 9. A negatively sloped individual demand curve indicates that the quantity purchased is inversely related to price.

_____ 10. A decrease in the price of a good will result in an increase in real income for consumers of that good.

_____ 11. If one were constructing a demand curve, a change in income would be a violation of the *ceteris paribus* assumption.

_____ 12. An increase in the price of a good causes a decrease in demand for its complement.

_____ 13. An increase in the cost of production typically results in a decrease in the quantity supplied.

_____ 14. A price floor sets a minimum price at which a good may be legally sold.

_____ 15. An increase in income causes a decrease in demand for an inferior good.

_____ 16. A free market is one in which the equilibrium price is $0.

_____ 17. The quantity sold is always the same as the quantity purchased.

_____ 18. A positively sloped supply curve can be explained by changes in profit at different prices.

_____ 19. Excess demand at a given price is equivalent to a shortage at that price.

_____ 20. If, at a price of $2 per unit, there is a surplus of 100 units, there is an excess supply of 100 units.

_____ 21. Once attained, the equilibrium price in a free market never changes.

_____ 22. An increase in the price of shoes is likely to result in a decrease in demand for the shoes, *ceteris paribus*.

_____ 23. A decrease in the supply of shoes, *ceteris paribus*, is likely to result in a decrease in the demand for shoes.

_____ 24. Because demand and supply are likely to change over time, equilibrium may be best thought of as a moving target.

_____ 25. The quantity demanded at a given price is the number of units that the consumer would like to have even though he or she may not be able to afford them.

_____ 26. In constructing the graph of a market, economists plot price on the vertical axis and quantity on the horizontal axis.

_____ 27. When the market price is below the equilibrium price, there will be an excess demand for the good and a tendency for the price to increase.

_____ 28. Price is a rationing device.

_____ 29. Price is the only rationing device available in a market.

_____ 30. Aggregate supply is a macroeconomic concept dealing with the total output of a particular industry.

_____ 31. Macroeconomic equilibrium occurs when all markets are in equilibrium.

Multiple Choice   Choose the *one best* answer in each of the following cases:

_____ 1. According to the law of demand,
   a. the demand curve is positively sloped.
   b. price and demand are directly related.
   c. price and the quantity demanded are inversely related.
   d. the quantity purchased is equivalent to the quantity demanded.
   e. there is a negative relationship between price and demand.

_____ 2. The equilibrium point is characterized by
   a. the equality of prices in all markets.
   b. an excess demand for goods in short supply.
   c. the intersection of price and the quantity traded.
   d. a surplus of the good at the market-determined price.
   e. an equality between quantity demanded and quantity supplied.

_____ 3. At any given price in a free market, the quantity traded is
   a. determined by the government.
   b. equal to the sum of the quantity demanded and the quantity supplied.
   c. equal to the difference between the quantity demanded and the quantity supplied.
   d. equal to the greater of the two: excess demand or excess supply.
   e. equal to the smaller of the two: the quantity demanded or the quantity supplied.

_____ 4. An increase in demand for a good may be caused by a decrease in the price of
a. the good.
b. a complement.
c. a substitute good.
d. all of the above.
e. none of the above.

_____ 5. The income effect of a price change is the change in
a. quantity sold caused by a change in money income.
b. real income created by a change in the demand for a good.
c. the quantity demanded because of a change in real income that results from a price change.
d. the quantity demanded, from a change in money income caused by a price change.
e. the quantity purchased because of the change in real income that results from a price change.

_____ 6. The substitution effect of a price change measures the change in
a. demand caused by a change in the demand for a substitute.
b. demand from a change in the prices of substitutes.
c. the quantity purchased because of a change in the relative prices of substitutes.
d. the quantity demanded caused by a change in the relative prices of substitutes.
e. the equilibrium quantity created by a change in the relative prices of substitutes.

_____ 7. The law of supply is reflected by
a. a shift in the supply curve.
b. a supply curve that is positively sloped.
c. an inverse in supply in response to an increase in profits.
d. an inverse relationship between price and the quantity supplied.
e. a direct relationship between the quantity supplied and the quantity sold.

_____ 8. Which one of the following effects would be most closely associated with a decrease in supply?
a. a change in consumer incomes
b. a decrease in the price of the good
c. a leftward shift in the supply curve
d. the existence of a surplus in the market
e. an increase in the price of a substitute good

_____ 9. Of the following combinations of goods, which is most likely to be representative of complements?
a. a camera and film
b. hot tea and iced tea

   c. pencils and pens
   d. a record and a cassette tape
   e. peanuts and cashews

Use the following table to answer questions 10 through 12.

	Market for X	
Price of X	Quantity Demanded	Quantity Supplied
$20	250	425
15	305	400
10	355	355
5	420	300

10. Consider the market described in the preceding table. If the current market price of good X is $15,
   a. the quantity sold is 400 units.
   b. the quantity demanded is 305 units.
   c. there is a shortage of 95 units.
   d. there will be a tendency for the price to increase.
   e. both a and b are true.

11. In the market described in the table above, the quantity traded at equilibrium is
   a. 250 units.
   b. 300 units.
   c. 355 units.
   d. 420 units.
   e. impossible to determine from the information given.

12. Consider the market described in the table above. Assume that the government imposes a price ceiling at $5 per unit. Which one of the following conclusions is appropriate?
   a. The quantity purchased will be 420 units.
   b. There will be an increase in demand.
   c. There will be a decrease in supply.
   d. There will be a shortage of 120 units.
   e. There will be a tendency for the price to decrease.

13. Assume that the government imposes a price ceiling at $5 per unit in a market for which the equilibrium price is $7 per unit. Which of the following effects is most likely to occur?
   a. There will be a shortage of the good.
   b. There will be an increase in the supply of the good.
   c. There is likely to be an excess supply of the good.
   d. The price will decrease further when the price control is relaxed.
   e. Suppliers will collude to cut supply.

Use the following graph to answer questions 14 through 16.

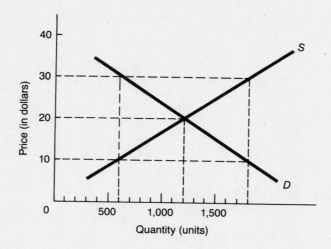

_____ 14. In the market described by the preceding graph, the equilibrium price and quantity, respectively, are
   a. $10 and 600 units.
   b. $10 and 1,200 units.
   c. $20 and 1,200 units.
   d. $20 and 1,800 units.
   e. $30 and 1,800 units.

_____ 15. Consider the free market described by the graph. If the current price is $10 per unit,
   a. the quantity sold is 1,200 units.
   b. the market is in equilibrium.
   c. there is an excess supply of the product.
   d. there will be a tendency for demand to increase.
   e. there will be a tendency for the price to increase.

_____ 16. Consider the market described by the graph. Assume that the government imposes a price floor at $30 per unit. What will be the consequence of the price control?
   a. The quantity sold will be 1,800 units.
   b. A shortage of 1,200 units will develop.
   c. There will be a surplus of 1,800 units.
   d. The quantity traded will be 1,200 units.
   e. There will be an excess supply of 1,200 units.

_____ 17. If, at the same market price, a firm is willing to make 200 units available now rather than the 100 units it was willing to make available last year, one could most accurately conclude that
   a. demand has increased.
   b. supply has increased.
   c. quantity demanded has increased.
   d. the equilibrium price will increase.
   e. the supply curve has shifted to the left.

_____ 18. Last summer, Bobby was able to sell 20 glasses of lemonade a week at a price of 10 cents per glass. This year Bobby finds that he can still sell 20 glasses of lemonade a week, even though he has doubled his price to 20 cents apiece. Most likely there has been
   a. a violation of the law of demand.
   b. an increase in quantity supplied.
   c. an increase in quantity demanded.
   d. an increase in supply of lemonade.
   e. an increase in demand for lemonade.

_____ 19. At $1 per unit, people will buy 50 units of product T. When the price of T is raised to $1.50 per unit, only 35 units are purchased. We can conclude that
   a. product T should be sold for $1 per unit.
   b. the demand curve for product T is positively sloped.
   c. the supply curve for product T is negatively sloped.
   d. the demand for product T is consistent with the law of demand.
   e. the supply of product T is consistent with the law of supply.

_____ 20. A simultaneous decrease in demand and supply will always result in
   a. a decrease in the equilibrium price.
   b. an increase in the equilibrium price.
   c. a decrease in the equilibrium quantity.
   d. an increase in the equilibrium quantity.
   e. a decrease in both equilibrium price and quantity.

Use the following graph to answer question 21.

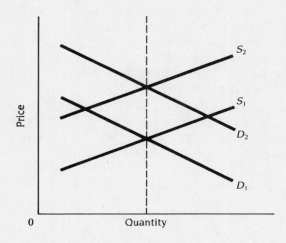

_____ 21. Consider the market described in the preceding graph in which
D_1 and S_1 represent the initial demand and supply curves,
respectively, and D_2 and S_2 represent the final demand and
supply curves, respectively. Which one of the following statements most accurately describes this graph?
a. Demand has decreased.
b. Supply has increased.
c. The equilibrium price has increased.
d. The final equilibrium price is indeterminate.
e. The final equilibrium quantity is indeterminate.

_____ 22. Knowing that the quantity bought is equivalent to the quantity
sold in a free market enables us to conclude that
a. the market is in equilibrium.
b. there will be no change in price.
c. the quantity demanded is equivalent to the quantity supplied.
d. all of the above are true.
e. none of the above is true.

_____ 23. Though the price of widgets has decreased significantly over the
past year, the manufacturer finds he continues to sell only 200
widgets per week. This situation suggests that
a. a widget is an inferior good.
b. the supply of widgets has decreased.
c. the demand for widgets has decreased.
d. the market is not in equilibrium.
e. there is a collusion in the market.

_____ 24. Assume that goods M and N are substitutes and that the price of M increases. Which one of the following statements is accurate?
   a. The demand for both M and N will increase.
   b. The demand for both M and N will decrease.
   c. The quantity demanded of M will decrease and the demand for N increase.
   d. The quantity demanded of M will decrease and the demand for N decrease.
   e. The demand for M will decrease and the supply of N increase.

_____ 25. Which one of the following situations best illustrates the role of price as a rationing device?
   a. a shift of the demand curve
   b. a shift of the supply curve
   c. the imposition of a price floor
   d. bidding for a good at an auction
   e. reserving output for a preferred customer

_____ 26. Which of the following changes would cause a decrease in the demand for math textbooks?
   a. an increase in the price of math textbooks, *ceteris paribus*
   b. a decrease in the supply of math textbooks, *ceteris paribus*
   c. a relaxation of the math requirement for graduation
   d. all of these changes.
   e. none of these changes.

_____ 27. Which of the following conditions would cause an increase in the supply of Florida oranges?
   a. an increase in the price of oranges, *ceteris paribus*
   b. an increase in the demand for orange juice, *ceteris paribus*
   c. a mild winter in Florida
   d. a decrease in the number of citrus farms in Florida, *ceteris paribus*
   e. a, b, and c only

_____ 28. Last year Firm X made 200 units of good X available at a price of $2 per unit. This year the firm will still make 200 units available—but only if the price rises to $3 per unit. What has most likely happened?
   a. demand has decreased
   b. demand has increased
   c. supply has increased
   d. supply has decreased
   e. the quantity supplied has decreased

_____ 29. Although the price of good W has increased significantly over the last few months, the supplier finds that she is still able to sell 1000 units per month. Evidently there has been
   a. a decrease in demand.
   b. an increase in demand.
   c. a decrease in supply.
   d. a decrease in the quantity supplied.
   e. collusion in the market for W.

_____ 30. Last week, the Shrinkets Shop sold 1,000 shrinkets at a price of $3 each. This week the shop finds it can sell only 600 shrinkets at that price. What has most likely happened?
   a. Demand has increased.
   b. Supply has increased.
   c. Supply has decreased.
   d. The quantity supplied has decreased.
   e. None of the above has occurred.

_____ 31. Last year, the Zee Corporation made 500 zeegs available for sale at $10 each. This year the corporation will make 500 zeegs available, even if it can get only $8 per zeeg. What has most likely happened?
   a. Demand has increased.
   b. Supply has increased.
   c. Supply has decreased.
   d. The quantity demanded has decreased.
   e. The quantity supplied has decreased.

_____ 32. The inverse relationship between price and the quantity demanded may be explained most adequately by
   a. substitution and income effects.
   b. the relationship of income to the quantity purchased.
   c. the concept of equilibrium in a free market.
   d. the concept of disequilibrium.
   e. the concept of equilibrium as a moving target.

_____ 33. Aggregate demand and aggregate supply
   a. are the macroeconomic equivalents of market demand and market supply.
   b. are relationships involving the market price of a good and the total output of that good.
   c. are both direct relationships.
   d. are both inverse relationships.
   e. differ from market demand and market supply in that there is no concept of equilibrium at the macro level.

_____ 34. Assume that aggregate demand decreases with no change in aggregate supply. Which of the following conditions is most likely to occur?
   a. inflation and decreased output
   b. inflation and increased output
   c. deflation and rising unemployment
   d. deflation and increased output
   e. inflation and deflation

_____ 35. Assume that aggregate supply increases with no change in aggregate demand. Which of the following situations is most likely to occur?
   a. inflation and rising unemployment
   b. inflation and increased employment
   c. deflation and rising unemployment
   d. deflation and increased employment
   e. no change in the general price level and no change in output

_____ 36. Inflation is most likely to be the result of
   a. an increase in the market demand for, and market supply of, a specific service.
   b. a decrease in the market demand for, and market supply of, a specific service.
   c. an increase in the market demand for, and a decrease in the market supply of, a specific service.
   d. a decrease in aggregate supply.
   e. a decrease in aggregate demand.

_____ 37. Deflation is most likely to be the result of
   a. an increase in the market supply of a specific good.
   b. a decrease in the market demand for a specific good.
   c. a decrease in the market demand for, and an increase in the market supply of, a specific good.
   d. all of the above.
   e. none of the above.

Discussion Questions

1. Assume that one pound of steak costs $3 and a pound of hamburger costs $1. How would your purchases of steak and hamburger change if the price of steak goes down to $1 a pound and the price of hamburger does not change? Which reason for expecting the law of demand to hold does this support?

2. Assume that your income is $100 per week and does not change. The price of a theatre ticket used to be $5 and you used to spend $10 per month going to the movies. How many tickets were you able to purchase? Now the price of tickets has decreased to $2 each. If you continue to spend $10 per month

going to the movies, how many tickets can you afford? What has happened to your real income? Which reason for expecting the law of demand to hold does this support?

3. What would you expect to happen to the demand for a product that becomes a fad overnight? Why?

4. Assume that last year Company V was able to sell (that is, customers actually purchased) 15,000 units of its product at a price of $1 per unit. This year Company V has already sold 20,000 units of its product at the higher price of $1.50 per unit. Explain why this situation is not an exception to the law of demand. Give a possible rationale.

5. What would happen to the equilibrium price and quantity of good X if there were an increase in the cost of producing it?

6. What would happen to the equilibrium price and quantity of good X if the price of good Y (a substitute for it) increased?

7. What would you expect to happen to the equilibrium price and quantity if consumers in the market for beef engage in a successful boycott? Explain.

8. Quantities bought and sold are always equal. Why, then, aren't markets always in equilibrium?

9. The imposition of a price ceiling in the market for gasoline results in a shortage of gasoline. With this relationship in mind, provide a rationale for establishing the price ceiling.

10. Other than price, what are some rationing devices that might be used to allocate a good for which there is a shortage?

Answers   *Problems and Applications*

1. a. 1, 5, 1, shortage, 4, increase
   b. 4, 2, 2, surplus, 2, decrease
   c. The equilibrium price is $6; the equilibrium quantity is 3 units.

2. a. normal; shift the demand curve to the left
   b. inferior; shift the demand curve to the right
   c. increase

3. a. The quantity demanded decreases; law of demand; movement along the demand curve
   b. The demand for margarine increases; shift the demand curve to the right

4. a. The quantity demanded decreases; law of demand; movement
        along the demand curve
    b. The demand for polish remover decreases; shift the demand
        curve to the left

5. The demand curve shifts to the left (D_2 represents new demand);
    the equilibrium price decreases; the equilibrium quantity
    decreases.

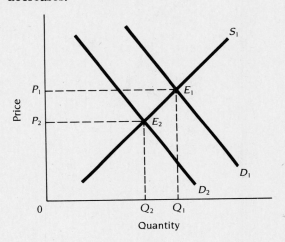

6. The supply curve shifts to the right (S_2 represents new supply);
    the equilibrium price decreases; the equilibrium quantity
    increases.

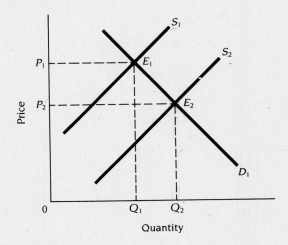

7. a. see point E_1 in the graph below
   b. increase
   c. increase
   d. see point E_2 in the graph below
   e. price decreases
   f. quantity increases

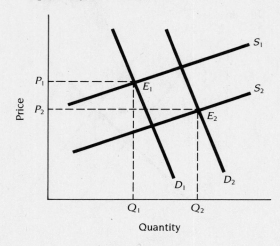

8. 1,300 units; 400 units; 400 units; a shortage; 900 units

True-False

1. T.
2. F. According to the law of supply, price and the quantity supplied are directly related.
3. T.
4. F. An increase in price will typically result in a decrease in the quantity demanded.
5. T.
6. F. An increase in supply is represented by a shift in the supply curve to the right.
7. F. According to the substitution effect, people tend to buy fewer units of a good that has become relatively more expensive.
8. T.
9. F. A negatively sloped individual demand curve indicates that the quantity demanded is inversely related to price.
10. T.
11. T.
12. T.

13. F. An increase in the cost of production typically results in a decrease in supply.
14. T.
15. T.
16. F. A free market is one in which the equilibrium price is determined by the interplay of demand and supply.
17. T.
18. T.
19. T.
20. T.
21. F. The equilibrium price in a free market is likely to change with changes in supply and/or demand.
22. F. An increase in the price of shoes is likely to result in a decrease in the quantity of shoes demanded, *ceteris paribus*.
23. F. A decrease in the supply of shoes, *ceteris paribus*, is likely to result in an increase in the price of shoes, which will then lead to a decrease in the quantity of shoes demanded.
24. T.
25. F. The quantity demanded at a given price is the number of units that the consumer is willing and able to buy at that price.
26. T.
27. T.
28. T.
29. F. Price is one of many rationing devices.
30. F. Aggregate supply is a macroeconomic concept dealing with the monetary value of the total output of the economy.
31. F. Macroeconomic equilibrium occurs at the output level that equates aggregate demand and aggregate supply.

Multiple Choice

1. c	2. e	3. e	4. b	5. c
6. d	7. b	8. c	9. a	10. b
11. c	12. d	13. a	14. c	15. e
16. e	17. b	18. e	19. d	20. c
21. c	22. e	23. c	24. c	25. d
26. c	27. c	28. d	29. b	30. e
31. b	32. a	33. a	34. c	35. d
36. d	37. e			

6 Unemployment and Inflation

Summary

Unemployment and inflation are among the most important economic problems. As such they are the subject of a considerable amount of public policy and deserve serious attention.

To the economist, unemployment refers to a situation in which a person is spending less time in wage-earning endeavors than desired. From the standpoint of a labor-supply curve, a person is fully employed at a given real wage rate if he or she is operating on the curve. For any given wage, if the individual is working fewer hours than the quantity indicated on the labor-supply curve, he or she is unemployed or underemployed. For any given wage, if the quantity of hours worked is greater than the quantity indicated on the labor-supply curve, the individual is overemployed.

For official purposes, in order for a person to be counted as unemployed he or she must be a nonworking member of the labor force who is actively seeking work. To the extent that people claim to be looking for work when in fact they are not, unemployment statistics overstate the problem. On the other hand, if people become discouraged and quit looking for work, they are no longer counted as part of the labor force and hence are not unemployed from an official standpoint. Unemployment statistics, then, tend to understate the problem to the extent of this discouraged-worker effect.

Economists generally classify unemployment as seasonal, frictional, structural, or cyclical. Seasonal unemployment is associated with jobs that require workers during only part of the year. It may be related to climatic conditions, holidays, or any number of seasonal factors. Frictional unemployment is short-term unemployment associated with the costs of information and mobility. It typically includes people who are between jobs or who are new labor-force entrants (or reentrants). Because we value freedom of choice in decision making, frictional unemployment is not generally considered to be a problem; in fact, to some extent frictional unemployment is considered desirable. Structural unemployment is the type of unemployment that arises when people's qualifications do not match the requirements of existing jobs. This type of unemployment is often associated with technological change and tends to single out certain groups of people in the economy. Cyclical unemployment, on the other hand, tends to affect workers throughout the economy. Cyclical unemployment is the unemployment associated with general downturns in economic activity, that is, with recessions and depressions. With cyclical unemployment, there are few job vacancies; by contrast, the job vacancies associated with structural unemployment cannot be filled by those in search of a job.

Inflation may be defined as an increase in general price levels. It becomes a problem when the increase is significant and sustained. The rate of inflation is the rate of change in whatever index number is being used to measure the general price level. For the United States, this is typically the GNP price deflator or the Consumer Price Index.

The economic, social, and personal costs of unemployment and inflation can be sizable. In economic terms, the cost of unemployment is the output that is not produced as a result of the unemployment. This foregone output can never be recovered. Unemployment, depending on its extent and its concentration, may also be associated with public health problems, the deterioration of neighborhoods, increases in violence and crime, and other problems that grow out of poverty. For the unemployed individual, unemployment not only results in a loss of income but also tends to be demoralizing and may lead to a deterioration of human skills.

Inflation, too, is associated with significant costs. The most important of these is likely to be the inclusion of an adjustment factor in economic decision making. This tendency to make adjustments for inflation affects household consumption, saving, and labor-supply decisions; it affects business hiring, investment, and pricing decisions; and it affects government budgeting and policy decisions. In addition, inflation tends to redistribute income and wealth; it may lead to insecurity and may even result in a return to barter exchange.

Major Objectives   After you have finished this chapter, you will be able to do the following:

1. Describe the major characteristics of bullionism and mercantilism.
2. Identify Karl Marx and briefly discuss his predictions about the future of capitalism.

3. Specify the time period associated with the Great Depression and the major problem associated with it.
4. Describe the major contribution of John Maynard Keynes.
5. Discuss the major economic problem of the 1970s.
6. Define unemployment as used for official purposes and as defined by economists, and distinguish between them.
7. Define and distinguish between microeconomic and macroeconomic unemployment.
8. Identify the relationships expressed by labor-supply and demand curves and describe the nature of these relationships.
9. Distinguish between real and nominal wage rates.
10. Use the concept of wages as being the opportunity cost of leisure to explain the positive slope of the labor-supply curve.
11. Define underemployment, overemployment, and full employment, and illustrate their meanings in terms of individual and aggregate labor-supply curves.
12. Explain negative slope in the demand curve for labor.
13. Distinguish between a movement along a labor demand or supply curve and a shift of the curve, identify the factors responsible for each, and describe these concepts.
14. Identify the equilibrium point in the labor market and explain the process whereby a market adjusts to equilibrium.
15. Define labor force and identify its participants.
16. Define, distinguish, and calculate the unemployment rate, the employment rate, and the labor-force participation rate.
17. Explain how the U.S. unemployment rate is determined.
18. Define what is meant by a discouraged worker.
19. Identify and explain the consequences of changing the age requirement in the definition of the labor force.
20. Identify and explain the consequences of including discouraged workers in the labor force.
21. Discuss the historical pattern of unemployment and inflation for the United States.
22. Define, distinguish, and classify examples of unemployment as representative either of seasonal, frictional, structural, or cyclical unemployment.
23. Explain why it is difficult to separate structural and cyclical unemployment.
24. Identify the basic types of programs designed to deal with each type of unemployment.
25. Discuss the incidence of unemployment in the U.S. economy by sex, race, and age groups.
26. Identify the costs of unemployment.
27. Identify and discuss the economic and social consequences of unemployment and inflation.

28. Define, calculate, and utilize index numbers.
29. Distinguish between real and nominal values.
30. Describe and distinguish the Consumer Price Index (CPI), the CPI-W, and the CPI-U.
31. Distinguish between the Gross National Product deflator and the CPI.
32. Calculate, interpret, and utilize price index numbers, the implicit price deflator for the GNP, and CPI numbers.
33. Estimate the present purchasing power of the dollar.
34. Identify and explain biases that overstate and understate inflation.
35. Explain the importance of the CPI.
36. Recognize and explain the importance of special index numbers and deflators.
37. Define, calculate, interpret, utilize, and explain the importance of the inflation rate.
38. Define and explain the importance of disinflation.
39. Identify and explain the consequences of inflation.
40. Identify and discuss the relationships between inflation and wages, inflation and wealth, and inflation and political stability.
41. Explain how inflation redistributes wealth.

Review Terms

macroeconomics
aggregate
stabilization function of government
inflation
unemployment
communism
capitalism
three basic economic questions
microeconomics vs. macroeconomics
microeconomic unemployment
macroeconomic unemployment
supply

demand
real vs. nominal values
positive vs. negative slopes
opportunity cost
market
equilibrium
disequilibrium
movement along a curve vs. shift of a curve
production possibilities
price control
shortage
wealth
economic growth

Important Terms and Concepts

bullionism
mercantilism
business cycle
Karl Marx
recession
the Great Depression

John Maynard Keynes
Keynesian theory
labor-supply curve
real wage rate
nominal wage rate
underemployment

overemployment
full employment
demand curve for labor
unemployment rate
labor force
job search
discouraged worker
seasonal unemployment
frictional unemployment
structural unemployment
cyclical unemployment
seasonally adjusted data
employment rate
labor-force participation rate
inflation
index number
base point
general price level

Gross National Product (GNP)
current dollars
nominal values
implicit price deflator for GNP
deflator
current-dollar GNP
constant-dollar GNP
real values
Consumer Price Index (CPI)
CPI-U
CPI-W
purchasing power of the dollar
reciprocal
cost-of-living adjustment (COLA)
buyer-response bias
inflation rate
disinflation
deflation

Completion

Labor, unemployment rate

In terms of the monthly statistics computed by the U.S. Department of _____ , the _____ is the percentage of the labor force that is unemployed. In order to be counted among the unemployed, a person must be a member of the

labor force

_____ . This means that he or she must be nonin-

16

stitutionalized, at least _____ years of age, and working or

actively seeking work

_____ . Any member of the labor force who is working regularly, part time or full time, is

employed

counted as _____ . A person who is not working and who has given up looking for a job, a labor-force dropout, is

discouraged worker, is not

called a _____ and _____ (is/is not) counted as unemployed.
    Economists typically classify unemployment into four groups:

seasonal, frictional, structural

_____ , _____ , _____ ,

cyclical

and _____ . The Santa Clauses and Easter bunnies hired by department stores for holiday periods are apt to experience

seasonal

_____ unemployment at other times of the year.

can

Because this type of unemployment follows a pattern, it _____ (can/cannot) be predicted fairly accurately. Short-term unemploy-

frictional	ment associated with information and mobility costs is _____ unemployment. Because this type of unemployment is experienced when people first enter (or reenter) the labor market or are changing
is not	jobs, it _____ (is/is not) considered to be a problem. Unemployment associated with technological change or changes in the
structural	specific goods and services that people buy is called _____
microeconomic	unemployment. This type of _____ (microeconomic/macroeconomic) unemployment comes about when specific jobs become obsolete or when people do not meet the requirements for existing jobs. Since structural unemployment affects unskilled
training	workers, one approach to reducing it is through _____
is not	programs. Structural unemployment _____ (is/is not) limited
can also	to unskilled workers; it _____ (can also/can never) affect skilled workers. Finally, when unemployment affects the entire economy rather than particular industries or groups it is
cyclical	_____ unemployment. This type of unemployment
macroeconomic	is _____ (microeconomic/macroeconomic).

The government publishes other important employment data in addition to the unemployment rate. Civilian employment as a percentage of the total noninstitutionalized population, or the

employment	_____ rate, may be less ambiguous than the unemployment rate, because it does not require the determination of
actively seeking work	whether an individual is _____ . Changes in the percentage of the total noninstitutionalized popula-
labor-force participation	tion that is working or looking for work, the _____ rate, help explain how employment and unemployment can increase at the same time.

When economists refer to the problem of inflation they mean a

increase in the general price level	significant and sustained _____ .

When prices, income, and the value of output are reported in current dollars we are dealing with

nominal	rent dollars we are dealing with _____ (nominal/real)
real	values. In order to determine _____ (nominal/real)
general price level	values, we must correct for changes in the _____ .
average	To do this, we must first measure _____ prices and
index number	then compare these values using an _____ system. To
current price	compute a price index number, divide the _____ by

base period price   the _____ and then multiply
by 100.

The index number used to compare current-dollar Gross National Product expenditures with the amount that would have been needed to purchase the same goods at base-year prices is called the

implicit price
deflator for GNP   _____ . The
index number that is generally used to reflect the cost of living is

Consumer Price
Index   called the _____ . The reciprocal of this

purchasing power
of the dollar   index number is used to estimate the _____
for consumer goods.

Inflation tends to redistribute income and wealth as well as to create insecurity. But, in terms of economic analysis, perhaps the most significant consequences arise when people feel they have to

price level change
factor   incorporate a _____
in their daily economic decisions. Because labor is the main input in

wage   production, this adjustment factor is often included in _____
negotiations. The adjustment factor is incorporated in investment

real   spending when the business person compares the _____ rate

real   of return with the _____ rate of interest. Household consumption and saving decisions are also likely to be adjusted as a result of inflation. If households anticipate continued inflation, they may be inclined to buy before the anticipated price increases. This type of

additional   response tends to result in _____ (additional/less) inflation in the future. The increase in consumption means that

decrease   saving will _____ (increase/decrease), perhaps leading to a decrease in investment. If investment decreases, there may be a decrease in production and economic growth in the long run. Of course, households may respond to inflation by consuming less and

more   saving _____ (more/less). This behavior is likely to

counteract   _____ (reinforce/counteract) inflationary pressure. Finally, government is also affected by inflation and must attempt to make adjustments for the price increases. With progressive income taxes, higher nominal incomes push taxpayers into higher tax-rate

bracket creep   brackets. This process is referred to as _____ .

indexed   It can be eliminated if the tax system is _____ . Without

loss of   indexing, taxpayers experience a _____ (gain in/loss of) real income.

Problems and Applications

Use the following graph to answer problem 1.

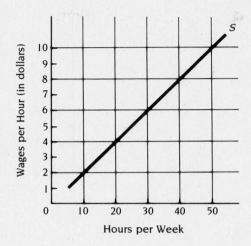

1. Consider an individual's supply of labor as given in the preceding graph.
   a. How many hours per week would this individual be available for work at a wage of $6 per hour?
   b. If, at a wage of $8 an hour, an employer insisted that the individual work 45 hours per week, would the individual be underemployed, fully employed, or overemployed?
   c. If, at a wage of $10 per hour, an employer would hire this worker for 40 hours per week, would the individual be underemployed, fully employed, or overemployed?
   d. Assume that the individual has just moved and really needs additional income to afford a new home. Draw the individual's new labor supply curve (S_1) if at any given wage the individual will now work 10 more hours per week than before. Is this an increase or a decrease in supply? If the wage is $8 an hour and the employer insists that the individual work 45 hours per week, would the individual be underemployed, fully employed, or overemployed?
   e. Assume that the individual has just graduated from college and believes that for any number of hours she should be paid $2 more per hour than on the original supply curve. Draw the individual's new labor supply curve (S_2). Is this an increase or a decrease in supply?

Use the table below to answer problem 2.

Wages per Hour	Number of Workers Demanded	Number of Workers Supplied
$2	175	20
4	125	50
6	75	75
8	20	150

2. Consider the labor market described in the table above.
   a. How many people will be demanded for work if the wage is $2 per hour? $6 per hour? $8 per hour?
   b. How many people will be available for work if the wage is $2 per hour? $6 per hour? $8 per hour?
   c. How many people will be employed if the wage is $2 per hour? $6 per hour? $8 per hour?

Use the following graph to answer problem 3.

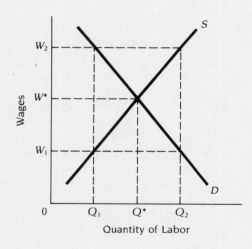

3. Consider the labor market described in the preceding graph.
   a. What is the equilibrium wage? How many units of labor will be hired at equilibrium?
   b. If the wage is W_1, what is the quantity of labor demanded? What is the quantity supplied? How many units of labor will be hired at W_1?

c. If the wage is W_2, what quantity of labor is demanded? What quantity of labor is supplied? How many units of labor will be hired at a wage of W_2?

Use the following graph to answer problem 4.

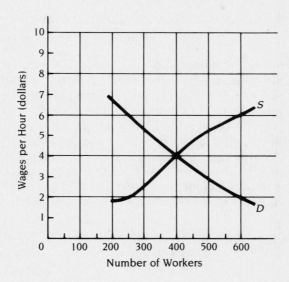

4. Consider the labor market described in the graph above.
    a. What is the equilibrium wage? How many people will be employed at the equilibrium wage?
    b. If the wage is $2 per hour, how many people will be available for work? How many jobs will be available? How many people will be employed? Is there a shortage, or a surplus of labor? Interpret this shortage or surplus of labor in terms of unemployment or job vacancies.
    c. If the wage is $6 per hour, how many people will be available for work? How many jobs will be available? How many people will be employed? Is there a shortage, or a surplus of labor? Interpret this shortage or surplus of labor in terms of unemployment or job vacancies.

Use the following table to answer problems 5 and 6.

1970 Data for Economy X

Noninstitutionalized population	400
Size of labor force	300
Number of people employed full time	150
Number of people employed part time	50
Number of discouraged workers	25

5. Consider Economy X, described in the preceding table.
    a. How many people in Economy X would be unemployed from an official standpoint? What is the official unemployment rate?
    b. What is the employment rate?
    c. What is the labor-force participation rate?
    d. Assume that the discouraged workers have started looking for jobs but have not as yet found employment. What is the new size of the labor force? What is the labor-force participation rate? What is the unemployment rate? What is the employment rate?

6. Consider Economy X as originally described in the above table. By 1980 there had been an increase in population of 100, of which 60 were employed and 30 unemployed. In 1980, what was the size of the labor force? What was the labor-force participation rate? What was the employment rate? What was the unemployment rate?

7. Assume that the 1970 current-dollar GNP was $200 and the 1980 current-dollar GNP was $400.
    a. What was the 1970 nominal GNP?
    b. What was the 1980 nominal GNP?
    c. If prices remained constant between 1970 and 1980, what happened to real GNP?
    d. If prices doubled between 1970 and 1980, what happened to real GNP?
    e. If prices more than doubled between 1970 and 1980, what happened to real GNP?

Use the table below to answer problem 8.

Products	Prices per Unit		Production	
	1972	1974	1972	1974
X	$1	$1	15	20
Y	$1	$2	5	8
Z	$2	$4	10	11

8. Consider the economy described in the table above. Assume that for the years given, the economy produced only products X, Y, and Z.
   a. Compute the economy's 1972 current-dollar GNP.
   b. Compute the economy's 1974 current-dollar GNP.
   c. What is the economy's 1972 nominal GNP?
   d. What is the economy's 1974 nominal GNP?
   e. Compute the economy's 1972 constant-dollar GNP with 1972 as the base year.
   f. Compute the economy's 1974 constant-dollar GNP with 1972 as the base year.
   g. Explain what happened to real GNP between 1972 and 1974.

Use the table below to answer problem 9.

Products	Prices per Unit		Production
	Base Year	Current Year	Current Year
P	$1	$2	150
Q	$3	$3	100
R	$6	$7	50

9. Consider the economy described in the table above. Assume that, for the years indicated, the economy produced only products P, Q, and R.
   a. Compute the economy's current-dollar GNP.
   b. Compute the economy's constant-dollar GNP.
   c. What is the economy's nominal GNP?
   d. What is the economy's real GNP?
   e. What is the implicit price deflator?

Use the following table to answer problem 10.

Product	Prices per Unit Base Year	Prices per Unit Current Year
X	$1.00	$3.50
Y	$1.50	$3.00
Z	$2.00	$5.50

10. Consider an economy in which the representative market basket of consumer goods and services contains 100 units of X, 200 units of Y, and 100 units of Z. Assume the base year and current year prices indicated in the table above.
   a. Compute the Consumer Price Index based on the representative market basket indicated above.
   b. What does this index number mean? By how much has the cost of living increased?
   c. What is the purchasing power of the dollar?

11. Consider the following table, indicating the Consumer Price Index for Economy X between 1975 and 1980:

Year	CPI	Year	CPI
1975	91	1978	105
1976	97	1979	107
1977	100	1980	110

   a. What was the rate of inflation between 1977 and 1979?
   b. What was the purchasing power of a 1977 dollar in 1979?
   c. What was the rate of inflation between 1975 and 1976?
   d. What was the rate of inflation between 1978 and 1980?

True-False   Indicate whether each of the following statements is basically true or false. If the statement is false, rewrite it so that it is true.

_____ 1. Bullionism was a form of macroeconomics concerned with how to accumulate treasure.

_____ 2. Mercantilism was concerned with regulating foreign trade in an effort to strengthen an economy.

_____ 3. Changes in economic activity over time are measured by business cycles.

_____ 4. Karl Marx argued that business cycles, which he claimed were inherent in capitalism, would prevent the downfall of capitalist economic systems.

_____ 5. Keynesian economics developed during the 1970s to explain the major economic problem of the decade, which was rising unemployment accompanied by inflation.

_____ 6. In official terms, someone is unemployed whenever he or she is not working.

_____ 7. Macroeconomic unemployment singles out certain groups or occupations in an economy.

_____ 8. Microeconomic unemployment is unemployment associated with answers to the basic economic questions of what and how to produce goods.

_____ 9. Appropriate training and relocation of the unemployed are likely to be successful remedies for macroeconomic unemployment.

_____ 10. To an economist, unemployment or underemployment occur when a person spends less time in wage earning than desired at the going wage rate.

_____ 11. If the nominal wage rate were to remain constant, inflation would cause the real wage rate to increase.

_____ 12. A positively sloped labor-supply curve suggests that people are less willing to sacrifice leisure time as the real wage rate increases.

_____ 13. A wage represents the opportunity cost of leisure.

_____ 14. When wages rates are high, leisure time is relatively cheap.

_____ 15. A person's labor-supply curve indicates that person's willingness to exchange leisure time for income.

_____ 16. At a given real wage rate, a person is underemployed if she is working fewer hours than desired at that wage or if her training and skills are not fully utilized.

_____ 17. At a given real wage rate, a person is overemployed if he is enjoying less leisure time than desired at that wage.

_____ 18. A demand curve for labor indicates the willingness of employers to hire workers.

_____ 19. Equilibrium in a labor market occurs at full employment, regardless of one's definition of full employment.

_____ 20. The unemployment rate is equal to the number of unemployed persons divided by the number of persons in the labor force.

_____ 21. During the Great Depression, the official unemployment rate approached 25%.

_____ 22. In terms of official statistics, a discouraged worker is counted as unemployed.

_____ 23. If an unemployment statistic is seasonally adjusted, seasonal unemployment has been added to it so that the statistic will measure full or total unemployment.

_____ 24. Frictional unemployment is not considered to be a serious problem.

_____ 25. During good economic times, a factory worker who loses a job to automation is most likely cyclically unemployed.

_____ 26. Cyclical unemployment is microeconomic in nature, because it singles out particular industries.

_____ 27. The unemployment rate is highest for teenagers (especially for members of minorities) and lowest for white adult males.

_____ 28. The economic cost of unemployment is the lost output that can never be replaced.

_____ 29. The employment rate and the unemployment rate cannot increase simultaneously.

_____ 30. The labor-force participation rate is the percentage of the total noninstitutionalized population that is working or looking for work.

_____ 31. Recent population statistics suggest that, by the end of the century, the ratio of workers to retirees will decline.

_____ 32. Inflation is said to exist when relative prices are rising.

_____ 33. Inflation occurs whenever there has been a significant and sustained increase in the general price level.

_____ 34. An index number measures a change or deviation from some reference point.

_____ 35. The nominal GNP is measured in base-period prices.

_____ 36. The implicit price deflator for the GNP is an index number.

_____ 37. The Consumer Price Index is an index number used to measure changes in the cost of purchasing a specific group of consumer goods and services.

_____ 38. The estimated purchasing power of the dollar for consumer goods is the sum of the CPI-W and the CPI-U.

_____ 39. The buyer response bias and the quality bias both tend to overstate the impact of inflation on the cost of living.

_____ 40. There are a number of special-purpose index numbers that are used to predict future changes in consumer prices.

_____ 41. The index number for any given base year is 100.

_____ 42. If the price index number of period two is 190, prices have increased by 190%.

_____ 43. In terms of the Consumer Price Index, the rate of inflation for a given time period is the rate of change in the CPI for that time period.

Multiple Choice   Choose the *one best* answer in each of the following cases:

_____   1. Which of the following is true of the Great Depression?
  a. The major economic problem was unemployment.
  b. Keynesian economics provided a theoretical explanation of the causes of unemployment under capitalism.
  c. The Depression was basically limited to the U.S. economy.
  d. all of the above
  e. a and b above

_____   2. During the 1970s, most major industrial countries experienced
  a. full employment and inflation.
  b. full employment and deflation.
  c. rising unemployment and inflation.
  d. rising unemployment and deflation.
  e. rising unemployment and stable prices.

_____   3. An individual's labor-supply curve most likely shows the number of hours per week that the person
  a. is actually working.
  b. is available for work at different real wage rates, *ceteris paribus.*
  c. would be hired to work at different real wage rates, *ceteris paribus.*
  d. would be hired to work at different nominal wage rates, *ceteris paribus.*
  e. has to work in order to earn different levels of income, *ceteris paribus.*

_____   4. The supply curve of labor
  a. may be negatively sloped at the microeconomic level.
  b. may be positively sloped at the microeconomic level.
  c. is likely to be positively sloped at the macroeconomic level.
  d. all of the above
  e. both b and c above

Use the graph below to answer questions 5 and 6.

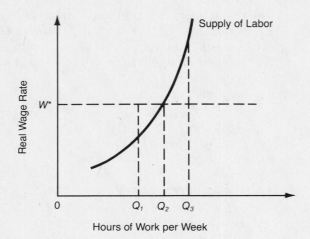

5. Consider the individual labor-supply curve in the graph above. At a real wage rate of W* the individual will be
   a. employed for Q_1 hours of work per week.
   b. employed for Q_2 hours of work per week.
   c. fully employed if he is working Q_2 hours per week.
   d. underemployed if he is working Q_2 hours per week.
   e. b and c above

6. According to the individual labor-supply curve in the graph above, the individual
   a. is willing to sacrifice more leisure time for income as the real wage rate increases.
   b. will attempt to work overtime when the real wage rate declines.
   c. does not consider the real wage rate to be the opportunity cost of leisure.
   d. will be hired to work more hours per week as the real wage rate increases.
   e. none of the above

7. For any given real wage rate, a person is
   a. fully employed whenever he is on his labor demand curve.
   b. fully employed whenever she is on her labor supply curve.
   c. unemployed whenever he is not on his labor demand curve.
   d. unemployed whenever she is not on her labor supply curve.
   e. both b and d above

_____ 8. The event that is *least* likely to cause a shift in the demand curve
for labor is a change in
a. the real wage rate.
b. the productivity of labor.
c. the availability of substitute resources.
d. demand for the good being produced by the labor.
e. none of the above

_____ 9. Equilibrium in a given labor market occurs
a. whenever there is equilibrium in the economy.
b. only when there is equilibrium in the economy.
c. only when there is full employment in the economy.
d. whenever there is equilibrium in the associated product
markets.
e. none of the above

_____ 10. If the current real wage rate exceeds the equilibrium real wage
rate in a specific labor market, one can accurately conclude that
a. there is unemployment.
b. there are job vacancies.
c. the government has set a minimum wage.
d. the government should set a wage ceiling.
e. the equilibrium real wage rate will decrease.

_____ 11. If the equilibrium real wage rate exceeds the current real wage
rate, one can accurately conclude that
a. there is unemployment.
b. there are job vacancies.
c. the government has set a minimum wage.
d. the government should set a wage ceiling.
e. the equilibrium real wage rate will decrease.

Use the graph below to answer questions 12 and 13.

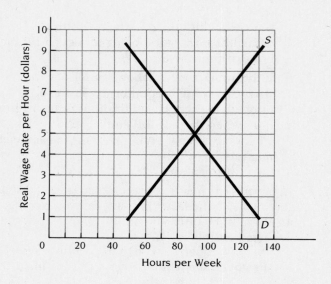

12. Consider the labor market described by the graph above. When the market is in equilibrium the real wage rate will be
   a. $1 per hour and there will be no unemployment.
   b. $9 per hour and there will be no unemployment.
   c. $5 per hour and 90 hours of labor per week will be hired.
   d. $5 per hour and there will be 40 hours of unemployed labor.
   e. impossible to determine, but there will be no unemployment.

13. Which of the following statements is true of the labor market described by the graph above.
   a. At a wage of $1 per hour, 130 hours of labor will be hired.
   b. At a wage of $2 per hour, 120 hours of labor will be available for work.
   c. At a wage of $7 per hour, 70 hours of labor will be hired.
   d. At a wage of $8 per hour, 90 hours of labor will be hired.
   e. At a wage of $8 per hour, 60 hours of labor will be hired and there will be a shortage of 60 hours of labor.

Use the graph below to answer question 14.

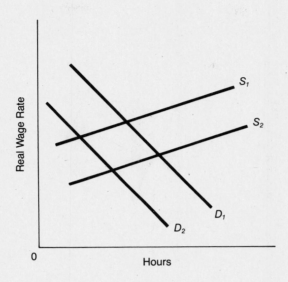

_____ 14. Consider the labor market described by the graph above. Assume that the original demand and supply curves are given by D_1 and S_1, respectively, and that the current demand and supply curves are given by D_2 and S_2, respectively. Given this, which of the following statements is true?

a. The supply of labor has decreased.

b. The equilibrium real wage rate has decreased.

c. For any given real wage rate, employers will be willing and able to hire more hours of labor now than before.

d. both a and b above

e. all of the above

Use the graph below to answer questions 15 and 16.

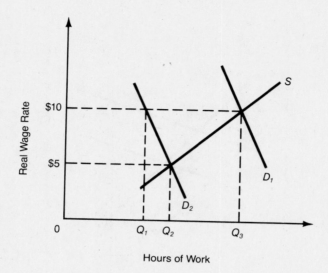

15. Consider the labor market described in the graph above. Assume
    that the market is initially in equilibrium with a real wage rate of
    $10 per hour and Q_3 hours of work hired. If the demand for
    labor shifts from D_1 to D_2,
    a. the supply of labor will decrease to Q_1.
    b. the supply of labor will decrease to Q_2.
    c. the quantity of labor supplied will eventually decrease to Q_2
       if the new equilibrium wage rate of $5 is established.
    d. the quantity of labor supplied will decrease to Q_2 regardless
       of what happens to the real wage rate.
    e. c and d above

16. Consider the labor market described by the graph above. Assume
    that the market is initially in equilibrium with a real wage rate of
    $10 per hour and Q_3 hours of work hired. If the demand for
    labor shifts from D_1 to D_2, there will be
    a. unemployment of $(Q_3 - Q_2)$ hours of work if the wage drops
       to $5.
    b. unemployment of $(Q_3 - Q_1)$ hours of work if workers refuse
       to accept a wage cut.
    c. unemployment of $(Q_2 - Q_1)$ hours of work if workers refuse
       to accept a wage cut.
    d. full employment, regardless of the workers' willingness to
       accept a wage cut.
    e. none of the above.

_____ 17. Which of the following individuals would be counted as part of a labor force?
  a. a discouraged worker
  b. a prisoner who makes license plates for the state
  c. a 14-year-old girl with a paper route
  d. a housewife looking for a job outside the home
  e. a househusband who prefers not to work outside the home

_____ 18. According to the official statistics, in order for a person to be counted as unemployed, that person must be
  a. at least 18 years old.
  b. less than 65 years old.
  c. part of the labor force.
  d. all of the above
  e. none of the above

_____ 19. Seasonal unemployment is
  a. macroeconomic unemployment.
  b. the type of unemployment associated with business cycles.
  c. a result of the costs associated with acquiring information.
  d. common in occupations where workers are needed only part of each year.
  e. difficult to predict with accuracy, since seasonal needs tend to change throughout the year.

_____ 20. The short-term unemployment experienced by an individual between jobs is
  a. cyclical unemployment.
  b. frictional unemployment.
  c. intermediate unemployment.
  d. seasonal unemployment.
  e. structural unemployment.

_____ 21. Frictional unemployment is
  a. likely to be severe because it is of long duration.
  b. the subject of a considerable amount of public policy.
  c. likely to lead to cyclical unemployment if it lasts long enough.
  d. a result of imperfect information and mobility.
  e. macroeconomic or microeconomic unemployment, depending on the number of people involved.

_____ 22. Structural unemployment is
   a. likely to decrease during times of great technological change.
   b. unemployment that occurs when worker qualifications do not match job requirements.
   c. unemployment that is limited to the housing and building industries.
   d. generally considered desirable, since it is most often associated with voluntary job changes.
   e. likely to increase with improvements in the collection and dissemination of job information.

_____ 23. Which of the following is correct with respect to structural unemployment?
   a. It may be the result of discrimination.
   b. It is generally considered to be a more serious problem than frictional unemployment.
   c. It may be reduced by on-the-job training programs.
   d. It may be reduced by policies to relocate workers.
   e. all of the above

_____ 24. Cyclical unemployment is
   a. microeconomic unemployment.
   b. neither microeconomic nor macroeconomic unemployment.
   c. associated with recessions and depressions.
   d. unemployment that occurs in isolated sectors or industries in the economy.
   e. accurately measured by measuring the duration of unemployment.

_____ 25. Unemployment statistics for the United States from 1970 through 1980 reveal that
   a. unemployment rates tend to be highest for persons sixteen to nineteen years old.
   b. during bad economic times, unemployment rates tend to increase among all groups except adult males.
   c. during good economic times, unemployment rates tend to decrease among all groups except black females.
   d. all of the above
   e. unemployment tends to be spread equally among different groups in the economy.

_____ 26. The costs of unemployment
   a. tend to be insignificant for structural unemployment.
   b. tend to be microeconomic rather than macroeconomic in nature.
   c. tend to be macroeconomic rather than microeconomic in nature.

    d. include the output that is not produced as a result of the unemployment.

    e. tend to be insignificant because any losses during periods of unemployment can be recouped during better economic times.

_____ 27. The employment rate is

    a. 1 – unemployment rate.

    b. 1/(unemployment rate).

    c. (total employment)/(total population).

    d. (civilian employment)/(civilian labor force).

    e. none of the above

_____ 28. The labor force participation rate is

    a. the same as the employment rate.

    b. the percentage of the labor force that is working.

    c. both a and b above

    d. the percentage of the total noninstitutionalized population that is working.

    e. equal to the civilian labor force divided by the noninstitutionalized population.

_____ 29. Inflation may be defined as

    a. high prices.

    b. an increase in the money supply.

    c. an increase in the general price level.

    d. a permanent increase in relative prices.

    e. a temporary increase in relative prices.

_____ 30. The general price level is

    a. the average price.

    b. the current price.

    c. the base-period price.

    d. an index number.

    e. a and d above.

_____ 31. Deflation is

    a. defined as low prices.

    b. never considered a serious economic problem.

    c. likely to result in an increase in the purchasing power of the dollar.

    d. not likely to redistribute income and wealth in an economy.

    e. likely to occur whenever there are changes in the relative prices of goods.

_____ 32. Assume that the index number for the base period is 1. To calculate the base-year equivalent of a particular price, one should
a. divide the price by its index number.
b. multiply the price by its index number.
c. add the price to its index number.
d. add the price to its index number and divide by 100.
e. divide the price by 100.

_____ 33. Assume that the index number for the base period is 1. If the price of a good is $12 in time period five and the index number for period five is 6, the base-year equivalent price of the good is
a. $0.50.
b. $2.00.
c. $18.00.
d. $36.00.
e. $72.00.

_____ 34. Assume that the index number for the base period is 100. If the index number in period two is 150, then, on average, prices in period two are
a. $0.50 higher than in the base period.
b. $0.75 higher than in the base period.
c. $1.50 higher than in the base period.
d. 50% higher than in the base period.
e. 150% higher than in the base period.

_____ 35. Assume that the index number for the base period is 100. If the current price of good X is $10, the index number is
a. 200 if the base-period price was $5.
b. 200 if the base-period price was $20.
c. 10, regardless of the base-period price.
d. 110, regardless of the base-period price.
e. none of the above.

_____ 36. Assume that the index number for the base period is 100. If the current price of a good is $5 and the base-period price of the good was $20, the index number for the current period is
a. 4.
b. 5.
c. 25.
d. 400.
e. 500.

_____ 37. Price index numbers
   a. require the selection of a base period.
   b. may be used to convert nominal prices to real prices.
   c. may be used to compare prices between two time periods.
   d. are equal to 100 times the current price divided by the base period price.
   e. all of the above

_____ 38. The implicit price deflator for the GNP
   a. is useful only in times of deflation.
   b. converts constant dollars to real dollars.
   c. compares current-dollar GNP with the amount that would have been needed to purchase the same goods at prices existing in some base year.
   d. is determined by dividing real GNP by the expenditure that would have been required to purchase the same goods and services in the base period.
   e. all of the above

_____ 39. If current-dollar GNP is $500 and base-year GNP is $250, what is the implicit price deflator for GNP?
   a. 50
   b. 150
   c. 200
   d. 1250
   e. It cannot be determined from the information given.

_____ 40. Consider an economy that only produces goods X, Y, and Z. During the current year, the economy will produce 100 units of X, 50 units of Y, and 150 units of Z. The current-year prices for X, Y, and Z are $3, $2, and $2, respectively. The base-year prices for X, Y, and Z are $2.50, $2, and $1, respectively. Which of the following is correct?
   a. Current-dollar GNP is $700.
   b. Constant-dollar GNP is $500.
   c. Nominal GNP is $700.
   d. The implicit price deflator for GNP is 140.
   e. all of the above

_____ 41. In general, nominal values are
   a. real values.
   b. constant-dollar values.
   c. current-dollar values.
   d. inflated values.
   e. base-year values.

_____ 42. In general, constant-dollar values are
   a. real values.
   b. nominal values.
   c. current-dollar values.
   d. deflated values.
   e. none of the above

_____ 43. Which of the following is true with respect to real and nominal values?
   a. When prices are rising, real GNP must also rise.
   b. Real national income must rise when nominal GNP is rising.
   c. An increase in nominal values implies an increase in real values.
   d. An increase in real values implies an increase in nominal values.
   e. Constant dollar GNP is a real GNP concept, whereas current-dollar GNP is a nominal concept.

_____ 44. The Consumer Price Index is
   a. equivalent to the purchasing power of the dollar.
   b. an index number used to measure changes in the cost of living.
   c. based on the collection of goods and services actually purchased by U.S. households in the previous year.
   d. all of the above.
   e. based on the same collection of goods and services as the GNP deflator.

_____ 45. If the current-year cost of a typical market basket is $400 and the base-year cost of the same basket is $500, the Consumer Price Index is
   a. 80.
   b. 100.
   c. 125.
   d. 200.
   e. impossible to determine from the information given.

_____ 46. If the CPI-U is 150, one can conclude that
   a. the purchasing power of the dollar is $0.67.
   b. the cost of the market basket in the current year is 1.5 times its cost in the base year.
   c. the cost of living has increased 50%.
   d. all of the above
   e. none of the above

_____ 47. Which of the following is true regarding the Consumer Price Index?
  a. It fails to recognize that consumers respond to changes in relative prices.
  b. To the extent that there is a quality bias, it tends to understate the actual impact of inflation.
  c. There are actually two indexes, one based on purchases by wage earners and clerical workers (the CPI-W) and one based on purchases by adult consumers (the CPI-A).
  d. all of the above
  e. none of the above

_____ 48. Historical data for the U.S. economy indicate that the
  a. GNP deflator more than tripled between 1965 and 1980.
  b. longest period of serious inflation was between 1965 and 1980.
  c. longest period of serious inflation was between 1940 and 1948.
  d. longest period of serious inflation was between 1909 and 1929.
  e. both a and b above

_____ 49. Disinflation refers to
  a. a decreasing rate of inflation.
  b. a decrease in the general price level.
  c. index numbers less than 100.
  d. a period in which the average price is falling.
  e. none of the above

_____ 50. The consequences of inflation may include
  a. a redistribution of income and wealth.
  b. an adjustment for inflation in daily economic decisions.
  c. bracket sweep if progressive income taxes are not indexed.
  d. additional inflation if people build expectations of continued inflation into their economic decisions.
  e. all of the above

_____ 51. Inflation that is not anticipated or that is greater than anticipated tends to redistribute income and wealth in favor of people
  a. who owe money.
  b. who lend money.
  c. with money in savings accounts.
  d. living on fixed nominal incomes.
  e. none of the above

Discussion Questions

1. In microeconomics you will learn that part of an individual's labor-supply curve may have a negative slope. Can you think of any reasons why this might be the case?

2. Your text illustrates how a decrease in the demand for labor can result in unemployment if workers refuse to accept a wage cut or fail to realize that the equilibrium wage rate has decreased. (See Figure 6-2.) Explain how an inmigration of workers may similarly result in unemployment if workers refuse to accept a wage cut or fail to realize that the equilibrium wage has decreased.

3. Explain how a person who works forty hours per week might be overemployed. Conversely, explain how someone working forty hours per week might be underemployed.

4. a. Do you think discouraged workers should be counted in computing the unemployment rate? What differences would this make?
   b. Do you think the discouraged-worker effect is more or less pronounced if there is greater unemployment? Why?

5. a. Do you think we should increase the minimum age associated with defining the labor force? What differences would this make?
   b. Do you think there should be a maximum age associated with a definition of the labor force? What differences would it make? What are the implications for public policy?

6. With the rise of automated production processes, we have commonly heard that "automation does not lead to unemployment. Someone has to produce the machines that replace the workers." Analyze this statement in terms of what you have learned about unemployment.

7. Do you think unemployment imposes fewer hardships today than it did in the 1930s? Explain.

8. Is it possible for the unemployment rate and the employment rate to increase simultaneously? Why or why not? Which do you think is a better measure of the economic state of the labor market? Explain.

9. How do you think the population makeup of the unemployed will change over the next fifty years? Explain.

10. Discuss the problems associated with attempting to compare the GNP of an economy from one time period with that of another. How might you avoid some of these problems?

11. Do you think unemployment or inflation imposes the greatest costs on society? Would your answer differ with different rates

of unemployment and inflation? Would your answer be different
if you were unemployed?

12. In Chapter 5 you studied the meaning and effects of price controls. What do you think of using price controls as a way to
fight inflation? What problems would you foresee with this
approach?

Answers   *Problems and Applications*

1. a. 30 hours   b. overemployed   c. underemployed
   d. increase in supply; underemployed
   e. decrease in supply

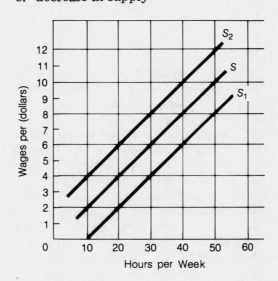

2. a. 175; 75; 20   b. 20; 75; 150   c. 20; 75; 20
3. a. $W*$; $Q*$ b. Q_2; Q_1; Q_1 c. Q_1; Q_2; Q_1
4. a. \$4; 400
   b. 250; 600; 250; shortage of labor; 350 job vacancies
   c. 600; 250; 250; surplus of labor; 350 people unemployed
5. a. 100; 33.3%   b. 50%   c. 75%
   d. 325; 81.25%; 38.5%; 50%
6. 390; 78%; 52%; 33%
7. a. \$200   b. \$400   c. It doubled.
   d. It remained the same.
   e. It decreased.

8. a. $40   b. $80   c. $40   d. $80   e. $40   f. $50
   g. Real GNP increased. Constant-dollar GNP is a real GNP statistic, and it increased from $40 to $50. Also, actual production levels in the two years show that production increased for all three products.

9. a. $950   b. $750   c. $950   d. $750   e. 126.7

10. a. 250
    b. The representative market basket costs 2.5 times what it cost in the base year. The cost of living has increased 150%.
    c. $0.40

11. a. 7%   b. $0.93   c. 6.6%   d. 4.8%

True-False

1. T.
2. T.
3. T.
4. F. Karl Marx argued that business cycles, which he claimed were inherent in capitalism, would eventually lead to the downfall of capitalist economic systems. The downfall would occur when recessions became so severe that the rising number of unemployed would overthrow the system.
5. F. Keynesian economics developed during the 1930s when there was widespread unemployment; Keynes did not address the major economic problem of the 1970s—rising unemployment accompanied by inflation.
6. F. In official terms, someone is unemployed if that person is a member of the labor force and is not working but is actively seeking work.
7. F. Macroeconomic unemployment tends to affect the entire economy rather than singling out certain groups or occupations in the economy.
8. T.
9. F. Appropriate training and relocation of the unemployed are likely to be successful remedies for microeconomic unemployment.
10. T.
11. F. If the nominal wage rate remains constant, inflation would cause the real wage rate to decrease.
12. F. A labor-supply curve that is positively sloped suggests that people are more willing to sacrifice leisure time as the real wage rate increases.
13. T.

14. F. When wage rates are high, leisure time is relatively expensive.
15. T.
16. T.
17. T.
18. T.
19. F. Equilibrium in a labor market occurs at the intersection of the labor demand and supply curves.
20. T.
21. T.
22. F. In terms of official statistics, a discouraged worker is not counted as unemployed, because when someone quits looking for a job that person ceases to be part of the labor force.
23. F. If an unemployment statistic is seasonally adjusted, the seasonal component has been smoothed out so that direct month-to-month or year-to-year comparisons can be made for other types of unemployment.
24. T.
25. F. During good economic times, a factory worker who loses a job to automation is most likely structurally unemployed.
26. F. Cyclical unemployment is macroeconomic in nature, because it tends to affect the entire economy rather than singling out particular industries.
27. T.
28. T.
29. F. The employment rate and the unemployment rate can increase simultaneously.
30. T.
31. T.
32. F. Inflation exists when the general price level rises.
33. T.
34. T.
35. F. The nominal GNP is measured in current prices.
36. T.
37. T.
38. F. The estimated purchasing power of the dollar for consumer goods is the reciprocal of the CPI or, more specifically, the reciprocal of the CPI-U.
39. T.
40. T.
41. T.
42. F. If the price index number for period two is 190, prices have increased by 90%.
43. T.

Multiple Choice

1. e	2. c	3. b	4. d	5. c
6. a	7. b	8. a	9. e	10. a
11. b	12. c	13. c	14. b	15. c
16. b	17. d	18. c	19. d	20. b
21. d	22. b	23. e	24. c	25. a
26. d	27. e	28. e	29. c	30. a
31. c	32. a	33. b	34. d	35. a
36. c	37. e	38. c	39. c	40. e
41. c	42. a	43. e	44. b	45. a
46. d	47. a	48. b	49. a	50. e
51. a				

7 *National Income Accounting*

Summary

The U.S. Department of Commerce is responsible for the collection, refinement, and dissemination of national income and product data for the United States. The national income accounting system divides the data into three major sections: the national product section, the national income section, and the personal income section.

National product reports the total amount of money spent for all goods and services produced in the economy during a given time period. The most familiar statistic in this section is the Gross National Product, which includes personal consumption spending, investment spending, government purchases, and net exports. (It is important to note the differences between government spending, government purchases, and government transfer payments. Government purchases refers to government spending to buy goods and services. Government transfer payments are a different form of government spending, in which no goods or services are directly exchanged.) The potential problem of double counting is avoided by using final sales values or value-added data. Another important statistic in the national product section is the net national product, which estimates the net gain from all production during a given time period.

National income reports income earned by the owners of resources used in producing goods and services during a given time period. This income is tabulated to reflect compensation of employees, proprietors' income, rental income of persons, corporate profits, and net interest.

The personal income section of the national income accounting system reports data to indicate the amount of money received by households during a given time period. Earned income and money received are distinguished in accordance with whether or not the households allowed resources they owned to be used in the production of goods and services. The personal income section also reports a statistic called disposable personal income, which is personal income minus personal taxes. Disposable personal income is further described in terms of how it is used: personal consumption, personal saving, and personal transfer payments (interest paid to business and transfers to foreigners).

There are a number of problems associated with our national income accounting system. For example, most do-it-yourself and underground productive activities are not included, even though they result in the production of goods and services. And since the national accounts are measured in accordance with market values, changes in prices over time can also create complications. Additional problems arise when one attempts to find a measure of social welfare and progress. One of the major concerns in this area deals with environmental issues. The economy has not progressed by as much as it might seem if, for example, much of the productive output of the economy is used to clean up pollution. Production associated with war and violence causes similar concerns. These issues are particularly difficult to resolve because of their normative nature.

Major Objectives   After you have finished this chapter, you will be able to do the following:

1. Identify and describe the three major sections of the national income accounting system.
2. Define Gross National Product (GNP) and its four components.
3. Define multiple counting and indicate its importance in national income accounting.
4. Define value added and distinguish it from value of output.
5. Define and describe net national product (NNP) and distinguish it from GNP.
6. Define, describe, and recognize examples of transfer payments, capital consumption allowance, net investment, and indirect business taxes and subsidies.
7. Describe the role of the statistical discrepancy adjustment in national income accounting.
8. Define national income (NI) and describe its five components.
9. Define personal income (PI).
10. Define disposable personal income (DPI) and indicate its disposition.

11. Describe the relationships among the five major national income accounts and indicate the importance of each as a measure of aggregate economic activity.

12. Identify and describe the major shortcomings of the national income accounting system and in each case indicate whether the accounts are likely to be overstated or understated as a result.

Review Terms

unemployment
unemployment rate
inflation
inflation rate
microeconomics
aggregate
investment

capital goods
input or factor of production
macroeconomics
business cycles
capitalism
socialism
per capita

Important Terms and Concepts

national income and product accounts
national product section of national income accounts
national income section of national income accounts
personal income section of national income accounts
Gross National Product (GNP)
Simon Kuznets
"value" of production
consumption (C)
investment (I)
government spending
government purchases (G)
transfer payments
net exports (X-Im)
exports (X)
imports (Im)
multiple counting (double counting)
net inventory change
intermediate goods
value added
value of output
net national product (NNP)

depreciation
capital consumption allowance
gross investment (I_g)
net investment (I_n)
indirect business taxes and subsidies
statistical discrepancy
national income (NI)
compensation of employees
proprietors' income
rental income of persons
corporate profits
net interest
fringe benefits
personal income (PI)
disposable personal income (DPI)
personal taxes
earnings not received
receipts not earned
personal consumption
personal saving
personal transfer payments
correlated
Y as a symbol for national income and product
long-run economic welfare

short-run economic welfare

consumer expenditures

necessary consumption

discretionary ("supernumerary")
     income

durable goods

final buying income

do-it-yourself economy

less-developed country (LDC)

more-developed country (MDC)

underground economy

barter

bracket creep

ecosystem

bads vs. goods

measure of economic welfare
     (MEW)

net national welfare (NNW)

Completion

national product

national income

personal income

The three major sections of the national income accounting system

are the _____ section, the

_____ section, and the

_____ section.

    The national product section of our national income accounting system divides spending into four categories, the sum of which is

Gross National Product

equal to the _____ . Spending by households to buy currently produced goods and services is referred

consumption

to as _____ spending. Business purchases of new

investment

capital goods and changes in inventories are counted as _____

does not

spending. Investment spending _____ (does/does not) include purchases of stocks and bonds. Government purchases in-

spending to buy goods and services

cludes government _____ ;

are not

government transfer payments _____ (are/are not) in-

net exports

cluded. Finally, international spending is recorded in _____ .

capital consumption allowance

    Gross National Product minus the _____

is equal to net national product. The capital consumption allowance is

depreciation and obsolescence

a measure of the _____ of capital goods used in producing GNP.

    To get national income from NNP we must subtract

indirect business taxes and subsidies

_____ and the

statistical discrepancy

_____ . National income can also be cal-

compensation of employees

culated by adding _____ ,

proprietors' income, rental income of persons

corporate profits
net interest

personal income

unreceived earnings

unearned receipts

Social Security taxes

government transfer payments

personal income

personal taxes

personal consumption

multiple counting

value added

are not

_____ , _____ ,

_____ , and _____ .
     To determine the amount of money that is available to people, we must look at _____ . This is computed as national income minus _____ plus _____ . The biggest component of unreceived earnings is _____ , and the biggest component of unearned receipts is _____ .

Disposable personal income is equal to _____ minus _____ . Most disposable personal income is used for _____ .
     If the national income accounts included values for both intermediate and final goods, we would be guilty of _____ . To avoid this problem, the national accounts use the _____ system. Other problems are not so easily avoided. For example, most do-it-yourself and underground productive activities _____ (are/are not) included.

Problems and Applications

1. The following table describes the production of a doodad.

Stages of Production	Sales Value	Value Added
1. Raw materials	5 cents	
2. Construction	11 cents	
3. Packaging	14 cents	
4. Retailing	19 cents	
	49 cents	

   a. Complete the third column of the table above by determining the value added in each stage of production
   b. How much income is earned by the owner(s) of the raw materials used in the production of one doodad?
   c. What does a doodad sell for in the marketplace?

d. If you were to include a doodad in the GNP, how much would you add?

e. If you were to include 100 doodads in the GNP, by how much would the GNP increase?

f. What would be wrong with adding 49 cents to the GNP for each doodad produced?

2. Consider the following data for Economy X in 1980:

National Income Data for Economy X (1980)

Personal consumption expenditures	$100
Government purchases of goods and services	20
Government transfer payments	15
New capital goods: residential	4
New capital goods: nonresidential	6
Increases in inventories	7
Exports	8
Imports	5

a. What is the 1980 gross investment for Economy X?

b. Calculate net exports for Economy X in 1980.

c. Compute Economy X's 1980 Gross National Product.

3. Consider the following data describing Economy Y in 1980:

National Data for Economy Y (1980)

Net exports	$ 20
Net investment	40
Net interest	10
Indirect business taxes and subsidies	15
Capital consumption allowance	30
Government purchases of goods and services	70
Government transfer payments	30
Statistical discrepancy	25
Personal consumption spending	100

a. What is the 1980 gross investment for Economy Y?

b. What is the 1980 Gross National Product for Economy Y?

c. What is the 1980 net national product for Economy Y?

d. What is the 1980 national income for Economy Y?

4. Consider the following data describing Economy Z in 1985:

National Data for Economy Z (1985)

Gross investment	$ 500
Imports	50
Exports	70
Consumption spending	1,400
Personal saving	30
Unreceived earnings	35
Unearned receipts	25
Indirect business taxes and subsidies	15
Personal tax payments	20
Gross National Product	2,250
Disposable personal income	1,550
Capital consumption allowance	100
Statistical discrepancy	30

a. How much did the government of Economy Z spend to purchase goods and services produced in 1985?

b. What was the net investment of Economy Z in 1985?

c. What was the net national product of Economy Z in 1985?

d. What was the national income in 1985 for Economy Z?

e. What was the personal income in 1985 for Economy Z?

f. How much did the citizens of Economy Z spend for nontax payments like traffic fines, penalties, and charges for government services in 1980?

g. How much did the citizens of Economy Z spend for personal transfer payments in 1980?

5. Consider the following national income data for Incomeland in 1980:

National Income Data for Incomeland (1980)

Compensation of employees	$1,255
Money wages paid to employees	945
Proprietors' income	145
Rental income of persons	30
Rental income of unincorporated businesses	25
Profits of unincorporated businesses	55
Corporate profits	180
Net interest	130
Income earned but not received	250
Unearned receipts	260
Personal tax and nontax payments	275

a. How much money did employers spend for social insurance and fringe benefits in Incomeland in 1980?
b. What was the 1980 labor income of proprietors and partners?
c. Calculate the 1980 national income for Incomeland.
d. Calculate personal income for Incomeland in 1980.
e. What was the 1980 disposable personal income in Incomeland?

6. Match each of the following data series on the left with the most accurate description of them on the right.

——— Gross National Product

_____ Net national product

_____ National income

_____ Personal income

_____ Disposable personal income

a. A measure of short-run economic welfare

b. A rough measure of long-run economic welfare

c. The major determinant of consumption spending

d. Closely related to measured employment and unemployment

e. A measure of Y, the economist's general symbol for national income and product

7. For each of the following, identify whether or not the activity *should* be included in the GNP as it is defined and whether or not the activity *is* included in the GNP.
   a. spending for national defense
   b. $10,000 robbed from a bank
   c. $10,000 spent by a local government to fight crime
   d. purchase of food by a family
   e. purchase of ten shares of stock in a corporation
   f. construction of a new apartment complex
   g. three dollars in spending money given to a thirteen-year old
   h. purchase of materials for the construction of a public highway
   i. the price paid for a stolen car
   j. increases in inventories
   k. the tomatoes grown by an accountant
   l. the tomatoes grown and taken to market by a farmer
   m. the tomatoes grown by a farmer and eaten by his family
   n. the price paid by a Canadian businessman for an American computer
   o. a $100 donation to your college alumni fund
   p. the price paid by an American citizen for a Japanese car
   q. the addition of a new wing to a factory
   r. the growth, harvesting, and processing of tobacco by a tobacco company
   s. the illegal growth, harvesting, and processing of marijuana
   t. a $100 unemployment compensation check
   u. the monthly rent paid for an apartment
   v. an estimated rental equivalent for an owner-occupied townhouse
   w. the purchase of an old vase at a garage sale
   x. the deposit of $100 in a savings account
   y. the payment of a broker's fee on a stock transaction
   z. a businessman's purchase of an old factory building

True-False

Indicate whether each of the following statements is basically true or false. If the statement is false, rewrite it so that it is true.

_____ 1. Consumption spending refers to household purchases of currently produced goods and services.

_____ 2. In terms of the national income accounts, investment spending refers to purchases of stocks and bonds.

_____ 3. Gross National Product is the sum of personal consumption expenditures, investment spending, government expenditures, and net exports.

_____ 4. The GNP is calculated by the Department of Commerce with information from tax returns, surveys, and other data sources.

_____ 5. Veterans' benefits, Social Security benefits, and welfare payments are examples of government transfer payments.

_____ 6. The value-added approach to computing the GNP results in a higher figure than the "value of output" approach, *ceteris paribus.*

_____ 7. Investment spending is part of net inventory change.

_____ 8. Net investment is gross investment minus the capital consumption allowance.

_____ 9. The capital consumption allowance is a depreciation allowance.

_____ 10. $GNP = C + I_n + G + X - Im.$

_____ 11. $NNP = C + I_g + G + X - Im.$

_____ 12. Net national product is the sum of personal consumption expenditures, net investment, government purchases, and net exports.

_____ 13. National income is equal to net national product minus additions to inventories.

_____ 14. National income measures income that is generated in producing the national product.

_____ 15. Personal income = national income + (money received but not earned) – (income earned but not received).

_____ 16. Disposable personal income excludes nontax payments such as traffic fines.

_____ 17. Consumption expenditures are primarily determined by disposable personal income.

_____ 18. Disposable personal income is basically equivalent to personal income minus necessities.

_____ 19. The national income accounting statistics include estimated values for most do-it-yourself activities.

_____ 20. As the underground economy grows in importance, measured GNP automatically decreases.

_____ 21. The inclusion of intermediate as well as final goods in a national income statistic would illustrate the problem of double counting.

_____ 22. The inclusion of do-it-yourself activities in calculating income per capita would most likely decrease the discrepancy between the standard of living in the more-developed countries and the less-developed countries.

_____ 23. The purpose of computing MEW and NNW statistics has been to eliminate environmental damage and wartime destruction from the national accounts.

Multiple Choice   Choose the *one best* answer in each of the following cases:

_____ 1. Which of the following is true of the U.S. national income accounting system?
   a. It uses double-entry bookkeeping.
   b. It was developed during the 1920s by the National Bureau of Economic Research, a private research agency.
   c. Today, the collection, analysis, and publication of the data is the responsibility of the Department of Commerce.
   d. It is composed of three major sections: the national product section, the national income section, and the personal income section.
   e. all of the above

_____ 2. The national product section of the U.S. national accounting system measures production during a given time period by recording the
   a. monetary transactions during the indicated time period.
   b. total domestic purchases during the indicated time period.
   c. quantities of goods produced during the indicated time period.
   d. value of goods and services produced during the indicated time period.
   e. total costs associated with the production of final goods, regardless of when the costs were incurred.

_____ 3. The Gross National Product statistic *excludes*
   a. exports.
   b. transfer payments.
   c. local government purchases.
   d. net additions to inventories.
   e. household spending to purchase services.

_____ 4. In terms of the national accounting system, investment spending includes the purchase of
   a. a new home.
   b. undeveloped land.
   c. a government savings bond.
   d. stock in an American corporation.
   e. none of the above

_____ 5. Double counting is
   a. desirable and should be used whenever possible.
   b. avoided by the use of a measure called value of output.
   c. the productive use of recycled goods and services.
   d. advisable if the sales value of a good exceeds the value added.
   e. avoided by counting only the amount paid in the final sale of a good or service.

_____ 6. Net national product is equal to
   a. Gross National Product minus imports.
   b. Gross National Product minus net exports.
   c. net investment plus the capital consumption allowance.
   d. gross investment minus the capital consumption allowance.
   e. Gross National Product minus the capital consumption allowance.

_____ 7. The statistical discrepancy adjustment in the national income accounting system is
   a. necessary because people do not report their true incomes to the Internal Revenue Service.
   b. equal to the difference between the estimates for Gross National Product and national income.
   c. placed in the national income section because the national product estimates are usually more accurate than the national income estimates.
   d. all of the above
   e. none of the above

_____ 8. The "compensation of employees" component of the national income statistic includes
   a. unemployment compensation.
   b. only the money wages and salaries of employees.
   c. Social Security benefits, excluding Social Security taxes.
   d. expenditures by employers for fringe benefits and social insurance.
   e. all forms of monetary payments to employees, excluding all nonmonetary benefits.

_____ 9. The national income statistic excludes
   a. net interest.
   b. welfare benefits.
   c. corporate profits.
   d. proprietors' income.
   e. rental income of persons.

_____ 10. Proprietors' income includes
   a. profits and unincorporated businesses.
   b. rental income of unincorporated businesses.
   c. labor income of unincorporated businesses.
   d. all of the above
   e. none of the above

_____ 11. Net interest is
   a. total interest income of households, business, and government.
   b. interest that households pay to businesses.
   c. interest that the government pays on U.S. Savings Bonds.

    d. a government transfer payment.

    e. none of the above

12. Personal income includes
   a. undistributed corporate profits.
   b. the capital consumption allowance.
   c. indirect business taxes.
   d. an estimate for barter income.
   e. none of the above

13. Disposable personal income basically measures
   a. household spending.
   b. all monetary payments to workers.
   c. compensation to employees minus income tax deductions.
   d. the difference between personal income and personal taxes.
   e. the amount of money households have for spending after contractual obligations.

14. The U.S. national income accounting system *fails* to count
   a. exports.
   b. most services.
   c. rent on owner-occupied homes.
   d. most do-it-yourself production.
   e. all of the above

15. Items that *should be* counted as part of the national income and product accounts but that *are not* include
   a. imports.
   b. transfer payments.
   c. the purchase of used goods.
   d. the purchase of stocks in American corporations.
   e. currently produced goods and services exchanged through barter.

16. Do-it-yourself activities
   a. are typically included in the calculation of national income.
   b. are typically included in the calculation of national income for the LDCs but not the MDCs.
   c. are typically included in the calculation of national income for the MDCs but not the LDCs.
   d. are likely to be more important in the MDCs than the LDCs.
   e. none of the above

_____ 17. If income and production refer to positive contributions to welfare and the standard of living, then the U.S. national income accounting system
a. tends to be misleading, because it includes most illegal activity.
b. might better measure productive activity if we netted out an environmental consumption allowance.
c. tends to understate income and production, because we do not include productive efforts associated with the clean-up and repair work that follow a natural disaster.
d. tends to overstate income and production to the extent that much of our measured productive activity involves efforts to correct for environmental damage done in the process of producing our national output.
e. both b and d above

_____ 18. Which of the following is likely to result in an increase in measured GNP?
a. an increase in bartering
b. an increase in tax evasion
c. more women entering the labor force and finding employment outside the home
d. people retiring at younger ages
e. all of the above

Discussion Questions

1. Comment on the accuracy of the following statements:
a. "The GNP is equivalent to the total sales in an economy."
b. "The GNP is equivalent to the total spending in an economy."
c. "The GNP is equivalent to the total monetary transactions in an economy."
d. "The GNP is an accurate measure of an economy's well being."
e. "Economic growth is indicated by an increase in the GNP."

2. New residential construction is included in the GNP as a form of investment spending. Rental payments and estimated rental equivalents are also included in the GNP. Why doesn't this constitute double counting?

3. Explain why the international spending component of the GNP includes net exports rather than total exports.

4. Explain the advantage to separating government purchases into two categories, public consumption and public investment.

5. Discuss the effect of current trends in labor-force participation on do-it-yourself activity and the national income accounting system.

6. What would happen to U.S. national income and product statistics if the United States adopted a Marxist approach with respect to the measurement of services? Would this result in a more or a less accurate statistic? Why? Given current trends, what would be the consequences for measured GNP in the future if the United States did adopt a Marxist approach?

7. Discuss the problems associated with attempting to compare the GNP statistics of two different economies.

Answers

Problems and Applications

1. a.

Stage	Value Added
1	5 cents
2	6 cents
3	3 cents
4	5 cents

   b. 5 cents   c. 19 cents   d. 19 cents   e. $19

   f. It would involve double counting. The 5 cents' worth of raw materials, for example, would be counted four times.

2. a. $17   b. $3   c. $140

3. a. $70   b. $260   c. $230   d. $190

4. a. $330   b. $400   c. $2,150   d. $2,105
   e. $2,095   f. $345   g. $120

5. a. $310   b. $65   c. $1,740   d. $1,750   e. $1,475

6. d, e, b, a, c

7. a. should be, is
   b. should not be, is not
   c. should be, is
   d. should be, is
   e. should not be, is not
   f. should be, is
   g. should not be, is not
   h. should be, is
   i. should not be, is not
   j. should be, is
   k. should be, is not
   l. should be, is
   m. should be, is

   n. should be, is
   o. should not be, is not
   p. should not be, is not
   q. should be, is
   r. should be, is
   s. should be, is not
   t. should not be, is not
   u. should be, is
   v. should be, is
   w. should not be, is not
   x. should not be, is not
   y. should be, is
   z. should not be, is not

True-False

1. T
2. F. In terms of the national income accounts, investment spending refers to purchases of new capital goods (residential and nonresidential) and net additions to inventories.
3. F. Gross National Product is the sum of personal consumption expenditures, investment spending, government purchases, and net exports.
4. T.
5. T.
6. F. The value-added approach to computing the GNP results in a lower figure than the "value of output" approach, *ceteris paribus.*
7. F. Net inventory change is part of investment spending.
8. T.
9. T.
10. F. GNP = C + I_g + G + X – Im.
11. F. NNP = C + I_n + G + X – Im.
12. T.
13. F. National income is equal to net national product minus indirect business taxes and subsidies and minus the statistical discrepancy; alternatively, national income is equal to compensation of employees plus proprietors' income plus rental income of persons plus corporate profits plus net interest.
14. T.
15. T.
16. T.
17. T.
18. F. Disposable personal income is equivalent to personal income minus personal taxes and certain small nontax items.
19. F. The national income accounting statistics exclude most do-it-yourself activities except food grown by a farmer and retained for personal use and an estimated rent for owner-occupied housing.
20. T.
21. T.
22. T.
23. T.

Multiple Choice

1. e	2. d	3. b	4. a	5. e
6. e	7. e	8. d	9. b	10. d
11. e	12. e	13. e	14. d	15. e
16. e	17. e	18. c		

8 The Circular Flow and Macroeconomic Equilibrium

Summary

Economists often use a circular flow model to depict the macroeconomic functioning of a system. This model shows how resources and goods and services flow through the system. It also shows how money flows through the system in response to this real flow of resources and goods and services. Money spent to buy goods and services provides revenues for business firms. Business firms use their revenues to meet the costs of production, that is, to pay for the resources used in producing goods and services. These payments constitute income to the owners of the resources. And these income payments provide a source of funds for the purchase of goods and services.

In its simplest form, the circular flow model considers only the household and business sectors of an economy and assumes that households use all their income for consumption spending. Households own the productive resources; businesses use these resources to produce the goods and services demanded by households. Households receive income in return for their resources and use this income to purchase the goods and services produced by the business sector.

The model can be made more realistic by recognizing additional uses for the funds of households. These uses are saving, payment of taxes (net taxes), and the purchase of imports. The recognition of these additional uses for household funds suggest that the circular flow model be expanded to include financial markets, government, and foreign markets. With this expansion one is able to consider the role of investment spending, government purchases, and exports in the economy. The circular flow, then, shows the relationships among many of the components of the national income and product accounts.

The circular flow model can be used to explain concepts of equilibrium and disequilibrium within individual spending flows, as well as for the economy as a whole. Equilibrium for the economy as a whole requires that total planned expenditure equals the total value of goods and services that business plans to sell. Alternatively, macroeconomic equilibrium occurs when total planned injections (investment spending, government purchases, and exports) equal total planned leakages (saving, net taxes, and imports). Macroeconomic equilibrium does not require equilibrium in each of the separate paths of the circular flow.

Major Objectives After you have finished this chapter, you will be able to do the following:

1. Construct and describe the consumption-only circular flow model, identifying the functions of households and business firms.
2. Indicate the relationship of the consumption-only circular flow model to the national income accounting system.
3. Define macroeconomic equilibrium.
4. Describe the concept of macroeconomic equilibrium in terms of the consumption-only circular flow.
5. Define disequilibrium.
6. Construct and describe the circular flow model with financial markets, government, and foreign markets.
7. Identify the four uses for household income, describe their patterns of movement in the circular flow, and indicate their relationship to the national income accounts.
8. Define saving.
9. Explain the potential role of depreciation in the circular flow and reconcile it with the national income accounts.
10. Identify the function of financial markets and list their major participants.
11. Distinguish between *ex ante* and *ex post.*
12. Identify and describe the conditions leading to disequilibrium in financial markets.
13. Describe the consequences of a difference in planned investment and planned saving.
14. Define net taxes.
15. Describe the role of government in the circular flow.
16. Identify and describe the conditions leading to disequilibrium in the government sector.
17. Describe the consequences of a difference between net taxes and government purchases.

18. Explain the important differences between an imbalance in the government and the financial paths of the circular flow in terms of ability to control the flow of funds.
19. Describe the activity associated with the international sector and its relationship to the national income accounts.
20. Explain the causes of disequilibrium in the international sector and discuss the similarities with disequilibrium in the financial markets.
21. Describe the relationship between the government and the financial markets and indicate the effect of government budget policy in terms of the national debt and the availability of funds for investment.
22. Discuss the concept of crowding out and explain its importance.
23. Explain the connections between the foreign markets and the financial markets.
24. Recognize that activity in one path of the circular flow may reinforce or counteract activity in the other paths and that public fiscal, monetary, and foreign trade policies may be used deliberately for such a purpose.
25. Identify the conditions for macroeconomic equilibrium.
26. Identify the conditions that give rise to disequilibrium situations and explain the adjustment process whereby the economic activity expands or contracts in a move toward equilibrium.
27. Explain why disequilibrium conditions are difficult to detect.
28. Define leakages and injections and identify their components.
29. Identify the following symbols: C, I, G, X, S, T_n, and Im.
30. Identify the following symbols: C_d, I_d, and G_d.
31. Define equilibrium in the circular flow in terms of leakages and injections.
32. Explain how equilibrium can exist in an economy without having equilibrium in each separate path of the circular flow.
33. Using injections and leakages, explain how disequilibrium in the economy will result in an expansion or contraction of economic activity in a move toward equilibrium.
34. Reconcile the two basic approaches (the total-planned-expenditure approach and the leakages-injections approach) to explaining equilibrium and disequilibrium.

Review Terms

macroeconomic
national income
national product
consumption (C)
investment (I)
government purchases (G)

exports (X)
imports (Im)
net exports (X-Im)
factors of production
compensation of employees
proprietors' income

rental income of persons
corporate profits
net interest
equilibrium
transfer payments
wealth
depreciation
net national product

Gross National Product
market
inventory
government spending
national income and
    product (Y)
capitalism
socialism

Important Terms and Concepts

circular flow model
consumption-only circular flow
    model
macroeconomic equilibrium
disequilibrium
financial markets
net taxes (T_n)
saving (S)
financial market
ex ante
ex post
disinvestment in inventory
negative taxes
budget surplus

budget deficit
foreign exchange rate
national debt
crowding out
equilibrium national income
    and product (Y^*)
total planned expenditure
expansion
expansionary disequilibrium
contraction
contractionary dis-
    equilibrium
leakages
injections

Completion

consumption expenditures

supplying the resources

suppliers

demanders

demanders

suppliers

In the simplest circular flow model, households use all their income

for _____ . Households earn their

income by _____ used in the pro-
duction of the goods and services they purchase. Households are the

_____ (demanders/suppliers) of resources and the

_____ (demanders/suppliers) of goods and services;

business firms are the _____ (demanders/suppliers) of

resources and the _____ (demanders/suppliers) of
goods and services.

use the money to consume goods and services, save, pay taxes

   A more realistic circular flow model recognizes four uses for the

funds of households. Households may _____

_____ , _____ , _____ ,

purchase imports

and/or _____ . Household spending to buy goods and services represents consumption expenditures; saving flows

financial

from households to the _____ markets and emerges as

investment

_____ spending; net taxes are paid to governments

government purchases

and emerge as _____ ; and money spent

foreign

for the purchase of imports flows through _____ markets

finance the purchase of our exports

and is used to _____ .
These four flows of funds correspond to the four components of

national product

_____ ; similarly, the payments to households for the use of their resources correspond to the components of

national income

_____ .

equal

Ex post, saving and investment must be _____ , though this need not be true *ex ante*. There will be disequilibrium in the financial

planned saving

markets when _____ does not equal

planned investment

_____ . An excess of planned saving over

accumulation

planned investment will lead to an unintended _____ (accumulation/depletion) of inventories, resulting in a tendency for

lower

firms to _____ (raise/lower) their production plans and/or to

lower

_____ (raise/lower) their prices in the next time period. An excess of planned investment over planned saving will lead to an unin-

depletion

tended _____ (accumulation/depletion) of inventories,

raise

resulting in a tendency for firms to _____ (raise/lower) their

raise

production plans and/or to _____ (raise/lower) their prices in the next time period.

Disequilibrium may also occur in the government box of the circu-

net taxes do not equal government purchases

lar flow model. This occurs when _____ .
If net taxes exceed government purchases, there is a budget

surplus

_____ (surplus/deficit) as far as the income and product

accumulation

accounts are concerned. This leads to an unintended _____

lower

(accumulation/depletion) of inventories, resulting in a _____ (higher/lower) national output in the future. If government purchases

deficit

exceed net taxes, there is a budget _____ (surplus/deficit), as far as the income and product accounts are concerned. This will

depletion

result in an unintended inventory _____ (accumulation/

increase

depletion) and a tendency for national output to _____
(increase/decrease) in the future.

When there is a surplus in the government income and product

decreased

budget, the national debt is _____ (increased/decreased)

into

and money flows _____ (into/out of) the financial markets.
Alternatively, when there is a deficit in the government income and

increased

product budget, the national debt is _____ (increased/

out of

decreased) and money flows _____ (into/out of) the financial
markets.

When exports exceed imports, there is disequilibrium in the

foreign

_____ market. Imports will finance the purchase of
some of the exports; the rest may be financed with funds from U.S.

from

financial markets. This represents a flow of funds _____

to

(from/to) the U.S. financial markets _____ (from/to)
foreign markets. Similarly, when imports exceed exports, there is

foreign

disequilibrium in the _____ market. American dollars

accumulate

will tend to _____ in foreign markets and may flow

into

_____ (out of/into) the U.S. financial markets if the foreign
owners of these funds want to earn interest on them.

does not

Equilibrium for the economy as a whole _____ (does/does
not) require equilibrium in each of the separate paths of the circular
flow. For the economy as a whole, equilibrium requires that

total planned
expenditure

_____ equal the value of goods

companies plan
to sell

and services that _____ . If total
planned expenditure exceeds the value of goods and services that

depletion

companies plan to sell, there will be an unintended _____
(accumulation/depletion) of inventories and a corresponding ten-

expansion

dency for _____ (expansion/contraction) of the
economy in the future. Alternatively, if total planned expenditure
falls short of the value of goods and services that business plans to

accumulation

sell, there will be an unintended _____ (accum-
ulation/depletion) of inventories and a corresponding tendency for

contraction

_____ (expansion/contraction) of the economy
in the future.

	Equilibrium for the economy as a whole can also be defined as an
injections	equality between total planned _____ and total
leakages	planned _____ . Expenditures on currently produced goods and services, except those for domestic consumption, are
injections	called _____ . Uses of funds that take them out of
leakages	the direct consumption expenditure flow are called _____ .
leakages	Saving, net taxes, and imports are examples of _____ ; investment, government purchases, and exports are examples of
injections	_____ .

Problems and Applications

1. Complete the circular flow diagram on the opposite page by identifying the
   a. components that make up the flow of funds into the household sector.
   b. national income account represented by the oval feeding into the household sector.
   c. flow of funds from households directly to firms.
   d. markets that are connected to households, business firms, government, and foreign markets.
   e. flow of funds into the government box.
   f. flow of funds out of the government box.
   g. flow of funds into the foreign markets.
   h. flow of funds out of the foreign markets.

2. Identify each of the following as either an *ex ante* or an *ex post* concept:
   a. intended saving
   b. unintended inventories
   c. actual expenditures
   d. planned leakages
   e. realized investment spending

3. Consider an economy described by the following data:

Saving	$65
Planned investment spending	50
Government purchases	75
Net taxes	50
Exports	20
Imports	15
Consumption expenditures	90

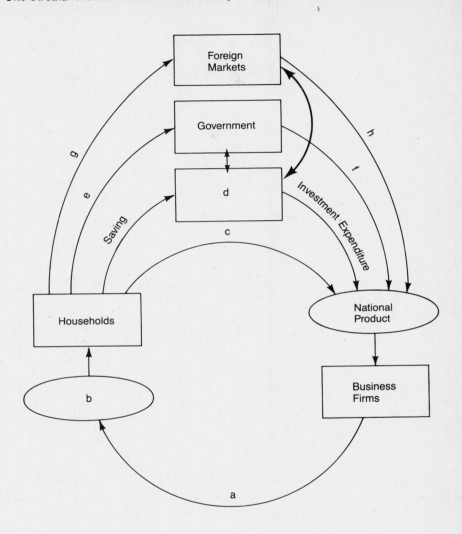

a. What is the actual level of investment spending in the economy?
b. What is the value of net exports?
c. What is the value of total planned injections?
d. What is the value of total planned leakages?
e. What is the value of total planned expenditure?
f. Is there equilibrium in the path through saving–financial markets–investment of the circular flow? Considering this path alone, would you expect to see an unintended accumulation or a depletion of inventories?
g. Is there equilibrium in the government box of the circular flow? If not, is there a surplus or a deficit in the government budget in terms of the income and product accounts?

    h. Is there equilibrium in the foreign markets box of the circular flow model?

    i. Is the economy as a whole in equilibrium? How do you know?

4. Consider the economy described by the data below:

Total planned expenditure	$190
Planned saving	30
Planned investment spending	40
Government purchases	25
Government transfer payments	20
Total taxes	45
Exports	55
Imports	65

    a. What is the value of total planned injections?

    b. What is the value of total planned leakages?

    c. What is the value of planned consumption expenditures?

    d. Is there equilibrium in the path through saving–financial markets–investment of the circular flow? Considering this path alone, would you expect to see an unintended accumulation or depletion of inventories?

    e. If there equilibrium in the government box of the circular flow? If not, is there a surplus or a deficit in the government income and product budget?

    f. Is there equilibrium in the foreign markets box of the circular flow model?

    g. Is the economy in macroeconomic equilibrium? How do you know?

True-False   Indicate whether each of the following statements is basically true or false. If the statement is false, rewrite it so that it is true.

_____ 1. In the simplified consumption-only circular flow model, the function of households is to consume; businesses serve a dual function as producers and as owners of resources.

_____ 2. Macroeconomic equilibrium is always a characteristic of the simplified consumption-only circular flow.

_____ 3. The flow of payments from businesses to households includes wages and salaries, rent, interest, and profits, which together essentially represent national income in the national income accounting system.

_____ 4. Equilibrium is a state of balance among opposing forces such that there is no tendency for change, whereas disequilibrium is a state of imbalance among opposing forces such that there is some tendency for change.

_____ 5. In general, there are two ways households may use their money: they may spend it to buy consumer goods and services and/or they may save it.

_____ 6. Household saving includes undistributed corporate profits that businesses reinvest on behalf of stockholders.

_____ 7. Financial markets consist of banks, savings and loan associations, credit unions, stock and bond brokerage firms, and insurance companies.

_____ 8. The function of financial markets is to bring savers and investors together.

_____ 9. The term *ex post* refers to plans or intentions, and the term *ex ante* refers to accomplishments or actual deeds.

_____ 10. There is equilibrium in the financial markets whenever actual saving and actual investment are equal.

_____ 11. When planned saving exceeds planned investment, business firms tend to have cash flow problems.

_____ 12. Crowding out occurs when firms sell more of their inventories than planned.

_____ 13. Net taxes are the total amount of personal and business taxes minus government expenditures.

_____ 14. It is impossible to have disequilibrium in the government box of the circular flow.

_____ 15. Since consumption, investment, and government purchases include imports, the international section of the national income accounting system records net exports only.

_____ 16. If actual exports are not equal to planned exports, there is disequilibrium in foreign markets.

_____ 17. If U.S. exports exceed imports, funds are likely to flow from U.S. financial markets to foreign markets.

_____ 18. A major reason for disequilibrium in financial and foreign markets is that separate decision-making units make decisions that are not always consistent.

_____ 19. Disequilibrium in individual paths of the circular flow is difficult to detect, one major reason for this difficulty being that, *ex post*, saving equals investment.

_____ 20. Disequilibrium in the aggregate economy occurs whenever there is an inequality in any of the paths of the circular flow.

_____ 21. If total planned expenditure exceeds the total value of goods and services that businesses plan to sell, the actual level of inventories will exceed the level of inventories planned by businesses, resulting in a tendency toward economic expansion.

_____ 22. Leakages include all uses of household funds other than domestic consumption spending; injections include all expenditures on currently produced goods and services except those for domestic consumption.

_____ 23. Equilibrium exists in the economy when total planned injections and total planned leakages are equal.

_____ 24. The economy is in a disequilibrium state whenever imports and exports are not equal.

_____ 25. Macroeconomic equilibrium occurs whenever total actual purchases equal total actual sales.

_____ 26. Macroeconomic equilibrium is always desirable.

Multiple Choice   Choose the *one best* answer in each of the following cases:

_____ 1. The circular flow model
  a. is a microeconomic model.
  b. in its most simplified form shows how government influences households and businesses.
  c. may be used to illustrate relationships between many components of the national income and product accounts.
  d. may be useful in describing an economy at equilibrium but is unable to illustrate disequilibrium situations.
  e. all of the above

_____ 2. In the consumption-only circular flow model,
  a. it is assumed that households spend their money to buy goods and services or to pay taxes.
  b. business firms sell goods, services, and resources to households, government, and/or other businesses.
  c. households are assumed to spend all their income to buy goods and services produced by businesses.
  d. business firms buy resources from households and sell goods and services to households, government, and/or other businesses.
  e. both c and d above

3. In general, households may
    a. save income, which represents a flow of money from business firms to households through the financial markets.
    b. spend their money for imports, which represents a flow of money to foreigners, who use the money to buy our exports.
    c. pay taxes, which represents a flow of money from business firms to government through both financial and government sectors.
    d. spend their income to buy goods and services, which represents a flow of money from households to firms by way of the financial markets.
    e. all of the above

4. Household saving includes
    a. disposable personal income that is not spent.
    b. undistributed corporate profits reinvested on behalf of stockholders.
    c. depreciation allowances when dealing with Gross National Product but not when dealing with net national product.
    d. all of the above
    e. both a and b above

5. Which of the following is true of financial markets?
    a. They channel saving into investment spending.
    b. They are limited to banks and savings and loan associations.
    c. They are in equilibrium when actual saving and investment are equal.
    d. They remove savings from the circular flow so that it has no influence on national product.
    e. They do not include insurance companies, even though many insurance policies have savings features.

6. Saving and investment
    a. must be equal *ex post.*
    b. must be equal *ex ante.*
    c. may be unequal *ex post*, in which case the financial markets are in a disequilibrium state.
    d. both b and c above
    e. none of the above

7. If planned saving exceeds planned investment,
    a. interest rates will probably rise.
    b. there is unplanned inventory accumulation.
    c. *ex post* saving will exceed *ex post* investment.
    d. households are spending more than business anticipated.
    e. business firms will have more cash on hand than they would like.

_____   8. An excess of planned investment over planned saving is
   a. likely to result in an accumulation of inventories.
   b. likely to result in an increase in production and possibly in prices.
   c. unlikely, since households and businesses make these decisions jointly.
   d. likely to result in equilibrium in financial markets if actual saving and investment are equal.
   e. all of the above

_____   9. According to the circular flow, which of the following is true with respect to the government box?
   a. It represents budgetary decisions by the federal government only.
   b. Government expenditures flow into the box and net tax revenues flow out.
   c. Disequilibrium arises when net taxes and government purchases are unequal and may be a deliberate result of policy.
   d. The flow of funds into and out of the box are both completely controlled by government, so there is no distinction between *ex ante* and *ex post* amounts.
   e. all of the above

_____   10. The connection between government and the financial markets is such that
   a. funds may flow in either direction.
   b. a budget surplus may result in the government retiring bonds.
   c. savings may be used for government spending rather than for investment spending.
   d. in the case of a budget deficit the government may obtain funds by selling bonds in the financial markets.
   e. all of the above

_____   11. Crowding out most likely occurs when
   a. net taxes exceed government purchases.
   b. total taxes exceed government spending.
   c. there is a budget surplus in the government path of the circular flow.
   d. the government budget is balanced in terms of national income and product accounts.
   e. the government budget is in deficit in terms of national income and product accounts.

_____   12. According to the circular flow, which of the following is true with respect to foreign markets?
   a. *Ex ante* and *ex post* amounts may differ.
   b. They are not connected to financial markets.
   c. They are directly connected to the government.

d. Disequilibrium is impossible, since these markets deal only with net exports.

e. Changes in foreign exchange rates assure that each of these markets will be in equilibrium at any point in time.

_____ 13. Disequilibrium in the foreign trade path of the circular flow

a. may be reinforced or counteracted by actions taken in the financial markets.

b. is unimportant because foreign markets are not connected to other markets in the economy.

c. results only when governments interfere with the determination of foreign exchange rates.

d. never results in a flow of funds from U.S. financial markets to foreign borrowers.

e. is unlikely, since plans are made jointly by American importers, foreign purchasers of American goods, and American producers of these goods.

_____ 14. In terms of the circular flow,

a. disequilibrium in foreign markets arises because of an imbalance between imports and exports.

b. disequilibrium in financial markets arises because planned saving and planned investment are not equal.

c. disequilibrium in the entire circular flow need not result just because of imbalances within the separate paths of the circular flow.

d. disequilibrium in the government path arises because the government does not have a balanced budget in terms of the income and product accounts.

e. all of the above

_____ 15. Equilibrium in an economy

a. is rare, since it requires equilibrium in all sectors of the economy.

b. exists whenever total planned leakages equal total planned injections.

c. exists if total expenditures in the economy equal total sales in the economy.

d. generally exists, since equilibrium for an economy as a whole does not require equilibrium in all sectors of the economy.

e. both a and c above

_____ 16. Which of the following is true with respect to leakages and injections?
   a. They both include domestic consumption expenditures.
   b. Leakages include net taxes, net exports, and savings.
   c. Injections are limited to domestic consumption spending, investment spending, and government purchases.
   d. Leakages refers to uses of household funds other than for domestic consumption spending; injections are expenditures on currently produced goods and services except those for domestic consumption.
   e. Leakages include uses of funds that remove these funds from the circular flow; injections include all expenditures on goods and services that enter the circular flow.

Discussion Questions

1. Explain the difference between *ex ante* and *ex post*, and demonstrate the importance of this distinction in terms of investment spending. Which component of investment spending accounts for *ex ante* and *ex post* differences in this variable?

2. What is the significance of using net taxes and government purchases as the flows into and out of the government box in the circular flow diagram?

3. Explain the connections between the financial markets and each of the following sectors of the economy: households, business firms, government, and the international sector.

4. Explain how government action can reinforce or counteract a disequilibrium in the financial markets.

5. Explain how an imbalance in the foreign markets can reinforce or counteract activity in the financial markets.

6. Show how an equality between total planned expenditure and the value of goods and services that businesses plan to sell is equivalent to an equality between total planned injections and total planned leakages.

Answers   *Problems and Applications*

1. a. wages, salaries, rents, interest, and profits
   b. national income
   c. consumption expenditures
   d. financial markets
   e. net taxes
   f. government purchases
   g. imports
   h. exports

2. a. *ex ante*   b. *ex post*   c. *ex post*
   d. *ex ante*   e. *ex post*

3. a. $65   b. $5   c. $145
   d. $130   e. $220   f. no; accumulation
   g. no; deficit h. no
   i. no; planned injections exceed planned leakages

4. a. $120   b. $120   c. $135
   d. no; depletion e. yes   f. no
   g. yes; planned injections equal planned leakages

True-False

1. F. In the simplified consumption-only circular flow model, households are consumers and owners of the resources, and businesses are producers and purchasers of resources.
2. T.
3. T.
4. T.
5. F. In general, there are four ways households may use their money: they may spend it to buy domestically produced consumer goods and services, save it, pay taxes, and/or spend it to buy imported goods and services.
6. T.
7. T.
8. T.
9. F. The term *ex ante* refers to plans or intentions. *Ex post* refers to accomplishments or actual deeds.
10. F. *Ex post*, saving and investment are equal by definition; there is equilibrium in the financial markets when planned saving and planned investment are equal.
11. T.

12. F. Disinvestment occurs when firms sell more of their inventories than planned; crowding out occurs when household saving is used to finance deficit spending by government and is therefore less available for investment.

13. F. Net taxes are the total amount of personal and business taxes minus government transfer payments.

14. F. There is disequilibrium in the government box of the circular flow when net taxes and government purchases are unequal.

15. T.

16. T.

17. F. If U.S. exports exceed imports, funds are likely to flow from U.S. financial markets to foreign markets.

18. T.

19. T.

20. F. Disequilibrium in the aggregate economy occurs whenever there is an inequality between total planned expenditure and the value of goods and services that firms plan to sell; alternatively, disequilibrium in the aggregate economy occurs whenever there is an inequality between planned injections and planned leakages.

21. F. If total planned expenditure exceeds the total value of goods and services that businesses plan to sell, the actual level of inventories will fall below the level planned by businesses, resulting in a tendency toward economic expansion.

22. T.

23. T.

24. F. The economy may be in equilibrium with an imbalance between imports and exports; disequilibrium for the economy as a whole occurs when total planned expenditure and the total value of goods and services that businesses plan to sell are unequal or when total planned injections and total planned leakages are unequal.

25. F. Total actual purchases and total actual sales are always equal. Macroeconomic equilibrium occurs when total planned expenditure equals total planned sales. Alternatively, macroeconomic equilibrium occurs when total planned injections equal total planned leakages.

26. F. Macroeconomic equilibrium in itself is neither desirable nor undesirable.

Multiple Choice

1. c	2. c	3. b	4. d	5. a
6. a	7. b	8. b	9. c	10. e
11. e	12. a	13. a	14. e	15. b
16. d				

9 The Keynesian Model

Summary

Neoclassical economists believed that the price system would operate in all markets to ensure the smooth flow of money, goods, services, and resources in the economy, as indicated by the circular flow diagram. Neoclassical theory is sometimes summarized in Say's Identity: supply creates its own demand. A major conclusion of the neoclassical theory held that the economy would reach a full-employment equilibrium.

The persistent high levels of unemployment during the 1930s led to the development of a new economic theory, Keynesian economics. Keynesian theory criticized the neoclassical theory, maintaining that modern economic systems do not follow competitive pricing practices. Consequently, argued Keynes, the economy might come to equilibrium at any level of employment, and government intervention might be necessary for the economy to reach a full-employment equilibrium.

The Keynesian model of income and output determination is built on a theory of household consumption behavior. According to this theory, consumption spending and saving are determined primarily by income. Using the concept of disposable personal income, saving is defined to be income that is not spent. Hence, $DPI = C + S$. Using the concept of national income and product (Y), $Y = C + S + T_n$.

The marginal propensity to consume (MPC) measures the change in planned consumption spending that results from a unit change in income, and the marginal propensity to save (MPS) measures the change in planned saving that results from a unit change in income. The MPC and MPS also measure the slopes of the consumption and saving functions, respectively. Since disposable income can only be spent or saved, any additional disposable income must be spent or saved. Hence, for any given change in disposable income, $MPC + MPS = 1$.

The permanent income hypothesis places emphasis on whether income changes are perceived by households to be permanent or transitory. Consumption spending changes in response to changes in permanent income. As income increases, households first respond as though the increase is largely transitory, saving a relatively large proportion of the additional income. Over time, a greater proportion of the additional income is perceived to be permanent and so a larger proportion of it is spent, giving rise to a larger MPC over time.

Nonincome determinants of consumption and saving include the stock of durable goods, wealth, and expectations. Whereas a change in income leads to a movement along a consumption function, a change in a nonincome determinant of consumption leads to a shift in the consumption function.

Planned investment expenditure is another important component in the development of the Keynesian theory of national income and product. Planned investment will be undertaken when the expected rate of return on the investment is equal to or greater than the rate of interest associated with borrowing the money to finance the investment. The demand curve for planned investment is typically negatively sloped. Whether planned investment spending changes with changes in the level of national income and product is a very complex issue. For simplicity, it is assumed that planned investment spending will not change with changes in national income and product.

In addition to planned consumption expenditures and planned investment expenditures, two additional spending streams are needed to make up total planned expenditure: government purchases and net exports. Again, for simplicity, it is assumed that neither government purchases nor net exports are affected by changes in national income.

Total planned expenditure is the sum of planned consumption expenditures, planned investment expenditures, government purchases, and net exports. The economy is in equilibrium when total planned expenditure is equal to national income (or national output). Alternatively, equilibrium occurs at the level of national income where total planned leakages and total planned injections are equal.

When total planned expenditure is greater than national income or national product, total leakages are less than total injections, actual inventory holdings decrease, and production and/or prices increase. When total planned expenditure is less than national output, total leakages exceed total injections, actual inventory holdings increase, and production and/or prices decrease.

Both neoclassical and Keynesian theories suggest an adjustment process whereby an economy will more toward a state of equilibrium from any disequilibrium state. In neoclassical theory, the competitive price system provides the adjustment mechanism. In Keynesian theory, the accumulation or depletion of inventory holdings provides the stimulus. A primary difference between the neoclassical and Keynesian views of equilibrium is the neoclassical prediction of a full-employment equilibrium. In Keynesian theory, equilibrium may be associated with any level of employment. As a consequence, government intervention might be indicated if the economy is to reach full employment.

Major Objectives   After you have finished this chapter, you will be able to do the following:

1. Describe Keynesian economics as a demand-side approach and explain what this means.
2. Describe neoclassical economics as a supply-side approach and explain what this means.
3. Quote and explain Say's Identity.
4. Briefly describe the neoclassical school of thought and indicate the adjustment mechanism and the important conclusion of this theory with regard to employment.
5. Explain the importance of the Great Depression of the 1930s in terms of the development of macroeconomic theory.
6. Identify the major contribution of John Maynard Keynes to macroeconomics, indicating his assessment of the shortcomings of the neoclassical school of thought.
7. Explain what is meant by the consumption and saving functions.
8. Identify the primary determinant of consumption and saving.
9. Explain the meaning of autonomous consumption expenditure.
10. Distinguish the Keynesian cross from the Marshallian cross.
11. Draw and explain the significance of the forty-five degree line.
12. Define saving, breakeven, and dissaving.
13. Given a consumption function, develop the associated saving function, and vice versa.
14. Given a graph of a consumption function, identify the levels of income associated with positive, negative, and zero saving.
15. Draw a graph of a consumption function and the associated saving function.
16. Define, interpret, and calculate the marginal propensities to consume and to save, and explain the relationship between them.
17. Discuss the importance of time as it relates to the consumption and saving functions.

18. Summarize the permanent income hypothesis.
19. Compare the permanent income hypothesis to the concepts of short-run and long-run consumption functions.
20. Explain the concept of a lump-sum tax.
21. Convert consumption and saving functions based on disposable personal income to corresponding functions based on national income and product, assuming a lump-sum tax.
22. Explain why it is helpful to express the consumption and saving functions in terms of national income and product.
23. Identify at least three nonincome determinants of consumption and saving and explain the effect of a change in one of the nonincome determinants on these functions.
24. Explain the relationship between planned investment expenditure and the interest rate.
25. Develop a graph of and explain the demand curve for planned investment.
26. Identify and explain at least four factors, other than the interest rate, that influence the volume of planned investment.
27. Explain and draw graphs of autonomous planned investment expenditure, autonomous government purchases, and autonomous net exports.
28. Write the equation for total planned expenditure and graph it.
29. Define and locate the equilibrium level of national income and product and, using total planned expenditure, explain the process whereby the economy adjusts to equilibrium.
30. Using leakages and injections, define and locate the equilibrium level of national income and product and explain the process whereby the economy adjusts to equilibrium.
31. Compare and contrast the total-planned-expenditure approach with the injections-leakages approach to determining the equilibrium level of national income and product.
32. Compare and contrast the neoclassical and Keynesian theories with respect to the equilibrium adjustment process and the characteristics of equilibrium, national income, and product.

Review Terms

macroeconomics
circular flow
national income
national product
consumption (C)
saving (S)
investment (I)
net taxes
government purchases (G)

imports
exports
net exports (X-Im)
financial markets
foreign markets
full employment
Great Depression
inflation
disposable personal income (DPI)

real values as opposed to
  nominal values
ex ante
ex post
slope
aggregate
net national product (NNP)
national income (NI)
national income and product (Y)
durable goods
shortages
wealth
dependent variable
independent variable
saving–financial markets–
  investment path of the
  circular flow

capital good
inventory
net investment
gross investment
capitalist market system
interest rate
opportunity cost
ceteris paribus
equilibrium
macroeconomic equilibrium
import–foreign markets–export
  path of the circular flow
normal good
expansion
contraction
leakages
injections

Important Terms and Concepts

Keynesian economics
demand-side approach
John Maynard Keynes
neoclassical economics
supply-side approach
Jean Baptiste Say
Say's Identity
time lag
full-employment equilibrium
flexible prices and wages
stagflation
consumption function
disposable personal income
  (DPI; Y_d)
autonomous consumption
  expenditure
marginal propensity to
  consume (MPC)
marginal propensity to save
  (MPS)

the Keynesian cross graph
forty-five degree line
breakeven point
dissaving
short-run consumption function
long-run consumption function
permanent income hypothesis
permanent or long-run income
temporary or transitory income
lump-sum tax
shifts in the consumption and
  saving functions
movements along the consumption and saving functions
shift variables
rate of return on an investment
planned investment demand
equilibrium national income and
  product (Y*)
econometrics

Completion

neoclassical

The macroeconomic component of _____ economic theory may be summarized as Say's Identity. Briefly, Say's Identity

supply creates its own demand

maintains that _____ . The neoclassical economists believed that price adjustments would

all

occur in _____ markets, thus ensuring the smooth flow of money, goods, services, and resources in the economy as indicated by

circular flow

the _____ diagram. Neoclassical economists concluded that the economy would come to equilibrium with

full employment

_____ .

A new theory developed in response to the Great Depression of

John Maynard Keynes

the 1930s. Named after _____ , followers

Keynesian

of this school of thought are referred to as _____ economists. Essentially, Keynes maintained that modern economies

do not

_____ (do/do not) follow competitive pricing practices. His

government

conclusions suggested that _____ involvement in the economy might be indicated for the economy to reach a full employment equilibrium.

consumer

Keynesian economics is based on a theory of _____ behavior. According to the Keynesian theory, consumption spending

income

and saving are determined primarily by _____ . Using the concept of disposable personal income, and assuming that

consumption, saving

_____ and _____ are the only two uses for this income, it must follow that disposable personal income is

sum

equal to the _____ of consumption and saving.

The percentage of an extra dollar of income that will be spent is

marginal propensity to consume

called the _____ ; the percentage of an extra dollar of income that will be saved is called

marginal propensity to save

the _____ .

In graphing the consumption function based on disposable personal

consumption spending

income, economists measure dollars of planned _____

disposable personal income

on the vertical axis and dollars of _____ on the horizontal axis. The slope of the consumption function is the

planned consumption spending	change in _____
DPI, *MPC*	associated with a change in _____ . But this is simply the _____ .
	In graphing the consumption function, economists generally begin
forty-five degree	by drawing a straight line from the origin at a _____
	angle. If the units of measurement are the same on both the vertical
forty-five degree	and the horizontal axes, the _____ line connects all
equal	points at which the value measured on one axis is _____ to
	the value measured on the other axis. Hence, the forty-five degree
	line can be used as an alternative measure of the variable measured
horizontal	on the _____ (horizontal/vertical) axis. In terms of
	the graph of the consumption function, this means that the forty-five
income	degree line can be used as a measure of _____ .
	When the consumption function crosses the forty-five degree line,
equal	consumption and disposable income are _____ ; this indi-
zero	cates _____ (positive/zero/negative) saving and is
breakeven	called the _____ point. When the consumption
	function lies above the forty-five degree line, consumption is
greater than	_____ (greater than/equal to/less than)
negative	income, saving is _____ (positive/zero/negative), or
dissaving	there is _____ . When the consumption function lies be-
less than	low the forty-five degree line, consumption is _____
	(greater than/equal to/less than) income, and saving is
positive	_____ (positive/zero/negative). Furthermore, for
	any given level of disposable personal income, the vertical distance
	between the consumption function and the forty-five degree line in-
	dicates the amount of saving.
	In a relatively short time period, a change in income will bring
small	about a relatively _____ (large/small) change in planned
small	consumption, resulting in a relatively _____ (large/small)
small	*MPC* and in a consumption function with a relatively _____
	(large/small) slope. The consumption function associated with a
short-run	relatively short response time is a _____ consumption
	function. When the response time is allowed to increase until all
	potential response can be realized, the resulting consumption func-

long-run	tion is called the _____ consumption function. This
high	consumption function will have a relatively _____ (high/low)
large	*MPC* and a correspondingly _____ (large/small) slope.
	According to the permanent-income hypothesis, a household's consumption spending is a fixed proportion of what it believes to be
permanent	its _____ or long-run income level. The permanent income hypothesis places emphasis on whether income changes are
permanent, transitory	perceived by households to be _____ or _____ . Changes in consumption spending are the result of changes in the
permanent income	perceived level of _____ . Income that
transitory	is perceived to be temporary or _____ is
saved	_____ . As real income increases, households first respond
transitory	as though the increase is largely _____ (permanent/ transitory). Hence, a relatively large proportion of the additional
saved	income is _____ (spent/saved). As a consequence, the
low	short-run *MPC* will tend to be relatively _____ (high/low). As the time period lengthens, a greater proportion of additional
permanent	income is perceived to be _____ (permanent/transitory). Consequently, as the time period increases, a greater proportion of the additional income will be spent, indicating that the *MPC* will
increase	_____ (increase/decrease).
	It is possible to reconstruct the consumption and saving functions so that they are based on national income and product (NI or NNP)
disposable personal income	rather than on _____ . If the difference between disposable personal income and national income is a lum-sum tax, the new consumption and saving functions
the same	will have _____ (smaller/the same/larger) slopes as the original consumption and saving functions. The consumption and saving functions, based on national income and product, are the
right	original consumption and saving functions shifted to the _____
the lump-sum tax	(right/left) by the amount of _____ .
	Whether or not a particular investment project should be under-
rate of return	taken by a firm depends on how the expected _____ on the investment compares with the cost of borrowing the money to
interest rate	finance the investment, that is, the _____ . Planned investment will be undertaken when the rate of return from the

greater

investment is expected to be equal to or _____ (greater/ less) than the rate of interest. This typically gives rise to a demand

negatively

curve for planned investment that is _____ (positively/ negatively) sloped.

Four spending streams make up total planned expenditure:

consumption, investment, government purchases

_____ , _____ , _____ ,

net exports, sum

and _____ . Total planned expenditure is the _____ of these four components. Note that these spending streams are the

planned

_____ (planned/actual) streams.

When total planned expenditure is greater than national income or

decrease

product, actual inventory holdings _____ (increase/

increase

decrease) and production and/or prices _____ (increase/ decrease). When total planned expenditure is less than national in-

increase

come and product, actual inventory holdings _____

decrease

(increase/decrease) and production and/or prices _____ (increase/decrease). Only when total planned expenditure and

equal

national income and product are _____ will there be no incentive for a change in production and/or prices. Hence, it is only when total planned expenditure and national income and product are

equilibrium

equal that the economy is in _____ .

Referring to the Keynesian cross, equilibrium occurs at the

intersection, total-planned-expenditure

_____ of the _____

forty-five degree

curve and the _____ line. Recall, how-

is not necessarily

ever, that in the Keynesian model, equilibrium _____ (is/is not necessarily) associated with full employment.

An alternative approach to determining the equilibrium level of

leakages

national income and product relies on a comparison of _____

injections, saving

and _____ . Leakages include _____ ,

net taxes, imports

_____ and _____ ; injections

planned investment, government purchases

include _____ , _____ ,

exports

and _____ . Equilibrium occurs when total leakages

equal

_____ total injections. When total leakages are less

decrease

than total injections, actual inventories _____

an increase

(increase/decrease) giving rise to _____ (an
increase/a decrease) in production and/or prices. When total leakages

increase

are greater than total injections, actual inventories _____

a decrease

(increase/decrease) giving rise to _____ (an increase/
a decrease) in production and/or prices.

**Problems and
Applications**

1. Consider the graph of the consumption function below. Identify
    the breakeven point, the region in which dissaving takes place, and
    the region in which saving occurs. Draw the saving function that
    goes with the consumption function.

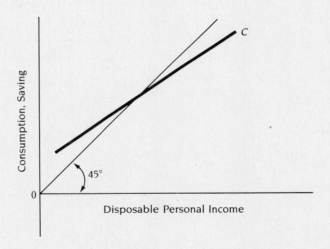

2. a. Determine the saving function that corresponds to the consumption function described by the schedule below. Determine the marginal propensities to consume and to save. What is the relationship between them? Graph both functions on the grid below.

Y_d	C	S
$100	$140	$
200	200	
300	260	
400	320	
500	380	
600	440	
700	500	

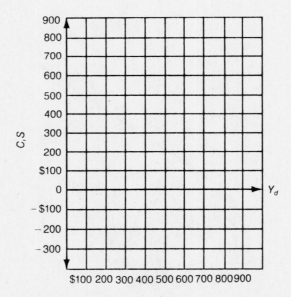

b. Assume that for every level of disposable income, households plan to consume $100 more. Develop and graph the new consumption function on the grid above. What has happened to the consumption function? Develop and graph the saving function for this new consumption function. What has happened to saving?

c. What do you think would happen to saving if the consumption function shifted upward by $200 at every level of disposable income? What would happen to consumption if the saving function shifted upward by $200? (If you cannot answer these questions directly, draw graphs of each situation and describe the results.) What can you conclude regarding changes in consumption and saving?

3. Assume that the consumption function is given as $C = 500 + .75Y_d$.
   a. What is autonomous consumption?
   b. What is the marginal propensity to consume?
   c. What is the marginal propensity to save?
   d. What is planned household spending when disposable personal income is $2,000?
   e. What is household saving when disposable personal income is $2,000?
   f. What is the breakeven level of disposable personal income?

4. In addition to the information contained in the consumption table below, assume that the government purchases $60 worth of goods and services, there are no government transfer payments, planned investment spending is $40, the value of exports is $80, and the value of imports is $30.

NI	DPI	C
$150	$100	$150
250	200	225
350	300	300
450	400	375
550	500	450
650	600	525
750	700	600
850	800	675

   a. Draw the consumption and saving functions based on disposable personal income.
   b. Draw the consumption and saving functions based on national income and product.
   c. Compare the graph of the consumption function based on national income and product with that based on disposable personal income. What happens to the slope of the consumption function? What happens to the position of the consumption function?
   d. Compare the graph of the saving function based on national income and product with that based on disposable personal income. What happens to the slope of the saving function? What happens to the position of the saving function?
   e. What is the amount of the lump-sum tax?
   f. What is the value of net exports?

g. Compute the marginal propensities to consume and save for the consumption function based on DPI.

h. What is the value of total planned injections?

i. Identify the breakeven level of disposable personal income.

j. Identify the equilibrium values of national income and disposable personal income.

k. What are the equilibrium values of consumption, saving, total injections, total leakages, and total planned expenditure?

l. Assume that full employment occurs at a level of national income and product equal to $850. What is the implication for equilibrium?

5. In addition to the information contained in the saving-function table below, assume that lump-sum net taxes are $40, the government purchases $30 worth of goods and services, planned investment spending is $40, the total value of exports is $20, and the total value of imports is $30.

Y	Y_d	C	S
	$100		$-20
	200		0
	300		20
	400		40
	500		60
	600		80
	700		100

a. Complete the schedule, indicating the amount of consumption that occurs at each level of disposable personal income (Y_d) and the level of national income (Y) associated with each level of disposable income.

b. What is the value of net exports?

c. Compute the marginal propensities to consume and save based on disposable personal income.

d. What is the total value of planned injections?

e. What is the breakeven level of consumption spending?

f. Determine the equilibrium levels of national income and disposable personal income.

g. At equilibrium, what are the values for each of the following: consumption, saving, total injections, total leakages, total planned expenditure?

h. If the full-employment level of consumption is $280, what is the full-employment level of national income and product? What can you conclude with respect to equilibrium?

True-False   Indicate whether each of the following statements is basically true or false. If the statement is false, rewrite it so that it is true.

_____ 1. Say's Identity essentially says that "demand creates its own supply."

_____ 2. Neoclassical economists believed that an economy would always operate at full employment.

_____ 3. The Keynesian model as described in the text is based on nominal values.

_____ 4. Wealth is the primary determinant of household spending.

_____ 5. DPI = $C + S$.

_____ 6. The breakeven point occurs at the level of disposable personal income that equates the amount consumed by households with the amount saved by households.

_____ 7. The marginal propensity to consume measures the percentage of income that is spent.

_____ 8. The marginal propensity to save measures the amount of extra income that is saved.

_____ 9. If consumption spending decreases by $70 when disposable personal income falls by $100, the *MPC* is 0.7 or 70%.

_____ 10. The Keynesian cross is a graph of consumption and saving, whereas the Marshallian cross refers to a graph of demand and supply.

_____ 11. The long-run consumption function, as compared to a short-run consumption function, has a relatively higher *MPC* and steeper slope.

_____ 12. The *MPC* is likely to be greater the shorter the time period under consideration.

_____ 13. Transitory income is income that is perceived to belong to someone else.

_____ 14. The difference between national income and disposable personal income is net taxes.

_____ 15. Equilibrium national income and product occurs at the intersection of the consumption function and the forty-five degree line.

_____ 16. Historically, planned investment expenditure appears to have been the most volatile component of total planned expenditure.

_____ 17. Equilibrium national income and product occurs at the level of national income where leakages equal injections.

_____ 18. According to Keynesian economics, prices adjust until the economy reaches a full-employment equilibrium.

_____ 19. Unlike neoclassical economics, Keynesian economics suggests that government intervention may be necessary for the economy to reach a full-employment equilibrium.

Multiple Choice   Choose the *one best* answer in each of the following cases:

_____ 1. Dissaving occurs
   a. whenever C exceeds S.
   b. whenever S = DPI – C.
   c. whenever the *MPC* exceeds the *MPS*.
   d. at disposable incomes less than the breakeven level of DPI.
   e. at any income level less than the equilibrium level.

Use the following graph to answer questions 2 and 3.

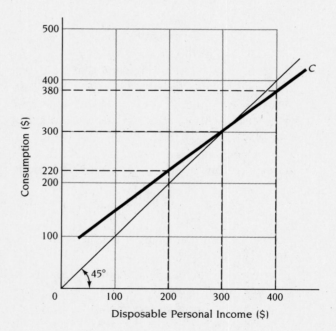

_____ 2. With regard to the consumption function in the graph above, which one of the following conclusions about the marginal propensities to consume and save is correct?
   a. The *MPC* is 4/5 and the *MPS* is 1/5.
   b. The *MPC* plus the *MPS* must equal $300.
   c. The *MPC* and the *MPS* vary with varying levels of DPI.

d. The *MPC* is equal to the slope of the consumption function, but the *MPS* cannot be determined.

e. Neither the *MPC* nor the *MPS* can be determined from the information given.

3. If the consumption function in the graph were reconstructed on a national income base, the
   a. *MPS* would increase.
   b. *MPC* would increase.
   c. *MPC* would decrease.
   d. forty-five degree line would be steeper.
   e. none of the above

4. Which one of the following statements is accurate with respect to a comparison of Keynesian and neoclassical economics?
   a. In both Keynesian and neoclassical economics, a full-employment equilibrium is the result of appropriate wage adjustments in labor markets.
   b. In Keynesian economics the economy might come to equilibrium at any level of employment, whereas in neoclassical economics the economy always comes to a full-employment equilibrium.
   c. In Keynesian economics full employment is associated only with equilibrium, whereas in neoclassical economics full employment exists whether or not the economy is in equilibrium.
   d. In Keynesian economics the economy might not reach full employment, but in neoclassical economics the economy is always characterized by full employment.
   e. Neither Keynesian nor neoclassical economics guarantees a full-employment equilibrium.

5. Which one of the following statements is accurate with respect to a comparison of the appropriate role of government in Keynesian versus neoclassical economics?
   a. Neither Keynesian nor neoclassical economics deals with the issue of government intervention in the economy.
   b. Both Keynesian and neoclassical economics conclude that government intervention is unnecessary and may even be detrimental to the goal of full employment.
   c. Keynesian economics concludes that government intervention may be helpful in assuring a full-employment equilibrium, whereas neoclassical economics concludes that government intervention is unnecessary.
   d. Keynesian economics concludes that government intervention may be helpful in assuring a full-employment equilibrium, whereas neoclassical economics concludes that govern-

ment intervention is essential if the economy is ever to reach full employment

e. Both Keynesian and neoclassical economics conclude that government intervention is essential if the economy is to reach full-employment equilibrium.

6. Keynes and the neoclassical economists agreed in thinking that
   a. prices and wages could be guaranteed to change in accordance with the dictates of supply and demand.
   b. in the midst of a drop in sales, big nusiness would prevent price cuts by laying off workers until unplanned inventories were used up.
   c. powerful labor unions might successfully prevent wage cuts.
   d. both b and c above
   e. none of the above

7. Assume that the breakeven level of disposable personal income is $100,000 and that the MPC is 9/10. What is planned consumption spending at an income of $200,000?
   a. $90,000
   b. $180,000
   c. $190,000
   d. $200,000
   e. It cannot be determined from the information given.

8. What is the MPC if planned household spending is $500 when disposable personal income is $700 and $650 when disposable personal income is $900?
   a. $150
   b. 150%
   c. $75
   d. 0.75
   e. 0.15

9. If planned household spending increases by $80 when disposable personal income increases from $200 to $300, the MPC is
   a. $20.
   b. $80.
   c. 0.80.
   d. 0.20.
   e. It cannot be determined from the information given.

10. If households plan to save an additional $20 when disposable personal income increases from $200 to $300, the MPS is
    a. $20.
    b. $80.
    c. 0.80.
    d. 0.20.
    e. It cannot be determined from the information given.

_____ 11. If planned household spending is $80 when disposable personal income is $100, the *MPC* is
   a. $20.
   b. $80.
   c. 0.2.
   d. 0.8.
   e. It cannot be determined from the information given.

_____ 12. If households plan to save $20 when disposable personal income is $100, the *MPS* is
   a. $20.
   b. $80.
   c. 0.2.
   d. 0.8.
   e. It cannot be determined from the information given.

_____ 13. According to the permanent income hypothesis,
   a. the *MPC* tends to decrease over time as income becomes permanent.
   b. households tend to spend a relatively large proportion of transitory income.
   c. households perceive increases in income as transitory and decreases in income as permanent.
   d. if an increase in income is perceived to be temporary, households will tend to save it.
   e. permanent income is that proportion of total income that a household saves, whereas transitory income is the proportion that is spent.

_____ 14. Under which one of the following circumstances is a consumption function *least* likely to shift?
   a. when there is a change in wealth
   b. when there is a change in income
   c. when there is a change in expectations
   d. when there is a change in the stock of durable goods
   e. both a and b above

_____ 15. Which one of the following is an accurate statement with respect to planned investment spending?
   a. Profit expectations are a primary determinant of planned investment.
   b. Planned investment is a major component of planned consumption expenditures.
   c. Unlike most demand curves, the demand curve for planned investment is positively sloped.
   d. Planned investment spending includes all purchases of stocks and bonds as well as acquisitions of new capital goods.

e. Planned investment spending includes business purchases of stocks and bonds but excludes these purchases when made by households.

_____ 16. Under which one of the following circumstances is the investment demand curve *least* likely to shift?
a. when there is a technological change
b. when there is a change in operating costs
c. when there is a change in the interest rate
d. when there is a change in government policies
e. when there is a change in expected business conditions

_____ 17. If I, G, and X-Im are all autonomous, what is the slope of the total-planned-expenditure curve?
a. the slope of the consumption function
b. the slope of the saving function
c. the slope of the investment function
d. the slope of the government purchases function
e. the slope of the net exports function

_____ 18. When total planned expenditure is greater than national income and product, which of the following tends to decrease?
a. prices
b. production
c. employment
d. actual inventory holdings
e. planned consumption spending

_____ 19. According to Keynesian economics, equilibrium national income occurs
a. whenever full employment is reached.
b. whenever inventory holdings are eliminated.
c. whenever total leakages equal total injections.
d. at the intersection of the consumption and saving curves.
e. at the intersection of the planned consumption spending curve and the forty-five degree line.

_____ 20. When total leakages exceed total injections
a. the economy is in disequilibrium.
b. there will be a tendency for prices to increase.
c. actual inventory holdings are less than intended.
d. there will be a tendency for production to increase.
e. all of the above

_____ 21. If national income, national product, and total planned expenditure all equal $1,000 and full employment occurs at a level of national income equal to $1,500, then
a. the economy will not reach equilibrium.
b. at full employment, total leakages will exceed total injections.

c. at equilibrium, total planned expenditure will be less than national income and product.

d. at full employment, the actual level of inventory holdings is less than the planned level.

e. national income and product will have to increase by $500 in order for the economy to reach equilibrium.

Use the following table to answer questions 22 through 26.

NI	DPI	C
$400	300	300
500	400	375
600	500	450
700	600	525
800	700	600
900	800	675

In addition to the information contained in the consumption schedule above, it is known that the government purchases $100 worth of goods and services, there are no government transfer payments, planned investment spending is $50, the value of exports is $60, and the value of imports is $35.

22. What is the equilibrium level of national income and product for the economy described in the table above?
    a. $300
    b. $400
    c. $600
    d. $700
    e. $900

23. If the economy described in the table is in equilibrium, what is the value of total leakages?
    a. $65
    b. $75
    c. $135
    d. $210
    e. $260

24. For the economy described in the table, if disposable personal income is $700, then
    a. leakages total $210.
    b. net taxes are $50.
    c. planned injections total $210.
    d. net exports are indeterminate.
    e. total planned expenditure is $810.

_____ 25. Consider the economy described in the table. Which one of the following statements correctly describes this economy if the full-employment level of national income and product is $900?
a. At equilibrium, net taxes are $200.
b. The economy will not reach equilibrium.
c. The economy will come to equilibrium with unemployment.
d. At full employment, total injections exceed total leakages.
e. At full employment, total planned expenditure exceeds national income.

_____ 26. Which one of the following statements is accurate with respect to the economy described in the table?
a. When based on national income, the *MPC* is 3/5.
b. When based on national income, the *MPS* is 2/5.
c. When based on disposable personal income, the *MPC* is 75.
d. When based on disposable personal income, the *MPS* is 25.
e. When based on disposable personal income, the *MPS* is 1/4.

Discussion Questions

1. Explain why each of the four curves on the graph below is not a realistic consumption function.

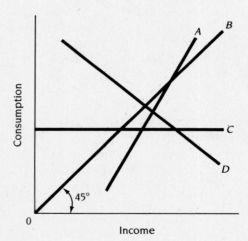

2. Explain what is likely to happen to total planned expenditure if consumers expect continued inflation?

3. What is likely to happen to consumption if there is a tightening of credit conditions? What is the consequence for total planned expenditure and for the equilibrium levels of national income and national product? Explain.

4. Explain what happens to the saving function if there is an increase in the consumption function.

Answers

Problems and Applications

1. Regions of dissaving and saving are shown by the shaded areas in the graph below.

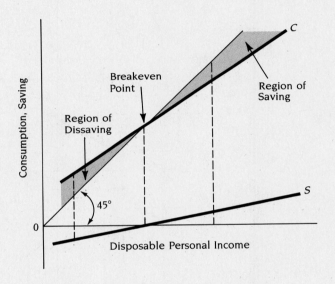

2. a.

Y_d	C	S
$100	$140	$-40
200	200	0
300	260	40
400	320	80
500	380	120
600	440	160
700	500	200

MPC = 0.6 or 3/5
MPS = 0.4 or 2/5
For every particular change in Y_d, *MPC* + *MPS* = 1.

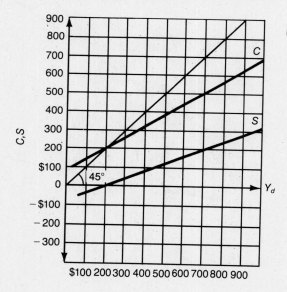

b.

Y_d	C	S
$100	$240	$-140
200	300	-100
300	360	-60
400	420	-20
500	480	20
600	540	60
700	600	100

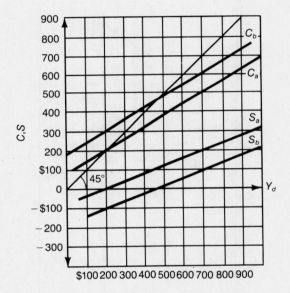

The consumption function shifts upward by $100. The saving function shifts downward by $100.

c. Saving would shift downward by $200. Consumption would shift downward by $200. For every change in consumption (represented by a shift in the consumption function), the saving function will change in the opposite direction by an equal amount.

3. a. $500   b. 0.75   c. 0.25   d. $2,000
   e. $0   f. $2,000

4. a.

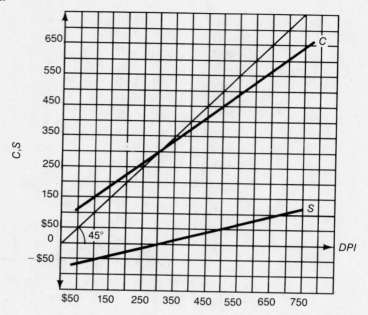

b.

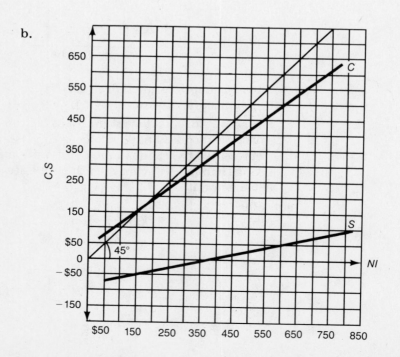

    c. Nothing; the consumption function shifts to the right by the amount of the lump-sum tax ($50, in this case).

    d. Nothing; the saving function shifts to the right.

    e. $50

    f. $50

    g. 0.75; 0.25

    h. $180

    i. $300

    j. $750; $700

    k. $600; $100; $180; $180; $750

    l. The economy will come to equilibrium with unemployment.

5. a.

Y	Y_d	C	S
$140	$100	$120	$-20
240	200	200	0
340	300	280	20
440	400	360	40
540	500	440	60
640	600	520	80
740	700	600	100

    b. -$10

    c. $MPC = 4/5 = 80\%$; $MPS = 1/5 = 20\%$

    d. $90

    e. $200

    f. $340; $300

    g. $280; $20; $90; $90; $340

    h. $340; the economy will come to a full-employment equilibrium.

True-False

1. F. Say's Identity essentially says that "supply creates its own demand."

2. F. Neoclassical economists believed that an economy would be characterized by a full-employment equilibrium.

3. F. The Keynesian model as described in the text is based on real values.

4. F. Income is the primary determinant of household spending.

5. T.

6. F. The breakeven point occurs at the level of disposable personal income at which the amount consumed by households is just equal to disposable personal income; alternatively, the breakeven point occurs at the level of disposable personal income at which the amount saved by households is zero.

7. F. The *MPC* measures the percentage of additional income that is spent.
8. F. The *MPS* measures the percentage of extra income that is saved.
9. T.
10. T.
11. T.
12. F. The *MPC* is likely to be greater the longer the time period under consideration.
13. F. Transitory income is income that is perceived to be temporary.
14. T.
15. F. Equilibrium national income and product occurs at the intersection of the total planned expenditure line and the forty-five degree line.
16. T.
17. T.
18. F. According to neoclassical economics, prices adjust until the economy reaches a full-employment equilibrium.
19. T.

Multiple Choice

1. d	2. a	3. e	4. b	5. c
6. e	7. c	8. d	9. c	10. d
11. e	12. e	13. d	14. b	15. a
16. c	17. a	18. d	19. c	20. a
21. b	22. d	23. d	24. c	25. c
26. e				

10 *The Multiplier and Business Fluctuations*

Summary

One of the most important contributions of Keynesian economics has been an explanation of how a relatively small change in planned expenditure can lead to a much larger change in national income and product. This is the multiplier concept. If we assume that planned investment, government purchases, and net exports are not altered in the short run by changes in national income, then the multiplier is equal to the reciprocal of $(1 - MPC)$; that is, the multiplier is equal to $\frac{1}{MPS}$.

The multiplier concept may be helpful in explaining business fluctuations, that is, changes in economic activity over time. Economists refer to two cumulative phases of business fluctuations, the expansion and contraction phases, and to two turning points, the upper and lower turning points. Though business fluctuations are recurrent, they do not recur in a uniform fashion. Analysts have identified several cyclical patterns for the U.S. economy. These include, in order of length, the Kitchin cycle, the Juglar cycle, the Kuznets cycle, and the Kondratieff cycle.

The cumulative phases of the business cycle are initiated by changes in planned expenditure, which give rise to a multiplier process. The multiplier gives these phases a time dimension as well as their cumulative character. In addition, other forces may add to the cumulative character of the expansion or contraction phases. For example, there may be additional changes in total planned expenditure caused by psychological responses to the expansion or contraction.

The upper and lower turning points of a business cycle exist because the expansion and contraction phases cannot continue indefinitely. The upper turning point may be reached simply because resource limitations have been reached or because bottlenecks arise in some sectors of the economy; other factors may also be involved. The lower turning point of the cycle will be reached, if for no other reason, because there is some floor below which planned expenditure will not fall. This floor is defined by requirements for survival. Once a turning point is reached, a combination of accelerator and multiplier effects causes the economy to move into a new cumulative phase.

Keynesian economics came about as a result of the Great Depression of the 1930s. As a consequence, the theory offers insight into the problems of the 1920s that led to the Great Depression, and it provides some explanations for the delayed recovery.

In addition to Keynesian theory, there are many other theories of business cycles. One of these is Karl Marx's theory that capitalism will lead to increasingly severe depressions until finally the capitalist system will be overthrown and replaced by socialism. An alternative theory was offered by Joseph Schumpeter. In Schumpeter's view, the success (rather than the failure) of capitalism will lead to its downfall. Capitalist innovations will raise living standards to such an extent that attention will no longer be focused on production but on the distribution of income and wealth.

The Great Depression of the 1930s and Roosevelt's New Deal enable us to investigate Keynesian economics further. The extent to which New Deal policies were successful is still subject to question.

Major Objectives

After you have finished this chapter, you will be able to do the following:

1. Identify the major nonincome variables that influence planned consumption and planned saving, planned investment, government purchases, and net exports.
2. Explain and show graphically how a change in one or more components of total planned expenditure will affect the equilibrium level of national income and product.
3. Define, calculate, and use the simple multiplier.
4. Use the concepts of marginal propensities and induced expenditures to explain the multiplier process.
5. Explain how time affects the multiplier process.
6. Distinguish between changes that initiate the multiplier process and responses that are induced as a result of it.
7. Recognize and explain the fact that the *MPS* is equal to one minus the *MPC*.
8. Define business cycle and business fluctuation, and describe the major characteristics of business fluctuations.

9. Identify and describe the phases of a business fluctuation.
10. Describe how business fluctuations are measured and the problems associated with their measurement.
11. Trace the steps involved in statistically identifying business cycles.
12. Distinguish the following business cycles in terms of their causes and their lengths: Kitchin, Juglar, Kuznets, Kondratieff.
13. Discuss the interaction of relatively short and long business cycles.
14. Use the multiplier principle to provide a simple explanation for the cumulative phases of business cycles.
15. Identify forces other than the multiplier that affect the cumulative phases of business cycles.
16. Use the concept of an accelerator effect to explain the turning points in business cycles.
17. Identify the primary objectives of business-cycle policy.
18. Discuss the role of business-cycle theory and its consequences for capitalism.
19. Discuss Joseph Schumpeter's explanation of business cycles and its consequences for capitalism.
20. Describe the economic and political climate preceding and during the Great Depression of the 1930s.
21. Discuss the three major economic policies of the New Deal.
22. Explain the concept of priming the pump and the role of this technique in the 1930s.

Review Terms

Keynesian economics
total planned expenditure
macroeconomic equilibrium
equilibrium national income
  and product (Y*)
ceteris paribus
marginal propensity to consume
marginal propensity to save
a shift in a curve vs. a movement
  along a curve
planned consumption expenditure
income vs. wealth
real vs. nominal values
planned investment expenditure
demand curve for planned
  investment spending
rate of interest

rate of return
government purchases
net exports
foreign exchange rates
general vs. partial equilibrium
  analysis
Keynesian cross
net taxes
expansion
contraction
reciprocal
index number
inventory
innovation
disequilibrium
resources or inputs or factors
  of production

capital good	durable goods
net investment	"rest of the world"
gross investment	balanced budget
capitalism	neoclassical economics
socialism	budget deficit
stock exchange	stagnation
inflation	dividends

Important Terms and Concepts

multiplier	Juglar cycle
induced expenditure	Kuznets cycle
the nth round or limit	Kondratieff cycle
initiating changes vs. induced changes	"prime the pump"
business cycles	bottlenecks
business fluctuations	accelerator effect
cumulative	idle capacity
upper turning point	Karl Marx
lower turning point	Joseph Schumpeter
expansion phase	Black Thursday
contraction phase	installment credit
length of a fluctuation	agricultural fundamentalism
amplitude	international fundamentalism
trend line	maldistribution
leading indicator	overspeculation
lagging indicator	hoard
seasonal variation	deflationist
time-series data	liquidate
time-series graph	New Deal
Kitchin cycle	Social Security
	Federal Reserve Board

Completion

A change in total planned expenditure that comes about because of a

shift in

change in some nonincome variable is represented by a _____
(shift in/movement along) the total-planned-expenditure curve. This
change in total planned expenditure will cause a change in the

equilibrium,
national income and
product

_____ level of _____ .
The resulting change in equilibrium national income and product will

same

be in the _____ (same/opposite) direction as the initi-

larger than

ating change in total planned expenditure and will be _____
(larger than/equal to/less than) the change in total planned expendi-

multiplier process

ture. That is, a _____ is operative. The

change in equilibrium national income	multiplier is equal to the ratio of the _____
change in total planned expenditure	to the _____ .
the reciprocal of (1 – *MPC*)	Alternatively, the multiplier is equal to _____
the reciprocal of *MPS*	or _____ .

Expansions and contractions in the volume of economic activity

business cycles	that alternate with some regularity are referred to as _____ . Since there is much irregularity in these expansions and contractions,
fluctuations	it may be preferable to refer to them as business _____ .
expansion	There are two cumulative phases to a business cycle: the _____
contraction	phase and the _____ phase. The cumulative phases are
changes in planned expenditure	initiated by _____ ,
multiplier	which give rise to a multiplier process. The _____ gives these phases a time dimension as well as their cumulative character.
two	There are also _____ turning points in a business cycle. The
upper, lower	_____ and _____ turning points exist because the expansion and contraction phases cannot continue indefinitely. The
upper	_____ (upper/lower) turning point may be reached because resource limitations have been reached or because bottlenecks arise in some sectors of the economy. At some point there will be a slow-
contraction	down in the rate of expansion, which will lead to a(n) _____ (expansion/contraction) in capital goods industries. This is called an
accelerator	_____ effect. The reduced demand for resources by
multiplier	the capital goods industries starts a _____ process in
lower	the downward direction. The _____ (upper/lower) turning point will be reached, if for no other reason, because there is some floor below which planned expenditure will not fall. This floor is de-
survival	fined by requirements for _____ . When reserves of idle machinery are used up and capital equipment must again be pro-
expansion	duced, the rise in capital goods production will start a new _____ (expansion/contraction) in the economy. Alternatively, the upturn
innovation	may begin with a successful _____ , an increase in

foreign,
government

_____ demand, or an increase in _____ spending.

The prosperity of the 1920s was characterized by increased invest-

a few

ment in _____ (many/a few) industries, resulting in multiplier effects in the economy at large. Among the important growth indus-

urban housing,
automobile

tries were _____ , the _____ ,

radio

and the _____ . Another important development,

installment credit

_____ , allowed people to buy durable consumption goods before they had saved the money to pay for them. Two areas of particular weakness in the American economy were

agriculture, export
trade

_____ and _____ .

There are a number of theories to explain the stock market crash, most of which are not mutually exclusive. One theory concentrates

multiplier effects

on the _____ of slowdowns in leading industries.

agricultural funda-
mentalism

Another blames _____ , seeing the failure in the inability of agricultural purchasing power to absorb the in-

International
fundamentalism

creased production of urban goods. _____ focuses on the spread of worldwide difficulties to the United States. Wages failed to keep pace with average labor productivity, and the

income distribution

_____ of the 1920s seems to have shifted

overspeculation

against labor. Finally, _____ resulted in a shift in income away from the purchase of currently produced goods in favor of the purchase of assets such as real estate, art works, antiques, and stocks. Such a decrease in expenditure on current output initi-

multiplier, down-
ward

ates _____ effects in a(n) _____ (upward/downward) direction.

Franklin Roosevelt's New Deal involved three sets of economic

increase

policies. One was to _____ (increase/decrease) prices in advance of production costs. Roosevelt was especially interested in

farm, increase

_____ prices. A second policy was to _____

before

(increase/decrease) wages _____ (before/after) prices. The

redistribution

third policy was general reform, including a _____

break-up

of income and wealth, the _____ (encouragement/

strengthening

break-up) of monopolies, the _____ (strengthening/

expanded

weakening) of farm and labor organizations, and a(n) _____

(expanded/contracted) role for government in the emerging "welfare state."

depression

Because of a severe secondary _____ in 1937–1938, many people have concluded that the New Deal was a failure and

World War II

that recovery was brought about by _____ . There are several causes for the secondary depression. One of these was the

priming the pump

failure of the New Deal process of _____ , which was supposed to encourage investment and shift the planned investment curve. In addition, wage gains in trade unions were passed

inflation

on in the form of higher prices, resulting in a fear of _____ .

tight

This led to a(n) _____ (easy/tight) money policy on the part of the Federal Reserve System. Finally, corporations had to pay both a

corporate income, undistributed profits

_____ tax and an _____

decrease

tax. This led to a(n) _____ (increase/decrease) in private investment spending.

Problems and Applications

1. For each of the following cycles on the left, give the length of the cycle and match it with its description on the right.

   _____ Juglar cycle

   _____ Kitchin cycle

   _____ Kondratieff cycle

   _____ Kuznets cycle

   a. associated with inventory changes
   b. perhaps associated with major technological innovations (e.g., railroads and automobiles)
   c. of debatable cause; the Great Depression came between the upper turning points on either side of one of these cycles
   d. associated with the duration of buildings and transportation facilities; perhaps related to population waves set in motion by birthrate changes following wars

2. Determine the multiplier for each of the following scenarios:
   a. A $400 increase in total planned expenditure causes a $1,200 increase in equilibrium national product.
   b. The *MPC* is 7/8.
   c. The *MPC* is 5/8 and planned investment, government purchases, and net exports are not altered in the short run by changes in national income.

  d. Equilibrium national income decreases by $25,000 as a result of a $5,000 decrease in total planned expenditure.
  e. Equilibrium national product increases by $2,000 as a result of a $500 increase in planned investment spending.
  f. The *MPS* is 1/4.
  g. The *MPS* is 2/5.

3. Will a larger *MPC* result in a larger or a smaller multiplier?

4. Assuming that the multiplier is 3, indicate the effects of each of the following on total planned expenditure and on equilibrium national income and product:
  a. Consumption spending increases by $20,000.
  b. Planned investment spending decreases by $1,000.
  c. Government purchases increase by $300.
  d. *C* increases by $100 and *I* increases by $100.
  e. *C* increases by $100, *I* increases by $200, and *G* decreases by $100.
  f. *C* decreases by $100, *I* decreases by $400, and *G* increases by $200.
  g. Government purchases increase by $400 and planned investment decreases by $500.

5. Consider the economy described by the schedule below.

Y	C	Total Planned Expenditure
$ 400	500	700
600	640	840
800	780	980
1,000	920	1,120
1,200	1,060	1,260
1,400	1,200	1,400
1,600	1,340	1,540
1,800	1,480	1,680

  a. Identify the following: the equilibrium level of national income and product, the *MPC*, the *MPS*, and the multiplier.
  b. What will happen to total planned expenditure if consumption increases by $30? What will happen to national income and product? What will the new equilibrium level of national income be?
  c. What will happen to total planned expenditure if planned investment spending decreases by $30? What will happen to national income and product? What will the new equilibrium level of national income be?

d. What will happen to total planned expenditure if government purchases decrease by $33? What will happen to national income and product? What will the new equilibrium level of national income be?

6. Consider the economy described by the total-planned-expenditure curves in the graph below. Curve I represents the initial planned-expenditure curve; Curve II represents the final planned-expenditure curve.

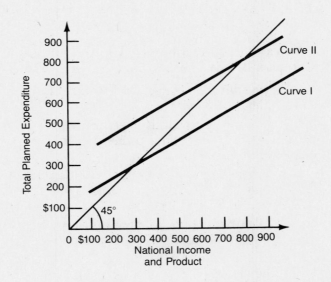

a. Initially, what was the level of equilibrium national income and product?
b. What has happened to total planned expenditure? (Be specific: in what direction did it change, and by how much?)
c. If the change in total planned expenditure was caused by a change in planned investment spending, what was the change in planned investment spending? (Be specific: in what direction did it change, and by how much?)
d. What is the new level of equilibrium national income and product?
e. What happened to equilibrium national income and product? (Be specific: in what direction did it change, and by how much?)
f. What was the multiplier?
g. What is the *MPS*?
h. What is the *MPC*? Is this *MPC* consistent with the total-planned-expenditure curves? How do you know?

7. If out of every income level, people save $100 more, what happens to
   a. consumption?
   b. total planned expenditure?
   c. equilibrium national income if the multiplier is 5/2?

8. Assume that, initially, equilibrium national income is $2,000. Given a multiplier of 4, determine the effect of a $100 increase in planned investment spending on equilibrium national income. What will be the new level of equilibrium national income?

True-False   Indicate whether each of the following statements is basically true or false. If the statement is false, rewrite it so that it is true.

_____ 1. The multiplier concept is an important part of neoclassical economic theory.

_____ 2. A change in wealth is likely to cause a movement along the consumption function and therefore a movement along the total-planned-expenditure curve.

_____ 3. A change in expectations about the state of the economy may cause a shift in the consumption function and a corresponding shift in the saving function.

_____ 4. A significant improvement in technology is likely to cause a downward shift in the total planned expenditure curve, because investment spending will decline.

_____ 5. The multiplier process suggests that an increase in equilibrium national income will cause a larger increase in total planned expenditure.

_____ 6. The multiplier works for decreases in total planned expenditure as well as for increases.

_____ 7. The multiplier process works instantaneously.

_____ 8. The full effects of the multiplier will be experienced within about one year.

_____ 9. If equilibrium national income decreases by $3,000 as a result of a $1,000 decrease in total planned expenditure, the multiplier is 1/3.

_____ 10. The multiplier is $1/(1 - MPC)$.

_____ 11. Business cycles measure changes in economic activity over time.

_____ 12. Business cycles tend to be of uniform length and are measured from an upper turning point to a lower turning point.

_____ 13. The cumulative phases of the business cycle can be explained, in part, by the multiplier.

_____ 14. The trend line measures the seasonal changes in economic activity.

_____ 15. President Hoover believed that the stock market crash had no effect on the real economy, so he expected prosperity to continue at the lower level of stock prices.

_____ 16. The New Deal called for a decrease in prices followed by a decrease in wages.

_____ 17. Pump-priming under the New Deal was supposed to encourage an upward shift in the investment curve so that government spending would not have to continue.

Multiple Choice   Choose the *one best* answer in each of the following cases:

_____ 1. Which of the following would be *least* likely to cause a shift in the consumption curve?
a. a change in income
b. a change in wealth
c. a change in saving
d. a change in expectations
e. a change in household stocks of durable goods

_____ 2. A shift in the planned investment curve may be caused by a change in
a. taxes, whereas a movement along the curve is caused by a change in government regulations.
b. technology, whereas a movement along the curve is caused by a change in consumption spending.
c. stock market activity, whereas a movement along the curve is caused by a change in interest rates.
d. anticipated business conditions, whereas a movement along the curve is caused by a change in national income.
e. all of the above

_____ 3. According to the multiplier principle,
a. an upward shift in the consumption function will cause a multiplied increase in equilibrium national income.
b. equilibrium national income will decrease by a multiplied amount when the total-planned-expenditure curve shifts downward.
c. an increase in planned saving, represented by an upward shift in the planned saving curve, will result in a multiplied decrease in equilibrium national income.
d. both a and b above.
e. all of the above.

_____ 4. Assume that the *MPC* is 3/5. What is the multiplier?
  a. 5
  b. 5/2
  c. 5/3
  d. 3/5
  e. 2/5

_____ 5. If the multiplier is 4, a $100 decrease in government purchases will cause a
  a. $25 decrease in taxes.
  b. $400 decrease in taxes.
  c. $25 decrease in equilibrium national income.
  d. $400 decrease in equilibrium national income.
  e. $400 increase in investment spending.

_____ 6. If the *MPC* is 4/5, then a
  a. $400 increase in total planned expenditure will result in a $500 increase in equilibrium national income.
  b. $200 increase in total planned expenditure will result in a $1,000 increase in equilibrium national income.
  c. $100 increase in equilibrium national income will result in an $80 increase in total planned expenditure.
  d. $400 increase in equilibrium national income will result in a $2,000 increase in total planned expenditure.
  e. none of the above

_____ 7. Assume that the multiplier is 3 and that net exports decrease by $300. Total planned expenditure will probably
  a. decrease by $100.
  b. decrease by $300.
  c. decrease by $900.
  d. increase by $900.
  e. not change.

_____ 8. If planned consumption expenditure decreases by $500, planned investment spending increases by $700, and the multiplier is 3, then total planned expenditure will
  a. not change, but national income will increase by $200.
  b. increase by $200 and national income will increase by $600.
  c. decrease by $500 and national income will decrease by $1,500.
  d. decrease by $1,200 and national income will decrease by $3,600.
  e. increase by $600 and national income will increase by $200.

_____ 9. Assume that the equilibrium level of national income is $30,000 and that the *MPC* is 2/3. What is the new equilibrium level of national income if planned consumption spending increases by $3,000?
   a. $2,000
   b. $9,000
   c. $23,000
   d. $32,000
   e. $39,000

_____ 10. Assume that a given economy is in equilibrium with national income of $10,000. What is the new equilibrium level of national income if the *MPS* is 2/5 and total planned expenditure decreases by $1,000?
   a. $7,500
   b. $9,400
   c. $9,600
   d. $10,400
   e. $12,500

_____ 11. Which of the following statements is true with respect to the multiplier process?
   a. It may be initiated by a change in national income.
   b. It is sometimes referred to as the accelerator concept.
   c. It works for increases in spending but not for decreases.
   d. It involves movements along the total-planned-expenditure curve after a shift in that curve has caused a disequilibrium.
   e. all of the above

_____ 12. Business cycles and fluctuations are
   a. sometimes called trend lines.
   b. designed to show seasonal variations in data series.
   c. characterized by three cumulative phases, the upper phase, the intermediate phase, and the lower phase.
   d. characterized by a turning point called the pivot.
   e. none of the above

_____ 13. The cumulative phases of business cycles
   a. offset each other exactly.
   b. tend to recur in a uniform fashion.
   c. always result in an upward-sloping trend line.
   d. are set in motion by changes in the flow of planned expenditure.
   e. all of the above

_____ 14. Which of the following might trigger one of the cumulative phases of a business cycle?
a. a change in consumption
b. a change in planned investment
c. a change in government purchases
d. a change in net exports
e. all of the above

_____ 15. Several cyclical patterns have been identified for the U.S. economy. These include the
a. cabinet cycle, sometimes called the inventory cycle, lasting 1 to 3 years.
b. Jaguar cycle, caused by major changes in transportation systems, lasting 5 to 10 years.
c. Kuznets cycle, sometimes called the building cycle, lasting from 15 to 25 years.
d. Klondike cycle, caused by major wars, lasting in excess of 25 years.
e. all of the above

_____ 16. Forces that contribute to the cumulative character if the expansion and contraction phases of business cycles may include
a. the multiplier process.
b. the accelerator effect.
c. changes in planned expenditure caused by changes in expectations and attitudes that result from the expansion or contraction itself.
d. all of the above
e. both a and c above

_____ 17. The accelerator principle is illustrated by which of the following?
a. an increasing rate of growth during an expansion
b. an increase in total planned expenditure leading to a multiplied increase in national income and product
c. a decrease in demand that gives rise to declining prices and production, potentially leading to a collapse of the stock market
d. the need to produce new capital goods toward the end of a contractionary period when capital goods wear out and replacements cease to be available
e. all of the above

_____ 18. The accelerator effect
a. relates investment to rate of change of national income.
b. can be used to explain the turning points in business cycles.
c. may contribute to the cumulative phases of business cycles.

    d. can be used to explain how a slowdown in the rate of economic expansion can lead to a contraction in investment.

    e. all of the above

_____ 19. The upper turning point of a business cycle

    a. need never occur if the expansion phase of the cycle lies entirely above the trend line.

    b. is likely to be the result of idle capacity.

    c. may be the result of bottlenecks (limitations) in some resources.

    d. occurs, if for no other reason, because there is a lower limit on planned expenditure.

    e. all of the above

_____ 20. The lower turning point of a business cycle

    a. tends to create excess capacity.

    b. may be eliminated through the use of idle machinery.

    c. may come about after reserves of idle machinery are exhausted and new investment begins.

    d. requires a leveling off of the expansion phase and a general downturn in economic activity.

    e. none of the above

_____ 21. Explanations for the stock market crash include the

    a. decrease in output in urban areas.

    b. expansion in American export trade.

    c. growing shortage of housing in urban areas.

    d. failure of wages to keep pace with average labor productivity.

    e. increase in expenditure on current output and its associated multiplier effects.

_____ 22. Which of the following is descriptive of the Hoover administration?

    a. continued warnings about the declining economic activity

    b. incentives for business leaders to increase prices and decrease wages

    c. an increase in tax rates and a cut in government spending in an attempt to balance the budget

    d. a belief that investment spending would decline as a result of the impact of the stock market crash on profit expectations

    e. a recognition that the decrease in wealth associated with the stock market crash would result in a decrease in consumption spending

_____ 23. Which of the following is characteristic of the New Deal?
   a. It was successful in priming the pump.
   b. It sought to weaken labor organizations.
   c. It led to a slow but consistent recovery.
   d. It sought to redistribute income and wealth.
   e. all of the above

_____ 24. Which of the following is true of a comparison of the theories of Karl Marx and Joseph Schumpeter?
   a. Both welcomed the end of capitalism.
   b. Both were concerned about the exploitation of labor that results under capitalism.
   c. Both concentrated on the role of innovations in promoting economic growth and stability.
   d. Marx thought capitalism was a necessary step in the development of a socialist state, whereas Schumpeter thought socialism would lead to capitalism.
   e. none of the above

Discussion Questions

1. Identify three nonincome determinants of consumption spending. Explain how a change in each of these variables would affect saving. Also explain how a change in each of these would lead to a change in total planned expenditure and therefore to a change in equilibrium national income and product.

2. Identify three nonincome determinants of investment spending. Explain how a change in each of these variables would affect investment spending. Then explain how the change in investment spending would affect total planned expenditure and equilibrium national income and product.

3. Utilize the meaning of the *MPC* to explain why there is a direct relationship between the size of the *MPC* and the multiplier.

4. What difference would it make if a change in total planned expenditure is for one time period only rather than a continuing change?

5. Explain the importance of time in the multiplier process. Why is the multiplier effect never fully realized?

6. Explain the difference between a trend line and a business cycle.

7. Explain the difference between a seasonal variation and a business cycle.

8. Explain how a change in the rate of economic expansion can lead to an absolute contraction in capital goods industries. What is this called?

Answers   *Problems and Applications*

1. Juglar cycle: 7 to 11 years; c
   Kitchin cycle: 3 to 5 years; a
   Kondratieff cycle: 30 to 50 years; b
   Kuznets cycle: 15 to 25 years; d

2. a. 3   b. 8   c. 8/3   d. 5
   e. 4   f. 4   g. 5/2

3. larger

4. a. Total planned expenditure increases by $20,000;
      equilibrium national income and product increase by $60,000.
   b. Total planned expenditure decreases by $1,000;
      equilibrium national income and product decrease by $3,000.
   c. Total planned expenditure increases by $300;
      equilibrium national income and product increase by $900.
   d. Total planned expenditure increases by $200;
      equilibrium national income and product increase by $600.
   e. Total planned expenditure increases by $200;
      equilibrium national income and product increase by $600.
   f. Total planned expenditure increases by $300;
      equilibrium national income and product decrease by $900.
   g. Total planned expenditure decreases by $100;
      equilibrium national income and product decrease by $300.

5. a. $1,400; 0.7; 0.3; 10/3
   b. increase by $30; increase by $100, $1,500
   c. decrease by $30; decrease by $100, $1,300
   d. decrease by $33; decrease by $110, $1,290

6. a. $300
   b. increased by $200
   c. increased by $200
   d. $800
   e. increased by $500
   f. 5/2
   g. 0.4
   h. 0.6, yes, the slope of the planned expenditure curves is 0.6.

7. a. decreases by $100
   b. decreases by $100
   c. decreases by $250

8. Equilibrium national income will increase by $400; the new level
   of equilibrium national income will be $2,400.

True-False

1. F. The multiplier concept is an important part of Keynesian theory.
2. F. A change in wealth is likely to cause a shift in the consumption function and therefore a shift in the total-planned-expenditure curve.
3. T.
4. F. A significant improvement in technology is likely to cause an upward shift in the total-planned-expenditure curve because investment spending will tend to increase.
5. F. The multiplier process suggests that an increase in total planned expenditures will cause a larger increase in equilibrium national income.
6. T.
7. F. Approximately three months are needed for one complete round of the multiplier process.
8. F. The full effects of the multiplier will never be experienced, but the major consequences will occur in the early rounds of the process.
9. F. If equilibrium national income decreases by $3,000 as a result of a $1,000 decrease in total planned expenditure, the multiplier is 3.
10. T.
11. T.
12. F. Business cycles are of varying lengths. They are measured from one upper turning point to the next or from one lower turning point to the next.
13. T.
14. F. The trend line measures the long-term growth path of an economy.
15. T.
16. F. The New Deal called for an increase in prices in advance of production costs and an increase in wage rates ahead of prices.
17. T.

Multiple Choice

1. a	2. d	3. e	4. b	5. d
6. b	7. b	8. b	9. e	10. a
11. d	12. e	13. d	14. e	15. c
16. d	17. d	18. e	19. c	20. c
21. d	22. c	23. d	24. e	

11 Fiscal Instruments

Summary   Macroeconomic policy goals can be expressed, in part at least, as a
target level for national income. In the United States, national income and product targets emerge as part of the budget-making
process. The target level of national income and product is typically
set to achieve high-level employment and stable prices. A problem
exists when the expected performance of the economy does not
match the target that has been set. A contractionary gap is said to
exist when the equilibrium level of national income is less than the
target level; an expansionary gap is said to exist when the equilibrium level of national income is greater than the target level.

A contractionary gap is associated with a problem of unemployment and calls for an expansionary fiscal policy to stimulate economic activity. Keynesian economic theory developed in response
to this particular problem. The Keynesian policy prescription would
call for an increase in total planned expenditure by increasing government spending and/or cutting taxes. Because there is a multiplier
effect, a relatively small change in total planned expenditure will
cause a larger change in equilibrium national income.

An expansionary gap is associated with inflation and calls for a
policy that will stimulate production and curtail spending. Because
it may involve both demand-side and supply-side approaches, the
policy to close an expansionary gap is more complicated than that
for closing the contractionary gap. An expansionary gap may be
closed from the demand side through a decrease in total planned
expenditure and/or from the supply side through increased production capabilities that move the target to a higher level of national
income and output.

Fiscal instruments of macroeconomic policy operate through the government budget and are important for both the demand-side and the supply-side approaches. Demand-side instruments basically concentrate on government purchases and net tax collections, though they also include changes in regulations governing tax policies and changes in the structure of tax rates. Changes in government purchases and net tax collections cause changes in total planned expenditure and, therefore, multiplied changes in equilibrium national income.

In addition to the deliberate policy actions of the government, some automatic stabilizers have been built into our tax and spending laws. These built-in stabilizers tend to moderate contractionary and expansionary gaps without requiring the enactment of new policies.

Because fiscal policy operates through the government's budget, there are important implications for the national debt. Though the U.S. national debt has grown steadily in dollar amount, recent years show no clear trend in terms of its growth as a percentage of GNP.

Major Objectives   After you have finished this chapter, you will be able to do the following:

1. Define and indicate the importance of target levels of national income and product and explain how these levels are set.
2. Identify and describe, verbally and graphically, the contractionary and expansionary gaps.
3. Associate each of the problems of unemployment, idle production capacity, inflationary pressures, and shortages with one of the two gaps.
4. Describe the appropriate Keynesian policy for closing each type of gap.
5. Characterize the economic conditions of the 1970s and the events that created these conditions.
6. Identify the fiscal instruments and indicate their importance for demand-side applications.
7. Explain verbally and graphically how a change in government purchases can be used to close both a contractionary gap and an expansionary gap.
8. Explain and identify examples of displacement effects.
9. Describe and explain the implications of a change in net taxes on total planned expenditure.
10. Explain, verbally and graphically, how a change in net tax collections can be used to close both a contractionary gap and an expansionary gap.

11. Explain why, dollar for dollar, changes in net tax collections have less impact on equilibrium national income than do changes in government purchases.
12. Define, calculate, and utilize the tax-change multiplier.
13. Define, explain, and use the balanced budget multiplier.
14. Define, provide examples of, and illustrate the use of automatic stabilizers.
15. Explain the concept of a full-employment balanced budget.
16. Explain and provide examples of the regulatory features of the tax and expenditure fiscal instruments.
17. Define national debt and explain how it is affected by fiscal policy.
18. Discuss the implications of and interaction between fiscal policy and the financial markets.
19. Explain how the national debt is created.
20. Discuss the size (in dollar amounts and as a percentage of GNP) of the national debt from a historical perspective.
21. Discuss the effects of unstable prices on the national debt.
22. Discuss the national debt in terms of bankruptcy, de facto bankruptcy, and its burden on future generations.

Review Terms

Keynesian economics
business cycles
aggregate
market economy
neoclassical theory
Great Depression
inflation
macroeconomic equilibrium
macroeconomic unemployment
frictional unemployment
structural unemployment
total planned expenditure
forty-five degree line
equilibrium national income and product (Y*)
shortage
stagflation
government purchases (G)
circular-flow model
government transfer payments
net taxes (T_n)
multiplier

substitute good
planned consumption expenditure (C)
planned saving (S)
marginal propensity to consume (*MPC*)
marginal propensity to save (*MPS*)
autonomous
balanced budget
real vs. nominal values
indexing
lump-sum tax
depreciation
planned investment expenditure
budget deficit
budget surplus
crowding out
financial markets
per capita
GNP
opportunity cost

Important Terms and Concepts

fiscal instruments
monetary instruments
target level of national income
  and product (Y_T)
contractionary gap
expansionary gap
"full" employment
price stability
supply-side of the economy
demand-side approach
Organization of Petroleum
  Exporting Countries (OPEC)
displacement effect
tax-change multiplier (K_{Tn})
"change in" (Δ)

balanced-budget multiplier
automatic built-in stabilizers
progressive income tax
tax-bracket push
full-employment balanced budget
depreciation allowances
capital gain
capital loss
national debt
government bonds and securities
Treasury Department
securities markets
non-interest-bearing debt
bankruptcy
debt financing

Completion

gap

contractionary

unemployment

expansionary

inflation

contractionary gap

increase

increases

decreases

demand-side

demand-side

decrease

When the predicted level of equilibrium national income does not

equal the target level, a _____ is said to exist. The gap is

_____ (expansionary/contractionary) when
the equilibrium level of national income is less than the target level.

This is associated with a problem of _____ (unemploy-

ment/inflation). The gap is _____ (expansionary/
contractionary) when the equilibrium level of national income
exceeds the target level. This is associated with a problem of

_____ (unemployment/inflation).
  One of the costs of unemployment is the output of goods and
services that could have been produced but that will not be produced
because of the unemployment. The dollar value of this lost output

can be measured by the _____
  The Keynesian policy to close a contractionary gap is one that will

_____ (increase/decrease) total planned expenditure.

Hence, the appropriate fiscal policy would be one that _____

(increases/decreases) government purchases and/or _____

(increases/decreases) net taxes. This is a _____
(demand-side/supply-side) approach.

  The Keynesian or _____ (demand-side/supply-

side) policy to close an expansionary gap is one that will _____
(increase/decrease) total planned expenditure. This suggests a fiscal

decreases

increases

policy that _____ (increases/decreases) government
purchases and/or _____ (increases/decreases) net taxes.

As discussed in Chapter 5, an especially difficult problem arose in
the United States during the 1970s with the coexistence of high inflation, widespread unemployment, and sluggish growth. This combina-

stagflation

increase

tion of problems is known as _____. From a Keynesian
perspective, unemployment calls for a(n) _____ (increase/
decrease) in total planned expenditure, whereas the problem of infla-

decrease

tion calls for a(n) _____ (increase/decrease) in total
planned expenditure. That is, a Keynesian would use essentially

opposite

_____ (the same/opposite) approaches to deal with
the two problems. It was the unexpected occurrence of the simultaneous problems of unemployment and inflation, coupled with the
policy dilemma associated with trying to solve these problems, that
gave rise to a new approach to macroeconomic problem solving, the

supply-side

_____ approach.

Fiscal instruments are those that operate through the

government budget

government pur-
chases

net tax collections

_____ . Changes in the annual flow of
_____ and in the annual flow of
_____ are basically demand-side
applications of the fiscal instruments. Fiscal instruments

can also

_____ (can also/cannot) have supply-side effects.

equivalent

A change in government purchases causes a(n) _____
(larger/equivalent/smaller) change in total planned expenditure in the

same

_____ (same/opposite) direction. This change in total

larger

planned expenditure will lead to a(n) _____ (larger/
equivalent/smaller) change in equilibrium national income and

same

product in the _____ (same/opposite) direction. The
change in equilibrium national income and output will be larger than

multiplier

the change in planned expenditure because of the _____
effect.

A change in net tax collections causes a change in the amount of
after-tax spending power available to the private sector. If the tax is

consumption

saving

on household incomes, it will affect _____ and
_____ . The change in consumption associated with a

opposite

change in net taxes will be in the _____ (same/opposite)

smaller than

direction and will be _____ (larger than/equal to/ smaller than) the change in net taxes, with the amount determined

MPC

by the _____ . The change in consumption causes a(n)

equivalent

_____ (larger/equivalent/smaller) change in

larger

total planned expenditure and a(n) _____ (larger/ equivalent/smaller) change in equilibrium national income and

also

product. There is _____ (also/not) a multiplier for tax changes. But since only a portion of a tax change affects consumption spending, the multiplier associated with a tax change is

smaller than

_____ (larger than/equivalent to/smaller than) the multiplier associated with a change in purchases. The tax-change

the simple multiplier minus one

multiplier is equal to _____ .
   The Keynesian fiscal policy to close a contractionary gap is

deficit

typically associated with a budget _____ (surplus/deficit), whereas the policy to close an expansionary gap is typically associ-

surplus

ated with a budget _____ (surplus/deficit). It is possible to avoid deficit spending or a budget surplus by changing gov-

the same direction

ernment purchases and net taxes in _____

the same

(the same direction/different directions) by _____ (the same/different) amounts. If government purchases and net taxes are changed in the same direction and by the same amounts, equilib-

same

rium national income will change in the _____ (same/

the same

opposite) direction and by _____ (the same/a different)

balanced-budget

amount. This change occurs because of the _____

1

multiplier, which is equal to _____ .

Problems and Applications

1. Assume that the *MPC* is 4/5 for everyone in a given economy. Indicate the effects of each of the following on total planned expenditure and on equilibrium national income and product.
   a. Government purchases increase by $100.
   b. Net tax collections increase by $100.
   c. Government purchases increase by $100 and net tax collections increase by $100.
   d. Transfer payments increase by $100.
   e. Total tax collections increase by $100 and government transfer payments increase by $100.

f. Total tax collections increase by $100 and government transfer payments decrease by $100.

2. For each of the policies in problem 1, indicate the consequence for an otherwise balanced budget (that is, is the policy associated with deficit spending, a budget surplus, or a balanced budget?).

3. Consider the economy described by the graph below. Assume that the economy is in equilibrium and that the target level of national income and product is $1,000.

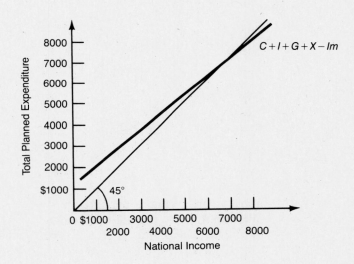

a. What is the actual dollar value of output for this economy?
b. What kind of economic problem is the economy experiencing (a contractionary or an expansionary gap)?
c. How much should you change total planned expenditure, and in what direction, to eliminate the gap?
d. If you were going to use government purchases to eliminate the gap, what would your policy be? (Determine the direction and the amount of change needed in government purchases.)
e. If you were required to use a balanced budget policy, what would it be? (Determine the specific policy.)

4. Consider the economy described by the graph below. Assume that the economy is in equilibrium and that the target level of national income and product is $4,000.

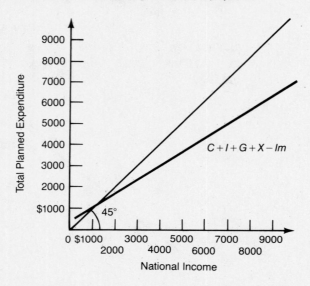

a. What is the actual dollar value of output for this economy?
b. What kind of economic problem is the economy experiencing (a contractionary or an expansionary gap)?
c. How much should you change total planned expenditure, and in what direction, to eliminate the gap?
d. If you were going to use government purchases to eliminate the gap, what would your policy be? (Determine the direction and the amount of change needed in government purchases.)
e. If you were required to use a balanced budget policy, what would it be? (Determine the specific policy).

5. Assume that Economy X is currently in equilibrium. The target level of national income is $1,000, and the equilibrium level of national income is $600. The *MPC* is 3/4. Answer questions a through e in problem 4 for Economy X. (You may find it helpful to approach the problem graphically.)

6. Assume that Economy Y is currently in equilibrium with national income of $800 and a target level of national income equal to $300. The *MPC* is 4/5. Answer questions a through e in problem 4 above for Economy Y.

7. Economy Z is in equilibrium. The target level of national income is $1,800, and the equilibrium level of national income is $1,000. The marginal propensity to save is 1/4. Answer questions a through e in problem 4 above for Economy Z.

8. Consider Economy XX, which is currently in equilibrium with consumption spending of $300, investment spending of $100, government purchases of $200, and net exports of $200. The target level of national income is $2,400 and the *MPC* is 7/8.
   a. What is the equilibrium total planned expenditure for the economy?
   b. What is the actual dollar value of output for the economy?
   c. What kind of problem is Economy XX experiencing (a contractionary or an expansionary gap)?
   d. How much and in what direction should you change total planned expenditure to eliminate the gap?
   e. If you were going to use government purchases to eliminate the gap, what would your policy be? (Determine the direction and the amount of change in government purchases.)
   f. If you were required to use a balanced budget policy, what would it be? (Determine the specific policy.)

9. What is the effect on equilibrium national income and product of an increase in government purchases coupled with an equivalent increase in net taxes? Explain.

10. What is the effect on equilibrium national income and product of an increase in government transfer payments coupled with an equal increase in total taxes? Explain.

True-False

Indicate whether each of the following statements is basically true or false. If the statement is false, rewrite it so that it is true.

_____ 1. The identification of target levels of national income and product suggests a belief that government intervention in the economy can be useful in reaching economic goals.

_____ 2. Neoclassical economics is especially concerned with setting target levels of national income and product because of its anticipation of high levels of unemployment.

_____ 3. A contractionary gap occurs when the target level of national income is less than the equilibrium level.

_____ 4. An expansionary gap is associated with unemployment and therefore suggests that government policy should be used to stimulate the economy.

_____ 5. The Keynesian demand-side approach to fiscal policy calls for increased government spending and/or decreased taxes to fight unemployment.

_____ 6. A supply-side approach to closing an expansionary gap would most likely include attempts to shift the planned expenditure curve downward.

_____ 7. Stagflation refers to a situation of high inflation, widespread unemployment, and sluggish growth.

_____ 8. The fiscal instruments of macroeconomic policy include government spending and taxation programs and may have both demand-side and supply-side effects.

_____ 9. An increase in government purchases causes a multiplied increase in national income and may be used to close a contractionary gap.

_____ 10. A displacement effect occurs when a change in one component of aggregate planned expenditure is offset by an opposite change in another component.

_____ 11. An increase in government purchases that results in a budget deficit and increased interest rates may be partly displaced by a decrease in private-sector planned investment spending.

_____ 12. A cut in taxes that results in an increase in disposable personal income will tend to cause households to spend more and save less.

_____ 13. According to Keynesian economics, a $100 increase in government purchases is equivalent to a $100 decrease in net taxes.

_____ 14. According to Keynesian economics, an increase in taxes has a smaller impact on equilibrium national income than an equivalent decrease in government purchases because a portion of the taxes will be paid for by reductions in saving.

_____ 15. During inflationary times, a Keynesian demand-side approach to fiscal policy might call for increases in net taxes to discourage private-sector spending.

_____ 16. According to the balanced budget multiplier principle, an increase in government purchases accompanied by an equivalent increase in net tax collections will leave equilibrium national income unchanged.

_____ 17. The automatic stabilizing feature of the progressive income tax would be enhanced by indexing.

_____ 18. The concept of a full-employment balanced budget relies on automatic stabilizers to guarantee an annually balanced budget.

_____ 19. An increase in capital gains taxes will tend to result in a decrease in planned investment spending.

_____ 20. Quicker deductions for depreciation will typically result in an increase in planned investment spending.

_____ 21. The Treasury Department finances a budget deficit by printing money.

Multiple Choice   Choose the *one best* answer in each of the following cases:

_____   1. National income targets are
   a. not generally important in command economies.
   b. determined in accordance with purely economic concerns and typically raise no real political problems.
   c. generally necessary if the economy is going to reach an equilibrium characterized by full employment and stable prices, according to Keynesian economics.
   d. essential to ensure full employment and the smooth functioning of an economy, according to neoclassical economic theory.
   e. all of the above

_____   2. A contractionary or expansionary gap
   a. occurs when the predicted level of national income and product differs from the target level.
   b. exists whenever there is a difference between national income and total planned expenditure.
   c. is the difference between the actual level of national income and the predicted level of national income.
   d. measures the extent to which the actual level of national income differs from the equilibrium level of national income.
   e. both b and c above

_____   3. In a Keynesian model
   a. a contractionary gap is associated with a problem of unemployment, whereas an expansionary gap is associated with inflation.
   b. a contractionary gap is associated with a problem of inflation, whereas an expansionary gap is associated with unemployment.
   c. a contractionary gap is associated with a problem of stagflation, whereas an expansionary gap is associated with depression.
   d. a contractionary gap is associated with a problem of inflation; an expansionary gap is not likely to occur.
   e. an expansionary gap is associated with a problem of depression; a contractionary gap is not likely to occur.

Use the graph below to answer questions 4 and 5.

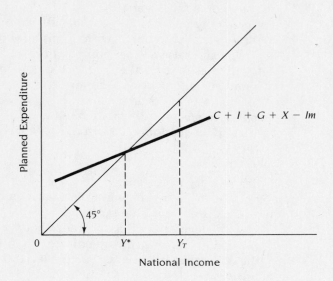

_____ 4. Which of the following statements is accurate with respect to
the economy described by the graph above? (Assume Y_T represents the target level of national income.)
  a. The economy will not reach equilibrium.
  b. The economy will reach equilibrium at Y_T.
  c. The economy will reach a full-employment equilibrium.
  d. The economy will come to equilibrium with unemployment.
  e. The economy will reach equilibrium only if total planned
     expenditure is increased.

_____ 5. Assuming that Y_T represents the target level of national income
and product, which of the following statements is accurate with
respect to the economy described by the graph?
  a. There is a contractionary gap, which is likely to result in
     unemployment.
  b. The existence of an expansionary gap suggests that Y_T should
     be reduced.
  c. The economy will experience inflation unless the contrac-
     tionary gap is closed.
  d. According to Keynesian theory, the economy cannot reach
     the target level of national income and product.
  e. According to neoclassical theory, the expansionary gap can
     be eliminated through increases in government purchases
     or decreases in taxes.

_____ 6. An expansionary gap
   a. is likely to result in inflation.
   b. occurs when the equilibrium level of national income is higher than the target level of national income.
   c. may be eliminated by cuts in government purchases and/or increases in net taxes according to demand-side policy approaches.
   d. all of the above
   e. none of the above

_____ 7. According to Keynesian economics, which of the following policies might be appropriate for closing a contractionary gap?
   a. deficit spending
   b. budget surpluses
   c. increases in net taxes
   d. decreases in government purchases and increases in taxes
   e. none of the above

_____ 8. Fiscal instruments
   a. include government spending and taxation programs.
   b. may include regulatory, as well as financial, aspects.
   c. are those that operate through the government budget.
   d. may have both demand-side and supply-side consequences.
   e. all of the above

_____ 9. If the marginal propensity to consume is 3/4, a
   a. $400 decrease in net taxes will result in a $1,600 increase in national output.
   b. $400 increase in taxes will result in a $300 increase in total planned expenditure.
   c. $400 cut in government purchases will result in a $300 decrease in national income.
   d. $400 increase in government transfer payments will result in a $1,600 increase in national income.
   e. none of the above

_____ 10. Displacement effects
   a. may limit the effectiveness of Keynesian fiscal policy.
   b. help eliminate the national debt.
   c. measure the effect of decreased total planned expenditure on unemployment.
   d. measure the costs of unemployment.
   e. are the budget deficits associated with increases in government transfer payments.

_____ 11. Given a marginal propensity to consume of 4/5, a $100 increase in tax collections will cause a(n)
a. increase in equilibrium national income.
b. $500 decrease in equilibrium national income.
c. $80 decrease in aggregate planned expenditure.
d. $100 decrease in aggregate planned expenditure.
e. $500 decrease in aggregate planned expenditure.

_____ 12. Which of the following policies would have the greatest impact on equilibrium national income?
a. a $100 increase in government purchases
b. a $100 decrease in net taxes
c. a $100 increase in government purchases coupled with a $100 decrease in net taxes
d. a $100 increase in government purchases coupled with a $100 increase in net taxes
e. both a and b above, since they have the same impact on equilibrium national income

_____ 13. If the *MPC* is 2/3 and tax collections decrease by $3 billion, equilibrium national income will
a. decrease by $2 billion.
b. decrease by $6 billion.
c. decrease by $9 billion.
d. increase by $6 billion.
e. increase by $9 billion.

_____ 14. According to Keynesian economics, the multiplier associated with tax change is
a. always equal to 1.
b. equivalent to the multiplier associated with changes in government purchases.
c. smaller than the multiplier associated with changes in government purchases.
d. larger than the multiplier associated with changes in government purchases.
e. equivalent to the balanced-budget multiplier.

_____ 15. The budget surplus necessary to close an expansionary gap will need to be larger if the gap is to be closed using an increase in tax collections rather than a decrease in government purchases because
a. there are no displacement effects associated with changes in government purchases.
b. the multiplier associated with budget surpluses is larger than the multiplier associated with deficits.
c. only a portion of the money to pay the increased taxes comes from household consumption spending, with the remainder taken from saving.

d. the increase in taxes will have no effect on the economy.

e. none of the above

_____ 16. From a demand-side perspective, choosing between the government-purchases instrument and the tax-change instrument

a. may be as much a political decision as an economic one.

b. is likely to be unimportant, since the consequences are typically identical.

c. may involve a consideration of the relative effects of the two instruments on the provision of public and private goods.

d. both a and c above

e. all of the above

_____ 17. The balanced-budget multiplier

a. is equal to zero.

b. increases with increases in the *MPC*.

c. decreases with increases in the *MPC*.

d. depends on the size of the federal budget.

e. none of the above

_____ 18. Given an *MPC* of 4/5 and an equal decrease in government purchases and net tax collections, a Keynesian would predict that there would be

a. no change in equilibrium national income.

b. an increase in equilibrium national income equal to the decrease in government purchases.

c. a decrease in equilibrium national income equal to the decrease in government purchases.

d. a decrease in equilibrium national income five times the change in government purchases.

e. a decrease in equilibrium national income equal to the sum of the decrease in government purchases and tax collections.

_____ 19. Automatic stabilizers

a. are specific features built into some government spending and taxation programs that are automatically activated and that tend to moderate contractionary and expansionary gaps.

b. include the progressive income tax, the corporate income tax, Social Security taxes, and unemployment taxes.

c. include certain transfer payment programs such as Social Security, unemployment compensation, and welfare.

d. are features that tend to create budget deficits during periods of unemployment and budget surpluses during periods of inflation.

e. all of the above

_____ 20. The enactment of a full-employment balanced-budget policy would
   a. eliminate the need for automatic stabilizers.
   b. result in a balanced budget only when there was full employment.
   c. assure that budget deficits were paid for by compensating surpluses during periods of full employment.
   d. all of the above
   e. guarantee an annually balanced budget.

_____ 21. Which of the following would be an example of crowding out?
   a. an increase in planned investment spending as a result of a cut in the tax rate for capital gains
   b. a decrease in planned investment spending as a result of stiffer rules regarding depreciation allowances
   c. an increase in private-sector planned investment spending as a result of increased public expenditures on highways
   d. a decision on the part of a corporation to build a new hospital because the county hospital is not centrally located
   e. an increase in interest rates for financing investment spending because of increased deficit spending on the part of the federal government

_____ 22. Which of the following statements is true with regard to deficit spending and the national debt?
   a. The government prints money to pay for deficit spending.
   b. In real terms, inflation tends to increase the size of the national debt.
   c. The Treasury Department finances a budget deficit by issuing bonds and government securities.
   d. It is generally agreed that deficit spending burdens future generations and should therefore be discouraged at all times.
   e. A sizable national debt will ultimately lead to bankruptcy, regardless of the health and stability of the government and the economy involved.

Discussion Questions

1. Why would national income targets have no place in neoclassical economic theory?

2. Demonstrate the contradiction between the Keynesian model and stagflation.

3. Explain the policy dilemma associated with trying to address the problem of stagflation with a Keynesian demand-side approach.

4. Explain the importance of the distinction between government purchases and transfer payments for weighing the consequences of a particular policy for the economy.

5. Explain why the multiplier effect is smaller for changes in net taxes than for changes in government purchases.

6. Explain how displacement effects associated with household consumption might lessen the impact of a change in government purchases. What are the consequences for the mix between public and private goods?

7. Explain how the connection between the government and the financial markets might result in displacement effects.

8. If a change in government purchases coupled with an equivalent change in net taxes in the same direction is a balanced budget policy, why doesn't it leave equilibrium national income unchanged? Explain fully.

9. Discuss the opportunity cost associated with utilizing Keynesian fiscal policy to fight unemployment.

10. Discuss the opportunity cost associated with utilizing Keynesian fiscal policy to fight inflation.

Answers

Problems and Applications

1. a. increase by $100; increase by $500
   b. decrease by $80; decrease by $400
   c. increase by $20; increase by $100
   d. increase by $80; increase by $400
   e. no change; no change
   f. decrease by $160; decrease by $800

2. a. deficit spending   b. surplus
   c. balanced budget   d. deficit spending
   e. balanced budget   f. surplus

3. a. $6,000   b. expansionary
   c. decrease by $1,000   d. decrease G by $1,000
   e. decrease government purchases and net taxes by $5,000

4. a. $1,000   b. contractionary
   c. increase by $1,000   d. increase G by $1,000
   e. increase government purchases and net taxes by $3,000

5. a. $600   b. contractionary
   c. increase by $100   d. increase G by $100
   e. increase government purchases and net taxes by $400

6. a. $800   b. expansionary
   c. decrease by $100   d. decrease G by $100
   e. decrease government purchases and net taxes by $500

7. a. $1,000
   b. contractionary
   c. increase by $200
   d. increase *G* by $200
   e. increase government purchases and net taxes by $800

8. a. $800
   b. $800
   c. contractionary
   d. increase by $200
   e. increase *G* by $200
   f. increase government purchases and net taxes by $1,600

9. An equal increase will result in equilibrium national income and product; increasing government purchases and net taxes in the same direction by the same amount is an application of the balanced-budget multiplier.

10. No change will occur in equilibrium national income or product; when transfer payments are increased by an amount equal to the change in total taxes, there will be no change in net taxes and therefore no change in equilibrium national income or product.

True-False

1. T.
2. F. Keynesian economics is especially concerned with setting target levels of national income and product because of the possibility of high levels of unemployment; neoclassical economics anticipates a full-employment equilibrium.
3. F. A contractionary gap occurs when the equilibrium level of national income is less than the target level.
4. F. An expansionary gap is associated with inflation and calls for a policy that discourages spending and encourages production.
5. T.
6. F. A demand-side approach to closing an expansionary gap would most likely include attempts to shift the planned-expenditure curve downward.
7. T.
8. T.
9. T.
10. T.
11. T.
12. F. A cut in taxes that results in an increase in disposable personal income will tend to cause households to spend more and to save more.
13. F. According to Keynesian economics, a $100 increase in government purchases will have a greater effect on total planned expenditure and equilibrium national income than a $100 decrease in net taxes.

14. T.
15. T.
16. F. According to the balanced-budget multiplier principle, an increase in government purchases accompanied by an equivalent increase in net tax collections will result in an equivalent increase in equilibrium national income.
17. F. The automatic stabilizing feature of the progressive income tax would be lessened by indexing.
18. F. The concept of a full-employment balanced budget relies on automatic stabilizers to create budget deficits in response to contractionary gaps and budget surpluses in response to expansionary gaps. With a full-employment balanced budget, the budget will be balanced only when the economy is operating at full employment and stable prices.
19. T.
20. T.
21. F. The Treasury Department finances a budget deficit by issuing bonds and other securities and offering them for sale in the securities market.

Multiple Choice

1. c	2. a	3. a	4. d	5. a
6. d	7. a	8. e	9. e	10. a
11. c	12. c	13. d	14. c	15. c
16. d	17. e	18. c	19. e	20. b
21. e	22. c			

12 *Money and Banks*

Summary

Money may be defined as something that serves as a medium of exchange, a unit of account, a store of purchasing power, and a standard of deferred payment. To say that money is a medium of exchange indicates that it must be generally acceptable in trade. This is the most important function of money. As a unit of account, money provides a way of comparing the values of different items. That is to say, money serves as a common denominator of expressing value. As a store of purchasing power, money provides a way of holding assets or wealth for use at a later time. In times of inflation, money is not a particularly good store of purchasing power; likewise, in times of deflation, the value of money increases and so it is a good store of purchasing power. Finally, as a standard of deferred payment, money provides a standard way to specify the amount of a payment that is due at a later date.

The medium of exchange function of money suggests that money should be something that is spendable. For this reason, the most generally used concept of the money supply includes coins and currency in circulation plus demand deposit balances. In the United States, we actually have four different measures of the money supply. M1 includes coins plus currency in circulation and balances in demand deposits and other checkable accounts. The other measures of the money supply, M2, M3, and L, include progressively less liquid assets and are sometimes referred to as near money.

As organized in the United States, banks are profit-seeking businesses. A bank charter, the legal authority to engage in banking, may be issued by federal as well as state governments. Using money from depositors and shareholders, banks earn income by lending money and by purchasing and holding interest-bearing securities. The ability to lend money results from the fact that the U.S. banking system is a partial or fractional reserve system. This means that a bank need not keep enough cash or immediately available funds on hand to completely fulfill its promises to its depositors. The official reserves of a bank include its vault cash and funds on deposit with its Federal Reserve Bank. The bank is required to keep some percentage of its deposits on reserve; any official reserves above those required reserves are called excess reserves. Excess reserves give banks their lending ability.

Because banks can lend out their excess reserves, they are able to increase the money supply. The deposit expansion factor, which indicates the extent to which the banking system can expand the money supply, is equal to the reciprocal of the reserve ratio. It is important to note, however, that just as the banking system can create money by creating demand deposits, it also may have to contract the money supply when deposits are withdrawn from the system.

The size of the money supply is controlled by regulations stipulating the reserve requirement. These regulations affect both the amount of excess reserves that will be created by a deposit and the deposit expansion multiplier. But since banks may not always meet the reserve requirement exactly, the ability to control changes in the money supply is not exact.

Major Objectives

After you have finished this chapter, you will be able to do the following:

1. Identify and explain the four functions of money.
2. Define and describe barter.
3. Define money and identify the important characteristics associated with a substance that becomes money.
4. Identify the basic forms of money in the United States.
5. Cite and explain Gresham's Law.
6. Define bank note and discuss the historical importance of bank notes in the development of currency in the United States.
7. Describe the concept of legal tender.
8. Define demand deposit, explain how most demand deposits are created, and explain why many people regard most of our money supply as monetized debt.
9. Distinguish between checks and bank notes.
10. Identify, discuss the composition of, and compare the four alternative measures of the money supply as established by the Federal Reserve System.
11. Define liquidity and near money.

12. Discuss the organization of banks, noting the importance of charters and the differences in types of charters.
13. Explain the concept of partial or fractional reserves, their role in banking, and their relationship to bank failures.
14. Discuss the role of bank examiners, deposit insurance, and the size of bank reserves in providing for bank safety.
15. Describe the balance sheet of a bank, indicating the assets and liabilities.
16. Define reserve ratio, reserve requirement, and excess reserves, and be able to perform calculations involving these concepts.
17. Explain the process by which the money supply is expanded or contracted by the banking system.
18. Define, calculate, and utilize the deposit expansion factor.
19. Discuss the limitations associated with controlling the actual deposit expansion factor.

Review Terms	circular flow	barter
	disequilibrium	index number
	equilibrium level of national income and product (Y*)	wealth
		balance sheet
	inflation	assets
	deflation	liabilities
	real vs. nominal values	net worth
	general price level	

Important Terms and Concepts	money	Federal Reserve System
	velocity of circulation	liquid
	medium of exchange	money supply
	unit of account	M1
	store of purchasing power	M2
	standard of deferred payment	M3
	coins	L
	Gresham's Law	negotiable order of withdrawal (NOW)
	base money vs. dear money	
	currency	automatic transfer service (ATS)
	bank note	share draft accounts
	Federal Reserve Note	Eurodollars
	fiat money	near money
	legal tender	bank charter
	demand deposits	partial or fractional reserves
	monetize	run on a bank

bank examiner
deposit insurance
Federal Deposit Insurance
    Corporation (FDIC)
Federal Savings and Loan
    Insurance Corporation
    (FSLIC)
National Credit Union
    Administration (NCUA)
reserves
reserve requirement

deposit expansion process
loan
securities
savings deposit
time deposit
certificate of deposit
borrowings
reserve ratio
excess reserve
deposit contraction process
desired excess reserves

Completion

medium of exchange

generally accepted

unit of account

store of purchasing
power

standard of
deferred payment

M1, coins

currency

checking accounts

less

M2, M3, L

near

partial or fractional

fraction

is

bank examiners

deposit insurance

The most important function of money is that it serves as a
_____ . This means that money should
be _____ in exchange for goods and services.
In addition, money should serve as a _____ ,
as a _____ , and as a
_____ .
   The most widely accepted and frequently used definition of the
U.S. money supply is called _____ and includes _____
and _____ in circulation and balances in
_____ . The definition of the money supply
may be broadened to include assets that are _____ (more/less)
liquid. In order of liquidity, these alternative measures of the money
supply are called _____ , _____ , and _____ ; sometimes
they are simply called _____ money.
   The U.S. banking system is a _____
reserve system. This means that banks are required to keep only a
_____ of any deposit on reserve. Consequently, a run on a
bank _____ (is/is not) possible. In an attempt to prevent bank
failures, official _____ investigate banking
operations. In addition, most banks purchase _____ ,
which protects bank deposits up to $100,000 per deposit.
   A bank often holds more reserves than are required; such reserves

excess reserves	are called _____ . These are available for
expand	lending and make it possible for banks to _____ the money supply. In order to demonstrate the deposit expansion capabilities of the banking system, assume that all banks meet a reserve requirement of 20 percent and lend out any excess reserves whenever they accumulate. Consider a situation in which $1,000 in cash is deposited in National Bank. The official reserves of National Bank increase by
$1,000	_____ as a result of the deposit. This means that National
$800	Bank has excess reserves in the amount of _____ . Hence,
$800	National Bank can increase the money supply by _____ if
lends out	it _____ its excess reserves. Because the deposit expan-
the reciprocal of the reserve ratio	sion factor is equal to _____ , the banking system as a whole can increase the money supply by a
5, $4,000, maximum	factor of _____ , or by _____ . This is the _____ (maximum/minimum) by which the money supply can expand. In order for the expansion to be this great, all excess reserves must be
lent out, cash	_____ and there can be no leakages into _____ . Just as a bank deposit can lead to an expansion of demand
contraction	deposits, a withdrawal can lead to a _____ of the money supply. The maximum potential contraction of the money supply associated with a withdrawal is determined by the
deposit contraction process	_____ . The money supply can con-
reciprocal of the reserve ratio	tract by a factor equivalent to the _____ .

Problems and Applications

1. Identify which measure of the money supply is being described by each of the following:
   a. It includes U.S. Savings Bonds.
   b. It includes small but not large time deposits.
   c. It is the most widely used definition of the money supply.
   d. It is essentially equal to M2 plus large time deposits and term repurchase agreements.

2. National Bank currently has reserves totaling $40,000 and deposit liabilities of $100,000. Assume a reserve requirement of 25 percent.
   a. What is National Bank's actual reserve ratio?
   b. How much is National Bank required to hold on reserve?

   c. Does National Bank have any excess reserves? If so, in what amount?

   d. By how much could National Bank increase the money supply?

   e. By how much could the banking system increase the money supply?

3. National Bank is just meeting its reserve requirement of 20 percent when a new customer deposits $5,000 in cash in the bank.

   a. What happens to the official reserves of National Bank?

   b. What happens to the required reserves of National Bank?

   c. By how much can National Bank increase the money supply?

   d. By how much can the banking system increase the money supply?

   e. What is the total amount of deposits that can be supported by $5,000?

4. Assume that the reserve requirement is 20 percent. National Bank has just created a new checking account for Mr. X as a result of granting him a loan of $10,000.

   a. By how much has National Bank increased the money supply as a result of the loan?

   b. By how much can the banking system increase the money supply as a result of the loan?

True-False

Indicate whether each of the following statements is basically true or false. If the statement is false, rewrite it so that it is true.

_____ 1. The most basic requirement of money is that it be backed by a precious metal such as gold or silver.

_____ 2. As a store of purchasing power, money is the common denominator that enables people to compare values of different items.

_____ 3. The basic forms of money in the United States today are coins and currency in circulation and demand deposit balances.

_____ 4. According to Gresham's Law, dear money will drive base money out of circulation.

_____ 5. Fiat money is legal tender.

_____ 6. A bank note is a payment order to a bank backed by a checking account.

_____ 7. A check is a payment order to a bank signed by a person or business with rights to a checking account.

_____ 8. Demand deposits are savings accounts.

_____ 9. The M1 measure of the money supply includes coins and currency in circulation, demand deposit balances, and balances in other accounts that offer check-writing services.

_____ 10. Since M2 includes savings accounts, it is more liquid than M1.

_____ 11. The major difference between M2 and M3 is large time deposits.

_____ 12. Near money is easily converted into money or can be spent directly.

_____ 13. The opportunity cost of liquidity is the general price level.

_____ 14. The L measure of the money supply includes forms of wealth, such as U.S. Savings Bonds, which are near money.

_____ 15. A business must have a federal bank charter in order to operate legally as a bank.

_____ 16. A primary difference between state and federal bank charters is that federal charters require that the bank be a member of the Federal Reserve System.

_____ 17. One of the requirements set by bank charters is that banks must keep enough cash or immediately available funds on hand to fulfill all promises to depositors.

_____ 18. Though banks lend money, they are prevented by charter from borrowing money.

_____ 19. A bank's reserve ratio is the amount of demand deposits in the bank divided by the cash and official reserves of the bank.

_____ 20. The reserve requirement establishes the minimum allowable reserve ratio for a bank.

_____ 21. Excess reserves consist of all official reserves over and above the reserves that banks are required to keep.

_____ 22. The deposit expansion factor indicates the maximum potential by which the money supply can be expanded or contracted.

_____ 23. The U.S. Treasury Department, the nation's central bank, is responsible for controlling the deposit expansion factor and the actual amount of reserves in the banking system.

Multiple Choice   Choose the *one best* answer in each of the following cases:

_____   1. Which of the following statements is true with respect to the functions of money?
        a. Money serves as a unit of account only when it is backed by gold.
        b. Money is the unit of account in a society that relies solely on barter.
        c. As a medium of exchange, money determines the deposit expansion factor.
        d. To the extent that there are increases in the general price level, money may not be a good store of purchasing power.
        e. Because it is a medium of exchange and a unit of account, money always serves as the best store of purchasing power.

_____   2. In an economy that relies on barter,
        a. money is the medium of exchange.
        b. coins are used to facilitate trade.
        c. fractional reserve banking is common.
        d. goods and services are traded directly for each other.
        e. the money supply consists entirely of coins and currency.

_____   3. Which of the following would *not* be considered money?
        a. a bad check
        b. the reserves of a bank
        c. a checking account balance of $500
        d. both a and b above
        e. all of the above

_____   4. According to Gresham's Law,
        a. base money would never be acceptable as a medium of exchange.
        b. dear money would be hoarded and base money would circulate.
        c. base money would cease to circulate, being replaced by dear money.
        d. in time, all money made out of base metal would become dear money.
        e. none of the above

_____   5. Currency in the U.S. economy today
        a. includes private bank notes.
        b. is legal tender for all private and public debts.
        c. is no longer a form of fiat money, though it used to be.
        d. all of the above
        e. none of the above

_____ 6. Demand deposits are
   a. demonetized debt.
   b. checking account balances.
   c. included in the M1 measure of the money supply but not in the other measures.
   d. a store of purchasing power and a unit of account but not a medium of exchange.
   e. all of the above

_____ 7. Which of the following is true with regard to the U.S. money supply?
   a. It includes bank reserves.
   b. The most widely used measure of it is M1.
   c. The broadest, most inclusive measure of it is M3.
   d. When measured by L it includes only assets that are perfectly liquid.
   e. It may be measured by M2, which consists entirely of savings accounts and small time deposits.

_____ 8. Which of the following statements is true of bank charters?
   a. They are issued by state and local governments.
   b. They represent legal authority to engage in banking as a business.
   c. They typically stipulate that banks must be nonprofit enterprises.
   d. They require all banks to become members of the Federal Reserve System.
   e. all of the above

_____ 9. A partial or fractional reserve system of banking
   a. reduces the liquidity of M1.
   b. eliminates the possibility of runs on banks.
   c. means that all reserves will be excess reserves.
   d. means that banks will never have excess reserves.
   e. enables the banking system to expand or contract the money supply.

_____ 10. Which of the following is generally used by the banking system as a way of promoting bank safety?
   a. deposit insurance on deposits up to $100,000 per deposit through the Federal Deposit Insurance Corporation
   b. deposit insurance on deposits in excess of $100,000 through the Federal Excess Deposits Association
   c. a 100 percent reserve requirement
   d. all of the above
   e. both a and b above

_____ 11. Which of the following is *not* true with regard to the balance sheet of a bank?
   a. Reserves are assets.
   b. Loans are assets.
   c. Demand deposits are liabilities.
   d. Savings accounts are liabilities.
   e. Net worth is equal to bank reserves.

_____ 12. Official bank reserves
   a. include vault cash.
   b. may be required or excess.
   c. include deposits with Federal Reserve Banks.
   d. both a and c above
   e. all of the above

_____ 13. The deposit expansion process
   a. requires a 100 percent reserve requirement.
   b. enables banks to create demand deposits out of required reserves.
   c. is illegal and may result in revocation of a bank's charter.
   d. may work in reverse and result in a contraction of the money supply.
   e. none of the above

_____ 14. The deposit expansion factor is equal to
   a. 1/(reserve ratio).
   b. 1/(excess reserves).
   c. 1/(official reserves).
   d. (excess reserves)/(official reserves).
   e. (excess reserves)/(required reserves).

_____ 15. Assume that $100 in cash is used to open a new checking account at National Bank, that National Bank holds the $100 as vault cash, and that prior to the deposit National Bank was meeting the reserve requirement of 25 percent but had no excess reserves. As a result of the deposit, National Bank's official reserves
   a. increase by $25.
   b. increase by $75.
   c. increase by $100.
   d. increase by $400.
   e. remain unchanged.

_____ 16. Consider the situation described in question 15. As a result of the deposit, National Bank's required reserves
a. increase by $25.
b. increase by $75.
c. increase by $100.
d. increase by $400.
e. remain unchanged.

_____ 17. Consider the situation described in question 15. As a result of the deposit, National Bank's excess reserves
a. increase by $25.
b. increase by $75.
c. increase by $100.
d. increase by $400.
e. remain unchanged.

_____ 18. Consider the situation described in question 15. National Bank can now expand the money supply by a maximum of
a. $25.
b. $75.
c. $100.
d. $300.
e. $400.

_____ 19. Consider the situation described in question 15. The banking system as a whole can now expand the money supply by a maximum of
a. $25.
b. $75.
c. $100.
d. $300.
e. $400.

_____ 20. A single bank in a system of banks can expand the money supply by an amount equal to
a. the bank's excess reserves.
b. the bank's required reserves.
c. the bank's official reserves.
d. its total demand deposit liabilities.
e. a multiple of the bank's excess reserves.

_____ 21. A banking system can expand the money supply by an amount equal to
a. the excess reserves in the system.
b. a multiple of the excess reserves.
c. the official reserves in the system.
d. the required reserves in the system.
e. the demand deposit liabilities in the system.

_____ 22. The actual expansion of the money supply may be limited by
    a. the deposit of borrowed money in a checking account.
    b. a bank's failure to lend out all of its excess reserves.
    c. a bank's loan of excess reserves to a preferred customer.
    d. a bank's loan to a risky customer at a high interest rate.
    e. both a and b above

Discussion Questions

1. You are to choose something to serve as money for an economy. In addition to serving the four functions of money, what characteristics would you like your money to have?

2. What determines the value of money? Do you think it makes a difference if money is backed by a precious metal? Explain.

3. Distinguish between money and near money.

4. What are the implications for deposit expansion by the banking system of each of the following:
    a. an increase in the reserve requirement
    b. a general decrease in the reserve ratios of banks
    c. leakages into cash
    d. a generally pessimistic outlook with respect to growth and expansion in the economy
    e. concern among bankers about an increase in defaults on loans

5. What would be the effect of a 100 percent reserve requirement on each of the following:
    a. excess reserves
    b. the deposit creation capability of the banking system

Answers

Problems and Applications

1. a. L   b. M2   c. M1   d. M3
2. a. 40%   b. $25,000
    c. yes; $15,000   d. $15,000   e. $60,000
3. a. increases by $5,000   b. increases by $1,000
    c. $4,000   d. $20,000   e. $25,000
4. a. $10,000
    b. $40,000, in addition to the $10,000 created by National Bank

True-False

1. F. The most basic requirement of money is that it be generally acceptable in trade.

2. F. As a unit of account, money is the common denominator that enables people to compare values of different items.
3. T.
4. F. According to Gresham's Law, base money will drive dear money out of circulation.
5. T.
6. F. A bank note is a promise to pay that is issued by a bank.
7. T.
8. F. Demand deposits are checking accounts.
9. T.
10. F. Since M2 includes savings accounts, it is less liquid than M1.
11. T.
12. F. Near money is easily converted into money but cannot be spent directly.
13. F. The opportunity cost of liquidity is the foregone interest earnings.
14. T.
15. F. A business must have a state or federal bank charter in order to operate legally as a bank.
16. T.
17. F. Our fractional reserve system of banking means that banks are not required to keep enough cash or immediately available funds on hand to fulfill all promises to depositors.
18. F. Banks lend money but also borrow money, sometimes from other banks, sometimes from nonfinancial corporations, and sometimes from Federal Reserve Banks.
19. F. A bank's reserve ratio is the official reserves (including cash) of the bank divided by the amount of demand deposits in the bank.
20. T.
21. T.
22. T.
23. F. The Federal Reserve System, the nation's central bank, is responsible for controlling the deposit expansion factor and the actual amount of reserves in the banking system.

Multiple Choice

1. d	2. d	3. d	4. b	5. b
6. b	7. b	8. b	9. e	10. a
11. e	12. e	13. d	14. a	15. c
16. a	17. b	18. b	19. d	20. a
21. b	22. b			

13 The Federal Reserve System and Monetary Instruments

Summary

The Federal Reserve System serves as the central bank of the United States. In addition, its twelve district banks hold reserves, clear checks, conduct bank examinations, and lend money to member banks. These district banks are owned by member banks in each district.

Policy for the Federal Reserve System is set by the Board of Governors, which consists of seven members appointed by the president with Senate approval. These seven governors have primary responsibility for controlling the money supply and determining the monetary policy of the United States. The governors are responsible for setting the reserve requirement and the discount rate. Though changes in the discount rate may not have much direct effect on banks, such changes provide a valuable signal indicating potential future policy. Changes in the reserve requirement, on the other hand, can be extremely effective, since the reserve requirement not only affects the extent to which there are excess reserves in the system, but also the deposit-expansion factor. Because changes in the reserve requirement are so powerful, the requirement is seldom changed.

The seven governors, along with five representatives from District Banks, also serve on the Federal Open Market Committee. This committee is responsible for open market operations, that is, the buying and selling of government securities. Open market operations, the most frequently used tool of the system, provide another means by which the reserves of the banking system can be influenced by the Fed.

In exercising its responsibility for monetary policy, the Fed attempts to control the monetary base and the money multiplier. The monetary base consists of bank reserves and coins and currency in circulation. The Fed attempts to control it through open market operations and its ability to lend to banks. Control is not perfect, however, since outside forces can also bring about a change in the monetary base. The money multiplier is the ratio of the amount of money in the economy to the size of the monetary base. Unfortunately, the money multiplier has not proven to be constant, making monetary policy all the more difficult a job.

Since its creation in 1913, Fed policy has generally, though not always, been consistent with the fiscal policy undertaken by the president and the Congress. The policy has often been controversial.

Major Objectives

After you have finished this chapter, you will be able to do the following:

1. Discuss the problems that gave rise to the establishment of the Federal Reserve System as the central bank of the United States and the primary functions it was created to serve.
2. Explain the structure of the Federal Reserve System, including the role and composition of the Board of Governors and the Federal Open Market Committee as well as the Federal Reserve District Banks.
3. Describe the ownership and functions of the Federal Reserve District Banks.
4. Identify the major asset and liability entries on a Federal Reserve Bank balance sheet.
5. Identify and describe the major instruments of monetary policy, specifically including the reserve requirement, open market operations, and the discount rate.
6. Identify and explain the importance of the regulatory powers granted to the Board of Governors as a result of the Monetary Control Act of 1980.
7. Explain how open market transactions are indicated on the balance sheets of Federal Reserve Banks and the banks in the commercial banking system.
8. Sketch the history and explain the importance of open market operations and the discount rate as instruments of monetary policy.
9. Discuss the relationship between changes in the discount rate and interest rates.
10. Define federal funds and the federal funds rate and explain their roles in banking.
11. Define margin and margin requirement and explain their roles, historically and currently, in controlling stock market activity.

12. Identify the major change brought about by the Depository Institutions Deregulation Act of 1980.
13. Define and explain the role of moral suasion in the U.S. banking system.
14. Describe the monetary base and explain why the Fed may not be able to control it exactly.
15. Define the money multiplier and explain why it may fluctuate.
16. Sketch the history of the Fed from its creation in 1913 to the present, noting the problems faced by the monetary authorities, important legislative changes, the policy measures taken, and the reactions to these policies.

Review Terms

partial or fractional reserve system
macroeconomics
fiscal policy
equilibrium national income and product (Y*)
real vs. nominal values
shortage
currency
reserves
Federal Reserve Note
national bank
balance sheet
asset
national debt
liability
legal tender

reserve requirement
official reserve
reserve ratio
deposit-expansion process
demand deposit
excess reserves
stock market
run on a bank
inflation
price controls
recession
Keynesian economic theory
budget deficit
Organization of Petroleum Exporting Countries (OPEC)
demand-side approach

Important Terms and Concepts

Federal Reserve System (Fed)
monetary instruments
central bank
National Banking System
pyramiding of reserves
Federal Reserve Bank
Board of Governors
monetary policy
Federal Open Market Committee (FOMC)
lender of last resort
discounting
discount rate

debt instrument
short-term securities
Monetary Control Act of 1980
depository institutions
transactions accounts
open market operations
open market purchases
open market sales
discount rate signals
federal funds
federal funds rate
tightening of the money market
easing of the money market

margin   contractionary
margin requirements   gold standard
trading "on margin"   bank holiday
Depository Institutions   Glass-Steagall Act
  Deregulation Act of 1980   bond market
Garn-St. Germaine Depository   the "accord" of 1951
  Institutions Act of 1982   "leaning against the wind"
moral suasion   "war on poverty"
monetary base   disintermediation
money multiplier   stagflation
expansionary   "Whip Inflation Now" (WIN)

Completion

Federal Reserve System

The central bank for the United States is the _____ .

twelve

The country is divided into _____ districts, with a Federal Reserve Bank in each district. Policy for the Fed is determined by the

Board of Governors, seven

_____ . This Board consists of _____

the president, Senate

members appointed by _____ with _____ confirmation. The Board of Governors is responsible for determining

monetary

_____ policy in the United States.

    Among the tools of monetary policy, the most powerful is the

reserve requirement

ability to set the _____ . Because this

seldom

tool is so powerful, the reserve requirement is _____ (often/seldom) changed.

discount rate

    The Board of Governors also determines the _____ , that is, the rate of interest charged to a member bank when it bor-

last resort

rows from the Fed. The Fed is a lender of _____ , so banks are encouraged to look elsewhere for loans. One alternative is to look to banks that have excess reserves in their accounts with the

federal funds

Fed. Balances in these accounts are called _____ and the rate of interest charged on these loans is the

federal funds rate

_____ .

    The Open Market Committee is also an important body of the Fed.

open market operations

This committee has responsibility for _____ ,

government securities

that is, for the buying and selling of _____ .

The first real test of the Fed's ability to stabilize the economy through the exercise of its monetary powers came in 1921 when the

recession

economy experienced a short but severe _____ . Critics of

lower

the Board cite its failure to _____ (raise/lower) reserve requirements and engage in open market operations.

The Fed did show concern for the increased speculation in the stock market in the late 1920s. However, power to regulate stock

margin requirements

market trading directly by setting _____ was not given to the Governors until the 1930s. As an alternative, the

moral suasion

Fed utilized its persuasive powers or _____ in an attempt to convince people not to buy so extensively on margin. The Fed also attempted to reduce stock market speculation by

restraining

_____ (encouraging/restraining) the growth of the money supply, but when the stock market crashed the Board

reversed

_____ (continued/reversed) this policy.

In 1931, in an attempt to avoid further reductions in their holdings

raised

of commercial paper, the Fed _____ (raised/lowered) discount

further tightening of

rates and allowed _____ (growth in/ further tightening of) the money supply. This led to numerous bank

bank holiday

closings and the declaration of a nationwide _____ by President Roosevelt.

Passage of the Glass-Steagall Act in 1932 allowed the Fed to use

government bonds

_____ to back Federal Reserve notes and

Federal Open Market

established the _____ Committee.

In 1933, the United States followed other countries in refusing to back its paper currency with a fixed amount of gold. That is, the

gold standard

United States went off the _____ and remained off this standard for nearly two years. In 1934, the gold standard

into

was reestablished in modified form and gold flowed _____ (into/out of) the U.S. banking system. This strengthened the reserve position of the Fed. Excess reserves in commercial banks increased

inflation

sizably. By 1936, fearing _____ (inflation/deflation), the

increased

Fed dramatically _____ (increased/decreased) reserve requirements and used open market operations to counteract the

contributed to

effect of gold imports. This policy _____ (helped delay/contributed to) the recession of 1937.

Fed policy during World War II relied primarily on

open market opera-
tions

_____ to assure the government adequate financing for the war. More specifically, the Fed, interested

preventing

in _____ (promoting/preventing) an increase in interest

bought

rates, _____ (bought/sold) government securities on the

expansion

open market. This led to a sizable _____ (expansion/ contraction) of the money supply, coupled with government-imposed

price and wage
controls

_____ as well as

rationing

_____ of goods and services.

     After World War II, the Fed bowed to the pressures of the U.S.

purchases

Treasury and continued open market _____ (purchases/

higher

sales) to support the bond market, relying on _____ (higher/ lower) discount rates and reserve requirements to fight inflation. This decision no doubt contributed to a worsening inflation.

     U.S. involvement in the Korean War in the 1950s caused a recur-

inflation

rence of _____ (inflation/deflation) and war-related problems. The Treasury wanted the Fed to continue open market purchases to support the bond market. The Fed responded by

asserting its inde-
pendence from

_____ (recognizing its dependence on/asserting its independence from) the U.S. Treasury,

freed from

and open market operations were _____ (more securely bound to/freed from) a commitment to support the bond market. In 1951, the Treasury and the Fed publicly

reached an accord

_____ (reached an accord/ recognized their discord).

     Monetary policies operated fairly smoothly during the 1950s and 1960s. In an attempt to encourage production and reduce unemploy- ment in the early 1970s under the Nixon administration, the Fed

bought, lowered

_____ (bought/sold) on the open market and _____ (raised/lowered) the discount rate. During the Ford administration,

tight

the Fed followed a(n) _____ (easy/tight) monetary policy

increased

to fight inflation, and unemployment _____ (increased/ decreased) The election of Carter signaled support for economic ex-

increase

pansion and the Fed allowed the money supply to _____ (increase/decrease). But the high rates of inflation finally resulted in restrictive

a(n) _____ (easy/restrictive) monetary policy, which helped bring the inflation rate down during the Reagan administration.

Problems and Applications

1. Assume that National Bank is just meeting a reserve requirement of 10 percent when the Open Market Committee purchases $100 worth of government securities from the bank.
   a. How would this transaction be reflected on the balance sheet for National Bank?
   b. How would this transaction be reflected on the balance sheet for the Federal Reserve Banks?
   c. What happens to the required reserves of National Bank as a result of the open market transaction?
   d. What happens to the excess reserves of National Bank as a result of the open market transaction?
   e. By how much can National Bank increase the money supply?
   f. By how much can the banking system increase the money supply?

2. Answer questions a through f in problem 1 above, assuming that National Bank is just meeting a reserve requirement of 25 percent.

3. National Bank currently has reserves totaling $30,000 and deposit liabilities of $100,000. The reserve requirement is 10 percent. National Bank is contemplating the purchase of $5,000 worth of government securities from the Fed (that is, the Open Market Committee is selling securities).
   a. What will happen to the reserves of National Bank if it buys the securities?
   b. Does National Bank have sufficient excess reserves to purchase the securities?
   c. What would be National Bank's reserve ratio after the transaction?

4. Answer questions a through c in problem 3, assuming that the reserve requirement is 20 percent.

5. Consider an economy described by the following data:

Coins and currency in circulation	$100,000
Demand deposit liabilities of the banking system	$500,000
Excess reserves in the banking system	$40,000
Reserve requirement	20 percent

   a. What is M1 for the economy?
   b. How much is the banking system holding in official reserves?

c. What is the economy's monetary base?

d. Using M1 as the definition of the money supply, calculate the money multiplier.

True-False Indicate whether each of the following statements is basically true or false. If the statement is false, rewrite it so that it is true.

_____ 1. The Federal Reserve System is a branch of the Treasury Department.

_____ 2. The National Banking System permitted a pyramiding of reserves in which a large part of the reserves of small banks were held as deposits in banks in larger cities; these banks, in turn, held reserves as deposits in banks in a few major cities.

_____ 3. The Federal Open Market Committee (FOMC) of the Fed is responsible for setting the reserve requirement.

_____ 4. The Federal Reserve District Banks are owned by the state and local governments within each district.

_____ 5. On the balance sheet of a Federal Reserve Bank, the reserve accounts of member banks and Federal Reserve Notes circulating in the economy are listed as liabilities.

_____ 6. Changing the reserve requirement is such a powerful instrument of monetary policy that it is the most frequently used of all the available tools.

_____ 7. Open market operations consist of the buying and selling of government securities by the Open Market Committee.

_____ 8. When the FOMC purchases $100 worth of government securities on the open market, the reserves of the bank involved will decrease by $100.

_____ 9. FOMC sales tend to contract the money supply.

_____ 10. The discount rate is the interest rate that one bank charges on a loan to another bank.

_____ 11. Changes in the discount rate have a direct effect on general interest rates in the economy, with interest rates changing by the same amount and in the same direction as any change in the discount rate.

_____ 12. Margin requirements specify the percentage of a stock purchase that must be paid for with unborrowed funds.

_____ 13. The Depository Institutions Deregulation Act of 1980 gave the Fed the authority to set upper limits on interest rates.

_____ 14. The monetary base consists of coins and currency in circulation, demand deposits, and bank reserves.

_____ 15. The money multiplier is the ratio of the monetary base to the money supply.

_____ 16. Disintermediation occurs when depositors withdraw funds from financial institutions in order to obtain higher interest rates elsewhere.

Multiple Choice   Choose the *one best* answer in each of the following cases:

_____ 1. The Federal Reserve System
   a. relies on the pyramiding of reserves.
   b. replaced the National Banking System.
   c. was started by an Act of Congress in 1913.
   d. both b and c above
   e. all of the above

_____ 2. The pyramiding of reserves under the National Banking System
   a. led to repeated nationwide bank panics.
   b. referred to the requirement of a higher reserve ratio as the size of deposits increased.
   c. was one of the advantages of the system that Congress included in the Federal Reserve System.
   d. meant that a few large banks determined the reserve requirement for a large number of smaller banks.
   e. none of the above

_____ 3. The Federal Reserve Act provided for the establishment of a Federal Reserve Bank in
   a. Washington, D.C., operated by the Treasury Department.
   b. each of four regions, with branch banks in the capitals of each state in the region.
   c. each state, with each bank overseeing the commercial banks within the state.
   d. each state, with each bank directly responsible to the governor of the state.
   e. each of twelve districts, in order to recognize the diverse interests of different parts of the country.

_____ 4. The members of the Board of Governors of the Federal Reserve System
   a. are appointed by the president to serve fourteen-year terms.
   b. must include at least two Senators and one Representative among its seven members.
   c. make recommendations with respect to monetary policy but have no direct control.
   d. primarily serve as economic (money and banking) advisors to the president.
   e. all of the above

_____ 5. The Open Market Committee of the Fed
   a. maintains and monitors the reserves of member banks.
   b. is responsible for buying and selling government securities.
   c. has twelve members, who must be current or past presidents of the district banks.
   d. served in the capacity of Board of Directors when the Fed was created in 1913.
   e. meets in New York City and has direct control over stock market activity as a result of its ability to set margin requirements.

_____ 6. The Federal Reserve Banks are owned by
   a. the U.S. government.
   b. the state governments within each district.
   c. private, nonbanking business firms within each district.
   d. member banks, which include all national and some state banks.
   e. the individual shareholders who have checking and savings accounts with the Federal Reserve Banks.

_____ 7. The Federal Reserve District Banks
   a. provide for bank examinations.
   b. serve as a clearinghouse for checks.
   c. serve as banks for the federal government.
   d. provide many services for commercial banks that commercial banks provide for the general public.
   e. all of the above

_____ 8. Federal Reserve Banks make loans to member banks
   a. as a lender of last resort.
   b. whenever member banks request such loans.
   c. primarily for the purpose of earning profits.
   d. only when such banks are holding excess reserves.
   e. only when such banks are having long-run difficulties.

_____ 9. The asset side of a balance sheet for the district banks of the Federal Reserve System would include
   a. U.S. government securities.
   b. the vault cash of member banks.
   c. the deposit of the U.S. Treasury.
   d. Federal Reserve Notes in circulation.
   e. the reserve deposit accounts of commercial banks.

_____ 10. An increase in the reserve requirement will most likely lead to a(n)
   a. increase in the actual reserve ratio maintained by banks and a corresponding increase in the deposit-expansion factor.
   b. increase in the actual reserve ratio maintained by banks and a corresponding decrease in the deposit-expansion factor.

    c. decrease in the actual reserve ratio maintained by banks and a corresponding decrease in the deposit-expansion factor.

    d. decrease in the actual reserve ratio maintained by banks and a corresponding increase in the deposit-expansion factor.

    e. increase in the actual reserve ratio maintained by banks, with no change in the deposit-expansion factor.

_____ 11. The Monetary Control Act of 1980
    a. extended the powers of the Board of Governors to include regulatory control over all depository institutions.
    b. broadened the powers of the Board of Governors to include all transactions accounts, all savings accounts, U.S. Savings Bonds, and Treasury Bills.
    c. severely limited the powers of the Board of Governors by requiring presidential approval of any changes in the reserve requirement or the discount rate.
    d. limited the powers of the Board of Governors by excluding from regulatory control all depository institutions except banks that are members of the Fed.
    e. both c and d above

_____ 12. Open market operations
    a. refer to purchases and sales of stock in member banks.
    b. provide a way to control trading on the stock exchange.
    c. affect the quantity of reserves in the banking system.
    d. include the public forums held by the Board of Governors.
    e. none of the above

_____ 13. Open Market Committee purchases of securities
    a. cause bank reserves to increase.
    b. always decrease the money supply.
    c. generally decrease the money supply.
    d. are designed to increase trading on the stock exchange.
    e. none of the above

_____ 14. The discount rate is the rate of interest
    a. banks charge on loans for stock purchases.
    b. banks charge to their preferred customers.
    c. the Fed pays when it borrows from the Treasury.
    d. charged to banks when they borrow from the Fed.
    e. charged to banks when the borrow the excess reserves of other banks.

_____ 15. An increase in the discount rate
      a. tends to create excess reserves.
      b. would be a signal that the Fed wanted to decrease the money supply.
      c. directly affects all member banks by reducing their reserve accounts.
      d. means that there would be an increase in all interest rates in the economy.
      e. none of the above

_____ 16. Which of the following actions is most likely to lead to an increase in the money supply?
      a. an increase in the reserve requirement
      b. an increase in the discount rate
      c. an increase in margin requirement
      d. a decrease in margin requirement
      e. FOMC purchases of government securities

_____ 17. The federal funds rate
      a. determines the discount rate.
      b. is the rate of interest charged on government loans.
      c. must decrease when the Fed engages in a restrictive monetary policy.
      d. is determined by the U.S. Treasury but must exceed the discount rate.
      e. tends to rise when economic activity and bank lending are expanding more rapidly than the money supply.

_____ 18. The monetary base
      a. may be affected by changes in interest rates.
      b. is primarily used to determine the reserve requirement.
      c. cannot exceed the amount of gold owned by the government.
      d. measures the amount of cash in existence inside and outside the banking system.
      e. is completely controlled by the Fed and is therefore the most useful measure of the money supply.

_____ 19. The money multiplier is
      a. the ratio of excess reserves to total reserves.
      b. the ratio of excess reserves to required reserves.
      c. the ratio of money in the economy to the monetary base.
      d. a constant determined by the reserve requirement.
      e. both c and d above

Discussion Questions

1. Name and describe two ways the Fed can create excess reserves. Is one preferable to the other? If so, in what way(s)?

2. If the Fed serves as lender of last resort for member banks, where else might a bank turn if it needs or wants to build up its reserves?

3. Does the creation of excess reserves in a bank guarantee an increase in the money supply? If not, what must happen before the money supply actually increases?

4. Would you expect the Fed to be more successful when it attempts to increase or to decrease the money supply? Why?

5. Explain why changes in the money supply constitute a demand-side policy approach.

Answers

Problems and Applications

1. a. The transaction would increase the reserves of National Bank and decrease the bank's securities by $100 each. These are both entries on the assets side of the bank's balance sheet.
   b. On the assets side of the balance sheet, securities would increase by $100; on the liabilities side, reserve deposits would increase by $100.
   c. nothing   d. increase by $100
   e. $100   f. $1,000

2. a. The transaction would increase the reserves of National Bank and decrease the bank's securities by $100 each. These are both entries on the assets side of the bank's balance sheet.
   b. On the assets side of the balance sheet, securities would increase by $100; on the liabilities side, reserve deposits would increase by $100.
   c. nothing   d. increase by $100
   e. $100   f. $400

3. a. decrease by $5,000   b. yes   c. 25 percent

4. a. decrease by $5,000   b. yes   c. 25 percent

5. a. $600,000   b. $140,000   c. $240,000
   d. 5/2, or 2.5

True-False

1. F. The Federal Reserve System is independent of the Treasury Department.
2. T.
3. F. The FOMC of the Fed is responsible for the buying and selling of government securities on the open market.

4. F. The Federal Reserve District Banks are owned by banks within each district, with all nationally chartered banks required to be member-owners and state chartered banks allowed to become member-owners.
5. T.
6. F. Changing the reserve requirement is such a powerful instrument of monetary policy that it is rarely used.
7. T.
8. F. When the FOMC purchases $100 worth of government securities on the open market, the reserves of the bank involved will increase by $100.
9. T.
10. F. The discount rate is the interest rate that Federal Reserve Banks charge on loans to member banks.
11. F. Changes in the discount rate have only an indirect effect on interest rates in the economy; thus, the Fed is unable to determine general interest rates in the economy directly.
12. T.
13. F. The Depository Institutions Deregulation Act of 1980 phases out, over a period of six years, the Fed's ability to set interest rate limits.
14. F. The monetary base consists of coins and currency in circulation and bank reserves.
15. F. The money multiplier is the ratio of the money supply to the size of the monetary base.
16. T.

Multiple Choice

1. d	2. a	3. e	4. a	5. b
6. d	7. e	8. a	9. a	10. b
11. a	12. c	13. a	14. d	15. b
16. e	17. e	18. a	19. c	

14 Monetary Economics and Monetarism

Summary

Monetarism focuses on the importance of the supply of money in determining an economy's equilibrium level of national income and output. Like Keynesians, monetarists are concerned with the effect of changes in total planned expenditure on the equilibrium level of national income and product. But whereas a Keynesian would use government budgetary action to reach a particular target level of national income, a monetarist would see such an approach as uncertain at best.

The distinction between nominal and real values is particularly important in monetary theory. Thus far, we have dealt primarily with real values, on the assumption that people base their behavior on real values.

The quantity theory of money provides a relatively simple approach to investigating the role of money in an economy. The quantity theory is based on the equation of exchange, which merely expresses the equality between the total money spent by purchasers and the total money received by sellers. If the velocity of circulation of money is stable and predictable as maintained by quantity theorists, then changes in the money supply will cause predictable changes in the nominal value of national income. But unless additional assumptions are made, it is impossible to determine the extent to which these changes represent changes in real production as opposed to changes in the general price level.

In order to better understand the relationship between the money supply and national income, modern monetary theory concerns itself with the determination of interest rates. Long-run real interest rates in the economy are basically determined by the productivity of capital and the willingness of some to postpone the use of their wealth. Short-run rates, on the other hand, are likely to be influenced by other factors. One of these may be the supply of money. To investigate this possibility, economists look at the demand for and supply of money.

In dealing with the demand for money, quantity refers to the amount of their assets people will hold in liquid (money) form as opposed to less liquid forms. The interest rate reflects the opportunity cost of liquidity and so is the price of holding money. The demand for money is composed of a speculative demand, a transactions demand, and a precautionary demand. Because the speculative demand, the transactions demand, and precautionary demand curves for money are all negatively sloped, the demand curve for money will be negatively sloped. The location of this demand curve is significantly influenced by the level of national income. A change in national income is likely to cause a shift in the money demand curve in the same direction.

The money supply curve represents the amount of money available in the economy at different real rates of interest. Banks are more willing to lend as real interest rates rise, so the money supply curve is positively sloped. The location of the money supply curve, in nominal terms, at least, may be influenced by monetary policy. If, however, monetary policy results in a change in the price level, the real money supply curve may not change in the manner intended by policy.

The extent to which monetary policy results in a change in the real money supply is very important for assessing the consequences of the policy. Assuming there is no change in the demand for money, a change in the real money supply causes a change in the real interest rate. The change in the interest rate causes a change in the level of planned investment spending. This change in planned investment spending calls forth a change in total planned expenditure and a corresponding (multiplied) change in real national income and product.

When monetary policy is successful in changing the real value of equilibrium national income, there will be feedback effects to the demand for money. These feedback effects arise because the demand for money is influenced by the level of national income. The feedback effects will tend to moderate the changes in income and product.

There is much uncertainty about interest-rate determination in the market for liquidity, with much of the uncertainty centering around inflationary expectations associated with changes in the money supply. There is less uncertainty in interest-rate determination in the market for loanable funds, where modern monetarists believe long-run real interest rates are determined. Modern monetarists believe that neither the demand for nor the supply of loanable funds is significantly affected by central bank policy. Hence, in the long run the real interest rate will not be affected by changes in the money supply. If the real interest rate is not affected by changes in the money supply, the volume of production will likewise not be affected.

Major Objectives   After you have finished this chapter, you will be able to do the following:

1. State and explain the equation of change.
2. Define velocity of circulation.
3. State and explain the quantity theory of money, indicating the major assumptions and conclusions.
4. Discuss the predictability of the velocity variable and its importance in the quantity theory of money.
5. Define and distinguish between nominal values and real values.
6. Determine one of the following three variables, given the other two: real value, nominal value, a change in the general price level.
7. State and use the rule regarding the difference between real and nominal interest rates.
8. Identify and describe the components of the demand for money and use these components to explain the slope and location of the demand curve.
9. State, explain, and utilize the present value formula.
10. Explain the consequences of a change in income or wealth on the demand for money.
11. Describe and explain the slope and location of the money supply curve.
12. Identify the equilibrium interest rate, given money demand and supply curves, and explain the process whereby this rate is established.
13. Explain how a given Federal Reserve policy is likely to change the real money supply curve under the assumption that no price-level change is expected.
14. Explain the process of adjustment to a new equilibrium in the money market resulting from a change in the real money supply.
15. Explain how a change in the real money supply and the resulting change in the real interest rate affect planned investment spending and equilibrium national income (the Keynesian transmission mechanism).
16. Explain the direct transmission mechanism, by which a change in the money supply works directly through consumption spending to cause changes in national income.

17. Describe the process whereby a change in the real money supply could lead to a change in the demand for money and therefore to further changes in the real interest rate, planned investment, and equilibrium national income.
18. Explain the various consequences of a change in the money supply, given a variety of expectations about inflation.
19. Explain modern monetarist thinking with regard to the market for loanable funds and the determination of long-run real interest rates.
20. Identify and describe the major factors influencing the effectiveness of monetary instruments in changing equilibrium national income.

Review Terms

real vs. nominal values
national income and product (Y)
general price level (P)
Gross National Product
  (GNP = PQ)
M1
M2
equilibrium national income
  and product (Y*)
interest rate
investment
Keynesian model
macroeconomic equilibrium
demand curve for planned
  investment expenditure
index number
wealth
consumption function
purchasing power

supply
demand
GNP deflator
income vs. wealth
liquidity
opportunity cost
movement along a curve vs. shift
  in a curve
deposit-expansion process
reserve requirement
excess reserves
monetary instruments of the Fed
open market operations
discount rate
equilibrium
total planned expenditure
  (C + I + G + X – Im)
multiplier
capital

Important Terms and Concepts

monetarist approach
quantity theory of money
equation of exchange
velocity of circulation (V)
money supply or quantity of
  money (M)
quantity of real output (Q)
identity
nominal value
real value

real interest rate
nominal interest rate
money market
money supply (MS)
demand for money (MD)
speculation
speculative demand for money
transactions demand for money
precautionary demand for money
present value

liquidity demand
expansionary policy
restrictive policy
contractionary policy
Keynesian transmission
  mechanism
liquidity trap

effective full employment
direct transmission mechanism
feedback to the demand for
  money
inflationary expectations
loanable funds market

Completion

Modern monetary theory is interested in determining the effect of a change in the money supply on real income and product. In order to investigate this relationship, monetarists focus on the determination

interest rates

of real _____ . This requires a study of the de-

money

mand for and supply of _____ .

inverse

    The demand for money is a(n) _____ (direct/inverse)

interest rate

relationship between the _____ , or opportunity cost of money, and the amount of assets people will hold in money

speculative

form. It is made up of a _____ demand, a

transactions,
precautionary

_____ demand, and a _____ demand.
    The speculative demand for money reflects a desire to hold assets

money

in the form of _____ in order to take advantage of

interest rate

changes in the _____ . The connection between the interest rate and the value of a particular asset is indicated by the

(expected annual
income flow)/
(interest rate)

present value formula: present value = _____

_____ . When interest rates are relatively low, the present value or price of bonds, for example,

high

will be relatively _____ (low/high). Since people will antici-

decrease

pate a(n) _____ (decrease/increase) in the price of

will

bonds as interest rates rise, they _____ (will/will not) want to hold money when interest rates are relatively low. On the other hand, when interest rates are relatively high, the price of bonds will

low, less

be relatively _____ (low/high). People will be _____ (less/more) likely to want to hold money, anticipating a(n)

increase

_____ (decrease/increase) in the price of bonds as inter-est rates fall. This means that the speculative demand curve for

negatively

money is _____ (positively/negatively) sloped.

transactions

The _____ demand for money arises because money facilitates trade, that is, because money serves as a medium of

interest rate

exchange. If the _____ represents the opportunity cost of money, the transactions demand curve for money will be

negatively

_____ (positively/negatively) sloped. A change in national income has a significant effect on the transactions demand for

shift in

money, causing a _____ (movement along/shift in) the demand curve for money. The relationship between the

positive

demand for money and national income is a _____ (positive/negative) one.

precautionary

The _____ demand for money arises because people want to be prepared for the unexpected. As with the transactions motive, this motive for holding money is also represented by a

negative

_____ (positive/negative) relationship between the amount of money and the interest rate. The precautionary demand

is also

for money _____ (is also/is not) affected by changes in national income, with changes in national income affecting the

location

_____ (slope/location) of the curve.

The supply of money is a relationship showing the amount of

interest rates

money that will be available at different _____ . The

direct

relationship is _____ (direct/inverse), since banks will be

rise

willing to make more loans as interest rates _____ (rise/fall).

Equilibrium in the money market occurs at the intersection of the

money demand
and supply

_____ curves. The equilibrium

interest

rate of _____ is the rate that equates the amount of money demanded with the amount supplied. When the actual rate of interest is greater than the equilibrium rate, people find they are holding

more

_____ (more/fewer) of their assets in money form than they

buy

would like. As they attempt to _____ (buy/sell) nonmoney assets (such as stocks, bonds, and real estate) the prices of these assets

rise, drop

_____ (fall/rise). This leads to a _____ (drop/rise) in the rate of interest, moving the market toward the equilibrium point. On the other hand, when the actual rate of interest is less than the

less

equilibrium rate, people find they are holding _____ (more/

sell

less) money than they would like. As they attempt to _____

fall   (buy/sell) nonmoney assets, the prices of these assets _____

rises   (rise/fall) and the interest rate _____ (rises/falls). Again, the market moves toward the equilibrium point.

supply of money   Monetary policy is used to change the _____ .

increase   An expansionary monetary policy will tend to _____ (increase/decrease) the nominal supply of money, and a contraction-

decrease   ary monetary policy will tend to _____ (increase/decrease) the nominal supply of money. But in order for monetary policy to affect real interest rates (and therefore to influence investment spending and real national income), a change in the nominal money supply

real   must result in a change in the _____ money supply. Whether a change in the nominal money supply results in a change in the real money supply depends on the extent of associated changes in the

general price level   _____ .

When a change in the nominal supply of money does not lead to a

will   change in the price level, the real money supply _____ (will/will not) change with the nominal money supply. Given the demand curve for money, a change in the real money supply results in a

real interest rate   change in the _____ .

Changes in the real interest rate cause changes in the level of

investment   planned _____ spending. A change in the level of planned investment spending, then, leads to an equivalent change in

total planned expenditures   _____ . A change in total planned expenditures causes a multiplied change in equilibrium

national income   _____ . Because the demand for money changes with changes in national income, there are likely to be

feedback   _____ effects that cause a shift in the demand

moderate   curve for money. These feedback effects tend to _____ (magnify/moderate) the change in national income.

Recall, however, that for any of these changes to occur there has to be a change in the real money supply. If a change in the nominal

general price level   money supply causes a change in the _____ that offsets the change in money supply, any change in the real

temporary   money supply would be _____ (temporary/perma-nent). In such an event, a change in the real interest rate would also

temporary   be _____ (temporary/permanent). Consequently, there would be no permanent effect on the level of planned investment spending and hence no permanent effect on equilibrium national income.

Problems and Applications

1. a. Assume that prices are rising by 8 percent and the nominal interest rate is 15 percent. What is the real interest rate?
    b. Assume that prices are falling by 10 percent and the nominal interest rate is 13 percent. What is the real interest rate?

2. a. Assume that prices are rising by 6 percent and the real interest rate is 8 percent. What is the nominal interest rate?
    b. Assume that prices are falling by 3 percent and the real interest rate is 9 percent. What is the nominal interest rate?

3. a. Assume that a nominal interest rate of 12 percent is equivalent to a real interest rate of 5 percent. What is the change in prices?
    b. Assume that a nominal interest rate of 11 percent is equivalent to a real interest rate of 14 percent. What is the change in prices?

4. Assume that an economy produces 200 units of goods and services, the average price is $3 per unit, and the money supply is $120.
    a. What is the velocity of circulation of money?
    b. Assuming that velocity and output remain constant, what happens if you double the money supply?
    c. Assuming that velocity and output remain constant, what happens if you triple the money supply?
    d. Assuming that velocity and output remain constant, what happens if you cut the money supply in half?

5. Recall that in neoclassical economic theory, the economy would automatically reach a full-employment equilibrium. The neoclassical economists also believed that the velocity of circulation of money was constant. What are the implications of these assumptions for the quantity theory of money? (First determine the implication for Q of an economy operating at a full-employment equilibrium.)

6. a. What is the present value of a bond that pays $100 a year indefinitely if the interest rate is 10 percent? What is the price of this bond?
    b. What is the present value of a bond that pays $100 a year indefinitely if the interest rate is 20 percent? What is the price of this bond?
    c. What is the present value of a bond that pays $100 a year indefinitely if the interest rate is 5 percent? What is the price of this bond?

    d. What is the nature of the relationship (direct or inverse) between the interest rate and the price of a bond?

7. If the present value of a bond that pays $20 a year indefinitely is $200, what is the interest rate?

8. What is the expected annual income flow from a bond selling for $500 today if the interest rate is 10 percent?

Use the graphs below to answer problems 9 and 10.

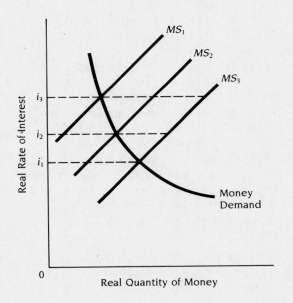

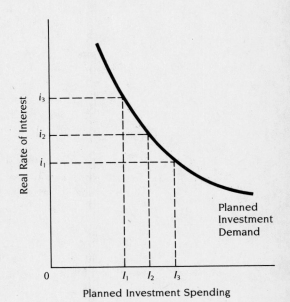

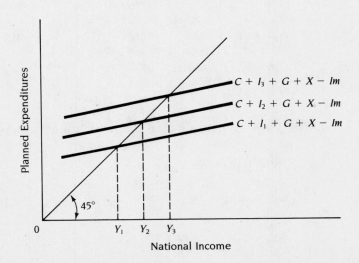

9. Consider the economy described in the graphs on page 265.
   a. Assume that the money supply curve for the economy is MS_2. What is the equilibrium real rate of interest? What is the level of planned investment spending? What is the equilibrium level of national income? What is the equilibrium level of national product?
   b. Assume that the money supply curve shifts from MS_2 to MS_1. What has happened to the money supply? What happens to the equilibrium real rate of interest? What happens to the equilibrium level of planned investment spending? What happens to the equilibrium level of national income?
   c. Assume that the money supply curve shifts from MS_2 to MS_3. What has happened to the money supply? What happens to the equilibrium real rate of interest? What happens to the equilibrium level of planned investment spending? What happens to the equilibrium level of national income?
   d. In problems 9b and 9c, you have traced the effects of a change in the money supply on national income and product via the real interest rate and planned investment expenditure. What is this process called? What would be the consequence of feedback effects to the demand for money?

10. Consider the economy described by the graphs on page 265. Assume that the current real money supply is given by MS_2 and that the economy is currently in equilibrium.
   a. If Y_1 represents the target level of national income and product, what kind of Keynesian gap exists? In order to close this gap, would you increase or decrease the real money supply? By how much?
   b. If Y_3 represents the target level of national income, what kind of Keynesian gap exists? In order to close this gap, would you increase or decrease the real money supply? By how much?

True-False

Indicate whether each of the following statements is basically true or false. If the statement is false, rewrite it so that it is true.

_____ 1. Real and nominal values are distinguished by whether there has been an adjustment for price changes.

_____ 2. The real cost of borrowing money is measured by the nominal interest rate.

_____ 3. The difference between real and nominal interest rates can be measured by the discount rate.

_____ 4. The quantity theory of money is the equation of exchange.

_____ 5. The velocity of circulation of money is the rate at which money is borrowed from the banking system.

_____ 6. In the equation of exchange, *PQ* represents GNP.

_____ 7. A quantity theorist is likely to contend that, in the long run, the velocity of circulation of money is absolutely constant.

_____ 8. To speculate means to act on the basis of expected future changes in the market value of an asset.

_____ 9. People may hold money as an asset for speculative, transactions, and precautionary reasons.

_____ 10. The speculative demand for liquidity refers to money held in anticipation of a reduction in the price of nonmoney assets.

_____ 11. A person who expects an increase in the value of nonmoney assets is likely to want to hold more money for speculative reasons.

_____ 12. The present value of a bond is the rate of interest times the expected annual income flow.

_____ 13. The speculative motive for holding money suggests that the demand curve for money will be positively sloped.

_____ 14. The transactions demand for money is likely to increase as a result of an increase in national income.

_____ 15. The transactions demand for money exists because of unexpected events that alter a person's income and/or expenditure patterns.

_____ 16. A change in income or wealth is likely to change the slope of the demand curve for money.

_____ 17. Monetary policy involves attempts to shift the money supply curve.

_____ 18. Assuming that there is no change in the general price level, an increase in the supply of money will cause a rise in the real interest rate.

_____ 19. A change in the real money supply that results in a new real rate of interest may cause a change in planned investment spending and therefore a change in total planned expenditure.

_____ 20. The effects of a change in the real money supply via the Keynesian transmission mechanism are magnified if there are feedback effects to the demand for money.

_____ 21. An expansionary monetary policy will always cause an increase in the real money supply, and as a consequence the real interest rate will fall.

_____ 22. When people believe that an increase in the money supply is the cause of inflation, the real interest rate is likely to rise while the nominal interest rate stays the same.

_____ 23. Monetary policy, like Keynesian fiscal policy, is a demand-side approach.

Multiple Choice   Choose the one *best answer* in each of the following cases:

_____ 1. To determine the real values, given nominal values, one would be most interested in knowing
a. the current interest rate.
b. the current monetary policy.
c. the rate of change in the price level.
d. how monetary policy has changed over time.
e. the average number of times each dollar is used per year.

_____ 2. An increase in nominal value always implies a(n)
a. increase in the price level.
b. decrease in real value when the price level rises.
c. increase in real value when the price level rises.
d. decrease in real value when there is no change in the price level.
e. none of the above

_____ 3. Assume that you purchased a $600 bond ten years ago. During the past ten years, the general price level has risen by 20 percent. Which one of the following statements accurately reflects your situation?
a. The bond is now worth $720.
b. You have suffered a real loss of $120.
c. In terms of the old price level, the real value of the bond is now $500.
d. The real value of the bond has risen with the rise in the price level.
e. The nominal value of the bond has declined with the rise in the price level.

_____ 4. Which of the following equations is consistent with the simple rule for finding the real rate of interest, given the nominal rate of interest and the rate of change in the price level?
a. real rate = nominal rate + rate of change in prices
b. real rate = nominal rate − rate of change in prices
c. real rate = rate of change in prices − nominal rate
d. real rate = (nominal rate) × (rate of change in prices)
e. real rate = (nominal rate)/(rate of change in prices)

_____   5. The velocity of circulation of money is
    a. equal to GNP times the money supply.
    b. equal to GNP divided by the money supply.
    c. equal to the money supply divided by GNP.
    d. definitely constant in the short run, though it may vary considerably in the long run.
    e. definitely constant in the long run, though it may vary in the short run.

_____   6. In the equation of exchange,
    a. Q represents the quantity of money.
    b. V represents the velocity of circulation.
    c. P represents the production of goods and services.
    d. all of the above
    e. none of the above

_____   7. The equation of exchange
    a. relies on the stability and predictability of the velocity of circulation.
    b. shows the identity between the total money spent by purchasers and the total money received by sellers.
    c. establishes the causal relationship between a change in the money supply and the equilibrium level of national income.
    d. verifies that an increase in the quantity of money in an economy results in an increase in the level of real output.
    e. all of the above

_____   8. The modern version of the quantity theory of money
    a. is based on the equation of exchange.
    b. acknowledges that velocity may fluctuate in the short run.
    c. relies on the stability and predictability of the velocity of circulation in the long run.
    d. establishes a causal relationship between changes in the money supply and changes in nominal national income.
    e. all of the above

_____   9. According to the quantity theory of money, the
    a. nominal value of the GNP is determined by the quantity of money in an economy.
    b. velocity of circulation of money is determined by the quantity of money in an economy.
    c. quantity of money in an economy is determined by the velocity of circulation of money.
    d. quantity of money in an economy is determined by the real value of output in the economy.
    e. none of the above

_____ 10. Using the M1 definition of the money supply, U.S. data for 1960 through 1980 show that
   a. the velocity of circulation was constant.
   b. the velocity of circulation decreased consistently.
   c. though the velocity of circulation increased only slightly, the increases were consistent.
   d. though the changes were not consistent, the velocity of circulation increased substantially.
   e. the velocity of circulation cannot be computed in the real world.

_____ 11. Long-run real interest rates are determined by the
   a. productivity of capital.
   b. willingness of some to postpone the use of their wealth.
   c. interplay of a demand for and a supply of money for loans.
   d. all of the above
   e. amount of money in the economy at a given point in time.

_____ 12. According to the present value formula, present value is equal to
   a. (expected annual income flow)/(interest rate).
   b. (interest rate)/(expected annual income flow).
   c. (expected annual income flow) × (interest rate).
   d. (real value + nominal value)/(rate of change in prices).
   e. (nominal value − real value)/(rate of change in prices).

_____ 13. When people hold money in order to take advantage of a change in interest rates, they are said to have a
   a. supply of liquidity.
   b. speculative supply of money.
   c. speculative demand for money.
   d. precautionary demand for money.
   e. transactions demand for liquidity.

_____ 14. The demand curve for money
   a. is primarily determined by Federal Reserve policy.
   b. tends to be positively sloped, because of the speculative demand for money.
   c. typically arises because of transactions, precautionary, and speculative motives.
   d. all of the above
   e. shows the relationship between the quantity of money a person has and the value of his or her nonmonetary assets.

_____ 15. The transactions demand for money
   a. determines the amount of cash in circulation.
   b. would generally decrease with increases in wealth.
   c. is likely to be affected by the level of national income.
   d. arises because people want to be prepared for the unexpected.
   e. enables people to take advantage of changes in the interest rate.

_____ 16. When money is demanded for precautionary reasons, the
a. demand is highly dependent on the reserve ratio, because banks must meet a reserve requirement.
b. demand is negatively related to the speculative demand for money, because most people cannot afford both.
c. demand is positively related to the discount rate, because banks will take greater precautions when it costs them more to borrow from the Fed.
d. quantity demanded is negatively related to income and wealth, because richer people do not need to worry so much about unforeseen problems.
e. quantity demanded is negatively related to the interest rate, because the interest rate reflects the opportunity cost of holding the money.

_____ 17. The money supply curve tends to be
a. nonexistent during times of inflation.
b. positively sloped, because banks will be willing to lend more as interest rates rise.
c. negatively sloped, because banks will borrow more from the Fed and from other banks as interest rates decline.
d. horizontal, because the treasury can always print additional money.
e. vertical, because it is determined entirely by the amount of cash in circulation in the economy.

_____ 18. When the money market is in equilibrium, the
a. velocity of circulation must be constant.
b. Fed would never change its monetary policy.
c. amount of money supplied is equal to the amount demanded.
d. all of the above
e. none of the above

_____ 19. Monetary policy of the Federal Reserve System may include
a. a reduction in the discount rate in order to increase the demand for money.
b. a reduction in the reserve requirement primarily for the purpose of increasing the demand for money.
c. a reduction in the discount rate in an attempt to decrease the supply of money.
d. Fed purchases on the open market for the purpose of increasing the supply of money.
e. both a and b above

_____ 20. Assuming there is no change in the general price level, an expansionary monetary policy will most likely increase the
a. nominal money supply and the real money supply.
b. nominal money supply, while decreasing the real money supply.
c. real money supply, while decreasing the nominal money supply.
d. nominal money supply, but leave the real money supply unchanged.
e. real money supply, but leave the nominal money supply unchanged.

_____ 21. According to the direct transmission mechanism, an increase in the supply of money causes a(n)
a. decrease in planned consumption spending and a multiplied decrease in national income.
b. increase in planned consumption spending and a multiplied increase in national income.
c. decrease in planned investment spending and a multiplied decrease in national income.
d. decrease in government purchases and a multiplied decrease in national income.
e. increase in government purchases and a multiplied increase in national income.

Use the graph below to answer questions 22 and 23.

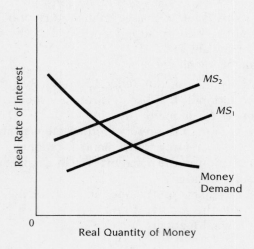

_____ 22. Consider the money market described by the graph above. Assume that MS_1 was the original money supply curve and MS_2

is the current money supply curve. Note that all variables are measured in real terms. Which of the following conclusions is accurate?

a. The real money supply has increased.

b. The equilibrium real rate of interest has increased.

c. People now find they have more money than they want at the original equilibrium interest rate.

d. As people attempt to convert money to less liquid forms of wealth, they will bid up the interest rate to the new equilibrium level.

e. all of the above

_____ 23. Consider the real money market described by the graph, assuming that the real money supply curve has shifted from MS_1 to MS_2. Which of the following statements best describes the effect of this change in the money supply on planned investment spending and equilibrium national income?

a. The increase in the real interest rate will tend to cause an increase in the amount of planned investment spending and a multiplied increase in equilibrium national income.

b. The increase in the real interest rate will tend to cause a decrease in the amount of planned investment spending and a multiplied decrease in equilibrium national income.

c. The increase in the real interest rate will tend to cause a decrease in the amount of planned investment spending, but the effect on equilibrium national income cannot be determined without knowing what happens to the nominal interest rate.

d. The decrease in the real interest rate will tend to cause a decrease in the amount of planned investment spending and a multiplied decrease in equilibrium national income.

e. The decrease in the real interest rate will tend to cause an increase in the amount of planned investment spending, but the effect on equilibrium national income cannot be determined without knowing what happens to the nominal interest rate.

_____ 24. According to modern monetarists,

a. monetary policy has a pronounced effect on the volume of output in the long run.

b. monetary policy has little effect on the general price level over the long run.

c. monetary policy is a major determinant of the supply of loanable funds in the long run.

d. real interest rates are, in the long run, determined in the market for loanable funds.

e. all of the above

Discussion Questions

1. Identify and discuss several factors that might cause a change in velocity of circulation.

2. What is the importance of the stability of velocity for the quantity theory? Show how the reliability of monetary policy is influenced by the stability of the velocity of circulation.

3. What is the significance for an expansionary monetary policy if people hoard money during a recession? What is the significance for a contractionary monetary policy if people increase their spending in anticipation of continued inflation?

4. Use demand-and-supply analysis to show how long-run interest rates are determined.

5. Discuss the differences between the determination of real interest rates in the long run and in the short run.

6. The interest rate is the "opportunity cost for holding money." Explain.

7. Explain the transmission mechanisms linking monetary changes to changes in equilibrium national income.

8. How do you think a change in interest rates affects household consumption spending? Do you think the effect of a change in interest rates on consumption spending is more or less significant than the effect on investment spending? If ou think the effect on consumption is less significant, what is the difference between the nature of consumption and investment spending that causes consumption to be relatively insensitive to changes in interest rates? If the effect of a change in interest rates on consumption were significant, what would be the consequences for equilibrium national income?

9. The use of monetary policy is complicated by feedback effects on money demand. Discuss and demonstrate this complication graphically.

10. Over time, an increase in the nominal money supply may, but does not necessarily, result in an increase in the real money supply. What does it depend on?

Answers

Problems and Applications

1. a. 7%   b. 23%
2. a. 14%   b. 6%
3. a. rising by 7%   b. falling by 3%
4. a. 5
   b. prices double; average price rises to $6 per unit

    c. prices triple; average price rises to $9 per unit

    d. prices are halved; average price falls to $1.50 per unit

5. At equilibrium, Q is constant at the full-employment level; any change in the money supply causes a proportional change in P, the general price level.

6. a. $1,000; $1,000   b. $500; $500

   c. $2,000; $2,000   d. inverse

7. 10%

8. $50

9. a. i_2; I_2; Y_2; Y_2

   b. money supply decreases; increases to i_3; decreases to I_1; decreases to Y_1

   c. money supply increases; decreases to i_1; increases to I_3; increases to Y_3

   d. the Keynesian transmission mechanism; changes in national income and product would be moderated.

10. a. expansionary gap; decrease the real money supply to MS_1.

    b. contractionary gap; increase the real money supply to MS_3.

True-False

1. T.

2. F. The real cost of borrowing money is measured by the real interest rate.

3. F. The difference between real and nominal interest rates can be measured by the rate of change in the general price level.

4. F. The quantity theory of money is based on the equation of exchange.

5. F. The velocity of circulation of money is the average number of times per year that a dollar is used.

6. T.

7. F. A quantity theorist is likely to contend that, in the long run, the velocity of circulation of money is fairly stable and predictable.

8. T.

9. T.

10. T.

11. F. A person who expects an increase in the value of nonmoney assets is likely to want to hold less money for speculative reasons.

12. F. The present value of a bond is the expected annual income flow divided by the rate of interest.

13. F. The speculative motive for holding money suggests that the demand curve for money will be negatively sloped.

14. T.
15. F. The precautionary demand for money exists because of un-expected events that alter a person's income and/or expenditure patterns.
16. F. A change in income or wealth is likely to change the location of the demand curve for money.
17. T.
18. F. Assuming that there is no change in the general price level, an increase in the supply of money will cause a decline in the real interest rate.
19. T.
20. F. The effects of a change in the real money supply via the Keynesian transmission mechanism are moderated if there are feedback effects to the demand for money.
21. F. When an expansionary monetary policy results in an increase in the general price level, the real money supply might not in-crease and consequently the real interest rate might not fall.
22. F. When people believe that an increase in the money supply is the cause of inflation, the real interest rate is likely to stay the same while the nominal interest rate rises.
23. T.

Multiple Choice

1. c	2. e	3. c	4. b	5. b
6. b	7. b	8. e	9. a	10. d
11. d	12. a	13. c	14. c	15. c
16. e	17. b	18. c	19. d	20. a
21. b	22. b	23. b	24. d	

15 *Aggregate Demand and Aggregate Supply*

Summary

Aggregate demand in an economy is the relationship between the general price level and the amount of real national income and product demanded. Like other demand curves, the aggregate demand curve is negatively sloped. The inverse relationship between the price level and real national income and product can be explained with the interest rate theory or with the real balances theory. The interest rate theory recognizes that an increase in the general price level results in a decrease in the real money supply. This causes an increase in real interest rates and a decrease in planned investment spending. The decrease in planned investment spending causes a decline in total planned expenditure and therefore a decrease in real national income. The real balances theory argues that an increase in the price level causes reductions in the real wealth of people who hold money or who have assets whose values are given in fixed nominal amounts. The decrease in wealth will cause a decline in consumption and therefore a decline in total planned expenditure. This decrease in total planned expenditure leads to a reduction in real national income and product.

Aggregate supply is a relationship between the price level and the real national income and output of an economy. Modern macroeconomic theory recognizes the influences of a wage-cost lag and money illusion on productive behavior. Aggregate supply is short run if wage and cost changes lag behind changes in the general price level and if behavior is influenced by money illusion. Aggregate supply is long run if sufficient time has elapsed for wages and costs to adjust to price level changes and for money illusion to have been eliminated.

The short-run aggregate supply curve can be divided into three segments: a nearly horizontal "depression" segment at relatively low price levels; a positively sloped "normal times" segment; and a vertical "absolute full-employment" segment. In the depression segment, an increase in aggregate demand calls forth an increase in real output with little or no increase in the price level. In the normal times segment, a rise in aggregate demand calls forth an increase in the price level as well as in real output. In the absolute full-employment segment, a rise in aggregate demand causes an increase in the price level but no additional real output.

An economy will be in short-run macroeconomic equilibrium at the intersection of the aggregate demand and short-run aggregate supply curves. At price levels below the equilibrium level, more real goods and services will be demanded than are available and the price level will be bid up. At price levels above the equilibrium level, more real goods and services will be available than people will buy, so the price level will fall.

The recession–deflation model illustrates the problem of unemployment and declining prices. A decrease in aggregate demand results in a new short-run equilibrium position associated with decreased output and a lower price level. As wage-cost lags are reduced and money illusion wears off, short-run aggregate supply increases and a new equilibrium is established at a lower price level.

Another model, the expansion–inflation model, illustrates low unemployment and a rising price level. In this model an increase in aggregate demand causes an increase in real output and the price level. As wage-cost lags are reduced and money illusion evaporates, short-run aggregate supply decreases and a new equilibrium is established at a higher price level.

Long-run aggregate supply is a relationship between the price level and real national product, assuming that there is no change in the physical production capabilities of the economy and that sufficient time has elapsed for people to adapt completely to the existing price level. Economists do not agree as to the slope of the long-run aggregate-supply curve: some assume that it is vertical; others use a real balances approach to arrive at a positively sloped curve. The long-run aggregate-supply curve shifts to the right with increases in production capabilities and to the left with decreases in production capabilities. Cultural and institutional factors may also influence the location of the long-run aggregate-supply curve.

The rate of unemployment that prevails in long-run equilibrium is called the natural rate of unemployment. To say that it is the natural rate of unemployment does not mean there is no unemployment, nor does it mean that the unemployment rate is desirable, nor that the rate is as low as possible. The natural rate of unemployment, which includes frictional, seasonal, and structural unemployment but not cyclical unemployment, is also referred to as effective full employment.

Major Objectives   After you have finished this chapter, you will be able to do the following:

1. Define aggregate demand and distinguish it from total planned expenditure.
2. Explain the slope of the aggregate demand curve using the interest rate theory and the real cash balances theory.
3. Distinguish between a movement along the aggregate demand curve and a shift in the curve, identify the causes of each, and describe each.
4. Define aggregate supply and distinguish it from total production.
5. Distinguish between demand-side and supply-side economics.
6. Explain the wage-cost lag theory.
7. Define money illusion and explain the money-illusion theory.
8. Distinguish between the short-run aggregate supply curve and the long-run aggregate supply curve.
9. Identify and explain the three segments of the short-run aggregate supply curve and, for each segment, indicate the effects of a change in aggregate demand on the general price level and on output.
10. Distinguish between a movement along the aggregate supply curve and a shift in the curve, identify the causes of each, and describe each.
11. Discuss the relationship between the aggregate supply curve and a wage-cost lag and explain how the aggregate supply curve shifts in accordance with changes in the wage-cost lag.
12. Discuss the relationship between the aggregate supply curve and money illusion, and explain how the aggregate supply curve shifts in accordance with changes in the extent of money illusion.
13. Identify the short-run macroeconomic equilibrium point and explain the process whereby the economy reaches this point.
14. Explain the recession–deflation model by showing how a decrease in aggregate demand leads to a new short-run equilibrium, then explain the adjustment process that yields long-run equilibrium.
15. Identify and explain the Keynesian view of the demand shock that occurred in the Great Depression.
16. Identify and characterize the monetarist view of the demand shock that occurred in the Great Depression.
17. Define and describe the process of hyperdeflation.
18. Identify and explain the "deflationist" solution to recession.
19. Define and describe reflation.

20. Identify and explain the "reflationist" solution to recession.
21. Explain the expansion–inflation model by showing how an increase in aggregate demand leads to a new short-run equilibrium, then explain the adjustment process that yields long-run equilibrium.
22. Define and describe hyperinflation.
23. Define and describe stagflation.
24. Identify and explain the conditions associated with long-run equilibrium.
25. Define and develop the long-run aggregate supply curve.
26. Distinguish between the conditions giving rise to a vertical long-run aggregate-supply curve and those leading to a positively sloped long-run aggregate-supply curve.
27. Identify factors that might result in a shift in the long-run aggregate-supply curve.
28. Define and explain the natural rate of unemployment, and identify the types of unemployment associated with this rate.
29. Distinguish between absolute full employment and effective full employment.
30. Explain the relationship between the natural rate of unemployment and effective full employment.
31. Identify factors that might lead to a change in the natural rate of unemployment.
32. Identify tools that might be used to reduce the natural rate of unemployment.
33. Explain the concept of a supply shock.
34. Distinguish between an expansionary supply shock and a contractionary supply shock and recognize examples of each.

Review Terms

unemployment
inflation
Keynesian model
monetarist model
recession
deflation
national income and product (Y)
general price level (P)
index number
real vs. nominal values
total planned expenditure
  (C + I + G + X – Im)
movement along a curve vs.
  shift in the curve

ceteris paribus
positive vs. negative slope
direct vs. inverse relationship
dependent vs. independent
  variable
money supply curve
transmission mechanism
investment demand curve
planned investment spending (I)
demand-side
wealth
planned consumption
  expenditure (C)
fiscal policy

monetary policy
expansionary policy
contractionary policy
resources
cyclical unemployment
macroeconomic unemployment
bottlenecks in production
frictional unemployment
structural unemployment
macroeconomic equilibrium
deflation

disequilibrium
inventories
deficit spending
New Deal
planned vs. actual levels of
  variables
technology
labor force
microeconomy
individual labor-supply curve

Important Terms and Concepts

aggregate demand (AD)
aggregate supply (AS)
interest rate theory
  ("Keynes effect")
real balances theory
  ("Pigou effect")
short-run aggregate supply
  (SRAS)
supply-side economics
wage-cost lag theory
money illusion
money illusion theory
depression segment of the
  SRAS curve
normal times segment of the
  SRAS curve
absolute full employment
absolute full employment
  segment of the SRAS curve
excess capacity
full capacity

"reopener" provision
cost of living adjustment (COLA)
short-run macroeconomic
  equilibrium
recession–deflation process
expansion–inflation process
demand-side shock
hyperdeflation
deflation
deflationist solution to recession
reflation
reflationist solution to recession
hyperinflation
stagflation
long-run aggregate supply
  (LRAS)
long-run equilibrium
the natural rate of
  unemployment
effective full employment
supply shock

Completion

general price level

negatively

the price level

real national income
and product

Aggregate demand is a relationship between the _____

_____ and the amount of real national

product demanded. The curve is _____ (positively/

negatively) sloped, with _____ plotted on

the vertical axis and _____

plotted on the horizontal axis. Two theories explain the negative

interest rate	slope: the _____ theory and the
real cash balances	_____ theory.
interest rate	The _____ theory is based on the fact that
decreases	an increase in the price level _____ (increases/decreases)
	the real quantity of money in the economy. A reduction in the real
increase	money supply leads to a(n) _____ (increase/decrease) in
fall	real interest rates and therefore a _____ (rise/fall) in the
	amount of planned investment spending. This change in planned in-
decrease	vestment spending causes an equivalent _____ (increase/
lower	decrease) in total planned expenditure, leading to a _____
	(higher/lower) level of equilibrium national income. The original in-
decrease	crease in the price level, then, has resulted in a(n) _____
	(increase/decrease) in the level of real national income and product.
	The extent of the change in the level of real national income and
	product will depend, in part, on the steepness of the demand curves
money, planned investment spending	for _____ and for _____ .
	It will also depend on whether the change in the price level causes a
money demand	shift in the _____ curve. Nonetheless, we
negatively	still expect to get a _____ (positively/negatively)
	sloped aggregate demand curve.
real balances theory	The _____ recognizes that an in-
decrease	crease in the price level will _____ (increase/decrease)
real wealth	the _____ of people who hold money and assets
	whose values are given in fixed nominal amounts. A reduction in
decrease	wealth causes a(n) _____ (increase/decrease) in con-
	sumption and therefore in total planned expenditure. Hence, the
fall	equilibrium level of national income will _____ (rise/fall).
	The net strength of the real balances effect is likely to be quite
small	_____ (large/small); therefore, the aggregate demand
steep	curve is likely to be fairly _____ (steep/flat) but with a
negative	_____ (positive/negative) slope nonetheless.
supply	Aggregate _____ is a relationship between the price
	level and the real national product that will be made available. In
	dealing with aggregate supply, economists distinguish between the

short run, long run	_____ and the _____ . Behavior in the
short run	_____ may be influenced by money illusion; in the
long run	_____ , all money illusion has worn off and there is no
nominal, real	confusion between _____ and _____ values.

Behavior in the short run may also be influenced by the effects of

wages, costs	lags in _____ and _____ . In the long run,
price level	people will have completely adjusted to the existing _____ .
recession–deflation	The _____ model describes how an

economy can experience a period of high unemployment and defla-

decline	tion after a _____ (rise/decline) in aggregate demand.

The analysis begins with the economy in equilibrium in the

normal times	_____ segment of the short-run aggregate

supply curve. It is assumed that this equilibrium has lasted long

well adjusted to it	enough so that people have become _____ .
decline	Then there is a _____ (rise/decline) in aggregate demand,

which results in a new short-run equilibrium associated with a

lower	_____ (higher/lower) level of real national income and a
lower	_____ (higher/lower) price level.

When sufficient time has elapsed for the effects of

wage-cost lags, money illusion	_____ and _____

to disappear, the short-run aggregate supply curve will shift to the

right, increase	_____ (right/left), indicating a(n) _____

(increase/decrease) in supply. A new equilibrium will be reached at a

higher	_____ (higher/lower) level of real national income and
lower	a _____ (higher/lower) price level. Whether the econ-

omy will return to the original equilibrium level of real output is
debatable. At any rate, this new equilibrium represents a point on

long-run aggregate supply	the _____ curve,

since it is associated with behavior after people have adjusted to the
existing price level.

The expansion–inflation model begins after the economy has been

adjusted to it	in equilibrium long enough for people to have _____ .
low	It describes how an economy may experience a period of _____
rising	(high/low) unemployment and _____ (rising/falling) price
increase	levels as a result of a(n) _____ (increase/decrease) in

increase

aggregate demand. The _____ (increase/decrease) in aggregate demand results in a new short-run equilibrium position

higher

associated with a _____ (higher/lower) level of real national

higher

income and product and a _____ (higher/lower) price level.
When sufficient time has elapsed for the effects of

wage-cost lags, money illusion

_____ and _____

short-run aggregate supply

to disappear, the _____ curve

left, fall

shifts to the _____ (right/left), indicating a _____
(rise/fall) in supply. This occurs as people realize that real wages have

increased

not _____ (increased/decreased) as much as they

short-run aggregate supply

had thought. Again, it is debatable whether the _____
curve shifts enough to realize an equilibrium at the original level of
real national income and product. Nonetheless, the new equilibrium

long-run aggregate supply

represents a point on the _____
curve, since it is the level of output that will be made available at the
particular price level after all wage-cost lags and money illusion have
evaporated.

Problems and Applications

Use the following graph to answer problems 1 and 2.

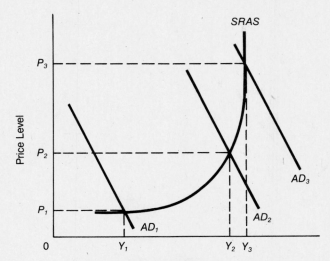

1. Use the graph above to identify the three segments of the short-run aggregate supply curve.
   a. What economic condition is described by the nearly horizontal segment?
   b. What economic condition is described by the positively sloped segment?
   c. What economic condition is described by the vertical segment?
2. Use the graph to answer the following questions:
   a. What are the equilibrium values of the general price level and real national income if aggregate demand is AD_1? What happens to these values if aggregate demand increases but stays within the nearly horizontal segment?
   b. What will happen to the general price level if it is currently P_1 and aggregate demand is AD_2? Why? What will happen to the general price level if it is currently P_3 and aggregate demand is AD_2? Why? What are the equilibrium values of the general price level and real national income if aggregate demand is AD_2? What happens to the equilibrium values of the price level and real national income if aggregate demand is originally at AD_2 and then increases?
   c. What are the equilibrium values of the general price level and real national income if aggregate demand is AD_3? What happens to these values if aggregate demand increases?

Use the graphs below to answer problem 3.

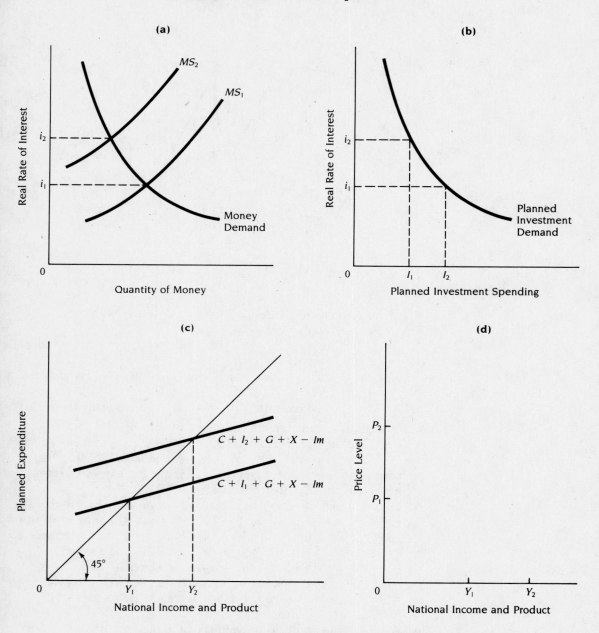

(a)

(b)

(c)

(d)

3. Consider the economy described by the graphs above. Assume that a general price level of P_1 (in panel d) is associated with the real money supply curve MS_1 (in panel a), that a general price

level of P_2 (in panel d) is associated with the real money supply curve MS_2 (in panel a), and that P_2 exceeds P_1 (as indicated in panel d).

a. What happens to the real money supply when there is a rise in the general price level from P_1 to P_2 with no change in the nominal money supply? Is this consistent with the real money supply curves that are drawn in panel a?

b. What is the equilibrium value of the real interest rate when the general price level is P_1? What is the level of planned investment spending at this interest rate? What is the corresponding value of national income and product?

c. What is the equilibrium value of the real interest rate when the general price level is P_2? What is the level of planned investment spending at this interest rate? What is the corresponding value of national income and product?

d. Panel d is designed so that you can draw the aggregate demand curve for the economy described. Do so. (First, trace back through problems 3b and 3c, recording your answers in panel d.)

True-False   Indicate whether each of the following statements is basically true or false. If the statement is false, rewrite it so that it is true.

_____ 1. Aggregate demand is a relationship between the general price level and the amount of real national product demanded.

_____ 2. Both the interest rate theory and the real balances theory suggest that the aggregate-demand curve will be negatively sloped but very flat.

_____ 3. The negative slope of the aggregate-demand curve can be explained by the interest rate theory, which recognizes that a rise in the price level causes a decrease in the real money supply and therefore a decrease in the equilibrium real interest rate.

_____ 4. The real balances theory explains the negative slope of the aggregate-demand curve by reasoning that a rise in the price level results in an increase in real wealth for people who hold money or assets whose values are given in fixed nominal amounts.

_____ 5. Expansionary fiscal and monetary policies tend to shift the aggregate-demand curve to the right, representing an increase in aggregate demand.

_____ 6. A short-run aggregate-supply curve is influenced by the effects of wage-cost lags.

_____ 7. A short-run aggregate-supply curve reflects behavior influenced by money illusion.

_____ 8. The short-run aggregate-supply curve is positively sloped, though nearly vertical, throughout its entire length.

_____ 9. In the normal times segment of the short-run aggregate-supply curve, an increase in aggregate demand will increase both real national income and the general price level.

_____ 10. A change in labor force participation causes a movement along the short-run aggregate-supply curve.

_____ 11. Short-run macroeconomic equilibrium occurs at the intersection of the aggregate-demand and short-run aggregate-supply curves.

_____ 12. Over time, as money illusion wears off, the short-run aggregate-supply curve will shift.

_____ 13. As people become more experienced with respect to changes in the general price level, the short-run aggregate-supply curve becomes flatter.

_____ 14. In the recession–deflation model, the initial shock to the system is on the demand side of the economy; in the expansion–inflation model it is on the supply side.

_____ 15. According to the deflationist solution to the problem of depression, wage reductions will become acceptable to workers as money illusion wears off.

_____ 16. The reflation solution to depression is to increase aggregate demand.

_____ 17. A technological improvement is an example of a supply-side shock that would tend to shift the short-run aggregate-supply curve to the right.

_____ 18. The long-run aggregate-supply curve reflects the relationship between the general price level and the real national product after all wage-cost lags and money illusion have disappeared but before there is a change in physical production capabilities.

_____ 19. The long-run aggregate-supply curve is negatively sloped.

_____ 20. The natural rate of unemployment is the unemployment rate when the economy is in long-run equilibrium.

_____ 21. The natural rate of unemployment is the rate associated with absolute full employment.

_____ 22. At effective full employment there is no macroeconomic unemployment.

Multiple Choice   Choose the *one best* answer in each of the following cases:

_____   1. Aggregate demand is the
    a. total-planned-expenditure curve.
    b. relationship between the price level and the amount of real national product demanded.
    c. relationship between total planned expenditure and real national income and product.
    d. total-planned-expenditure curve in the short run and real national income in the long run.
    e. none of the above

_____   2. The interest rate theory
    a. is sometimes called the Pigou effect.
    b. can be used to explain the negative slope of the total-planned-expenditure curve.
    c. is based on the fact that a rise in the price level causes a decrease in the real money supply.
    d. relies on the fact that a rise in real interest rates tends to increase the volume of planned investment.
    e. reasons that a rise in the price level will reduce the real wealth of people who hold money and assets whose values are given in fixed nominal amounts.

_____   3. The real balances theory
    a. shows how a rise in the price level will cause a decrease in the real national product demanded.
    b. suggests that the aggregate-demand curve will be negatively sloped and relatively flat.
    c. relies on the fact that reductions in real wealth tend to cause the total-planned-expenditure curve to shift upward.
    d. all of the above
    e. none of the above

_____   4. Short-run aggregate supply
    a. reflects behavior that is influenced by money illusion.
    b. assumes there is no confusion between nominal and real values.
    c. is represented by the forty-five degree line of the Keynesian cross diagram.
    d. is a relationship between real national product and real national income.
    e. is distinguished from long-run aggregate supply in Keynesian economics but is not distinguished from long-run aggregate supply in modern macroeconomic theory.

_____   5. The short-run aggregate-supply curve is
   a. nearly vertical at relatively low prices, positively sloped during normal times, and nearly horizontal at relatively high prices.
   b. vertical at absolute full employment, reflecting the fact that a rise in aggregate demand causes an increase in the price level and no change in output.
   c. negatively sloped throughout, reflecting the fact that a rise in aggregate demand causes a decrease in the price level and an increase in output.
   d. negatively sloped at relatively low prices, reflecting the fact that a rise in aggregate demand causes an increase in the price level and a decrease in national output.
   e. positively sloped and very steep during depression periods, reflecting the fact that a rise in aggregate demand causes an increase in the price level and in national output.

_____   6. Which of the following is *least* likely to cause a shift in the short-run aggregate-supply curve?
   a. a natural disaster
   b. a technological discovery
   c. a change in the price level
   d. the disappearance of money illusion
   e. a change in labor force participation

_____   7. Which of the following statements is true with regard to an economy in the short run?
   a. Production of the equilibrium real national product requires full employment.
   b. Short-run macroeconomic equilibrium occurs at the intersection of aggregate demand and short-run aggregate supply.
   c. At price levels below the equilibrium price level, more will be offered for sale than can be sold at that price level.
   d. At price levels above the equilibrium price level, people will want to buy more real goods and services than are available.
   e. all of the above

_____   8. In the first phase of the recession–deflation model, the new short-run equilibrium is associated with
   a. a rise in unemployment and a decline in wage rates.
   b. a rise in unemployment and a rise in wage rates.
   c. a decrease in unemployment and a rise in wage rates.
   d. a decrease in unemployment and a decrease in wage rates.
   e. a decrease in unemployment and no change in wage rates.

_____ 9. In phase one of the recession–deflation model, the economy moves to a new short-run equilibrium position. This new short-run equilibrium will be associated with greater unemployment when the
    a. short-run aggregate-supply curve is relatively flat.
    b. short-run aggregate-supply curve is relatively steep.
    c. shift in the aggregate-supply curve is relatively small.
    d. shift in the aggregate-supply curve is relatively large.
    e. shift in the aggregate-demand curve is relatively small.

_____ 10. According to the recession–deflation model,
    a. an increase in aggregate demand results in disequilibrium unemployment.
    b. short-run aggregate supply eventually decreases as money illusion wears off.
    c. as long as there is money illusion, the economy operates at absolute full employment.
    d. the pessimism caused by the initial shift in aggregate demand may cause further shifts in aggregate demand, resulting in hyperdeflation.
    e. none of the above

_____ 11. The recession–deflation model may be used to analyze the Great Depression of the 1930s. Which of the following statements is consistent with the model and its application to this 1930s experience?
    a. Keynesians attribute the change in aggregate demand to a fall in planned investment spending.
    b. Keynesians attribute the change in aggregate supply to poor business prospects after the stock market crash.
    c. Monetarists attribute the change in aggregate demand to a rise in the money supply.
    d. Monetarists attribute the change in aggregate supply to bank failures and the hoarding of cash.
    e. Both Keynesians and monetarists attribute the change in aggregate demand to the elimination of money illusion.

_____ 12. In the first phase of the expansion–inflation model,
    a. the initiating event comes from the supply side.
    b. money illusion causes a decrease in aggregate demand.
    c. fiscal and monetary policies may cause the initial increase in aggregate demand.
    d. the new short-run equilibrium is associated with lower output and a higher price level.
    e. the initial increase in short-run aggregate supply results in a higher output and a lower price level.

_____ 13. In phase two of the expansion–inflation model,
   a. short-run aggregate supply increases as wage rates rise.
   b. people realize that wages have increased more than they thought.
   c. both a and b above
   d. short-run aggregate supply decreases as money illusion wears off.
   e. none of the above

_____ 14. If there is no change in aggregate demand, a contractionary supply-side shock will cause
   a. hyperdeflation.
   b. a rise in equilibrium real national income.
   c. a rise in the equilibrium price level.
   d. the short-run aggregate supply curve to shift to the right.
   e. both a and b above

_____ 15. A long-run aggregate-supply curve
   a. assumes that enough time has passed to eliminate money illusion.
   b. assumes that there is no change in physical production capabilities.
   c. is made up of points associated with short-run macroeconomic equilibrium.
   d. is a relationship between the general price level and real national product.
   e. all of the above

_____ 16. The long-run aggregate-supply curve will
   a. be vertical if the price level is constant.
   b. likely be horizontal at relatively high price levels.
   c. be positively sloped if higher price levels result in money illusion.
   d. shift to the left as money illusion is eliminated.
   e. shift if there is a change in the production capabilities of the economy.

_____ 17. An increase in long-run aggregate supply
   a. is represented by a rightward shift in the curve.
   b. is indicated by a movement upward along the curve.
   c. may be caused by an increase in the general price level.
   d. may be caused by a decrease in the general price level.
   e. both b and c above

_____ 18. The natural rate of unemployment is
   a. associated with effective full employment.
   b. the rate that prevails in long-run equilibrium.
   c. both a and b above
   d. the minimum unemployment rate for an economy.
   e. the unemployment rate associated with money illusion.

Discussion Questions

1. Is the aggregate demand curve likely to be relatively steep or flat? Explain.

2. Identify factors that affect the duration of money illusion.

3. As people become more experienced with respect to changes in the price level due to changes in aggregate demand, the short-run aggregate supply curve will become steeper. Explain.

4. What are the consequences for the recession–deflation model of a growing awareness and experience with changes in price level? What are the consequences for the expansion–inflation model?

5. Economists are not in agreement about the slope of the long-run aggregate supply curve. It may be either vertical or positively sloped. Explain the two possibilities.

6. Is it possible to reduce the unemployment rate below the natural rate of unemployment? If so, how? In what sense is the unemployment rate "natural"?

7. Distinguish between demand-side and supply-side shocks. Discuss the implications of each for unemployment and the general price level.

8. Explain why monetary policy is a demand-side approach to fighting unemployment and inflation.

Answers

Problems and Applications

1. a. depression   b. normal times
   c. absolute full employment

2. a. P_1, Y_1; the price level stays the same or rises slightly; real national income and product increase.
   b. The price level will rise because, at P_1, the aggregate quantity demanded exceeds the aggregate quantity supplied. The price level will fall to P_2 because, at P_3, the aggregate quantity supplied exceeds the aggregate quantity demanded. P_2, Y_2; the price level and real national income both increase.
   c. P_3, Y_3; the price level increases, real national income and product remain the same.

3. a. real money supply decreases; yes
   b. i_1; I_2; Y_2
   c. i_2; I_1; Y_1
   d.

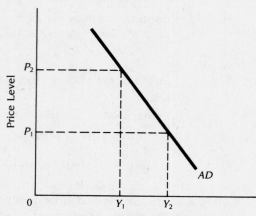

True-False

1. T.
2. F. Both the interest rate theory and the real balances theory suggest that the aggregate demand curve will be negatively sloped but very steep.
3. F. The negative slope of the aggregate demand curve can be explained by the interest rate theory, which recognizes that a rise in the price level causes a decrease in the real money supply and therefore a rise in the equilibrium real interest rate.
4. F. The real balances theory explains the negative slope of the aggregate demand curve by reasoning that a rise in the price level results in a decrease in real wealth for people who hold money or assets whose values are given in fixed nominal amounts.
5. T.
6. T.
7. T.
8. F. The short-run aggregate supply curve is made up of three basic segments: a nearly horizontal "depression" segment, a positively sloped "normal times" segment, and a vertical "absolute full employment" segment.
9. T.
10. F. A change in labor force participation causes a shift in the short-run aggregate-supply curve.

11. T.
12. T.
13. F. As people become more experienced with respect to changes in the general price level, the short-run aggregate supply curve becomes steeper.
14. F. In both the recession–deflation and the expansion–inflation models, the initial shock to the system is on the demand side of the economy.
15. T.
16. T.
17. T.
18. T.
19. F. Some economists argue that the long-run aggregate-supply curve is vertical, and others believe that it is positively sloped.
20. T.
21. F. The natural rate of unemployment is the rate associated with effective full employment.
22. T.

Multiple Choice

1. b	2. c	3. a	4. a	5. b
6. c	7. b	8. a	9. a	10. d
11. a	12. c	13. d	14. c	15. e
16. e	17. a	18. c		

16 *Macroeconomic Policy: Demand Side*

Summary

Keynesian economics grew out of the Great Depression of the 1930s. It focuses attention on the demand side of the economy, placing primary importance on total planned expenditure. High and lasting unemployment, such as that which characterized the Great Depression, would result from insufficient aggregate demand. The unemployment could be eliminated by increasing aggregate demand. Keynesian economics relies on government budgetary action, or fiscal policy, to stimulate the economy, suggesting that monetary policy is likely to be ineffective. Though Keynesian economics was influential during the 1930s, much of the actual policy did not fully apply Keynesian principles. And in fact the economy did not completely recover until World War II, when wartime expenditures caused the kind of increase in aggregate demand that Keynesian economics had called for.

Prior to the Great Depression and Keynesian economics, economic theory had not generally recommended direct government action in times of unemployment. After World War II, however, two major pieces of legislation, the Employment Act of 1946 and the Full Employment and Balanced Growth Act of 1978, made the federal government responsible for promoting full employment and price stability.

Monetarism, another important school of thought, focuses attention on the role of changes in the money supply in promoting our economic objectives. Like Keynesians, monetarists are demand-side oriented. In general, however, monetarists argue that fiscal policy is neither necessary nor effective in promoting effective full employment. Monetarists generally maintain that changes in the money supply have greater impact on national income and product than do changes in government spending and taxation policy.

There are several major issues in the Keynesian–monetarist debate. One of these deals with the influence of real interest rates on planned investment. Keynesians argue that planned investment is not very sensitive to changes in real interest rates; rather, they argue, it is determined primarily by expected consumer spending on final goods. Hence, a Keynesian would view the planned investment demand curve as relatively steep. A monetarist, on the other hand, would expect the planned investment demand curve to be relatively flat, reflecting the importance of changes in real interest rates on the amount of planned investment spending. Monetarists are inclined to think of investment as a long-run decision in which the time-related variable, the real interest rate, tends to be important.

Monetarists also argue that changes in the money supply need not operate through planned investment spending to have an important effect on national income and output. Changes in the money supply are believed to affect consumer spending directly.

Another major issue in the Keynesian–monetarist debate addresses the problem of crowding out. According to the monetarists, a change in national income (due to the implementation of fiscal policy) is likely to be moderated by feedback effects to the demand for money. A change in the demand for money tends to cause a change in the real interest rate, with a subsequent change in the amount of planned investment spending. Of course, the extent to which private investment spending will be crowded out by government action depends on the sensitivity of planned investment to changes in the real interest rate.

The extent of crowding out also depends on the slope of the demand curve for money. When this demand curve is fairly steep, as monetarists maintain, a change in money demand will result in a relatively large change in the interest rate. Keynesians argue that the money demand curve is relatively flat and therefore when it changes it has relatively little impact on the interest rate.

Monetarists also argue that a decision on the part of monetary authorities with regard to accommodation can enhance or negate any particular fiscal policy measure. The importance of accommodation depends on the slopes of the demand curves for planned investment and money.

Finally, Keynesians and monetarists disagree in their approaches to policy making. Keynesians tend to favor fine tuning or discretionary use of fiscal powers. Monetarists, on the other hand, tend to prefer limited government involvement beyond the application of fixed rules. Two such rules are the full-employment balanced-budget rule and the monetary growth rule. The full-employment balanced-budget rule would require a balanced budget when the economy is operating at effective full employment. The monetary growth rule would have changes in the money supply tied to the long-run growth trend of the economy.

Monetary and fiscal approaches, both demand side in orientation, seem to suggest that there is a tradeoff between unemployment and inflation. This notion of a tradeoff between the two was further evidenced by early Phillips curves, which specify the relationship between rates of unemployment and inflation. By the 1970s, however, the Phillips relationship began to appear as a series of loops, and the notion of a clear tradeoff has come under question. Today economists recognize that supply-side influences may be as important as those on the demand side. Though this suggests that it may be possible to reduce both unemployment and inflation, it does not identify the specific policies that would do so.

Major Objectives   After you have finished this chapter, you will be able to do the following:

1. Name Keynes's book published in 1936.
2. Verbally and graphically identify and explain the policy implications of Keynesian economics.
3. Describe the manner and extent to which Keynesian theory was applied in the 1930s.
4. Cite the causes of the inflation that followed World War II.
5. Describe the major provisions of the Employment Act of 1946, name and describe the two government agencies created by the act, and indicate the importance of the act.
6. Describe the major provisions of the Full Employment and Balanced Growth (Humphrey-Hawkins) Act of 1978.
7. Identify and explain the issues addressed by and the major positions on each side of the Keynesian–monetarist debate.
8. Identify the important contributions of Irving Fisher and Milton Friedman.
9. Verbally and graphically explain the concept of crowding out.
10. Describe the concept of a liquidity trap and explain its significance.
11. Define and explain the policy of accommodation or validation and indicate circumstances in which it has been or might be used.
12. Explain how accommodation can be used to strengthen or weaken fiscal policy.
13. Explain the concept of fine tuning.
14. Describe the full-employment balanced-budget rule, indicate how it could be used with accommodation to reach the target level of national income, and explain its appeal.

15. Describe the monetary growth rule and explain the theoretical basis for it.
16. Identify and explain areas of agreement between Keynes and the monetarists.
17. Describe the relationship demonstrated by the Phillips curve, indicate and explain the policy implications of the curve, and discuss its application and reliability from a historical standpoint.

Review Terms

theory
Keynesian economics
demand-side economics
macroeconomics
Say's Identity
neoclassical theory
cyclical unemployment
aggregate demand (AD)
total planned expenditure
  (C + I + G + X – Im)
consumption (C)
planned investment (I)
government purchases (G)
exports (X)
imports (Im)
net taxes (T_n)
marginal propensity to
  consume (*MPC*)
multiplier
contraction
expansion
fiscal policy
macroeconomic unemployment
depression
aggregate supply (AS)
short-run macroeconomic
  equilibrium
short-run aggregate supply (SRAS)
general price level (P)
real vs. nominal values
wealth vs. income
New Deal
effective full employment
pump priming
wage-cost lag
money illusion

budget deficit
absolute full employment
price controls
near money
Federal Reserve System
open market operations
price stability
economic growth
the accord of 1951
monetarism
monetary policy
equation of exchange
money supply (MS)
transmission mechanisms
real interest rate
equilibrium national income
  and product (Y*)
demand for money (MD)
planned investment demand
  curve
slope
long-run real interest rate
feedback to the demand for
  money
Board of Governors of the
  Fed
transactions demand for
  money
precautionary demand for
  money
speculative demand for money
market for loanable funds
crowding out
Organization of Petroleum Exporting Countries (OPEC)
supply-side shocks

transfer payments   business cycle
balanced budget   velocity of circulation
automatic stabilizers   stagflation

Important Terms and Concepts

National Industrial Recovery   Irving Fisher
  Act of 1933 (NIRA)   Milton Friedman
"codes of fair competition"   liquidity trap
Employment Act of 1946   accommodation or validation
Council of Economic Advisers   fine tuning
Joint Economic Committee   discretionary policy
Full Employment and Balanced   recognition lag
  Growth (Humphrey-Hawkins) decision-making lag
  Act of 1978   implementation lag
Keynesian–monetarist debate   full-employment balanced-
fiscalist   budget rule
neo-Keynesian   monetary growth rule
post-Keynesian   Phillips curve

Completion

demand-side

Keynesians and monetarists rely on _____ (demand-side/supply-side) approaches to dealing with economic issues. But

Keynesian

whereas a _____ (Keynesian/monetarist) would favor

monetarist

government involvement in economic matters, a _____ (Keynesian/monetarist) is more likely to prefer the laissez-faire approach of the neoclassical economists. Much of the debate between the two schools of thought centers around the question of whether

fiscal, monetary

_____ or _____ instruments are more effective in promoting our macroeconomic objectives. There are several specific points of disagreement between the two schools.

    The effectiveness of monetary policies depends in part on the steepness of the investment demand curve. Keynesians tend to see

steep

this curve as relatively _____ (steep/flat) and therefore con-

will not

clude that changes in the real interest rate _____ (will/will not) significantly influence the level of planned investment spending.

long-term

Monetarists emphasize _____ (short-term/long-term)

are

investment decisions and maintain that such decisions _____ (are/are not) sensitive to time-related variables such as interest rates. Hence, monetarists view the investment demand curve as relatively flat

_____ (steep/flat). They argue that changes in the real inter-

are

est rate _____ (are/are not) likely to influence the level of planned investment spending.

Even without the interest rate linkage, monetarists believe that changes in the money supply will affect aggregate expenditures by

consumer

affecting _____ spending. When the money supply is

consumption

increased, they argue, _____ spending will rise.

A change in equilibrium national income will tend to cause a

same

change in the demand for money in the _____ (same/opposite) direction. This phenomenon is referred to as the

feedback mechanism to the demand for money

_____ . A change in the demand for money calls forth a change in real interest rates.

sensitive

If planned investment spending is _____ (sensitive/insensitive) to changes in real interest rates, as monetarists believe, then the original change in equilibrium national income will be

crowding out

moderated by this _____ process. Monetarists argue that crowding out makes the use of fiscal policy

less

_____ (more/less) effective than Keynesians believe it to be.

Partly because they view planned investment spending as insensi-

interest rates, do not

tive to changes in _____ , Keynesians _____ (do/do not) perceive crowding out to be a problem. In addition,

flat

Keynesians view the demand curve for money as relatively _____ (steep/flat). If this is the case, then changes in the demand for money

small

result in relatively _____ (large/small) changes in the real interest rate. Monetarists, who tend to view the demand curve for

steep

money as relatively _____ (steep/flat), expect changes in this curve to have pronounced effects on the real interest rate. This

more

makes the problem of crowding out all the _____ (more/less) important.

accommodation

The monetary policy of _____ calls for shifts in the money supply curve so that shifts in the demand curve for money do not cause changes in the interest rate. If crowding out is likely, accommodation could be used to prevent it, making fiscal policy

more

_____ (more/less) effective. On the other hand, if crowding out is a problem and monetary authorities refuse to accommodate,

less

they make fiscal policy _____ (more/less) effective.

Keynesians and monetarists also disagree on whether policy makers should be allowed discretion in determining policy or should set certain rules and stick with them. Keynesians favor the use of

discretion

_____ (discretion/rules), which is also called

fine tuning

_____ . Monetarists, on the other hand, are more

rules

apt to support the use of _____ (discretion/rules).

Problems and Applications

1. Summarize the Keynesian-monetarist debate by answering each of the following questions, first as a Keynesian and then as a monetarist.

Topic of debate	Keynesian	Monetarist
a. Is the real interest rate an important determinant of investment spending?		
b. Is the planned investment demand curve relatively steep or relatively flat?		
c. Is crowding out likely to be a problem?		
d. Is the money demand curve relatively steep or relatively flat?		
e. Is accommodation or failure to accommodate likely to be important?		
f. Which is preferable, rules or discretion in policy making?		
g. Is your approach demand side or supply side?		

Use the following graph to answer problem 2.

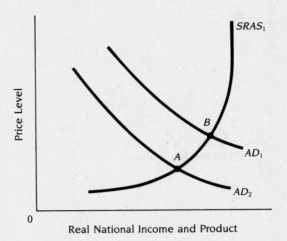

2. Consider the economy described by the graph above. Assume
   initially that the economy is in equilibrium at point A with
   aggregate demand and short-run aggregate supply described by
   curves AD_1 and $SRAS_1$, respectively. Now let aggregate demand
   shift to AD_2.
   a. Identify the new short-run equilibrium point. What happens
      to the equilibrium values of the price level, real national
      income and product, employment, and unemployment?
   b. How would a Keynesian respond to the shift in aggregate
      demand?
   c. If you were going to change the money supply to decrease
      the unemployment, would you increase or decrease the
      money supply? Which curve (aggregate demand or aggregate
      supply) would you expect this to affect?
   d. How would a monetarist who supports the monetary growth
      rule respond to the decrease in aggregate demand?

Use the graph below to answer problems 3 and 4.

3. Consider the money market described in the graph above. What would be the effect of an increase in the money supply on the following:
   a. the equilibrium real interest rate.
   b. the level of planned investment spending.
   c. the equilibrium national income level.

4. What problem is illustrated by the graph? Would a change in the money supply have a larger or smaller impact on equilibrium national income if you were operating in the steeper portion of the money demand curve? Why?

Use the graphs below to answer problems 5 and 6.

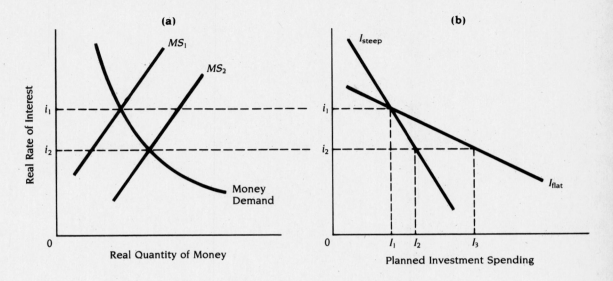

5. Notice that there are two planned investment demand curves in graph (b) above, one curve drawn by a Keynesian and one drawn by a monetarist.
   a. Identify the planned investment demand curve associated with a Keynesian viewpoint and the one associated with a monetarist viewpoint, and cite the reasons for the differences in their slopes.
   b. Assume an increase in the real money supply from MS_1 to MS_2. What is the consequence of this change for the real interest rate? What is the consequence for planned investment spending according to the Keynesian? What is the consequence for planned investment spending according to the monetarist?
   c. Would the Keynesian or the monetarist expect the change in the real money supply to have a greater impact on equilibrium national income? Why?
6. Consider the money market described in graph (a) above. Assume that monetary policy causes the nominal money supply curve to shift from MS_1 to MS_2. What must be true in order for this to represent a shift in the real money supply curve? If the price level increases as a result of the monetary policy, what happens to MS_2?

Use the graph below to answer problem 7.

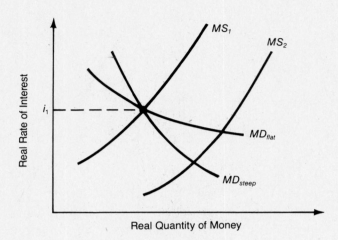

7. Notice that there are two demand-for-money curves in the graph above, one curve drawn by a Keynesian and one drawn by a monetarist.
    a. Identify the demand-for-money curve associated with a Keynesian viewpoint and the one associated with a monetarist viewpoint.
    b. If the money supply is MS1 and the economy is in equilibrium, what is the real interest rate?
    c. Assume that there is an increase in the money supply from MS1 to MS2. What is the consequence of this change for the real interest rate? On what does the specific answer depend? Which demand-for-money curve results in the largest change in the real interest rate?
    d. What difference does the extent of a change in the real interest rate make in terms of selecting and evaluating fiscal policy?

True-False   Indicate whether each of the following statements is basically true or false. If the statement is false, rewrite it so that it is true.

_____ 1. One of the important conclusions of Keynesian economics is that government budgetary action might be justified if the economy is to reach full employment.

_____ 2. A fiscalist is one who believes that fiscal instruments are more effective than monetary instruments in carrying out macroeconomic policy.

_____ 3. Monetarism grew out of Keynesian economics and the work of Irving Fisher.

_____ 4. Keynesian economics is demand-side oriented, whereas monetarism is supply-side oriented.

_____ 5. The equation of exchange was devised by Irving Fisher.

_____ 6. Milton Friedman is the best-known contributor to neo-Keynesian economics.

_____ 7. Both Keynesians and monetarists see macroeconomic unemployment as temporary.

_____ 8. One of the major concerns in the Keynesian–monetarist debate is the effectiveness of fiscal versus monetary instruments of macroeconomic policy.

_____ 9. Keynesians tend to view the investment demand curve as relatively flat in comparison with monetarists, who see it as relatively steep.

_____ 10. Many monetarists believe that long-run real interest rates are not affected by changes in the money supply.

_____ 11. Keynesians tend to believe that changes in the money supply affect consumer spending directly.

_____ 12. Monetarists argue that expansions started through fiscal policy may be less effective than Keynesians expect because of crowding out.

_____ 13. Monetary tools are effective in changing real interest rates only in the case of a liquidity trap.

_____ 14. Accommodation is a monetary policy that calls for changes in the money supply so that changes in the demand for money will not cause changes in the interest rate.

_____ 15. In questions of policy, monetarists favor fine tuning, whereas Keynesians would rely on discretionary fiscal policy.

_____ 16. The monetary growth rule calls for the Fed to increase the money supply by an amount equal to the growth rate of the economy.

_____ 17. The Phillips curve shows the relationship between the rate of inflation and the employment rate.

_____ 18. The experience of the 1970s seemed to verify the Phillips curve suggestion that there is a tradeoff between unemployment and inflation.

Multiple Choice   Choose the *one best* answer in each of the following cases:

_____   1. Neoclassical economic theory
   a. recommends the involvement of government when prices and wages fluctuate.
   b. maintains that a general glut can be eliminated through government intervention.
   c. suggests that cyclical unemployment can exist only if wages are too high and inflexible.
   d. supports the idea that widespread unemployment is the result of too little aggregate demand.
   e. both a and b above

_____   2. Which of the following is associated with Keynes and Keynesian economics?
   a. concern with the problem of crowding out
   b. a relatively flat investment demand curve
   c. *The General Theory of Employment, Interest, and Money*
   d. a belief that the economy would reach a full-employment equilibrium
   e. all of the above

_____   3. In the Keynesian model, total planned expenditure
   a. excludes the international sector.
   b. consists entirely of private sector spending.
   c. should never deliberately be altered by government policy.
   d. plays a major role in determining the income and output level of an economy.
   e. consists of household consumption spending, investment demand, government purchases, net taxes, and the money supply.

_____   4. With respect to the role of government in the economy, Keynes basically
   a. agreed with the neoclassical economists in supporting a limited role for government in the economy.
   b. agreed with the neoclassical economists by recognizing the need for government in assuring full employment.
   c. disagreed with the neoclassical economists when he recommended government budgetary action to influence economic performance.
   d. disagreed with the neoclassical economists, who believed in government budgetary action to assure maintenance of a full-employment equilibrium.
   e. none of the above

_____ 5. The Great Depression of the 1930s was the result of
   a. excess aggregate demand.
   b. a decrease in aggregate demand.
   c. an increase in aggregate demand.
   d. a decrease in long-run aggregate supply.
   e. a decrease in short-run aggregate supply.

_____ 6. Which of the following is consistent with a Keynesian approach to fighting the depression of the 1930s?
   a. a decrease in aggregate demand
   b. an increase in aggregate demand
   c. a decrease in aggregate supply
   d. an increase in aggregate supply
   e. both b and c above

_____ 7. Which of the following statements is true with respect to the application of Keynesian economics in the 1930s?
   a. New Deal policy was entirely consistent with Keynesian theory.
   b. Keynesian economics did not influence actual policy until after World War II.
   c. Keynesian economics was influential, but actual policy did not apply it fully.
   d. Priming the pump was the only complete application of Keynesian economics.
   e. Except for the policy of priming the pump, Keynesian economics formed the basis of policy in the 1930s.

_____ 8. The National Industrial Recovery Act
   a. was passed in 1943.
   b. encouraged price increases.
   c. was an example of Keynesian economics at its best.
   d. eliminated industries' "codes of fair competition."
   e. both c and d above

_____ 9. During World War II,
   a. deflation continued to be a problem.
   b. budget surpluses were used to finance the war.
   c. large budget deficits stimulated aggregate demand.
   d. the government failed to address the major problem of inflation.
   e. households spent their money on war bonds, thus creating surpluses of goods and services.

_____ 10. After World War II,
   a. price controls were imposed to prevent the anticipated inflation.
   b. the Fed expanded the money supply by buying securities on the open market.
   c. the decrease in military spending caused an overall decrease in aggregate demand.
   d. all of the above
   e. none of the above

_____ 11. The Employment Act of 1946
   a. is also called the Humphrey–Hawkins Act.
   b. called for the federal government to promote full employment.
   c. replaced the Joint Economic Committee with the Council of Economic Advisers.
   d. all of the above.
   e. recognized the importance of full employment but prevented federal government involvement.

_____ 12. The Full Employment and Balanced Growth Act of 1978
   a. set goals for unemployment and inflation rates.
   b. created the Joint Economic Committee and the Council of Economic Advisers.
   c. concerned itself with employment and economic growth but did not address the issue of price stability.
   d. limits federal government involvement in macroeconomic affairs by requiring an annually balanced budget.
   e. called for the government to promote economic growth but did not involve itself with international problems.

_____ 13. Which of the following statements is true with respect to monetarism?
   a. It recommends the use of discretionary fiscal policy.
   b. Its advocates are often referred to as post-Keynesians.
   c. Unlike Keynesian economics, it is a supply-side approach.
   d. It is closer to neoclassical economics than to Keynesian economics.
   e. It generally recognizes the likelihood of a macroeconomic equilibrium characterized by considerable unemployment.

_____ 14. Which of the following is _least_ likely to be associated with monetarism?
   a. the work of Irving Fisher
   b. the work of Milton Friedman
   c. the quantity theory of money
   d. a distinction between nominal and real values
   e. a reliance on fine tuning as opposed to a monetary growth rule

_____ 15. Keynesians argue that real interest rates
    a. are of primary importance in determining planned investment spending.
    b. have little influence on planned investment, because the investment demand curve is relatively flat.
    c. have little influence on planned investment, because the investment demand curve is relatively steep.
    d. have considerable influence on planned investment, because the investment demand curve is relatively flat.
    e. have considerable influence on planned investment, because the investment demand curve is relatively steep.

_____ 16. Monetarists argue that real interest rates
    a. are unimportant in decisions regarding planned investment.
    b. are the only link between changes in the money supply and economic activity.
    c. play an important role in decisions regarding long-term investments.
    d. have considerable influence on planned investment, because the investment demand curve is relatively steep.
    e. are more likely determined by the money supply than by the productivity of capital and the time preferences of lenders in the long run.

_____ 17. In contrast to Keynesians, monetarists believe that changes in the money supply
    a. have no effect on consumer spending.
    b. affect consumer spending directly.
    c. have an inverse effect on consumer spending.
    d. affect consumer spending indirectly by influencing nominal interest rates.
    e. none of the above

_____ 18. Which of the following statements is true with respect to crowding out?
    a. Keynesians are likely to see it as an important reason for relying on fiscal as opposed to monetary policy.
    b. Keynesians are not likely to see it as important, because they view the investment demand curve as relatively flat.
    c. Monetarists are likely to see it as an important limitation of fiscal policy.
    d. Monetarists are not likely to see it as important, because they view the investment demand curve as relatively flat.
    e. Neither Keynesians nor monetarists see it as an important issue.

_____ 19. Which of the following statements is true with regard to the demand curve for money?
   a. Both Keynesians and monetarists see it as vertical.
   b. Both Keynesians and monetarists see it as relatively flat.
   c. Both Keynesians and monetarists see it as relatively steep.
   d. Keynesians see it as relatively flat, and monetarists see it as relatively steep.
   e. Keynesians see it as relatively steep, and monetarists see it as relatively flat.

_____ 20. Which of the following statements is true with respect to accommodation?
   a. Keynesians see it as necessary to prevent crowding out.
   b. Keynesians see it as a reasonable alternative to validation.
   c. Monetarists see it as an important way of preventing crowding out.
   d. Monetarists see it as preferable to validation and as helpful in promoting crowding out.
   e. Monetarists do not see it as important, since they do not expect crowding out to be a problem.

_____ 21. The concept of fine tuning
   a. calls for discretion in the use of fiscal and monetary policy.
   b. is consistent with reliance on the full-employment balanced-budget rule.
   c. is based on the belief that the economy will reach a full-employment equilibrium.
   d. suggests that fiscal and monetary tools are ineffective in promoting our economic objectives.
   e. none of the above

_____ 22. The monetary growth rule
   a. is considered too rigid a policy by monetarists.
   b. is inconsistent with the quantity theory of money.
   c. is the same as the full-employment balanced-budget rule.
   d. would increase the money supply by an amount equal to the long-run growth rate of the economy.
   e. all of the above

_____ 23. The Phillips curve
   a. shows that stagflation is inevitable.
   b. originally suggested a tradeoff between inflation and the unemployment rate.
   c. shows the tradeoff between the use of monetary and fiscal policy.
   d. has never been viewed as important in the formation of economic policy.
   e. all but c above

**Discussion
Questions**

1. The authors make the observation that theory informs policy. Is the reverse also true? If so, can you cite examples?

2. Keynesian economics recommended an increase in aggregate demand to counter the decreased aggregate demand that resulted in the Great Depression. It is possible for a change in aggregate supply to offset the output and employment consequences of decreased aggregate demand. What problems would have been associated with such an approach in the 1930s?

3. Why would a Keynesian see a fairly steep investment demand curve and a monetarist see a fairly flat one? Of what significance is the difference?

4. If the slope of the planned investment demand curve is steep, as suggested by Keynes, a monetarist would still prefer monetary policy to fiscal policy. Explain why.

5. Keynesians tend to view the demand curve for money as relatively flat. But even if it were found to be relatively steep, a Keynesian is not likely to abandon his or her preference for fiscal policy. Why?

6. a. What is the significance of the liquidity trap?
   b. What does it mean if the demand curve for money is flat at some relatively low rate of interest?
   c. Explain the importance of the liquidity trap for determining the effectiveness of monetary policy.

7. Explain how accommodation can be used to prevent crowding out. Would a Keynesian think accommodation was necessary? Explain.

8. Explain how accommodating an expansionary fiscal policy can lead to inflation.

9. Discuss the importance of time in Keynesian economics and in monetarism. (For example, how does one's perspective on time influence one's view of the investment demand curve; how does time affect the multiplier; does a concern with time alter one's assessment of fine tuning?)

10. Explain the relationship between the monetary growth rule and the quantity theory of money.

11. Identify areas of agreement between Keynesians and monetarists. Explain why both are considered demand-side approaches.

Answers   *Problems and Applications*

1.   Keynesian   Monetarist

   a. no   yes
   b. steep   flat
   c. no   yes
   d. flat   steep
   e. no   yes
   f. discretion   rules
   g. demand side   demand side

2. a. *B*; price level decreases; real national income and product decrease; employment decreases; unemployment increases
   b. increase aggregate demand (i.e., shift the aggregate demand curve back to the right)
   c. increase money supply; aggregate demand
   d. A monetarist would not change the policy but would continue to increase the money supply in accordance with the real growth trend for the economy.

3. a. no change   b. no change   c. no change

4. a liquidity trap; a larger impact, because a change in the money supply would cause a change in the real interest rate

5. a. The steep investment demand curve is associated with a Keynesian viewpoint; the flat investment demand curve is associated with a monetarist viewpoint. Keynesians deal with a relatively short time horizon, view interest costs as a small part of the total costs of investment projects, and/ or consider a relatively small backlog of investment projects; monetarists consider a longer time horizon with a larger backlog of investment projects and view interest costs as a significant part of the costs of investment.
   b. real interest rate decreases from i_1 to i_2; planned investment spending increases to I_2; planned investment spending increases to I_3
   c. The monetarist would expect a greater impact, because the monetarist expects a greater change in planned investment spending.

6. There must be no change in the general price level; MS_2 would shift to the left, indicating a decrease in the real money supply.

7. a. flat; steep
   b. i1
   c. the real interest rate will decrease; whether the demand-for-money curve is relatively steep or flat; the steep one, that is, the curve assumed by the monetarists

     d. the greater the change in the real interest rate, the greater will be the effect on planned investment spending; the change in planned investment spending changes total planned expenditure and therefore affects aggregate demand

True-False

1. T.
2. T.
3. F. Monetarism grew out of neoclassical economics and the work of Irving Fisher.
4. F. Both Keynesian economics and monetarism are demand-side oriented.
5. T.
6. F. Milton Friedman is the best-known contributor to modern monetarist theory.
7. F. Monetarists see macroeconomic unemployment as temporary, whereas Keynesians believe that the economy can come to equilibrium with any level of employment (and therefore with unemployment).
8. T.
9. F. Keynesians tend to view the investment demand curve as relatively steep by comparison to how monetarists see it, as relatively flat.
10. T.
11. F. Monetarists tend to believe that changes in the money supply affect consumer spending directly.
12. T.
13. F. Monetary tools are not effective in changing real interest rates in the case of a liquidity trap.
14. T.
15. F. In questions of policy, Keynesians favor fine tuning or the use of discretionary fiscal policy, whereas monetarists prefer to rely on specific rules.
16. T.
17. F. The Phillips curve shows the relationship between the rate of inflation and the unemployment rate.
18. F. The experience of the 1960s seemed to suggest a tradeoff between unemployment and inflation, but in the 1970s the Phillips relationship no longer suggested such a tradeoff.

Multiple Choice

1. c	2. c	3. d	4. c	5. b
6. b	7. c	8. b	9. c	10. b
11. b	12. a	13. d	14. e	15. c
16. c	17. b	18. c	19. d	20. c
21. a	22. d	23. b		

17 *Macroeconomic Policy: Supply Side*

Summary

Supply-side economics concentrates on shifts in the aggregate-supply curve. The aggregate-supply curve can shift for a number of reasons: supply shocks, inflationary expectations, wage and price controls, supply-side economic policies.

Supply shocks change short-run and long-run aggregate supply. The shocks are caused by exogenous forces and may result in increases or decreases in aggregate supply. If there is no change in aggregate demand, a supply shock will result in new equilibrium price and real national income and product levels. Supply shocks also typically result in changes in relative prices. Policy responses include both demand-side and supply-side approaches.

The inflationary expectations model explains how the expectation of continued inflation can be self-fulfilling. Consider the expansion–inflation model with inflation created by an increase in aggregate demand. As wage-cost lags diminish and money illusion wears off, short-run aggregate supply decreases. If people expect future inflation, short-run aggregate supply will decrease even more. The additional change in aggregate supply puts upward pressure on the general price level. If the change in aggregate supply is accommodated by a change in aggregate demand, the economy can return to effective full employment, but the inflationary expectations will be confirmed. If the change in supply is not accommodated, the economy will experience unemployment in excess of the natural rate, but the inflationary expectations will not be completely confirmed.

The inflationary expectations model can be extended to consider additional aspects in the study of inflation. One of these is the theory of accelerating inflation, which suggests that unemployment can be kept below its natural rate if we are willing to allow ever-increasing rates of inflation. The theory of rational expectations, however, argues that people learn so much about inflation that they will respond immediately to expansionary attempts to reduce unemployment. As a consequence, expansionary policies only create additional inflation. The theory of decelerating inflation suggests that the rate of inflation can be slowed if policy makers would refuse to accommodate inflationary expectations. Unemployment will rise above the natural rate but should fall again when people adjust their expectations to the new lower rate of inflation. Finally, inflationary expectations could be built into agreements through indexing. Indexing remains a controversial issue. Some people maintain that it would mean people no longer create additional inflation simply because they expect it; others believe it amounts to giving up without a fight.

Wage and price controls are another way that policy attempts to make supply-side adjustments. These controls typically impose limits on increases in wages and prices. Upper limits on prices tend to create shortages, necessitating some form of rationing.

Supply-side economic policies attempt to increase both long-run and short-run aggregate supply. The tools to do so include deregulation of business and tax cuts for corporations and for higher-income people. The intention is to stimulate innovation and investment; tax cuts for higher-income people are justified as a way of increasing saving in order to provide the funds for increased investment spending. Critics of supply-side economic policies argue that it essentially amounts to a reassertion of Say's Identity. They also maintain that tax cuts will lead to deficit spending. Many supply-siders respond to the suggestion of increased deficits by referring to the Laffer curve. This curve assumes that, after a point, increases in the average net tax rate cause decreases in net tax revenues. The belief is that if our tax rate is "too" high, we can increase tax revenues by reducing the tax rate.

The three mainstream schools of modern macroeconomic thought are Keynesian economics, monetarism, and supply-side economics. Keynesian economics and monetarism are both demand-side approaches. Supply-side economics had its roots in neoclassical economics; monetarism grew out of neoclassical economics. Monetarism generally supports little or no government involvement; supply-side economics tends to support deregulation; Keynesians generally favor active government involvement in the form of fine tuning.

Major Objectives   After you have finished this chapter, you will be able to do the following:

1. Define, recognize, and provide examples of supply shocks.
2. Identify and explain the appropriate policy responses to supply shocks.
3. Explain the dilemma associated with attempting to use demand-side strategies to deal with stagflation.
4. Explain why supply shocks tend to create frictional and structural unemployment.
5. Use the expansion–inflation model to explain inflationary expectations.
6. Explain the role of accommodation in the inflationary expectations model.
7. Discuss the importance of time in dealing with inflationary expectations.
8. Explain the concept of adaptive expectations and indicate its relationship to the inflationary expectations model.
9. Explain the theory of accelerating inflation and discuss the implications of the theory for unemployment.
10. Explain the theory of rational expectations and discuss its implications as they relate to the use of accelerating inflation as a tool to fight unemployment.
11. Explain the theory of decelerating inflation.
12. Define and describe indexing and indicate its relationship to theories of inflationary expectations.
13. Explain the concept of indexing and discuss the pros and cons of it.
14. Discuss the various types of wage and price controls, their relationship to an incomes policy, their relationship to supply-side economics, historical experience with them, and problems associated with their use.
15. Identify the major objectives of supply-side economics.
16. Identify the tools associated with supply-side economics and, from a theoretical standpoint, explain how they are expected to operate.
17. Describe the problems associated with supply-side economics and cite the arguments used against these criticisms.
18. Explain in what sense supply-side economics is both the oldest and the youngest school of thought in macroeconomics.
19. Explain how monetarism is a "halfway house" between demand-side and supply-side macroeconomic policy.
20. Describe Milton Friedman's monetarist position and indicate the role he sees for government.
21. Describe Reaganomics in relation to the three major macroeconomic schools of thought.

Review Terms

wage-cost lag
money illusion
Organization of Petroleum
    Exporting Countries (OPEC)
expansion–inflation model
aggregate supply
short-run aggregate supply
    (SRAS)
long-run aggregate supply
    (LRAS)
aggregate demand
short-run macroeconomic
    equilibrium
real national income and
    product
contractionary
stagflation
target level of national income
    and product
expansionary
general price level (P)
demand-side economics
monetary tools
fiscal tools
frictional unemployment
structural unemployment

subsidies
GNP deflator
inflation rate
accommodate
effective full employment
natural rate of unemployment
deflation
price stability
long-run macroeconomic
    equilibrium
real vs. nominal values
cost of living adjustment
planned vs. market economy
shortages
Say's Identity
deficit
crowding out
net taxes
Keynesian
monetarism
neoclassical theory
foreign markets
financial markets
imports
exports
monetary growth rule

**Important Terms
and Concepts**

supply shock
exogenous
relative prices
supply-side instruments
inflationary expectations
adaptive expectations
accelerating inflation
decelerating inflation
rational expectations
indexing

wage and price controls
wage and price guidelines
incomes policy
rationing
supply-side economics
demand-pull inflation
Laffer curve
Reaganomics
Gramm-Rudman Act

Completion

exogenous

aggregate supply

income and product

general price level

relative

growth

targets

long-run aggregate supply

as well as

short-run aggregate supply

left

wage-cost lags

money illusion

future inflation

upward

price level

exceed

will not

will

adaptive

initiate

sustained inflation

A supply shock is an independent or _____ event that shifts the _____ curve. It can result in an increase or a decrease in aggregate supply, and it typically causes a change in real national _____ and in the _____ . In addition to changing the price level, a supply shock also tends to change _____ prices. In formulating policy responses to supply shocks, the first step would be to ascertain the _____ rate of the economy and to identify policy _____ . In order to do so, it is necessary to determine whether the supply shock has shifted the _____ curve. Once this has been done, programs must be formulated and implemented. Responses may include supply-side _____ (as well as/but not) demand-side instruments.

The _____ curve may also be shifted by inflationary expectations. In the inflationary expectations model, the short-run aggregate supply curve shifts to the _____ as _____ disappear, as _____ wears off, and because of expectations of _____ . This shift in the short-run aggregate supply curve puts _____ (upward/downward) pressure on the _____ . If the aggregate demand curve does not shift, the unemployment rate will _____ fall short of/exceed) the natural rate and the expected rate of inflation _____ (will/will not) be confirmed. If, however, monetary and fiscal policies accommodate the expected inflation and shift the aggregate demand curve so that the economy achieves effective full employment, the inflationary expectations _____ (will/will not) be confirmed.

The inflationary expectations model is one of _____ expectations, since the expectations do not _____ the original inflation. Further, it usually takes several years of _____ before people develop really firm expectations.

The theory of accelerating inflation is an extension of the inflationary expectations model. It suggests that the unemployment rate

temporarily   might be _____ (permanently/temporarily) reduced

natural   below the _____ rate if the real rate of inflation were pushed

above   _____ (above/below) the expected rate. The theory of

rational expectations _____ argues that it is not possible to reduce unemployment below the natural rate, because people

learn   soon _____ to make immediate adjustments to monetary and fiscal policies designed to reduce the unemployment rate.

Another extension of the inflationary expectations model, the

decelerating   theory of _____ inflation, explains how to achieve downward movements of the price level or slower rates of inflation.

decrease   Deflation requires a(n) _____ (increase/decrease) in aggregate demand; a slowdown in the rate of inflation requires a

refusal   _____ (policy/refusal) to accommodate inflationary expectations.

indexed   If financial agreements were _____ , an automatic adjustment for inflation would be built into the agreements. As an example, consider an indexed savings account that pays 5 percent. With a 10 percent rate of inflation, a balance of $100 would auto-

110   matically increase to $ _____ and the interest rate would increase

5.5   to _____ percent. At the end of the year, with no withdrawals,

115.50   there would be $ _____ in the account.

Wage and price controls also work through the supply side of the economy. These controls may be mandatory or voluntary; when they

guidelines   are voluntary they are sometimes called _____ . The

incomes   controls become part of an _____ policy when they are used throughout the economy and coordinated to reach certain goals.

Wage and price controls are usually imposed after the economy

demand   has experienced an expansionary shock from the _____ (demand/supply) side. As wage-cost lags diminish and money illusion

short-run aggregate starts to wear off, the _____
supply

left   curve begins to shift to the _____ (right/left), reducing

output, prices   _____ (output/prices) and raising _____ (output/prices). Wage and price controls try to solve the problem by flattening

_____ (steepening/flattening) the

short-run aggregate supply

_____ curve and

preventing

by _____ (encouraging/preventing) the shift in the

short-run aggregate supply

_____ curve that would otherwise occur as wage-cost lags disappear and money illusion wears off.

increase

     In general, supply-side economists attempt to _____

short run and the long run

(increase/decrease) aggregate supply in the _____ (short run/long run/short run and the long run). In order to do so,

decrease

they would _____ (increase/decrease) taxes and

deregulate

_____ (regulate/deregulate) business in an attempt to

investment, innovation

encourage _____ and _____ . Indi-

high

vidual tax reductions would favor relatively _____ (high/low)

saving

income groups with the intention of encouraging _____ (consumption/saving) to help provide funds for the increased investment.

**Problems and
Applications**

Use the graph below to answer problems 1 and 2.

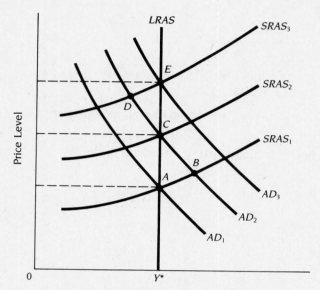

Real National Income and Product

1. Consider the economy described in the graph above. Assume
   initially that the economy is in equilibrium at point A with
   aggregate demand and short-run aggregate supply described by
   curves AD_1 and $SRAS_1$, respectively.
   a. What income and product level is associated with effective
      full employment? What income and product level is associated
      with the natural rate of unemployment?
   b. Let aggregate demand shift to AD_2. Identify the new short-run
      equilibrium point. What happens to the equilibrium values of
      the price level, real national income and product, employment,
      and unemployment?
   c. Now assume that the short-run aggregate supply curve shifts to
      $SRAS_2$ as wage-cost lags disappear and money illusion wears
      off. Identify the new equilibrium point. Compare the new equi-
      librium price level with the original price level. What is the new
      equilibrium employment level? What is the new equilibrium
      rate of unemployment?

2. Consider the expansion–inflation process described by problem 1
   and the graph. Aggregate demand and supply for the economy
   are currently described by AD_2 and $SRAS_2$, respectively.

a. What will happen if people expect inflation to continue and adjust their behavior accordingly?

b. Assume that inflationary expectations cause the short-run aggregate supply curve to shift to $SRAS_3$. Identify the new short-run equilibrium point if aggregate demand remains stable. Are the inflationary expectations confirmed? What happens to the employment level?

c. Assume that inflationary expectations cause the short-run aggregate supply curve to shift to $SRAS_3$. What will happen if monetary and fiscal policies accommodate the expected inflation? What is the new equilibrium point? Are the inflationary expectations confirmed? Why would monetary and fiscal authorities accommodate the inflationary expectations?

True-False   Indicate whether each of the following statements is basically true or false. If the statement is false, rewrite it so that it is true.

_____ 1. A supply shock is any change that causes the economy to move along its aggregate supply curve.

_____ 2. Policy responses to supply-side shocks must be supply-side responses.

_____ 3. In the inflationary expectations model, the short-run aggregate supply curve shifts to the left when people expect additional inflation.

_____ 4. Inflationary expectations will be confirmed if monetary and fiscal policy accommodate the expected inflation.

_____ 5. The theory of accelerating inflation suggests that unemployment can be temporarily reduced below its natural rate if the rate of inflation is pushed above its expected level.

_____ 6. The theory of rational expectations suggests that unemployment can be permanently reduced below its natural rate if the rate of inflation is pushed above its expected level.

_____ 7. A policy of decelerating inflation might be used to create deflation or to stabilize the price level.

_____ 8. Wage and price controls are a demand-side policy approach because they occur after the economy has had a demand-side shock.

_____ 9. An incomes policy is an alternative to price and wage controls.

_____ 10. Because wage and price controls tend to create shortages of goods and services, we often see some form of rationing system implemented along with the controls.

_____ 11. The major objective of supply-side economics is to increase short-run and long-run aggregate supply.

_____ 12. Supply-side economists would use tax cuts for relatively low income groups to encourage consumption.

_____ 13. The Laffer curve shows a positive relationship between net tax revenues and the average net tax rate.

_____ 14. Milton Friedman, the best-known spokesperson for monetarism, is opposed to fine tuning and supports the implementation of a monetary growth rule.

_____ 15. Reaganomics is a mixture of several macroeconomic policy approaches.

_____ 16. The Gramm-Rudman Act of 1985 required a balanced budget by 1986 and established procedures to achieve it.

Multiple Choice   Choose the *one best* answer in each of the following cases:

_____ 1. A supply shock
    a. could be the result of a natural disaster.
    b. causes a movement along the aggregate supply curve.
    c. may cause aggregate supply to fall but never to rise.
    d. changes the general price level but not relative prices.
    e. changes relative prices but not the general price level.

_____ 2. Which of the following will happen to the short-run equilibrium price level and real product when a supply shock results in an increase in short-run aggregate supply?
    a. The price level and real product will rise.
    b. The price level and real product will fall.
    c. The price level will rise and real product will fall.
    d. The price level will fall and real product will rise.
    e. It is impossible to determine what will happen to the price level and real product from the information given.

_____ 3. What is the consequence of a contractionary supply shock if there is no subsequent change in aggregate demand?
    a. a decrease in real national income and product and a decrease in the general price level
    b. a decrease in real national income and product and an increase in the general price level
    c. an increase in real national income and product and a decrease in the general price level
    d. an increase in real national income and product and an increase in the general price level
    e. a decrease in real national income and product with no change in the general price level

____ 4. The problem of stagflation
   a. requires a demand-side solution.
   b. was large in the 1930s.
   c. is equivalent to cost-push inflation.
   d. is treated easily with Keynesian fiscal policy.
   e. is the combination of rising prices, declining output, and rising unemployment.

____ 5. In developing a policy response to supply shocks, one should
   a. rely entirely on supply-side approaches.
   b. rely primarily on monetary, rather than fiscal, instruments.
   c. determine whether the supply shock has shifted the long-run aggregate supply curve.
   d. concentrate on the short-run aggregate supply curve, ignoring any potential changes in long-run aggregate supply.
   e. none of the above

____ 6. In the inflationary expectations model,
   a. the short-run aggregate-supply curve shifts to the right as wage-cost lags disappear and money illusion wears off.
   b. the short-run aggregate-supply curve shifts to the right, reflecting people's anticipation of future inflation.
   c. short-run aggregate supply changes by more than enough to correct for wage-cost lags and money illusion.
   d. all of the above
   e. inflationary expectations are always fulfilled.

____ 7. Inflationary expectations are
   a. "obstructive" expectations in the sense that they prevent future inflation.
   b. "illusionary" expectations in the sense that they arise out of money illusion.
   c. "initiating" expectations in the sense that they create the initial inflationary pressure.
   d. "adaptive" expectations in the sense that people adapt their behavior to the rate of inflation they experience.
   e. "adoptive" expectations in the sense that people modify their lifestyles so that inflation ceases to concern them.

____ 8. In the inflationary expectations model, accommodating demand-side policies
   a. are needed to confirm the expectations fully.
   b. must be continued if they are to eliminate the expectations.
   c. are designed to prevent additional inflationary expectations.
   d. increase unemployment in order to prevent the expected inflation.
   e. tend to decrease aggregate demand in order to eliminate the expectations.

9. Which of the following statements is true with respect to the theory of accelerating inflation?
    a. Unemployment can be reduced to a level below the natural rate.
    b. Accelerating inflation tends to create additional unemployment.
    c. Unemployment can be reduced, but never to less than the natural rate of unemployment.
    d. In order for unemployment to be reduced, money illusion would have to be eliminated.
    e. The real rate of inflation would have to be less than the expected rate in order for the unemployment rate to be reduced permanently.

10. According to the theory of rational expectations,
    a. people never learn to adjust their inflationary expectations accurately.
    b. accelerating inflation can be successful in reducing unemployment only in the long run.
    c. in the long run, demand-side attempts to reduce unemployment below the natural rate will result only in greater inflation.
    d. it is possible to keep the actual rate of inflation above the expected rate only after people learn to adjust their inflationary expectations accurately.
    e. demand-side attempts to reduce unemployment below the natural rate will be successful only after people learn to adjust their inflationary expectations accurately.

11. According to the theory of decelerating inflation,
    a. deflation requires that unemployment permanently rise above the natural rate.
    b. inflationary expectations must be accommodated if the price level is to fall.
    c. contractionary demand-side policies might be used to reduce the rate of inflation.
    d. unemployment above the natural rate will be eliminated only when people's behavior is influenced by money illusion.
    e. none of the above

12. The practice of indexing
    a. prevents all cost-of-living adjustments.
    b. essentially denies the existence of inflation.
    c. causes people to operate under money illusion.
    d. is generally recommended as a way of eliminating inflation.
    e. automatically builds an inflation adjustment into financial agreements.

_____ 13. Wage and price controls
   a. are part of supply-side economics.
   b. have rarely been used in the real world.
   c. attempt to decrease short-run aggregate supply.
   d. attempt to steepen the short-run aggregate supply curve.
   e. are generally used after a contractionary demand-side shock.

_____ 14. Rationing
   a. is likely to result from wage and price controls.
   b. is likely to be the result of illegal markets.
   c. is the consequence of a surplus.
   d. is illegal.
   e. requires the use of coupons.

_____ 15. Supply-side economists tend to
   a. favor tax cuts for corporations and high-income persons.
   b. concentrate on short-run, rather than long-run, remedies.
   c. support increased government regulation of the private sector.
   d. minimize the importance of innovation and investment spending.
   e. use tax cuts for the primary purpose of encouraging consumption spending.

_____ 16. Supply-side economics
   a. generally accepts deficit spending as inevitable.
   b. denies the possibility of changes in aggregate demand.
   c. has been criticized for failing to utilize Say's Identity.
   d. attempts to increase both short-run and long-run aggregate supply.
   e. both c and d above

_____ 17. The Laffer curve
   a. proves Say's Identity.
   b. suggests that deficit spending is inevitable.
   c. proves that increased tax rates cause deficit spending.
   d. proves that supply-side policies will not result in deficit spending.
   e. is a relationship between net tax revenues and average net tax rates.

_____ 18. Which of the following statements is true of the three main-stream schools of modern macroeconomic thought?
   a. Monetarism is a branch of supply-side economics.
   b. Supply-side economics has its roots in classical economics.
   c. They are neoclassical economics, monetarism, and supply-side economics.
   d. Monetarism, as represented by Milton Friedman, would increase the money supply in order to reduce unemployment.
   e. all of the above

_____ 19. Reaganomics is
   a. a pure application of supply-side economics.
   b. basically supported by those opposed to inflation, high taxes, and high interest rates.
   c. both a and b above
   d. a completely new school of thought in macroeconomics.
   e. none of the above

Discussion Questions

1. Explain the problems associated with attempting to use demand-side policies to deal with stagflation.

2. Identify supply-side instruments for dealing with frictional and structural unemployment.

3. Explain the importance of time in the model of inflationary expectations.

4. In what sense is the inflationary expectations model a situation of adaptive expectations?

5. Discuss the relationship of indexing to inflationary expectations.

6. Explain the importance of changes in relative prices in adjusting to changes in market demand and supply conditions. Explain how wage and price controls affect relative prices.

7. Explain why supply-side economics tends to adopt a long-run point of view.

8. Discuss the role of Say's Identity in supply-side economics.

Answers

Problems and Applications

1. a. Y^*, Y^*
   b. the new short-run equilibrium point is B; price level increases; income and product increase; employment increases, unemployment decreases
   c. C; price level increases; effective full employment; natural rate of unemployment

2. a. Short-run aggregate supply will shift to the left.
    b. D; no; employment decreases
    c. Aggregate demand will shift to AD_3; E; yes; to attain effective full employment (decrease unemployment to the natural rate)

True-False

1. F. A supply shock is an exogenous event that shifts the aggregate supply curve.
2. F. Policy responses to supply-side shocks may be demand-side or supply-side responses.
3. T.
4. T.
5. T.
6. F. The theory of rational expectations suggests that unemployment cannot be reduced below its natural rate by increases in aggregate demand, because people learn to adjust their inflationary expectations almost immediately.
7. T.
8. F. Wage and price controls are a supply-side policy approach, because they are intended to shift the short-run aggregate supply curve.
9. F. Incomes policies use price and wage controls.
10. T.
11. T.
12. F. Supply-side economists would use tax cuts for relatively high income groups to encourage saving.
13. F. The Laffer curve shows a positive relationship between net tax revenues and the average net tax rate only up to a point; at some point, increases in the average net tax rate cause net tax revenues to decline.
14. T.
15. T.
16. F. The Gramm-Rudman Act of 1985 required a balanced budget by 1991 and established procedures to achieve it.

Multiple Choice

1. a	2. d	3. b	4. e	5. c
6. c	7. d	8. a	9. a	10. c
11. c	12. e	13. a	14. a	15. a
16. d	17. e	18. b	19. b	

18 International Macroeconomics: Exchange Rates and the Balance of Payments

Summary

For simplicity, economists often assume they are working with a closed economic system. A closed economy is one that does not interact with other economies. More realistically, economies are open. That is, real-world economies interact with each other. These economic interactions are the subject of international trade and finance. International trade and finance often have significant political and social consequences that make them even more important than their dollar amounts would suggest.

Monies of different countries, called foreign exchange, are traded in foreign exchange markets. When a free foreign exchange market determines the value of a money, the exchange rate is said to be free, floating, or flexible. When a government determines the exchange rate and supports it at a given level, the exchange rate is said to be fixed. Historically, most economies relied on the gold standard, which is essentially a fixed exchange rate system. The International Monetary Fund, set up after World War II, established gold and the U.S. dollar as joint monetary standards. Other monies were fixed in relation to the dollar. In 1971, the United States refused to continue to exchange gold for dollars with foreign governments. Today, most economies tend to rely on a mixed system wherein governments intervene to influence a market-determined rate. Such a system is called a dirty float.

Advocates of flexible exchange rates maintain that free markets are better at allocating resources and determining prices than are governments. Advocates of fixed rates emphasize the uncertainty that goes with flexible rate systems and the importance of fixed rates for long-term international lending. Whether fixed or flexible rates best protect internal autonomy in policy making depends on the specific instrument and the policy objective.

International financial transactions are recorded in a country's balance of payments account. A particular transaction is recorded as a credit or a positive item if it leads to a demand for domestic currency or a supply of foreign currency. The transaction is a debit or a negative item if it leads to a demand for foreign currency or a supply of domestic currency. There is no official way of organizing the entries in international accounts. Your text provides an example of one approach.

The balance of trade is the amount by which the value of an economy's exports of goods exceeds the value of its imports of goods. The balance on current account adds the invisible items to the balance of trade. These items are investment income payments, transactions in services, and unilateral transfers. The balance on capital account is the balance between capital outflows or purchases of foreign assets (which are debit items) and capital inflows or purchases of domestic assets by foreigners (which are credit items). Finally, the errors and omissions entry records estimates of transactions that escape the official reporting process and is used to balance the current and capital accounts.

A country's balance of trade and capital movements generally go through several stages of balance and imbalance in the growth and development of the economy. One theory identifies five stages in this process: immature debtor, mature debtor, intermediate stage, immature creditor, and mature creditor.

An active, positive, or surplus balance of trade or payments is sometimes referred to as a favorable balance, and a passive, negative, or deficit balance is said to be unfavorable. These terms, which came into use with the mercantilists, suggest that a positive balance is preferable to a negative balance. This may be true under certain economic conditions, for example when the primary macroeconomic objective is to achieve and maintain high employment. But when the economy is primarily concerned with inflation, a negative balance may be preferable.

A country is said to have a balance of payments problem when the international situation puts it under pressure to change its economic policies. This would occur when its negative balance is so large, relative to its reserves, that it cannot continue to settle its deficits with reserves of gold or currencies that other countries will accept. There are eight types of solutions for payments problems. These are generally used in combination, though they need not be. Five of these approaches, the price-specie flow, depreciation or devaluation, absorption, protectionism, and countertrade (or barter), operate primarily on the current account. The monetary approach operates primarily on the capital account. All six of these approaches involve action initiated by the country with the payments problem. The other two approaches are passive in that they require policy changes by the country's trading partners. These two approaches are passivity and renegotiation, and locomotive theory.

Major Objectives   After you have finished this chapter, you will be able to do the following:

1. Discuss the importance of international trade and finance in terms of world politics and in terms of current income, output, and employment measures.
2. Define tariff.
3. Define foreign exchange and describe the purpose of foreign exchange markets.
4. Develop and explain a two-country model of foreign exchange.
5. Extend the two-country model of foreign exchange to handle multilateral trade.
6. Explain how the foreign exchange value of the dollar can increase while the value of the dollar is decreasing in terms of some specific currency.
7. Identify and explain the slope of the supply curve of a currency.
8. Identify and explain the slope of the demand curve for a currency.
9. Identify and explain the circumstances that might give rise to a vertical currency demand or supply curve.
10. Define and distinguish between an overvalued dollar and an undervalued dollar, and between depreciation and appreciation of a dollar.
11. Define interest rate parity.
12. Define purchasing power parity.
13. Identify the equilibrium condition for a free international exchange market and explain the process of adjustment toward equilibrium.
14. Define and distinguish between free, floating, or flexible foreign exchange rates and fixed foreign exchange rates.
15. Verbally and graphically explain how an exchange value may be fixed.
16. Define exchange controls and inconvertible currency.
17. Cite the arguments for and against flexible exchange rates.
18. Cite the arguments for and against fixed exchange rates.
19. Identify and explain an economy's preference for flexible versus fixed exchange rates with respect to the issue of internal policy autonomy.

20. Provide a brief history of exchange systems, being sure to define and/or explain the gold standard, the Bretton Woods system or the International Monetary Fund, and Eurocurrencies.
21. Identify and explain the relationship between the value of an economy's currency and the economy's price level.
22. Identify the conditions required for the smooth functioning of a gold standard.
23. Identify and explain the problems associated with a gold standard.
24. Define devaluation and indicate its purposes.
25. Define competitive depreciation.
26. Explain what is meant by a dirty float system.
27. Identify and explain the advantages of Eurocurrencies.
28. Define European Currency Unit and explain its advantage.
29. Define balance of payments account.
30. Define and distinguish between positive, active, credit, or favorable transactions and negative, passive, debit, or unfavorable transactions.
31. Identify the major sections of the balance of payments account and indicate the entries in each section.
32. Define and identify the makeup of a balance of trade, a balance on current account, a balance on capital account, an official settlements balance, and an errors and omissions entry.
33. Identify and describe five balance of payments stages and explain how an economy might move from one stage to another in the course of its growth and development.
34. Distinguish between a favorable and an unfavorable balance and indicate the derivation of the concepts.
35. Describe and explain the mercantile theory and indicate its relationship to the problems of unemployment and inflation.
36. Explain the concept of a balance of payments problem.
37. Identify the eight groups of remedies for payments problems, indicate which accounts they affect, explain how they correct a payments problem, and discuss their use.
38. Explain the meaning of Special Drawing Rights (SDRs) or paper gold.
39. Discuss the use of payments solutions by the United States.

Review Terms	export	index number
	import	base year
	resources	positive vs. negative slope
	market demand	free market
	market supply	fiscal policy
	market equilibrium	monetary policy

expansionary policy
budget deficit
contractionary policy
direct vs. inverse relationship
recession
money supply
price level
Great Depression
inflation
deflation
reflate
transfers
real capital
private sector
public sector
economic growth and
    development
aggregate demand
aggregate supply

stagflation
monetary base
wage-cost lag
money illusion
accommodate
accelerating inflation
national income and product (Y)
consumption (C)
investment (I)
government purchases (G)
net exports (X – Im)
rationing
subsidies
open market operation
reserve requirement
discount rate
barter
OPEC

**Important Terms
and Concepts**

international trade
international finance
tariff
Hawley-Smoot tariff
Imperial Preference
foreign exchange
foreign exchange markets
multilateral trade
foreign exchange value of the
    dollar
trade-weighted
overvalued dollar
depreciate
undervalued dollar
appreciate
interest rate parity
purchasing power parity
free, floating, or flexible
    foreign exchange rates
fixed foreign exchange rates
exchange controls
inconvertible currency
quota
internal policy autonomy

gold standard
gold inflows
distress goods
protectionist
deflationary bias
to "go off gold"
competitive depreciation
to export unemployment
Bretton Woods system
International Monetary Fund
    (IMF)
Eurocurrencies
devaluation
competitive devaluations
pegged
dirty float system
Eurodollar
European Currency Unit (ECU)
European Currency Union
balance of payments account
positive, active, credit, or
    favorable transaction
negative, passive, debit, or
    unfavorable transaction

balance of trade
current account
balance on current account
invisible items in current
  account
capital account
balance on capital account
capital exports or outflows
capital imports or inflows
net repatriation
official reserves account
official settlements balance
errors and omissions entry
balance of payments stages
immature debtor stage
mature debtor stage
intermediate debtor stage
immature creditor stage
mature creditor stage
original flow
return flow
active, positive, surplus, or
  favorable balance
passive, negative, deficit, or
  unfavorable balance
mercantilist theory
balance of payments problem

classical medicine or price-specie
  flow
absorption
open vs. closed economy
protectionism
tariff factories
generalized (macroeconomic)
  protection
interest-equalization tax
foreign exchange taxes
exchange controls
exchange rationing
passivity
renegotiation
debt repudiation
Marshall Plan for Western Europe
World Bank (formerly the International Bank for Reconstruction and Development)
Special Drawing Rights (SDRs)
  or paper gold
locomotive theory
countertrade
bilateral balancing
"swing credit"
multilateralism
transactions costs

Completion

foreign exchange

foreign exchange
markets

their own

positively

sensitive

more than

Currencies of different countries, called _____ ,
are traded in _____ . These markets
are needed because people who sell goods typically want to be paid
in the currency of _____ (their own/the buyer's)
country.

    In a foreign exchange market for the dollar, the supply curve is
usually _____ sloped. This typical situation requires that
those who supply dollars be _____ (sensitive/insensitive)
to changes in its exchange value. In fact, they must be so aware of
these changes that their response in terms of actual buying and investment decisions is _____ (more than/exactly/less than)

proportional to the change in the dollar's exchange value. When the actual response is just proportional to the change in the dollar's ex-

vertical   change value, the supply curve will be _____ .

In a foreign exchange market for the dollar, the demand curve is

negatively   usually _____ sloped. This requires that those who de-

sensitive   mand dollars are _____ (sensitive/insensitive) to changes in its exchange value. When people's response to changes in the dollar's exchange value is just proportional to the changes, the

vertical   demand curve will be _____ .

Equilibrium in a foreign exchange market for the dollar occurs at

demand, supply the intersection of the _____ and _____ curves. When equilibrium exists in a free international exchange market, the real purchasing power of the dollar in international trade is

the same as   _____ (greater than/the same as/less than) at home.

purchasing power parity   This is referred to as a situation of _____ .

At any exchange rate above the equilibrium exchange rate, the

overvalued   dollar is _____ (overvalued/undervalued). This means

less   that the dollar will buy _____ (more/less) at home than in

overpriced   foreign countries. American goods are _____ (over-

supply of   priced/underpriced) in international trade. The excess _____

downward   (demand for/supply of) dollars will put _____ (upward/ downward) pressure on the exchange value, causing the dollar to

depreciate   _____ (appreciate/depreciate).

When the exchange rate is below the equilibrium rate, the dollar is

undervalued   _____ (overvalued/undervalued). That is, the

more   dollar will buy _____ (more/less) at home than in foreign

underpriced   countries. American goods are _____ (overpriced/

demand for   underpriced) in international trade. The excess _____ (demand for/supply of) the dollar will tend to result in a(n)

appreciation   _____ (appreciation/depreciation) of the dollar.

Foreign exchange rates that are determined by the free interplay

free, floating of supply and demand are called _____ or _____

flexible   or _____ . When a government controls the exchange value

fixed   of its currency, the exchange rate is said to be _____ .

In order to influence or fix exchange rates, governments hold

reserves, gold,
monies
_____ of _____ and _____ . When a
government wants to maintain the exchange value of its currency

buys
above the free market equilibrium rate, it _____ (buys/sells)

supply
the excess _____ (demand/supply) that exists at the con-

demand
trolled rate. In essence, this makes the _____ (demand/

horizontal
supply) curve _____ (horizontal/vertical) at the
controlled rate. If a government wants to force the exchange value of

sells
its currency below the free market equilibrium rate, it _____

demand
(buys/sells) an amount equal to the excess _____ (demand/
supply) that exists at the controlled rate. This essentially makes the

supply, horizontal
_____ (demand/supply) curve _____
(horizontal/vertical) at the controlled rate.

Most governments value autonomy in implementing domestic economic policy. Neither a floating nor a fixed rate always results in the
greatest autonomy. Expansionary monetary policy is best protected

flexible
under _____ rates, whereas expansionary fiscal policy is

fixed
best protected under _____ rates; contractionary mone-

fixed
tary policy is best protected under _____ rates, whereas

flexible
contractionary fiscal policy is best protected under _____
rates. Consider, for example, the consequences of each type of exchange rate for expansionary fiscal policy. Expansionary fiscal policy

deficit
is typically associated with a budget _____ (surplus/deficit).

higher
This typically results in _____ (higher/lower) interest rates.

inflow
With floating rates, the _____ (inflow/outflow) of capital

appreciation
brings about an _____ (appreciation/depreciation)

fall
of the country's currency. This is likely to cause a _____

rise
(rise/fall) in exports and a _____ (rise/fall) in imports.

less
Hence, the expansionary fiscal policy is _____ (more/less)

inflows
effective. With fixed rates, however, the additional capital _____

outflows
(inflows/outflows) and the curtailment of capital _____
(inflows/outflows) do not alter the exchange rate, so they do not
cause adverse trade balances.

fixed

Historically, _____ (fixed/floating) rate systems have been more common. Probably the best-known fixed rate system is

gold

the _____ standard, under which countries promise to back their own money with a fixed amount of gold. Price levels in gold-standard countries are linked to each other. A country with a low-valued

high

money would have a _____ (high/low) price level; a country

low

with a high-valued money would have a _____ (high/low) price level. The differences in price levels would tend to result in

purchasing power parity

_____ .

A gold standard creates problems in times of rapidly changing economic conditions. For example, consider an economy in a recession with falling prices. If prices have not fallen elsewhere, there

exports

would be an increase in _____ (imports/exports) for the

rise

country experiencing the recession, the price level would _____

inflows

(rise/fall) as a result of gold _____ (inflows/outflows), and the economy would recover. But trading partners would experience

falling, rising

_____ (rising/falling) exports and _____

out of

(rising/falling) imports; gold would flow _____ (into/out of) these economies; and they might experience deflation and recession. These difficulties would tend to be worse when prices and wages

slowly

change _____ (quickly/slowly).

The gold standard began to break down after World War I with the worldwide spread of recession. Countries renounced their guarantees to exchange gold for their currency or tried to lower the exchange value of their currency by reducing the amount of gold that they would exchange for it. The purpose of this latter process, called

devaluation, increase

_____ , was to _____ (increase/decrease)

decrease

exports and _____ (increase/decrease) imports in order to reduce domestic unemployment. The collapse of the gold standard

competitive depreciation

led to _____ , trade wars, and restrictions that contributed to World War II.

International Monetary Fund

Shortly before the end of World War II, the _____ was set up at a meeting of central bankers and finance ministers in Bretton Woods, New Hampshire. The major goal of the IMF was to

competitive devaluations

avoid _____ . Gold and the U.S. dollar

joint monetary
standards

were established as _____ ; the
exchange values of other currencies were fixed in relation to the

dollar

_____ . The IMF also set up a fund using contributions from
the major trading countries. The IMF could then make loans from

fixed exchange rate

the fund to help countries maintain the _____ .
If, for example, a country's equilibrium exchange rate fell below its

reserves

fixed rate and if the country did not have sufficient _____
to support the fixed rate, an IMF loan could be made, the IMF could

devalue

allow the country to _____ its currency, or the IMF could
set conditions for its assistance.

Since 1971, when the United States ceased to exchange gold for
dollars with foreign governments, there have been no fixed ratios.
Instead, a weak imitation of the fixed rate system has developed.

dirty float

Called a _____ , it occurs when a government
attempts to influence the exchange value of its money by trading
large amounts of foreign exchange.

Problems and Applications

1. Consider the following graph as the foreign exchange market for Starland's currency. Assume that Starland uses stars (*) for money just as the United States uses dollars, Japan uses yen, or Britain uses pounds.

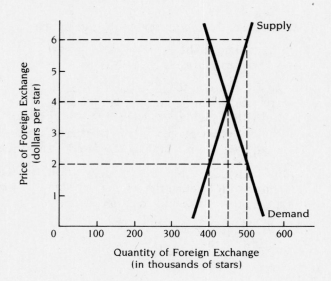

Quantity of Foreign Exchange
(in thousands of stars)

  a. Assuming that the foreign exchange rate is determined by the free market, what would be the equilibrium exchange rate between dollars and stars? At this rate, what would you have to pay in U.S. dollars for a souvenir priced at *3 in Starland? If a star were worth $6, what would you have to pay in U.S. dollars for the souvenir? At an exchange rate of $6 per *1, is the star overvalued or undervalued? At an exchange rate of $6 per *1, are you more or less inclined to buy the souvenir?

  b. Assume that the government of Starland wanted to maintain an exchange rate of $6 per *1. Should Starland buy or sell stars? How many?

  c. Assume that the government of Starland wanted to maintain an exchange rate of $2 per *1. Should Starland buy or sell stars? How many?

2. For each of the following transactions, indicate whether it is a credit or a debit.

  a. A U.S. citizen buys souvenirs while on vacation in Europe.

  b. A Japanese citizen buys a product made in the United States.

  c. An African visitor flies from New York to Los Angeles.

  d. A foreign citizen buys stock in IBM.

  e. IBM pays dividends to the foreign owner of the stock.

    f. A U.S. citizen buys a Japanese car.

    g. A British citizen buys a Mickey Mouse cap at Disneyland.

    h. A U.S. citizen buys stock in a foreign corporation.

    i. A U.S. citizen sends money to his grandchild in South America.

    j. A U.S. citizen receives money from her grandmother in Israel.

    k. A U.S. citizen receives a dividend payment from a company overseas.

True-False

Indicate whether each of the following statements is basically true or false. If the statement is false, rewrite it so that it is true.

1. About one out of six U.S. workers owe their jobs to exports and about 20 percent of our industrial output is exported.

2. Foreign exchange refers to the money of another country.

3. Foreign exchange markets are markets in which people of one country exchange goods with people from another country.

4. If the foreign exchange value of the dollar rises, then the value of the dollar with respect to any particular money must also rise.

5. Equilibrium in the foreign exchange market for dollars occurs at the exchange rate that equates quantity of dollars demanded with quantity of dollars supplied.

6. Assuming free markets, purchasing power parity refers to a situation in which the real purchasing power of a money is the same in domestic and international trade.

7. When interest rate parity value and the purchasing power parity value differ, there is neither interest rate parity nor purchasing power parity.

8. When the actual foreign exchange rate for the dollar is greater than the equilibrium rate, the dollar is undervalued, meaning that it will buy less in international trade than it will buy at home.

9. When the foreign exchange value of a currency rises, the currency appreciates.

10. To say that foreign exchange rates float means that they are determined by market forces.

11. In order to fix the foreign exchange rate of its money, a government may have to take part in the buying and selling of the money.

12. When a government imposes exchange controls, it is fixing exchange rates.

13. Exchange rates are fixed under a gold standard.

_____ 14. In the Great Depression of the 1930s, no major country went off the gold standard.

_____ 15. Under the International Monetary Fund, gold and the U.S. dollar were established as joint monetary standards.

_____ 16. Eurodollars are dollars printed by European governments.

_____ 17. A country's balance of payments account simply records the value of that country's imported and exported goods.

_____ 18. In the U.S. record of international transactions, capital inflows or imports refers to imports of capital goods, whereas capital outflows or exports refers to exports of capital goods.

_____ 19. Capital might flow from poor countries to rich countries if outstanding loans come due and new loans are not forthcoming.

_____ 20. A deficit or passive balance of trade is always undesirable and so is often called an unfavorable balance of trade.

_____ 21. The terms _favorable_ and _unfavorable_ balance of trade were developed by mercantilists and may not accurately evaluate all situations.

_____ 22. According to mercantile theory, an economy should attempt to gain and keep positive international balances and accumulate treasure.

_____ 23. Most economists would say that a country has a balance of payments problem when its balance of payments becomes negative.

_____ 24. Countertrade, or barter, is especially important between countries with payments deficits.

_____ 25. A country may temporarily solve a balance of payments problem by a grant of special drawing rights (or paper gold) from the International Monetary Fund.

_____ 26. U.S. trade problems in the early 1980s have been problems with the balance of payments as a whole.

Multiple Choice   Choose the _one best_ answer in each of the following cases:

_____ 1. International trade and finance are
   a. generally unimportant in the less-developed countries.
   b. important only in relatively small economies that must import necessities.
   c. relatively unimportant in the United States, since only about one out of a thousand jobs is tied to exports.
   d. perhaps more important for political reasons than for reasons associated with production, employment, and consumption.
   e. both c and d above

_____ 2. In a two-country foreign exchange market for the dollar,
a. the price of the dollar is expressed in dollars.
b. part of the demand for dollars may come from foreigners who want to sell their goods to Americans.
c. part of the demand for dollars may come from foreign investors who want to purchase stocks and bonds in the United States.
d. part of the supply of dollars may come from foreigners who want to buy American goods.
e. part of the supply of dollars may come from the foreign government if it wishes to increase its official dollar reserves.

_____ 3. In a foreign exchange market for dollars, the supply curve of the dollar will be
a. negatively sloped if people are relatively sensitive to changes in its exchange value.
b. negatively sloped if people are insensitive to changes in its exchange value.
c. horizontal if people are not sensitive to changes in its exchange value.
d. positively sloped if people are relatively sensitive to changes in its exchange value.
e. both c and d above

_____ 4. In a foreign exchange market for dollars, the demand curve for the dollar will be
a. positively sloped if people are relatively sensitive to changes in its exchange value.
b. positively sloped if people are insensitive to changes in its exchange value.
c. horizontal if people are insensitive to changes in its exchange value.
d. negatively sloped if people are relatively sensitive to changes in its exchange value.
e. both c and d above

Use the following graph to answer questions 5 and 6.

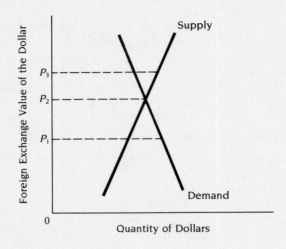

5. Consider the graph above, representing a foreign exchange market for dollars. Assume that the demand and supply curves are the result of free international trade. At an exchange rate of
   a. P_1 the dollar is overvalued.
   b. P_2 the market is in equilibrium.
   c. P_3 the dollar is undervalued.
   d. all of the above
   e. none of the above

6. In the graph, assume that the demand and supply curves are the result of free international trade. At an exchange rate of
   a. P_1 a dollar will buy more at home than it will in foreign markets.
   b. P_1 American goods are overpriced in international trade.
   c. P_3 a dollar will buy less in international trade than it will at home.
   d. P_3 American goods are underpriced in international trade.
   e. all of the above

Use the graph below to answer questions 7 and 8.

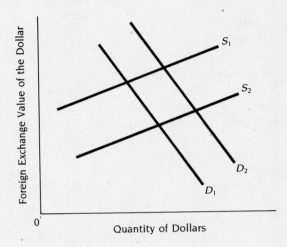

7. Consider the graph above, representing a foreign exchange market for dollars. Assume that the demand and supply curves are the result of free international trade, with D_1 and S_1 representing the initial demand and supply conditions and D_2 and S_2 representing current conditions. One could accurately say that
   a. the demand for dollars has increased.
   b. the supply of dollars has decreased.
   c. both a and b above
   d. the decrease in the supply of dollars could be the result of a decrease in foreign demand for American goods.
   e. all of the above

8. In the graph, assume that the demand and supply curves are the result of free international trade, with D_1 and S_1 representing the initial demand and supply conditions and D_2 and S_2 representing current conditions. With freely floating exchange rates, one could accurately say that
   a. fewer dollars will be traded now than before.
   b. at the original equilibrium price, the dollar would now be undervalued.
   c. at the original equilibrium price, there is now purchasing power parity.
   d. the changes in demand and supply will lead to a depreciation of the dollar.
   e. the changes in demand and supply will lead to an appreciation of the dollar.

_____ 9. If the United States wanted to fix the exchange value of the dollar above the equilibrium value determined by the free market, it could
   a. buy dollars at the desired exchange value.
   b. sell dollars at the desired exchange value.
   c. sell dollars at the free market exchange value.
   d. buy foreign money at the desired exchange value.
   e. buy foreign money at the free market exchange value.

_____ 10. In order to fix the exchange rate of the dollar below the free market equilibrium rate, the United States should
   a. buy dollars at the desired exchange rate.
   b. sell dollars at the desired exchange rate.
   c. buy dollars at the free market exchange rate.
   d. sell foreign money at the desired exchange rate.
   e. none of the above

_____ 11. The government might want to fix the exchange rate of the dollar below the free market equilibrium rate in order to
   a. promote exports.
   b. encourage imports.
   c. create purchasing power parity.
   d. appreciate the value of the dollar.
   e. increase the price of U.S. goods to foreign buyers.

_____ 12. Advocates of flexible exchange rates are most likely to assert that
   a. flexible rates ensure the government's autonomy in making domestic policy.
   b. flexible rates eliminate the influence of changing supply and demand conditions.
   c. free markets do a better job of setting prices and allocating resources than do governments.
   d. flexible rates tend to reduce the risks associated with long-term international transactions.
   e. fixed rates enable speculators to destabilize exchange markets deliberately for their own gain.

_____ 13. Advocates of fixed exchange rates are most likely to assert that
   a. flexible rates increase the likelihood of government intervention.
   b. fixed rates ensure the government's autonomy in making domestic policy.
   c. flexible rates prevent speculation in exchange markets for personal gain.
   d. fixed rates tend to reduce the risks associated with long-term international transactions.
   e. all of the above

_____ 14. Autonomy in domestic macroeconomic policy is best protected when
a. exchange rates are fixed.
b. exchange rates are flexible.
c. expansionary monetary policy is used with fixed exchange rates.
d. expansionary fiscal policy is used with flexible exchange rates.
e. contractionary monetary policy is used with fixed exchange rates.

_____ 15. Historically, fixed exchange rates
a. have been more common than floating rates.
b. often resulted in the imposition of a gold standard.
c. were pegged to the dollar under the Bretton Woods system.
d. all of the above
e. none of the above

_____ 16. The gold standard
a. was initially set up by the International Monetary Fund.
b. generally prevents purchasing power parity in international trade.
c. requires that a country back its money with a fixed amount of gold per unit of money.
d. became stronger during the worldwide depression following World War I.
e. all of the above

_____ 17. For a gold standard to work smoothly
a. no country may be permitted to allow increased international reserves to exert inflationary effects on domestic prices.
b. no participating country may be permitted to implement a contractionary monetary policy in order to maintain its gold reserves.
c. at least one major participating country must create a market for goods exported by deficit countries unless it is to damage its own domestic import-competing markets.
d. at least one major participating country must create a market for goods exported by deficit countries even if in doing so it damages its own domestic import-competing markets.
e. at least one participating country must be willing to implement a contractionary monetary policy in order to maintain its gold reserves unless such a policy creates contractionary pressures domestically.

_____ 18. The International Monetary Fund
   a. replaced the Bretton Woods system.
   b. set up a type of fixed exchange rate.
   c. was set up jointly by the United States and the U.S.S.R.
   d. was set up to encourage competitive depreciations and devaluations.
   e. was established in the early 1970s when the United States refused to exchange gold for dollars.

_____ 19. Dirty float
   a. is another term for devaluation.
   b. is a system in which money is backed by Eurocurrency.
   c. has been illegal since the establishment of the International Monetary Fund.
   d. refers to government interference in an otherwise floating exchange rate system.
   e. occurs when governments on a fixed exchange system refuse to back their money at the fixed rate.

_____ 20. The Eurocurrency system
   a. refers to European monies.
   b. was begun by the International Monetary Fund.
   c. attempted to establish a single worldwide currency.
   d. imposed a rigid set of exchange requirements on monies that make up the system.
   e. none of the above

_____ 21. The European Currency Unit
   a. is the Eurodollar.
   b. is the U.S. dollar.
   c. circulates only in Europe.
   d. is fixed relative to the dollar.
   e. is a weighted average of the values of a number of European community monies.

_____ 22. In terms of our international accounts,
   a. transactions that lead to a demand for our money are recorded as debits.
   b. transactions that add to our accumulation of foreign money are called positive.
   c. both a and b above
   d. imports are called active.
   e. exports are considered passive.

_____ 23. A country's balance of trade
  a. refers to the amount by which the value of its exported goods exceeds the value of its imported goods.
  b. includes transactions in services as well as tangible goods.
  c. both a and b above
  d. will be negative if the value of a country's exports exceeds the value of its imports.
  e. all of the above

_____ 24. The balance on current account
  a. consists entirely of credit items.
  b. adds the invisible items to the balance of trade.
  c. is the balance of trade minus service transactions.
  d. includes the capital account and the official reserves account.
  e. includes long-term (but not short-term) net private capital exports.

_____ 25. In terms of our international accounts, invisible items include
  a. errors and omissions.
  b. investment income payments.
  c. the value of smuggled goods.
  d. official government reserves.
  e. false valuations of goods and services.

_____ 26. Balance of payments stages in the course of economic growth and development are likely to include a(n)
  a. intermediate stage with a positive trade balance and a net export of capital.
  b. mature debtor stage with a negative trade balance and positive capital account.
  c. mature creditor stage characterized by a positive trade balance and a negative balance on capital.
  d. immature debtor stage characterized by a surplus in the balance of trade and in the current account balance.
  e. none of the above

_____ 27. A positive balance of trade or payments is
  a. always preferable to a negative balance.
  b. either active or passive, depending on the specific entries.
  c. generally considered favorable when the economy wants to promote domestic employment.
  d. generally considered favorable when the economy is experiencing inflation as a result of insufficient aggregate domestic supply.
  e. all of the above

_____ 28. An economy has a balance of payments problem whenever
   a. it has a deficit balance.
   b. it has a passive balance.
   c. it has an unfavorable balance.
   d. the international situation puts it under pressure to change its economic policies.
   e. all of the above

_____ 29. The price-specie flow
   a. is also called the classical medicine.
   b. automatically (though not necessarily immediately) corrects a payments problem.
   c. relies on the operation of the gold standard to solve a balance of payments problem.
   d. tends to result in a decrease in the monetary base of a country with a negative balance.
   e. all of the above

_____ 30. Which of the following statements is true with respect to potential solutions to balance of payments problems?
   a. The monetary approach is a passive form of renegotiation.
   b. Absorption asks domestic consumers and producers to bear the burdens of the problem by reducing domestic expenditures.
   c. Depreciation or devaluation of a country's currency is a more effective solution if it is accompanied by domestic inflation.
   d. Protectionism attempts to encourage exports and imports through the use of subsidies, tariffs, and regulations affecting foreign exchange activity.
   e. The locomotive theory requires deflation in foreign countries and may be considered active or passive depending on how a country attempts to implement it.

Discussion Questions

1. What are the important differences between domestic trade and international trade?

2. Identify factors that influence the demand and supply curves for foreign exchange.

3. Explain the slopes of the demand and supply curves for foreign exchange. Identify and explain situations that would give rise to vertical demand and supply curves.

4. Explain how a government maintains a fixed exchange rate above the free market equilibrium rate. Explain how a government maintains a fixed exchange rate below the free market equilibrium rate.

5. Explain how the gold standard results in a fixed exchange system.

6. Distinguish between the depreciation and devaluation of a currency.

7. The depreciation of an economy's currency may result in inflationary pressures at home. Explain.

8. Compare fixed and floating exchange rate systems in terms of their influence on internal policy autonomy.

9. Explain how a negative balance of trade might be beneficial to an economy.

10. Explain the price-specie flow as a mechanism for correcting a balance of payments problem.

Answers

Problems and Applications

1. a. $4 = *1; $12; $18; overvalued; less
   b. buy; 100,000 stars
   c. sell; 100,000 stars

2. a. debit   b. credit   c. credit   d. credit
   e. debit   f. debit   g. credit   h. debit
   i. debit   j. credit   k. credit

True-False

1. T.
2. T.
3. F. Foreign exchange markets are markets in which currencies of different countries are traded.
4. F. The foreign exchange value of the dollar may rise while the value of the dollar with respect to any particular single currency is rising, falling, or constant.
5. T.
6. T.
7. T.
8. F. When the actual foreign exchange rate for the dollar is greater than the equilibrium rate, the dollar is overvalued, meaning that it will buy more in foreign countries than it will buy at home.
9. T.
10. T.
11. T

12. F. When a government imposes exchange controls it is limiting the ability of individuals to engage in international transactions.
13. T.
14. F. In the Great Depression of the 1930s, major countries (including the United States and Great Britain) went off the gold standard in the sense that they would not exchange gold for currency.
15. T.
16. F. Eurodollars are dollar accounts held in European banks.
17. F. A country's balance of payments account is a record of transactions affecting the international demand and supply for that country's currency.
18. F. In the U.S. record of international transactions, capital inflows or imports refers to purchases of American assets by foreigners, whereas capital outflows or exports refers to U.S. purchases of foreign assets.
19. T.
20. F. A deficit or passive balance of trade might be beneficial if, for example, the economy is experiencing inflation.
21. T.
22. T.
23. F. A country has a balance of payments problem when its negative balance is so large, relative to its reserves, that it cannot continue to settle its deficits with reserves of gold or currencies that other countries will accept.
24. T.
25. T.
26. F. U.S. trade problems in the early 1980s have been problems with the trade and current accounts rather than the balance of payments as a whole.

Multiple Choice

1. d	2. c	3. d	4. d	5. b
6. a	7. a	8. d	9. a	10. b
11. a	12. c	13. d	14. e	15. d
16. c	17. d	18. b	19. d	20. e
21. e	22. b	23. a	24. b	25. b
26. a	27. c	28. d	29. e	30. b

Study Guide material for *Chapter 18, Appendix*, follows.

Appendix: Summary

A country's involvement in international trade and financial activities affects the macroeconomic conditions of the economy. The relationship between internal and external equilibriums may be illustrated with the concepts of the macrodot, payments equilibrium, and the balance of payments line. A macrodot identifies a level of real national income and real interest rate associated with internal macroeconomic equilibrium. Payments equilibrium occurs when a country's balance on current account is matched by an equal but opposite balance on capital account. A balance of payments line identifies combinations of real income and product and real interest rates associated with payments equilibrium.

When an economy's balance of payments line passes through a macrodot, the economy will experience both internal and external equilibrium when it is operating at the macrodot. If the economy's balance of payments line lies above the macrodot, the economy experiences a balance of payments deficit when it is operating at the macrodot. In this situation, achievement of payments equilibrium requires a higher interest rate and/or lower national income. When the balance of payments line lies below the macrodot, an economy that is actually operating at the macrodot will experience a balance of payments surplus. This may be corrected by a declining interest rate and/or a rising national income.

Appendix: Major Objectives

After you have finished this appendix, you will be able to do the following:

1. Verbally and graphically define and explain the concepts of payments equilibrium and macrodot.
2. Explain the positive or horizontal slope of the balance of payments line, indicating the circumstances that give rise to each.
3. Explain the relationship between the location of the balance of payments line and the macrodot, indicating verbally and graphically the circumstances that give rise to a payments surplus and a payments deficit.
4. Explain how an economy might reach internal macroeconomic equilibrium and payments equilibrium by changes in the real interest rate and/or in real national income and indicate the likely consequences of such changes.

Appendix: Review Terms

aggregate
real national income and
    product
real interest rate

macroeconomic equilibrium
total planned expenditure
    (C + I + G + X – Im)
Keynesian cross diagram

**Appendix:
Important Terms
and Concepts**

payments equilibrium
macrodot
balance of payments line (*BP*)

**Appendix:
Completion**

macro

current

capital

balance of payments

real national income

real interest rate

internal

internal, external

deficit

low

surplus

higher

lowering

rise

Achieving and maintaining a balance of payments equilibrium is one

of the _____ (micro/macro) problems facing an economy.

Payments equilibrium occurs when a country's balance on _____

account is matched by an equal but opposite balance on its _____
account. Combinations of real income and interest rates that are
associated with payments equilibrium are identified by a

_____ line.

   A macrodot identifies the level of _____

and the _____ associated with

_____ equilibrium. When the balance of payments
line passes through the macrodot, an economy operating at the

macrodot is in _____ and _____
equilibrium.
   When an economy is in internal equilibrium with its balance of
payments line above the macrodot, the economy is experiencing a

payments _____ . This suggests that the economy's interest

rate is too _____ (high/low) to attract enough capital inflow
to offset its negative balance on current account. Similarly, when the
balance of payments line is below the macrodot, an economy at in-

ternal equilibrium is experiencing a payments _____ . In
this case, internal equilibrium is associated with an interest rate that

is _____ (higher/lower) than that needed for payments
equilibrium.
   Payments problems might be corrected by changing the level of
real income and product rather than the real interest rate. Assuming
a balance of payments deficit at internal equilibrium, an economy

could achieve payments equilibrium by _____ (raising/
lowering) real income. A surplus balance of payments at internal

equilibrium could be eliminated with a _____ (rise/fall) in
real income.

**Appendix:
Problems and
Applications**

Use the following graph to answer problems 1 and 2.

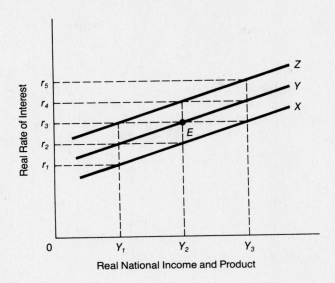

1. Assume that the economy described by the graph above is in internal equilibrium with the macrodot at E and balance of payments line X.
   a. What is the economy's current level of real national income?
   b. What is the economy's current real rate of interest?
   c. Is the economy experiencing a payments surplus or a deficit?
   d. What interest rate would enable the economy to achieve payments equilibrium without a change in national income?
   e. What level of real income would enable the economy to achieve payments equilibrium without a change in the real interest rate?

2. Assume that the economy described by the graph is in internal equilibrium with the macrodot at E and balance of payments line Z.
   a. What is the economy's current level of real national income?
   b. What is the economy's current real rate of interest?
   c. Is the economy experiencing a payments surplus or a deficit?
   d. What interest rate would enable the economy to achieve payments equilibrium without a change in national income?
   e. What level of real income would enable the economy to achieve payments equilibrium without a change in the real interest rate?

Appendix:
True-False

Indicate whether each of the following statements is basically true or false. If the statement is false, rewrite it so that it is true.

_____ 1. Payments equilibrium is any situation in which a country's balance on current account is matched by an equal but opposite balance of trade.

_____ 2. The real interest rate associated with a macrodot is such that total planned expenditure is equal to real production and the demand for the economy's stock of money is equal to its supply.

_____ 3. The balance of payments line identifies the amount of payments surplus or deficit associated with different levels of real national income.

_____ 4. If the balance of payments line lies above an economy's macrodot, a payments deficit is incurred at the income level and interest rate associated with the macrodot.

_____ 5. If the balance of payments line lies below the macrodot, payments balance requires either a lower real interest rate or a higher level of real national income.

Appendix:
Multiple Choice

Choose the _one best_ answer in each of the following cases:

_____ 1. Payments equilibrium is a situation associated with
   a. domestic equilibrium.
   b. a basic balance of zero.
   c. a trade balance of zero.
   d. all of the above
   e. none of the above

_____ 2. When an economy is operating at a macrodot, the economy must be
   a. at full employment
   b. experiencing payments equilibrium.
   c. in internal macroeconomic equilibrium.
   d. operating at its target level of national income.
   e. all of the above

_____ 3. The real interest rate at a macrodot
   a. guarantees payments equilibrium.
   b. equates total planned expenditure with aggregate supply.
   c. equates the quantity of money demanded with the stock of money.
   d. equates the demand for foreign exchange with the supply of foreign exchange.
   e. both c and d above

_____ 4. When a balance of payments line passes through a macrodot, the economy must be in
   a. internal and external equilibrium.
   b. external equilibrium with full employment.
   c. internal equilibrium with full employment.
   d. internal equilibrium with a balanced federal budget.
   e. none of the above

_____ 5. Generally, the balance of payments line is
   a. vertical.
   b. positively sloped.
   c. negatively sloped.
   d. positively sloped at relatively low income levels and negatively sloped at relatively high income levels.
   e. negatively sloped at relatively low income levels and positively sloped at relatively high income levels.

_____ 6. When an economy is so small with respect to the rest of the world that it is unable to influence its interest rate significantly, the economy
   a. will not have a macrodot.
   b. will not have a balance of payments line.
   c. can never achieve full employment and stable prices.
   d. is likely to have a horizontal balance of payments line.
   e. can never experience internal and external equilibrium.

_____ 7. When an economy is in internal equilibrium, with its balance of payments line above the macrodot, the economy must be experiencing
   a. inflation.
   b. unemployment.
   c. a payments surplus.
   d. a payments deficit.
   e. full employment and stable prices.

_____ 8. When an economy is at internal equilibrium, with a payments deficit, the economy can balance its payments by
   a. allowing its interest rate to rise.
   b. allowing its interest rate to fall.
   c. expanding real national income.
   d. both a and c above
   e. both b and c above

_____ 9. If an economy is operating at a macrodot with its balance of payments line below the macrodot, the economy
   a. is experiencing a payments deficit.
   b. is in internal and external equilibrium.
   c. is experiencing a payments equilibrium but is not in internal equilibrium.
   d. can achieve payments equilibrium by allowing a decrease in real national income.
   e. none of the above

Appendix: Discussion Questions

1. Is it possible for an economy to be operating at a macrodot and not at its targeted level of national income? Explain.

2. Assume that an economy is operating at a macrodot with a balance of payments surplus. What might the economy do to achieve payments equilibrium? Explain verbally and graphically.

3. Explain why the balance of payments line is likely to have a positive slope. Under what circumstances would the balance of payments line be horizontal? Explain.

Appendix: Answers

Problems and Applications

1. a. Y_2 b. r_3 c. payments surplus   d. r_2 e. Y_3
2. a. Y_2 b. r_3 c. payments deficit   d. r_4 e. Y_1

True-False

1. F. Payments equilibrium is any situation in which a country's balance on current account is matched by an equal but opposite balance on capital account.
2. T.
3. F. The balance of payments line identifies combinations of real national income and real interest rates associated with payments equilibrium.
4. T.
5. T.

Multiple Choice

1. e   2. c   3. c   4. a   5. b
6. d   7. d   8. a   9. e

19 Economic Growth and Development

Summary

Economic growth and development do not refer to the same thing, and either may occur without the other. Growth is measured in terms of real GNP, either total or per capita. Development, on the other hand, refers to progress or improvement.

The First World is composed of the non-Communist more-developed countries (MDCs); the Second World includes the Communist countries; and the Third World refers to all other countries, although the poorest of these are sometimes referred to as the Fourth World. There are considerable differences in income and living standards in the different "worlds." For example, in 1978, the First World countries received over five-eighths of the estimated total income, although they had less than one-sixth of the population.

There are a number of theories of economic development. Adam Smith wrote of the "natural course of things" in which a country progresses from agriculture to manufacturing to foreign trade. Marxism, which is based on the proposition that all value comes from labor, predicts the downfall of capitalism. Although the specifics differ, Marxian theories generally see capitalism leading to stagnation, imperialism, and then revolution. The dependencia theories are forms of neo-Marxism. These theories attempt to explain the underdevelopment of less-developed countries (LDCs) by going back to mercantilist times when present-day MDCs used their superiority in military technology to gain control. Later, the advocates of the dependencia theory maintain, labor movements continued to support neomercantilist ideals. Walt Rostow argued against Marxism with his institutional stage theory. According to him, there are five stages of development: traditional society, preconditions for takeoff,

takeoff, drive to maturity, and maturity itself. Once maturity is reached, it can be used in one or more of three ways: militarism and imperialism, the welfare state, and high mass consumption.

Theories of growth focus on determining the growth rate of an economy. The neoclassical theory is a supply-side explanation. According to this theory, economic growth is a weighted sum of the growth rates of the quantity and quality of an economy's inputs plus a factor reflecting technical progress. Keynesian theories of growth are demand side in approach. These theories are exemplified by one of Sir Roy Harrod's early models in which the growth rate is the economy's saving rate divided by its capital/output ratio.

There are a number of advantages associated with economic growth. In addition to fairly obvious advantages, such as increased consumption, there may be less obvious advantages associated with growth. One of these is the potential to raise the standard of living for those at the lowest levels without an absolute loss to those at the upper levels.

Economic growth is not always seen as advantageous. Antigrowth arguments date back at least to David Ricardo, who feared that growth would lead to a stationary state. Not all antigrowth theorists are concerned about a stationary state, though. John Stuart Mill defended the stationary state but attacked growthmanship, the overemphasis on measured economic growth. Some antigrowth authors concentrate on the consequences of growth for the environment, for a population's mental and physical health, and for the quality of life. Other authors focus on the limits of growth and predict catastrophe if population growth continues.

Major Objectives

After you have finished this chapter, you will be able to do the following:

1. Define and distinguish between economic growth and economic development.
2. Explain the basic human needs approach to development.
3. Distinguish and compare the First, Second, Third, and Fourth World countries.
4. Explain what is meant by the widening gap between First or Second World countries and Third World countries.
5. Describe, explain, and evaluate Adam Smith's development theory.
6. Describe and explain Marxian theories of development including the rise and fall of imperialism as viewed by Vladimir Lenin and Rosa Luxemburg.
7. Describe and explain dependencia theories of underdevelopment.

8. Describe and explain Walt Rostow's institutional stage theory.
9. Describe and explain the neoclassical theory of growth.
10. Describe and explain the Harrod growth model.
11. Cite and discuss arguments for and against economic growth.
12. Identify and discuss the limits to growth.
13. Discuss the relationship between growth and income distribution.
14. Explain the concept of economic dualism.

Review Terms

economic growth
economic development
GNP
per capita
capitalism
capital
tariffs
saving
investment

neoclassical
supply-side economics
productive inputs
productivity
automation
full employment
microeconomic
macroeconomic
stagnation

Important Terms and Concepts

less developed countries (LDCs)
more developed countries (MDCs)
economic growth
economic development
basic human needs approach (BHN)
First World
Second World
Third World
Fourth World
widening gap
Adam Smith's development theory
Marxian theories of development
exploitation of labor
imperialism
liberation movements
dependencia theories of development
mercantilism
neomercantilism
redeployment

Rostow's institutional stage theory
traditional society
preconditions for takeoff
takeoff
drive to maturity
high mass consumption
social overhead capital
maturity
neoclassical theory of growth
resource reallocations
Harrod growth model
saving rate
capital/output ratio
economic growth rate
stationary rate
diminishing returns
dismal science
growthmanship
"appropriate technology"
the Club of Rome
the Kuznets hypothesis
economic dualism

Completion

is not	Economic growth _____ (is/is not) equivalent to economic
Growth	development. _____ (Growth/Development) refers to
real	increases in _____ (real/nominal) GNP or GNP per capita,
development	whereas _____ (growth/development) more likely refers
is not	to an improved standard of living. Growth _____ (is/is not)
is not	essential for development; development _____ (is/is not)

essential for growth.

There are a number of theories of development and underdevelopment. One of these is Adam Smith's "natural course of things," in

agriculture	which an economy progresses from _____ to
manufacturing, foreign trade	_____ to _____. Smith
did not	_____ (did/did not) mention potential problems associated with

population explosion and a need to obtain resources outside the boundaries of the economy.

Marxian theories of development predict the eventual downfall of

capitalism	_____ . A major proposition of Marxian economics is
labor	that all value comes from _____ . Any profits associated with
exploitation of labor	capitalism result from the _____ .

Since capitalist profits are reinvested in machinery, production be-

capital	comes increasingly _____-intensive. Hence there are
decreasing	_____ (increasing/decreasing) opportunities to
profit	exploit labor. The result is a falling rate of _____ . Rather
consumption	than increasing their _____ as classical economists
continue	expected, Marxists contend that capitalists will _____

(continue/discontinue) accumulating and simply hoard money or cash balances. This will result in stagnation and unemployment, and eventually in the downfall of capitalism.

imperialism	Lenin theorized about _____ . He predicted that
Third World	as capital accumulated it would be exported to _____

countries where the exploitation of labor would continue. This imperialism could slow down or reverse the predicted stagnation.

would not	The LDCs _____ (would/would not) grow and develop;

profits earned in the LDCs would go mainly to residents in the

MDCs
_____ .
Not all Marxists saw the same role for imperialism. According to

markets
Luxemburg, for example, LDCs would be acquired as _____
for the products of the MDCs. In order to pay for these products,

land, mineral
resources
LDCs would sell their _____ and _____.
Both Lenin and Luxemburg predicted that the end would come

limited in size
because the Third World was also _____ .

Dependencia
_____ theories of underdevelopment come
primarily from Latin American LDCs. These theories go back to

mercantile
_____ times, when the goal of a country's economic

political (military)
power
activity was to strengthen its _____ .
Mercantilists attempted to acquire colonies first as a source of

precious metals,
industrial raw
materials
_____ and _____
for the mother country, and second to keep such riches away from

not
their rivals. Colonies were _____ (expected/not) to develop

not
modern industry; they also were _____ (expected/not) to
develop an economic base for independent political existence.

has never
According to the dependencia theories, mercantilism _____
(has/has never) died. As labor movements developed, skilled workers

neomercantilism
came to support _____ . Workers and unions

wages
demanded protection against low _____ in LDCs.
Dependency is more than a political or economic issue. It has

psychological
_____ aspects as well. Europeans and their descen-

managerial
dants took over most _____ jobs in the modern
sectors of the LDCs. The result is that many natives still doubt their
ability to run their own affairs.
Furthermore, technical progress has had different effects on LDCs

higher
and MDCs. In LDCs, progress led to _____ (higher/lower)

lower
output and _____ (higher/lower) prices on competitive ex-

higher
port markets. In MDCs, progress resulted mainly in _____
(higher/lower) profits and wages while prices remained steady or

increased
_____ (increased/decreased).

Rostow's
The institutional stage theory is exemplified by _____

five	*Stages of Economic Growth.* According to him, there are _____
traditional	stages of economic growth. The first stage, _____ society, may last a long time. In this stage, economic activity is limited to
farming, handicrafts	_____ and _____ . Stage two is
preconditions for takeoff	associated with the _____ . In this stage, countries may have accumulated roads, schools, and
social overhead capital	public health facilities, referred to as _____ . They also may have one or more leading industries. The third stage,
takeoff, one	the _____ , is quite sudden, covering about _____ generation(s). This stage is characterized by the spread of
modern methods, leading	_____ from the _____ sectors
rest of the economy	to the _____ and a sharp rise in
saving, investment	_____ and _____ , often aided by an
influx of foreign capital	_____ . After stage three,
drive to maturity	the _____ begins. This fourth stage is likely to be easier if the gains from takeoff are
reinvested, maturity	_____ . The fifth stage, _____ , is characterized by higher average labor skills and a shift in economic leadership to professionally trained managers. Once stage five is reached, it can be used in some combination of the following three
militarism and imperialism, welfare state	ways: _____ , the _____ ,
high mass consumption	and _____ .
neoclassical	Two important theories of growth are the _____
Keynesian	theory, which is a supply-side theory, and the _____ , which is a demand-side theory. According to the neoclassical theory,
weighted sum	a country's growth rate is the _____ of the
growth rates	_____ of the quantity and quality of each
inputs, technical progress	of its _____ plus a factor reflecting _____ .
Keynesian	According to an early Harrod model, which exemplifies the _____

saving rate

capital/output ratio

theory, the economic growth rate is equal to the _____

divided by the _____ .

**Problems and
Applications**

1. Economic growth can be measured as an increase in real GNP or
   as an increase in real GNP per capita. Assume that the GNP
   increases from $100 in 1900 to $120 in 1901.
   a. What was the rate of growth, according to real GNP?
   b. Calculate real GNP per capita for 1900 and for 1901 if there
      were 10 people in the economy in both 1900 and 1901. What
      was the rate of growth in population? What was the rate of
      economic growth according to real GNP per capita?
   c. Calculate real GNP per capita for 1900 and for 1901 if there
      were 10 people in the economy in 1900 and 12 people in the
      economy in 1901. What was the population growth rate?
      What was the economic growth rate according to real GNP
      per capita?
   d. Calculate real GNP per capita for 1900 and 1901 if there were
      10 people in the economy in 1900 and 20 people in the econ-
      omy in 1901. What was the population growth rate? Did the
      economy grow according to real GNP per capita?
   e. Does an increase in real GNP necessarily mean that there is an
      increase in real GNP per capita? What must be true for an
      increase in real GNP to result in an increase in real GNP per
      capita?

2. a. Assume that Economy X saves 20 percent of its national
      income and that it takes five units of capital to produce one
      more unit of output. What is the saving rate for the economy?
      What is the capital/output ratio? What is the growth rate?
   b. If the saving rate for Economy X increases to 30 percent with
      no change in the capital/output ratio, what is the growth rate?
   c. If the saving rate for Economy X is 20 percent and the
      capital/output ratio decreases from 5 to 4, what happens to
      the growth rate?

3. In general, what is the effect on economic growth of a change in
   an economy's saving rate? Explain. (Refer to problem 2 above.)

4. What is the effect on economic growth of a change in the capital/
   output ratio? Explain. (Refer to problem 2 above.)

True-False

Indicate whether each of the following statements is basically true or false. If the statement is false, rewrite it so that it is true.

_____ 1. According to the basic human needs approach, GNP must increase in order for there to be economic development.

_____ 2. Per-capita income differences between MDCs and LDCs probably exaggerate differences in living standards to the extent that people in LDCs produce relatively more "do-it-yourself" services that are not included in their GNP.

_____ 3. According to Adam Smith's theory of development, economies progress from agriculture to manufacturing to foreign trade.

_____ 4. According to Marxian economics, development ultimately leads to increased consumption and the rise of imperialism.

_____ 5. Dependencia theories of development come primarily from Latin America and are basically consistent with neoclassical theories.

_____ 6. Dependencia theories are likely to support redeployment of manufacturing capacity to LDCs.

_____ 7. Rostow's five stages of growth begin with a traditional society that advances through a takeoff stage and eventually results in maturity.

_____ 8. According to Rostow, the five stages of growth are inevitable and must occur in order.

_____ 9. Neoclassical growth theory assumes full employment of labor and capital.

_____ 10. The capital/output ratio is the amount of additional capital needed for a one-unit increase in output.

_____ 11. Neoclassical and Keynesian theories of economic growth are both demand-side theories.

_____ 12. Lester Thurow's _Zero-Sum Society_ argues that doing something about poverty is more costly to the rich and the middle class when the country's per capita income is stagnant than when it is growing.

_____ 13. Economics got its reputation as the "dismal science" from Ricardo's prediction that growth would end in a stationary state with net saving and investment of zero.

_____ 14. Growthmanship refers to the promotion of economic growth.

_____ 15. The Club of Rome refers to an international group of engineers and scientists who promote economic growth.

_____ 16. According to Kuznets, economic growth causes ever-increasing income inequality.

_____ 17. The coexistence of a modern, technologically advanced sector and a traditional, technologically retarded sector may be referred to as dualism.

Multiple Choice   Choose the *one best* answer in each of the following cases:

_____ 1. If an economy's GNP increases while its income distribution becomes more uneven, one could most reasonably conclude that the economy has experienced
a. economic growth but not economic development.
b. economic development but not economic growth.
c. both economic growth and economic development.
d. neither economic growth nor economic development.
e. economic development, but no conclusion can be drawn with respect to economic growth.

_____ 2. The basic human needs approach to development requires that
a. GNP rise over time.
b. per capita GNP rise over time.
c. everyone have the basic necessities.
d. a steadily falling percentage of the population lacks good food and decent shelter.
e. both a and b above

_____ 3. Economic development
a. always accompanies economic growth.
b. can take place even when there is no economic growth.
c. cannot exist without economic growth, although growth can exist without development.
d. exists only when real GNP is rising.
e. exists only when per capita GNP is rising.

_____ 4. Which of the following statements is true with respect to the countries that make up the four "worlds"?
a. The First World countries consist of the Communist and non-Communist MDCs.
b. The First World countries received over three-fourths of the estimated total income in 1983.
c. In 1983, more than half of the world's population lived in Second World, that is, Communist, countries.
d. Third World income is growing more rapidly than that of either the First or the Second World.
e. The Fourth World consists of the oil-exporting countries that used to be considered Third World countries.

_____ 5. Theories of development and underdevelopment include
   a. Adam Smith's theory of the "natural course of things," which emphasizes the need for natural resources.
   b. Marxian theories, which predict the downfall of capitalism.
   c. Luxemburg's theory, which predicts the triumph of imperialism.
   d. all of the above
   e. none of the above

_____ 6. According to Marxian theories of development,
   a. all value comes from capital.
   b. the profits of capitalism come from the exploitation of labor.
   c. as production becomes increasingly capital intensive, the rate of profit increases.
   d. as the rate of profit increases, capitalists increase their consumption.
   e. all of the above

_____ 7. Which of the following statements is true with respect to the role of imperialism in Marxian theories of development?
   a. Imperialism did not enter into Lenin's theory of development.
   b. According to Lenin, MDCs would be interested in Third World countries as a source of relatively cheap labor.
   c. According to Lenin, but not Luxemburg, MDCs would acquire LDCs in order to have markets for their goods.
   d. According to Luxemburg, but not Lenin, the downfall of capitalism would come because the Third World is limited in size.
   e. According to both Luxemburg and Lenin, liberation movements would begin in the imperialist countries and spread to the Third World.

_____ 8. Dependencia theories of underdevelopment
   a. tend to promote capitalism.
   b. tend to be optimistic about the future of capitalism.
   c. see Western European and U.S. labor movements as supportive of neomercantilism.
   d. refer primarily to psychological, as opposed to economic or political, dependency.
   e. generally maintain that at the start of the mercantilist age the present LDCs were undeveloped and the present MDCs were developed, giving present MDCs long-standing advantages.

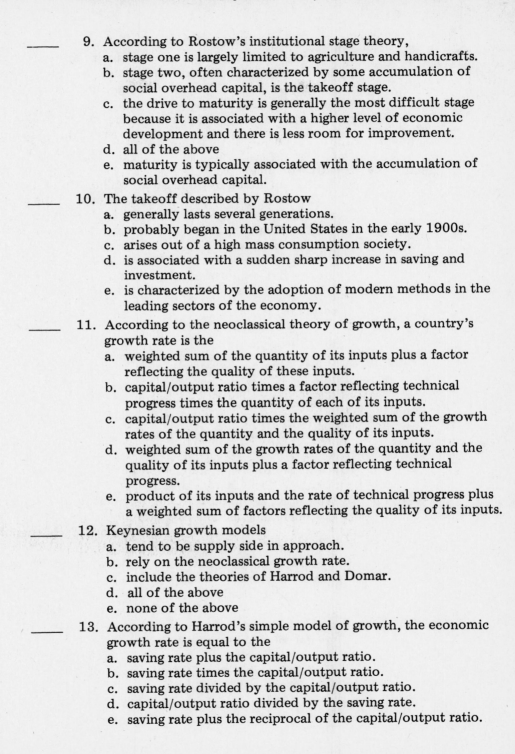

_____ 9. According to Rostow's institutional stage theory,
   a. stage one is largely limited to agriculture and handicrafts.
   b. stage two, often characterized by some accumulation of social overhead capital, is the takeoff stage.
   c. the drive to maturity is generally the most difficult stage because it is associated with a higher level of economic development and there is less room for improvement.
   d. all of the above
   e. maturity is typically associated with the accumulation of social overhead capital.

_____ 10. The takeoff described by Rostow
   a. generally lasts several generations.
   b. probably began in the United States in the early 1900s.
   c. arises out of a high mass consumption society.
   d. is associated with a sudden sharp increase in saving and investment.
   e. is characterized by the adoption of modern methods in the leading sectors of the economy.

_____ 11. According to the neoclassical theory of growth, a country's growth rate is the
   a. weighted sum of the quantity of its inputs plus a factor reflecting the quality of these inputs.
   b. capital/output ratio times a factor reflecting technical progress times the quantity of each of its inputs.
   c. capital/output ratio times the weighted sum of the growth rates of the quantity and the quality of its inputs.
   d. weighted sum of the growth rates of the quantity and the quality of its inputs plus a factor reflecting technical progress.
   e. product of its inputs and the rate of technical progress plus a weighted sum of factors reflecting the quality of its inputs.

_____ 12. Keynesian growth models
   a. tend to be supply side in approach.
   b. rely on the neoclassical growth rate.
   c. include the theories of Harrod and Domar.
   d. all of the above
   e. none of the above

_____ 13. According to Harrod's simple model of growth, the economic growth rate is equal to the
   a. saving rate plus the capital/output ratio.
   b. saving rate times the capital/output ratio.
   c. saving rate divided by the capital/output ratio.
   d. capital/output ratio divided by the saving rate.
   e. saving rate plus the reciprocal of the capital/output ratio.

_____ 14. The advantages of growth may include
   a. consumption advantages associated with higher income.
   b. increased security if crime and pollution can be controlled.
   c. additional aid to LDCs, even though they may not be experiencing similar growth.
   d. potential advantages for those at the lowest standards of living without absolute loss to those at higher standards.
   e. all of the above

_____ 15. Antigrowth arguments
   a. include an attack by John Stuart Mill on the stationary state.
   b. date back to David Ricardo, who introduced the concept of the zero-sum society.
   c. may involve a concern for the environment, as in the case of Ezra Mishan's work.
   d. can be found in the work of Erich Schumacher, who opposes growth but supports growthmanship.
   e. all of the above

_____ 16. The Club of Rome
   a. is an international group of scientists who support economic growth.
   b. recommends an ever-increasing growth rate as a way of preventing catastrophe.
   c. predicts disaster if population growth is not limited drastically in the near future.
   d. believes there is a limit to growth but does not predict doom as long as real income levels continue to rise.
   e. none of the above

_____ 17. Which of the following statements is true with respect to economic growth and income distribution?
   a. According to Simon Kuznets, economic growth leads to ever-increasing income inequality.
   b. According to the basic human needs approach, economic growth will inevitably lead to development.
   c. According to the World Bank, redistribution with growth may be possible with "appropriate technology" and an "appropriate product mix."
   d. According to Simon Kuznets, continual increases in population growth rates eventually result in decreased wages and greater income inequality.
   e. According to Harry G. Johnson, an economy that wants to experience rapid growth should insist on policies that would ensure economic equality.

_____ 18. Which of the following statements is true regarding dualism?
   a. It may be technological or regional.
   b. It is a distribution problem that may accompany economic growth.
   c. It may be a distribution problem between large cities and rural areas.
   d. It may refer to the coexistence of an agricultural and an industrial sector.
   e. all of the above

Discussion Questions

1. Explain how it is possible to have economic development without economic growth.
2. Evaluate Adam Smith's development theory from the viewpoint of a Third or Fourth World citizen.
3. Compare Walt Rostow's institutional stage theory with Marxian and dependencia theories of development.
4. Describe the development of the U.S. economy in terms of Rostow's stages.
5. Explain how economics came to be called the dismal science.
6. Do you think economic dualism increases or decreases with economic growth? Do you think economic dualism increases or decreases with economic development? Do your answers change if you begin with economic systems at different stages in their growth and development?

Answers

Problems and Applications

1. a. 20%
   b. $10; $12; 0%; 20%
   c. $10; $10; 20%; 0%
   d. $10; $6; 100%; no, real GNP per capita declined
   e. No; the population growth rate must be less than the growth in real GNP.
2. a. 20%; 5; 4%   b. 6%   c. increases from 4% to 5%
3. A change in the saving rate causes a proportional change in the growth rate in the same direction; an increase in saving makes more money available to finance investment, which increases the stock of physical capital and promotes growth.
4. A change in the capital/output ratio causes the growth rate to change in the opposite direction; a decrease in the capital/output ratio implies an increase in the productivity of capital.

True-False

1. F. According to the basic human needs approach to economic development, a country is developing only if a steadily falling percentage of its population lacks good food, clean water, decent shelter, basic health care, elementary education, and a means of presenting views to the government.
2. T.
3. T.
4. F. According to Marxian economics, development leads to stagnation, the rise and fall of imperialism, then revolution and the downfall of capitalism.
5. F. Dependencia theories of development come primarily from Latin America and are basically neo-Marxist.
6. T.
7. T.
8. F. According to Rostow, there is nothing inevitable about the five stages of growth.
9. F. Neoclassical growth theory does not assume full employment of labor and capital.
10. T.
11. F. The neoclassical theories of economic growth are supply-side explanations, and Keynesian theories are demand-side explanations.
12. T.
13. T.
14. F. Growthmanship refers to an overemphasis on measured economic growth.
15. F. The Club of Rome refers to an international group of engineers and scientists responsible for the best-known "model of doom" expressed in their publication *Limits to Growth*.
16. F. According to Kuznets, economic growth initially causes greater income inequality, but this tendency is reversed as growth progresses.
17. T.

Multiple Choice

1. a	2. d	3. b	4. b	5. b
6. b	7. b	8. c	9. a	10. d
11. d	12. c	13. c	14. e	15. c
16. c	17. c	18. e		

20 *A New International Economic Order? North-South Confrontation*

Summary

Economic relations between the First World (the North, or MDCs) and the Third World (the South, or LDCs) have deteriorated in recent decades. LDCs tend to believe that the MDCs have grown and developed because of the cheap labor and raw materials available in the LDCs. Consequently, countries of the Third World have called for a New International Economic Order (NIEO).

The specifics of the NIEO change over time, and not all LDCs support all aspects of it. Nonetheless, the major concerns of the NIEO can be expressed in fourteen proposals. Four of the fourteen proposals relate to international trade. These have to do with granting LDCs preferential access to MDC markets, the stockpiling of LDC exports, the development of LDC cartels, and redeployment of world industrial capacity to LDCs. Another four proposals deal with international financial obligations. The South is demanding additional financial reparations, an increase in concessional loans, debt renegotiation, and issuance of special drawing rights on the basis of development financing. Two of the NIEO proposals deal with internal economic policies. These relate to the development of appropriate technology and the control of multinational corporations located within LDC borders. The remaining four of the fourteen NIEO proposals deal with essentially political issues. These include demands for international control of the open sea, greater LDC input in World Bank and IMF decision making, recognition of LDC sovereignty, and MDC disarmament.

MDC responses to the call for a NIEO have ranged from acceptance to outright rejection. Most MDCs have made only token concessions to what they view as one-sided demands. As a consequence, some LDC leaders threaten to use "self-reliance." By this they mean an economic boycott of most of the First World by most of the Third World. Such a boycott would undoubtedly hurt both the North and the South.

Major Objectives　　After you have finished this chapter, you will be able to do the following:

1. Distinguish between the "North" and the "South."
2. Describe the conflict surrounding the proposal of a New International Economic Order (NIEO).
3. Identify the fourteen major proposals of the NIEO.
4. Identify and describe reactions to the NIEO.
5. Discuss the economic merits of the individual proposals of the NIEO.
6. Verbally and graphically explain the effect of preferential trade agreements for LDCs on wages, employment, income distribution, and prices.
7. Define and explain the consequences of being monocultural.
8. Explain the Prebisch thesis.
9. Define and explain the objective of cartels and the four main reasons for their failure.
10. Explain the concept and consequences of redeployment of industries.
11. Describe the Brandt Report and discuss it in terms of dependencia theory.
12. Identify and compare the attitudes of the LDCs and the MDCs toward aid.
13. Define concessional loan and indicate the primary sources of such loans.
14. Explain the concept of self-liquidating loans.
15. Identify and discuss the issues surrounding debt renegotiation.
16. Explain the concept of paper gold.
17. Discuss the issues associated with the transfer of technology under the NIEO proposal.
18. Identify and discuss the problems associated with multinational corporations as perceived by LDCs.
19. Identify and discuss the political demands in the NIEO proposal.
20. Explain why the North might be inclined to accept the NIEO proposals.

Review Terms

First World
Third World
economic growth
development
more developed countries
  (MDCs)
less developed countries
  (LDCs)
protectionism
International Monetary Fund
  (IMF)
capital
human capital
trade balance
imports
exports
real vs. money wage rates

factors of production
change in quantity demanded vs.
  change in demand
business cycles
foreign exchange
OPEC
redeployment
transfer payments
dependencia theory
liquidity
international reserve accounts
balance of payments deficit
balance of payments surplus
Special Drawing Rights (SDRs)
  or paper gold
appropriate technology

**Important Terms
and Concepts**

"North"
"South"
North–South conflict
New International Economic
  Order (NIEO)
World Bank or International
  Bank for Reconstruction and
  Development
brain drain
"East"
"West"
tokenism
buck passing
splitting the LDC bloc
preferential access
light manufactures
labor intensive
subsistence
stockpiles or buffer stocks
monocultural
Prebisch thesis
price parity

collective bargaining
collusive bargaining
Common Fund
cartel
Brandt Report
reparations
tied grant
concessional loan
self-liquidating loan
recycled deposits
debt renegotiation
multinational corporation (MNC)
patent
neocolonialism
destabilization
law of the sea
European Economic Community
  (EEC)
sovereignty
boycott
disarmament
self-reliance

Completion

do not	As part of the NIEO, LDCs generally _____ (do/do not)
preferential access	promote free trade. Most of them want _____
do not	to MDC markets; in return, they _____ (do/do not) propose
	to give MDCs preferential access to their markets.
unskilled	LDC labor is primarily _____ (skilled/unskilled) and
low	hence earns _____ (high/low) wages. With freer trade, LDCs
light manufactures	would probably produce _____ for export,
labor	because these industries tend to be _____-intensive. If the
	LDCs could export these goods, demand for their workers would
increase	_____ (increase/decrease), as would the wages paid to
	these workers. Of course, this means that demand for low-skilled
decrease	MDC workers is likely to _____ (increase/decrease),
fall	causing their wages to _____ (rise/fall). Freer trade, then, would
decrease	tend to _____ (increase/decrease) differences in real
	wage rates for these workers.
	In terms of world income distribution, the freer access would lead
less	to _____ (greater/less) inequality. In terms of income distribu-
inequality	tion within MDCs, however, there is likely to be greater _____
	(equality/inequality). This is because the increased trade would dis-
unskilled	place _____ (skilled/unskilled) workers who already
disadvantage	have a(n) _____ (advantage/disadvantage) in the
	labor force of the MDCs.
gain	MDC consumers of the goods involved would _____ (gain/lose)
	as a result of the trade, since MDC prices of these goods would tend
fall	to _____ (rise/fall). LDC consumers of these goods would end
higher	up paying _____ (higher/lower) prices than before the trade.
LDCs	The NIEO also proposes that the storable exports of _____
stockpiled	(MDCs/LDCs) be _____ by an internationally financed
	organization. Surplus goods would be bought and stored during MDC
recessions, boom years	_____ and be sold during MDC _____ .
LDC	The purpose of this stockpiling would be to assure that _____

stable, profitable

(MDC/LDC) producers would have _____ and _____ prices, regardless of the economic conditions in MDCs.

The NIEO proposes that the several stockpiling plans of the South

Common Fund

be brought together in a _____ so that net losses on one good could be covered by net profits on other goods. The Fund

United Nations

would be financed by the _____ , largely out of

MDC taxpayers

money provided by _____ . If the Common Fund

low-interest loans

has enough resources, it would provide _____ to LDCs.

Problems and Applications

1. a. Assume that the graph below represents a market for LDC labor before preferential access to MDC markets. What is likely to happen in this market if preferential access is granted? What is the consequence for the real wage rate and employment in the LDC?

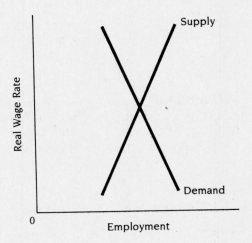

b. Assume that the graph above represents a market for MDC labor before LDCs are given preferential access to MDC markets. What is likely to happen in this market if preferential access is given to LDCs? What is the likely consequence for the real wage rate and employment in the MDC?

2. a. Assume that the graph below represents a market for a good that is typically produced by LDCs and exported to MDCs. What is likely to happen to supply in this market if the LDCs form a cartel for this product? Assuming that MDCs do not currently have appropriate substitutes for this good, what is likely to happen to the price of this good and the quantity traded?

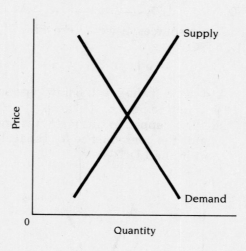

   b. What is likely to happen in the market above if the MDCs develop substitutes for the good? What is likely to happen to the price of this good and the quantity traded? (Answer in terms of the post-cartel price and quantity.)

True-False   Indicate whether each of the following statements is basically true or false. If the statement is false, rewrite it so that it is true.

_____   1. Economic relations between the North and the South have generally improved since 1960.

_____   2. The NIEO demands include proposals that relate to international economic issues, internal economic issues, and political issues.

_____   3. NIEO demands have increased over time, both in number and in variety.

_____   4. The "brain drain" is another term for Third World Human capital.

_____   5. The MDCs have met as an international group and coordinated their replies to the NIEO demands so that they respond in a uniform fashion.

_____ 6. Reaction to NIEO proposals seems to depend, in part, on the state of East–West relations: when such relations improve, each side seems less interested in LDC problems; in contrast, the cold war seems to mean competition to win over the LDCs.

_____ 7. The NIEO demands call for free trade.

_____ 8. A labor-intensive production process uses a lot of labor for each unit of output.

_____ 9. The South tends to support international stockpiling of its storable goods.

_____ 10. LDCs are generally not monocultural.

_____ 11. A country is monocultural when its source of foreign exchange is the export of a good whose world markets are sensitive to cyclical problems in the buying countries.

_____ 12. The Prebisch thesis maintains that the market system has developed in a manner that is unfair to agricultural and raw materials producers.

_____ 13. In their demand for redeployment of industries, the South proposes that unskilled-labor-intensive industries be located in LDCs.

_____ 14. The Brandt Report recommends that foreign aid to LDCs continue but does not recommend any specific levels of aid.

_____ 15. After allowing for inflation, interest rates on concessional loans are often negative.

_____ 16. The total of all LDC debts, new and old, was estimated at nearly $1 trillion in 1985.

_____ 17. Special drawing rights are sometimes referred to as "paper gold."

_____ 18. The NIEO proposes that all patents be abolished.

_____ 19. One of the NIEO demands is for the establishment of a U.N. agency that would have exclusive rights to license and/or carry on seabed exploration.

_____ 20. Among the essentially political issues raised by the NIEO is the demand for unconditional recognition of LDC sovereignty over natural resources and capital located within their borders.

Multiple Choice   Choose the *one best* answer in each of the following cases:

_____   1. NIEO refers to
     a. New International Economic Order.
     b. New International Energy Organization.
     c. National Involvement in Energy-Related Occupations.
     d. National–International Economic Organization.
     e. Network of International Economic Organizations.

_____   2. The NIEO is
     a. generally supported in full by the MDCs.
     b. a set of proposals voiced mainly by LDCs.
     c. evidence of improvement in North–South relations.
     d. a list of fourteen demands, all of which directly relate to international trade.
     e. all of the above

_____   3. In discussing the NIEO, the North–South conflict essentially refers to the conflict between
     a. North and South America.
     b. Yankees and Confederates.
     c. the First and Third Worlds.
     d. North Dakota and South Dakota.
     e. countries separated by the Equator.

_____   4. NIEO proposals
     a. are not supported by any MDC.
     b. are generally voiced through the United Nations.
     c. currently include an international tax.
     d. deal primarily with East–West relations.
     e. seek to unite First and Second World countries.

_____   5. MDC strategies for responding to the NIEO demands have included
     a. "tokenism."
     b. "buck passing."
     c. "splitting" the LDC bloc.
     d. all of the above
     e. none of the above

_____   6. With respect to trade balance issues, LDCs generally support
     a. free trade throughout the world.
     b. free trade between MDCs and LDCs.
     c. preferential access to MDC markets for LDCs.
     d. preferential access to LDC markets for MDCs.
     e. both c and d above

_____ 7. In terms of world production, LDCs
   a. have nothing to contribute.
   b. typically specialize in the provision of services.
   c. should attempt to acquire heavy-manufacturing industries.
   d. have relatively low wages.
   e. are likely to excel when it comes to capital-intensive production.

_____ 8. The NIEO recommends international stockpiling
   a. except when a country is monocultural.
   b. to stabilize the prices of LDC exports.
   c. only when MDCs are experiencing prosperity.
   d. to protect MDCs from changes brought about by business cycles.
   e. of perishable necessities so that they will be available for LDCs.

_____ 9. In general, international cartels
   a. for copper, tin, and rubber have been successful.
   b. attempt to lower the prices of controlled commodities.
   c. are less successful when production is geographically widespread.
   d. are more successful when there are natural substitutes for the controlled commodities.
   e. are more successul when there are manufactured substitutes for the controlled commodities.

_____ 10. In their support of redeployment, the South recommends
   a. that new capacity be concentrated mainly in the LDCs.
   b. the physical movement of existing plant and equipment.
   c. that unskilled-labor-intensive industries be moved to the MDCs.
   d. all of the above
   e. none of the above

_____ 11. The Brandt Report recommends that
   a. military spending be increased.
   b. the dependencia theory be disregarded.
   c. capital-intensive industries be redeployed.
   d. foreign aid from each MDC increase to 1.0 percent of GNP per year by the year 2000.
   e. foreign aid decrease steadily with the intention that it be eliminated entirely by the year 2000.

_____ 12. MDC objections to foreign aid are *least* likely to include the argument that
   a. the aid is tied to specific uses.
   b. the aid fails to reach its targets.
   c. LDCs do not show sufficient gratitude.
   d. they (the MDCs) have domestic uses for the funds.
   e. LDC production competes with production in the granting country.

_____ 13. With regard to concessional loans, the South would generally like to see them
   a. abolished entirely.
   b. replace grants-in-aid.
   c. continued at higher interest rates.
   d. discontinued in favor of short-term loans.
   e. freed from any requirement that recipients must make profits.

_____ 14. To say that a loan is self-liquidating means that the loan is
   a. made in cash form.
   b. unlikely to be repaid.
   c. to be used to establish a financial institution.
   d. to be repaid out of revenues from projects it supported.
   e. made in reparation for war damages and mercantilistic practices.

_____ 15. Proposals for debt renegotiation on the part of the non-oil-producing countries of the Third World
   a. often amount to a decrease in real interest rates.
   b. are designed to cause formal repudiation or default.
   c. generally recommend an increase in nominal interest rates.
   d. generally recommend shortening the life of outstanding loans.
   e. all of the above

_____ 16. With respect to SDRs, the NIEO proposes that
   a. the number of issues be decreased.
   b. they be eliminated in favor of paper gold.
   c. the South receive the major portion of each new issue.
   d. they be brought under the control of the International Monetary Fund.
   e. none of the above

_____ 17. Which of the following is true with respect to technology?
   a. The South prefers technology that is not economically efficient.
   b. Most Northern technology has been designed for use by unskilled labor.
   c. According to the South, "appropriate technology" is capital intensive.

    d. The NIEO proposes that the North actually develop capital-intensive technology for the South.

    e. none of the above

_____ 18. Multinationals

    a. are sometimes larger than LDC governments.

    b. may be involved in neocolonialist situations.

    c. often give development aid to their LDC host countries.

    d. may encourage their home governments to engage in destabilization policies.

    e. all of the above

_____ 19. With respect to the voting rights of the World Bank and the IMF, the NIEO would change them

    a. in favor of present and potential debtor countries.

    b. in order to tie voting rights to financial contribution.

    c. both a and b above

    d. in order to give veto power to the European Economic Community.

    e. under no circumstances.

_____ 20. When "self-reliance" is suggested as an economic weapon in the North–South conflict, it typically refers to

    a. the termination of trade between First World countries.

    b. an economic boycott of most of the Third World by most of the First World.

    c. an economic boycott of most of the First World by most of the Third World.

    d. the termination of international relations between countries of the Third World.

    e. none of the above

Discussion Questions

1. On what grounds do the LDCs base their claims against the MDCs? In general, do you think the South is justified in its call for a new international economic order?

2. Which of the fourteen main NIEO proposals would you support? Why?

3. What type of preferential trade agreements for LDCs would you support? Why? Would your position change if your job and/or income changed? If so, explain why.

4. Evaluate foreign aid according to the dependencia theory.

5. Do LDCs benefit when multinational corporations locate within their borders? Why do LDCs complain about multinational corporations?

6. Explain why the North might be willing to accept the NIEO proposals.

7. Do you think self-reliance on the part of the South would be sufficiently damaging that the North should respond more favorably to the NIEO proposals? What would be the harmful repercussions of self-reliance for the North? What would be the harmful repercussions of self-reliance for the South?

Answers

Problems and Applications

1. a. demand for labor will rise; real wage rate will rise; employment will rise
   b. demand for labor will fall; real wage rate will fall; employment will fall
2. a. supply will fall; price will rise; quantity traded will fall
   b. demand will fall; price will fall; quantity traded will fall

True-False

1. F. Economic relations between the North and the South have deteriorated since about 1960.
2. T.
3. T.
4. F. The "brain drain" occurs when people educated in Third World countries live and work in the First World.
5. F. The MDC response to the NIEO demands varies within countries as well as from country to country.
6. T.
7. F. The NIEO demands call for LDCs to have preferential access to MDC markets, though there is no proposal for special reciprocal treatment for MDCs.
8. T.
9. T.
10. F. Many LDCs are monocultural.
11. T.
12. T.
13. T.
14. F. The Brandt Report recommended that foreign aid rise to 0.7 percent of GNP a year by 1985 and to 1.0 percent by the year 2000.
15. T.
16. T.
17. T.

18. F. The NIEO proposes licensing of MDC patents to an international agency that would act on behalf of LDCs.
19. T.
20. T.

Multiple Choice

1. a	2. b	3. c	4. b	5. d
6. c	7. d	8. b	9. c	10. a
11. d	12. a	13. e	14. d	15. a
16. c	17. e	18. e	19. a	20. c

21 *Consumer Choice*

Summary

Utility refers to expected satisfaction. When it is assumed to be measurable, a unit of utility is called a util. Total utility associated with the consumption of a good, then, would be the total number of utils associated with that consumption. Marginal utility is the change in total utility associated with the consumption of an additional unit.

Utility analysis enables us to explain the law of demand and to construct demand curves. In order to do so, we make six assumptions. Consumers are assumed to be rational. This means that they attempt to maximize utility subject to their incomes. Utility is assumed to be measurable. As consumption of a good increases, total utility is assumed to increase and marginal utility is assumed to diminish. Finally, consumers are assumed to have limited incomes and to know the prices of all the goods and services they might buy. These limited incomes and prices serve to constrain consumer behavior.

A rational consumer will be in equilibrium when he or she maximizes utility subject to the income constraint. This will occur when the marginal utility per dollar spent is the same for all goods purchased.

When a consumer experiences diminishing marginal utility for a good and is charged a uniform price, he or she receives a consumer surplus. This is the difference between what the consumer would be willing to pay for the good and what he or she has to pay.

Often we observe people paying lower prices for "necessities" than for "luxuries." Utility theory can help us understand this paradox of value. Total utility represents the value in use associated with the consumption of a good. The value in exchange is associated with the marginal utility. With diminishing marginal utility and uniform prices, value in exchange is typically less than value in use. This difference between value in use and value in exchange is also what gives rise to the consumer surplus.

Major Objectives   After you have finished this chapter, you will be able to do the following:

1. State the law of demand and briefly explain it, using the concepts of substitution and income effects.
2. Define utility and marginal utility.
3. State and explain the six assumptions of utility analysis.
4. Define util and explain its importance in utility analysis.
5. Discuss the problems associated with making interpersonal utility comparisons.
6. State and explain the principle of diminishing marginal utility.
7. Identify and discuss exceptions to the principle of diminishing marginal utility.
8. Construct marginal utility schedules and curves, identify the nature of the relationship between the quantity of a good and marginal utility, and explain this relationship.
9. Construct total utility schedules and curves, given information reflecting marginal utility.
10. Identify and explain the nature of the relationship between the quantity of a good and total utility.
11. Discuss the possibility and meaning of declining total utility and its implications for marginal utility.
12. Explain how a rational individual decides what to purchase, given necessary information about utility, income, and prices.
13. Define consumer equilibrium.
14. Identify and explain the conditions for consumer equilibrium.
15. Determine the equilibrium position for a consumer, given necessary information about utility, prices, and income.
16. Derive consumer demand schedules and curves, given necessary information about utility, prices, and income.
17. Define and discuss the validity and importance of the assumption of consumer sovereignty.
18. Discuss the relationship between consumer sovereignty and utility analysis.
19. Define consumer surplus.
20. Calculate the total utility and the consumer surplus associated with a particular purchase, given a marginal utility curve and a uniform price.

21. Graphically illustrate the total utility and the consumer surplus associated with a particular purchase, given a marginal utility curve and a uniform price.
22. Calculate the amount a consumer would be willing to pay and the total expenditure, given a demand curve and a uniform price.
23. Graphically illustrate the amount a consumer would be willing to pay and the total expenditure, given a demand curve and a uniform price.
24. Calculate the consumers' surplus associated with a particular purchase, given a demand curve and a uniform price.
25. Graphically illustrate the consumers' surplus associated with a particular purchase, given a demand curve and a uniform price.
26. Identify and explain the two economic principles that give rise to consumers' surplus.
27. Define, explain, and graphically illustrate (on a marginal utility curve) the concepts of value in use and value in exchange.
28. State, explain, and resolve (verbally and graphically) the paradox of value.

Review Terms

microeconomics
individual demand
inverse relationship
quantity demanded
law of demand
ceteris paribus
income effect
substitution effect
real income

substitute goods
theory
economic rationality
marginal
negative vs. positive slope
equilibrium
market-capitalist system
positive vs. normative economics

Important Terms and Concepts

utility analysis
utility
marginal utility
commodity
total utility
util
subjective
conspicuous consumption
diminishing marginal utility
addiction
set completion
increasing total utility
income
"living within one's income"

saving
future income
transaction prices
marginal utility per dollar
   expenditure
consumer equilibrium
consumers' sovereignty
"perfect conditions"
consumer surplus
uniform market price
paradox of value
value in use
value in exchange

Completion

expected satisfaction

utils

increase

decrease

income, prices

rational

maximize utility

income

equilibrium

marginal utility

dollar spent

more

less

decreases

increases

diminishing marginal utility

equals

equilibrium

decreases

no longer

buy fewer units of good I

There are six assumptions associated with utility analysis. Utility, meaning _____ , is assumed to be measurable. When we make this assumption, utility is measured in _____ . As the consumption of a good increases, total utility is assumed to _____ (increase/decrease) and marginal utility is assumed to _____ (increase/decrease). Consumers are assumed to have limited _____ and to know the _____ of all goods and services they might purchase. Finally, consumers are assumed to be _____ . This means that consumers will attempt to _____ subject to their _____ constraints.

A rational consumer will be in _____ when he or she has maximized utility, subject to the appropriate income constraint. This condition requires that the _____ per _____ be the same for all goods purchased.

Consider a situation in which a consumer has quantities of two goods I and J such that the marginal utility per dollar spent on good I exceeds the marginal utility per dollar spent on good J. In such a circumstance the consumer could increase utility by buying _____ (more/less) of good I and _____ (more/less) of good J. When the consumer puts back units of J in order to purchase additional units of I, the marginal utility per dollar spent on I _____ (increases/decreases) and the marginal utility per dollar spent on J _____ (increases/decreases). This is due to _____ . The consumer should continue in this fashion until the marginal utility per dollar spent on good I _____ the marginal utility per dollar spent on J.

Now that the consumer is in _____ , assume that the price of good I increases. When the price of good I increases, the marginal utility per dollar spent on I _____ (increases/decreases). The consumer is _____ (still/no longer) in equilibrium. In order to maximize utility, the consumer should _____ (do nothing/buy more units of good I/buy fewer units of good I). That is, when the price of good I increases, *ceteris paribus*, the quantity demanded

decreases, is   of good I _____ (increases/decreases). This _____ (is/is not) consistent with the law of demand.

Problems and Applications

1. The following two schedules show the total utility a consumer would get from consuming various quantities of products M and N. Assume that it is impossible to buy partial units of M and N.

Units of M	Total Utility	Marginal Utility	Units of N	Total Utility	Marginal Utility
1	178		1	182	
2	202		2	210	
3	218		3	234	
4	230		4	254	
5	240		5	266	
6	248		6	276	
7	254		7	284	

a. Complete the schedules above by determining the marginal utility associated with the consumption of additional units of M and N.

b. Are the utility schedules of M and N consistent with the principle of diminishing marginal utility?

c. If the consumer has a budget of $20 to spend on M and N and if the prices of M and N are $4 each, what combination of M and N will maximize the consumer's utility? What will be the consumer's total utility if he makes this purchase?

d. If the price of M is $4 and the price of N is $2 and if the consumer has $18 to spend on M and N, how many units of each will be purchased by a rational consumer? What will be the consumer's total utility if he makes this purchase?

e. If the prices of M and N are $4 and $2, respectively, and if the consumer has $26, how many units of M and N will be purchased at equilibrium? What will be the consumer's total utility if he makes this purchase?

2. Consider the following marginal utility schedules for goods X and Y. Assume that a rational consumer has $20 to spend on the goods and that it is impossible to buy partial units.

Quantity of Good	Marginal Utility of X	Marginal Utility of Y
1	18	30
2	16	25
3	12	20
4	10	15
5	8	13
6	6	10

a. If the prices of X and Y are $2 each, how many units of X and Y will be purchased? What will be the consumer's total utility from this purchase?

b. What combination of X and Y will be purchased if the price of Y increases to $3 with no change in the price of X? How much utility will be associated with this purchase.

c. Construct a demand schedule for good Y. What assumption had to be made in order to construct the demand schedule? Was this requirement satisfied? Explain.

3. Consider the marginal utility curve in the graph below. Assume that the consumer purchases 100 units of the good at a uniform price.

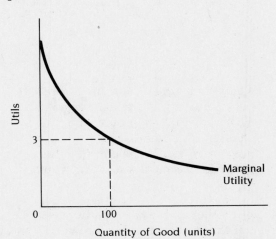

a. What is the marginal utility of the 100th unit of the good?

b. Graphically identify the total utility associated with this purchase.

c. Graphically identify the value in use associated with consumption of the 100 units.

    d. Graphically identify the value in exchange associated with consumption of the 100 units.

    e. Graphically identify the consumers' surplus associated with this purchase (measuring consumers' surplus in utils).

4. Consider the demand curve in the graph below. Assume a uniform market price of $6 per unit.

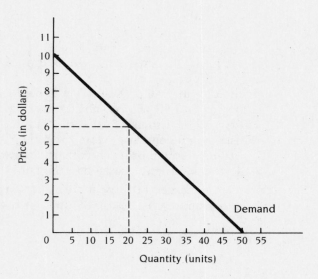

    a. How many units will be purchased at this price?

    b. What will be the total expenditure? Represent the total expenditure as an area on the graph.

    c. What is the dollar amount of consumer surplus? Graphically represent this amount.

    d. How much would the consumer be willing to pay for the good? Represent this amount graphically.

True-False

Indicate whether each of the following statements is basically true or false. If the statement is false, rewrite it so that it is true.

_____ 1. Utility refers to the usefulness of a good.

_____ 2. Consumer rationality means that the consumer attempts to maximize utility, subject to existing constraints.

_____ 3. Most modern economists would agree that interpersonal utility comparisons are not valid.

_____ 4. Marginal utility is the change in total utility associated with consuming an additional unit of a good.

_____ 5. If the total utility associated with consuming 3 units of a good is 14 and the total utility associated with consuming 4 units of the good is 18, the marginal utility of the fourth unit of the good is 1.

_____ 6. If total utility is increasing, marginal utility must be increasing.

_____ 7. When marginal utility is positive and diminishing, total utility is positive and diminishing.

_____ 8. Utility analysis assumes diminishing marginal utility.

_____ 9. Linder's book *The Harried Leisure Class* suggests that people's consumption has reached the point of not only diminishing but also negative marginal utility.

_____ 10. A consumer is in equilibrium when marginal utility per dollar spent is maximized.

_____ 11. Consumer sovereignty means that the consumer rules, that, within constraints, the consumer makes the decisions.

_____ 12. Consumers' surplus is the difference between what you would be willing to pay for a good and what you have to pay.

_____ 13. Value in use is measured by the marginal utility of the last unit purchased.

_____ 14. The paradox of value refers to the improbability of consumer surplus.

Multiple Choice   Choose the *one best* answer in each of the following cases:

_____ 1. It is typical for a demand curve to be
   a. vertical.
   b. horizontal.
   c. negatively sloped.
   d. positively sloped.
   e. indeterminant in slope.

_____ 2. Substitution and income effects are usually used to explain
   a. consumer surplus.
   b. the law of demand.
   c. the paradox of value.
   d. negative total utility.
   e. the principle of diminishing marginal utility.

_____ 3. Utility is best defined as
   a. usefulness.
   b. consumer surplus.
   c. the price of a good.
   d. expected satisfaction.
   e. value in exchange minus value in use.

_____ 4. Which of the following is *not* consistent with utility analysis?
  a. knowledge of prices
  b. consumer rationality
  c. increasing total utility
  d. diminishing marginal utility
  e. objectivity in determining utility

_____ 5. When we assume that utility is measurable, we measure it in
  a. tilis.
  b. utils.
  c. inches.
  d. measures.
  e. none of the above

_____ 6. Consumer rationality means that a consumer
  a. is always in equilibrium.
  b. has perfect information about the market.
  c. seeks to maximize utility, subject to constraints.
  d. always pays more for necessities than for luxuries.
  e. all of the above

_____ 7. Marginal utility is equal to
  a. 1/(total utility).
  b. (total utility)/(quantity).
  c. (quantity)/(total utility).
  d. (change in total utility) X (quantity).
  e. (change in total utility)/(change in quantity).

_____ 8. The marginal utility of a good refers to the
  a. total utility of the good prior to consumption of the last unit.
  b. extra utility associated with consuming another unit of the good.
  c. utility associated with consuming an alternative good.
  d. consumer surplus associated with the consumption of an alternative good.
  e. difference between total utility and the utility associated with an additional unit of the good.

_____ 9. When total utility is positive, we know that marginal utility is
  a. positive.
  b. increasing.
  c. both a and b above
  d. greater than total utility.
  e. none of the above

_____ 10. Negative marginal utility implies that
   a. total utility is negative.
   b. total utility is diminishing.
   c. marginal utility is diminishing.
   d. both a and b above
   e. all of the above

_____ 11. When total utility is increasing at a decreasing rate, we know that marginal utility is
   a. positive.
   b. negative.
   c. diminishing.
   d. both a and c above
   e. both b and c above

_____ 12. Economists generally assume that consumption of additional units of the same good during a specified time period eventually result in
   a. negative total utility.
   b. decreasing total utility.
   c. negative marginal utility.
   d. increasing marginal utility.
   e. decreasing marginal utility.

_____ 13. Exceptions to the principle of diminishing marginal utility
   a. are called "bads."
   b. may include cases of addiction and set completion.
   c. are fairly common, but utility analysis disregards them.
   d. demonstrate the notion that "variety is the spice of life."
   e. all of the above

_____ 14. In utility analysis, income and prices
   a. constrain the consumer.
   b. are unknown to the consumer.
   c. are unimportant in decision making.
   d. reflect the consumer's subjective evaluation of the circumstances.
   e. none of the above

_____ 15. Consider a consumer who has a fixed budget, all of which is spent on goods X and Y. If the prices of X and Y are P_X and P_Y, respectively, the consumer will be in equilibrium when
   a. $(MU_X)/(P_X) = (MU_Y)/(P_Y)$.
   b. $(TU_X)/(P_X) = (TU_Y)/(P_Y)$.
   c. $(MU_X) \times (P_X) = (MU_Y) \times (P_Y)$.
   d. $(TU_X) \times (P_X) = (TU_Y) \times (P_Y)$.
   e. $(MU_X) - (P_X) = (MU_Y) - (P_Y)$.

_____ 16. Mary is about to purchase 3 units of A and 2 units of B. The total utility associated with the 3 units of A is 12 and the total utility associated with the 2 units of B is 8. Assume that A and B are both priced at $1 per unit and that Mary has $5 to spend on A and B. Which of the following conclusions could you accurately draw from the information given?
   a. Mary is in equilibrium.
   b. In order to maximize utility, Mary should buy more of A and less of B.
   c. In order to maximize utility, Mary should buy more of B and less of A.
   d. Given another dollar, Mary should buy an additional unit of B.
   e. none of the above

_____ 17. Mary is about to purchase 3 units of A and 2 units of B. The marginal utility of A is 12 and the marginal utility of B is 8. Assume that A and B are both priced at $1 per unit and that Mary has $5 to spend on A and B. Which of the following conclusions could you accurately draw from the information given?
   a. Mary is in equilibrium.
   b. In order to maximize utility, Mary should buy more of A and less of B.
   c. In order to maximize utility, Mary should buy more of B and less of A.
   d. Given another dollar, Mary should buy an additional unit of B.
   e. none of the above

_____ 18. Tom is planning to purchase 3 units of good X and 5 units of good Y. Assume that the marginal utility of X is 18 and the marginal utility of Y is 30. The price of good X is $2 per unit and the price of good Y is $3 per unit. Which of the following conclusions could you accurately draw from the information given?
   a. Tom currently has a total utility of 48.
   b. In order to maximize utility, Tom should buy more X and less Y.
   c. If Tom wants to maximize utility, he should not make any changes.
   d. both a and c above
   e. none of the above

_____ 19. A consumer with a fixed income will maximize utility when each good is purchased in amounts such that the
   a. total utility is the same for all goods.
   b. marginal utility is the same for each good.

  c. marginal utility of each good is maximized.
  d. marginal utility per dollar expenditure is the same for all goods.
  e. marginal utility per dollar expenditure is maximized for each good.

_____ 20. Consumer sovereignty means that
  a. there is no advertising.
  b. there are no constraints on consumers.
  c. consumers make all the decisions in an economy.
  d. all of the above
  e. none of the above

_____ 21. If you would be willing to pay $50 for a good and have to pay only $40 for it, you would have
  a. value in use of $40.
  b. a consumer surplus of $10.
  c. a marginal utility of $10.
  d. illustrated the paradox of value.
  e. a total utility of 50 and a marginal utility of 10.

_____ 22. Consumer surplus can be measured by the
  a. marginal utility of the last unit purchased.
  b. degree of consumer sovereignty in the marketplace.
  c. difference between regular price and sale price.
  d. difference between value in use and value in exchange.
  e. none of the above

_____ 23. Diminishing marginal utility is useful in explaining
  a. the existence of consumer surplus.
  b. the paradox of value.
  c. the law of demand.
  d. all of the above
  e. consumer sovereignty.

Discussion Questions

1. Provide some examples illustrating the influence of environment on utility.

2. If we assume that interpersonal utility comparisons are legitimate, the progressive income tax can be justified on the grounds of diminishing marginal utility. Explain.

3. How would you define a "bad" (the opposite of a good) in terms of utility? Is declining total utility sufficient? What does declining total utility indicate?

4. What is the utility-maximizing condition if a consumer derives utility out of holding money? (Consider what the price is of holding $1 of money.)

5. Explain how the *ceteris paribus* assumption is upheld when using utility theory to construct a demand relationship.

6. Use utility analysis to verify the law of demand.

7. Does utility analysis require perfect information? Explain.

8. Identify real-world pricing schemes that diminish or eliminate the consumers' surplus. Explain.

9. State and resolve the paradox of value.

Answers

Problems and Applications

1. a.

Marginal Utility of M	Marginal Utility of N
178	182
24	28
16	24
12	20
10	12
8	10
6	8

  b. yes

  c. 2 units of M and 3 units of N; 436 utils

  d. 2 units of M and 5 units of N; 468 utils

  e. 3 units of M and 7 units of N; 502 utils

2. a. 4 units of X and 6 units of Y; 169 utils

  b. 4 units of X and 4 units of Y; 146 utils

  c.

Price of Y	Quantity of Y
$2	6
$3	4

the *ceteris paribus* assumption; yes; income and the price of good X were held constant while the price of good Y changed.

3. a. 3 utils
   b. shaded area in graph below
   c. shaded area in graph below
   d. area in graph below marked by horizontal lines
   e. area in graph below marked by vertical lines

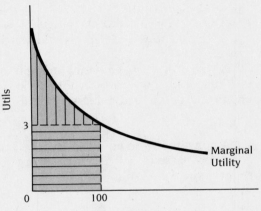

4. a. 20
   b. $120; area on graph below marked by horizontal lines
   c. $40; area on graph below marked by vertical lines
   d. $160; shaded area on graph below

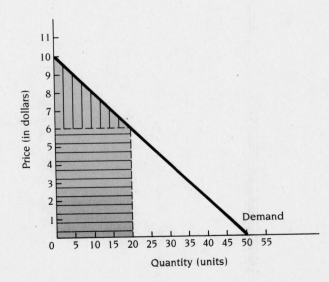

True-False

1. F. Utility refers to expected satisfaction.
2. T.
3. T.
4. T.
5. F. If the total utility associated with consuming 3 units of a good is 14 and the total utility associated with consuming 4 units of the good is 18, the marginal utility of the fourth unit of the good is 4.
6. F. If total utility is increasing, marginal utility must be positive.
7. F. When marginal utility is positive and diminishing, total utility is increasing at a decreasing rate.
8. T.
9. T.
10. F. A consumer is in equilibrium when the combination of goods purchased is such that the marginal utility per dollar spent is the same for all goods.
11. T.
12. T.
13. F. Value in use is measured by total utility; value in exchange is measured by the marginal utility of the last unit purchased.
14. F. The paradox of value refers to the fact that consumers often pay higher prices for "luxuries" than for "necessities."

Multiple Choice

1. c	2. b	3. d	4. e	5. b
6. c	7. e	8. b	9. e	10. b
11. d	12. e	13. b	14. a	15. a
16. e	17. b	18. e	19. d	20. e
21. b	22. d	23. d		

Study Guide material for *Chapter 21, Appendix,* follows.

Appendix: Summary

Indifference curve analysis is another approach to studying consumer behavior. It couples an indifference map with a budget line to determine a rational consumer's equilibrium purchase combination. The indifference map is a collection of indifference curves that define the consumer's preference system. An indifference curve shows the various combinations of two goods that the consumer finds equally satisfactory. The budget line shows those combinations of the two goods that the consumer is able to purchase with a given money income and the prices of the goods. Equilibrium occurs at a point of tangency between an indifference curve and the budget line.

Indifference curve analysis requires that the consumer be able to rank his or her preferences. But, unlike utility analysis, it does not require that one measure utility. In this sense it is superior to utility analysis. Like utility analysis, indifference analysis can be used to construct demand curves.

Appendix: Major Objectives

After you have finished this appendix, you will be able to do the following:

1. State and explain the assumptions underlying indifference curve analysis and compare these to the assumptions associated with utility analysis.
2. Explain the meaning of indifference curves, graphically represent them, and explain their shape.
3. Define and construct indifference maps.
4. Evaluate an indifference map in terms of the indicated preferences.
5. Explain why two indifference curves cannot intersect.
6. Discuss and compare the meanings of indifference curves that are negatively sloped, positively sloped, horizontal, and vertical.
7. Discuss and compare the meanings of indifference curves that are bowed in and bowed out.
8. Define perfect substitutes in terms of indifference curve analysis.
9. Define and graphically construct the budget line.
10. Identify the combinations that an individual is able to buy, given a budget line.
11. Indicate the effect on a budget line of an income or price change.
12. Identify the objective and the subjective components of indifference curve analysis.
13. Identify and explain the utility-maximizing or equilibrium position using indifference curve analysis.
14. Express and explain the behavioral opposition to the rationality assumption in consumer decision making.

Appendix: Review Terms	utility analysis util origin of a graph negative slope positive slope	diminishing marginal utility substitute consumer equilibrium rationality

Appendix:
Important Terms
and Concepts
	indifference curve analysis
	indifference curve
	rank goods in order of
	    preference
	indifferent
	indifference map
	bowed inward toward (or
	    convex to) the origin
		a "bad"
		tradeoff
		perfect substitute
		constraint
		budget line
		tangent to
		behavioral opposition
		aspiration level

Appendix:
Completion

indifference map   A series of indifference curves is called an _____ .

subjective   The indifference curves represent the _____ (objective/ subjective) part of indifference curve analysis. Two points that lie on

utility   the same indifference curve provide the same _____ . Higher

greater utility   indifference curves indicate _____ . Hence, a

highest   consumer would like to reach the _____ (highest/lowest) indifference curve possible.

As with utility analysis, the consumer is constrained by income and the prices of the goods. In indifference curve analysis this con-

budget line   straint is represented by a _____ .

Given an indifference map and a budget line, a consumer maxi-

tangency   mizes utility by consuming at the point of _____

indifference curve   between an _____ and the

budget line   _____ . This point represents

equilibrium   _____ for a rational consumer.

Appendix:
Problems and
Applications

1. The following graph is Dr. Indifferent's indifference map for goods X and Y.

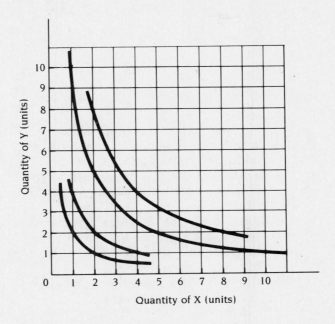

a. Assume that the prices of goods X and Y are $1 each and that Dr. Indifferent has a budget of $4 to spend on X and Y. Draw the budget line. Identify the equilibrium point on the graph. How many units of each good will be purchased at equilibrium?

b. Assume that Dr. Indifferent's budget increases to $8. What happens to the budget line? What combination of goods X and Y will maximize Dr. Indifferent's utility?

c. Let the price of X be $2 per unit and the price of Y be $1 per unit. If Dr. Indifferent has a budget of $4, how many units of X and Y will she buy? Construct Dr. Indifferent's demand schedule for good X, assuming a budget of $4 and a price of $1 per unit for good Y.

d. Let the price of X be $1 per unit and the price of Y be $2 per unit. If Dr. Indifferent has $4 to spend on X and Y, how many units of each will she buy? Construct Dr. Indifferent's demand schedule for good Y assuming a budget of $4 and a price of $1 per unit for good X.

2. The indifference schedule below identifies combinations of goods A and B between which Mr. Maximizer is indifferent:

Indifference Schedule

Good A	Good B
1	36
2	18
3	12
4	9

a. Assume that Mr. Maximizer has one unit of good A. How many units of good B would he give up in order to get an additional unit of good A without losing any utility?

b. If Mr. Maximizer has two units of good A, how many units of good B would he be willing to give up to get an additional unit of A?

c. What happens to Mr. Maximizer's willingness to give up good B for good A as he acquires more units of A? Is this pattern consistent with a desire for variety? Is the pattern consistent with diminishing marginal utility?

d. Graph Mr. Maximizer's indifference schedule. What is the shape of the curve? Is this shape consistent with the typical indifference curve?

3. Consider the following graph showing one of Professor Preference's indifference curves for goods and services.

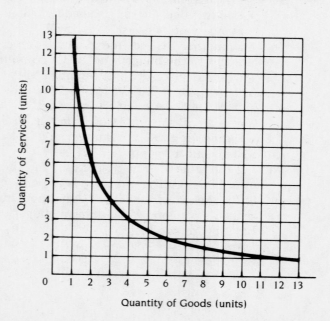

Quantity of Services (units)

Quantity of Goods (units)

a. Assume that Professor Preference currently has two units of the good. How many units of service would he give up in order to get an additional unit of the good and not lose any utility?

b. If the Professor currently has three units of the good, how many units of service would he be willing to give up to get an additional unit of the good?

Appendix:
True-False

Indicate whether each of the following statements is basically true or false. If the statement is false, rewrite it so that it is true.

_____ 1. Indifference curve analysis is like utility analysis in that it assumes that preferences can be measured in utils.

_____ 2. All points along an indifference curve represent the same level of utility.

_____ 3. Indifference curves cross each other at the equilibrium point.

_____ 4. Indifference curves are generally bowed inward toward the origin.

_____ 5. A positively sloped indifference curve would indicate that one of the items was a "bad" rather than a good.

_____ 6. An indifference map is a collection of indifference curves.

_____ 7. The budget line identifies bundles of two goods that an individual wants to buy at given prices and a given level of income.

_____ 8. A budget line would shift outward parallel to the original line as a result of an increase in the price of one good.

_____ 9. The equilibrium point for a rational consumer will occur at the point of tangency between an indifference curve and the budget line.

_____ 10. Indifference curve analysis can be used to construct demand curves only when one assumes that the utility associated with the indifference curves is measurable.

Appendix:
Multiple Choice

Choose the *one best* answer in each of the following cases:

_____ 1. Indifference curve analysis
a. requires that utility be measured.
b. assumes that preferences can be ordered.
c. is generally more restrictive than utility analysis.
d. assumes that consumers are indifferent between goods.
e. is preferable to utility analysis, because indifference curve analysis is entirely objective.

_____ 2. An indifference curve for an individual includes all combinations of two goods that
   a. the individual will purchase.
   b. are available to the individual.
   c. maximize the individual's utility.
   d. satisfy the individual equally well.
   e. the individual is able to purchase at given income and prices.

_____ 3. An individual's indifference map for two goods contains
   a. intersecting indifference curves for those two goods.
   b. an infinite number of indifference curves for those two goods.
   c. only those indifference curves that are objectively determined.
   d. only those indifference curves that the consumer is able to reach.
   e. none of the above

_____ 4. Indifference curves are generally
   a. negatively sloped straight lines.
   b. negatively sloped and bowed outward from the origin.
   c. negatively sloped and bowed inward toward the origin.
   d. positively sloped and bowed outward from the origin.
   e. positively sloped and bowed inward toward the origin.

_____ 5. Indifference curves that are horizontal indicate that
   a. the two goods are "bads."
   b. one of the two goods is a "bad."
   c. the two goods are substitutes.
   d. the two goods are complements.
   e. the individual does not care about the good measured on the horizontal axis.

_____ 6. Indifference curves that are negatively sloped straight lines indicate that the
   a. two goods are "bads."
   b. two goods are substitutes.
   c. two goods are complements.
   d. prices of the two goods are the same.
   e. individual does not care about one of the goods.

_____ 7. An indifference curve that is negatively sloped suggests that
   a. the consumer will not reach equilibrium.
   b. less of a good is preferred to more of it.
   c. the budget line will be positively sloped.
   d. the consumer will trade off units of both of the two goods in order to save money.
   e. the consumer can trade off units of one good to get additional units of the other good and maintain the same level of utility.

_____ 8. When an individual's indifference curve is convex to the origin, we would expect that
   a. total utility is diminishing.
   b. marginal utility is increasing.
   c. the individual desires variety.
   d. the individual is not rational.
   e. the individual will not reach equilibrium.

_____ 9. According to the indifference map graphed below, the consumer
   a. will buy bundle *D*.
   b. prefers bundle *B* to bundle *A*.
   c. prefers bundle *C* to bundle *B*.
   d. is indifferent between bundles *A* and *C*.
   e. is indifferent between bundles *A* and *D*.

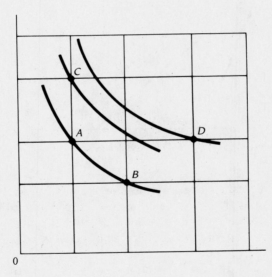

_____ 10. Given a budget and the prices of the goods, a budget line shows combinations of two goods that an individual
   a. will purchase.
   b. is able to purchase.
   c. would like to purchase.
   d. will purchase at equilibrium.
   e. none of the above

_____ 11. Which of the following would cause an individual's budget line
to move?
a. a change in prices
b. a change in the individual's income
c. a change in the individual's tastes and preferences
d. both a and b above
e. all of the above

Use the following graph to answer questions 12 and 13.

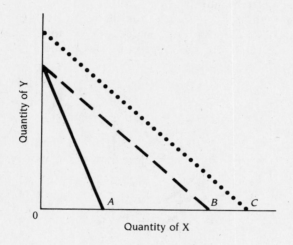

_____ 12. Consider the graph above, showing several budget lines. Assume
that the budget line moves from line A to line B. Which of the
following is consistent with such a move?
a. a decrease in the price of good X with no change in the price
of good Y
b. a decrease in the price of good Y with no change in the price
of good X
c. an increase in the price of good X with no change in the price
of good Y
d. an increase in the price of good Y with no change in the price
of good X
e. an increase in income with no change in the prices of the two
goods

_____ 13. Assume that the budget line in the graph moves from line B to
line C. Which of the following is consistent with such a move?
a. a decrease in the price of good X with no change in the price
of good Y

b. a decrease in the price of good Y with no change in the price of good X
c. an increase in the price of good X with no change in the price of good Y
d. an increase in the price of good Y with no change in the price of good X
e. an increase in income with no change in the prices of the two goods

_____ 14. In terms of indifference curve analysis, consumer equilibrium occurs at the point where
a. the budget line intersects the vertical axis.
b. the budget line intersects the horizontal axis.
c. an indifference curve is tangent to the budget line.
d. the highest indifference curve intersects the vertical axis.
e. the highest indifference curve intersects the horizontal axis.

_____ 15. "Behavioral" opposition in consumer theory would
a. question the assumption of consumer rationality.
b. expect a consumer to follow an established routine.
c. employ the concept of a consumer's "aspiration" level.
d. not necessarily expect a consumer to purchase at the point of tangency of an indifference curve and a budget line.
e. all of the above

Appendix: Discussion Questions

1. Compare and contrast utility analysis and indifference curve analysis.
2. Explain why indifference curves cannot intersect.
3. Discuss the shape of indifference curves in terms of opportunity cost.
4. Identify and explain the equilibrium condition in indifference curve analysis.
5. Discuss the behavioral objections to indifference curve analysis.

Appendix:
Answers

Problems and Applications

1. a. At equilibrium, 2 units of X and 2 units of Y will be purchased.

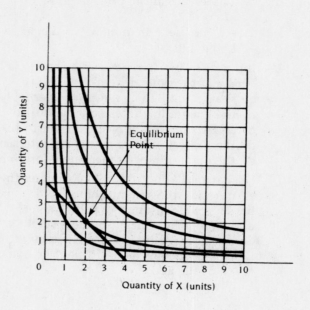

b. the budget line shifts out parallel to the original budget line; 4 units of good X and 4 units of good Y

c. 1 unit of X and 2 units of Y:

Price of Good X	Quantity of Good X
$1	2
2	1

d. 2 units of X and 1 unit of Y:

Price of Good Y	Quantity of Good Y
$1	2
2	1

2. a. 18
    b. 6
    c. willingness diminishes; yes; yes
    d. curve is bowed inward toward (convex to) the origin; yes

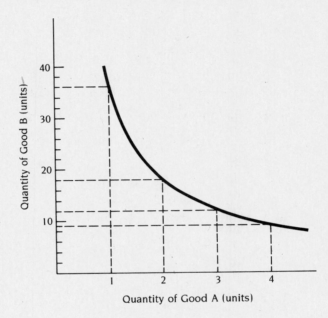

3. a. 2
    b. 1

True-False

1. F. Indifference curve analysis, unlike utility analysis, does not
    assume that preferences can be measured.
2. T.
3. F. Indifference curves cannot cross each other.
4. T.
5. T.
6. T.
7. F. The budget line identifies bundles of two goods that an
    individual is able to buy at given prices and a given level of
    income.
8. F. A budget line would shift outward, parallel to the original
    line, as a result of an increase in income.

9. T.
10. F. Indifference curve analysis can be used to construct demand curves, whether or not one assumes that the utility associated with the indifference curves is measurable.

Multiple Choice

1. b	2. d	3. b	4. c	5. e
6. b	7. e	8. c	9. c	10. b
11. d	12. a	13. e	14. c	15. e

22 *Market Demand and Elasticity*

Summary

The market demand for a good is the sum of all individual demands for the good. Like individual demand, market demand is typically an inverse relationship between price and quantity demanded. The determinants of market demand include consumer preferences, income and the distribution of income, the prices of related goods, and the number of consumers.

Elasticity is a way of measuring the responsiveness of one variable to a change in another variable. Price elasticity of demand is the absolute value of the percentage change in quantity demanded due to a percentage change in price.

When the coefficient of elasticity is less than 1, demand is inelastic. A given percentage change in price will result in a smaller percentage change in quantity demanded. In the extreme, when the coefficient of elasticity is zero, demand is said to be perfectly inelastic. In such a case, a change in the price of the good causes no change in the quantity demanded, and the demand curve will be vertical.

When the coefficient of elasticity is equal to 1, demand is unitary elastic. A given percentage change in price causes an equivalent percentage change in quantity demanded. When the demand curve is a rectangular hyperbola, demand is unitary elastic at all prices.

When the coefficient of elasticity is greater than 1, demand is elastic. In this case, the percentage change in quantity demanded is greater than the percentage change in price. In the extreme, when the coefficient of elasticity is infinity, demand is said to be infinitely elastic or perfectly elastic. In the infinitely elastic case, the demand curve will be horizontal.

Price elasticity of demand has important implications for total revenue. If demand is elastic, a change in price will cause total revenue to change in the opposite direction. If demand is inelastic, a change in price will cause total revenue to change in the same direction. In the case of unitary elasticity, a change in price will cause no change in total revenue.

Cross-elasticity of demand enables us to distinguish between substitutes and complements. Cross-elasticity is measured by the percentage change in the quantity demanded of one good divided by the percentage change in the price of the other good. A positive coefficient indicates that the two goods are substitutes; a negative coefficient indicates that the two goods are complements.

Income elasticity of demand enables us to distinguish between normal goods and inferior goods. Income elasticity is the percentage change in the quantity demanded of a good due to a percentage change in income. If the coefficient of income elasticity is positive, the good is normal; if the coefficient is negative, the good is inferior.

Major Objectives

After you have finished this chapter, you will be able to do the following:

1. Derive market demand schedules and curves from individual demand relationships.
2. Distinguish between a change in quantity demanded and a change in demand, graphically represent each, and indicate the causes of each.
3. Explain the meaning of elasticity.
4. Define, explain, calculate, and interpret the price elasticity of demand.
5. Distinguish price elasticity of demand from the slope of the demand curve.
6. Calculate elasticity coefficients.
7. Identify, interpret, and explain the five different degrees of elasticity and indicate the consequences of each for the graph of the demand curve.
8. Identify and explain the determinants of price elasticity of demand.
9. Define and compute total revenue.
10. Identify, explain, and demonstrate graphically the relationship between price elasticity of demand and the effect of a price change on total revenue.
11. Define, distinguish between, and provide examples of substitutes and complements.
12. Define, calculate, and interpret cross-elasticity of demand.

13. Define, distinguish between, and provide examples of normal and inferior goods.
14. Define, calculate, and interpret income elasticity of demand.
15. Indicate the determinants of income elasticity of demand.

Review Terms

demand
individual demand
negative relationship
law of demand
change in quantity demanded
    vs. change in demand

ceteris paribus
substitute
complement
slope

Important Terms and Concepts

market demand
number of consumers
income distribution
elasticity
price elasticity of demand (E_D)
percentage change vs. absolute
    change
change in quantity demanded
    (ΔQ_D)
change in price (ΔP)
average quantity demanded
    (Q_D)
average price (P)
elasticity coefficient
absolute value
inelastic

elastic
perfectly inelastic
infinitely elastic
perfectly elastic
infinity
rectangular hyperbola
determinants of elasticity
total revenue (TR)
cross-demand
cross-elasticity of demand (E_C)
income demand
income elasticity of demand
    (E_y)
normal good
inferior good

Completion

inverse

quantity demanded

increases

movement along

quantity demanded

demand

According to the law of demand, there is an _____ rela-tionship between price and _____ . If the price of a good decreases, the quantity demanded _____ . This means that when the price of a good decreases, there will be a _____ (shift in/movement along) the market demand curve for the good. This is referred to as a change in _____ (demand/quantity demanded).

    A change in _____ (demand/quantity demanded) is caused by a violation of the *ceteris paribus* assumption. Such a

shift in

change is represented by a _____ (shift in/ movement along) the market demand curve. The market demand curve may shift as a result of a change in consumer preferences, a

distribution

change in income and in the _____ of income, a

related goods

change in the prices of _____ , and a change in the

number

_____ of consumers.

The sensitivity of one variable to a change in another variable is

elasticity

measured by _____ . The price elasticity of demand is

percentage

the absolute value of the _____ change in

quantity demanded

_____ due to a

percentage, price

_____ change in _____ . The coefficient can be calculated from a demand schedule by the following formula:

difference in quan- tities demanded

sum of quantities demanded

difference in prices

sum of prices

$$\frac{(\ D_1 - D_2 \qquad)/(\ D_1 + D_2 \qquad)}{(\ P_1 - P_2 \qquad)/(\ P_1 + P_2 \qquad)}$$

The determinants of price elasticity of demand include the avail-

substitute

ability of _____ goods, the proportion of consumers'

incomes

_____ spent on the good, whether the good is a

necessity, time

_____ or a luxury, and the length of _____ consumers have to adjust to the price change.

Problems and Applications

1. Individual demand schedules for product M are given in the table below. Assuming that there are only the four potential buyers in the market, determine the market demand schedule for product M. Are the individual and market demand relationships consistent with the law of demand? Draw the individual and market demand curves on one grid.

Price per Unit	Buyer A	Buyer B	Buyer C	Buyer D	Market
$.10	5	6	3	7	21
.20	4	4	2	6	16
.30	3	2	1	4	10
.40	2	0	1	3	6

2. Consider the demand schedule in the table below:

Demand for Googoos

Price	Quantity
$ 2	100
4	90
6	70
8	40
10	0

a. What is the elasticity of demand for googoos for price changes between $2 and $4?

b. What is the elasticity of demand for googoos for price changes between $4 and $2?

c. What is the elasticity of demand for googoos for price changes between $6 and $8?

d. What is the elasticity of demand for googoos for price changes between $8 and $10?

e. As price increases, does demand become more or less elastic?

f. In the price range between $4 and $6, what happens to quantity demanded if price increases by 8 percent?

g. In the price range between $6 and $8, what happens to quantity demanded if price decreases by 11 percent?

h. In the price range between $8 and $10, what happens to quantity demanded if price increases by 10 percent?

i. What is the total revenue associated with a price of $6?

j. What is the total expenditure associated with a price of $8?

k. What is the relationship between total revenue and total expenditure?

l. What is the total revenue associated with a price of $10?

3. What is the elasticity of demand if a price change causes no change in the quantity demanded?

4. What is the elasticity of demand if a price change causes no change in total revenue? What is the elasticity of demand if a price change causes no change in total expenditure?

5. What is the elasticity of demand if you always budget a fixed number of dollars for the purchase of a good?

6. What is the elasticity of demand if you always purchase a fixed amount of a good?

7. Is demand elastic or inelastic if a slight price increase causes you to quit consuming a product?

8. What is the elasticity of demand if a price increase of any amount causes you to quit consuming a product?

9. Consider the demand curve drawn in the graph below. Graphically indicate the total revenue associated with a price of $1.
Graphically indicate the total revenue associated with a price of
$2. What happens to total revenue when the price increases from
$1 to $2? Is demand elastic or inelastic in this price range?
(Remember that the product of two adjacent sides of a rectangle
is the area of the rectangle.)

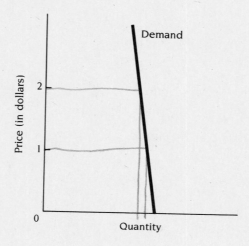

10. Consider the demand curve drawn in the graph below. Graphically indicate the total revenue associated with a price of $100. Graphically indicate the total revenue associated with a price of $101. What happens to total revenue when the price increases from $100 to $101? Is demand elastic or inelastic in this price range?

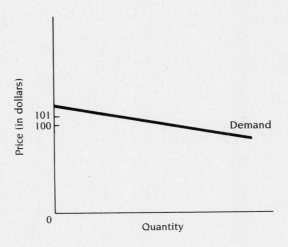

True-False

Indicate whether each of the following statements is basically true or false. If the statement is false, rewrite it so that it is true.

_____ 1. A market demand curve is the sum of all individual demand curves for a particular good in a particular area.

_____ 2. Unlike individual demand curves, market demand curves tend to be positively sloped.

_____ 3. A shift in the market demand curve for a good is likely to be caused by a change in the price of the good.

_____ 4. Price elasticity of demand measures the change in price due to a change in quantity demanded.

_____ 5. A price elasticity of demand equal to 3/5 indicates that a 5 percent increase in the price of a good causes a 3 percent decrease in quantity demanded.

_____ 6. When the price elasticity of demand is equal to 3/5, demand for the good is said to be inelastic.

_____ 7. Unitary elasticity refers to a situation where there is only one elasticity of demand.

_____ 8. When demand is inelastic, the percentage change in price is less than the percentage in quantity demanded.

_____ 9. Demand is said to be infinitely elastic when a price change causes no change in quantity demanded.

_____ 10. Demand is said to be infinitely elastic when the demand curve is a horizontal line.

_____ 11. When the demand curve is a rectangular hyperbola, demand is unitary elastic.

_____ 12. Over time, price elasticity of demand is likely to decrease.

_____ 13. Price elasticity of demand will tend to be greater the more substitutes there are for the good in question.

_____ 14. If a price change causes no change in total revenue, the price elasticity of demand is zero.

_____ 15. When demand is elastic, a price increase will cause an increase in total revenue.

_____ 16. Cross-demand is a relationship between the quantity demanded of one good and the price of a different good.

_____ 17. Cross-elasticity of demand enables us to distinguish normal goods from inferior goods.

_____ 18. Income demand is a relationship between quantity demanded of a good and the income of consumers.

_____ 19. In the mid-1950s, the Du Pont Company argued successfully in the Supreme Court that it was not monopolizing cellophane production, based on the high and positive cross-elasticity of demand.

_____ 20. A negative income elasticity of demand for a good indicates that the good is a necessity.

_____ 21. If X is inferior, the demand for X will increase when income decreases.

Multiple Choice

Choose the *one best* answer in each of the following cases:

_____ 1. The market demand curve for a good
   a. often violates the law of demand.
   b. will usually be positively sloped.
   c. is a relationship between price and quantity demanded.
   d. all of the above
   e. identifies how many units of the good will be sold in the market.

_____ 2. Which of the following is *least* likely to cause a shift in the market demand curve for a good?
   a. a change in consumer incomes
   b. a change in the price of the good
   c. a change in consumer tastes and preferences
   d. a change in the distribution of consumer incomes
   e. none of the above

_____ 3. Assume that goods X and Y are substitutes. An increase in the price of good X will result in a(n)
   a. decrease in demand for X.
   b. decrease in demand for Y.
   c. increase in demand for X.
   d. increase in demand for Y.
   e. decrease in quantity demanded of Y.

_____ 4. Price elasticity of demand is the absolute value of the
   a. average quantity demanded divided by average price.
   b. change in quantity demanded divided by change in price.
   c. change in price divided by change in quantity demanded.
   d. percentage change in quantity demanded divided by percentage change in price.
   e. percentage change in price divided by percentage change in quantity demanded.

_____ 5. A price elasticity of demand equal to 7/5 means that
   a. a 7 percent increase in price causes a 5 percent decrease in quantity demanded.
   b. a 5 percent decrease in price causes a 7 percent increase in quantity demanded.
   c. quantity demanded will increase by 5 percent when price increases by 7 percent.
   d. quantity demanded will increase by 7 units when price decreases by $5.
   e. a $7 increase in price will cause quantity demanded to decrease by 5 units.

_____ 6. Assume that the price elasticity of demand for good X is 3. What would be the consequence of a 10 percent increase in the price of X?
   a. quantity demanded would decrease by 3 percent
   b. quantity demanded would decrease by 30 percent
   c. quantity demanded would decrease by one-third
   d. quantity demanded would increase by 30 percent
   e. quantity demanded would increase by one-third

_____ 7. Assume that the coefficient of elasticity of a certain good is 1/5.
A $5 increase in price will result in
a. a $1 increase in quantity demanded.
b. a $1 decrease in quantity demanded.
c. a $0.20 decrease in quantity demanded.
d. a 1 percent decrease in quantity demanded.
e. an indeterminate effect.

_____ 8. Assume that a price rise of 30 cents causes the quantity
demanded to decrease by 300 bushels. From this one can conclude that the
a. price elasticity of demand is 1/10.
b. price elasticity of demand is 10.
c. demand is unitary elastic in the indicated price range.
d. law of demand is violated.
e. none of the above

_____ 9. If a price increase from $1 to $3 causes the quantity demanded
to decrease from 90 to 30 units, the coefficient of elasticity is
a. 1/30.
b. 1/2.
c. 1.
d. 2.
e. 30.

_____ 10. Which of the following statements is true of elasticity?
a. Elasticity is always greater than 1.
b. Elasticity cannot be compared for different goods.
c. Elasticity is equivalent to the slope of the demand curve.
d. Elasticity uses percentage changes so that it will be independent of the units of measurement.
e. all of the above

_____ 11. When the price elasticity of demand is greater than zero but
less than 1, demand is
a. elastic.
b. inelastic.
c. unitary elastic.
d. infinitely elastic.
e. perfectly inelastic.

_____ 12. When the demand curve is a vertical line, the coefficient of
elasticity is
a. one.
b. zero.
c. infinity.
d. greater than one.
e. nonexistent.

_____ 13. If the coefficient of elasticity is 2/3, demand is
      a. elastic.
      b. inelastic.
      c. unitary elastic.
      d. infinitely elastic.
      e. perfectly inelastic.

_____ 14. If the coefficient of elasticity is zero, demand is
      a. elastic.
      b. unitary elastic.
      c. infinitely elastic.
      d. perfectly inelastic.
      e. nonexistent.

_____ 15. When demand is unitary elastic, the coefficient of elasticity is
      a. one.
      b. zero.
      c. negative.
      d. infinity.
      e. indeterminate.

_____ 16. Total revenue is
      a. equal to total expenditure.
      b. equal to price times quantity traded.
      c. both a and b above
      d. unrelated to elasticity of demand.
      e. equal to price when demand is unitary elastic.

_____ 17. When demand is unitary elastic
      a. the demand curve is a vertical line.
      b. the demand curve is a horizontal line.
      c. a change in price causes no change in total revenue.
      d. a change in price causes an equivalent change in total revenue.
      e. none of the above

_____ 18. If a price increase causes a decrease in total revenue, demand is
      a. elastic.
      b. inelastic.
      c. unitary elastic.
      d. perfectly inelastic.
      e. inconsistent with the law of demand.

_____ 19. If the elasticity of demand is greater than 1, a price decrease will result in
      a. a decrease in total revenue.
      b. an increase in total revenue.
      c. no change in total expenditure.
      d. a decrease in total expenditure.
      e. none of the above

_____ 20. Demand is likely to be the most elastic when there are
    a. good substitutes, when the good is relatively expensive, and when the good is a luxury.
    b. good substitutes, when the good is relatively inexpensive, and when the good is a luxury.
    c. no good substitutes, when the good is relatively expensive, and when the good is a luxury.
    d. good substitutes, when the good is relatively expensive, and when the good is a necessity.
    e. good substitutes, when the good is relatively inexpensive, and when the good is a necessity.

_____ 21. Which of the following goods would be expected to have the lowest price elasticity of demand?
    a. milk
    b. food
    c. candy
    d. hamburger
    e. a McDonald's hamburger

_____ 22. A negative cross-elasticity of demand indicates that
    a. the good is normal.
    b. the good is inferior.
    c. the two goods are substitutes.
    d. the two goods are complements.
    e. a price change causes a decrease in total revenue.

_____ 23. When two goods are substitutes, the
    a. elasticity of demand will be zero.
    b. cross-elasticity of demand will be zero.
    c. cross-elasticity of demand will be positive.
    d. the price elasticity of demand will be the same for the two goods.
    e. both c and d above

_____ 24. Income elasticity of demand is equal to the
    a. change in income associated with a change in quantity demanded.
    b. change in quantity demanded associated with a change in income.
    c. percentage change in income associated with a percentage change in demand.
    d. percentage change in demand associated with a percentage change in income.
    e. average change in quantity demanded associated with the average change in income.

_____ 25. Negative income elasticity of demand indicates that a good is
  a. normal.
  b. superior.
  c. inferior.
  d. a necessity.
  e. a luxury item.

Use the table below to answer questions 26 through 29.

	Quantity Demanded of		
PA	A	B	C
$1	5	3	10
$2	3	8	7

_____ 26. Consider the table above. Good A has a price elasticity of demand equal to
  a. 0.75.
  b. 1.33.
  c. 2.
  d. 1.
  e. indeterminate.

_____ 27. In the table, goods A and B are
  a. substitutes.
  b. complements.
  c. both normal goods.
  d. both inferior goods.
  e. normal and inferior, respectively.

_____ 28. In the table, goods A and C are
  a. substitutes.
  b. complements.
  c. both normal goods.
  d. both inferior goods.
  e. normal and inferior, respectively.

_____ 29. In the table, which of the following is correct?
  a. Good B is inferior.
  b. Good B violates the law of demand.
  c. The cross-elasticity of demand for good C is 9/17.
  d. The income elasticity of demand for good A is indeterminate.
  e. all of the above

**Discussion
Questions**

1. Explain why elasticity concepts use percentage changes rather than absolute changes.

2. Of what importance is information about the price elasticity of demand to a business?

3. Assume that your local mass transit system discovers that a rate hike results in decreased revenues. What does this suggest about the price elasticity of demand for mass transit? What are the characteristics of mass transit that give rise to this elasticity?

4. Provide examples of how a business might use information about cross-elasticity of demand in marketing.

5. Identify some goods for which your income elasticity of demand is negative. What does this mean in terms of your consumption of these goods? Do you think everyone would agree with your choices? Would you change your answer if you were considerably poorer? Would you change your answer if you were considerably richer?

6. What would be meant by the advertising elasticity of demand? How might a business firm use this concept?

Answers

Problems and Applications

1.

Price per Unit	Market Quantity
$.10	21
.20	16
.30	10
.40	6

Yes.

1. (Continued)

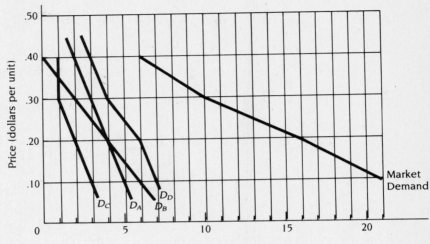

2. a. 3/19   b. 3/19   c. 21/11   d. 9
   e. more elastic   f. decreases by 5%
   g. increases by 21%   h. decreases by 90%
   i. $420   j. $320   k. they are equal   l. $0

3. 0   4. unitary elastic; unitary elastic

5. unitary elastic   6. 0

7. elastic   8. infinitely elastic

9. total revenue (PQ_D) at a price of $1 is indicated by the shaded
   area; total revenue at a price of $2 is the area indicated by vertical
   lines; comparing the two rectangular areas, observe that total
   revenue increases; demand is inelastic

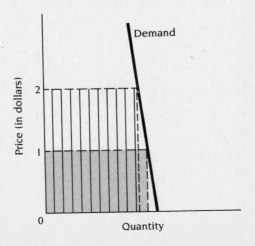

10. total revenue at a price of $100 is the area indicated by vertical lines; total revenue at a price of $101 is indicated by the shaded area; total revenue decreases; demand is elastic

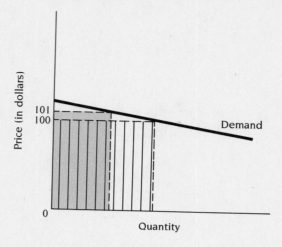

True-False

1. T.
2. F. Like individual demand curves, market demand curves tend to be negatively sloped.
3. F. A change in the price of a good causes a movement along the market demand curve for that good; a shift in the demand curve is caused by a violation of the *ceteris paribus* assumption.
4. F. Price elasticity of demand measures the percentage change in quantity demanded due to a percentage change in price.
5. T.
6. T.
7. F. Unitary elasticity refers to a situation where the price elasticity of demand is equal to 1.
8. F. When demand is inelastic, the percentage change in price is greater than the percentage in quantity demanded.
9. F. Demand is said to be perfectly inelastic when a price change causes no change in quantity demanded.
10. T.
11. T.
12. F. Over time, price elasticity of demand is likely to increase.
13. T.

14. F. If a price change causes no change in total revenue, the price elasticity of demand is 1.
15. F. When demand is elastic, a price increase will cause a decrease in total revenue.
16. T.
17. F. Cross elasticity of demand enables us to distinguish substitutes from complements.
18. T.
19. T.
20. F. A negative income elasticity of demand for a good indicates that the good is inferior.
21. T.

Multiple Choice

1. c	2. b	3. d	4. d	5. b
6. b	7. e	8. e	9. c	10. d
11. b	12. b	13. b	14. d	15. a
16. c	17. c	18. a	19. b	20. a
21. b	22. d	23. c	24. d	25. c
26. a	27. a	28. b	29. d	

23 Business Firm Choice

Summary

Rationality on the part of a business firm requires that the firm attempt to maximize profits. In order to do so the firm must make decisions with regard to what and how much to product. In part, these decisions will be based on the firm's production function. This function identifies the technically efficient input combinations associated with a given level of output. For any given output level, a profit-maximizing firm would want to adopt the technically efficient method associated with the lowest cost. This is the condition for economic efficiency.

Firms must make decisions for three time spans: the short run, the long run, and the very long run. The short run is a time period so short that at least one input is fixed. In the long run, no inputs are fixed, but the firm cannot alter its production function. In the very long run, technological change is permitted so that the firm's production function can be changed.

In the short run, a firm's product curves show relationships between variable inputs and output. The three product curves are total product, average product, and marginal product. There is an important principle of production in the short run known as the principle of diminishing marginal returns. According to this principle, when additional units of a variable input are added to some fixed inputs, marginal product may increase at first, but eventually it will diminish and may even become negative.

A firm that attempts to maximize profits will want to produce any given level of output at the lowest possible cost. The economist is typically concerned with nonmonetary outlays as well as with actual monetary payments. Hence the economist is concerned with implicit as well as explicit costs.

In the short run, costs may be separated into those associated with hiring fixed inputs and those associated with hiring variable inputs. Total cost is the sum of total fixed cost and total variable cost. Total fixed cost is constant; total variable cost increases as output rises. Average cost is total cost divided by output. Average total cost is equal to the sum of average fixed cost and average variable cost. Marginal cost is the change in total cost associated with the production of an additional unit of output. As output rises, the average variable cost and average total cost curves decrease, reach a minimum, and then rise. Marginal cost may decrease initially, but eventually it rises, coming up through the minimum points on the average variable and average total cost curves.

In the long run, all costs are variable. Hence there are only three cost concepts: long-run total cost, long-run average cost, and long-run marginal cost. The long run is often thought of as a series of short-run situations. The long-run average-cost curve is made up of points from short-run average-cost curves. In particular, for any given output level, the firm is assumed to select the short-run plant that enables production of that output at the lowest per unit cost.

In the very long run, business decisions may affect the production function itself. Such decisions deal with research, development, invention, and innovation. The firm will attempt to make changes that increase productivity. Increases in productivity are generally associated with input substitution that results from technological progress and/or with improvements in the quality of inputs.

Major Objectives

After you have finished this chapter, you will be able to do the following:

1. Define and provide examples of inputs and outputs.
2. Define production and production function and express a production function in the form of a mathematical equation.
3. Define, explain, and distinguish between technical efficiency and economic efficiency.
4. Define, explain, and distinguish the short run, the long run, and the very long run.
5. Define and distinguish between fixed and variable inputs.
6. Define, explain, and calculate total product, marginal product, and average product, and describe the relationship between these three concepts.
7. Define, explain, and provide examples of increasing, diminishing, and negative returns.
8. Identify and explain the relationships between total product and marginal product and between average product and marginal product.

9. Construct and interpret graphs of the total, marginal, and average product relationships.
10. Identify and explain the three stages of production.
11. Define and explain the concept of cost.
12. Define, explain, and distinguish between implicit and explicit costs.
13. Calculate implicit costs from information regarding opportunity costs.
14. Define, explain, and calculate total cost, total fixed cost, and total variable cost.
15. Identify and explain the relationships between total cost, total fixed cost, and total variable cost.
16. Construct and interpret graphs of the total cost, total fixed cost, and total variable cost relationships.
17. Identify and explain the relationship between total variable cost and marginal returns.
18. Define, explain, and calculate average total cost, average fixed cost, and average variable cost.
19. Identify and explain the relationships between average total cost, average fixed cost, and average variable cost.
20. Construct and interpret graphs of the average cost relationships.
21. Identify and explain the relationship between average variable cost and average product.
22. Define, explain, calculate, and graph marginal cost.
23. Identify and explain the relationships between marginal cost and each of the following: marginal product, total cost, total variable cost, and average total cost.
24. Define, explain, calculate, and graph long-run total cost, long-run average cost, and long-run marginal cost.
25. Define plant.
26. Define, explain, and cite examples of economies of scale (increasing returns to scale), constant returns to scale, and diseconomies of scale (decreasing returns to scale).
27. Graph long-run total cost, long-run average cost, and long-run marginal cost under conditions of increasing, constant, and decreasing returns to scale.
28. Verbally and graphically explain the relationship between long-run average cost and the short-run average-cost relationships that make up the long run.
29. Define and distinguish between invention and innovation.
30. Define the very long run and discuss its relationship to invention and innovation.
31. Define productivity and explain the increases in productivity that have characterized most industrialized countries.
32. Explain how productivity might decrease.

33. Define technological progress.
34. Describe and explain changes in productivity in the United States during the twentieth century.

Review Terms

supply
rationality
inputs
labor

natural resources
capital
opportunity cost
standard of living

Important Terms and Concepts

production
outputs
technically efficient
production function
economic efficiency
short run
long run
very long run
fixed input
variable input
total product
marginal product
average product
increasing returns
diminishing returns
negative returns
stages of production
cost
explicit cost
implicit cost
profit
total cost (TC)
total fixed cost (TFC)

total variable cost (TVC)
average total cost (ATC)
average fixed cost (AFC)
average variable cost (AVC)
marginal cost (MC)
long-run total cost (LRTC)
long-run average cost (LRAC)
long-run marginal cost (LRMC)
plant
scale
economies of scale or increasing
    returns to scale
constant returns to scale
diseconomies of scale or de-
    creasing returns to scale
specialization
tangent
invention
innovation
productivity
input substitution
technological progress

Completion

inputs

outputs, maximum

minimum

Production refers to the transformation of _____ into _____ . A production function shows the _____ output that can be obtained from given amounts of inputs. Alternatively, a production function shows the _____ amount of inputs needed to support a given level of output. Economists often assume that a firm has knowledge of its production function.

may not

In reality, business firms _____ (must/may not) know their actual production function.

short run

The three time spans for decision making are the _____ ,

long run, very long run

the _____ , and the _____ .

are not

These time spans _____ (are/are not) associated with specific amounts of time. The short run is a time period such that at least

fixed, fixed

one input is _____ . Hence there will be _____ costs. In addition to its fixed inputs, the short run is typically char

variable

acterized by one or more _____ inputs. This means that

variable

there are likely to be _____ costs. In the long run, all

variable

inputs are _____ . Hence, in the long run all costs are

variable

_____ . The long run is a time period sufficiently long to

not

permit firms to enter or exit an industry. It is _____ (also/not) long enough to permit a change in the production function. When the time period is long enough to permit a whole new technology,

very long run

we are talking about the _____ .
Production costs need not be associated with actual outlays of money. When money payments are actually made, the costs are said

explicit

to be _____ . When no actual payment is made, the

implicit

costs are _____ .
The firm's cost functions include short-run and long-run total costs, average costs, and marginal costs. Average cost is equal to

total, output

_____ cost divided by _____ . Marginal cost is

change in total cost

the _____ divided by the

change in output

_____ . Except in the case of

falls

average fixed cost, which _____ (rises/falls) as output in

fall

creases, average cost tends to _____ (rise/fall) initially,

minimum

reach a _____ (maximum/minimum), and then

rise, below

_____ (rise/fall). Marginal cost lies _____ (above/below) average cost when the average is falling. Marginal cost lies

above

_____ (above/below) average cost with the average is rising.

equal to

Hence, marginal cost is _____ average cost at the extreme point on the average curve.

Problems and Applications

1. Consider the total product information given in the table below. Assume that there is only one variable input. Complete the marginal and average product schedules

Variable Input	Total Product	Marginal Product	Average Product
0	0	0	0
1	10	10	10
2	22	12	11
3	33	11	11
4	40	7	10
5	45	5	9

2. In the graph below, sketch in a marginal product curve that is consistent with the total product and average product curves. Identify the three stages of production.

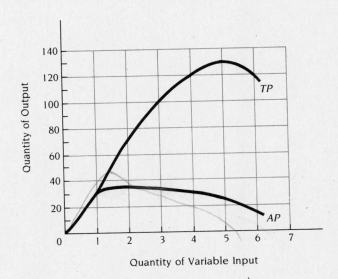

3. Use the short-run cost information below to complete the table.

TP	TFC	TVC	TC	AFC	AVC	ATC	MC
0	10	0	10	—	—	—	5
1	$10	$ 5	15	10	5	15	4
2	10	9	19	5	4.5	9.9	6
3	10	15	25	3.3	5	8.1	7
4	10	22	32	2.2	11	8	8
5	10	30	40	2	6	8	

4. In the graph below, sketch in a marginal cost curve that is consistent with the average total cost and average variable cost curves. Notice that curve *AVC* is not parallel to curve *ATC*. Why not?

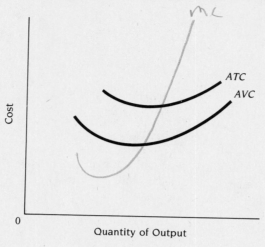

5. Consider a firm that is producing output Q′ as shown on the graph below.

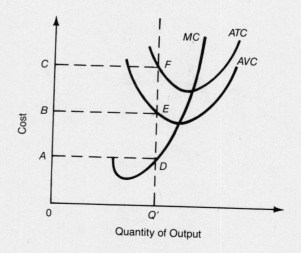

Find the following: average variable cost, average total cost, average fixed cost, marginal cost, total variable cost, total cost, and total fixed cost.

6. Consider the firm described by the table below.

Total Product	Total Variable Cost
0	$
2	30
4	60
6	90

Assume that the total fixed cost is $10. What is the total cost of producing nothing? What is the total cost associated with producing six units of output? What is the average total cost associated with producing two units of output? What is the marginal cost of the fourth unit of output? What is the marginal cost of the sixth unit of output?

True-False　　Indicate whether each of the following statements is basically true or false. If the statement is false, rewrite it so that it is true.

_____ 1. In business, rationality essentially means that the firm's objective is profit maximization.

_____ 2. Production is the transformation of inputs into outputs.

_____ 3. A production function shows the maximum output that can be obtained from the minimum amount of inputs.

_____ 4. To say that production is technically efficient implies that no resources are being wasted.

_____ 5. Economic efficiency may be achieved even if production is not technically efficient.

_____ 6. In the short run, all inputs must be fixed in amount.

_____ 7. The marginal product of a fourth worker is the output produced by that fourth worker.

_____ 8. The average product of four workers is the output produced by the fourth worker.

_____ 9. Negative returns occur when an additional unit of the variable input causes a decrease in total product.

_____ 10. When a firm is experiencing increasing returns in the short run, both total cost and total variable cost increase at a decreasing rate.

_____ 11. When a firm is experiencing diminishing returns in the short run, both total cost and total variable cost decrease.

_____ 12. Stage II begins at the level of variable input associated with maximum marginal product.

_____ 13. A cost associated with an actual outlay of money is called an explicit cost.

_____ 14. The total fixed cost curve is a horizontal line.

_____ 15. The average fixed cost curve is a horizontal line.

_____ 16. $ATC = AFC + AVC$

_____ 17. Total cost increases throughout all three stages of production, but this is not the case with total variable cost.

_____ 18. In Stage I when average product is increasing, average variable cost is decreasing.

_____ 19. Marginal cost is the change in total cost associated with the production of an additional unit of output.

_____ 20. Marginal cost is the change in total variable cost associated with the production of an additional unit of output.

_____ 21. A change in fixed cost causes an equivalent change in marginal cost.

_____ 22. When a firm is experiencing diminishing marginal returns in the short run, the firm's marginal cost curve is rising.

_____ 23. Economies of scale are associated with declining long-run average cost.

_____ 24. A plant is a production facility or factory in a particular geographic location.

_____ 25. The long run permits changes in all inputs as well as changes in the production function itself.

_____ 26. Invention refers to the discovery of a new product or new process; innovation refers to the development of an invention from the idea to practical use.

_____ 27. The productivity of labor is the amount of output produced by a worker during a given time period.

_____ 28. The United States has the highest productivity in the world and its growth in productivity is also the greatest.

Multiple Choice   Choose the *one best* answer in each of the following cases:

_____   1. A production function
    a. is a relationship between inputs and outputs.
    b. identifies input combinations that are technically efficient.
    c. shows the maximum output that can be produced with given amounts of inputs.
    d. shows the minimum amount of inputs needed to produce a given level of output.
    e. all of the above

_____   2. If production is technically efficient,
    a. the firm is operating at its lowest possible cost.
    b. it must also be economically efficient.
    c. no other method of production will yield the same output.
    d. no other method of production will yield the same output without more of all inputs.
    e. a given output level cannot be produced with less of an input unless more of another input is used.

_____   3. Economic efficiency for a given output level
    a. may occur even if the firm is not operating on its production function.
    b. means that a firm is using the technically efficient combination of inputs with the lowest cost.
    c. occurs only when no other method of production will yield the same output without increasing all inputs.
    d. both a and b above
    e. none of the above

_____   4. In the short run
    a. all costs are fixed.
    b. all inputs are fixed.
    c. all costs are variable.
    d. there may be fixed and variable inputs.
    e. all production decisions must be made on a daily basis.

_____   5. The long run is
    a. typically one year.
    b. long enough for all inputs to be variable.
    c. long enough for the introduction of new technology.
    d. both b and c above
    e. long enough for all inputs to be variable but not long enough for entry and exit of firms.

_____ 6. When marginal product is positive and increasing,
   a. average product exceeds marginal product.
   b. total product is increasing at a decreasing rate.
   c. total product is increasing at an increasing rate.
   d. both a and b above
   e. both a and c above

_____ 7. Diminishing returns
   a. characterize all stages of production.
   b. eventually occur in all short-run production situations.
   c. are always associated with declining average product in the short run.
   d. exist in the short run, because as additional units of an input are hired, the firm has to accept less satisfactory units.
   e. none of the above

_____ 8. Which of the following adages best illustrates the concept of diminishing marginal returns?
   a. "The more, the merrier."
   b. "Turn about is fair play."
   c. "All's well that ends well."
   d. "Two's company, three's a crowd."
   e. "It's not whether you win or lose, but how you play the game."

_____ 9. A negative marginal product
   a. is consistent with a falling total product.
   b. is associated with negative average product.
   c. may be consistent with rising or falling total product.
   d. indicates that total product is increasing at a decreasing rate.
   e. none of the above

_____ 10. In Stage II,
   a. marginal product is negative.
   b. only marginal product is declining.
   c. marginal and average product are declining.
   d. total product is increasing at an increasing rate.
   e. marginal, average, and total product are all declining.

_____ 11. Which of the following statements is true of short-run costs?
   a. They may include both implicit and explicit costs.
   b. They are implicit if they are associated with hiring fixed inputs.
   c. They are explicit if they are associated with using variable inputs.
   d. all of the above
   e. They are never implicit.

_____ 12. In the short run, when output is zero,
    a. total cost is zero.
    b. total fixed cost is zero.
    c. total variable cost is zero.
    d. average fixed cost is zero.
    e. average total cost is zero.

_____ 13. In the short run, total variable cost
    a. is nonexistent.
    b. is positive when output is zero.
    c. increases with increasing output.
    d. decreases when the firm is experiencing diminishing returns.
    e. decreases when the firm is experiencing increasing returns.

_____ 14. In the short run, the average variable-cost curve
    a. is rising when marginal cost is falling.
    b. is falling when average product is rising.
    c. is parallel to the average total cost curve.
    d. lies above the average total cost curve.
    e. lies above the marginal cost curve whenever the marginal curve is rising.

_____ 15. In the short run, marginal cost is equal to
    a. total variable cost.
    b. total variable cost divided by output.
    c. the change in total cost divided by the change in output.
    d. the change in total variable cost divided by the change in output.
    e. both c and d above

_____ 16. The marginal cost curve must be
    a. rising at all output levels.
    b. rising when total cost is rising.
    c. less than average fixed cost when the average curve is rising.
    d. greater than average total cost when the average curve is rising.
    e. falling when the average total cost curve lies below the marginal curve.

_____ 17. In the long run,
    a. total cost is zero when output is zero.
    b. marginal cost is equal to total variable cost.
    c. total fixed cost is positive even when output is zero.
    d. average fixed cost is positive and decreases with rising output.
    e. all of the above

_____ 18. Economies of scale
   a. are associated with decreasing returns in the long run.
   b. are associated with increasing returns in the short run.
   c. occur whenever an increase in inputs causes a rise in output.
   d. occur whenever an increase in inputs causes a more-than-pro-
      portionate rise in output.
   e. occur whenever the long-run marginal-cost curve lies above
      the long-run average-cost curve.

_____ 19. When a firm is experiencing increasing returns to scale, the firm's
   a. long-run total-cost curve is increasing.
   b. long-run average-cost curve is declining.
   c. long-run marginal-cost curve is below the long-run average-
      cost curve.
   d. all of the above
   e. none of the above

_____ 20. Constant returns to scale
   a. may occur in the short run but not in the long run.
   b. may occur in the very long run but not in the long run.
   c. occur when an increase in inputs results in an exactly propor-
      tionate increase in output.
   d. mean that the long-run total-cost curve is constant.
   e. mean that the average fixed-cost curve is constant.

_____ 21. Diseconomies of scale
   a. occur when the long-run average-cost curve is decreasing.
   b. mean that a firm is experiencing increasing returns to scale.
   c. occur when a firm's marginal-cost curve is declining.
   d. occur when a firm's marginal-cost curve is below its long-run
      average-cost curve.
   e. none of the above

_____ 22. As output increases, long-run decreasing returns may be
   a. caused by increased management costs.
   b. represented by declining long-run average cost.
   c. associated with economies of scale in the short run.
   d. consistent with rising or falling long-run average cost.
   e. the result of cost advantages associated with specialization.

_____ 23. The long-run average-cost curve is
   a. made up of points from short-run average total-cost curves.
   b. made up of the minimum points on the short-run average
      total-cost curves.
   c. tangent to points of minimum average cost on all short-run
      average-cost curves.
   d. tangent to points associated with declining short-run average
      cost when there are diseconomies of scale.
   e. both a and b above

____ 24. For a given level of output, the existence of economies of scale suggest that
    a. a firm would build a plant that is too big from a short-run efficiency standpoint.
    b. a firm would overutilize plant and capacity.
    c. marginal cost is negative.
    d. long-run average cost is negative.
    e. total fixed cost is constant.

____ 25. The very long run is a time period long enough for a change in
    a. technological progress.
    b. the productivity of labor.
    c. the quality of productive inputs.
    d. all of the above
    e. none of the above

Discussion Questions

1. Explain why the marginal product of a worker is not the output produced by that worker.

2. "In the short run, the marginal product of labor diminishes because each new worker hired is less skilled than previous workers." Do you agree? Explain.

3. Explain the relationship between total variable cost and marginal returns.

4. Short-run marginal cost is the change in total cost associated with the production of an additional unit of output. Alternatively, short-run marginal cost is the change in total variable cost associated with the production of an additional unit of output. Explain.

5. What do economists mean when they refer to the scale of operation?

6. Define increasing, constant, and decreasing returns to scale in terms of the relationship between changes in inputs and the corresponding changes in output.

7. Give at least two reasons for economies of scale and at least two reasons for diseconomies of scale.

Answers

Problems and Applications

1.

Variable Input	Marginal Product	Average Product
1	10	10
2	12	11
3	11	11
4	7	10
5	5	9

2.

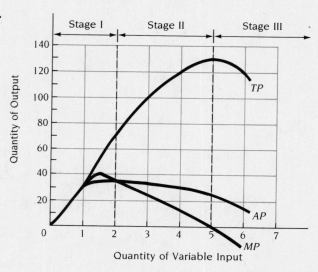

3.

TP	TFC	TVC	TC	AFC	AVC	ATC	MC
0	$10	$ 0	$10	—	—	—	—
1	10	5	15	$10	$5	$15	$5
2	10	9	19	5	4.5	9.5	4
3	10	15	25	3.3	5	8.3	6
4	10	22	32	2.5	5.5	8	7
5	10	30	40	2	6	8	8

4. The *AFC* is the difference between the *ATC* and the *AVC*. As output rises, *AFC* declines so the difference between *ATC* and *AVC* declines. That is, *ATC* and *AVC* get closer together as output rises.

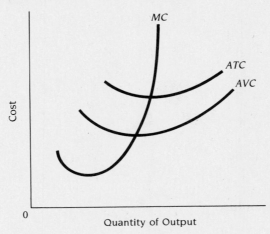

5. OB or Q′E; OC or Q′F; BC or EF; OA or Q′D; the area of rectangle OBEQ′; the area of rectangle OCFQ′; the area of rectangle BCFE.

6. $10; $100; $20; $15; $15

True-False

1. T.
2. T.
3. F. A production function shows the maximum output that can be produced from given amounts of inputs or it shows the minimum amount of inputs needed to produce a given level of output.
4. T.
5. F. Economic efficiency requires technical efficiency.
6. F. In the short run, at least one input is fixed.
7. F. The marginal product of the fourth worker is the extra output associated with employing that fourth worker.
8. F. The average product of four workers is the total output produced by four workers divided by four.
9. T.
10. T.
11. F. When a firm is experiencing diminishing returns in the short run, both total cost and total variable cost increase at an increasing rate.

12. F. Stage II begins at the level of variable input associated with maximum average product.

13. T.

14. T.

15. F. The average fixed-cost curve is negatively sloped.

16. T.

17. F. Both total cost and total variable cost increase throughout all three stages of production.

18. T.

19. T.

20. T.

21. F. A change in fixed cost causes no change in marginal cost.

22. T.

23. T.

24. T.

25. F. The long run permits changes in all inputs but not in the production function; the very long run permits changes in the production function.

26. T.

27. T.

28. F. The United States has the highest productivity in the world, but its growth in productivity has been less than that in other countries in the last two decades.

Multiple Choice

1. e	2. e	3. b	4. d	5. b
6. c	7. b	8. d	9. a	10. c
11. a	12. c	13. c	14. b	15. e
16. d	17. a	18. d	19. d	20. c
21. a	22. a	23. a	24. a	25. d

Study Guide material for *Chapter 23, Appendix* follows.

Appendix: Summary

It is possible to determine a firm's most profitable combination of inputs for a given output level by using isoquants and isocosts. An isoquant map is a graphic illustration of a production function. Any particular isoquant identifies technically efficient input combinations that yield the same output level. Isocost lines identify input combinations that cost the same for given input prices.

For any given output level, the profit-maximizing firm will attempt to select the combination of inputs that is economically efficient. For a particular output, an economically efficient input combination is both technically efficient and lowest in cost. This input combination can be located by finding the point of tangency between the appropriate isoquant and the isocost lines. Given the prices of the inputs, it is not possible for the firms to find a lower cost combination of inputs that will produce the output indicated by the isoquant.

Appendix: Major Objectives

After you have finished this appendix, you will be able to do the following:

1. Define and describe the characteristics of isoquants, an isoquant map, and isocost lines.
2. Construct and interpret graphs of isoquants and isocost lines, and determine the most profitable input combination.

Appendix: Review Terms

indifference curve analysis
slope

Appendix: Important Terms and Concepts

isoquant
isoquant map
isocost line

Completion

"same quantity"	The word *isoquant* means _____ . Economists
technically	use the term to refer to a curve that shows all _____
inputs	efficient combinations of _____ that yield a given level of
output	_____ . A collection of isoquants, called a(n)
isoquant map	_____ , is a way of representing a
production	_____ function.
"same cost"	The word *isocost* means _____ . Economists
inputs	use the term to refer to combinations of _____ that cost the
	same. The slope of an isocost line is given by the ratio of the
input prices	_____ ; the location of the line is determined by
	the total cost. Given the prices of the inputs, greater total cost is
right	indicated by a shift in the isocost to the _____ (right/left).

If the price of an input changes, the isocost will rotate, because of the change in its slope.

Assume that a firm has selected an output level. This output level

isoquant   can be represented graphically by a single _____ (isoquant/isocost). In order to maximize the profits associated with this particular output, the firm should select the input combination

lowest cost   that produces the output at _____ . This input

tangency   combination will be identified by a _____ between the isoquant and an isocost.

Appendix: Problems and Applications

1. Assume that the per-unit prices of labor and capital are $5 each.
   a. Draw the isocost associated with a total cost of $5.
   b. Draw the isocost associated with a total cost of $10.
   c. Let the price of capital rise to $10 per unit. Assuming a total cost of $10 and no change in the labor price, draw the new isocost line.
   d. Let the price of labor fall to $2 per unit. Still assuming a total cost of $10 and a capital price of $10, draw the new isocost line.

2. Assume that the per-unit prices of labor and capital are $5 each. The output level associated with the isoquant drawn on the graph below is 36 units. Identify the input combination that enables a firm to produce this output at the lowest cost. What is the total cost associated with your selection?

Appendix: True-False

Indicate whether each of the following statements is basically true or false. If the statement is false, rewrite it so that it is true.

_____ 1. For any given output level, the combination of inputs that is economically efficient is also the combination that maximizes profits.

_____ 2. Isoquants indicate output levels that are equally costly.

_____ 3. An isoquant map is a graphic representation of a firm's production function.

_____ 4. There is an isoquant for each output level.

_____ 5. Isoquants intersect at the economically efficient combination of inputs.

_____ 6. Isocosts indicate output levels that are equally costly.

_____ 7. For a given level of output, a profit-maximizing firm will hire equal amounts of capital and labor.

_____ 8. The profit-maximizing combination of inputs needed to produce any given level of output can be determined by the point of tangency of the isoquant and an isocost line.

Appendix: Multiple Choice

Choose the *one best* answer in each of the following cases:

_____ 1. An isoquant shows
    a. combinations of inputs that cost the same.
    b. combinations of outputs that are equally costly.
    c. combinations of inputs that are economically efficient.
    d. technically efficient combinations of inputs that produce a particular level of output.
    e. technically efficient combinations of outputs that are produced with equal amounts of inputs.

_____ 2. Two points on a given isoquant are associated with equal
    a. output levels.
    b. input levels.
    c. costs.
    d. utility.
    e. none of the above

_____ 3. An isoquant map is a collection of
    a. isoquants.
    b. intersecting isoquants.
    c. only economically efficient isoquants.
    d. the isoquants that a firm can afford to produce.
    e. none of the above

_____ 4. On an isoquant map, an increase in output level is best
represented by a
   a. higher isoquant.
   b. movement upward along a given isoquant.
   c. movement to the right along a given isoquant.
   d. movement along the isocost line.
   e. rightward shift in the isocost line.

_____ 5. An isocost line identifies combinations of
   a. inputs that are equally costly.
   b. outputs that are equally costly.
   c. inputs that are equally productive.
   d. inputs that are technically efficient.
   e. outputs that are technically efficient.

_____ 6. The slope of an isocost line is
   a. positive.
   b. indicated by the ratio of the input prices.
   c. dependent on the level of inputs.
   d. influenced by the technical efficiency of the firm.
   e. all of the above

_____ 7. For a given level of output, a firm will maximize profits by
selecting the input combination
   a. associated with lowest costs.
   b. that is economically efficient.
   c. identified by the tangency of the isoquant with an isocost.
   d. all of the above
   e. none of the above

Use the graph below to answer questions 8 through 13.

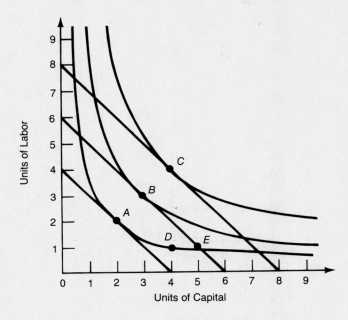

8. Which of the following is correct, according to the graph above?
   a. Output levels at points A and D are equivalent.
   b. Output levels at points A, B, and C are equivalent.
   c. Output levels at points B and E are equivalent.
   d. Output levels at points D and E cost the same.
   e. The output level associated with point E is greater than the output level associated with point B.

9. Which of the following is correct, according to the graph?
   a. Input combinations associated with points B and E cost the same.
   b. Input combinations associated with points A, B, and C cost the same.
   c. Input combinations associated with points A and D cost the same.
   d. The cost of the input combination associated with point E is less than the cost of the input combination associated with point A.
   e. none of the above

_____ 10. Referring to the graph, which of the following points is associated with the largest level of output?
           a. A
           b. B
           c. C
           d. D
           e. E

_____ 11. According to the graph, which of the following points is associated with the lowest total cost?
           a. A
           b. B
           c. C
           d. D
           e. E

_____ 12. Consider the isocost lines in the graph. If labor costs $1 per unit,
           then
           a. the capital cost is $1 per unit.
           b. the lowest isocost line shown is associated with a budget
               of $8.
           c. a profit-maximizing firm will hire two units of labor.
           d. a profit-maximizing firm will hire four units of capital.
           e. none of the above

_____ 13. If labor and capital each cost $1 per unit and a profit-
           maximizing firm has decided to produce the output level associated with point B, the firm will
           a. incur a total cost of $6.
           b. hire three units of labor.
           c. hire three units of capital.
           d. all of the above
           e. none of the above

Appendix:
Discussion
Questions

1. Explain why two isoquants could not intersect. Would greater
    output be associated with higher or lower isoquants? Explain.

2. Explain what happens to an isocost line when total
    increases. Explain what happens to an isocost line when total
    cost decreases. Explain what happens to an isocost line if the
    price of one input rises. Explain what happens to an isocost
    line if the price of one input falls.

3. Assume that a firm has a limited amount of money to spend on
    the production of a particular good. Explain how you could use
    an isoquant map to determine the maximum output possible at
    the given cost. Would your approach yield an economically
    efficient solution? Explain.

Appendix:
Answers

Problems and Applications

1. a. the isocost shown by the solid line on the graph below
   b. the isocost shown by the dashed line on the graph below
   c. the isocost shown by the dotted line on the graph below
   d. the isocost shown by the dotted-dashed line on the graph
      below

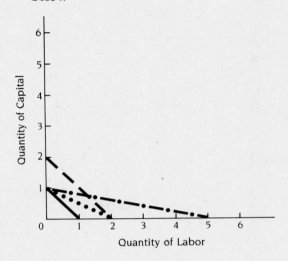

2. The least-cost input combination is 6 units of labor and 6 units
   of capital; the total cost is $60.

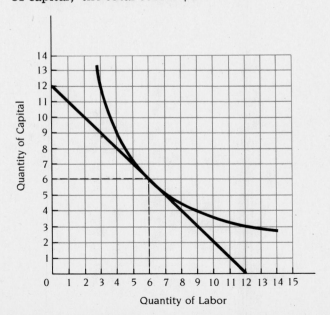

True-False

1. T.
2. F. Isoquants indicate technically efficient combinations of inputs that produce equal output levels.
3. T.
4. T.
5. F. Since each isoquant represents a different output level, it is not possible for isoquants to intersect.
6. F. Isocosts indicate combinations of inputs that are equally costly.
7. F. For a given level of output, a profit-maximizing firm will hire the input level associated with the point of tangency of the appropriate isoquant with an isocost line.
8. T.

Multiple Choice

1. d	2. a	3. a	4. a	5. a
6. b	7. d	8. a	9. a	10. c
11. a	12. a	13. d		

24 *Market Supply and Elasticity*

Summary

Rational business firms are assumed to be profit maximizers. In the real world, firms may have additional objectives. In fact, there is reason to believe and evidence that suggests that real-world firms do not always perceive profit maximization as their primary objective. Nonetheless, profit maximization is generally considered to be the single most appropriate motivating factor when studying a firm.

Profit is the difference between total revenue and total cost. Total revenue is a firm's total receipts from sales. For the economist, but rarely for the accountant, total cost includes implicit as well as explicit costs. Normal profit, the return to enterprise that will just keep the firm in business in the long run, is considered by the economist to be part of total cost. Economic profit, then, is revenue in excess of this and other costs. When economic profit is zero, the firm is said to break even and there will be sufficient revenue to pay normal profit. Negative economic profit is sometimes referred to as an economic loss. In this case, profit maximization is equivalent to loss minimization.

In maximizing profit, a producing firm produces the output level that generates the greatest positive difference between total revenue and total cost. This is equivalent to producing an output level such that marginal revenue is equal to rising marginal cost.

Marginal revenue is the extra revenue associated with selling the last or the next unit. Marginal cost is the extra cost associated with producing that last or next unit. If marginal revenue exceeds marginal cost, production of an additional unit adds more to revenue than to cost. A firm adds to its profit by producing the extra unit. This particular firm would continue to produce additional units as long as marginal revenue exceeds marginal cost. On the other hand, if marginal cost exceeds marginal revenue, the last unit adds more to the firm's cost than to its revenue. Thus, a profit-maximizing firm would cut back its production. This firm would continue to cut back as long as marginal cost exceeds marginal revenue. The firm will finally be in equilibrium when it produces the output such that marginal revenue is just equal to marginal cost.

There are some circumstances in which a profit-maximizing firm will decide not to produce. In the short run, a firm does not have the option of going out of business. The best a firm with losses can do is to minimize its losses. A firm will shut down its operation (produce nothing) when the price of the product is not sufficient to cover the firm's variable costs. Then the firm's losses will be limited to its fixed costs.

In the long run, a firm can enter or exit an industry. A firm that is incurring economic losses will go out of business in the long run. Note that a firm will be perfectly content to continue in operation when it is just breaking even. When a firm breaks even, it is earning a normal profit. Normal profit is the opportunity cost associated with enterprise. That is, it is an amount equivalent to what that enterprise could earn in its next best endeavor. Since no other endeavor will earn the firm a higher return on enterprise, there is no reason to go out of business.

Price elasticity of supply is a way of measuring the responsiveness of quantity supplied to a change in the price of a good. It is the percentage change in quantity supplied due to a percentage change in price.

When the coefficient of elasticity is less than 1, supply is inelastic. A given percentage change in price will result in a smaller percentage change in quantity supplied. In the extreme, when the coefficient of elasticity is zero, supply is said to be perfectly inelastic. In such a case, a change in the price of the good causes no change in the quantity supplied and the supply curve will be vertical.

When the coefficient of elasticity is equal to 1, supply is unitary elastic. A given percentage change in price causes an equivalent percentage change in quantity supplied. When the supply curve is a straight line through the origin, it will be unitary elastic at all prices.

When the coefficient of elasticity is greater than 1, supply is elastic. In this case, the percentage change in quantity supplied is greater than the percentage change in price. In the extreme, when the coefficient of elasticity is infinity, supply is said to be infinitely elastic. In the infinitely elastic case, the supply curve will be horizontal.

Elasticity of supply tends to increase over time as firms have greater opportunities to adjust to price changes. Elasticity of supply will also be influenced by the change in average cost incurred by a firm when it changes the quantity of its output.

Major Objectives After you have finished this chapter, you will be able to do the following:

1. Discuss the problems associated with the assumption of profit maximization in business decision making and also the appropriateness of such an assumption.
2. Define satisfice.
3. Discuss alternative goals of business.
4. Define total revenue and total cost.
5. Define profit and loss.
6. Define and distinguish accounting profit, normal profit, and economic profit.
7. Identify the breakeven output level and explain what it means to break even.
8. Identify the profit-maximizing output level given total revenue and total cost data.
9. State and explain the rule for determining the profit-maximizing or loss-minimizing output level.
10. Graph and explain the total revenue and total cost curves and the corresponding marginal revenue and marginal cost curves.
11. Identify output levels associated with economic loss, breakeven, and economic profit, using graphs of the total revenue and total cost curves.
12. Graphically identify and explain the profit-maximizing output level, using both the total revenue–total cost approach and the marginal revenue–marginal cost approach.
13. Identify and explain the conditions under which a firm will go out of business.
14. Identify and explain the conditions under which a firm will produce at a loss.
15. Identify and explain the conditions under which a firm will shut down.
16. Define, explain, calculate, and interpret price elasticity of supply.
17. State and explain the formula for price elasticity of supply and use it to calculate the coefficient of elasticity.
18. Identify, interpret, and explain the five different degrees of elasticity of supply and indicate the consequences of each for the graph of the supply curve.
19. Identify and explain the determinants of price elasticity of supply.

Review Terms

rationality
theory
long run
total revenue (TR)

total cost (TC)
implicit cost
explicit cost
opportunity cost

demand
increasing returns
diminishing returns
fixed cost
inventory
marginal cost (MC)
marginal revenue (MR)
short run
variable cost
supply
quantity supplied
positive slope
law of supply
elasticity
change in price (ΔP)
average price ($\overline{P}$)

coefficient of elasticity
inelastic
elastic
perfectly inelastic
perfectly elastic
infinitely elastic
infinity
unitary elasticity
rectangular hyperbola
origin of graph
average cost
substitutes
inputs
specialized resources
time

Important Terms and Concepts

profit maximization
loss minimization
uncertainty
probabilities
satisfice
profit
loss
accounting profit
normal profit
economic profit

economic loss
breakeven
"lumpy" data versus continuous
   data
exit vs. shut down
price elasticity of supply (E_S)
change in quantity supplied
   (ΔQ_S)
average quantity supplied ($\overline{Q}_S$)
productive capacity

Completion

maximize profit

The objective of a rational firm is to _____ .

total revenue

Profit is the difference between _____ and

total cost

_____ . Though an accountant is likely to consider only monetary costs, the economist includes both

implicit, explicit

_____ and _____ costs in determining a firm's profit. Economists include normal profit as part of total

cost, enterprise

_____ . Normal profit is the return to _____

in business

that is just sufficient to keep the firm _____ in the

long

_____ run.

   In order to maximize profit, a firm will produce that level of out-

marginal revenue, marginal cost	put that equates _____ and _____
below	so long as marginal cost intersects marginal revenue from _____ (above/below). A firm that is not producing this level of output is
equilibrium	not in _____ . That is, the firm will continue to make adjustments in its output. Consider, for example, a situation in which marginal revenue exceeds marginal cost. The firm can increase its
increasing	profit by _____ (increasing/decreasing) its output. Similarly, if marginal cost exceeds marginal revenue, the firm can in-
decreasing	crease its profit by _____ (increasing/decreasing) its output.
shut down	A firm that is losing money will _____ (exit/shut down) in the short run when the market price is not sufficient to
average variable cost	cover the firm's _____ . In the long run, a firm will go out of business when it has an eco-
less than	nomic profit _____ (equal to/less than) zero. An economic profit of zero means the firm is earning enough to cover
normal, is	its _____ profit. Normal profit _____ (is/is not) sufficient to keep the firm in business in the long run. The sensitivity of one variable to a change in another variable is
elasticity	measured by _____ . The price elasticity of supply is
percentage, quantity supplied	the _____ change in _____ due
percentage, price	to a _____ change in _____ . The coefficient can be calculated from a supply schedule by the following formula:
change in quantity supplied / sum of quantities supplied	(_____)/(_____)
change in price / sum of prices	(_____)/(_____)
	The determinants of price elasticity of supply include the length
time	of _____ suppliers have to adjust to the price change and the
substitute	availability of _____ resources, which is indicated
average cost	by the change in _____ that is incurred by a firm when it alters the quantity of its output.

Problems and Applications

1. Consider a profit-maximizing firm with the following marginal revenue and marginal cost data:

Output	Marginal Revenue	Marginal Cost
Q_1	15	18
Q_2	14	14
Q_3	13	10
Q_4	12	12
Q_5	11	15

   a. What is the equilibrium output level for the firm?

   b. Is the firm maximizing profit at an output of Q_2? If not, how could the firm increase its profit? Explain.

2. Consider a profit-maximizing firm with the marginal revenue and marginal cost curves described in the graph below.

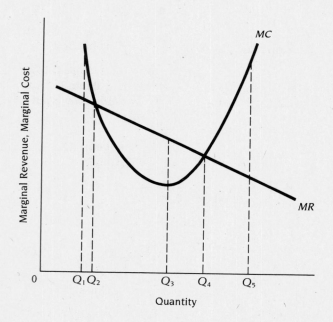

   a. What is the equilibrium output level for the firm?

   b. Is the firm maximizing profit at an output of Q_2? If not, how could the firm increase its profit? Explain.

   c. Why wouldn't a profit-maximizing firm be content with output Q_3?

3. Consider a profit-maximizing firm in the short run. Assume that $Q*$ is the output level at which marginal revenue equals rising marginal cost. At $Q*$, the firm's total fixed cost is $100 and its total variable cost is $80.

   a. What is the firm's total cost at $Q*$?
   b. What is the firm's total cost at zero units of output?
   c. Assume that the market price is such that total revenue is $200 at $Q*$. How much economic profit will be earned?
   d. Assume that the market price is such that total revenue is $180 at $Q*$. How much economic profit will be earned?
   e. Assume that the market price is such that total revenue is $150 at $Q*$. Will the firm produce $Q*$? How much economic profit will be earned?
   f. Assume that the market price is such that total revenue is $90 at $Q*$. Will the firm produce $Q*$? How much economic profit will be earned?
   g. Assume that the market price is such that total revenue is $70 at $Q*$. Will the firm produce $Q*$? How much economic profit will be earned?

4. Consider the supply schedule below:

Supply of Googoos

Price	Quantity
$2	100
4	150
6	250
8	400

   a. What is the elasticity of supply for googoos for price changes between $2 and $4?
   b. What is the elasticity of supply for googoos for price changes between $4 and $2?
   c. What is the elasticity of supply for googoos for price changes between $6 and $8?
   d. Is supply elastic or inelastic in the price range between $2 and $4?
   e. Is supply elastic or inelastic in the price range between $6 and $8?
   f. In the price range between $2 and $4, what happens to the quantity supplied if the price increases by 5 percent?
   g. In the price range between $2 and $4, what happens to the quantity supplied if the price decreases by 50 percent?
   h. In the price range between $6 and $8, what happens to the quantity supplied if the price increases by 13 percent?

5. Consider the following supply curves.

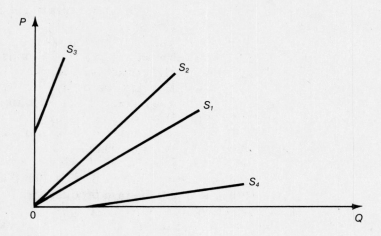

a. Which of the four supply curves is (are) unit elastic?
b. Which of the four supply curves is (are) relatively elastic?
c. Which of the four supply curves is (are) relatively inelastic?

True-False   Indicate whether each of the following statements is basically true or false. If the statement is false, rewrite it so that it is true.

_____ 1. A rational firm is in equilibrium when it is maximizing profit.

_____ 2. A rational firm will always make a positive profit.

_____ 3. Profit maximization is the only objective of real-world firms.

_____ 4. Profit maximization is typically easier in large, complex firms with many layers of management.

_____ 5. Profit is the difference between total revenue and total cost.

_____ 6. In calculating economic profit, economists consider only explicit costs.

_____ 7. A firm breaks even when total revenue equals total cost.

_____ 8. A profit-maximizing firm will typically produce the output level that equates marginal revenue with rising marginal cost.

_____ 9. If marginal revenue exceeds rising marginal cost, a rational firm will increase its output.

_____ 10. Normal profit is the return to enterprise that a firm must receive in order for the firm to be willing to continue in business in the long run.

_____ 11. In the short run, a firm that can cover its fixed cost will produce even at a loss.

_____ 12. When total cost exceeds total revenue, a profit-maximizing firm will shut down in the short run.

_____ 13. The price elasticity of supply is the percentage change in quantity supplied divided by the percentage change in price.

_____ 14. A perfectly inelastic supply curve is horizontal.

_____ 15. Any straight line drawn through the origin of a graph has a price elasticity of supply equal to 1.

_____ 16. When a 10 percent rise in price results in a 5 percent increase in quantity supplied, the price elasticity of supply is 2.

_____ 17. Over time, price elasticity of supply tends to decrease.

_____ 18. Price elasticity of supply is likely to be greater when there are relatively good substitute factors of production.

_____ 19. A supply curve will tend to be steeper in the long run than in the short run.

Multiple Choice   Choose the *one best* answer in each of the following cases:

_____ 1. Real-world uncertainty
   a. makes profit maximization more difficult.
   b. assures that firms will attempt to maximize profit.
   c. eliminates the possibility of satisficing behavior.
   d. all of the above
   e. none of the above

_____ 2. To satisfice means to
   a. maximize sales.
   b. maximize profit.
   c. minimize total cost.
   d. seek satisfactory profit.
   e. attempt to satisfy consumers.

_____ 3. The economist's definition of profit
   a. considers implicit as well as explicit costs.
   b. is likely to differ from the accountant's definition.
   c. both a and b above
   d. requires that firms actually make a monetary payment to cover implicit costs.
   e. all of the above

_____ 4. In economics, normal profit is
  a. considered to be a cost.
  b. always less than economic profit.
  c. zero when economic profit is zero.
  d. any revenue in excess of total cost.
  e. any revenue in excess of the implicit costs of the firm.

_____ 5. When a firm is breaking even, it must be true that its
  a. normal profit is zero.
  b. economic profit is zero.
  c. total revenue equals its explicit costs.
  d. both a and b above
  e. none of the above

_____ 6. In the short run, a firm that is earning less than normal profit
  a. will generally go out of business.
  b. will always shut down its operation.
  c. will attempt to minimize its losses.
  d. may still be covering its total costs.
  e. all of the above

_____ 7. In order to maximize profit, a firm will produce an output level that
  a. guarantees a normal profit of zero.
  b. equates total revenue and total cost.
  c. permits marginal revenue to exceed marginal cost.
  d. enables it to maximize the difference between marginal revenue and marginal cost.
  e. none of the above

_____ 8. When marginal cost is rising and is also greater than marginal revenue, a profit-maximizing firm will
  a. lose money.
  b. decrease its output.
  c. shut down in the short run.
  d. go out of business in the long run.
  e. all of the above

_____ 9. When marginal revenue equals rising marginal cost,
  a. the best a firm can do is break even.
  b. a firm should increase its production.
  c. a firm is always making a positive economic profit.
  d. total revenue exceeds total cost by the greatest amount.
  e. a firm should cut back its production by one unit so that marginal revenue will exceed marginal cost.

Use the following graph to answer questions 10 and 11.

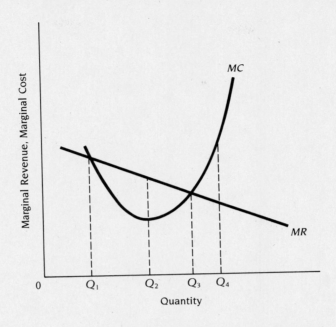

_____ 10. Consider the firm described by the marginal revenue and marginal cost curves in the graph above. If this firm is currently making positive economic profit by producing Q_2 units of output, then the firm
  a. could increase its profit by increasing its output.
  b. could maximize profit by decreasing its output to Q_1.
  c. maximizes profit by producing any output between Q_1 and Q_3.
  d. is maximizing profit, since marginal revenue exceeds marginal cost by the maximum amount.
  e. none of the above

_____ 11. Consider the firm described in the graph above. Which of the following conclusions is accurate with respect to this firm?
  a. The firm maximizes profit at output Q_3.
  b. The firm always earns a positive economic profit at output Q_3.
  c. The firm could not be earning a positive economic profit if it is producing Q_4.
  d. The firm is guaranteed a positive economic profit as long as it produces in the region between Q_1 and Q_3.
  e. all of the above

_____ 12. In the long run, a profit-maximizing firm will
   a. always earn positive economic profit.
   b. shut down when it is breaking even.
   c. go out of business when economic profit is zero.
   d. continue to produce even if it earns only normal profit.
   e. none of the above

_____ 13. In the short run, a profit-maximizing firm will
   a. always break even.
   b. shut down when it is breaking even.
   c. go out of business when economic profit is zero.
   d. continue to produce even if it earns only normal profit.
   e. none of the above

_____ 14. In the short run, a profit-maximizing firm will continue to produce at a loss
   a. whenever price exceeds marginal revenue.
   b. only if price exceeds average fixed cost.
   c. whenever price exceeds average variable cost.
   d. whenever marginal revenue exceeds marginal cost.
   e. whenever average variable cost exceeds average fixed cost.

_____ 15. Which of the following sayings most closely illustrates the shut-down point for a firm in the short run?
   a. "Don't cry over spilled milk."
   b. "A woman's work is never done."
   c. "The early bird catches the worm."
   d. "Do as I say, not as I do."
   e. "Home is where the heart is."

_____ 16. Elasticity of supply is the
   a. inverse of elasticity of demand.
   b. percentage change in cost divided by the percentage change in quantity supplied.
   c. percentage change in price divided by the percentage change in quantity supplied.
   d. percentage change in demand divided by the percentage change in quantity supplied.
   e. none of the above

_____ 17. Assume that a firm supplies 100 units at a price of $10 and 140 units at a price of $14. The price elasticity of supply is
   a. 0.
   b. 1/6.
   c. 1.
   d. 6.
   e. indeterminate.

_____ 18. If the price elasticity of supply is less than 1, the supply curve
   a. must be negatively sloped.
   b. must be a rectangular hyperbola.
   c. will be horizontal or nearly horizontal.
   d. will be a straight line through the origin.
   e. none of the above

_____ 19. Assume the current price is such that the elasticity of supply is equal to 1. Which of the following conclusions is accurate?
   a. The firm is breaking even.
   b. The firm is maximizing profit.
   c. The elasticity of demand is equal to 1.
   d. Quantity supplied is equal to quantity demanded.
   e. none of the above

_____ 20. If supply is perfectly inelastic and demand is relatively elastic, an increase in demand will result in
   a. a higher price and no change in quantity.
   b. a higher price and an increase in quantity.
   c. a lower price and an increase in quantity.
   d. a lower price and a decrease in quantity.
   e. a lower price and no change in quantity.

_____ 21. If supply is perfectly elastic, a decrease in demand will result in
   a. an increase in price and a decrease in quantity.
   b. an increase in price and no change in quantity.
   c. no change in price and no change in quantity.
   d. no change in price and a decrease in quantity.
   e. a decrease in price and no change in quantity.

_____ 22. An important determinant of both elasticity of demand and elasticity of supply is the
   a. total revenue of the firm.
   b. time period allowed for adjustment.
   c. degree of advertising in the market.
   d. availability of substitute resources.
   e. all of the above

_____ 23. Elasticity of supply tends to be greater when
   a. inputs are specialized.
   b. substitute resources are plentiful.
   c. demand for the product is inelastic.
   d. the time period for adjustment is fairly short.
   e. average cost increases sizably with rises in output.

Discussion Questions

1. It is not clear that firms always maximize profit.
   a. Provide examples of behavior that would seem to contradict the assumption of profit maximization.
   b. Suggest reasons why a firm might want to hold down profit deliberately.
   c. What might be alternative goals of real-world firms?

2. Distinguish the concepts of accounting profit, normal profit, and economic profit.

3. Explain the "marginal revenue–marginal cost" rule for profit maximization. Explain why a firm would not be profit maximizing if it stopped just short of the output at which marginal revenue equals rising marginal cost. Explain why the output at which marginal revenue equals declining marginal cost is not a profit-maximizing output.

4. Distinguish between shutting down and going out of business.

5. Explain why a profit-maximizing firm that is losing money might continue to produce in the short run. Why wouldn't the firm go out of business in the short run?

6. What is likely to happen to elasticity of supply, going from the short run to the very long run?

Answers

Problems and Applications

1. a. Q_4 b. no; increase output; marginal cost is falling

2. a. Q_4
   b. no; increase output; marginal cost is falling
   c. Marginal revenue exceeds marginal cost at Q_3. Hence, the firm can increase profit by producing more.

3. a. $180   b. $100   c. $20   d. $0
   e. yes; –$30   f. yes; –$90   g. no; –$100

4. a. 3/5   b. 3/5   c. 21/13   d. inelastic
   e. elastic   f. increases by 3%
   g. decreases by 30%   h. increases by 21%

5. a. S_1 and S_2
   b. S_3 (Note that any positively sloped straight-line supply curve that intersects the price axis is elastic.)
   c. S_4 (Note that any positively sloped straight-line supply curve that intersects the quantity axis is inelastic.)

True-False

1. T.
2. F. A rational firm will attempt to maximize profit or minimize loss.
3. F. Profit maximization may not be the major objective of a real-world firm; when it is, it need not be the only one.
4. F. Profit maximization may be more difficult in large, complex firms with many layers of management.
5. T.
6. F. In calculating economic profit, economists consider both implicit and explicit costs.
7. T.
8. T.
9. T.
10. T.
11. F. In the short run, a firm that can cover its variable cost will continue to produce, even at a loss.
12. F. When total cost exceeds total revenue, a profit-maximizing firm may or may not shut down in the short run; a shutdown occurs when price is less than average variable cost.
13. T.
14. F. A perfectly inelastic supply curve is vertical.
15. T.
16. F. When a 10 percent rise in price results in a 5 percent increase in quantity supplied, the price elasticity of supply is 1/2.
17. F. Over time, price elasticity of supply tends to increase.
18. T.
19. F. A supply curve will tend to be flatter in the long run than in the short run.

Multiple Choice

1. a	2. d	3. c	4. a	5. b
6. c	7. e	8. b	9. d	10. a
11. a	12. d	13. d	14. c	15. a
16. e	17. c	18. e	19. e	20. a
21. d	22. b	23. b		

25 *Pure Competition*

Summary

From the sellers' standpoint, there are four basic types of market structures: pure competition, pure monopoly, monopolistic competition, and oligopoly. This chapter concentrates on the first of these, pure competition.

Pure competition is a market structure characterized by a large number of sellers, all selling a standardized product, with no artificial restrictions and no barriers to entry. The exact number of firms is not important. There must be enough firms so that each individual firm believes it can sell its total output at the market-determined price. If a firm can sell its total ouput at the market price, the firm has no incentive to offer the product at a lower price. Furthermore, since the different firms sell identical units, a firm that attempts to raise its price will find that it sells nothing. This means that the demand curve facing any individual firm is infinitely elastic or horizontal at the market price.

For any given output, the demand curve identifies the highest price that people will pay per unit. This price is the same as the average revenue received by the firm. That is, the demand curve is the same as the average revenue curve. The demand and average revenue curves are the same for all firms, regardless of the market structure.

For the purely competitive firm, the demand curve is also the marginal revenue curve. Marginal revenue measures the extra revenue associated with selling an additional unit. The purely competitive firm also always sells an additional unit for the same price. Hence, that price is the marginal revenue.

By equating marginal revenue to marginal cost in an attempt to maximize profit, the purely competitive firm produces along its marginal cost curve. This is true as long as the price is sufficient to cover the variable costs of production. If the price drops below the average variable cost, the firm can minimize losses by shutting down. That portion of the marginal cost curve above average variable cost, then, is the short-run supply curve for the firm. The market supply curve is the sum of the various firms' supply curves.

In the long run, firms will enter a purely competitive market when there are positive economic profits to be earned. Firms that are losing will exit the industry. This entry and exit process continues until the remaining firms are earning just-normal profit.

The long-run expansion or contraction of output in the total market may lead to changes in the cost curves of the individual firms. Depending on how the cost curves shift, there are three possible cases: the constant-cost market, the increasing-cost market, and the decreasing-cost market. In the constant-cost market, long-run changes in market output do not affect the average cost of production. Hence, long-run prices do not change with changes in output, and the long-run market-supply curve is horizontal. In the case of increasing cost, increases in market output result in higher resource prices and therefore higher average costs. These increases in average cost are represented by upward shifts in the average cost curves of the firms. This means that as market output increases in the long run, prices will rise and the long-run market-supply curve will be positively sloped. Decreasing-cost markets are much less common. In this case, long-run increases in output lead to decreases in resource prices and therefore in average costs. Consequently, as market output increases, prices fall and the long-run market-supply curve is negatively sloped.

Pure competition is difficult to find in the real world, although there are markets that approach it. More importantly, pure competition is generally considered to be the ideal market structure. One of the desirable outcomes of this market structure is the fact that, at equilibrium, price is equal to marginal cost. This means that any consumer who will pay what it costs a firm to produce an additional unit of the good will find that unit forthcoming. Furthermore, in long-run equilibrium, firms earn just normal profit. That is, enterprise earns its opportunity cost. By just breaking even in long-run equilibrium, firms are operating at minimum average cost and there are no wasted resources. In addition, purely competitive firms do not use scarce resources in advertising. And, finally, purely competitive firms will adopt improved products and technology in order to keep up with rivals.

That purely competitive firms will adopt improvements does not mean that they are necessarily inclined to promote research and development. Since purely competitive firms just break even in the long run, they may not have sufficient incentive or funds to carry out research and development.

There are two other potential shortcomings of pure competition. To the extent that consumers value variety, the standardized output of the purely competitive industry may be less than ideal. In addition, in industries with significant economies of scale, one or a few large firms may be able to produce the output demanded at lower average cost than can the many small producers of the purely competitive industry. Therefore, though pure competition is often considered the ideal, it is unlikely that most would advocate an economy composed entirely of purely competitive markets.

Major Objectives

After you have finished this chapter, you will be able to do the following:

1. Identify the three bases for distinguishing among sellers' market structures.
2. Identify and describe the four sellers' market structures.
3. Define and explain the two concepts of competition as the term is used by economists.
4. Define *price taker* and explain the term as it relates to pure competition.
5. Identify and explain the four conditions for pure competition.
6. Identify the conditions for perfect competition.
7. Distinguish between a firm, an industry, and a market.
8. Explain how the equilibrium market output and price are determined in a purely competitive market.
9. Distinguish between the market demand curve and a firm's demand curve in the case of a purely competitive market.
10. Identify and explain the characteristics of the demand curve facing a purely competitive firm.
11. Define, calculate, and graphically represent each of the following for a purely competitive firm: total revenue, average revenue, and marginal revenue.
12. Explain the relationships between demand and average revenue and between demand and marginal revenue for a pure competitor.
13. Identify and explain, verbally and graphically, the profit-maximizing or equilibrium condition for a pure competitor.
14. Identify and explain, verbally and graphically, the short-run supply curve for a pure competitor.
15. Identify and explain, verbally and graphically, the short-run market-supply curve for a purely competitive industry.
16. Determine and graphically represent a purely competitive firm's short-run profit or loss.

17. Identify and explain the characteristics of long-run equilibrium under pure competition and describe, verbally and graphically, the process whereby the market adjusts to this equilibrium position.
18. Describe and construct the long-run market-supply curve in the case of a purely competitive market for a constant-cost market, an increasing-cost market, and a decreasing-cost market.
19. Identify conditions that are likely to give rise to constant-cost, increasing-cost, and decreasing-cost markets.
20. Discuss the purely competitive model in terms of its application to the real world.
21. Evaluate pure competition in terms of political and economic criteria, indicating both its advantages and shortcomings.

Review Terms

market
price controls
collusion
free market
short run
long run
market demand
negative slope
law of demand
substitution effect
income effect
supply
market supply
positive slope
law of supply
profit
market equilibrium
infinitely elastic demand curve
total revenue (TR)

marginal revenue (MR)
rational firm
total cost (TC)
marginal cost (MC)
equilibrium
profit-maximizing or equilibrium condition
shut down
average variable cost (AVC)
normal profit
opportunity cost
economic profit
economic loss
average total cost (ATC)
fixed cost
tangent
infinitely elastic supply curve
excess demand
excess supply

Important Terms and Concepts

sellers' market structures
pure competition
pure monopoly
monopolistic competition
oligopoly
number of sellers
differentiated products
standardized products
entry and exit conditions

rivalry
price taker
artificial restrictions
barriers to entry
perfect competition
perfect knowledge
perfect mobility
firm
industry

average revenue (AR)   constant-cost market
short-run market supply   decreasing-cost market
long-run market supply   invisible hand
long-run equilibrium   advertising
increasing-cost market

Completion

rivalry	The term *competition* has two different uses in economics. It is used to describe _____ between buyers or sellers. It also is used to describe a type of market structure that is characterized by a large number of sellers who believe they have no control over the price of
pure competition	their product. This market structure is called _____ .
many sellers	There are four basic conditions for pure competition: _____ ,
a standardized product, no artificial restrictions on price or quantity	_____ , _____ ,
easy entry and exit	and _____ .
	In a purely competitive market, there must be enough firms so that
it has no control over price	each firm believes that _____ .
market	The price is determined by the _____ . Since each firm takes the price as given, the purely competitive firm is said to be a
price taker	_____ .
	The condition that competitive firms sell standardized products
do not	means that consumers _____ (do/do not) have a preference for one seller as opposed to another. *Standardized* means that the
identical, consumer	units are _____ in the eyes of the _____ .
	In defining pure competition, artificial restrictions refer to
price controls, collusive	government-imposed _____ and _____
sellers	agreements among _____ . The impossibility of artificial restrictions prevents these outside forces from interfering with the
market	operation of the _____ .
	Requiring easy entry and exit is equivalent to saying that there
barriers	are no _____ to entry. A new firm in the industry must be able to sell its product as easily as an established firm. Firms will typically be inclined to enter markets in which they can earn

positive economic
profit

_____ .
    A purely competitive firm has no incentive to offer its product for a price below the market price because the firm believes it can sell

all it wants to

_____ at the market-determined price.

nothing

The firm also believes that if it raises its price it will sell _____ . Therefore, the demand curve facing the purely competitive firm is

infinitely elastic

_____ .
    In general, when firms face negatively sloped demand curves, the firm can sell additional units only by offering the product for a

lower

_____ price. Since the purely competitive firm can sell all it

market-determined

wants at the _____ price, the extra revenue associated with the sale of an additional unit will be equal to the

price, marginal
revenue

_____ . That is, _____ is equal to

price

the _____ .
    Assuming that marginal cost is rising, the firm will maximize profit

marginal revenue

by producing where _____ equals

marginal cost

_____ . This means that, for any price, the

marginal cost

competitive firm will produce along its _____ curve. This will be true as long as the price is sufficient to cover the

average variable cost

_____ . If price is not sufficient to do

shut down

so, the firm will _____ . Hence, the short-run supply curve

marginal cost

for the competitive firm is that portion of its _____

average variable cost

curve that lies at or above _____ .
    The firm will earn positive economic profit whenever price or

revenue, average
cost

average _____ is greater than _____ . The

average cost

firm will break even when price is equal to _____ .

average cost

If the price is below _____ , the firm will incur an economic loss.

exit

    In the long run, a firm will _____ the industry when it is

supply

incurring a loss. This will cause market _____ to

decrease, rise

_____ (increase/decrease) and price to _____ (rise/fall). Price will change until the least profitable firm is just

breaking even

_____ .

In the long run, if firms in the industry are earning positive

enter

economic profits, new firms will _____ the market. This is

no barriers to entry

possible because there are _____
in purely competitive markets. The entry of new firms will cause

supply, increase

market _____ to _____ (increase/decrease),

fall

causing the price to _____ (rise/fall). Price will change until

breaking even

the most profitable firm is just _____ .
At equilibrium in the long run, purely competitive firms will earn

just-normal, break
even

_____ profit. That is, they will just _____ .
This is considered to be one of the advantages of the purely competitive structure. It means that a firm's earnings are equal to its

opportunity cost

_____ .

In long-run equilibrium a firm will also be operating at the mini-

average cost

mum point on its _____ curve. This means that the

resources

least amount of _____ is being used to produce that

cannot

level of output. A purely competitive firm _____ (can
continue to/cannot) survive in the long run if it wastes resources.

revenue

Under pure competition, price is equal to marginal _____ .
Hence, when the firm maximizes profit it automatically produces an

cost

output such that price is equal to marginal _____ . This means
that any consumer who is willing and able to pay what it costs the

will

firm to produce an additional unit _____ (will/will
not necessarily) be able to buy one. In market structures other than

greater than

pure competition, firms typically charge a price that is _____
(greater than/equal to/less than) marginal cost.

**Problems and
Applications**

1. Consider the purely competitive firm described by the table
   below.

Quantity	Total Revenue	Total Cost
20	$40	$30
21	42	31
22	44	33
23	46	36
24	48	40

a. What is the market price of its product? What is its average revenue? Identify the profit-maximizing output level. How much profit will be earned by the firm?

b. Assume that the total cost increases by $11 at all output levels. What is the market price? What is the average revenue? Identify the profit-maximizing output level. How much profit will be earned by the firm? Will the firm produce this output level in the long run?

2. Consider the pure competitor described by the cost curves in the graph below. Assume that the firm is a profit maximizer.

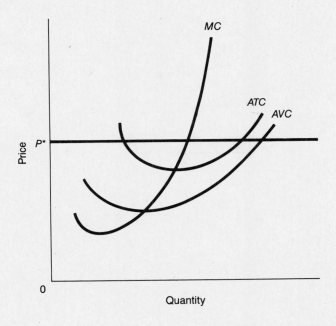

a. Identify the short-run supply curve for the firm.

b. Assume that the market price is P*. Identify the following curves for the firm: average revenue, marginal revenue, and demand. Find the profit-maximizing output level (Q*), the average total cost (ATC*) of producing this output level, and the average revenue (AR*) earned on sales. What is the per-unit profit?

c. Graphically indicate the total revenue, total cost, and economic profit associated with a price of P*.

3. Consider the pure competitor described by the cost curves in the graph below. Assume that the firm is a profit maximizer.

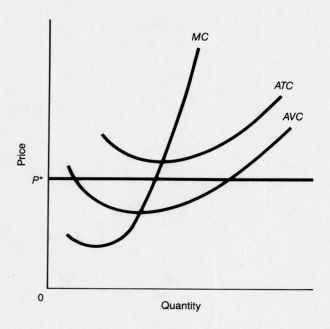

a. Identify the short-run supply curve for the firm.
b. Assume that the market price is P*. Identify the following curves for the firm: average revenue, marginal revenue, and demand. Find the profit-maximizing output level (Q*), the average total cost (ATC*) of producing this output level, and the average revenue (AR*) earned on sales. What is the per-unit profit?
c. Graphically indicate the total revenue, total cost, and economic profit associated with a price of P*.

4. Consider the pure competitor described by the cost curves in the graph below. Assume that the firm is a profit maximizer.

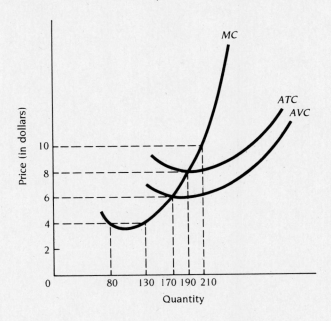

a. Assume that the market price is $10 per unit. What is the firm's average revenue? What is the marginal revenue? How many units of output will the firm produce?

b. Assume that the market price decreases to $8 per unit. What is the firm's average revenue? What is the marginal revenue? How many units of output will the firm produce? How much profit will the firm earn?

c. Assume that the market price decreases to $6 per unit. What is the firm's average revenue? What is the marginal revenue? How many units of output will the firm produce?

d. Assume that the market price decreases to $4 per unit. How many units of output will the firm produce?

e. At what price will the firm cease to earn positive economic profit? At what price will the firm shut down?

5. Consider a purely competitive firm that is in short-run equilibrium, operating at minimum average cost, and producing 100,000 units of output. The firm's average revenue is $10. (You may find it helpful to graph this problem; review the relationship between average and marginal curves.)

a. What is the market price?

b. What is the profit-maximizing output level?

c. What is the firm's marginal revenue at the profit-maximizing output? What would happen to marginal revenue if the firm increased its output? What would happen to marginal revenue if the firm decreased its output?

d. What is the firm's marginal cost at the profit-maximizing output?

e. How much profit is the firm earning?

f. Would this firm be content to remain in this industry in the long run?

True-False   Indicate whether each of the following statements is basically true or false. If the statement is false, rewrite it so that it is true.

_____ 1. Pure competition is characterized by a large number of firms and easy entry.

_____ 2. Monopolistic competition is characterized by a few firms and blocked entry.

_____ 3. Oligopolies in a given market must sell standardized products.

_____ 4. Entry into a pure monopoly market is blocked.

_____ 5. All markets in which there is rivalry are purely competitive.

_____ 6. Purely competitive firms are price takers.

_____ 7. In pure competition there must be at least 10,000 firms.

_____ 8. Perfect competition differs from pure competition in that perfectly competitive firms have perfect information and perfect mobility.

_____ 9. In pure competition, the market-demand curve is horizontal.

_____ 10. In pure competition, the market-supply curve is vertical.

_____ 11. In pure competition, price is determined by the interplay of market demand and market supply.

_____ 12. The total revenue curve for a purely competitive firm is horizontal.

_____ 13. In pure competition, average revenue or price is greater than marginal revenue.

_____ 14. A pure competitor's demand curve is perfectly inelastic.

_____ 15. A pure competitor maximizes profit at the output where marginal revenue exceeds marginal cost by the greatest amount.

_____ 16. The short-run supply curve for a pure competitor is that portion of its marginal cost curve at or above average variable cost.

_____ 17. The short-run market-supply curve under pure competition is the sum of the individual firms' short-run supply curves.

_____ 18. Under pure competition, firms always earn positive economic profit at short-run equilibrium.

_____ 19. In long-run equilibrium under pure competition, the entry and exit of firms will result in just-normal profits for firms in the industry.

_____ 20. In an increasing-cost market, long-run increases in output raise the average cost of production so that the price increases with increases in output.

Multiple Choice   Choose the *one best* answer in each of the following cases:

_____ 1. Pure competition is characterized by
   a. intense price wars.
   b. a standardized product.
   c. blocked entry and exit.
   d. a few extremely rivalrous firms.
   e. none of the above

_____ 2. Pure monopoly and pure competition
   a. are alike in that entry is easy in both.
   b. are alike in that entry is blocked in both.
   c. differ in terms of the number of firms in the industry.
   d. differ in that pure monopoly is associated with a standardized product and pure competition is associated with differentiated products.
   e. both c and d above

_____ 3. Pure competition differs from monopolistic competition in that pure competition is characterized by
   a. many sellers, whereas monopolistic competition is characterized by few sellers.
   b. few sellers, whereas monopolistic competition is characterized by many sellers.
   c. standardized products, whereas monopolistic competition is characterized by differentiated products.
   d. differentiated products, whereas monopolistic competition is characterized by standardized products.
   e. both a and c above

_____ 4. Oligopoly is a market structure characterized by
   a. a few firms.
   b. varying degrees of difficulty in entry.
   c. varying amounts of product differentiation.
   d. all of the above
   e. none of the above

_____   5. A purely competitive firm believes it can
    a. not influence the price of the product.
    b. obtain a higher price if it advertises.
    c. obtain a higher price if it improves its product.
    d. sell more units if it offers the product at a lower price.
    e. both b and c above

_____   6. To say that products are standardized means that they
    a. are similar, though not identical.
    b. meet government-established standards.
    c. are identical in the eyes of potential buyers.
    d. are identical in the eyes of potential buyers as well as being technically identical.
    e. are technically identical, though they need not be perceived as being identical by potential consumers.

_____   7. With respect to artificial restrictions, pure competition and perfect competition
    a. are similar in that artificial restrictions are absent in both.
    b. are similar in that artificial restrictions may be present in both.
    c. differ in terms of the extent to which artificial restrictions are permitted.
    d. differ in that the artificial restrictions in pure competition cannot exist in perfect competition.
    e. differ in that the artificial restrictions in perfect competition cannot exist in pure competition.

_____   8. Perfect competition requires
    a. perfect mobility.
    b. perfect information.
    c. all of the conditions required for pure competition.
    d. all of the above
    e. a larger number of sellers than the number required for pure competition.

_____   9. Under pure competition, the demand curve facing the market is generally
    a. horizontal, as is the demand curve facing the firm.
    b. negatively sloped, as is the demand curve facing the firm.
    c. vertical, whereas the demand curve facing the firm is horizontal.
    d. negatively sloped, whereas the demand curve facing the firm is horizontal.
    e. horizontal, whereas the demand curve facing the firm is negatively sloped.

_____   10. For a purely competitive firm, average revenue is
    a. the same as supply.
    b. equal to quantity sold.
    c. equal to marginal revenue.
    d. the total revenue divided by price.
    e. a straight line through the origin.

_____   11. Under pure competition, the firm's demand curve is
    a. infinitely elastic.
    b. the same as its average revenue curve.
    c. the same as its marginal revenue curve.
    d. horizontal at the market-determined price.
    e. all of the above

_____   12. A pure competitor maximizes profit by producing the output that
    a. equates price and average revenue.
    b. equates total revenue and total cost.
    c. equates average revenue and average total cost.
    d. equates marginal revenue and marginal cost.
    e. maximizes the difference between marginal revenue and marginal cost.

_____   13. A purely competitive firm that is in equilibrium will earn a positive economic profit whenever
    a. price exceeds average total cost.
    b. price exceeds marginal cost.
    c. price exceeds average revenue.
    d. price exceeds marginal revenue.
    e. marginal revenue exceeds marginal cost.

_____   14. When price is equivalent to a purely competitive firm's minimum average total cost, the firm will reach equilibrium with
    a. an economic loss.
    b. just-normal profit.
    c. positive economic profit.
    d. less than maximum profit.
    e. an indeterminate amount of profit.

_____   15. In the short run, when market price is less than a purely competitive firm's minimum total average cost, the firm
    a. should always shut down.
    b. should go out of business.
    c. will incur an economic loss.
    d. all of the above
    e. can earn just normal profit by following the rule for profit maximization.

_____ 16. A pure competitor will shut down in the short run whenever
   a. price is less than average total cost.
   b. price is less than average fixed cost.
   c. price is less than average variable cost.
   d. marginal revenue is less than marginal cost.
   e. average revenue is less than average total cost.

_____ 17. The short-run supply curve for a purely competitive firm is the firm's
   a. marginal revenue curve at or above its average-total-cost curve.
   b. marginal cost curve at or above its average fixed cost curve.
   c. marginal cost curve at or above its average variable cost curve.
   d. average cost curve at or above its marginal revenue curve.
   e. average cost curve at or above its minimum average variable cost curve.

_____ 18. In the long run, under pure competition, firms will
   a. exit the industry when price is equal to average cost.
   b. go out of business when price is less than average cost.
   c. shut down when price is less than average variable cost.
   d. all of the above
   e. none of the above

_____ 19. At equilibrium in the long run, purely competitive firms
   a. will just break even.
   b. will earn positive economic profit.
   c. may earn positive profit or break even.
   d. may earn positive profit or incur an economic loss.
   e. may earn positive, zero, or negative economic profit.

_____ 20. The long-run market-supply curve in a purely competitive industry
   a. will be horizontal.
   b. will be positively sloped.
   c. will be negatively sloped.
   d. may be positively sloped, horizontal, or negatively sloped.
   e. does not exist, since the industry is characterized by open entry and exit.

_____ 21. A constant-cost market is most likely characterized by
   a. specialized inputs that are relatively scarce.
   b. unspecialized inputs that are abundant in supply.
   c. a positively sloped long-run market-supply curve.
   d. decreases in average cost with the entry of new firms.
   e. none of the above

_____ 22. Under pure competition
   a. there is no advertising.
   b. long-run equilibrium is characterized by just-normal profits.
   c. firms produce at minimum average cost in long-run equilibrium.
   d. profit maximization results in a price that is just equal to marginal cost.
   e. all of the above

Discussion Questions

1. Identify some of the potential barriers to entry into a market.
2. Distinguish between pure and perfect competition.
3. Identify conditions that might give rise to positively sloped, horizontal, and negatively sloped long-run market supply curves.
4. Would a purely competitive firm advertise? Why or why not?
5. Explain how the existence of significant economies of scale might suggest that we would be better off with relatively few firms.
6. Pure competitors are price takers. They also do not advertise. Are they competitive in the ordinary sense of being rivalrous? Discuss.

Answers

Problems and Applications

1. a. $2; $2; between 21 and 22 units; $2; $11
   b. $2; $2; between 21 and 22 units; $2; $0; yes
2. a. The short-run supply curve is the firm's marginal-cost curve above its average variable cost.
   b. The average-revenue, marginal-revenue, and demand curves are indicated on the graph below. Q*, ATC*, and AR* are indicated on the graph below. Profit per unit is AR* - ATC*.
   c. Total revenue is the area shown by vertical lines on the graph below; total cost is the area shown by horizontal lines on the graph below; profit is the shaded area.

Graph for problem answer 2.

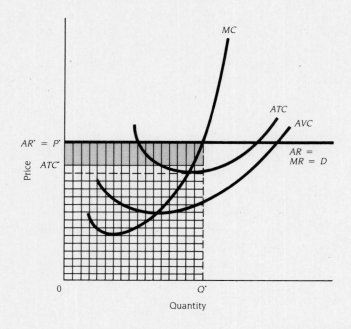

3. a. The short-run supply curve is a firm's marginal cost curve above its average variable cost.
   b. The average-revenue, marginal-revenue, and demand curves are indicated on the graph below. Q*, ATC*, and AR* are indicated on the graph below. Profit per unit is AR* − ATC*.
   c. Total revenue is the area shown by vertical lines on the graph below; total cost is the area shown by horizontal lines on the graph below; loss is the shaded area.

Graph for problem answer 3.

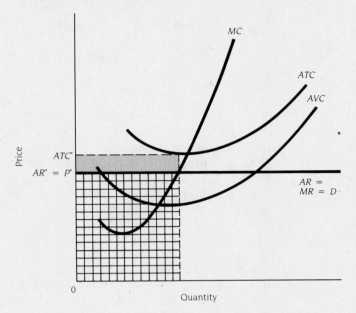

4. a. $10; $10; 210
   b. $8; $8; 190; $0
   c. $6; $6; 170
   d. 0
   e. $8; at or below $6

5. a. $10
   b. 100,000 units
   c. $10; remain the same; remain the same
   d. $10
   e. just-normal profit or zero economic profit
   f. yes

True-False

1. T.
2. F. Monopolistic competition is characterized by a large number
   of firms and easy entry.
3. F. Oligopolies in a given industry may sell standardized or differentiated products.
4. T.
5. F. Not all markets in which there is rivalry are purely
   competitive.

6. T.
7. F. In pure competition there are so many firms that each firm believes it cannot affect the market price by itself.
8. T.
9. F. In pure competition, the market-demand curve is generally negatively sloped.
10. F. In pure competition, the market-supply curve is generally positively sloped.
11. T.
12. F. The total revenue curve for a purely competitive firm is a straight line through the origin.
13. F. In pure competition, average revenue and marginal revenue are both equal to price.
14. F. A pure competitor's demand curve is infinitely elastic.
15. F. A pure competitor maximizes profit at the output where marginal revenue equals rising marginal cost.
16. T.
17. T.
18. F. Under pure competition, firms may earn positive economic profit at short-run equilibrium, but they may also just break even or even incur economic losses.
19. T.
20. T.

Multiple Choice

1. b	2. c	3. c	4. d	5. a
6. c	7. a	8. d	9. d	10. c
11. e	12. d	13. a	14. b	15. c
16. c	17. c	18. b	19. a	20. d
21. b	22. e			

26 *Monopoly*

Summary

Monopoly is a market structure in which there is only one firm. In other words, the monopoly firm is the industry. The monopoly is a pure monopoly when there are no acceptable substitutes for the firm's product. There is neither current nor anticipated rivalry in a pure monopoly. Like pure competition, pure monopoly is an extreme market type that does not exist in the real world. An actual monopoly, one that exists in the real world, is the only seller of a product for which there may be reasonable substitutes. Potential rivalry as well as government intervention in the form of protection and/or regulation may exist for the actual monopolist. An actual monopoly is government enforced if it owes its existence to some form of government protection, such as a franchise or a patent. Alternatively, an actual monopoly may arise because of economies of scale, in which case it is said to be a natural monopoly.

A firm has monopoly control or monopoly power when it has some influence over the price of its product. Any firm that faces a negatively sloped demand curve has monopoly control. Since only the pure competitor faces an infinitely elastic (horizontal) demand curve, it is the only type of firm that has no monopoly control. You will recall that the purely competitive firm is a price taker. The firm with monopoly control is a price searcher. A pure monopolist may be called a price maker, a term that implies full information and complete ability to act upon it.

A firm that faces a negatively sloped demand curve will have a negatively sloped marginal revenue curve that lies below the demand curve. From the relationship between price elasticity of demand and marginal revenue, we may note that marginal revenue will be positive when demand is elastic, zero when demand is unitary elastic, and negative when demand is inelastic.

Our assumption is that a rational firm is a profit maximizer. As with any firm, the pure monopolist maximizes profit at the output level that equates marginal revenue with rising marginal cost. The monopolist will charge the highest price people will pay for the output selected. This price is indicated by the demand curve. A pure monopolist may earn positive, zero, or negative economic profit. In the short run, a monopolist will shut down when price is not sufficient to cover average variable cost. In the long run, the monopolist will go out of business when it is incurring an economic loss.

Given the same market demand and cost conditions, an industry characterized by pure monopoly, as compared to pure competition, will produce less and charge a higher price in long-run equilibrium. Unlike the profit-maximizing purely competitive firm that charges a price equal to its marginal cost, the profit-maximizing monopolist will charge a price that is greater than marginal cost. In terms of average total cost, the promotion of progress, and equity, it is not clear exactly how the pure monopolist will behave.

A pure monopolist may engage in price discrimination in order to increase profit. Price discrimination occurs when price differentials for a given product are not justified by different costs. In order for price discrimination to be effective, the firm must have monopoly control, must be able to separate customers into different markets characterized by different elasticities of demand, and must be able to prevent resale of the product. Price discrimination may or may not be beneficial to society at large.

Major Objectives

After you have finished this chapter, you will be able to do the following:

1. Define, describe, and distinguish pure monopoly, actual monopoly, government-enforced monopoly, and natural monopoly.
2. Indicate the characteristics of a patent and explain its significance.
3. Define and describe the concept of monopoly control or monopoly power.
4. Identify and graphically construct the demand, average revenue, and marginal revenue curves for the pure monopolist.
5. Identify and explain, verbally and graphically, the relationship between marginal revenue, elasticity, and total revenue.
6. Identify elastic, inelastic, and unitary elastic regions on a straight-line negatively sloped demand curve.
7. Identify and describe, verbally and graphically, the profit-maximizing (equilibrium) output and price for the pure monopolist

in the short run under conditions of economic profit, just-normal profit, and economic loss.

8. Graphically indicate the profit or loss associated with short-run equilibrium for a monopolist under conditions of economic profit, just-normal profit, and economic loss.

9. Verbally and graphically describe the shutdown point for a pure monopolist.

10. Verbally and graphically describe the differences in the long-run conditions under pure monopoly and pure competition.

11. Identify and explain the relationships between price and marginal cost in the cases of pure competition and pure monopoly.

12. Identify and explain the welfare loss triangle associated with monopoly organization as compared to competitive organization.

13. Evaluate, verbally and graphically, and discuss the implications of a government action that would transfer resources from a purely competitive market to a purely monopolistic one.

14. Define and describe X-inefficiency, indicate its implications for average total cost, and explain why this may be a characteristic of pure monopoly but not of pure competition.

15. Indicate and discuss the implications of economies of scale for a comparison of the costs of production under monopoly versus pure competition.

16. Define progress, discuss the implications of progress for average total cost, and compare pure competition and pure monopoly in terms of the likelihood of progress.

17. Compare the pure monopoly and pure competition markets in terms of equity for consumers.

18. Define, distinguish between, and provide examples of price differentials and price discrimination.

19. Identify and explain the necessary conditions for price discrimination.

20. Define and cite examples of arbitrage.

21. Define and cite examples of dumping.

22. Explain how a monopolist can increase its profit by engaging in price discrimination when the necessary conditions exist.

23. Indicate the output and pricing decisions that would prevail under conditions of price discrimination and graphically illustrate them.

24. Evaluate price discrimination, indicating the harmful and beneficial effects.

25. Define and explain the basing-point system and indicate why it is a form of price discrimination.

Review Terms

pure competition
substitutes
competition
entry conditions
rival
average total cost
economies of scale
long-run average cost
price taker
perfectly inelastic demand
  curve
income effect
substitution effect
oligopoly
monopolistic competition
demand
negative slope
average revenue

marginal revenue
infinitely elastic
elasticity
total revenue
equilibrium
profit-maximizing or equilibrium
  condition
short run
long run
economic profit
economic loss
normal profit
shutdown
average variable cost
variable costs
opportunity cost
very long run
consumers' surplus

**Important Terms
and Concepts**

pure monopoly
actual monopoly
government-enforced monopoly
franchise
patent
natural monopoly
monopoly control or monopoly
  power
price maker
price searcher
welfare loss triangle

allocation of resources
X-inefficiency
progress
equity
price discrimination
price differentials
arbitrage
dumping
excess capacity
basing-point system

Completion

one

pure

substitutes

competition, are no

actual

one

A monopoly exists when there is _____ seller in a market. The
monopoly is a _____ monopoly when there are no acceptable
_____ for the product and no current or future
_____ . There _____ (are/are no)
real-world examples of pure monopoly. Monopolies that exist in the
real world are called _____ monopolies. In these monopolies,
there is _____ seller in the market, but other firms sell goods

substitutes

that may be reasonable _____ for the product sold by the monopoly.

equivalent to

The demand curve facing a firm is _____ the

negatively

average revenue curve. When the demand curve is _____ sloped, as in the case of a monopoly, the marginal revenue curve

lies below, negatively

_____ the demand curve and is _____

positive

sloped. When demand is elastic, marginal revenue is _____ (positive/zero/negative). When demand is inelastic, marginal revenue

negative

is _____ (positive/zero/negative). When demand is unitary

zero

elastic, marginal revenue is _____ (positive/zero/negative).

control

A firm is said to have monopoly _____ or monopoly

power

_____ when it has some control over the price of the product. This ability to influence price is characteristic of all firms that

negatively sloped

face a _____ demand curve. The only firms

purely competitive

that do not have monopoly control are _____

taker

firms. A pure competitor is said to be a price _____ . A pure

maker

monopoly is a price _____ , a term which implies that the

full information

firm has _____ and can act upon it in every case. Actual monopolies, and other firms with monopoly control, are more

searchers

appropriately called price _____ . This term implies

profit-maximizing

that the firm must search for the _____ price. In order to maximize profit, a pure monopolist will produce the

marginal revenue

output level at which _____ equals

rising marginal cost

_____ and charge the highest price that people will pay for that output, which is determined by the

demand

_____ curve. In the short run, the pure monopolist will produce that output so long as the price is sufficient to cover

average variable cost

_____ . When price is less than this,

shut down

the monopolist will _____ . In the long run the monopolist

average cost

will go out of business when the price does not cover _____ .

will

The pure monopolist _____ (will/will not) stay in business in the long run if it is earning just-normal profit.

Given the same market demand and cost conditions, a purely

larger

competitive industry will produce a _____ (larger/smaller)

lower

quantity of output and sell it for a _____ (higher/lower) price than will a pure monopoly. At equilibrium, under pure compe-

equal to

tition, price is _____ (greater than/equal to/less than) marginal cost. At equilibrium under pure monopoly, price is

greater than

_____ (greater than/equal to/less than) marginal cost. Since the demand curve is negatively sloped, the monopolist

higher

restricts output in order to be paid a _____ price. Con-sumers not only have to pay a higher price for what they buy, but they also are denied output. The amount of economic welfare that is lost as a result of this reduced output can be measured by the

welfare loss triangle

_____ .

prevents

A profit-maximizing pure monopolist _____ (permits/prevents) a socially desirable resource allocation. If government action forced a transfer of resources from a purely competitive market in long-run equilibrium to a pure monopoly in long-run equilibrium, the combined value of output produced by the two

increase

markets would _____ .
Pure monopolists may operate on higher average total cost curves than pure competitors, because they are not pushed by rivals to pro-duce at the lowest cost possible. This lack of motivational efficiency

X-inefficiency

is referred to as _____ . However, a monopolist may produce at lower average total cost than its counterparts in pure competition, because it is large enough to take advantage of

economies of scale

_____ .
The discovery and production of new and better products as well as the discovery and use of cost-saving technology is referred to as

progress, very long run

_____ . This is possible in the _____ (short run/long run/very long run). Since a pure monopolist is not

rivalry

faced with _____ , it may not promote progress. On the other hand, monopolists may be inclined to engage in progressive re-search and development projects because they have the incentive of

economic profit

long-run _____ and possibly the funds to do so.
In addition to decreasing consumer welfare by the amount of the welfare loss triangle, monopoly transfers welfare from buyers to the

consumer surplus

seller by transferring part of the _____ to the

not

monopolist. Under pure competition, such a transfer would _____ (also/not) take place.

Problems and Applications

1. Assume that a profit-maximizing monopolist faces the following total cost schedule:

Q	TC
1	$ 50
2	74
3	108
4	132
5	200

   a. Calculate the associated average and marginal cost schedules.
   b. Are the average and marginal cost schedules consistent with the average-marginal relationship? Explain.

2. Assume that a monopolist faces the following demand schedule for mmms:

Q	P
500	$9
600	8
700	7
800	6

   a. Calculate the associated total revenue and marginal revenue schedules for mmms.
   b. Assume that the marginal cost of producing mmms is $1, regardless of the level of output. Assuming that the monopolist is a profit maximizer, determine the output level and price.
   c. Assume that the marginal cost is always $3. What are the profit-maximizing levels of output and price?
   d. Given the following total cost schedule for mmms, calculate the associated average and marginal cost schedules:

Q	TC
500	$100
600	150
700	250
800	450

   e. Given this demand and cost schedule for mmms, determine the profit-maximizing output and price levels.
   f. Does the monopolist in part e above earn a positive, zero, or negative economic profit? Of how much?

3. Consider the following market demand curve for a product for which there are no close substitutes. Assume that a pure monopolist operates in this market.

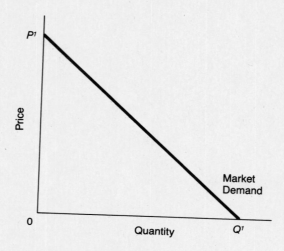

a. Identify the demand and average revenue curves facing the monopolist.

b. On the monopolist's demand curve, identify the regions of elastic, unitary elastic, and inelastic demand.

c. What is the basic shape of the monopolist's marginal revenue curve? On a graph showing the monopolist's demand curve, identify the point (Q) at which marginal revenue is zero. Using this information, sketch the marginal revenue curve.

4. Consider the following graph describing a pure monopoly
   market.

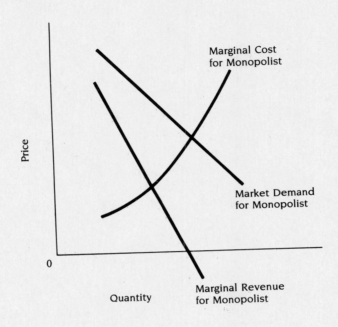

a. Identify the monopolist's equilibrium output (Q_M) and
   price (P_M).
b. Assume that the market demand curve is associated with a
   purely competitive market. What does the monopolist's
   marginal cost curve represent? Identify the equilibrium output
   (Q_C) and price (P_C) for the competitive market.
c. Identify the welfare loss triangle associated with a pure
   monopolist, as opposed to a purely competitive, market.

5. Assume that a monopoly firm is producing a profit-maximizing
   (that is, loss-minimizing) level of output in the short run with a
   price that is just sufficient to cover average variable cost.
   a. How much profit is the firm earning?
   b. How would the profit-maximizing output level and price
      change if the firm's fixed costs were higher? Explain. What
      would happen to the firm's profit?

True-False   Indicate whether each of the following statements is basically true or false. If the statement is false, rewrite it so that it is true.

_____ 1. Under pure monopoly, a single firm sells a product for which there are no substitutes, in a market characterized by a complete lack of competition.

_____ 2. A natural monopoly exists when a single seller is required for efficient production.

_____ 3. Monopoly control or monopoly power is measured by the number of firms in an industry.

_____ 4. Monopoly control exists only in the case of pure monopolies.

_____ 5. The demand curve facing a pure monopolist is perfectly inelastic.

_____ 6. In the case of monopoly, the firm's demand curve is equivalent to its average revenue curve.

_____ 7. In the case of monopoly, the firm's marginal revenue curve is equivalent to its average revenue curve.

_____ 8. Only the pure monopolist is a price maker.

_____ 9. Firms with monopoly control are said to be price searchers.

_____ 10. A profit-maximizing monopolist produces the output associated with the highest possible price.

_____ 11. A pure monopolist always earns a positive economic profit.

_____ 12. A pure monopolist will always shut down in the short run when it is incurring an economic loss.

_____ 13. In the long run, a pure monopolist will exit an industry if it is only breaking even.

_____ 14. _Ceteris paribus_, a pure monopolist tends to produce a smaller quantity and to charge a higher price than that which would be found in a purely competitive industry.

_____ 15. X-inefficiency occurs when a firm engages in high-cost internal practices like paying top management more than its opportunity cost.

_____ 16. Price discrimination occurs when a price differential is not justified by a cost difference.

_____ 17. Price discrimination requires that all consumers' demands have the same price elasticities.

_____ 18. Arbitrage is the purchase of a product in one market for the purpose of reselling it in another market at a higher price.

_____ 19. A basing-point system is a form of price discrimination.

_____ 20. Price discrimination may offer some benefits for society.

Multiple Choice   Choose the *one best* answer in each of the following cases:

_____ 1. A pure monopolist
   a. has no future competition.
   b. has no current competition.
   c. is concerned about rivals that sell close substitutes.
   d. all of the above
   e. both a and b above

_____ 2. An actual monopoly
   a. is generally a pure monopoly.
   b. is the only seller in its market.
   c. faces no current or future rivalry.
   d. all of the above
   e. both b and c above

_____ 3. A government-enforced monopoly
   a. may arise as a result of a patent.
   b. is not likely to be a pure monopoly.
   c. may arise as a result of a government franchise.
   d. may face rivalry from firms that sell substitutes.
   e. all of the above

_____ 4. A patent is
   a. valid in the United States for 25 years.
   b. a right of limited monopoly over a new product or process.
   c. a permanent right of monopoly over a new product or process.
   d. a temporary right of pure monopoly over a product or process.
   e. none of the above

_____ 5. In the case of a natural monopoly,
   a. there are significant economies of scale.
   b. additional firms would increase efficiency.
   c. monopoly power must be government enforced.
   d. entry of other firms is prohibited by government.
   e. minimum long-run average cost is associated with a relatively low output level.

_____ 6. Monopoly control refers to the
   a. size of a monopolist's market.
   b. degree of control a firm has over its price.
   c. extent to which a firm can differentiate its product.
   d. ability of a monopolist to block the entry of new firms.
   e. ability of a firm to influence the demand for its product.

_____ 7. Monopoly power is
   a. another term for monopoly control.
   b. limited to monopolies (pure or actual).
   c. greatest for firms that are price takers.
   d. measured by the profits of the monopolist.
   e. greater for actual monopolies than for pure monopolies.

_____ 8. The demand curve facing a monopoly firm is
   a. unitary elastic.
   b. infinitely elastic.
   c. perfectly inelastic.
   d. equivalent to the market demand.
   e. equivalent to its total revenue curve.

_____ 9. Typically, in order to sell an additional unit of output a pure monopolist must
   a. advertise.
   b. receive government approval.
   c. offer all units at a lower price.
   d. lower the price of the additional unit.
   e. simply be willing to sell the additional unit at the current market price.

_____ 10. In the case of a pure monopolist, marginal revenue is equivalent to
   a. demand.
   b. total revenue.
   c. average revenue.
   d. the change in revenue associated with the sale of an additional unit of output.
   e. all of the above

_____ 11. The marginal revenue curve for a monopolist
   a. is horizontal.
   b. is positively sloped.
   c. lies below the demand curve.
   d. coincides with the average revenue curve.
   e. intersects the demand curve at the profit-maximizing price.

_____ 12. Assuming that the demand curve facing the monopolist is a negatively sloped straight line, marginal revenue
   a. is positive at all output levels.
   b. increases with increases in output.
   c. is negative when the demand is price elastic.
   d. decreases with increases in the price elasticity of demand.
   e. is zero at the output associated with unitary elastic demand.

Use the graph below to answer questions 13 through 16.

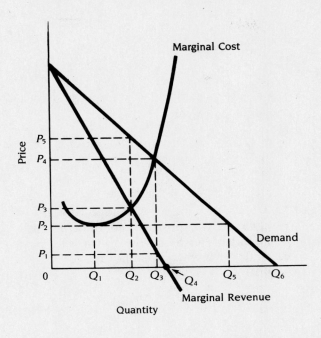

13. Assuming positive economic profit, the pure monopolist
    described in the graph above will maximize profit by producing
    output level
    a. Q_1.
    b. Q_2.
    c. Q_3.
    d. Q_4.
    e. Q_5.

14. The profit-maximizing monopolist described in the graph will
    charge a price of
    a. P_1.
    b. P_2.
    c. P_3.
    d. P_4.
    e. P_5.

_____ 15. If the market described in the graph were purely competitive,
the output level would be
  a. Q_1.
  b. Q_2.
  c. Q_3.
  d. Q_4.
  e. Q_5.

_____ 16. If the market described in the graph were purely competitive,
the price would be
  a. P_1.
  b. P_2.
  c. P_3.
  d. P_4.
  e. P_5.

_____ 17. In the short run, a pure monopolist will
  a. always earn a positive economic profit.
  b. go out of business whenever it is losing money.
  c. shut down when it cannot cover its average variable cost.
  d. both b and c above
  e. none of the above

Use the graph below to answer questions 18 through 20.

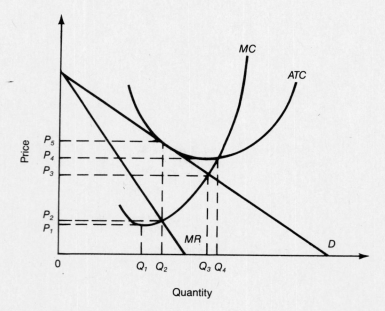

_____ 18. Consider the monopolist position described in the preceding graph. What is the profit-maximizing output level?

    a. 0

    b. q_1

    c. q_2

    d. q_3

    e. q_4

_____ 19. Consider the profit-maximizing monopolist described in the graph. What price will be charged?

    a. p_1

    b. p_2

    c. p_3

    d. p_4

    e. p_5

_____ 20. Consider the profit-maximizing monopolist in the graph. What would be the consequence of a decrease in fixed cost?

    a. The firm would produce the same output, charge the same price, but earn a positive economic profit.

    b. The firm would produce a larger output, charge the same price, and earn a positive economic profit.

    c. The firm would produce a larger output, charge a higher price, and earn a positive economic profit.

    d. The firm would produce a smaller output, charge a higher price, and earn a positive economic profit.

    e. none of the above

_____ 21. What can you correctly conclude if a monopolist is producing 50,000 units, earning a total revenue of $250,000, and has a marginal cost of $1?

    a. The monopolist is breaking even.

    b. The monopolist is maximizing profit.

    c. The monopolist could increase its profit by producing more.

    d. The monopolist could increase its profit by producing less.

    e. none of the above

_____ 22. If a monopolist is earning a positive economic profit, has a marginal revenue of $4, and has a marginal cost of $3, the monopolist could increase its profit by

    a. producing less and raising its price.

    b. producing less and lowering the price.

    c. producing more and lowering the price.

    d. continuing to produce its current output level and raising its price.

    e. none of the above

_____ 23. In long-run equilibrium, a pure monopolist will
   a. just break even.
   b. always earn a positive economic profit.
   c. go out of business when it is losing money.
   d. go out of business when it is earning just normal profit.
   e. both c and d above

_____ 24. Assuming identical market demand and cost conditions, a pure monopoly market (as compared to a purely competitive market) will tend to produce
   a. less and charge a lower price.
   b. more and charge a lower price.
   c. less and charge a higher price.
   d. more and charge a higher price.
   e. the same quantity and charge the same price.

_____ 25. At equilibrium, under pure monopoly,
   a. price exceeds marginal cost.
   b. price exceeds average revenue.
   c. price is equal to marginal cost.
   d. price is equal to marginal revenue.
   e. marginal revenue exceeds marginal cost.

_____ 26. In long-run equilibrium, a pure monopoly market
   a. uses society's resources more efficiently than does a purely competitive market.
   b. allocates too few resources to the production of the product to be efficient.
   c. allocates too many resources to the production of the product to be efficient.
   d. may or may not allocate resources efficiently, depending on the extent of the firm's profits.
   e. allocates the same amount of resources to the production of the product as would a purely competitive market.

_____ 27. X-inefficiency
   a. exists when a firm pays management its opportunity cost.
   b. occurs when a firm engages in high-cost internal practices.
   c. refers to a situation in which price equals marginal cost.
   d. is as likely to occur in pure competition as in pure monopoly.
   e. all of the above

_____ 28. Price discrimination occurs
   a. whenever there are price differentials.
   b. when identical prices are charged, despite cost differences.
   c. when price differentials are justified by differences in costs.
   d. all of the above
   e. none of the above

_____ 29. Effective price discrimination requires that a seller be able to
    a. have monopoly control.
    b. prevent resale of the product at a lower price.
    c. separate buyers into different markets with different price elasticities of demand.
    d. all of the above
    e. none of the above

_____ 30. Arbitrage refers to
    a. the practice of dumping.
    b. price discrimination in international trade.
    c. a basing-point system of price discrimination.
    d. purchase and resale of a product in order to take advantage of price differences.
    e. the separation of buyers into different markets in accordance with price elasticity of demand.

_____ 31. Price discrimination
    a. is illegal in the United States.
    b. may promote or reduce consumer welfare.
    c. interferes with a firm's ability to maximize profit.
    d. always increases rivalry among firms in an industry.
    e. prevents a firm from acquiring the buyers' consumer surplus.

Discussion Questions

1. Verbally and graphically identify the profit-maximizing output and price for a pure monopolist, indicating the shutdown point and the conditions under which the firm will go out of business. Explain your answers.

2. Identify the revenue-maximizing output for a pure monopolist facing a straight-line demand curve. Explain. (Review the relationship between price elasticity of demand and marginal revenue.)

3. Explain why a pure monopolist would be content to remain in an industry in the long run earning just-normal profit.

4. Explain why a firm with an infinitely elastic demand curve has no market control.

5. Explain why a basing-point system is a form of price discrimination.

6. Do you think a pure monopolist would ever advertise? Explain.

Answers

Problems and Applications

1. a.

Q	AC	MC
1	$50	—
2	37	$24
3	36	34
4	33	24
5	40	68

b. Yes: when average cost is decreasing, marginal cost is less than average cost; when average cost is rising, marginal cost is greater than average cost.

2. a.

Q	TR	MR
500	$4,500	—
600	4,800	$ 3
700	4,900	1
800	4,800	-1

b. 700 units at a price of $7 per unit

c. 600 units at a price of $8 per unit

d.

Q	AC	MC
500	$.20	—
600	.25	$ .50
700	.36	1.00
800	.56	2.00

e. 700 units at a price of $7 per unit

f. positive economic profit of $4,650

3. a. the monopolist's demand and average revenue curves are equivalent to the market demand curve

b.

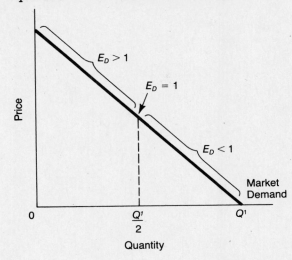

c. The marginal revenue curve is a negatively sloped line lying below the demand curve. Marginal revenue is equal to zero (that is, crosses the horizontal axis) at $Q^1/2$.

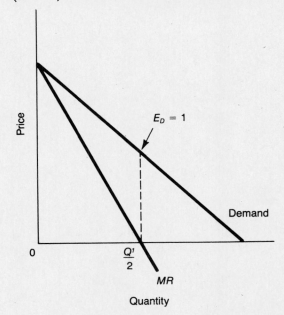

4. a. see the graph below
   b. the monopolist's marginal-cost curve represents market supply under pure competition; see the graph below
   c. the welfare loss triangle is the shaded area on the graph below

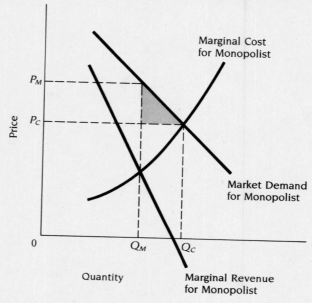

5. a. a negative profit or loss equivalent to total fixed cost
   b. Neither output nor price would change. A change in fixed costs does not affect variable costs; it also does not affect marginal cost. Hence, it does not affect price and output determinations. Profit would decrease; that is, the firm would lose more with the loss equivalent to the new, higher total fixed cost.

True-False

1. T.
2. T.
3. F. Monopoly control or monopoly power is the degree of control that a firm has over the price of its product.
4. F. Monopoly control exists to some extent in all but purely competitive firms.
5. F. The demand curve facing a pure monopolist is typically negatively sloped.
6. T.

7. F. In the case of monopoly, the firm's marginal revenue curve lies below its average revenue curve.
8. T.
9. T.
10. F. A profit-maximizing monopolist produces the output that equates marginal revenue with rising marginal cost.
11. F. A pure monopolist may earn a positive economic profit but may also just break even or incur an economic loss.
12. F. A pure monopolist will shut down in the short run when it cannot cover its variable costs.
13. F. In the long run, a pure monopolist will exit an industry if it is incurring an economic loss; a monopolist will continue to operate in an industry as long as it is earning normal profit.
14. T.
15. T.
16. T.
17. F. Price discrimination requires that the seller be able to divide buyers into two or more groups characterized by different price elasticities of demand.
18. T.
19. T.
20. T.

Multiple Choice

1. e	2. b	3. e	4. b	5. a
6. b	7. a	8. d	9. c	10. d
11. c	12. e	13. b	14. e	15. c
16. d	17. c	18. c	19. e	20. a
21. e	22. c	23. c	24. c	25. a
26. b	27. b	28. b	29. d	30. d
31. b				

27 Monopolistic Competition and Oligopoly

Summary

Real-world firms lie between the extremes of pure competition and pure monopoly. These firms are forms of imperfect competition, which includes monopolistic competition and oligopoly.

Monopolistic competition is characterized by a large number of independent firms selling differentiated products. Entry and exit are fairly easy in monopolistic competition. Advertising, as a means of product differentiation, is likely in this type of market. Though monopolistic competition would seem to be a realistic market type, the requirement that firms believe rivals will ignore each others' actions makes examples of this type of industrial organization difficult to cite.

Most real-world firms are oligopolies. This type of market is characterized by a few sellers of similar or differentiated products in industries with or without significant barriers to entry. The number of firms is not specified, but there must be enough so that the industry is characterized by interdependence in decision making. Unlike other firms, oligopolists consider the effects of rivals' expected responses. A number of different models have been developed to explain oligopolies. These include early duopoly models, which introduced the concept of reaction but disregarded the possibility of learning. Another important model of oligopoly is that of what is called the kinked demand curve. The kinked demand curve is useful in explaining the rigid prices of oligopolies, but it does not provide information as to how prices are established. Game theory focuses on the conflict relationship between oligopolists and demonstrates the incentives for cooperation. Finally, we may be better able to understand oligopolies by studying oligopolistic coordination.

Imperfect competitors (monopolistic competitors and oligopolists) tend to restrict output and charge higher prices than comparable firms under pure competition. In long-run equilibrium, monopolistic competitors are reduced to just-normal profits, and oligopolists may earn positive or zero economic profits.

There is likely to be considerable advertising in both monopolistic competition and in oligopoly. Advertising may be a means of product differentiation and is a likely form of nonprice competition.

Advertising is a controversial subject. It is often upheld as an important component of economic freedom and as an efficient source of information. Advocates claim that it encourages competition and enables firms to take advantage of economies of scale. Opponents, on the other hand, are likely to see advertising as a threat to consumer sovereignty and as more likely to persuade than to inform. Opponents would argue further that advertising tends to be self-canceling and creates substantial barriers to entry, thus reducing competition.

Major Objectives After you have finished this chapter, you will be able to do the following:

1. Identify and describe the two forms of imperfect competition.
2. Briefly discuss the historical development of models describing imperfect competition.
3. Explain the meaning of a large number of sellers in monopolistic competition.
4. Explain the meaning of product differentiation.
5. Explain the meaning of easy entry and exit in monopolistic competition.
6. Provide and recognize real-world examples of markets that approach the monopolistically competitive model.
7. Explain the role of advertising in monopolistic competition.
8. Identify and explain the major issues in the debate about advertising.
9. Identify and explain the probable slope of the demand or average revenue curve facing the monopolistic competitor.
10. Determine and graphically represent marginal revenue for the imperfect competitor when given a demand function.
11. Graphically represent the average total cost, average variable cost, and marginal cost functions for the imperfect competitor.
12. Identify the profit-maximizing (equilibrium) output level and price for the imperfect competitor under conditions of positive economic profit, normal profit, and economic loss.

13. Determine and graphically represent the level of short-run profit for an imperfect competitor under conditions of positive economic profit, normal profit, and economic loss.
14. Identify the conditions associated with positive economic profit, normal profit, and economic loss in the short run for the imperfect competitor.
15. Verbally and graphically describe the shutdown point for the imperfect competitor.
16. Describe, explain, and graphically represent the long-run conditions facing the monopolistic competitor.
17. Explain why the monopolistic competitor earns just-normal profit in long-run equilibrium.
18. Evaluate monopolistic competition in terms of its realism.
19. Evaluate monopolistic competition in comparison to pure competition.
20. Explain the meaning and realism of a few firms in the oligopoly structure.
21. Discuss the problems associated with developing demand curves for oligopolists.
22. Define, explain, and discuss the importance of experience variables in oligopoly.
23. Define duopoly.
24. Briefly describe the Cournot duopoly model and its refinements, and discuss the importance of the Cournot model.
25. Describe the kinked demand curve.
26. Explain the theory of the kinked demand curve, identifying the assumptions, conclusions, and limitations of the model.
27. Describe game theory and explain its relevance to the theory of oligopoly.
28. Explain the payoff matrix and solve simple game theory problems.
29. Identify three practices associated with oligopolistic coordination.
30. Define collusion and briefly discuss its role in oligopoly.
31. Define price leadership.
32. Cite and explain the reasons for price leadership.
33. Provide examples and explain the role of industry "conventions" or rules of thumb in coordinating the firms in an oligopoly.
34. Describe cost-plus pricing and explain its importance in oligopoly.
35. Describe the elasticity of demand for the oligopolist as compared to the monopolist and the monopolistic competitor.
36. Compare the profit-maximizing output level, price, and profit level under oligopoly as compared to pure competition, pure monopoly, and monopolistic competition.
37. Define price rigidity and explain its existence and role in industrial organization.

38. Evaluate oligopoly in terms of costs of production by comparison to those for the other forms of industrial organization.
39. Evaluate oligopoly in terms of research and development by comparison to those for the other forms of industrial organization.

Review Terms

pure competition
pure monopoly
price elasticity of demand
standardized product
barriers to entry
consumer sovereignty
economies of scale
long-run average total cost
economic profit
economic loss
normal profit
short run
demand curve

average revenue
negative slope
monopoly control
marginal revenue
average total cost
marginal cost
profit-maximization
equilibrium
average variable cost
long run
infinitely elastic
progress
very long run

Important Terms and Concepts

monopolistic competition
oligopoly
large number of sellers
product differentiation
entry and exit
advertising
self-canceling advertising
nonprice competition
price competition
a few firms
interdependence
rival
experience variables
duopoly

reaction
kinked demand curve
game theory
payoff matrix
strategy
oligopolistic coordination
collusion
price leadership
dominant-firm price leadership
barometric-firm price leadership
rules of thumb or industry
    "conventions" in oligopoly
cost-plus pricing
price rigidity

Completion

monopolistic competition

The market structure characterized by a large number of firms producing differentiated products is _____ .

independent

Firms in this type of industry are _____ (independent/interdependent). If there are so few firms that sellers are concerned

oligopoly

about the response of rivals, the industry is a(n) _____ .
Whereas monopolistically competitive firms within an industry

differentiated	produce _____ (identical/differentiated) products,
identical or differentiated	oligopolies within an industry produce _____
are no	products. Under monopolistic competition there _____ (are/are
may, but need not, exist	no) significant barriers to entry; barriers to entry _____ under oligopoly.
	Monopolistic competition and oligopoly are examples of
imperfect competition, do	_____ . These firms _____ (do/do not) have monopoly control. This means that the demand
negatively sloped	curves facing such firms will be _____ .
demand	The firms' average revenue curves will be _____ curves and
negatively sloped and lie below the demand curves	the marginal revenue curves will be _____ _____ .
	In the short run, assuming that price is sufficient to cover
average variable cost	_____ , the imperfectly competitive firm will maximize profit by producing the output that equates
marginal revenue, rising marginal cost	_____ with _____ . The firm will earn positive economic profit if price is greater than
average cost, normal	_____ ; the firm will earn just _____ profit when price is equal to average cost; and the firm will incur an
average cost	economic loss if price is less than _____ .
may	Whereas oligopolies _____ (may/may not) earn positive economic profit in long-run equilibrium, firms in monopolistic
just-normal	competition typically earn _____ profit. This is due
entry	in part to the _____ of new firms when positive profits are
exit	available and the _____ of losing firms. It may also be attrib-
cost	utable to shifts in the _____ curves of firms in the industry.
	In both monopolistic competition and oligopoly, equilibrium price
greater than	is _____ (greater than/equal to/less than) marginal
higher	cost. Firms in both types of industry tend to charge a _____ (lower/higher) price than similar firms in pure competition and to
smaller	produce a _____ (smaller/larger) output.
greater	Average and marginal costs tend to be _____ (greater/less) for the monopolistic competitor than for the pure competitor

advertising

variety

rivalry, can

are

because of _____ . Those who favor monopolistic

competition over pure competition believe that _____
justifies these cost differences.
   Average total cost may or may not be high in oligopoly, depending
on the extent of _____. Oligopolies typically _____
(can/cannot) take advantage of economies of scale and they _____
(are/are not) typically progressive.

**Problems and
Applications**

1. Consider the graph below describing the demand and cost conditions facing an imperfect competitor.

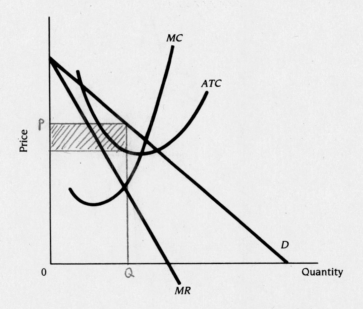

   a. Identify the profit-maximizing price (*P**) and output (*Q**).
      Does the firm earn positive, zero, or negative economic profit?
      Shade the area representing the firm's profit or loss.
   b. What would happen to the price and output decision of the
      firm if fixed cost were lower? What would happen to the
      firm's profit?

2. Consider the graph below, describing the demand and cost conditions facing an imperfect competitor. Identify the profit-maximizing price (P^*) and output (Q^*). Does the firm earn positive, zero, or negative economic profit? Shade the area representing the firm's profit or loss. At what point would a firm shut down when it is incurring a loss?

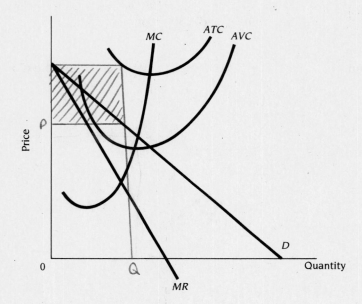

3. Consider the graph below, representing the average cost curves facing a firm before and after advertising (curves ATC_1 and ATC_2, respectively). Assume that, prior to advertising, the profit-maximizing output for the firm is 50 units. Advertising results in an increase in demand so that, with advertising, the firm's profit-maximizing output is 100 units. Should the firm advertise? Explain.

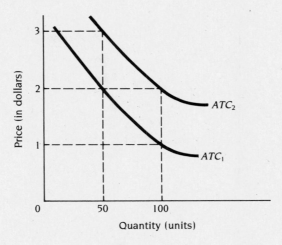

4. The payoff matrix below for firms A and B describes the payoffs associated with different pricing strategies: each duopolist can charge a price of either a nickel or a dime. (The first number represents the payoff to Firm A, the second the payoff to Firm B.)

		Firm B	
		nickel	dime
Firm A	nickel	$500, $500	$200, $800
	dime	$800, $200	$300, $300

a. What is the payoff to Firm A if both firms charge a nickel? What is the payoff to Firm B if it charges a dime and Firm A charges a nickel? If Firm B knows with certainty that Firm A will charge a dime, what price would Firm B choose in order to maximize its current payoff?

b. Assuming that each firm attempts to avoid the worst possible outcome, which pricing strategy will each firm choose? What will be the outcome for each firm?

c. If collusion is legal (and the firms have identical power), what strategy would you expect the firms to adopt? What would be the outcome for each firm?

5. The payoff matrix below for firms X and Y describes the payoffs associated with different advertising strategies: each duopolist must decide whether or not to advertise. (The first number represents the payoff to Firm X, the second the payoff to Firm Y.)

	Firm Y	
	advertise	do not advertise
Firm X — advertise	$200, $200	$900, $ 50
Firm X — do not advertise	$199, $800	$300, $300

a. What is the payoff to Firm X if both firms advertise? What is the payoff to Firm X if neither firm advertises?

b. Assuming that each firm attempts to avoid the worst possible outcome, which strategy will each firm choose? What will be the outcome for each firm?

True-False

Indicate whether each of the following statements is basically true or false. If the statement is false, rewrite it so that it is true.

_____ 1. Monopolistic competition refers to the whole range of market structures between pure competition and monopoly.

_____ 2. Edward Chamberlin was one of the economists who introduced a market model between pure competition and pure monopoly, which he referred to as monopolistic competition.

_____ 3. Monopolistic competition is like monopoly in that there are significant barriers to entry in each.

_____ 4. Monopolistic competition is like pure competition in that there are so many firms in the market that each firm believes that it alone cannot affect the product price.

_____ 5. An important distinction between pure and monopolistic competition is that under pure competition firms sell identical products, whereas under monopolistic competition firms sell differentiated products.

_____ 6. Product differentiation may amount to differences in sellers' characteristics rather than differences in the product itself.

_____ 7. There are no real-world examples of monopolistic competition.

_____ 8. To the extent that firms are concerned with the behavior of rivals, an industry is more likely to be monopolistically competitive.

_____   9. In *The Hidden Persuaders*, Vance Packard recognized advertising as a threat to consumer sovereignty.

_____   10. Over 2 percent of U.S. national income can be attributed to advertising.

_____   11. Advertising is a form of nonprice competition.

_____   12. The greater the amount of advertising, the more competitive an industry will be.

_____   13. Opponents of advertising might argue that it causes too large a percentage of a country's resources to be used for producing private, rather than public, goods.

_____   14. Costs of production under monopolistic competition are likely to be identical to those under pure competition.

_____   15. The demand curve facing a monopolistic competitor is negatively sloped, indicating that the firm has some monopoly control.

_____   16. A monopolistically competitive firm maximizes profit by producing at minimum average total cost.

_____   17. Monopolistic competition may be preferable to pure competition for one who values product differentiation.

_____   18. Oligopoly is a market structure characterized by a large number of firms, product differentiation, and significant barriers to entry.

_____   19. To say that oligopoly is characterized by a few firms means that there cannot be more than three firms.

_____   20. A duopoly is an industry in which there are two products.

_____   21. The kinked demand curve is more elastic at prices below the kink than at prices above the kink.

_____   22. Collusion refers to a situation in which firms get together to discuss ways of improving their mutual well-being.

_____   23. Adherence to a cost-plus pricing principle is an example of the utilization of a rule of thumb in oligopolistic coordination.

_____   24. For any given cost structure, the price charged by an oligopolist is likely to be higher than that charged by a pure competitor and lower than those charged by a monopolistic competitor and a monopolist.

Multiple Choice   Choose the *one best* answer in each of the following cases:

_____ 1. Which of the following is most closely associated with monopolistic competition?
   a. a few sellers
   b. Joan Robinson
   c. Alfred Marshall
   d. identical products
   e. all of the above

_____ 2. In terms of the number of sellers, monopolistic competition is characterized by
   a. one firm.
   b. two firms.
   c. a few firms.
   d. a large number of firms.
   e. both c and d above

_____ 3. Which of the following is an example of product differentiation?
   a. similar products perceived as identical by consumers
   b. identical products perceived as different by consumers
   c. products distinguished by consumers on the basis of packaging
   d. all of the above
   e. both b and c above

_____ 4. With respect to entry and exit, monopolistic competition is
   a. characterized by free entry and blocked exit.
   b. like pure competition in that entry and exit are free.
   c. characterized by easy (though not free) entry and exit.
   d. like pure monopoly in that entry is completely blocked.
   e. characterized by significant barriers, but entry is not completely blocked.

_____ 5. An advocate of advertising is most likely to argue that advertising
   a. diminishes consumer sovereignty.
   b. serves as a barrier to the entry of new firms.
   c. is an efficient means of providing information.
   d. prevents firms from taking advantage of economies of scale.
   e. is beneficial, because it tends to make a firm's demand curve more elastic.

_____ 6. Which of the following statements might be used to argue against advertising?
   a. Advertising promotes consumer sovereignty.
   b. Advertising makes demand curves perfectly inelastic.
   c. Advertising may be self-canceling so that firms' demand curves do not shift as intended.

d. Advertising is inefficient to the extent that it enables firms to take advantage of economies of scale.
e. none of the above

Use the following graph to answer questions 7 and 8.

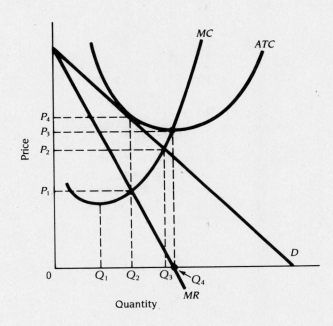

7. Consider the graph above describing a monopolistically competitive firm in the short run. At equilibrium, the firm will produce
   a. Q_1 units and charge P_1 per unit.
   b. Q_2 units and charge P_1 per unit.
   c. Q_3 units and charge P_2 per unit.
   d. Q_4 units and charge P_3 per unit.
   e. none of the above

8. Consider the graph in describing a monopolistically competitive firm in the short run. At equilibrium, the firm
   a. will produce nothing.
   b. incurs an economic loss.
   c. earns just-normal profit.
   d. earns a positive economic profit.
   e. both a and b above

_____   9. In the short run, a monopolistic competitor
        a. always earns just-normal profit.
        b. always earns positive economic profit.
        c. may earn positive, negative, or zero economic profit.
        d. will shut down whenever it is incurring an economic loss.
        e. will exit the industry whenever it is incurring an economic loss.

_____   10. In long-run equilibrium, a monopolistically competitive firm
        a. will just break even.
        b. earns positive economic profit.
        c. will exit the industry if it is just breaking even.
        d. will shut down whenever it is incurring an economic loss.
        e. none of the above

_____   11. By comparison to pure competition, monopolistic competition tends to produce
        a. less and charge a lower price.
        b. more and charge a lower price.
        c. less and charge a higher price.
        d. more and charge a higher price.
        e. the same quantity of output but charge a higher price.

_____   12. Most real-world firms are
        a. duopolies.
        b. oligopolies.
        c. natural monopolies.
        d. pure competitors.
        e. monopolistic competitors.

_____   13. In making production and output decisions, an oligopolist would be concerned about
        a. demand conditions.
        b. cost conditions.
        c. rivals' expected responses.
        d. experience variables.
        e. all of the above

_____   14. Which of the following is associated with early duopoly models?
        a. Cournot
        b. a recognition of the importance of learning
        c. continued reliance on output as the key decision variable
        d. a lack of appreciation for the importance of rivals' reactions
        e. all of the above

_____ 15. In the theory of the kinked demand curve, the kink occurs at the
   a. minimum price.
   b. maximum output.
   c. rival's output.
   d. current industry-wide price.
   e. current industry-wide output.

_____ 16. The kinked demand curve is based on the assumption that rivals will
   a. match price reductions but not price increases.
   b. match price increases but not price reductions.
   c. continue to charge the same price, regardless of a given firm's behavior.
   d. continue to produce the same output, regardless of a given firm's behavior.
   e. none of the above

_____ 17. Game theory
   a. is applicable to oligopoly.
   b. was developed by von Neumann and Morgenstern.
   c. can be used to analyze conflict relationships.
   d. explains why firms might have an incentive to cooperate.
   e. all of the above

_____ 18. Price leadership
   a. prevents firms from coordinating their pricing decisions.
   b. can take place only if firms engage in collusive behavior.
   c. is unlikely to occur when firms want to avoid price competition.
   d. is unlikely to occur if one firm is considered to be especially powerful.
   e. may occur when one firm's price changes are considered to be a good barometer of market conditions.

_____ 19. At equilibrium in the long run, oligopolies
   a. may just break even.
   b. may make positive economic profit.
   c. both a and b above
   d. always earn just-normal profit.
   e. always earn positive economic profit.

_____ 20. Oligopolies tend to be characterized by
   a. price rigidity.
   b. a lack of monopoly control.
   c. considerable independence in decision making.
   d. behavior that is inconsistent with progress.
   e. all of the above

Discussion Questions

1. Do you think advertising promotes or inhibits economic freedom? Explain.

2. In what ways might advertising provide an efficient approach to providing information?

3. Of what importance are economies of scale to advertising?

4. Identify and explain the shutdown point under monopolistic competition.

5. Do you think the variety provided by a monopolistically competitive industry as compared to a purely competitive industry is worth the cost? What is the cost?

6. Use the kinked demand curve to explain price rigidity in oligopoly. How is the price established in oligopoly?

7. The authors assert that, under oligopoly, demand is likely to be more elastic than in pure monopoly and more inelastic than in monopolistic competition. However, they note, the particular elasticity of demand at equilibrium varies considerably from one oligopolistic industry to another. Explain.

8. Explain why oligopolists are less likely to enjoy a prime competitive situation than are monopolists.

Answers

Problems and Applications

1. a. positive economic profit

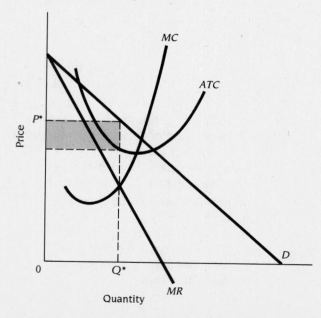

   b. nothing; a change in fixed cost does not affect marginal cost; hence, there is no change in either the pricing or output decisions; profit would increase, because average total cost would decrease.

2. economic loss; the firm would shut down when price no longer covered average variable cost.

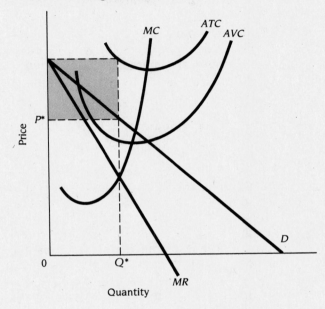

3. The firm should advertise. There are sufficient economies of scale and the additional demand is great enough so that the average cost of producing 100 units with advertising is equivalent to the average cost of producing 50 units without advertising.

4. a. $500; $800; a dime
   b. each firm will charge a dime; $300 each
   c. each firm will charge a nickel; $500 each

5. a. $200; $300
   b. both advertise; $200 each

True-False

1. F. Imperfect competition refers to the whole range of market structures between pure competition and monopoly.
2. T.
3. F. Monopolistic competition, unlike monopoly, is characterized by fairly easy entry and exit.

4. F. Monopolistic competition need not be characterized by as large a number of firms as pure competition; in monopolistic competition there must be so many firms that each one believes that the other firms will ignore its actions.

5. T.

6. T.

7. F. Some actual markets come close to being monopolistically competitive.

8. F. To the extent that firms are concerned with the behavior of rivals, an industry is less likely to be monopolistically competitive, because the characteristic of independent action is missing.

9. T.

10. T.

11. T.

12. F. A greater amount of advertising does not necessarily mean a more competitive industry.

13. T.

14. F. The costs of production under monopolistic competition are likely to be greater than those under pure competition, because of advertising costs.

15. T.

16. F. A monopolistically competitive firm maximizes profit by producing the output that equates marginal revenue and rising marginal cost.

17. T.

18. F. Oligopoly is a market structure characterized by a few firms, standardized or differentiated products, and easy or limited entry.

19. F. To say that oligopoly is characterized by a few firms means that there must be few enough firms so that they are interdependent in decision making.

20. F. A duopoly is an industry in which there are two sellers.

21. F. The kinked demand curve is more elastic at prices above the kink than at prices below the kink.

22. T.

23. T.

24. F. For any given cost structure, the price charged by an oligopolist is likely to be higher than those charged by both the pure competitor and the monopolistic competitor and lower than those charged by a monopolist.

Multiple Choice

1. b	2. d	3. e	4. c	5. c
6. c	7. e	8. c	9. c	10. a
11. c	12. b	13. e	14. a	15. d
16. a	17. e	18. e	19. c	20. a

28 Oligopoly: The Real World

Summary

Most real-world industries are oligopolies. They will differ in a number of specifics, one of which is the degree of competition or rivalry within the industry. Economic concentration is a measure used by economists to determine the degree of competition within an industry (called market concentration) as well as in an economy (called aggregate economic concentration). Though there are limitations in the use of economic concentration data, the assumption is that high levels of economic concentration are associated with relatively high levels of monopoly power and relatively little competition.

In computing concentration ratios to reflect market concentration, it is important to define adequately the market or industry under consideration. Industry definitions used by the U.S. Bureau of the Census are set forth in the Standard Industrial Classification (SIC) system. Concentration ratios based on this system may be misleading to the extent that the definition of an industry is too broad or too narrow, there is foreign competition, and the appropriate market is regional or local rather than national. The Herfindahl-Hirshman Index (HHI) is an alternative measure of market concentration that attempts to account for the distribution of market shares.

High levels of economic concentration are the result of both internal and external growth. Economists usually argue that internal growth is preferable in that firms must pass the test of the market.

There are three types of external growth or merger. In a horizontal merger, a firm acquires another firm in the same activity, on the same level, and serving the same geographic market. In a vertical merger, the two companies operate at different levels of a particular business activity. And in a conglomerate merger, the two firms operate in different industries.

There have been four major merger movements in the United States. The first, which occurred around the turn of the century, and the second, which occurred after World War I, primarily involved horizontal mergers. The third, which took place from 1967 to 1970, and the fourth, which began in 1976 and has continued into the 1980s, primarily involve conglomerate mergers. The Federal Trade Commission has estimated that of over 2,000 large mergers in the manufacturing and mining sectors during the 1948–1979 period, almost three-quarters were conglomerate mergers.

There are a number of advantages for the management of the acquiring firm in growth through merger. It may be the quickest way to increase plant capacity and meet excess demand for a firm's product. Growth through merger may be the most cost-effective way to grow and/or the easiest growth to finance. It may provide the least risk. It may be a way to capture speculative gains. Growth through merger may be pursued by managers (rather than owners) as a way of meeting personal goals. Finally, growth through merger may increase a firm's monopoly control by eliminating a competitor or potential competitor.

The degree of monopoly control in an industry is determined to a large extent by entry conditions into the industry. Potential entry is likely to be as important as actual entry in influencing what existing firms in an industry can and will do. Entry conditions vary considerably from industry to industry, depending on the extent of entry barriers. There are four types of barriers to entry: capital requirements, product differentiation, absolute cost differences, and minimum optimal scale effect.

Major Objectives

After you have finished this chapter, you will be able to do the following:

1. Define and explain the significance of economic concentration.
2. Define aggregate economic concentration.
3. Discuss the extent of aggregate economic concentration in the United States and among foreign firms and compare the two.
4. Discuss the extent of U.S. aggregate economic concentration from a historical perspective.
5. Define value added.
6. Define market concentration.
7. Define and interpret concentration ratios.
8. Explain the Standard Industrial Classification (SIC) system, discuss its use, identify its limitations, and discuss the implications

for figuring concentration ratios and using these ratios to measure economic concentration.

9. Explain the Herfindahl-Hirshman Index (HHI), compare it to the SIC system, and identify the advantages associated with its use.
10. Discuss the role of concentration ratios in analyzing an industry.
11. Define and distinguish between internal growth and external growth or merger, and discuss the merits of each for society.
12. Discuss the implications of internal growth for economic concentration (both market and aggregate).
13. Discuss the implications of external growth for economic concentration (both market and aggregate).
14. Define and distinguish between horizontal and vertical mergers.
15. Define conglomerate merger and identify and describe the three types of conglomerate merger.
16. Identify and describe the four chief merger movements in the United States.
17. Identify the government agency charged with the responsibility of maintaining competition in U.S. markets.
18. Identify and discuss the advantages associated with mergers.
19. Explain the meaning of the terms *hostile takeover*, *raider*, *greenmail*, and *reciprocal selling*.
20. Discuss the relationships between each of the three types of merger, economic concentration, and competition.
21. Define entry and condition of entry.
22. Discuss the importance of potential entry for decision making in an industry.
23. Identify, describe, and explain four kinds of barriers to entry.
24. Measure the absolute cost entry barrier faced by a potential entrant.
25. Define and distinguish between the minimum optimal scale and the minimum optimal scale effect.
26. Measure the minimum optimal scale effect of a potential entrant.
27. Discuss oligopoly in terms of social welfare.

Review Terms

pure competition
pure monopoly
monopolistic competition
oligopoly
competition
normative
aggregate

monopoly control
imports
collusion
product differentiation
entry conditions
complements
excess demand

<table>
<tr><td>long-run equilibrium</td><td>capital</td></tr>
<tr><td>interdependence</td><td>price elasticity of demand</td></tr>
<tr><td>patent</td><td>progress</td></tr>
<tr><td>average total cost</td><td>economies of scale</td></tr>
</table>

Important Terms and Concepts	economic concentration	Federal Trade Commission (FTC)
	concentration ratio	cost effective
	aggregate economic concentration	book value
	value added	diversify
	market concentration	"go-go" conglomerates of the late 1960s
	Standard Industrial Classification (SIC) system	price/earnings ratio
	Herfindahl-Hirshman Index	hostile takeover
	internal growth	raider
	external growth	greenmail
	merger	asset
	horizontal merger	reciprocal selling
	vertical merger	potential entry
	conglomerate merger	entry
	product extension conglomerate merger	condition of entry
	geographic market extension conglomerate merger	barriers to entry
	pure conglomerate merger	capital requirement entry barrier
	relatively pure conglomeration	absolute amount of cost difference
		minimum optimal scale effect
		minimum optimal scale

Completion

Control of an economic activity in terms of the number or percentage of companies in an industry, in a major part of an economy, in a whole economy, or in a region of the world can be measured by

economic concentration

_____ . Figures relating economic concentration offer a quantitative measure of potential

monopoly control

_____ . The assumption is that high economic

high

concentration is associated with a _____ (high/low) level of monopoly control. This is often assumed to imply that there is too

little

_____ (much/little) competition. A high level of con-

does not

centration _____ (does/does not) always indicate a lack of competition.

aggregate

An _____ economic concentration figure relates to the share of economic activity undertaken by the largest firms in a region of the world, in an economy, or in some major sector of the

do not

economy. Aggregate concentration data _____ (do/do not)

Market

focus on competing firms. _____ concentration measures the distribution by number and size of firms in a specific industry or market.

High levels of aggregate and market concentration may come

internal growth

about in two ways: through _____ and

external growth, building

_____ . Internal growth is growth by _____ ;

productive capacities

that is, by additions to firms' _____ .

merger

External growth is growth by _____ ; that is, by the acqui-

other firms

sition of _____ . Most economists would argue that

internal

_____ growth is preferable, because it must be accom-

competition

plished in the presence of _____ . Firms, on the

quicker

other hand, may prefer growth by merger because it may be _____

lower

(slower/quicker); it may be _____ (higher/lower) in cost; it

lower

may involve a _____ (higher/lower) risk; it may be a way to

speculative

capture _____ gains; it may suit the personal goals of

managers, owners

_____ as distinct from _____ of the firm; and

increase

it may _____ (increase/decrease) a firm's monopoly

competitor

control by eliminating a _____ or potential

competitor

_____ .

monopoly control

An important determinant of the extent of _____ in an industry is the condition of entry into that industry. Entry re-

capacity

quires an addition to industrial _____ as well as the

new firm

addition of a _____ to the industry. In addition to

potential entry

actual entry, the likelihood of entry or _____ will have an important effect on what established firms in an industry can and will do.

The extent to which existing firms in an industry can persistently

competitive

raise their prices above a _____ level without attracting

condition of entry

the entry of new firms is referred to as the _____ . This condition varies considerably from one industry to another

entry barriers

because of variations in the type and extent of _____ from industry to industry.

There are four basic kinds of barriers to entry:

capital requirements, product differentiation

_____ , _____ ,

absolute cost differences, minimal optimal scale effect

_____ , and _____ .

The capital requirement entry barrier refers to the amount of

money, capital

_____ needed to get the _____ goods for a new

risk

firm to compete adequately with existing firms. Given equal _____ ,

higher

the higher the capital requirement, the _____ (higher/lower) the entry barrier. In a study of twenty manufacturing industries, Joe Bain, in his work *Barriers to New Competition*, found the

product differentiation

_____ entry barrier to be greater than any other entry barrier. This barrier involves the extent to

differentiate

which companies _____ their products. The greater the degree of differentiation and consumer acceptance of established

higher

products, the _____ (higher/lower) the entry barrier. Another barrier is the absolute amount of cost difference between existing firms and potential entrants. This cost difference is measured

vertical, average total

by the _____ distance between the _____

lower

cost curves of the firms, assuming that existing firms have _____ (higher/lower) costs. Reasons for the cost differences may include

exclusive access

_____ on the part of existing firms to

patents

some inputs and/or highest-grade inputs, _____ held by

money

existing firms, and the ability of existing firms to raise _____ on relatively favorable terms. Finally, the minimum optimal scale

price

effect entry barrier is the effect on the _____ of the product that cannot be avoided when a new company enters an industry. The size of the price change is determined by the smallest addition to

output

industry _____ that the new firm must make if it is to survive in the industry. If the new entrant has to produce a large percentage of total industry output to keep its average cost low

competitive

enough to be _____ , it will add greatly to industry

supply

dustry _____ . With a given demand for the product, an

fall

    increase in supply will cause the equilibrium price to _____

both existing and
entering

(rise/fall). This new price would be faced by _____
(existing/entering/both existing and entering) firm(s). A potential
entrant attracted by a given profit and price before entry would have

fall

to anticipate the degree to which price and profit would _____
(rise/fall) as a result of entry.

**Problems and
Applications**

1. Consider the average total cost curves illustrated in the graph
below.
   a. What is the absolute cost entry barrier faced by the potential
   entrant if the entrant plans to produce 100 units of output
   per day?
   b. What is the absolute cost entry barrier faced by the potential
   entrant if the entrant plans to produce 200 units of output
   per day?

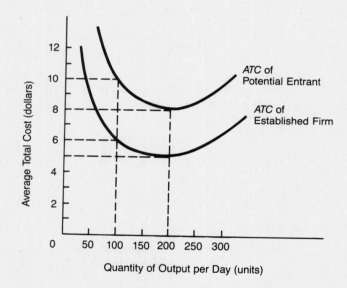

2. Consider the industry described by the long-run average cost curve
in the graph below.
   a. What is the minimum daily output level at which a potential
   entrant would be able to attain low enough average total cost
   to be competitive?
   b. What is the potential entrant's minimum optimal scale?

c. If the industry currently produces 2,000 units of output per day, what is the minimum optimal scale effect of the potential entrant?

d. If the industry currently produces 10,000 units of output per day, what is the minimum optimal scale effect of the potential entrant?

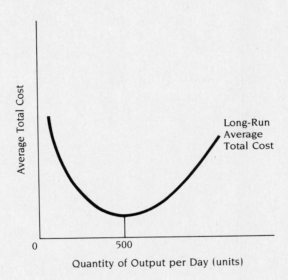

Long-Run Average Total Cost

Average Total Cost

0   500

Quantity of Output per Day (units)

3. Consider a market consisting of five firms with the following market shares: 50 percent, 30 percent, 10 percent, 5 percent, and 5 percent.

a. Calculate the four-firm concentration ratio.

b. Calculate the Herfindahl-Hirshman Index.

True-False   Indicate whether each of the following statements is basically true or false. If the statement is false, rewrite it so that it is true.

_____ 1. Aggregate concentration data focus on competing firms within an industry.

_____ 2. At the time of the Civil War in the United States, economic concentration was relatively low.

_____ 3. Value added is the additional value of a firm after a merger.

_____ 4. Market concentration relates to the distribution by number and size of the firms in a specific industry or market.

_____   5. In taking the Census of Manufactures, the U.S. Bureau of the Census uses the Manufacturing Concentration Measurement system.

_____   6. The most widely used SIC category is the six-digit product class code.

_____   7. The four-firm concentration ratio for an industry indicates the dollar value of output attainable to the four largest firms in the industry.

_____   8. An eight-firm concentration ratio for an industry of 95 indicates that the eight largest firms in the industry account for 95 percent of the industry's output.

_____   9. A Herfindahl-Hirshman Index of 10,000 indicates a monopoly.

_____   10. The omission of imports from the calculation of concentration ratios causes the extent of economic concentration to be overstated.

_____   11. A high concentration ratio always indicates a lack of competition.

_____   12. Economies with high levels of aggregate and market concentration have typically achieved their concentration through both internal and external growth.

_____   13. Internal growth is growth by merger.

_____   14. Internal growth is fairly commonplace, external growth relatively rare.

_____   15. External growth is generally considered to be better for society than internal growth.

_____   16. A merger between companies at different levels of a particular business activity is called a horizontal merger.

_____   17. A conglomerate merger takes place when one firm acquires another firm in a different industry.

_____   18. A relatively pure conglomerate merger occurs when the companies involved are engaged in different business activities with only some slight relationship between the firms.

_____   19. The Federal Trade Commission (FTC) is a government agency responsible for maintaining competition in U.S. markets.

_____   20. The ratio between the price of a share of a firm's stock and the earnings per share of that firm is called the price/earnings ratio.

_____   21. Greenmail is a result of "friendly" mergers.

_____   22. Mergers are typically very profitable for the long-term owners of the acquiring firms.

_____   23. Economists generally agree that conglomerate mergers reduce competition.

_____ 24. Potential entry, as well as actual entry, may have important consequences for decision making in an industry.

Multiple Choice   Choose the *one best* answer in each of the following cases:

_____ 1. Since the Civil War in the United States, the level of economic concentration has
a. increased greatly.
b. increased slightly.
c. decreased greatly.
d. decreased slightly.
e. remained about the same.

_____ 2. Aggregate concentration in U.S. manufacturing (measured in terms of value added)
a. has barely increased during the twentieth century.
b. has increased only moderately since the mid-1950s.
c. decreased in the years immediately following World War II.
d. has increased dramatically throughout the twentieth century.
e. has decreased dramatically throughout the twentieth century.

_____ 3. In the Standard Industrial Classification system, output is classified
a. according to inputs.
b. as fixed or variable.
c. into industry and product groupings.
d. in accordance with short-run and long-run production levels.
e. none of the above

_____ 4. According to the SIC system,
a. products are defined by seven-digit codes.
b. industries are defined by three-digit codes,
c. industry groups are defined by two-digit codes.
d. product classes are defined by four-digit codes.
e. major industry groups are defined by one-digit codes.

_____ 5. In terms of defining a group of competing firms, the four-digit industry code
a. always accurately reflects concentration.
b. may understate but never overstates actual concentration.
c. may overstate but never understates actual concentration.
d. will understate actual concentration if the four-digit definition is too broad.
e. will overstate actual concentration if the four-digit definition is too broad.

_____ 6. Assuming that an industry's four-firm concentration ratio is 10, it can be concluded that the
    a. four largest firms account for 10 percent of the industry output.
    b. four smallest firms account for 10 percent of the industry output.
    c. largest 4 percent of the firms account for 10 percent of the industry output.
    d. smallest 4 percent of the firms account for 10 percent of the industry output.
    e. four largest firms produce ten times the output of the remaining firms.

_____ 7. Consider an industry composed of 100 firms. Assuming that the industry's four-firm concentration ratio is 8 and that its eight-firm concentration ratio is 12, it can be concluded that the
    a. industry is highly concentrated.
    b. largest firm accounts for 2 percent of the industry's output.
    c. four largest firms account for 8 percent of the industry's output.
    d. fifth-largest firm accounts for 9 percent of the industry's output.
    e. eight smallest firms account for 12 percent of the industry's output.

_____ 8. U.S. concentration ratios based on SIC data understate the amount of concentration to the extent that
    a. imports are omitted.
    b. markets are defined too narrowly.
    c. markets are regional and/or local instead of national.
    d. all of the above
    e. none of the above

_____ 9. Internal growth of a firm
    a. always leads to higher market concentration.
    b. always leads to higher aggregate concentration.
    c. both a and b above
    d. has no effect on aggregate concentration.
    e. may lead to higher or lower concentration.

_____ 10. External growth of a firm
    a. has no effect on aggregate concentration.
    b. always leads to higher market concentration.
    c. always leads to higher aggregate concentration.
    d. both a and b above
    e. both b and c above

_____ 11. In a horizontal merger, a firm merges with another firm
    a. on the same level.
    b. in the same activity.
    c. serving the same geographic market.
    d. all of the above
    e. none of the above

_____ 12. A conglomerate merger is a(n)
    a. absolutely pure conglomerate merger when there is no relationship between the two firms involved.
    b. product extension conglomerate merger when a firm acquires another firm in the same industry, on the same level, serving the same market.
    c. geographic market extension conglomerate merger when a firm acquires another firm in a different business activity serving a different geographic market.
    d. horizontal conglomerate merger when a firm acquires another firm in the same business activity, at the same level, serving a different geographic market.
    e. all of the above

_____ 13. The first chief merger movement in the United States
    a. took place just prior to the Civil War.
    b. consisted primarily of conglomerate mergers.
    c. had little effect on industrial organization in the United States.
    d. saw the creation of Du Pont, General Electric, and U.S. Steel.
    e. resulted in diminished monopoly control by the newly created conglomerates.

_____ 14. The second chief merger movement in the United States
    a. took place at the turn of the century.
    b. consisted primarily of horizontal mergers.
    c. was characterized by a complete lack of conglomerate mergers.
    d. resulted in the "number one" giant firms, such as Standard Oil and Eastman Kodak, that continue to dominate American enterprise.
    e. none of the above

_____ 15. The third and fourth chief merger movements in the United States
    a. differed from the earlier two movements in that they involved mainly vertical mergers.
    b. differed from the earlier two movements in that they involved mainly conglomerate mergers.
    c. were similar to the earlier two movements in that they all involved mainly vertical mergers.

    d. were similar to the earlier two movements in that they all involved mainly conglomerate mergers.

    e. differed from each other in that the third movement involved mainly horizontal mergers and the fourth involved mainly conglomerate mergers.

_____ 16. External growth may be advantageous when
    a. there is excess demand for a firm's product.
    b. a firm wishes to increase its monopoly power.
    c. a firm's plant capacity needs to be increased.
    d. a firm wishes to diversify into a new product.
    e. all of the above

_____ 17. Horizontal mergers
    a. increase market concentration.
    b. decrease market concentration.
    c. increase competition in a market.
    d. decrease competition in a market.
    e. both a and d above

_____ 18. Vertical mergers generally
    a. increase market concentration.
    b. decrease market concentration.
    c. do not affect market concentration.
    d. increase competition in a market.
    e. both a and d above

_____ 19. Conglomerate mergers
    a. increase market concentration.
    b. increase aggregate concentration.
    c. increase competition in a market.
    d. both a and b above
    e. all of the above

_____ 20. Entry occurs in industry X when a(n)
    a. existing firm in that industry adds to its capacity.
    b. new firm in that industry adds to the capacity of the industry.
    c. firm in industry Y acquires the capacity of a firm in industry X but does not add to it.
    d. firm in industry X acquires the capacity of a firm in industry Y but does not add to it.
    e. all of the above

_____ 21. Joe Bain's work *Barriers to New Competition*
    a. extended the theory of oligopoly to include potential entrants.
    b. entirely neglected the condition of entry in studying oligopolies.
    c. concentrated on the factors that gave rise to monopolistic competition.

     d. concentrated on the factors that prevent the realization of pure monopoly.

     e. dealt only with actual (as opposed to potential) competition in oligopolies.

_____ 22. Barriers to entry may include

     a. capital requirements.

     b. product differentiation.

     c. absolute cost differences.

     d. minimum optimal scale effect.

     e. all of the above

Discussion Questions

1. Identify and discuss the problems associated with using the Standard Industrial Classification system.

2. Does a high concentration ratio always indicate a lack of competition? Explain.

3. Discuss the arguments in the debate about the effect of conglomerate mergers on competition.

4. Discuss the importance of potential entry for an oligopolist.

5. Explain what Joe Bain means by the condition of entry.

6. Explain how product differentiation may constitute a barrier to entry.

7. Explain the importance of the minimum optimal scale effect barrier to entry.

8. Identify factors that would enter into the evaluation of an oligopoly in terms of social welfare.

Answers

Problems and Applications

1. a. $4   b. $3

2. a. 500 units   b. 500 units   c. 25 percent   d. 5 percent

3. a. 95 percent   b. 3,550

True-False

1. F. Aggregate concentration data focus on firms in the same region of the world, or in the same economy, or in the same sector within a region or economy.

2. T.

3. F. Value added is the difference between the value of inputs that a firm buys and the value of its output.

4. T.
5. F. In taking the Census of Manufactures, the U.S. Bureau of the Census uses the Standard Industrial Classification (SIC) system.
6. F. The most widely used SIC category is the four-digit industry code.
7. F. The four-firm concentration ratio for an industry indicates the share of industry output attributable to the four largest firms in the industry.
8. T.
9. T.
10. T.
11. F. High concentration ratios may be associated with great differences in the amount of competition.
12. T.
13. F. Internal growth is growth by building; that is, by adding to firms' productive capacities; external growth is growth by merger.
14. F. Both internal and external growth are commonplace.
15. F. Internal growth is considered by many economists to be better for society than is external growth, because firms must pass the test of the market.
16. F. A merger between companies at different levels of a particular business activity is called a vertical merger.
17. T.
18. T.
19. T.
20. T.
21. F. Greenmail occurs when a raider buys up large quantities of a corporation's stock and then threatens a takeover in order to extract a premium price for the stock.
22. F. Many studies conducted during the past few decades have shown that mergers are not very profitable for the long-term owners of the acquiring firms.
23. F. Economists are not in agreement as to the effect of conglomerate mergers on competition.
24. T.

Multiple Choice

1. a	2. b	3. c	4. a	5. d
6. a	7. c	8. c	9. e	10. c
11. d	12. a	13. d	14. b	15. b
16. e	17. a	18. c	19. b	20. b
21. a	22. e			

29 Resource Supply and Demand

Summary

There are four categories of inputs or factors of production used by firms in the production of goods and services. The labor input includes most forms of human work. Natural resources consist of raw materials or gifts of nature. Capital resources are inputs that must first be produced. They include physical capital goods and human skills, called human capital. Entrepreneurship combines the other resources and coordinates the productive effort. Though we assume that resources can be neatly classified, in fact it is generally very difficult to do so. Most resources are hired in combination or in resource packages.

In considering the supply of resources, it is important to distinguish between the supply of a resource for all uses and the supply for a specific use. Both supply relationships specify the amount of a resource that is available at various prices. Both relationships tend to be positive. Furthermore, the price elasticity of supply in both relationships depends on the mobility of the resource and the length of time under consideration. Typically, however, the supply of a resource for all uses is greater than the supply for a specific use. The quantity of a resource available for all uses also tends to be less responsive to a change in the price of the resource. That is, the price elasticity of supply of a resource for all uses is less than for a specific use.

Resources are demanded for the purpose of producing goods and services. Hence, resource demand is said to be a derived demand. As with most demand relationships, the demand for resources is typically inverse. The price elasticity of demand for a resource is dependent on the elasticity of demand for the product itself, the proportion of the total production cost that is accounted for by the resource, the degree of competition in the product market, and the ease with which substitute resources may be used in the production of the good.

In determining the amount of a resource to hire, a profit-maximizing firm will hire the amount that equates marginal revenue product and marginal factor cost. (This is comparable to a profit-maximizing firm's producing the output level that equates marginal revenue with marginal cost.) In the case of a purely competitive input market, the marginal factor cost is equal to the price of the input. Hence, for any given factor price the firm will hire along the marginal revenue product curve. Consequently, the (declining) portion of the marginal revenue product curve is the demand curve for the input. (The rising portion of the marginal revenue product curve is associated with rising marginal physical product, and since profit-maximizing firms do not produce in this region, the firm will not hire inputs in this region.)

Equilibrium resource earnings may be thought of as a mix of transfer earnings and economic earnings. Transfer earnings are what the resource would earn in its next-best use. Any earnings in excess of transfer earnings are called economic earnings. Economic earnings, then, are payments in excess of what is required to keep a resource in its current use. You have already encountered an example with the payment to the entrepreneurial input. Normal profit is the opportunity cost of the entrepreneurial input; it is part of total cost and is a form of transfer earnings. Economic profit is a return to the entrepreneur in excess of what is required to keep the entrepreneurial input in its current use; it is a form of economic earnings.

Major Objectives

After you have finished this chapter, you will be able to do the following:

1. Identify, describe, and recognize examples of the four types of resources and the payments (or returns) to each.
2. Explain the concept of resource packages.
3. Explain the meaning of functional income distribution.
4. Identify major characteristics and trends in the functional income distribution for the United States.
5. Identify and explain the major problems in statistics that indicate relative resource shares in the functional income distribution.
6. Explain what is meant by the supply of resources.
7. Indicate whether the supply of resources is a positive or a negative relationship and explain why.
8. Distinguish between the supply of resources for all uses and the supply of resources for specific uses.

9. Identify and explain the determinants of the supply for all uses of labor.
10. Identify and explain the determinants of the labor force participation rate.
11. Define and discuss factors that determine working age.
12. Identify and explain the determinants of the supply for all uses of entrepreneurship.
13. Discuss and explain the turnover and varied stability of entrepreneurial business ventures.
14. Identify and explain the determinants of the supply for all uses of natural resources.
15. Distinguish between natural resources and exhaustible natural resources.
16. Identify and explain the determinants of the supply for all uses of capital.
17. Identify and explain the determinants of the supply of resources for specific uses.
18. Define, calculate, and identify the determinants of the price elasticity of supply of resources for all uses.
19. Define, calculate, and identify the determinants of the price elasticity of supply of resources for specific uses.
20. Compare the price elasticity of supply of resources for all uses with the price elasticity of supply of resources for specific uses and explain the differences.
21. Identify and explain the circumstances that give rise to a perfectly inelastic supply for all uses of natural resources.
22. Distinguish between demand for consumer goods and demand for resources.
23. Indicate whether the demand for resources is a positive or a negative relationship and explain why.
24. Identify and explain the determinants of the demand for resources.
25. Explain the concept of derived demand and discuss its importance in terms of the demand for resources.
26. Define, calculate, and identify the determinants of the price elasticity of demand for resources.
27. Define marginal factor cost and marginal revenue product and explain their significance in determining the quantity demanded of a resource.
28. Explain the difficulties in attempting to measure the marginal factor cost and marginal revenue product.
29. State and explain the equilibrium condition for hiring a resource.
30. Define, explain, and calculate marginal physical product.

31. Use marginal physical product data to determine marginal revenue product for a firm that sells its output in a purely competitive output market.
32. Use total revenue data to determine marginal revenue product for a firm that sells its output in a purely competitive output market.
33. Explain the significance of assuming a purely competitive output market for determining marginal revenue product.
34. Identify the conditions under which marginal revenue product will increase for a firm that sells its output in a purely competitive output market.
35. Identify the conditions under which marginal revenue product will decrease for a firm that sells its output in a purely competitive output market.
36. Determine the marginal factor cost for a factor that is traded in a purely competitive factor market.
37. Explain the significance of assuming a purely competitive input market in determining marginal factor cost.
38. Construct and interpret graphs of marginal revenue product and marginal factor cost curves under conditions of pure competition in both output and input markets.
39. Identify and explain the demand curve for a factor.
40. Use market demand and supply conditions for a resource to determine and explain the equilibrium price and quantity traded.
41. Define, explain, and distinguish between transfer earnings and economic earnings.
42. Discuss the implications of transfer earnings and economic earnings for resource allocation.
43. Identify, explain (verbally and graphically), and provide examples of transfer earnings, economic earnings, and total earnings under situations in which a resource is limited in supply and has only one use.
44. Identify, explain (verbally and graphically), and provide examples of transfer earnings, economic earnings, and total earnings under situations in which the supply of a resource is unlimited and the next-best use commands a price almost as high as the present use.
45. Identify, explain (verbally and graphically), and provide examples of transfer earnings, economic earnings, and total earnings under situations in which a resource has multiple uses and a slight reduction in price does not cause all of the resource to switch to the next-best use.
46. Identify and explain (verbally and graphically) the implications of changes in resource demand for transfer earnings, economic

earnings, and total earnings under situations in which a resource is limited in supply and has only one use.

47. Identify and explain (verbally and graphically) the implications of changes in resource demand for transfer earnings, economic earnings, and total earnings under situations in which the supply of a resource is unlimited and the next-best use commands a price almost as high as the present use.

48. Identify and explain (verbally and graphically) the implications of changes in resource demand for transfer earnings, economic earnings, and total earnings under situations in which a resource has multiple uses and a slight reduction in price does not cause all of the resource to switch to the next-best use.

49. Define and explain the significance of economic wages, economic rent, economic interest, and economic profit.

50. Explain and evaluate the reasoning behind Henry George's proposal of a single tax on economic rent.

Review Terms

output
input or factor of production
  or resource
national income
compensation of employees
proprietor's income
supply
positive relationship
price elasticity of supply
labor force
labor-force participation rate
substitution effect
income effect
opportunity cost
real income
productivity
competition
monopoly control
oligopoly
monopoly
monopolistic competition
pure competition
patent

depreciation
antitrust policy
entry conditions
perfectly inelastic
elastic
inelastic
unitary elastic
negative relationship
total cost
price elasticity of demand
profit maximization
marginal cost
marginal revenue
diminishing returns
increasing returns
total revenue
equilibrium
transfer payments
change in demand
infinitely elastic
economic profit
long-run equilibrium
normal profit

Important Terms and Concepts

labor resources
entrepreneurial resources
natural resources
capital resources
wages
profit
rent
interest
resource packages
functional distribution of income
supply for all uses of a resource
supply for a specific use of a resource
working age
Dun and Bradstreet

renewable natural resource
exhaustible natural resource
mobile resource
derived demand
price elasticity of resource demand
marginal productivity theory
marginal factor cost (MFC)
marginal revenue product (MRP)
marginal physical product (MPP)
transfer earnings
economic earnings
economic rent
economic wages
economic interest

Completion

labor, entrepreneurship	There are four categories of inputs: _____ , _____ ,
natural resources, capital	_____ , and _____ . Most forms of
labor	human work directed at production are _____ . The return to
wage	this factor is a _____ . One kind of human work is sometimes excluded from the labor category. That is the input we
entrepreneurship	call _____ . The entrepreneur seeks out the best opportunities for production and coordinates all
other resources	of the _____ in order to carry out the produc-
risk	tion. The entrepreneur is the _____ taker. If successful, the
profit	entrepreneur earns a _____ ; if unsuccessful, the entrepreneur
loss	incurs a _____ . Raw materials and gifts of nature used in pro-
natural	duction are _____ resources; they earn a return called
rent	_____ . Finally, inputs that must be produced in order to
capital	produce something else are referred to as _____ resources.
capital goods	These may be _____ like factories, machinery, and tools; they may also be in the form of skills called
human capital	_____ . The return to capital is
interest	_____ .

In order to determine how many units of a given input a profit-maximizing firm will hire, we must consider two variables: the con-

value

tribution that the resource makes to the _____ of the product

cost

that it helps to produce and the _____ of the resource. The extra revenue associated with selling the output produced by an addi-

marginal revenue
product

tional unit of an input is referred to as the _____ .

total revenue

It can be computed by dividing the change in _____

input

by the change in the quantity of _____ . In the case of a purely competitive output market, the marginal revenue product can be

marginal physical
product

computed by multiplying the _____

price, good

(or marginal product) by the _____ of the _____ . In

does not

a purely competitive output market, the price of the good _____ (does/does not) change with changes in output. The extra cost associated with hiring an additional unit of input is called the

marginal factor cost

_____ . It can be computed by dividing

total cost

the change in _____ by the change in the quantity of

input

_____ . In the case of a purely competitive input market, the

price, input

marginal factor cost is equal to the _____ of the _____ . In the purely competitive market, the price of the input is deter-

market, does not

mined by the _____ and _____ (does/does not) change with changes in the quantity of input.
    A profit-maximizing firm will hire units of a given input until the

marginal revenue
product

_____ equals the

marginal factor cost

_____ . A firm that is not hiring

equilibrium

this quantity of input is not in _____ . That is, the firm will continue to make adjustments in its hiring decisions. Consider, for example, a situation in which the marginal revenue product exceeds the marginal factor cost. The firm can increase its

increasing

profit by _____ (increasing/decreasing) the amount of input. Similarly, if marginal factor cost exceeds marginal revenue

decreasing

product, the firm can increase its profit by _____ (increasing/decreasing) the amount of input. The firm will continue to make adjustments in the amount of input it hires until the mar-

equal

ginal revenue product and marginal factor cost are just _____ .
In the case of a purely competitive input market, the marginal

price

factor cost is just equal to the _____ of the input. For any
given input price, then, the firm hires the quantity of input indicated

marginal revenue
product

by the declining portion of the _____
curve. Therefore, the declining portion of the marginal revenue prod-

demand

uct curve is the _____ curve for the input. The rising
portion of the marginal revenue product curve is associated with

rising marginal
physical product

_____ , where

output

marginal physical product is simply the extra _____ associ-

hiring, input

ated with _____ an additional unit of _____ . Since
profit-maximizing firms do not produce in the region of rising
marginal physical product, they do not hire inputs in the region of

rising

_____ (rising/falling) marginal revenue product.

Problems and Applications

1. Consider the following market demand and supply schedules for
   a particular resource that is traded under conditions of pure
   competition.

Factor Price	Quantity Demanded	Quantity Supplied
$1	100	40
2	80	50
3	60	60
4	40	75

   a. What is the equilibrium factor price?
   b. What is the marginal factor cost?
   c. Calculate the price elasticity of demand for a price change
      between $2 and $3.
   d. Calculate the price elasticity of supply for a price change
      between $2 and $3.

2. Consider the total product schedule below, describing a production situation characterized by pure competition in both the input and output markets. Assume that the factor price is $222 and that the product sells for $2 per unit.

Quantity of Input	Total Product
0	0
1	100
2	245
3	356
4	425
5	475

    a. Compute the marginal physical product, total revenue, and marginal revenue product schedules indicated by the production function above.

    b. What is the marginal factor cost?

    c. How many units of input will a profit-maximizing firm hire? What price will be paid for each unit of input? How many units of output will be produced? What price will be charged per unit of output?

3. Consider the marginal physical product schedule below. Assume purely competitive input and output markets. Calculate the marginal revenue product schedule if the product sells for $10 per unit.

Quantity of Input	Marginal Physical Product
1	6
2	10
3	8
4	6

4. Consider the schedule below facing a firm that operates in purely competitive input and output markets. Calculate the marginal revenue product schedule.

Quantity of Input	Total Revenue
0	$ 0
1	10
2	22
3	28
4	32

5. Consider the graph below describing the marginal revenue product curve facing a particular firm.
   a. If the marginal factor cost is $1, how many units of input will the firm hire?
   b. If the marginal factor cost is $2, how many units of input will the firm hire?
   c. If the marginal factor cost is $3, how many units of input will the firm hire?
   d. Identify the firm's demand curve for the input.

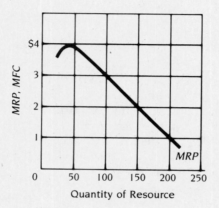

Quantity of Resource

6. Consider the following graphs, describing three different input markets. Assuming a market price of $1 in each of the three markets, graphically identify the total earnings, the economic earnings, and the transfer earnings in each case.

(a)

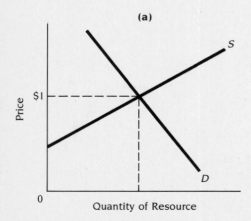

(b)

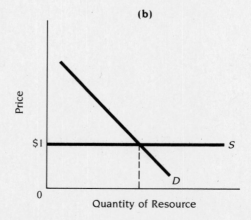

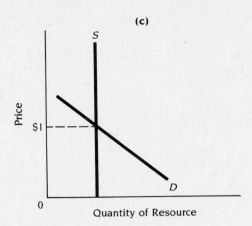

(c)

True-False

Indicate whether each of the following statements is basically true or false. If the statement is false, rewrite it so that it is true.

_____ 1. The return to the entrepreneurial input is a wage.

_____ 2. The management or administrative input in production is called entrepreneurship.

_____ 3. Capital includes raw materials and human skills.

_____ 4. There is a capital component in most resources.

_____ 5. Resource packages are combinations of resources.

_____ 6. The functional distribution of income refers to how income is divided among owners of different types of resources.

_____ 7. The supply of a resource is likely to be a negative relationship showing quantities of the resource that will be available at various prices.

_____ 8. Elasticity of supply for all uses of a resource is likely to decrease over time.

_____ 9. The substitution and income effects of a change in wages usually reinforce each other.

_____ 10. The income effect of a change in wages always outweighs the substitution effect.

_____ 11. In the very long run, increases in productivity may enable people to work fewer hours while receiving higher real incomes.

_____ 12. According to Dun and Bradstreet, managerial incompetence and lack of experience are major reasons for business failure.

_____ 13. If all uses of a certain resource are equally attractive to the owners of that resource, the return to the resource will tend to be the same in all uses.

_____ 14. The price elasticity of demand for a resource is the change in quantity demanded divided by the change in the price of the resource.

_____ 15. If the marginal physical product of the third unit of labor is 16 and the product sells in a purely competitive market for $2 per unit, the marginal revenue product is $8.

_____ 16. If total revenue increases from $15 to $25 when one more unit of input is hired, the marginal revenue product is $10.

_____ 17. Economic earnings are the part of the price or earnings of a resource that is equal to the price or earnings that this resource could command in its next-best use.

_____ 18. Economic earnings may take the form of economic rent when paid to natural resources, economic wages when paid to labor, economic profit when paid to entrepreneurship, and economic interest when paid to capital.

_____ 19. The lower the proportion of transfer earnings to economic earnings, the more likely it is that a resource will be transferred to another use.

_____ 20. A tax on economic rents, as proposed by Henry George, would cause landowners to shift the use of their land to uses associated with greater transfer earnings.

Multiple Choice   Choose the *one best* answer in each of the following cases:

_____ 1. Which of the following represents the return to natural resources?
   a. rent
   b. wages
   c. interest
   d. normal profit
   e. economic profit

_____ 2. Which of the following represents the return to capital?
   a. rent
   b. wages
   c. interest
   d. normal profit
   e. economic profit

_____ 3. Which of the following is *not* a factor of production?
   a. land
   b. labor
   c. money
   d. capital resources
   e. natural resources

_____ 4. Which of the following would be considered human capital?
     a. a surgeon
     b. a trained singer
     c. a natural talent
     d. both a and b above
     e. none of the above

_____ 5. Which of the following statements is true of the functional distribution of income in the United States.
     a. Compensation of employees makes up the largest share.
     b. Labor's share has decreased steadily over the past century.
     c. The proportion representing proprietors' income has grown steadily over the past century.
     d. all of the above
     e. both a and b above

_____ 6. In general, the supply of resources
     a. is perfectly inelastic.
     b. is absolutely fixed in amount.
     c. is characterized by a vertical supply curve.
     d. refers to the quantities that are available at various prices.
     e. all of the above

_____ 7. The supply of a resource for all uses and the supply of a resource for one specific use
     a. are usually the same.
     b. differ in that the supply for all uses is less responsive to a change in price than is the supply for a specific use.
     c. differ in that the supply for all uses is more responsive to a change in price than is the supply for a specific use.
     d. differ in that the supply for all uses is positively sloped and the supply for a specific use is generally negatively sloped.
     e. differ in that the supply for all uses is generally negatively sloped and the supply for a specific use is positively sloped.

_____ 8. The supply for all uses of labor
     a. may be permanently or temporarily affected by immigration.
     b. is negatively related to the labor-force participation rate.
     c. is not generally affected by the age distribution of the population.
     d. may be influenced by the labor-force participation rate but is not likely to be affected by the size and growth rate of the population itself.
     e. all of the above

_____ 9. Which of the following statements is true of the effect of changes in wages on labor-force participation rates?
a. Changes in wages have an income effect but no substitution effect.
b. Changes in wages have a substitution effect but no income effect.
c. Participation rates are expected to be positively related to changes in real income.
d. The substitution effect of a drop in wages is likely to cause people to stay in school longer, retire earlier, and so forth.
e. The income effect of a rise in wages measures the extent to which the increase in wages decreases the opportunity cost of labor.

_____ 10. An increase in wages is likely to result in
a. a decrease in the number of hours people are willing to work, due to the income effect.
b. an increase in the number of hours people are willing to work, due to the substitution effect.
c. both a and b above
d. a decrease in the number of hours people are willing to work, due to both the substitution and income effects.
e. an increase in the number of hours people are willing to work, due to both the substitution and income effects.

_____ 11. Working age
a. is defined as 16 to 65 years.
b. is any age greater than or equal to 16 years.
c. may be influenced by attitudes toward education.
d. is legally defined by the Social Security Act of 1935.
e. all of the above except a

_____ 12. The supply of entrepreneurs for all uses is generally
a. positively related to expected returns.
b. negatively related to the degree of monopoly control.
c. both a and b above
d. greater than the supply of labor for all uses.
e. not influenced by laws regulating patents, though it may be influenced by government antitrust policies.

_____ 13. The supply of natural resources for all uses
a. is perfectly inelastic.
b. can always be increased.
c. may be decreased in amount but cannot be increased.
d. is generally a positive relationship between quantity supplied and rent.
e. none of the above

14. The quantity of capital goods supplied for all uses is
    a. positively related to rental payments.
    b. positively related to interest payments.
    c. negatively related to the quantity of human capital available.
    d. affected by production of new capital but not by depreciation.
    e. affected by depreciation but not by production of new capital.

15. Differences in the returns to resources might be explained by differences in
    a. risk.
    b. location.
    c. working conditions.
    d. nonmonetary conditions of employment.
    e. all of the above

16. The price elasticity of resource supply is the
    a. change in quantity supplied divided by the change in price.
    b. change in price divided by the change in quantity supplied.
    c. percentage change in quantity supplied divided by the percentage change in price.
    d. percentage change in price divided by the percentage change in quantity supplied.
    e. percentage change in quantity supplied for a specific use divided by the percentage change in quantity supplied for all uses.

17. As the mobility of a resource increases, the
    a. supply of the resource increases.
    b. supply of the resource decreases.
    c. return to the resource decreases.
    d. more specialized the resource becomes.
    e. more easily the resource can change from one activity to another.

18. Demand for a resource is derived from the
    a. supply of the resource.
    b. elasticity of the resource.
    c. supply of the product it produces.
    d. demand for the product it produces.
    e. mobility of the product it produces.

19. The demand for a resource is likely to be more price elastic
    a. the more competition there is in the industry.
    b. the more difficult it is to use substitute resources.
    c. the smaller the price elasticity of demand for the final product

d. the smaller the proportion of the total production cost that is accounted for by the resource.

e. all of the above

_____ 20. The marginal factor cost is equal to the

a. price of the factor in a purely competitive input market.

b. additional cost associated with hiring one more unit of the factor.

c. change in total factor cost divided by the change in number of units of the factor hired.

d. all of the above

e. none of the above

_____ 21. The marginal revenue product is the

a. change in total revenue due to the hiring of an additional unit of input.

b. change in total revenue divided by the change in the number of units of input.

c. extra revenue associated with the sale of the output of an additional unit of input.

d. marginal physical product of the input times the price of the product when the product is sole in a purely competitive market.

e. all of the above

_____ 22. When the marginal revenue product for a specific resource exceeds the marginal factor cost, a profit-maximizing firm will

a. be maximizing profit.

b. lay off units of the resource.

c. hire additional units of the resource.

d. be earning a positive economic profit.

e. none of the above

Use the table below to answer questions 23 and 24.

Quantity of Input	Total Product
0	0
1	10
2	25
3	35
4	40
5	43

_____ 23. Consider the table above, describing a production situation characterized by pure competition in both input and output markets. From this schedule one can accurately conclude that

a. the marginal factor cost is 5.
b. a profit-maximizing firm will hire four units of input.
c. the marginal revenue product of the third unit of input is 10.
d. the marginal physical product of the fourth unit of input is 5.
e. all of the above

_____ 24. Consider the table on page 560. Assuming that the market-determined input price is $5 per unit and the market-determined product price is $1 per unit, one can conclude that
a. a profit-maximizing firm will hire four units of the input.
b. the total revenue product of three units of input is $10.
c. the marginal revenue product of the second unit of input is $25.
d. the marginal factor cost is $3 when the firm hires five units of input.
e. the firm will earn positive economic profit at the profit-maximizing output.

_____ 25. The declining portion of an input's marginal revenue product curve is
a. the supply curve of the input.
b. the firm's demand curve for the input.
c. equivalent to the input's marginal physical product curve.
d. the marginal factor cost in the case of a purely competitive input market.
e. none of the above

_____ 26. The equilibrium earnings of a resource
a. will be composed entirely of economic earnings when a resource has only one use.
b. are composed of three components: transfer earnings, economic earnings, and fixed earnings.
c. will consist entirely of fixed earnings when the supply of the resource is infinitely elastic.
d. will consist entirely of transfer earnings when the supply of the resource is perfectly inelastic.
e. will be equal to the economic earnings when a resource is put to a use for which it commands a price just barely above what it can command for its next-best use.

Discussion Questions

1. There are both substitution and income effects associated with a change in wages. Explain what these effects are and how they operate.
2. Identify the determinants of the supply of entrepreneurship for all uses.

3. Explain why supply curves for natural resources are not typically vertical.

4. Use the concept of derived demand to explain why the high price of land to grow wheat in early nineteenth-century England may have been the result of the high price of wheat rather than the cause of the high wheat price.

5. Discuss the importance of the extent of monopoly control for the price elasticity of demand for inputs.

6. The rule for determining the amount of an input to hire is analogous to the rule for determining the amount of a good to produce. Identify and compare the two rules.

7. Identify and derive the demand curve for a given resource.

8. Assume a purely competitive input market. How is the factor price determined? Identify and explain the derivation of the supply curve facing any single firm hiring inputs in the market.

9. Using the concepts of transfer earnings and economic earnings, explain when a worker would change jobs.

10. Explain the rationale underlying Henry George's proposal of a single tax on economic rent.

Answers

Problems and Applications

1. a. $3   b. $3   c. 5/7   d. 5/11

2. a.

Quantity of Input	MPP	TR	MRP
1	100	200	200
2	145	490	290
3	111	712	222
4	69	850	138
5	50	950	100

b. $222   c. 3 units; $222; 356 units; $2

3.

Quantity of Input	MRP
1	$ 60
2	100
3	80
4	60

4. | Quantity of Input | *MRP* |
   |:-:|:-:|
   | 1 | $10 |
   | 2 | 12 |
   | 3 | 6 |
   | 4 | 4 |

5. a. 200   b. 150   c. 100
   d. Input demand is the declining portion of the *MRP* curve.

6. In (a), economic earnings are shown by the area with horizontal lines and transfer earnings are shown by the shaded area. Total earnings are the sum of economic and transfer earnings. In (b), economic earnings are zero, and transfer earnings are shown by the shaded area. In (c), transfer earnings are zero, and economic earnings are shown by the area with horizontal lines.

(a)

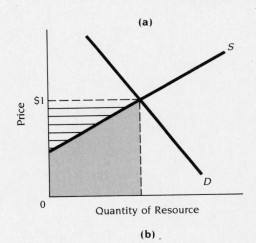

(b)

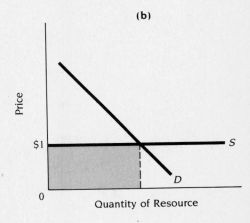

(b)

(c)

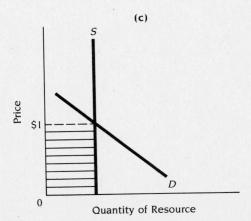

True-False

1. F. The return to the entrepreneurial input is a profit (or loss).
2. F. Most managerial and administrative jobs are considered to be labor.
3. F. Capital must be produced before it is available for use in further production; it includes human skills but not raw materials.
4. T.
5. T.
6. T.
7. F. The supply of a resource is likely to be a positive relationship showing quantities of the resource that will be available at various prices.
8. F. Elasticity of supply for all uses of a resource is likely to increase over time.
9. F. The substitution and income effects of a change in wages work against each other.
10. F. The income effect of a change in wages may, but does not necessarily, outweigh the substitution effect.
11. T.
12. T.
13. T.
14. F. The price elasticity of demand for a resource is the percentage change in quantity demanded divided by the percentage change in the price of the resource.
15. F. If the marginal physical product of the third unit of labor is 16 and the product sells in a purely competitive market for $2 per unit, the marginal revenue product is $32.
16. T.
17. F. Economic earnings are that part of the price or earnings of a resource that is not needed to keep that resource at its present use.
18. T.
19. F. The lower the proportion of transfer earnings to economic earnings, the less likely it is that a resource will be transferred to another use.
20. F. A tax on economic rents, as proposed by Henry George, would not cause landowners to shift the use of their land.

Multiple Choice

1. a	2. c	3. c	4. d	5. a
6. d	7. b	8. a	9. d	10. c
11. c	12. a	13. d	14. b	15. e
16. c	17. e	18. d	19. a	20. d
21. e	22. c	23. d	24. a	25. b
26. a				

30 Labor, Wages, and Collective Bargaining

Summary
Supply and demand conditions in a purely competitive labor market are similar to supply and demand conditions in a purely competitive product market, except that firms are the buyers and individual (potential) workers are the sellers. The market demand for labor is the sum of the individual firms' demand curves, and the supply of labor is the sum of individual workers' supply curves. Individual and market labor demand curves are typically negatively sloped, as in the case of the demand for goods. Like most supply curves, individual labor supply curves tend to be positively sloped at relatively low wages. However, individual labor supply curves tend to bend back at relatively high wages, becoming negatively sloped at these higher wages. Since not all individual labor supply curves bend back at the same wage and since additional individuals enter the labor market as the wage rises, the market supply curve of labor does not typically reveal this backward-bending portion.

In a purely competitive labor market, the market determines the equilibrium wage rate that individual buyers (firms) must accept as given. A firm can hire as much labor as it chooses at the market-determined wage but will find no labor available at lower wages. The labor supply curve facing the firm is therefore perfectly elastic (that is, horizontal). Furthermore, since the firm can hire additional workers at the same market-determined wage, the marginal factor cost is equal to the wage. As in the case of any resource market, a profit-maximizing firm hires the quantity of resources that equates marginal revenue product with marginal factor cost.

The firm that hires labor may sell its output in a purely competitive output market or in a monopolistic output market. For our purposes, the only essential difference in the two cases is in the marginal revenue product curve (and therefore the final profit-maximizing hiring level). The marginal revenue product is the change in total revenue associated with hiring an additional unit of labor. For a firm that sells its output in a purely competitive output market, the marginal revenue product is also equal to the marginal physical product times the output price. When the output market is characterized by monopoly control, the firm must lower the price of all output units in order to sell the additional output. Hence, the marginal revenue product curve declines faster for the firm selling under monopolistic conditions than for the one selling under pure competition. This means that the quantity of labor hired will be less when the firm sells its output under monopoly conditions than when it sells under competitive conditions. In the purely competitive labor market, both firms will pay the same market-determined wage.

When individual buyers (firms) in a labor market have some influence over the wage, the market is said to be monopsonistic. In this case, individual firms face positively sloped labor supply curves. In order to hire additional units of labor, the firm must typically pay all units a higher wage. This means that the marginal factor cost will be greater than the wage, and the marginal factor cost curve will be positively sloped and lie above the labor supply curve. Again, the profit-maximizing firm hires just enough labor to equate marginal revenue product with marginal factor cost. The firm will pay as low a wage as possible for the quantity of labor selected. Unless labor is organized, this wage is indicated by the labor supply curve.

In a monopsonistic labor market (with unorganized labor), the firm that sells its output under conditions of pure competition will hire a larger quantity of labor than does the firm that has some monopoly control in the product market. This is because the marginal revenue product is greater for the pure competitor. Since the pure competitor hires a greater quantity of labor, it also will have to pay a higher wage (to call forth the additional labor).

Labor market outcomes are likely to be different when labor is organized. In fact, when union labor operates in a monopsonistic labor market, the wage and quantity outcomes are indeterminate. The extreme case, called a bilateral monopoly, occurs when a single buyer confronts a single seller in the labor market. The specific outcome will depend on the strength of the union versus the strength of management.

Unions engage in collective bargaining in order to improve conditions of employment and to secure a more desirable relationship between union and management. In their attempts to raise wage rates, labor unions may attempt to increase demand for labor (that is, increase firms' marginal revenue product curves), restrict the supply of labor, and/or secure a higher-than-equilibrium wage. Increasing demand for labor has the advantage that it results in a higher wage as well as in greater employment.

The development of labor unions in the United States has certainly not been smooth. Unions were generally local until the American Federation of Labor was formed in 1886. General acceptance of unions did not come until the Great Depression. During this time two major pieces of legislation, the Norris-LaGuardia Act of 1932 and the Wagner-Connery Act, lent support to union activities. By the end of World War II, union membership had grown considerably. At the same time, public disfavor began to develop and led to the passage of the Taft-Hartley Act. This act identified and outlawed certain unfair labor practices. Soon after the American Federation of Labor and the Congress of Industrial Organizations merged in 1955, unions had to face the problem of corruption and racketeering. Public concern was so great that Congress passed the Landrum-Griffin Act, which established rules governing the relationship between union governments and union membership.

Government affects wages through legislation regarding unionization and collective bargaining, through changes in taxes on employers and employees, and through minimum-wage legislation. Minimum-wage legislation typically results in higher wages and reduced employment, because the markets affected are typically fairly competitive. Economic theory suggests that the imposition of a minimum wage in a monopsonistic labor market would result in a higher wage and greater employment. However, low-wage labor markets are not usually monopsonistic.

Economic theory suggests that the interaction of labor supply and demand determines an equilibrium wage rate. In fact, there are many factors that influence wages and create wage differentials. These basically center around differences in worker qualifications, in the desirability of jobs, and in institutions that surround labor markets.

Major Objectives   After you have finished this chapter, you will be able to do the following:

1. Define monopsonistic resource market.
2. Identify the three types of monopsonistic resource markets and compare them with the three types of monopolistic product markets.
3. Identify the major implications of hiring labor in a purely competitive input market.
4. Calculate and graph the marginal revenue product for a factor whose output is sold in a monopolistic product market.

5. Compare the marginal revenue product for a factor whose output is sold in a purely competitive product market with the marginal revenue product for a factor whose output is sold in a monopolistic product market.

6. Develop a purely competitive firm's demand curve for a factor that is hired in a purely competitive labor market.

7. Develop a monopoly firm's demand curve for a factor that is hired in a purely competitive labor market.

8. Compare the outcomes for labor hired in a purely competitive input market when the output is sold under conditions of pure competition versus monopoly control.

9. Develop individual labor supply curves and use the concepts of substitution and income effects to explain the backward-bending labor supply curve.

10. Develop the market demand curve for labor hired under purely competitive input conditions, given individual firms' demand curves.

11. Discuss the complications involved in developing the market supply curve of labor for a specific use.

12. Determine the equilibrium wage and quantity traded in a purely competitive labor market, given market demand and supply conditions.

13. Derive the supply curve of labor for an individual firm that hires labor in a purely competitive labor market.

14. Explain why a firm hiring in a monopsonistic labor market faces a positively sloped labor supply curve.

15. Define, calculate, and graph the marginal factor cost for a monopsonistic labor market.

16. Determine the profit-maximizing (or equilibrium) hiring position (quantity and wage) for a purely competitive firm that hires labor in a monopsonistic labor market.

17. Determine the profit-maximizing (or equilibrium) hiring position (quantity and wage) for a monopolist that hires labor in a monopsonistic labor market.

18. Compare the profit-maximizing positions for firms that hire labor in monopsonistic labor markets under product market conditions of pure competition and monopoly control.

19. Explain why workers in a purely competitive labor market are paid a wage rate equal to their marginal revenue product, whereas workers in a monopsonistic labor market are paid less than their marginal revenue product.

20. Identify the purposes of labor unions.

21. Define collective bargaining.

22. Briefly trace the history of the labor movement in the United States.

23. Identify and discuss the implications of major labor legislation in the United States.
24. Discuss the development of labor unions in the United States.
25. Define and distinguish between craft unions and industrial unions.
26. Explain the concept of business unionism.
27. Explain the provisions and significance of the Norris-LaGuardia Act of 1932, the National Labor Relations Act of 1935, the Labor-Management Relations Act of 1947, the Labor-Management Reporting and Disclosure Act, and the Civil Rights Act.
28. Explain the following concepts: yellow-dog contract, closed shop arrangement, secondary boycott, secondary strike, jurisdictional strike, featherbedding, union shop, and "right-to-work" laws.
29. Discuss the growth and make-up of union membership in the United States.
30. Identify the goal of and discuss the major issues in collective bargaining.
31. Explain the following concepts: wage issues, fringe benefits, work standards, job security, seniority rules, bargaining unit, shop stewards, checkoff, arbitration, lockout, strike, picketing, and boycott.
32. Verbally and graphically explain how a union raises the wage rate of its workers when the labor market is purely competitive.
33. Compare the results in terms of employment of a union that raises wages by restricting supply or securing a higher-than-equilibrium wage rate, as compared to one that raises wages by increasing demand.
34. Define and provide an example of a bilateral monopoly.
35. Verbally and graphically describe the bargaining process in a monopsonistic labor market.
36. Discuss the role of government in determining wages and employment levels, identify the specific instruments used by the government to influence these variables, and explain how these instruments work.
37. Analyze the effects of a minimum wage in a purely competitive labor market.
38. Analyze the effects of a minimum wage in a low-wage monopsonistic labor market.
39. Explain how the kinked labor supply curve and the discontinuous marginal factor cost curve are developed, and indicate the consequences for the equilibrium employment and wage levels.
40. Identify and discuss the major factors that give rise to wage differentials.

Review Terms

labor
demand
supply
pure competition
monopoly
wage
marginal productivity theory
marginal revenue product
marginal factor cost
monopolistic competition
oligopoly
marginal physical product
  or marginal product

substitution effect
income effect
productivity
derived demand
import quota
dumping
tariff
minimum wage
excess supply
human capital
free market

**Important Terms
and Concepts**

monopsonistic resource market
monopsonistic competition
oligopsony
monopsony
backward-bending labor supply
  curve
labor union
collective bargaining
craft union
industrial union
National Labor Union
Knights of Labor
American Federation of Labor
  (AF of L)
business unionism
Industrial Workers of the World
  (IWW)
Norris-LaGuardia Act of 1932
yellow-dog contract
National Labor Relations Act
  (Wagner-Connery Act of 1935)
National Labor Relations Board
Congress of Industrial Organizations (CIO)
Labor-Management Relations
  Act of 1947 (Taft-Hartley Act)
closed shop
secondary boycott
secondary strike

jurisdictional strike
featherbedding
union shop
"right-to-work" laws
AFL-CIO
Teamsters Union
Labor-Management Reporting
  and Disclosure Act
  (Landrum-Griffin Act)
Civil Rights Act of 1964
two-tier contracts
profit sharing
wage issues
fringe benefits
work standards
job security
seniority rules
bargaining unit
shop stewards
checkoff
arbitration
lockout
strike
picketing
boycott
bilateral monopoly
Davis Bacon Act of 1931
Fair Labor Standards Act of
  1938

kinked labor supply curve
discontinuous marginal factor
   cost curve
wage differential
compensating wage differential

labor market institutions
labor market discrimination
Equal Employment Opportunities Commission (EEOC)

Completion

A profit-maximizing firm hires the quantity of labor that equates

marginal revenue
product

_____ with

marginal factor cost

_____ . If the firm hires a smaller

greater

quantity of labor, the marginal revenue product will be _____
(greater/less) than the marginal factor cost, giving the firm an incen-

additional

tive to hire _____ (additional/fewer) workers. If the
firm hires more labor than that which equates the *MRP* with the

less

MFC, the *MRP* will be _____ (greater/less) than the *MFC*

fewer

and the firm will be inclined to hire _____ (additional/
fewer) workers.

demand

The marginal revenue product represents a firm's labor _____
curve. The marginal revenue product curve differs from firm to firm,

output

depending on the type of _____ (input/output) market

monopolist

they face. The marginal revenue product curve for a _____

pure competitor

lies below the marginal revenue product curve for a _____ .
That is, for any quantity of labor, the marginal revenue product is

monopolist, pure
competitor

less for a _____ than for a _____ .
Consequently, when the firm equates marginal revenue product with
the marginal factor cost to determine the quantity of labor to hire,

fewer

the monopolist hires _____ (fewer/more) workers than the
pure competitor.

purely competitive

In the case of a _____ labor market, any
individual firm hires such a small amount of the total labor available
that it can hire any amount at the market-determined wage. This
means that in order to hire an additional unit of labor, the firm must

the same

pay _____ (the same/a higher) wage. Hence, the mar-

equal to

ginal factor cost is _____ the wage and becomes the

supply

labor _____ curve facing the firm. The labor supply curve is

horizontal

_____ . The firm that hires labor in a

cannot

purely competitive labor market _____ (can/cannot) influence the wage.

By equating marginal revenue product and marginal factor cost, the firm that hires labor in a purely competitive labor market must

marginal revenue product

pay a wage equal to labor's _____ as well as the marginal factor cost. The only difference between the outcome under conditions of a purely competitive output market as

quantity of labor hired

compared to a monopolistic output market is in the _____ (wage/quantity of labor hired). For the pure competitor by compari-

the same

son to the monopolist, the wage will be _____ (less/the same/

greater

greater) and the quantity of labor hired will be _____ (less/ the same/greater).

monopsonistic

In a _____ labor market, firms can influence the wage. In order for a firm to hire additional labor units, the firm must

pay a higher wage

_____ . Hence, the individual

supply, positively

firm's labor _____ (demand/supply) curve is _____

positively

sloped. And the marginal factor cost curve will be _____

above

sloped and lie _____ (below/on/above) the labor supply curve. In a monopsonistic labor market, a firm hires labor such that

marginal revenue product

the _____ is equal to the

marginal factor cost

_____ . Assuming that workers do not bargain collectively, this quantity of labor can be hired for the

supply

wage indicated on the labor _____ curve. The wage will

less than

be _____ (less than/equal to/greater than) the marginal

less than

factor cost. Hence, labor will be paid _____ (less than/ the same as/more than) its marginal revenue product.

In a monopsonistic labor market, the outcome will differ depend-

purely competitive

ing on whether the firm sells its products under _____

monopolistic

or _____ conditions. Since for any quantity of

marginal revenue product

labor the _____ is less for the

fewer

monopolist, the profit-maximizing monopolist will hire _____

lower

(fewer/the same number of/more) workers and pay a(n) _____ (lower/equal/greater) wage.

Problems and Applications

Use the following tables to answer problems 1 and 2

Table A. Purely Competitive Labor Market

Wage Rate	Quantity Demanded	Quantity Supplied
$1	1250	114
2	1100	450
3	870	870
4	450	1076
5	200	1598

Table B. Firm X

Quantity of Labor	MRP
4	$6
5	5
6	4
7	3
8	2

1. Table A above describes a purely competitive labor market. Table B describes the marginal revenue product schedule for Firm X in that market.
   a. Use the information contained in the tables to determine the equilibrium wage and the marginal factor cost.
   b. Identify the labor supply curve facing Firm X and the firm's demand curve for labor.
   c. How many units of labor will be hired by Firm X? What wage will be paid?

2. If the government imposes a minimum wage of $4 in the market described in Table A above, how many workers will be hired? How many would like to work at this wage? Does the imposition of the minimum wage in a competitive labor market result in increased or decreased employment?

3. Graph (a) below describes a purely competitive labor market, and graph (b) describes the marginal revenue product curve for Firm X in that market.

   a. Use the information contained in the graphs to determine the equilibrium wage and the marginal factor cost.

   b. Identify the labor supply curve facing Firm X and the firm's demand curve for labor.

   c. How many units of labor will be hired by Firm X? What wage will be paid?

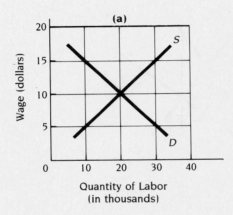

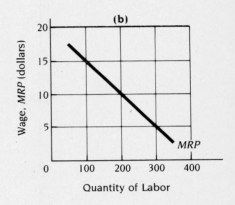

4. Is there any way to determine whether or not the firms described in problems 1 and 3 above sell their output in purely competitive product markets or under monopolistic conditions? If so, how? If not, would a worker have any preference between the two? Explain.

5. The table below describes the labor supply schedule facing a firm that hires labor in a monopsonistic labor market, as well as the marginal revenue product schedule for the firm.

Wage per Day	Quantity of Labor Supplied	MRP
$100	10	$245
105	11	205
110	12	165
115	13	120

   a. Use the information in the table above to determine the marginal factor cost schedule and the firm's demand curve for labor.

b. How many units of labor will be hired by the firm described? What wage will be paid?

6. The graph below describes the labor supply curve, marginal factor cost curve, and marginal revenue product curve for a firm that hires labor in a monopsonistic labor market. Assuming that labor is unorganized, determine the equilibrium wage and the quantity of labor hired.

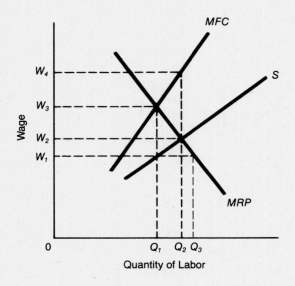

7. Consider the monopsonistic labor market described in the graph on page 577.
    a. What quantity of labor will the firm hire in the absence of unionization and government intervention? What wage would the firm pay?
    b. If the labor market described below is unionized and if the union agrees to the quantity of labor selected in paragraph 7. a., what wage will the union expect workers to be paid?
    c. Assume that the market is not unionized but that the government imposes a minimum wage of $2 per hour. How many workers will be hired? How many workers will be hired if the minimum wage is set at $3 per hour? How many workers will be hired if the minimum wage is set at $5 per hour?

Graph for problem 7.

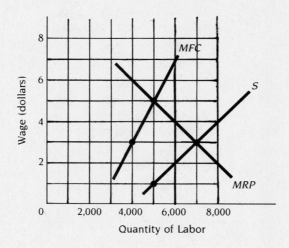

Quantity of Labor

True-False

Indicate whether each of the following statements is basically true or false. If the statement is false, rewrite it so that it is true.

_____ 1. A resource market is monopsonistic if individual buyers (that is, firms) can influence the price of the resource.

_____ 2. Firms in an oligopsonistic labor market face positively sloped supply curves.

_____ 3. In a purely competitive labor market, the interplay of market demand and supply determines the wage.

_____ 4. In a purely competitive labor market, the wage is equal to the marginal revenue product.

_____ 5. A profit-maximizing firm hires the amount of labor that equates marginal revenue product with marginal factor cost.

_____ 6. The marginal revenue product for a monopolist that faces a purely competitive labor market is equal to the marginal revenue product for a purely competitive firm that faces the same purely competitive labor market.

_____ 7. The marginal factor cost for a monopolist that faces a purely competitive labor market is equal to the marginal factor cost for a purely competitive firm that faces the same purely competitive labor market.

_____ 8. A profit-maximizing firm that hires labor in a purely competitive labor market will hire more workers and pay a higher wage if the firm sells its output in a purely competitive product market as compared to a monopolistic product market.

_____ 9. Individual labor supply curves are positively sloped throughout.

_____ 10. All individual labor supply curves bend backward at the same wage.

_____ 11. In a monopsonistic labor market, profit-maximizing firms will hire units of labor such that marginal revenue product equals marginal factor cost and will pay as low a wage as possible.

_____ 12. The major goals of labor unions are to improve the wages and working conditions of their members.

_____ 13. Labor unions originated in the United States.

_____ 14. An industrial union represents a certain kind of skilled worker.

_____ 15. Though generally unpopular, unions have found support in U.S. courts throughout their history.

_____ 16. A yellow-dog contract is an agreement that a worker will not join a union.

_____ 17. Union shops require business to hire union labor, and closed shops permit only nonunion employees.

_____ 18. A secondary boycott or strike is a boycott or strike against an employer other than the one with which the union has a dispute.

_____ 19. A jurisdictional strike is a strike called by a union against an employer who refuses to bargain.

_____ 20. Featherbedding is the practice of forcing an employer to pay for services that workers do not actually perform.

_____ 21. Unions have almost universally engaged in racial discrimination.

_____ 22. The 1980s have seen both increased confrontation and cooperation between labor and management.

_____ 23. Collective bargaining usually centers around conditions of employment and the relationship between a union and management.

_____ 24. The average wage in unionized industries is from 15 to 20 percent higher than the average wage in nonunionized industries.

_____ 25. Of the possible approaches to securing a higher wage rate for their members, industrial unions most often bargain for a wage rate that is higher than the competitive market equilibrium wage rate.

_____ 26. Decreasing the supply of labor in a competitive labor market results in a higher wage rate and employment level, whereas increasing the demand for labor results in a higher wage rate but a lower level of employment.

_____ 27. Unions are monopolistic sellers of labor.

_____ 28. A bilateral monopoly exists when a union represents all of the workers in an industry and only one firm hires these workers.

_____ 29. The substitution effect of a tax on employees' wages causes workers to consume more leisure.

_____ 30. Generally, firms in industries affected by minimum-wage laws are in monopsonistic labor markets.

_____ 31. As suggested by theory, studies have found that minimum-wage laws do tend to raise wage rates at the expense of some jobs.

Multiple Choice   Choose the *one best* answer in each of the following cases:

_____ 1. The marginal revenue product for a monopolist that faces a purely competitive labor market is equal to the
   a. wage times the marginal physical product.
   b. price of the product times the marginal physical product.
   c. change in total revenue associated with hiring an additional worker.
   d. change in total revenue associated with producing an additional unit of the product.
   e. both b and c above

_____ 2. The marginal factor cost for a monopolist that faces a purely competitive labor market is equal to the
   a. market-determined wage.
   b. change in total cost associated with hiring an additional unit of labor.
   c. change in total cost associated with producing an additional unit of output.
   d. both a and b above
   e. all of the above

_____ 3. A profit-maximizing firm that hires labor in a purely competitive labor market will
   a. hire the amount of labor that equates marginal revenue product with marginal factor cost.
   b. hire more workers if the firm sells its output in a monopolistic product market as compared to a purely competitive product market.
   c. pay a higher wage if the firm sells its output in a purely competitive product market as compared to a monopolistic product market.
   d. all of the above
   e. none of the above

_____ 4. Backward-bending individual labor supply curves
   a. tend to be negatively sloped throughout.
   b. will bend backward when the worker has worked an eight-hour day.
   c. will bend backward when the income effect of a wage change outweighs the substitution effect.
   d. will bend backward when the substitution effect of a wage change outweighs the income effect.
   e. tend to be positively sloped at relatively high wages and negatively sloped at relatively low wages.

_____ 5. Market demand for labor in a purely competitive labor market is equal to the
   a. sum of the marginal factor cost curves of all firms in the labor market.
   b. sum of the marginal revenue product curves of all firms in the labor market.
   c. intersection of the marginal revenue product curves with the marginal factor cost curves of all firms in the labor market.
   d. sum of the marginal factor cost curves of the firms in the labor market only if these firms sell their products in purely competitive output markets.
   e. sum of the marginal revenue product curves of the firms in the labor market only if these firms sell their products in purely competitive output markets.

_____ 6. The equilibrium wage in a purely competitive labor market determines the
   a. demand facing individual firms.
   b. marginal factor cost facing individual firms.
   c. marginal revenue product facing individual firms.
   d. all of the above
   e. none of the above

_____ 7. In a monopsonistic labor market,
   a. buyers face backward-bending demand curves.
   b. buyers face negatively sloped supply curves.
   c. sellers face negatively sloped supply curves.
   d. individual buyers of labor can influence the wage.
   e. individual buyers of labor take the wage as given by the market.

_____ 8. In a monopsonistic labor market, the marginal factor cost curve is
   a. horizontal and equal to the supply curve.
   b. positively sloped and equal to the supply curve.
   c. positively sloped and lying above the supply curve.
   d. positively sloped and lying below the supply curve.
   e. none of the above

9. At equilibrium in a monopsonistic labor market, the
   a. wage equals the marginal factor cost.
   b. wage equals the marginal revenue product.
   c. marginal revenue product equals the marginal factor cost.
   d. all of the above
   e. both a and c above

10. A profit-maximizing firm that hires labor in a monopsonistic labor market will
   a. hire the amount of labor that equates marginal revenue product with marginal factor cost.
   b. pay a wage that exceeds the marginal factor cost if the firm sells its output in a monopolistic product market.
   c. pay a wage that exceeds the maginal factor cost if the firm sells its output in a purely competitive product market.
   d. hire more workers if the firm sells its output in a monopolistic product market as compared to a purely competitive product market.
   e. pay a lower wage if the firm sells its output in a purely competitive product market as compared to a monopolistic product market.

11. In equilibrium, workers are paid a wage that is
   a. equal to their marginal revenue product in a monopsonistic labor market.
   b. less than their marginal revenue product in a monopsonistic labor market.
   c. equal to their marginal factor cost, regardless of the type of labor market.
   d. greater than their marginal revenue product in a monopsonistic labor market.
   e. greater than their marginal revenue product in a monopolistic output market.

12. Labor unions in the United States
   a. began as guilds in colonial America.
   b. went on strike as early as 1786.
   c. were almost exclusively craft unions prior to the 1820s.
   d. were sometimes national in scope by the 1850s.
   e. all of the above

13. The Knights of Labor
   a. began as a secret society.
   b. was the first federation of national unions in the United States.
   c. admitted all types and grades of labor, including lawyers, bankers, and doctors.

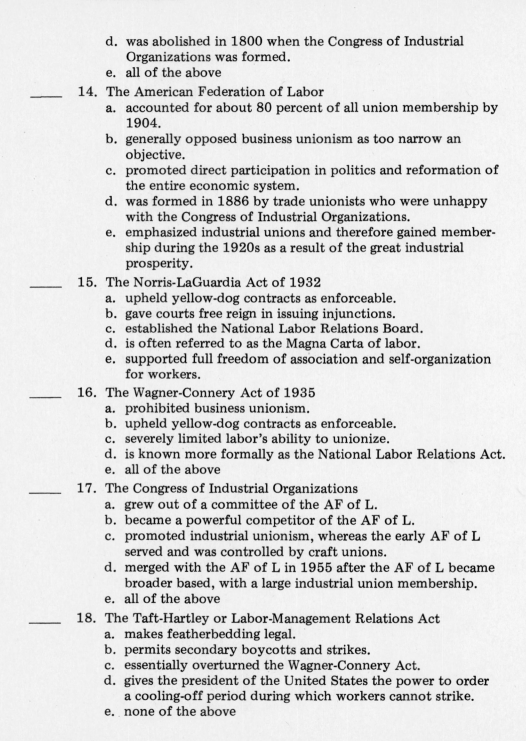

    d. was abolished in 1800 when the Congress of Industrial
       Organizations was formed.
    e. all of the above

____ 14. The American Federation of Labor
    a. accounted for about 80 percent of all union membership by
       1904.
    b. generally opposed business unionism as too narrow an
       objective.
    c. promoted direct participation in politics and reformation of
       the entire economic system.
    d. was formed in 1886 by trade unionists who were unhappy
       with the Congress of Industrial Organizations.
    e. emphasized industrial unions and therefore gained member-
       ship during the 1920s as a result of the great industrial
       prosperity.

____ 15. The Norris-LaGuardia Act of 1932
    a. upheld yellow-dog contracts as enforceable.
    b. gave courts free reign in issuing injunctions.
    c. established the National Labor Relations Board.
    d. is often referred to as the Magna Carta of labor.
    e. supported full freedom of association and self-organization
       for workers.

____ 16. The Wagner-Connery Act of 1935
    a. prohibited business unionism.
    b. upheld yellow-dog contracts as enforceable.
    c. severely limited labor's ability to unionize.
    d. is known more formally as the National Labor Relations Act.
    e. all of the above

____ 17. The Congress of Industrial Organizations
    a. grew out of a committee of the AF of L.
    b. became a powerful competitor of the AF of L.
    c. promoted industrial unionism, whereas the early AF of L
       served and was controlled by craft unions.
    d. merged with the AF of L in 1955 after the AF of L became
       broader based, with a large industrial union membership.
    e. all of the above

____ 18. The Taft-Hartley or Labor-Management Relations Act
    a. makes featherbedding legal.
    b. permits secondary boycotts and strikes.
    c. essentially overturned the Wagner-Connery Act.
    d. gives the president of the United States the power to order
       a cooling-off period during which workers cannot strike.
    e. none of the above

_____ 19. The Landrum-Griffin or Labor-Management Reporting and Disclosure Act of 1959
   a. offers a "bill of rights" for every union member.
   b. was passed in response to public concern with union corruption.
   c. provides strict penalties for any union official found guilty of mishandling union funds.
   d. contains a detailed set of rules governing the relationship between union governments and union membership.
   e. all of the above

_____ 20. Union membership
   a. has grown significantly since 1960.
   b. among public employees decreased during the 1960s and 1970s.
   c. includes only private employees, since public employees cannot unionize.
   d. as a percentage of the noninstitutionalized population, 16 years of age or older, doubled between 1970 and 1980.
   e. none of the above

_____ 21. Forms of compensation other than wages are called
   a. work standards.
   b. featherbedding.
   c. fringe benefits.
   d. bargaining units.
   e. compensating wage differentials.

_____ 22. Workers elected to represent a union on the job are called
   a. arbitrators.
   b. the checkoff.
   c. shop stewards.
   d. the seniority unit.
   e. the bargaining unit.

_____ 23. A procedure for settling differences between union and management by having a neutral outside party make a decision that will be binding on both sides is called
   a. a lockout.
   b. seniority.
   c. a checkoff.
   d. arbitration.
   e. a bargaining unit.

_____ 24. A work stoppage in which the company closes the plant to its workers is called a
a. picket.
b. strike.
c. boycott.
d. lockout.
e. checkoff.

_____ 25. If a purely competitive labor market is unionized, the union might try to raise the wage rate of its workers by
a. increasing market demand for the output of its members.
b. bargaining for a wage rate above the competitive market equilibrium wage rate.
c. decreasing the market supply of labor by restricting the number of people who can join the union.
d. decreasing the market supply of labor by pressuring employers for a shorter work week, early retirement, and longer vacations.
e. all of the above

_____ 26. In order to increase the demand for union workers, a union may attempt to
a. increase the productivity of union members.
b. increase the demand for the union-made product.
c. increase the union-labor component in production.
d. decrease competition from non-union-made goods.
e. all of the above

Use the graph below to answer questions 27 and 28.

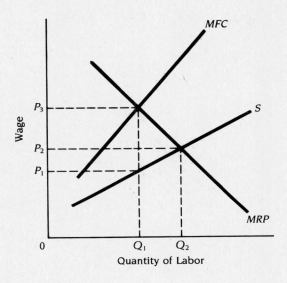

_____ 27. Consider the graph above, describing a bilateral monopoly. From the information given, one could accurately conclude that

    a. the equilibrium wage rate is P_2.

    b. at equilibrium, the firm will hire Q_2 workers.

    c. the firm would prefer to hire Q_1 workers and pay P_1.

    d. all of the above

    e. the equilibrium wage rate is P_1.

_____ 28. Consider the graph above, describing a union operating in a monopsonistic labor market. If Q_1 workers are hired, one could accurately conclude that

    a. the wage rate will be P_1.

    b. the wage rate will be P_3.

    c. the wage rate will be between P_1 and P_3.

    d. the union will attempt to get P_1 for its workers.

    e. union members will not work for less than P_3.

_____ 29. When the government imposes a tax on employers, the result will typically be a(n)

    a. decrease in the quantity of labor employed.

    b. decrease in the marginal factor cost of labor.

    c. increase in the marginal revenue product of labor.

    d. all of the above

    e. none of the above

Use the graph below to answer questions 30 and 31.

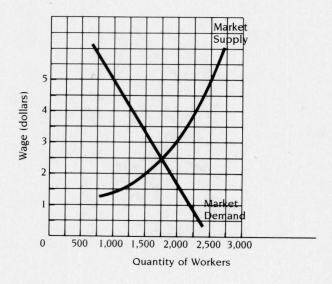

_____ 30. How many workers will be employed if a minimum wage of $5 per hour is imposed in the competitive labor market described in the graph above?
   a. 1,000
   b. 1,500
   c. 1,750
   d. 2,500
   e. 3,500

_____ 31. If a minimum wage of $5 per hour is imposed in the competitive labor market described in the graph,
   a. there will be full employment.
   b. 750 workers will be unemployed.
   c. 1,500 workers will be unemployed.
   d. 2,500 workers will be unemployed.
   e. none of the above

Use the graph below to answer question 32.

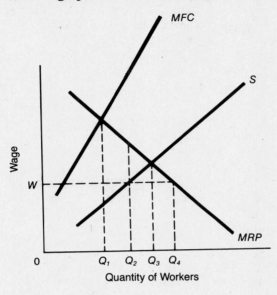

32. Consider the monopsonistic labor market described in the graph above. If a minimum wage is imposed at W, one could accurately conclude that
    a. the demand curve will be kinked at Q_2.
    b. Q_2 workers will be employed at the minimum wage.
    c. Q_4 people would be willing to work at the minimum wage.
    d. the marginal revenue product curve will be discontinuous at Q_2.
    e. all of the above

33. Wage differentials may be explained by
    a. discrimination.
    b. differences in worker qualifications.
    c. differences in the desirability of jobs.
    d. differences in the institutions that surround the labor market.
    e. all of the above

Discussion Questions

1. Use the concepts of income and substitution effects to explain the backward-bending individual labor supply curve.

2. Explain why the marginal factor cost curve represents the labor supply curve for a firm in a purely competitive labor market.

3. For a given quantity of labor, the marginal factor cost is greater than the wage in a monopsonistic labor market. Explain.

4. Workers in a purely competitive labor market are paid a wage equal to their marginal revenue product, whereas workers in a monopsonistic labor market are paid less than their marginal revenue product. Explain.

5. Analyze the effects of a minimum wage in a monopsonistic labor market. Does it matter where the wage is set? Explain. How realistic is this application?

Answers

Problems and Applications

1. a. $3; $3
   b. The labor supply curve is horizontal at a price of $3; the firm's demand curve for labor is the firm's *MRP* curve.
   c. 7; $3

2. 450 units; 1,076 units; decreased

3. a. $10; $10
   b. The labor supply curve is horizontal at a price of $10; the demand curve for labor is the firm's *MRP* curve.
   c. 200 units; $10

4. The character of the output market cannot be determined from the information given. The *MRP* curve of a monopolist in the output market is lower than the *MRP* curve of a pure competitor in the output market. Hence, for any given wage, more labor will be employed when the output market is purely competitive. A potential worker would have more likelihood of being employed under pure competition in the output market.

5. a.

Quantity of Labor	MFC
11	$155
12	165
13	175

   The demand curve for labor is the firm's *MRP* curve.
   b. 12; $110 per day

6. W_1; Q_1

7. a. 5,000; $1   b. $5   c. 6,000; 7,000; 5,000

True-False

1. T.
2. T.
3. T.
4. F. In a purely competitive labor market, the wage is equal to the marginal factor cost.
5. T.
6. F. The marginal revenue product for a monopolist that faces a purely competitive labor market is less than the marginal revenue product for a purely competitive firm that faces the same purely competitive labor market.
7. T.
8. F. A profit-maximizing firm that hires labor in a purely competitive labor market will hire more workers if the firms sells its output in a purely competitive product market as compared to a monopolistic product market; the two firms will pay the same wage.
9. F. Individual labor supply curves are likely to be positively sloped at relatively low wages but may bend backward at relatively high wages.
10. F. It is unlikely that all individual labor supply curves would bend backward at the same wage.
11. T.
12. T.
13. F. Labor unions date back at least as far as the medieval craft guilds of twelfth-century England.
14. F. A craft union represents a certain kind of skilled worker; an industrial union represents all the workers in an industry.
15. F. Throughout most of their early history, unions were generally unpopular and did not receive support in the courts until the passage of the Norris-LaGuardia Act of 1932.
16. T.
17. F. Closed shops require business to hire union labor; union shops permit business to hire nonunion employees but require that these employees join the union within thirty days.
18. T.
19. F. A jurisdictional strike is a strike called by a union against an employer who is already legitimately bargaining with another union.
20. T.
21. F. In the early 1960s, many unions became interested in the issue of racial discrimination and a number of industrial unions worked hard for passage of the Civil Rights Act of 1964.

22. T.
23. T.
24. T.
25. T.
26. F. Increasing the demand for labor in a competitive labor market results in a higher wage rate and employment level, whereas decreasing the supply of labor results in a higher wage rate but a lower level of employment.
27. T.
28. T.
29. T.
30. F. Generally, firms in industries affected by minimum-wage laws are in fairly competitive labor markets.
31. T.

Multiple Choice

1. c	2. d	3. a	4. c	5. b
6. b	7. d	8. c	9. c	10. a
11. b	12. e	13. a	14. a	15. e
16. d	17. e	18. d	19. e	20. e
21. c	22. c	23. d	24. d	25. e
26. e	27. c	28. c	29. a	30. a
31. c	32. b	33. e		

31 *Capital, Interest, and Investment*

Summary

A firm's decisions with respect to capital input are similar to its decisions with respect to other inputs. A firm will provide for the creation of new capital (invest) when the expected marginal revenue product is greater than or equal to the marginal factor cost.

There are, however, three major problems that are especially pronounced with the investment decision: the time problem, the obsolescence problem, and the derived demand problem. Because of these problems, an investment decision is typically characterized by greater risk and uncertainty than are decisions regarding the other inputs. Economists attempt to handle these problems by discounting.

Discounting is the process of calculating the present value of payments that are to be received in the future. A certain sum of money received now has greater value than that same sum of money to be received in the future. Hence, to determine the present value of a future sum of money, that sum of money must be discounted. The present value of a payment X to be received t years in the future when the discount rate is i is given by $X/(1 + i)^t$. For any given time period, the higher the interest rate, the lower the present value of a future payment; for any given interest rate, the further into the future a sum of money is to be received, the lower its present value.

In determining whether to undertake a particular investment, a firm compares the marginal factor cost with the appropriate marginal revenue product. The marginal factor cost of capital is the price of the capital good at the time it is purchased. The marginal revenue product of capital is more difficult to determine. It must be net of all operating costs. Since it tends to accrue over time, it must be discounted. A firm will undertake the investment only if the discounted marginal revenue product is greater than or equal to the marginal factor cost.

Interest rates are determined in the market for loanable funds. The demand for loanable funds is a negative relationship indicating the amount of money people want to borrow at different interest rates. This demand may consist of business demand for investment purposes, household demand, and government demand. The supply of loanable funds indicates the relationship between the amount of money that is available for loans and interest rates. As usual, the supply relationship is direct. The interaction of supply and demand determines the equilibrium interest rate.

As with other resource prices, there are many (rather than just one) interest rates. This is largely due to the existence of different levels of risk. Typically, a higher interest rate is charged on loans that involve greater risk.

Capital in the form of machinery, tools, and equipment is called physical capital. Capital associated with the productive power of people is referred to as human capital. The theory of investment in capital is applicable to both physical and human capital. Investment in human capital typically takes the form of education, training, and provision of health care. The returns to an investment in human capital may be psychic as well as monetary. They also may be social as well as private. Distinguishing a purchase as being for investment or consumption may be especially difficult in dealing with human capital. For example, the purchase of education is likely to have both consumption and investment components. Firms may be somewhat reluctant to invest in human capital, since employees may not remain with the firm after the investment.

Major Objectives   After you have finished this chapter, you will be able to do the following:

1. Define, distinguish between, and provide examples of physical and human capital.
2. Explain the concept of roundabout production and identify the expected advantages.
3. Define and explain the concepts of investment and an investment decision and compare the investment decision to other resource-hiring decisions made by a firm.
4. Identify and explain the three major problems associated with the investment decision.
5. Define and explain the importance of present value and discounting.
6. Identify and explain the relationship between present value and time.

7. Identify and explain the relationship between present value and the interest rate.
8. Cite and use the formulas for computing present value.
9. Explain what is meant by compounding interest and how it is accomplished.
10. Identify and explain the relationship between discount rates and the amounts of risk and uncertainty associated with an investment.
11. Explain how the marginal factor cost of capital is determined.
12. Identify the problems associated with determining the marginal revenue product of capital and explain how it is determined.
13. Determine whether a firm should undertake a specific investment, given the marginal factor cost, the marginal revenue product, and the discount rate.
14. Compare and contrast interest, rental, and wage rates.
15. Explain the concept of a breakeven interest rate.
16. Explain what is meant by the loanable funds market and identify the functions of this market.
17. Identify and explain the slopes of the demand and supply curves for loanable funds.
18. Explain the difference between and causes of a change in the demand for loanable funds and a change in the quantity of loanable funds demanded.
19. Identify the sources of demand for loanable funds.
20. Explain the difference between and causes of a change in the supply of loanable funds and a change in the quantity of loanable funds supplied.
21. Identify the sources of supply for loanable funds.
22. Locate the equilibrium point in a market for loanable funds and explain how the equilibrium is determined.
23. Explain why interest rates differ with different loans.
24. Define human capital and identify determinants of the productivity of people.
25. Explain what is meant by an investment in human capital.
26. Identify different kinds of returns to investment in human capital.
27. Identify potential costs and returns associated with an investment in education.
28. Explain the concept of psychic returns and identify different forms these might take.
29. Distinguish between investment and consumption components of individual investment-consumption decisions and discuss the difficulty of making such distinctions.
30. Identify reasons for, forms of, and problems associated with a firm's investment in human capital.

31. Identify important issues of concern in distinguishing between a firm's investment in human capital and physical capital.
32. Explain the meaning and forms of public investment in human capital and the reasons for it.
33. Identify and distinguish between private and social returns from investment.
34. Discuss research findings of studies dealing with the returns from education and the implications of these findings.

Review Terms

input or factor of production
   or resource
marginal productivity theory
capital
human capital
rationality
entrepreneur
natural resources
marginal revenue product
marginal factor cost
marginal product
diminishing marginal product
opportunity cost
derived demand
wage

rent
demand
supply
quantity demanded
quantity supplied
equilibrium
breakeven
change in demand vs. change in
   quantity demanded
inverse relationship
change in supply vs. change in
   quantity supplied
macroeconomics
scarcity

Important Terms and Concepts

physical capital
social capital
roundabout production
investment
investment decision
the time problem
obsolescence
the obsolescence problem
the derived demand problem
discounting
present value
discounted value
discount rate
compound interest
operating costs
interest rate

loanable funds
market for loanable funds
equilibrium interest rate
breakeven interest rate
investment demand for loanable
   funds
budget deficit
supply of loanable funds
investment in human capital
psychic returns
consumption decision
public investment in human
   capital
private returns
social returns

Completion

investment

marginal revenue
product

marginal factor cost

time, obsolescence

derived demand

time

before

durable

opportunity

obsolete, obso-
lescence

derived demand

price

long

increased

lower

risk

uncertainty

discounting

When a firm decides to provide money for the resources that are

needed to create new capital, the firm has made an _____

decision. As with other hiring decisions, the firm will undertake an

investment in capital as long as the _____

exceeds the _____ . Though the investment

decision is similar to decisions regarding other inputs, there are three
major problems that are especially pronounced when dealing with the

capital input. These are the _____ problem, the _____

problem, and the _____ problem.

The _____ problem arises because investment decisions
usually must be made before receiving all or a major part of the returns from these investments. Unlike other resources, capital is

usually purchased _____ (before/after) it is delivered or used.

Furthermore, capital is generally _____ (durable/nondur-
able) with returns accruing over a relatively long period. During the
time that a firm has invested funds but has received only part of its

return on the investment, it incurs an _____ cost.

When something is no longer useful or economically suited for its
intended purpose, even though it may still be in good working order,

it is said to be _____ . The _____ problem
arises because capital goods are expected to last for many years.

The _____ problem is based on the fact that
the demand for resources depends on the demand for the end products these resources help to produce. The expected return from an
investment is closely related to the firm's expectations about the

_____ of the product being produced. Since the return from

an investment generally accrues over a relatively _____ (short/

long) time period, there is _____ (decreased/increased)

probability that the product price will change. If the price is _____
(lower/higher) than expected, the return on the investment is likely
to be lower than had been expected.

The time, obsolescence, and derived demand problems help ex-

plain why investment decisions involve more _____ and

_____ than do most decisions about other inputs.

The process of _____ addresses these problems by

time

incorporating _____ into the evaluation of benefits. In making

present

an investment decision, the firm must determine the _____ value of the marginal revenue product that flows to it over a period

marginal factor cost

of time. This is then compared to the _____ , most or all of which is incurred at the beginning of the process.

discounted

Present value is the _____ value at the present time of a sum of money to be received in the future. The present value (PV) of a payment (X) to be received in one year, given the annual rate of interest (i) that could be earned on alternative uses of money

$X/(1 + i)$

that face the same risk, is determined by the formula PV = _____ . If the payment is to be received in t years, the present value is given

$X/(1 + i)^t$

by the formula PV = _____ . This formula assures that inter-

compounded

est will be _____ , since interest is earned on the principal amount of money and on interest paid at earlier dates.

Problems and Applications

1. Determine the present value of $1,000 to be paid one year from now if the interest rate is
   a. 5 percent.
   b. 10 percent.
   c. 15 percent.

2. What happens to the present value of a given sum when the interest rate rises?

3. Assuming that the discount rate is 10 percent, determine the present value of $1,000
   a. one year from today.
   b. two years from today.
   c. four years from today.

4. What happens to the present value of a given sum as the time period lengthens?

5. Assume that the cost of capital is $3,500, the discount rate is 12 percent, and the marginal revenue product (net of operating costs) is $4,000. This $4,000 is to be paid over four years at a rate of $1,000 per year. Would a profit-maximizing firm be willing to undertake this investment?

True-False   Indicate whether each of the following statements is basically true or false. If the statement is false, rewrite it so that it is true.

_____ 1. Physical capital refers to machinery, tools, and equipment that are produced for the purpose of producing something else.

_____ 2. Roundabout production refers to the production of goods in stages.

_____ 3. With roundabout production, some resources are initially diverted from the direct production of consumer goods to the production of capital goods.

_____ 4. The investment decision centers around a decision to provide for the creation of new capital.

_____ 5. During the time that a firm has invested funds but has received only part of its return on the investment, it is paid an opportunity return.

_____ 6. Obsolescence means that something (a machine, for example) no longer works.

_____ 7. Investment decisions involve more risk and uncertainty than do most decisions about other production inputs.

_____ 8. A dollar received today has greater value than a dollar to be received in the future.

_____ 9. The present value of a dollar to be received in the future is more than the value of a dollar to be received today.

_____ 10. For any given interest rate, the shorter the time period before the receipt of a dollar the lower its present value.

_____ 11. For any given time period, the higher the discount rate the higher the present value of the future payment.

_____ 12. Discounting is the process of determining the present value of payments that are to be received in the future.

_____ 13. A payment to be received one year from now is equal to the present value of the payment plus the interest that could be earned on that present value.

_____ 14. Higher interest rates are typically associated with greater risk and uncertainty.

_____ 15. At 10 percent interest, the present value of $1,000 to be received in three years is $1,331.

_____ 16. At 10 percent, $1,000 would have to be invested today in order to receive $1,331 three years from now.

_____ 17. The probability of obsolescence is determined by the formula $p = PV(1 + i)$, where p is the probability of obsolescence, PV is the present value of the investment, and i is the discount rate.

_____ 18. The marginal factor cost of capital purchased in a competitive market is the price of the capital good at the time of purchase.

_____ 19. Interest rates are determined in the market for loanable funds.

_____ 20. At any point in time, there are many different interest rates, primarily because of differences in risk.

Multiple Choice   Choose the *one best* answer in each of the following cases:

_____ 1. The concept of roundabout production
   a. was first described by Eugen von Bohm-Bawerk.
   b. means that resources are used to produce capital that is used to produce consumer goods.
   c. requires that some consumer goods be given up initially in order to produce capital goods.
   d. presumably results in greater efficiency in the production of goods through the use of capital goods.
   e. all of the above

_____ 2. The investment decision is
   a. like other business decisions in that the firm neglects any risk involved.
   b. like other resource-hiring decisions in that the firm compares the marginal factor cost with the marginal revenue product.
   c. unlike other business decisions in that the firm neglects any risk involved.
   d. unlike other business decisions in that it is not related to profit maximization.
   e. unlike other business decisions in that the firm cannot compare expected benefits with expected costs.

_____ 3. The time problem in investment decision making arises because capital goods usually are
   a. purchased before they are used in production.
   b. durable, so that the return accrues over time.
   c. both a and b above
   d. used intermittently.
   e. used concurrently with other resources.

_____ 4. Obsolescence is more likely to be a problem in the hiring of capital resources than other resources because capital is
   a. durable.
   b. discounted.
   c. compounded.
   d. subject to an opportunity cost.
   e. a form of roundabout production.

_____ 5. The concept of a derived demand for resources is
   a. of little importance in the case of capital, since capital is a durable good.
   b. of little importance in the case of capital, because of the problem of obsolescence.
   c. of little importance in the case of capital, since there is no opportunity cost associated with the use of capital.
   d. especially important in the case of capital, since there is no opportunity cost associated with the use of capital.
   e. especially important in the case of capital, since the expected return from an investment extends over a long period.

_____ 6. Present value refers to the
   a. value of the derived demand for a resource.
   b. current value of a sum of money received at the present time.
   c. value of a sum of money at some future time that is received at the present time.
   d. discounted value at the present time of a sum of money to be received in the future.
   e. none of the above

_____ 7. The present value of a future payment is
   a. greater the greater the interest rate.
   b. greater the further away the payment date.
   c. both a and b above
   d. lower the greater the interest rate.
   e. lower the greater the future payment.

_____ 8. If X represents the payment and i represents the annual rate of interest that could be earned on alternative uses of money that face the same risk, the present value of a payment to be made one year from now is equal to
   a. $X/(1 + i)$.
   b. $X/(1 - i)$.
   c. $i/(1 + X)$.
   d. $(X)(1 + i)$.
   e. $(i)(1 + X)$.

_____ 9. If X represents the payment and i represents the annual rate of interest that could be earned on alternative uses of money that face the same risk, the present value of a payment to be made t years from now is equal to
   a. $X/(1 + i)^t$.
   b. $X/(1 - i)^t$.
   c. $i/(1 + X)^t$.
   d. $(X^t)(1 + i)$.
   e. $(i^t)(1 + X)$.

_____ 10. At an interest rate of 20 percent, the present value of $600 to be received one year from today is
  a. $120.
  b. $500.
  c. $720.
  d. $750.
  e. $3,000.

_____ 11. At an interest rate of 10 percent, how much would have to be invested today to receive $5,000 two years from today?
  a. $2,272.73
  b. $2,500.00
  c. $4,132.23
  d. $6,172.84
  e. $9,090.91

_____ 12. The marginal revenue product of a machine would be the value that it adds to what it receives as inputs
  a. plus the cost of operating and maintaining the machine.
  b. minus the cost of operating and maintaining the machine.
  c. plus the cost of operating the machine minus the cost of maintaining the machine.
  d. minus the cost of operating the machine plus the cost of maintaining the machine.
  e. none of the above

_____ 13. Approximately how much would a profit-maximizing firm be willing to pay today for a machine if the discount rate is 10 percent and if the marginal revenue product (net of all operating costs) will be $1,200 received in an income stream of $400 per year for three years?
  a. $300
  b. $900
  c. $995
  d. $1,200
  e. $1,333

_____ 14. The loanable funds market
  a. determines the interest rate.
  b. is the market in which people borrow and lend money.
  c. both a and b above
  d. identifies the risk associated with an investment decision.
  e. all of the above

_____ 15. The demand for loanable funds is
   a. likely to change with changes in business expectations.
   b. the sum of business demand, household demand, and
      government demand.
   c. an inverse relationship between the interest rate and the
      quantity of money people want to borrow.
   d. all of the above
   e. a direct relationship between the interest rate and the
      quantity of money that people want to borrow.

_____ 16. The supply of loanable funds
   a. comes entirely from household savings.
   b. will change with changes in the interest rate.
   c. determines the quantity of loanable funds that people will
      want to borrow.
   d. is a direct relationship between the interest rate and the
      quantity of money that people make available for lending.
   e. none of the above

Use the following graph to answer question 17.

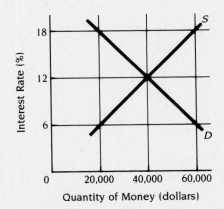

_____ 17. Consider the graph above, representing a market for loanable
   funds. In this market
   a. $60,000 will be borrowed at an interest rate of 6 percent.
   b. $60,000 will be borrowed at an interest rate of 18 percent.
   c. at an interest rate of 6 percent, more money will be available
      than people want to borrow.
   d. at an interest rate of 18 percent, people will want to borrow
      more money than is available.
   e. $40,000 worth of loans have returns at least high enough to
      cover their interest costs.

_____ 18. Differences in human capital are likely to be the result of differences in
   a. health.
   b. training.
   c. education.
   d. all of the above
   e. none of the above

_____ 19. Investment in human capital
   a. may be undertaken by a profit-maximizing firm.
   b. is identical to investment in physical capital.
   c. is undertaken by utility-maximizing individuals but not by profit-maximizing business firms.
   d. would be undertaken only when the expected monetary returns are greater than or equal to the monetary cost.
   e. both a and b above

_____ 20. Returns from an investment in human capital
   a. are always psychic.
   b. are always monetary.
   c. may be monetary and/or psychic.
   d. are typically less than the total costs.
   e. are typically less than the monetary costs.

_____ 21. Firms may be reluctant to invest in human capital when
   a. labor is highly mobile.
   b. the *MRP* exceeds the *MFC*.
   c. the returns are monetary as opposed to psychic.
   d. continued employment is guaranteed by a binding contract.
   e. the investment is in specialized training that is not transferable.

_____ 22. Research dealing with investment in education suggests that
   a. the returns are entirely monetary.
   b. the returns are both private and social.
   c. there is no consumption component in education.
   d. the returns increase with the level of education.
   e. the private rate of return has increased significantly in recent years.

Discussion Questions

1. Identify the three major problems associated with the investment decision and discuss how these problems might be handled by a firm.

2. Discuss the relationships between present value and time, present value and discount rates, and discount rates and risk.

3. Distinguish between the investment and consumption components of individual investment-consumption decisions and discuss the difficulty of making such distinctions. Provide specific examples.

4. To what extent is taking this course a consumption activity? To what extent are you investing in human capital? What are the expected returns to your investment?

5. If the returns to graduate study are as low as indicated by Ashenfelter and Mooney, why would people undertake graduate work?

6. We often think of education as being a form of investment in human capital. Why, then, do we find retirees going to school?

7. Assume that you are in charge of developing a training program for the employees of a firm. Would you be inclined to provide general or specific training? Why? Would your choice be affected by concerns with "obsolescence"?

Answers

Problems and Applications

1. a. $952.38   b. $909.09   c. $869.57
2. decreases
3. a. $909.09   b. $826.45   c. $683.01
4. decreases
5. no

True-False

1. T.
2. F. Roundabout production refers to the production of capital that is then used for further production.
3. T.
4. T.
5. F. During the time that a firm has invested funds but has received only part of its return on the investment, it incurs an opportunity cost.
6. F. Obsolescence means that something is no longer useful or economically suited for its intended purpose, even though it may still be in good working order.
7. T.
8. T.

9. F. The present value of a dollar to be received in the future is less than the value of a dollar to be received today.
10. F. For any given interest rate, the longer the time period before the receipt of a dollar, the lower its present value.
11. F. For any given time period, the higher the discount rate, the lower the present value of the future payment.
12. T.
13. T.
14. T.
15. F. At 10 percent interest, the present value of $1,000 to be received in three years is $751 and the present value of $1,331 to be received in three years is $1,000.
16. T.
17. F. There is no specific formula for determining the probability of obsolescence.
18. T.
19. T.
20. T.

Multiple Choice

1. e	2. b	3. c	4. a	5. e
6. d	7. d	8. a	9. a	10. b
11. c	12. b	13. c	14. c	15. d
16. d	17. e	18. d	19. a	20. c
21. a	22. b			

32 Government and Taxation

Summary

External costs or harmful externalities exist in the production or consumption of a good when costs accrue to individuals who have no voice in the market that generates these costs. Similarly, external benefits or beneficial externalities exist in the production or consumption of a good when benefits accrue to individuals who have no voice in the market that generates these benefits. Externalities result in a misallocation of society's resources.

When harmful externalities exist in a market, the market will tend to produce too much of the good. The amount of external cost associated with any output level can be measured by the difference between the social supply curve and the market supply curve. Government action in the form of corrective taxation and/or standards and controls may be used to encourage a more efficient allocation of resources. These regulatory instruments tend to result in higher prices for the goods involved and a corresponding decrease in the quantities demanded. Hence, to some extent at least, the externalities become internalized.

When beneficial externalities exist in a market, the market will tend to produce too little of the good. In the case of beneficial externalities in consumption, private demand for the good is less than the social demand for it. For any given quantity of the good, the amount of external benefit can be measured by the vertical distance between the social demand curve and the market demand curve. Government action to encourage production and/or consumption of the good may take the form of subsidies or direct regulation. Though subsidization may result in production and consumption of an efficient quantity of the good, it tends to have undesirable budget implications.

Collective goods are those provided directly by the government because markets fail to provide efficient quantities of them. Two characteristics of collective goods are especially important: (1) collective goods are nonrival in consumption and (2) the principle of nonexcludability is upheld. This combination of characteristics suggests that prices cannot and should not be used to finance collective goods. The nonexcludability feature of collective goods leads to the free rider problem in that people will not voluntarily pay for a good that they can receive free of charge. Consequently, collective goods are financed out of taxes.

Public choice addresses the problems associated with decision making in group situations, studies the effects of the political process on governmental decision making, and considers possible improvements in the provision of public programs. One of the major problem areas in public choice involves the collection of information about what the citizenry thinks the government should do. The difficulty in collecting this information stems partly from the fact that the information is typically gathered via the election process. Additional problems arise when the government attempts to design and implement programs to address the wishes of the citizenry. These attempts may be hindered by reliance on a complicated committee system to resolve differences with special-interest groups often able to wield considerable power. Program implementation may be more difficult due to government bureaucracies with rigid procedures, a resistance to change, and the absence of a profit incentive. Many people criticize the general fund system of financing programs as one that tends to result in waste and excessive spending. Furthermore, the short time horizon of elected officials may result in a bias toward programs that offer current benefits and delayed costs.

In order to carry out its functions, government collects and spends money. Expenditures are of two basic types: government purchases and transfer payments. Purchases are two-sided transactions in which the government receives goods or services in return for the expenditures; transfers are one-sided in that the government gives up money but receives no goods or services directly in exchange. Government receipts come primarily from individual income taxes, Social Security taxes, corporate income taxes, sales taxes, and property taxes. Individual and corporate income taxes are used at the federal and state and local levels; Social Security taxes are imposed by the federal government; and sales and property taxes are imposed at the state and local levels, although the federal government has imposed some excise taxes.

Major Objectives   After you have finished this chapter, you will be able to do the following:

1. Explain the importance and identify examples of market support activities.
2. Define and provide examples of market failure.
3. Define externalities, recognize examples of them, discuss how their existence results in market failure, and explain how the government might take corrective action.
4. Define, provide examples of, and distinguish social costs, private costs, and external costs.
5. Construct and explain the importance of a social supply curve.
6. Identify, distinguish between, and graphically represent the free market equilibrium output level in a competitive market with negative externalities and the efficient output level for society as a whole.
7. Define, provide examples of, and distinguish between private benefits and external benefits.
8. Construct and explain the importance of a social demand curve.
9. Identify, distinguish between, and graphically represent the free market equilibrium output level in a competitive market with beneficial externalities and the efficient output level for society as a whole.
10. Explain how government regulatory powers could be used to correct for negative externalities.
11. Explain how taxation could be used to correct for negative externalities.
12. Explain how government regulatory powers could be used to correct for positive externalities.
13. Define subsidy and explain how a subsidy could be used to correct for positive externalities.
14. Explain verbally and graphically how taxes and subsidies affect markets and the allocation of resources.
15. Explain and evaluate the voucher plan for subsidizing education.
16. Define, identify the characteristics of, and provide examples of collective goods and services.
17. Explain, identify the role of, and provide examples of excludability and nonexcludability.
18. Identify and explain the free rider problem.
19. Explain how the free rider problem can be used to justify the imposition of taxes to provide for collective goods and services.
20. Explain, identify the role of, and provide examples of rivalry and nonrivalry in consumption.
21. Explain how nonrivalry affects people's willingness to pay for collective goods and services.

22. Explain the meaning of public choice.
23. Explain the roles of and relationship between taxation and voting in democratic public choice models.
24. Explain and distinguish between the benefits-received and the ability-to-pay principles of taxation.
25. Identify the purpose of progressive taxation.
26. Identify the problems associated with allowing elected officials to make policy decisions.
27. Discuss the general fund method of government financing and the problems associated with it.
28. Discuss the role and consequences of special-interest groups being involved in policy making.
29. Discuss the role and consequences of government bureaucracies being involved in policy making.
30. Explain the purpose of, process of, and problems associated with cost-benefit analysis.
31. Explain and discuss the importance of the federal system of government and fiscal federalism.
32. Define, distinguish, and recognize examples of government expenditures, government purchases, and transfer payments.
33. Distinguish between conditional and unconditional grants-in-aid.
34. Identify, by level of government, the major areas of government spending and the major sources of government revenue.
35. Identify and discuss the major features of the individual income tax.
36. Define marginal tax rate and indicate its importance.
37. Explain the purpose and effects of indexing the income tax.
38. Explain the purpose of tax simplification.
39. Explain the flat tax.
40. Discuss the purpose and consequences of the Tax Reform Act of 1986.
41. Explain, identify the consequences of, and distinguish regressive, proportional, and progressive taxes.
42. Identify and discuss the major features of Social Security taxes.
43. Identify and explain, verbally and graphically, the economic effects of payroll taxes.
44. Identify and discuss the major features of the corporate income tax and its effects.
45. Explain the meaning and importance of tax shifting.
46. Identify and discuss the major features of sales and excise taxes and analyze their economic effects.
47. Identify and explain, verbally and graphically, the excess burden associated with sales and excise taxes.
48. Identify and discuss, verbally and graphically, the importance of price elasticity for sales and excise taxes.

49. Identify and discuss the major features of motor fuels taxes.
50. Explain and provide examples of user charges.
51. Identify and discuss the major features of property taxes and their effects.
52. Identify and explain the consequences of a reliance on property taxes to finance public education.

Review Terms

microeconomics
market vs. planned economy
capitalism vs. socialism
macroeconomics
demand and supply
resources
equilibrium in a market
changes in demand and supply
economic rationality
normative vs. positive
entrepreneur
discounting
aggregate demand

inflation
indexing
labor
corporation
pure competition
substitute
monopoly control
economic profit
shareholder
price elasticity
inelastic
elastic
complement

Important Terms and Concepts

market support activities
market failure
externalities
social supply curve
social costs
private costs
external costs
misallocation of resources
private benefits
external benefits
social demand curve
socially efficient quantity
regulatory approach
tax approach
subsidy
collective goods and services
nonrivalry
nonexcludability
free rider
public choice
benefits-received principle of taxation

ability-to-pay principle of taxation
progressive taxation
general fund system
interest groups
cost-benefit analysis
federal system
fiscal federalism
government expenditure
government transfer payments
government purchases
grants-in-aid
conditional vs. unconditional grants-in-aid
individual income tax
personal exemption
personal deduction
zero bracket amount
tax bracket
progressive tax
Tax Reform Act of 1986
marginal tax rate

bracket creep

burden of a tax

tax base

tax shifting

revenue neutral

sales tax

tax simplification

excise tax

flat tax

excess burden

Social Security taxes

motor fuels tax (gas tax)

payroll tax

user charge

proportional tax

property tax

regressive tax

millage

corporation income tax

Completion

government purchase

A form of government expenditure in which a good or service is provided in direct exchange for money is called a _____ .

more

State and local governments spend much _____ (more/less) on currently produced goods and services than the federal government spends.

transfer payment

A _____ is a form of government expenditure that is like a monetary gift from the government, since the government receives no good or service directly in return. Some-

entitlements

times called _____ , transfer payments amount

one-third

to over _____ of total government expenditures.

progressive

An income tax is said to be _____ if the tax rate increases as income increases. Alternatively, an income tax would be

regressive

_____ if the tax rate decreased as income increased. The federal income tax as well as most state income taxes are

progressive

_____ (progressive/regressive). A

marginal tax rate

person's _____ is the rate that applies to the highest tax bracket reached by that person.

net income or accounting profits

Corporation income taxes are based on the _____ _____ of corporations. In terms of the federal tax, most corporations fall into the highest bracket,

34 percent

which is taxed at a rate of _____ . The revenue that the

is

federal government collects from this tax _____ (is/is not) sensitive to the economic climate.

Generally, the burden of sales and excise taxes tends to be shifted

higher prices

to consumers in the form of _____ . Some of

the burden may be shifted to the owners of the resources used to pro-

decrease

duce the taxed good, since there is likely to be a(n) _____ (increase/decrease) in the quantity of the good that is finally traded. When the burden of a tax is greater in value than the amount of money collected by the government from the tax, there is said to be

excess burden

an _____ from the tax.

property

    The local tax imposed on a home is an example of a _____

local

tax. These taxes are a primary source of revenue for _____ governments. They differ from other taxes in that they are imposed even when there has been no transaction involving the property.

does not

Historically, the amount of tax _____ (does/does not) fluctuate with income or production from the property.

    Decision making in group situations, government decision making in particular, and the effects of the political process on this decision making, are likely to concern economists who study theories of

public choice

_____ .

Problems and Applications

1. Consider the graph below, describing a competitive market for a good characterized by harmful externalities. Curve S_s is the social supply curve; curve S_m is the market supply curve.
   a. At equilibrium, how many units of the good will be produced by the free market? What price will people pay?
   b. From the standpoint of society, what is the efficient quantity of the good?
   c. What is the external cost per unit of the good?
   d. If the government were to use corrective taxation to encourage production of the efficient quantity of the good, what per-unit tax would be appropriate?
   e. Graphically indicate the amount of revenue the corrective tax (as indicated in paragraph d above) would generate. What is the dollar amount of the revenue?

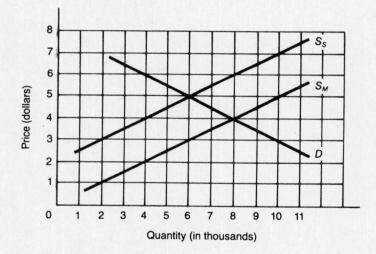

2. Consider the graph on page 613, describing a competitive market for a good characterized by beneficial externalities. Assume that the external benefit is $10 per unit of the good. Curve D_p is private demand.
   a. At equilibrium, how many units of the good will be traded by the free market? What price will people pay?
   b. From the standpoint of society, what is the efficient quantity of the good?
   c. If the government were to subsidize the consumption of the good to encourage production of the efficient quantity, what per-unit subsidy would be appropriate if all units are subsidized equally? Is it necessary that all units of the good be subsidized equally? Graphically indicate the total amount of subsidy paid

if all units are subsidized equally and if the subsidy is just sufficient to generate an efficient allocation of resources. Use curve D_s to show subsidized demand.

d. If the government were to subsidize the suppliers of the good to encourage production of the efficient quantity, what per-unit subsidy would be appropriate if all units are subsidized equally? How would you represent this subsidy graphically?

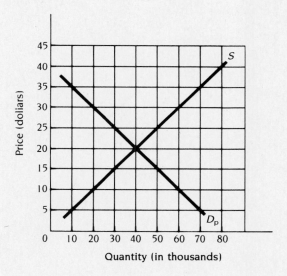

Quantity (in thousands)

3. For each of the following, indicate whether the tax is progressive, regressive, or proportional.
   a. The tax rate is an increasing percentage of the base.
   b. As the tax base increases, the tax rate decreases.
   c. A constant percentage of the base is paid into taxes.
   d. There is an inverse relationship between the tax base and the tax rate.
   e. An income tax such that everyone pays $100 per year regardless of income.
   f. An income tax such that a person with an income of $100 pays $10 in taxes and a person with an income of $1,000 pays $50 in taxes.

4. For each of the following, indicate whether or not the burden of the tax can be shifted. If the burden can be shifted, indicate how this is likely to be accomplished.
   a. personal income tax
   b. corporation income tax

    c. Social Security tax paid by employer
    d. Social Security tax paid by employee
    e. sales tax

5. Consider the market described by the demand and supply curves in the graph below.

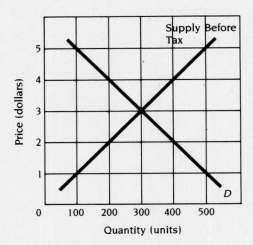

Assume that an excise tax of $1 per unit is imposed on the manufacturer of the good. What will be the effect of the tax? Specifically, show graphically any changes in demand and/or supply and identify the new equilibrium price and quantity traded. Also, show graphically the tax revenue collected by the government and the excess burden from the tax. What is the dollar amount of revenue collected?

6. Consider the market described by the demand and supply curves in the graph below.

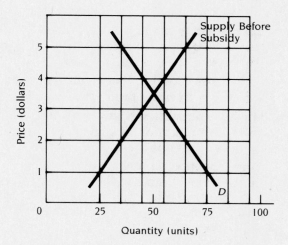

Assume that the government wants to encourage the manufacture of the product and does so by paying the supplier $1 per unit produced. What will be the effect of this subsidy on the supply curve? Show, on the graph, the consequences of the subsidy in terms of the new equilibrium price and quantity traded. What is the dollar amount of the total subsidy?

True-False   Indicate whether each of the following statements is basically true or false. If the statement is false, rewrite it so that it is true.

_____ 1. One of the advantages of the pure market system is that it always provides acceptable answers to the basic economic questions.

_____ 2. In a market-capitalist system, government may appropriately be involved in market-support activities as well as in cases of market failure.

_____ 3. Legal protection of private property rights is an example of a market-support activity on the part of a government in a market-capitalist system.

_____ 4. If in a capitalistic democracy the market system is deficient in some regard, the government will always be able to correct the problem adequately.

_____ 5. Externalities may exist when individuals are affected by actions over which they have no control.

_____ 6. Externalities result in an efficient allocation of resources from the standpoint of society at large.

_____ 7. Markets tend to produce too little of goods that are characterized by externalities.

_____ 8. Markets tend to underproduce goods characterized by negative externalities, because some of the costs of these goods are not recognized in the market.

_____ 9. Externalities may be either positive or negative and may be associated with either production or consumption.

_____ 10. Harmful externalities exist when people who pay for the production and consumption of a good are not allowed to enjoy the benefits of the good.

_____ 11. A corrective tax imposed on a good characterized by harmful externalities will cause the externalities to be internalized if the tax shifts the market supply curve so that it coincides with the demand curve.

_____ 12. The reallocation of resources that results from the corrective taxation of a good with negative externalities typically means that there will be additional jobs in the industry producing the good.

_____ 13. Beneficial externalities exist when people who have no voice in deciding about the production or consumption of a good are not allowed to enjoy the benefits of the good.

_____ 14. Subsidies to encourage production and/or consumption of goods with beneficial externalities often serve to redistribute income.

_____ 15. Government regulation may be used to decrease the quantity of goods characterized by harmful externalities but not to increase the consumption of goods characterized by beneficial externalities.

_____ 16. Voucher proposals for financing education are criticized because they would probably reduce competition among schools and therefore would probably reduce their efficiency.

_____ 17. The combination of nonrivalry and nonexcludability suggests that prices should not and cannot be charged to finance the production of collective goods.

_____ 18. Government purchases may include both government expenditures and transfer payments.

_____ 19. Government transfer payments are payments for which the government receives no good or service directly in return.

_____ 20. Education and national defense are the two largest categories of government purchases, with national defense being funded entirely by the federal government and most education being funded by state and local governments.

_____ 21. Even though the federal government is responsible for collecting almost two-thirds of all government revenues, some of this money is given back to state and local governments in the form of grants-in-aid.

_____ 22. The individual income tax, the largest source of government revenue, is used by federal, state, and local governments.

_____ 23. An income tax is said to be progressive if people with higher incomes are required to pay more dollars in taxes than people with lower incomes.

_____ 24. The Tax Reform Act of 1986 is based on the presumption that tax rates can be decreased without decreasing tax revenues, if special tax deductions and exclusions are eliminated.

_____ 25. A progressive income tax is based on the benefits-received principle of taxation.

_____ 26. The marginal tax rate for an individual is the tax rate that applies to the highest bracket reached by the individual.

_____ 27. The imposition of an excise tax can be represented as an increase in supply.

_____ 28. There is an excess burden from a tax when the total burden associated with the tax is greater in value than the revenue collected by the government.

_____ 29. Property taxes are like other taxes in that they are due after some kind of transaction has taken place, as for example, sale of the property.

_____ 30. Although there may be difficulties associated with the development and enactment of government programs, the election process assures that citizens' desires will be effectively communicated.

_____ 31. The portion of the Social Security tax paid by employers is likely to result in an increase in wages.

_____ 32. If a corporation is in long-run equilibrium in a purely competitive market when a corporate income tax is imposed, the firm may be able to shift the tax burden successfully to consumers if the other corporations in the industry are also made subject to the tax.

_____ 33. The imposition of an excise tax in a market with a perfectly elastic demand will result in a decrease in the quantity traded with no change in price.

_____ 34. The motor-fuels tax is based on the benefits-received principle of taxation.

Multiple Choice   Choose the *one best* answer in each of the following cases:

_____   1. Markets may fail to produce efficient results because of
         a. the existence of externalities.
         b. inaccurate or costly information.
         c. the existence of monopoly control.
         d. all of the above
         e. none of the above

_____   2. Positive and negative externalities
         a. always cancel each other out.
         b. are the result of business cycles.
         c. do not exist in pure market systems.
         d. are said to exist whenever government engages in production.
         e. may be exemplified by education and pollution, respectively.

_____   3. Beneficial externalities result in a(n)
         a. efficient allocation of resources, as do harmful externalities.
         b. efficient allocation of resources, whereas harmful externalities result in a misallocation of resources.
         c. efficient allocation of resources, whereas harmful externalities may result in an efficient or an inefficient allocation of resources.
         d. misallocation of resources, as do harmful externalities.
         e. misallocation of resources, whereas harmful externalities result in an efficient allocation of resources.

_____   4. When there are external benefits associated with the consumption of a good,
         a. the government should tax the good.
         b. the market places too great a value on this good.
         c. the market system allocates too many resources to its production.
         d. government intervention may be required to assure production of the optimal amount of the good.
         e. the market fails to recognize all of the costs associated with the consumption of this good.

_____   5. The existence of external costs in the production of a good suggests that
         a. the taxes are too high.
         b. not enough resources will be used in its production.
         c. the government should subsidize production of the good.
         d. both b and c above
         e. none of the above

_____ 6. Which of the following is *least* likely to generate external benefits?
   a. consumption of a hamburger
   b. landscaping your front yard
   c. education of the children in your community
   d. the location of a city park across the street
   e. an efficient mass transit system in your town

_____ 7. With regard to a good characterized by harmful externalities, one can conclude that correcting for the externality will
   a. result in the consumption of additional units of the good.
   b. result in the consumption of fewer units of other good(s).
   c. provide benefits to compensate the specific individuals who suffer losses incurred by the correction.
   d. all of the above
   e. none of the above

_____ 8. Which of the following is *not* likely to be a limitation of a program to correct for the misallocation of resources in the production of a good with negative externalities?
   a. The harmful effect may be direct and easily measurable.
   b. The harmful externality may not affect everyone equally.
   c. The harmful effect may exist only in certain circumstances.
   d. The connection between the use of a particular good and a subsequent harmful externality often is difficult to trace.
   e. The externality may be the result of combining several goods in particular ways, and it may be difficult to ascertain the extent to which one good is accountable.

_____ 9. The misallocation of resources associated with the existence of externalities
   a. requires a market solution.
   b. may be corrected by taxes or subsidies.
   c. is an example of government failure.
   d. cannot be corrected by government intervention.
   e. can be corrected only by government production of the good.

Use the following graph to answer questions 10 and 11.

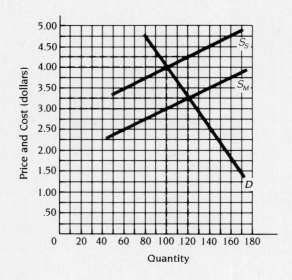

10. Consider the graph above, representing a purely competitive market for a good characterized by externalities. If S_m represents the market supply curve and S_s the social supply curve, one can accurately conclude that
    a. the market will tend to produce 120 units of the good.
    b. there are beneficial externalities associated with the good.
    c. the socially efficient output level is 120 units of the good.
    d. private consumers will buy 120 units at a price of $4 per unit.
    e. the market will tend to produce 20 fewer units than are socially desirable.

11. From the graph above, one can accurately conclude that a
    a. corrective tax of $1 per unit would result in the sale of an efficient quantity of the good at equilibrium.
    b. corrective subsidy would cause demand to decrease and thereby limit consumption and production of the good.
    c. subsidy to encourage additional consumption and production of the good would be an appropriate corrective action.
    d. corrective tax would cause the social supply curve to shift so as to coincide with the market supply curve.
    e. none of the above

Use the following graph to answer questions 12 and 13.

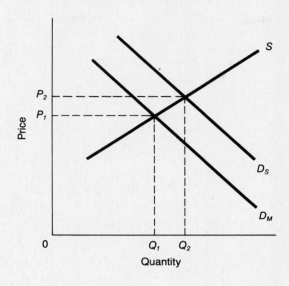

_____ 12. Consider the graph above, describing the competitive market for a good characterized by externalities. Assume that D_m and D_s represent the market and social demand curves, respectively. One can accurately conclude that
   a. the free market equilibrium price is P_1.
   b. from the standpoint of society at large, the efficient output level is Q_1.
   c. the sum of the private and the social demand curves reflects the total benefits to society.
   d. there are harmful as well as beneficial externalities associated with the consumption of the good.
   e. both a and c above

_____ 13. From the graph above, one can accurately conclude that
   a. the private market will tend to produce too few units of the good and charge too high a price.
   b. the private market will tend to produce too many units of the good and charge too high a price.
   c. the per-unit value of the external benefits is shown by the vertical distance between the social demand curve and the market demand curve.
   d. for any given price, the amount of external benefit is shown by the horizontal distance between the supply curve and the social demand curve.
   e. none of the above

_____ 14. To say that consumption of a good is nonrival means that
   a. no one consumes the good.
   b. only one person consumes the good.
   c. there are no reasonable substitutes for the good.
   d. there are no other goods that give as much utility per unit.
   e. one person's consumption of the good does not interfere with another person's consumption of it.

_____ 15. Nonexcludability in the consumption of a good means that
   a. everyone will buy the good.
   b. everyone is able to buy the good.
   c. minorities are able to buy the good.
   d. once the good is provided, it is not feasible to prevent someone from using it.
   e. once you begin consumption of the good you must consume additional units of it.

_____ 16. Collective goods are typically characterized by
   a. rivalry and excludability.
   b. rivalry and nonexcludability.
   c. nonrivalry and excludability.
   d. nonrivalry and nonexcludability.
   e. none of the above

_____ 17. The free rider problem in economics refers to the
   a. sale of an unpopular good with a popular one.
   b. sale of two complementary goods for the price of the more expensive one.
   c. fact that people will do whatever they can to avoid their tax responsibility.
   d. passage of unpopular legislation by adding it to a popular piece of legislation.
   e. fact that people will not voluntarily pay for a good if they believe they can have it without paying.

_____ 18. The study of public choice may be concerned with
   a. implementing government programs.
   b. how government collects information from citizens.
   c. designing programs consistent with citizen's desires.
   d. imperfections in the ability of governments to collect information and to design and implement programs.
   e. all of the above

_____ 19. Which of the following is true with regard to public choice?
  a. The evolution of the Social Security program illustrates the problem of a short time horizon.
  b. The election process assures the collection of information needed in providing public goods.
  c. General fund spending is likely to result in a reduction of programs for which total costs exceed total benefits.
  d. The short time horizon of elected officials probably works to assure that the total benefits and total costs of a program are equal.
  e. all of the above

_____ 20. Which of the following is true of government expenditures?
  a. They cannot exceed the tax revenues of government.
  b. They include both government purchases and transfer payments.
  c. When all levels of government are included, in 1980 they amounted to almost $1,000 per person.
  d. The federal government spends more on currently produced goods and services than do all state and local governments combined.
  e. They represent a two-sided transaction in which the government receives a good or service directly in exchange for the payment.

_____ 21. Which of the following is a transfer payment?
  a. salary paid to a senator
  b. tax revenue from sale of tires
  c. payments under the G.I. Bill
  d. spending associated with the construction of a state highway
  e. none of the above

_____ 22. Grants-in-aid are
  a. always tied to specific projects.
  b. said to be conditional when the money must be paid back by a certain date.
  c. unconditional when the receiving government may spend the money any way it wants.
  d. generally given by one governmental unit to a governmental unit at a higher level.
  e. all monetary transfers from one governmental unit to another with the exception of revenue sharing.

_____ 23. Fiscal federalism is
   a. the system of transfer payments implemented by the federal government.
   b. one of the major programs designed to fulfill the stabilization function of government.
   c. concerned with the utilization of taxes to eliminate negative externalities and the utilization of subsidies to create positive externalities.
   d. concerned with identifying the geographic area that benefits most from a collective good so that responsibility for provision of the good can be given to the appropriate level of government.
   e. a system of taxation by which the federal government collects income taxes and redistributes this money to state and local governments by way of a program of revenue sharing.

_____ 24. The individual income tax
   a. is the largest single source of government revenue.
   b. is used by state and local governments as well as by the federal government.
   c. is progressive as levied by the federal government and by most state governments.
   d. and the Social Security tax together represent over half of the receipts of governments in the United States.
   e. all of the above

_____ 25. Which of the following is true of the corporation income tax?
   a. It is used only by the federal government.
   b. The tax is based on total sales revenues of corporations.
   c. The revenue collected from this tax fluctuates greatly between good times and bad.
   d. The burden of the tax is borne entirely by stockholders in the form of decreased dividends.
   e. all of the above

_____ 26. The burden of sales and excise taxes may be
   a. shifted to consumers in the form of higher prices.
   b. shifted backward to the owners of the resources used in the production of the goods.
   c. greater in value than the amount of revenue collected by the government.
   d. both a and b above
   e. all of the above

_____ 27. The imposition of an excise tax
    a. may be the result of an attempt to correct for external benefits.
    b. is likely to be part of the stabilization function of government.
    c. may be graphically represented as a rightward (downward) shift in the supply curve.
    d. is perceived by the supplier of the good as an increase in the cost of producing the good.
    e. both c and d above

_____ 28. Property taxes are
    a. levied by the federal government.
    b. paid only when real estate is sold.
    c. one of the main sources of revenue for local governments.
    d. generally adjusted in accordance with the income of the property owner.
    e. unable to affect the profitability of owning land, since they are not based on the profits associated with land ownership.

_____ 29. In the case of collective goods, cost-benefit analysis is
    a. unlikely to involve discounting.
    b. likely to be easier than cost-benefit analysis applied to private goods.
    c. likely to be facilitated by the rivalry and excludability features of collective goods.
    d. likely to be complicated by the nonrivalry and nonexcludability features of collective goods.
    e. likely to be facilitated by the nonrivalry and nonexcludability features of collective goods.

Discussion Questions

1. Identify and discuss the limitations of using corrective taxation to deal with the problem of harmful externalities. What alternative measures might be employed to deal with these externalities? Which course of action would you find most appropriate for dealing with pollution? Would you favor the same approach for dealing with nuclear energy?

2. Would you prefer a system of public support for education in which the government was involved less in the actual production of education though perhaps no less involved in terms of the level of financial support? How might the government provide for the financing of public education without getting involved in the actual production of it?

3. Would you be willing to support a voucher plan to subsidize elementary education? Explain your reasons. Are your concerns purely economic in nature? Would your response differ for different levels of education?

4. Provide examples of goods traded in the marketplace that are
   a. nonrival in consumption.
   b. nonexcludable.

5. Explain why national defense is considered to be a nearly "pure" collective good.

Answers

Problems and Applications

1. a. 8,000; $4   b. 6,000   c. $2   d. $2
   e. Tax revenue is indicated by the shaded area in the graph below. The dollar amount of revenue is $12.

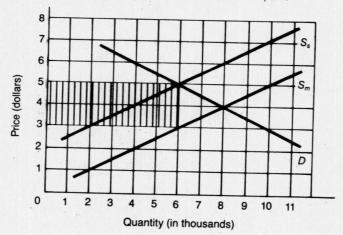

2. a. 40,000 units; $20 per unit   b. 50,000 units
   c. $10; no; in the graph on page 627, the total amount of the subsidy paid is shown by the shaded area.
   d. $10; shift the supply curve down (to the right) by a vertical distance of $10.

Graph for problem answer 2c.

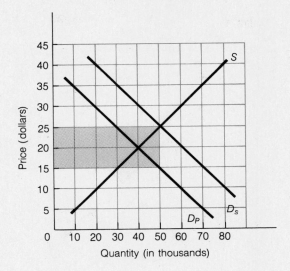

3. a. progressive   b. regressive   c. proportional
   d. regressive   e. regressive   f. regressive

4. a. cannot be shifted
   b. can be shifted; to consumers by higher product prices and/or to resource owners in the form of lower returns
   c. can be shifted; to consumers by higher product prices and/or to workers by lower wages
   d. cannot be shifted
   e. can be shifted; to consumers by higher product prices and/or to resource suppliers by smaller quantities

5. Originally, 300 units were traded at a price of $3 per unit. After the tax is imposed, the quantity traded is 250 units at a price of $3.50 per unit, $1 of which goes to the government for each unit traded. As shown in the graph below, the tax revenue collected by the government is the cross-hatched rectangular area and the excess burden from the tax is the shaded triangular area. The dollar amount of revenue collected is $250.

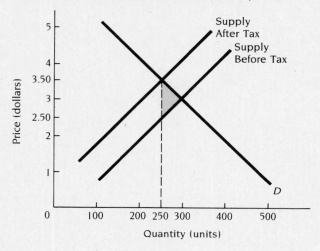

6. The subsidy essentially represents a decrease in costs of production; therefore, the supply curve will shift to the right, indicating an increase in supply. Originally, before the subsidy, 50 units were traded at a price of $3.50 per unit. After the subsidy, the price will fall to $3.00 per unit and 55 units will be traded. The dollar amount of the total subsidy is $55.

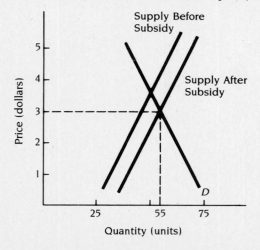

True-False

1. F. The pure market system provides answers to the basic economic questions, but there is no guarantee that these answers will be generally acceptable.
2. T.
3. T.
4. F. If the market system is deficient in some regard, the government may be able to correct the problem, but there is no guarantee.
5. T.
6. F. Externalities result in an inefficient allocation of resources from the standpoint of society at large.
7. F. Markets tend to produce too little of goods that are characterized by beneficial externalities and too much of goods that are characterized by harmful externalities.
8. F. Markets tend to overproduce goods with negative externalities, because some of the costs of these goods are not recognized in the market.
9. T.
10. F. Harmful externalities exist when people who have no voice in deciding about the production or consumption of a good incur some of the costs associated with production or consumption.
11. F. A corrective tax imposed on a good characterized by harmful externalities will cause the externalities to be internalized if the tax shifts the market supply curve so that it coincides with the social supply curve.
12. F. The reallocation of resources that results from the corrective taxation of a good with negative externalities typically means that there will be fewer jobs in the industry producing the good.
13. F. Beneficial externalities exist when people who have no voice in deciding about the production or consumption of a good enjoy some benefits of the good or would enjoy benefits if the good were produced.
14. T.
15. F. Government regulation is used to increase the quantity of goods characterized by beneficial externalities as well as to limit production and consumption of goods characterized by harmful externalities.
16. F. Those who support voucher proposals for financing education argue that they would increase competition among schools and therefore would increase their efficiency.
17. T.
18. F. Government expenditures include both government purchases and transfer payments.

19. T.
20. T.
21. T.
22. T.
23. F. An income tax is progressive if people with higher incomes are required to pay a higher percentage of their income in taxes.
24. T.
25. F. A progressive income tax is based on the ability-to-pay principle of taxation.
26. T.
27. F. The imposition of an excise tax can be represented as a decrease in supply.
28. T.
29. F. Unlike other taxes, property taxes are collected each year whether or not any transaction has occurred.
30. F. In the area of public choice, there are difficulties associated with the collection of information as well as with the development and enactment of programs that respond to citizens' desires.
31. F. The portion of the Social Security tax paid by employers is likely to result in a decrease in wages.
32. T.
33. T.
34. T.

Multiple Choice

1. d	2. e	3. d	4. d	5. e
6. a	7. e	8. a	9. b	10. a
11. a	12. a	13. c	14. e	15. d
16. d	17. e	18. e	19. a	20. b
21. c	22. c	23. d	24. e	25. c
26. e	27. d	28. c	29. d	

33 *Poverty and Income Distribution*

Summary

Poverty occurs when the real income or living standard of some members of society is lower than that which is considered acceptable. There are four concepts or criteria of poverty. The amenity criterion identifies persons as living in poverty if they have less than a certain level of key amenities, such as food and shelter. The proportionality criterion suggests that there will always be poverty except when there is absolute equality of income and wealth. This concept of poverty identifies those receiving the lowest incomes as poor, often specifying some particular percentage of the population. The budgetary criterion develops a minimum budget necessary to avoid poverty. This budget, which is typically based on the cost of a nutritive diet, identifies a poverty line. The newest concept of poverty utilizes the public opinion criterion. This approach involves a sample survey of a population to determine what it takes to "get by" in a particular place.

The incidence of poverty tends to be greatest among the following groups: nonwhites; the young and the elderly; the physically or psychologically handicapped; those who fail to secure regular employment; members of households headed by women; those with relatively little formal education; those with criminal records; and victims of racial, religious, and sexual discrimination. Also, those who grow up in areas with poor schools and poor opportunities for acquiring marketable skills are more likely to be poor.

Current antipoverty policies in the United States include Aid for Families with Dependent Children, food stamps, rent and medical subsidies, and a guaranteed minimum Social Security payment. These programs are highly criticized because of their costs, abuse, and failure to provide work incentives. The negative income tax system has been proposed as an alternative. It has the advantage of providing employment incentives. It also guarantees a minimum after-tax income. As generally proposed, the negative income tax could be carried out as part of our existing federal income tax program. However, there are conflicts among the key elements of any such program as well as potential political and administrative difficulties.

In addition to concerns with poverty per se, economists are also interested in the distribution of income and wealth. The functional distribution of income refers to the distribution among sources of income; the personal income distribution refers to the distribution of income among individuals.

Income inequality is generally measured by one of two indices: the Gini ratio, used in most countries of North America and Western Europe; and the quantile ratio, used in many socialist countries. The Gini ratio is based on the Lorenz curve. This curve illustrates inequality by recording the percent of total income received by successive percentages of the population. A Gini ratio of zero would be associated with absolute equality. The quantile ratio identifies some percentage of the population, k percent, and compares the percentage of total income received by the highest k percent of the population with the percentage of total income received by the lowest k percent. The higher the quantile ratio, the greater the inequality.

There are a number of reasons why inequality persists. These include genetic and environmental endowments, inheritances of wealth and opportunities, discrimination, economic change, and luck.

Maldistribution refers to excessive inequality (or equality) of personal income or wealth. It may be individual, economic, or ethical. There are many theories of what constitutes a "fair" or "just" distribution. Redistribution programs may provide a means for eliminating a maldistribution problem. Some redistribution programs that aim toward greater income equality are the progressive income tax, regressive government expenditures, price controls and rationing in some markets, and the socialization or taxation of wealth. Often these programs do not accomplish the type or extent of redistribution they intend.

Major Objectives

After you have finished this chapter, you will be able to do the following:

1. Explain the meanings of and distinguish between poverty and income distribution.
2. Identify and describe the four poverty criteria.
3. Define and provide examples of amenities.
4. Explain the meaning and importance of poverty lines and describe how they are developed.

5. Provide a basic profile of poverty for the 1980s in the United States.
6. Explain the concepts of "islands" of poverty and of "case" poverty.
7. Identify eight characteristics of poverty.
8. Distinguish between private charity and public charity and provide examples of each.
9. Describe the U.S. system of public welfare.
10. Explain what is meant by the "welfare mess" and by "regulating the poor."
11. Identify and discuss major elements of welfare reform.
12. Explain the concepts of a negative tax and a positive tax.
13. Describe and illustrate Milton Friedman's simple negative income tax proposal.
14. Define and calculate the breakeven point in a negative income tax system.
15. Identify, explain, and evaluate the appealing characteristics of the negative income tax system and compare these characteristics with those of the existing welfare system.
16. Explain the concept of the "working poor."
17. Identify the three key features of a negative income tax system, associate each feature with a policy objective, and explain the conflicts that arise among them.
18. Identify and discuss the administrative and political problems associated with a negative income tax system.
19. Define, explain, and distinguish between a functional income distribution and a personal income distribution.
20. Describe the functional and personal income distributions for the United States.
21. Distinguish between "workers" and "capitalists."
22. Show how the functional and personal income distributions are related.
23. Construct and describe a Lorenz curve.
24. Explain and compute the Gini ratio.
25. Cite, compare, and explain Gini ratios for the United States at different times in its history.
26. Identify and discuss the criticisms of the Gini ratio as a measure of inequality.
27. Explain and compute the quantile ratio, indicate its relationship to inequality, and identify its limitations.
28. Identify and discuss the major causes of income inequality.
29. Define discrimination and cite evidence of discrimination in the United States.
30. Explain the concepts of a "pink ghetto" and comparable worth.

31. Define and explain maldistribution, individual maldistribution, economic maldistribution, and ethical maldistribution.
32. Explain John Rawls's, Robert Nozick's, and John Bates Clark's concepts of ethical income distributions.
33. Explain Lester Thurow's recommended equity goal and compare this income distribution with the present distribution.
34. Relate the parable of the bamboo flute to concerns about income distribution.
35. Identify, explain, and evaluate the major methods of income redistribution aimed at equalizing incomes.
36. Explain the concept of the socialization of wealth and its consequences.

Review Terms

nonmoney income
subsidy
progressive (income) tax
aggregate
wealth vs. income
input or factor of production or resource
household
personal income
transfer payment
human capital
OPEC
equity
market economy
macroeconomics

microeconomics
marginal product
marginal productivity theory
physical capital
human capital
marginal revenue product
monopsony
progressive tax
minimum wage
price control
rationing
socialism
capitalism
production possibilities

Important Terms and Concepts

poverty
income distribution
amenity
amenity criterion
proportionality criterion
budgetary criterion
poverty line
public opinion criterion or survey research criterion
in-kind income
"islands" of poverty
"case" poverty
cumulative

private charity vs. public charity
Aid for Families with Dependent Children (AFDC)
food stamps
Social Security
"welfare mess"
"regulating the poor"
negative income tax
negative tax
positive tax
forty-five-degree line
breakeven point in a negative income tax system

incentive effects	robotization
the "working poor"	"headed by"
secondary workers	"pink ghetto"
flat-rate tax	comparable worth
functional income distribution	maldistribution
personal income distribution	individual maldistribution
quantile	economic maldistribution
"workers" vs. "capitalists"	underconsumption
Lorenz curve	ethical maldistribution
"line of equality"	the doctrine of "justice is
Gini ratio	fairness"
quantile ratio	relative income position
genetic endowments	the parable of the bamboo flute
environmental endowments	redistribution methods
inheritances	regressive expenditures
discrimination	socialization of wealth
automation	

Completion

<table>
<tr><td>greater</td><td rowspan="100">There are a number of personal characteristics that appear to be associated with poverty in the United States. The incidence of</td></tr>
</table>

Completion

greater — There are a number of personal characteristics that appear to be associated with poverty in the United States. The incidence of poverty is _____ (greater/less) for nonwhites than for

blacks, Indians — whites; it is especially great for _____ and _____

Orientals — but not as much for _____ . The young and the elderly

more — living alone tend to experience _____ (more/less) poverty

elderly — than the middled aged. However, poverty among the _____ (young/elderly) is likely to be exaggerated by official statistics, since many of these individuals own their homes. Individuals who are

handicapped — _____ by reason of present or recent-past deficiency, injury, or illness tend to have a relatively high incidence of poverty, as do members of households headed by women who are

unskilled laborers — employable only as _____ . Those who are

unemployed — _____ and intermittently employed, those with less than a high school education, and those who are functionally

illiterate, criminal — _____ in the English language, those with _____

unemployment — records, those with prolonged _____ , and victims

racial, religious, sexual — of _____ , _____ , and _____ discrimination are also relatively more likely to experience poverty.

cumulative — These characteristics tend to have a _____ effect, so

greater	that the likelihood of poverty is _____ (greater/less) when they appear in combination rather than individually.
	Among the major welfare programs in the United States are
Aid to Families with Dependent Children (AFDC)	_____ ;
food stamps	_____ , which allows people to buy food below
rent, medical care	market prices; subsidies for _____ and _____ ;
Social Security	and a guaranteed minimum _____ payment for low-income persons who might not qualify for the amount of benefit otherwise. Public assistance programs such as these are expensive and
"welfare mess"	controversial. Some critics refer to the _____ , pointing out that there is a lot of cheating by recipients, that the program is harsh, and that administrative costs are excessive. Others
expand	assert that welfare programs _____ (expand/contract) when the poor threaten to revolt and then systematically dehumanize the recipients when the threat is over. This is often referred to as
regulating	"_____ the poor." A more supportive view holds that though there are problems with our welfare system, it has been a tre-
completeness	mendous success when judged in terms of the _____
adequacy	of coverage for those who really need help and the _____ of the help they receive.
	Proposals for welfare reform often combine three concerns:
adequate	_____ payments to the poor, greater incentive for
employment, lower administrative costs	_____ , and _____ .
negative	One relatively popular proposal has been the _____ income tax system. Actually, there are a number of specific proposals that fall into this category. They are characterized by three key features:
minimum after-tax income	a poverty line or guaranteed _____ ,
negative tax, break-even income level	the rate of _____ , and the _____ , at which point a family neither pays nor receives money. Each of these features reflects a different policy objective in the system. The
goal of eliminating poverty	poverty line represents the _____ .
work incentive	The rate of negative tax represents the _____ feature,

greater   with _____ (less/greater) incentive associated with lower

cost   rates. The breakeven point influences the overall _____ of the
program. Unfortunately, these objectives conflict. There are also

administrative,   likely to be _____ and _____
political   problems with a negative income tax system.

    Inequality in the distribution of income is also considered by many
to be a major economic concern. There are a number of reasons why
incomes are not more equally distributed. One of these,

genetic endowments   _____ , refers to the fact that people
are born with different bodies, minds, and nervous systems. Differences in living conditions and facilities for health, education, safety,
and socialization explain some income inequality. These differences

environmental   are referred to as _____ . Another
endowments

inheritances   cause, _____ , refers to the fact that wealth can be
passed on after death to others and that opportunities for education,
training, and entry to certain jobs and professions can be passed on
to others. Inheritance can also produce a negative result. This occurs

discrimination   when there is _____ , that is, when different
economic opportunities are offered on the basis of personal charac-

Economic change   teristics. _____ , as, for example, when
an industry replaces workers with robots, may also cause inequality
in the distribution of income. Finally, one should also include

luck   _____ , elements of which are likely to be found in all of the
above.

Problems and Applications

1. Consider the following graph showing the effects of a negative income tax system. What is the guaranteed minimum after-tax income? Identify the breakeven income level. What is the negative tax rate?

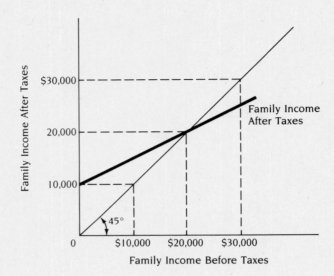

2. Assuming a negative income tax system, graph family income after taxes if the tax rate is 50 percent at all income levels and the breakeven income level is $12,000. What is the guaranteed minimum after-tax income?

3. Consider the following table, reflecting the personal income distribution for Poverty Peninsula.

Quantile	Percentage of Income
First (lowest)	2
Second	5
Third	13
Fourth	20
Fifth (highest)	60

    a. Draw the Lorenz curve for Poverty Peninsula. Identify the line of equality and the area of inequality.
    b. What is the quantile ratio for Poverty Peninsula?

True-False   Indicate whether each of the following statements is basically true or false. If the statement is false, rewrite it so that it is true.

_____ 1. Poverty exists when the real income or living standard of some members of the society is lower than is considered acceptable in that society.

_____ 2. According to the amenity criterion of poverty, a family is living in poverty if it has less than a certain income level.

_____ 3. A certain percentage of all families or individuals (those at the lowest income levels) are considered to be living in poverty, according to the proportionality criterion of poverty.

_____ 4. The dietary criterion of poverty indicates a poverty line based on a nutritious diet.

_____ 5. Poverty statistics for the United States indicate that in 1983 the same percentage of nonwhites and whites were poor.

_____ 6. Food stamps enable recipients to buy food below market prices.

_____ 7. Social Security is primarily an antipoverty program.

_____ 8. Under a negative income tax system, the breakeven point refers to the income level at which a family's negative tax and income are equal.

_____ 9. One of the drawbacks of negative income tax proposals is their lack of work incentives.

_____ 10. Experiments with the negative income tax clearly indicate that neither primary nor secondary workers quit work or reduce their hours of employment as a result of the program.

_____ 11. The functional income distribution refers to how income is distributed among the potential uses of that income (for example, to provide for shelter, food, taxes, and so forth).

_____ 12. The personal income distribution refers to how income is distributed among individuals by income size groups or brackets.

_____ 13. In 1983, the personal income distribution in the United States was such that over 40 percent of personal income went to the top fifth of the population and less than 5 percent went to the bottom fifth.

_____ 14. Work by Williamson and Lindert is consistent with the theory that income inequality decreases in the early stages of economic development and then increases later as physical capital accumulates and human capital becomes the key to further economic progress.

_____ 15. Socialist countries' income distribution statistics are criticized because they tend to compare family incomes rather than wage rates.

_____ 16. Discrimination occurs when different economic opportunities are offered to persons on the basis of their personal characteristics.

_____ 17. The median annual income of full-time female workers is significantly less than that of full-time male workers in both white collar and blue collar jobs.

_____ 18. The existence of a "pink ghetto" has led to a call for pay scales based on comparable worth.

_____ 19. Maldistribution generally implies the existence of too much inequality in the distribution of income or wealth but, according to supply-side economics, it could occur with too much equality.

_____ 20. Economic maldistribution refers to dissatisfaction about the particular people at the upper and lower ends of the income or wealth distribution.

_____ 21. Lester Thurow has suggested a compromise position to deal with ethical maldistribution by recommending that the income distribution be no more unequal than the current one for the earnings of fully employed white males.

Multiple Choice

Choose the *one best* answer in each of the following cases:

_____ 1. Poverty refers to
   a. the "welfare mess."
   b. the functional income distribution of a society.
   c. income inequality that results in a maldistribution of income.
   d. real income or living standards below what is considered acceptable for a particular society.
   e. none of the above

_____ 2. The amenity criterion of poverty is
   a. optimistic in that it assumes poverty can be eliminated.
   b. optimistic in that it assumes poverty has been eliminated.
   c. optimistic in that it assumes only a given percentage of the population will ever be in poverty.
   d. pessimistic in that it assumes poverty can never be eliminated.
   e. pessimistic in that it assumes only a small percentage of this type of poverty can be eliminated.

_____ 3. According to the proportionality criterion of poverty, poverty exists for a given percentage of the population at the lower end of the income spectrum
   a. regardless of the actual level of their income.
   b. only when their income level falls below the poverty line.

    c. only when their income level is less than a given amount specified by Congress.

    d. only when their income level is not sufficient to provide for certain amenities.

    e. only when their income level is less than an amount needed to feed a family of four.

4. The budgetary criterion of poverty
    a. is rarely used, since it requires excessive statistical analysis.
    b. typically identifies a poverty line based on provision of a nutritive diet.
    c. multiplies the cost of a nutritive diet by a factor of two when determining poverty lines for the United States.
    d. multiplies the cost of a nutritive diet by a factor of five when determining poverty lines for relatively low income countries.
    e. none of the above

5. Poverty is often defined in absolute terms. In the case of absolute poverty, specific measurable standards are predetermined, and those whose incomes or wealth do not permit them to meet these standards are considered poor. Which of the following concepts of poverty represent(s) absolute poverty?
    a. amenity
    b. budgetary
    c. proportionality
    d. both a and b above
    e. all of the above

6. Poverty is sometimes defined in relative terms. In this case, poverty is a matter of one's position in the income spectrum. That is, poverty is a matter of status; one is poor if one has less than most of the other members of society. Which of the following concepts of poverty represent(s) relative poverty?
    a. amenity
    b. budgetary
    c. proportionality
    d. both b and c above
    e. none of the above

7. The public opinion criterion of poverty
    a. is the oldest concept of poverty.
    b. relies on people's assessment of how much income a family needs to "get by."
    c. typically results in a measure of poverty that includes approximately 45 to 50 percent of the population.
    d. all of the above
    e. both b and c above

_____ 8. U.S. poverty statistics for 1983 indicate that
   a. for families, a higher percentage of nonwhites than whites
      are poor.
   b. for individuals, a higher percentage of nonwhites than whites
      are poor.
   c. single individuals, as compared to family units, are more
      likely to be poor.
   d. all of the above
   e. none of the above

_____ 9. Poverty estimates based on official poverty lines
   a. are often criticized for neglecting nonmoney income.
   b. would change little if nonmoney income were included.
   c. consider nonmoney income in determining the incidence of
      poverty.
   d. are criticized as being too low, as a result of relying on money
      incomes only.
   e. typically consider in-kind income from governmental units
      but not in-kind income from other sources.

_____ 10. The concept of islands of poverty
   a. places no importance on where an individual is raised.
   b. suggests that the poor never mingle with the rest of society.
   c. identifies the particular characteristics of individuals that
      appear to be associated with poverty.
   d. asserts that people who grow up in poverty areas are more
      likely to be poor than those who grow up elsewhere.
   e. none of the above

_____ 11. Case poverty
   a. suggests that poverty is very limited.
   b. suggests that the poor never mingle with the rest of society.
   c. asserts that there are no particular characteristics associated
      with poverty.
   d. is meaningful only when one is using the public opinion
      criterion of poverty.
   e. suggests that particular characteristics of individuals appear
      to be associated with poverty.

_____ 12. Which of the following characteristics appear to be associated
   with poverty?
   a. middle age
   b. Oriental heritage
   c. membership in households headed by women
   d. all of the above
   e. none of the above

_____ 13. The characteristics associated with poverty
    a. are mutually exclusive.
    b. have a cumulative effect.
    c. are based on the public opinion criterion.
    d. apply only in the case of the amenity criterion.
    e. none of the above

_____ 14. Those who complain about the "welfare mess" would be *least* likely to argue that
    a. programs overlap.
    b. coverage is too complete.
    c. administration tends to be harsh.
    d. administrative costs are excessive.
    e. there is considerable cheating by welfare recipients.

_____ 15. Those who describe welfare programs as "regulating the poor" assert that welfare programs
    a. offer complete and adequate coverage.
    b. expand when the poor threaten to revolt.
    c. systematically dehumanize recipients when they pose no threat to the society.
    d. both b and c above
    e. none of the above

_____ 16. Proposals for welfare reform are likely to be
    a. concerned with lowering administrative costs.
    b. concerned with assuring adequate payments to the poor.
    c. found on the right and the left of the political spectrum.
    d. concerned with providing incentives that encourage employment.
    e. all of the above

_____ 17. Negative income tax proposals
    a. guarantee a minimum after-tax income.
    b. guarantee that current welfare benefits would not be reduced.
    c. are typically meant to supplement rather than to replace the existing welfare system.
    d. require people at all income levels to make a positive tax payment to the government; recipients of the negative tax would receive a rebate from the government.
    e. all of the above

_____ 18. Milton Friedman's proposal of a simple negative income tax system would
   a. guarantee every family a minimum payment equal to the breakeven income level.
   b. supplement welfare payments with state and local tax rebates provided by income tax revenues.
   c. provide for a single payment equal to half of the difference between a family's income and its personal exemptions.
   d. create a Federal Negative Income Tax Commission that would operate independently of the Internal Revenue Service.
   e. provide an employment incentive by allowing recipients of the negative tax to keep 100 percent of money earned by working.

_____ 19. The Lorenz curve
   a. illustrates the functional distribution of income.
   b. is a straight line indicating the personal distribution of income.
   c. shows the relationship between the Gini ratio and the quantile ratio.
   d. identifies the quantile ratio associated with different income levels.
   e. lies below the line of equality when income is not equally distributed.

_____ 20. The Gini ratio
   a. has been rising in the United States since about 1929.
   b. would be zero if incomes were distributed equally.
   c. was estimated to be approximately 0.5 for the United States in 1983.
   d. would be –1 if incomes were distributed with perfect inequality.
   e. is the most frequently used measure of inequality in socialist countries.

_____ 21. The Gini ratio has been criticized because it
   a. does not include government transfers
   b. may be affected by changes in the racial mix of the population.
   c. may be affected by changes in the age distribution of the population.
   d. concentrates on the functional distribution of income rather than the personal distribution.
   e. a, b, and c above

_____ 22. A quantile ratio compares the percentage of total income received
   a. in the form of wages with the percentage received in the form of profits.
   b. in the form of wages with the percentage received in the form of property income.
   c. by the highest 20 percent of the population with the percentage received by the lowest 20 percent.
   d. by the lowest 20 percent of the population with the percentage received by the remaining 80 percent.
   e. by the highest 20 percent of the population with the percentage received by the remaining 80 percent.

_____ 23. A quantile ratio
   a. decreases as income inequality increases.
   b. ignores changes in income inequality among the middle income ranges.
   c. is used by socialist countries to measure the functional distribution of income.
   d. all of the above
   e. none of the above

_____ 24. The major causes of income inequality include
   a. luck.
   b. discrimination.
   c. economic change.
   d. environmental endowments.
   e. all of the above

_____ 25. Economic maldistribution theories
   a. are generally based on the doctrine that "justice is fairness."
   b. include that of John A. Hobson, who believed that business depressions were caused by overconsumption.
   c. suggest that the market economy may operate better under some distributions of income or wealth than under others.
   d. have become increasingly important since John M. Keynes suggested that government taxation and spending policy could be used to accomplish the goals of income redistribution programs.
   e. all of the above

_____ 26. Ethical arguments for specific distributions of income and wealth include
    a. John Rawls's underconsumption theory.
    b. Lester Thurow's parable of the bamboo flute.
    c. Robert Nozick's doctrine of "justice is fairness."
    d. John Bates Clark's application of the marginal productivity principle.
    e. John A. Hobson's goal of a distribution no more unequal than that which exists for the earnings of fully employed white males.

_____ 27. Methods used to redistribute income in the United States include
    a. socialization or taxation of wealth, which not only redistributes income and wealth but also clearly promotes economic growth.
    b. minimum wages, which tend to raise the wages of those poor workers who remain employed but which tend to reduce the number employed.
    c. government social and welfare expenditures that have the greatest equalizing effect when made available across the entire range of incomes.
    d. the progressive income tax, which has clearly redistributed income in favor of those at the lowest income levels at a cost to those at the highest levels.
    e. price controls and rationing in certain markets, which tend to be effective in practice but which provide assistance only to those at the very lowest income levels.

Discussion Questions

1. Which of the four poverty criteria do you find most reasonable from a public policy point of view? Why?

2. Of what value is the public opinion criterion of poverty?

3. Multiple choice questions 5 and 6 distinguish concepts of poverty as absolute or relative. Which concept of poverty do you find most acceptable? Why? What are the implications of each for the elimination of poverty?

4. Identify the eight characteristics that appear to be associated with poverty. What public policy programs attempt to correct for these?

5. Discuss the ethical merits of the bases of claim for the "bamboo flute." Discuss the economic merits of these bases of claim.

6. Do you think the distribution of income and wealth should be changed in the United States? If so, what ethical principle would guide your redistribution efforts? If not, would you eliminate current programs that tend to redistribute income and wealth? Explain.

7. Consider each of the following situations:

   (1) Every person has an income of $3,000 per year.
   (2) Every family has an income of $10,000 per year.
   (3) Income is at its present average level and distribution.
   (4) The real income of the poor is doubled and that of the nonpoor is tripled.

   a. Which of the above situations would you prefer? Why?
   b. Under which situation is poverty minimized? Explain.

8. Identify and discuss the social costs associated with poverty.

Answers

Problems and Applications

1. $10,000; $20,000; 50 percent
2. The guaranteed minimum after-tax income is $6,000.

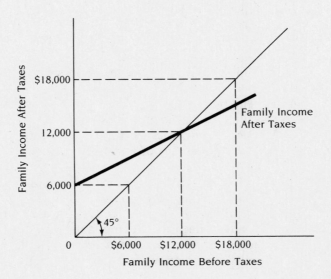

3. a. The **area of inequality** is shown by the shaded area in the graph below.

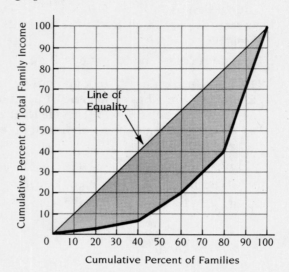

b. 30

True-False

1. T.
2. F. According to the amenity criterion of poverty, a family is living in poverty if it has less than a certain level of key amenities.
3. T.
4. F. The budgetary criterion of poverty identifies a poverty line based on a nutritious diet.
5. F. Poverty statistics for the United States indicate that in 1983 a higher percentage of nonwhites than whites were poor.
6. T.
7. F. Social Security is not primarily an antipoverty program; most people receiving Social Security benefits have qualified by reason of age, disability, or the death of a parent or spouse.
8. F. Under a negative income tax system, the breakeven point refers to the income level at which a family neither receives a negative tax payment from the government nor makes a positive tax payment.
9. F. One of the appeals of negative income tax proposals is their inclusion of work incentives.

10. F. Though the results are not entirely clear, experiments with the negative income tax suggest that primary workers are not likely to quit work or reduce their hours of employment as a result of the tax, but secondary workers may do so in order to receive further education and training and/or in order to care for children.
11. F. The functional income distribution refers to how income is distributed among sources of income (such as labor and property income).
12. T.
13. T.
14. F. Work by Williamson and Lindert is consistent with the theory that income inequality increases in the early stages of economic development and then decreases later as physical capital accumulates and human capital becomes the key to further economic progress.
15. F. Socialist countries' income distribution statistics are criticized because they tend to compare wage rates rather than family incomes.
16. T.
17. T.
18. T.
19. T.
20. F. Individual maldistribution refers to dissatisfaction about the particular people at the upper and lower ends of the income or wealth distribution.
21. T.

Multiple Choice

1. d	2. a	3. a	4. b	5. d
6. c	7. b	8. d	9. a	10. d
11. e	12. c	13. b	14. b	15. d
16. e	17. a	18. c	19. e	20. b
21. e	22. c	23. b	24. e	25. c
26. d	27. b			

34 Government Antitrust and Regulation Policy

Summary

There are three major pieces of antitrust legislation: the Sherman Antitrust Act passed in 1890, the Clayton Act of 1914, and the Federal Trade Commission Act of 1914. The Sherman Antitrust Act prohibited anticompetitive practices but was very general in its wording and was poorly enforced. The Clayton Act was more specific, concentrating on four potentially anticompetitive practices: price discrimination, mergers, exclusive dealing and tying arrangements, and interlocking directorates. The Federal Trade Commission Act prohibited unfair methods of competition among firms. It was later amended to cover unfair and deceptive practices toward consumers. The act also set up the Federal Trade Commission to supplement the Antitrust Division of the Justice Department. It is responsible for investigating and prosecuting cases of unfair competition.

In interpreting antitrust laws, the courts applied the "rule of reason" in the 1911 Standard Oil case and continued to focus on intent and conduct until the Alcoa case in 1945. The Alcoa case and several following cases overturned the rule of reason; in these cases monopolization itself was found to be illegal. With the mid-1950s came somewhat of a retreat from the "big is bad" attitude, though the rule of reason has not been fully reimplemented.

The Clayton Act and the Celler-Kefauver Amendment prohibit mergers that substantially lessen competition or that tend to create a monopoly. The courts have interpreted this legislation to cover horizontal and vertical mergers, but the Supreme Court has not yet heard a case in which it offered a clear statement on the inclusion of conglomerate mergers.

The courts have been most consistent in rulings regarding price fixing. In an 1897 precedent-setting case, the Supreme Court ruled that collusive agreements among competing firms to restrict output and fix prices were illegal per se.

A formal collusive arrangement among sellers with respect to output and price is called a cartel. Cartels may be national or international in scope. Their success depends on the willingness of the involved firms to give up independence in decision making. Cartels tend to be unstable because an individual firm can typically increase its profit by secretly breaking the agreement.

There are situations in which the government deems it desirable to grant monopoly status. For example, in order to promote research and development the government may grant patent protection. The government may also accept the existence of a natural monopoly because it is required for efficient production.

In addition, the government may own and operate a monopoly, as in a public enterprise. More often it regulates privately owned companies that have been given monopoly status. These are called public utilities. The question then arises as to whether and to what extent such monopolies should be regulated.

Industries that are granted monopoly status by the government, regulated industries, are governed by monopoly regulations as well as by the social regulations that affect most firms. Regulatory commissions operate at state and federal levels. The best-known federal regulatory bodies are the Interstate Commerce Commission, the Federal Communications Commission, the Federal Energy Regulatory Commission, and the Civil Aeronautics Board.

Regulatory commissions concern themselves with both the level and structure of rates. They typically seek a rate level that guarantees firms a "fair return" on invested capital. This usually means a normal profit on the replacement cost of the firm's capital. Commissions tend to support rate differentials based on cost differences but not price discrimination.

Since the 1960s, deregulation has become increasingly popular. Those in favor of deregulation offer several arguments. Some regulated industries have ceased to be natural monopolies as a result of technological change. Others that remain natural monopolies may be in contestable markets. In such cases, regulation may have prevented the entry of new firms offering improved quality and/or lower prices. Promoters of deregulation also cite studies showing that many public utilities invest in too much capital in order to broaden their rate base. Further, the public increasingly suspects that regulated firms have come to control their regulators.

Major Objectives

After you have finished this chapter, you will be able to do the following:

1. Describe the role of government in terms of competition and market regulation.
2. Identify the purposes of collusion and describe the market conditions that are likely to give rise to collusion.
3. Explain the purpose of antitrust policy.
4. Trace the history of major legislation prohibiting the restriction of competition and discuss the theory of its enforcement.
5. Define a trust and explain how it is used and for what purpose.
6. Discuss the purpose of and issues giving rise to the establishment of the Antitrust Division of the Department of Justice and the Federal Trade Commission.
7. Define, distinguish between, and provide examples of exclusive dealing arrangements and tying arrangements.
8. Define interlocking directorate and distinguish between direct and indirect interlocking directorates.
9. Define and explain predatory price cutting.
10. Define and explain the "rule of reason" and discuss its application in antitrust cases regarding monopolization.
11. Discuss the history of legislation and proposed legislation dealing with conglomerate mergers.
12. Define and explain the purpose of price fixing.
13. Identify and discuss the major Supreme Court antitrust decisions dealing with monopolization, mergers, and price fixing.
14. Discuss and explain the importance of the "great electrical conspiracy" of the 1950s.
15. Define, explain the purpose of, and provide examples of cartels.
16. Discuss the reasons for the instability of cartels.
17. Discuss the history of the OPEC cartel and its changing influence on the price of oil.
18. Discuss the reasoning behind government regulation of monopoly.
19. Distinguish between social regulation and monopoly regulation and explain what it means to be a regulated industry.
20. Define and explain the conditions that give rise to a natural monopoly.
21. Identify and discuss the problems associated with natural monopolies.
22. Define, provide examples of, and distinguish between a public enterprise and a public utility.
23. Provide and recognize examples of major regulatory bodies.
24. Define and compare replacement cost, original cost, and reproduction cost.

25. Explain what is meant by "a fair return on a fairly valued rate base" and "normal profit on replacement cost of capital" in regulating monopolies.
26. Identify the problems associated with regulation of the level of rates.
27. Define regulatory lag and explain its importance in rate regulation.
28. Define, explain, graphically illustrate, and compare and discuss the consequences of monopoly pricing, marginal cost pricing, and average cost pricing.
29. Define rate structure and discuss its relationship to price discrimination.
30. Briefly discuss the history of regulation and deregulation and provide arguments for each.
31. Define and explain the significance of contestable markets in terms of regulation.

Review Terms	competition
	monopoly control
	monopoly
	collusion
	oligopoly
	few firms
	pure competition
	monopolistic competition
	economic concentration
	barriers to entry
	merger
	price discrimination
	horizontal merger
	vertical merger
	conglomerate merger
	Herfindahl-Hirschman Index
	excess capacity
	actual monopoly
	patent

natural monopoly
government-enforced monopoly
economies of scale
long-run average cost (LRAC)
minimum optimal scale
capital
normal profit
opportunity cost
monopoly pricing
consumer welfare loss
economic loss
subsidy
short run
long run
average total cost
average variable cost
shutdown
price differentials
elasticity of demand

Important Terms and Concepts

anticompetitive practices
antitrust policy
Sherman Antitrust Act
Clayton Act
Robinson-Patman Act

Celler-Kefauver Antimerger Amendment to the Clayton Act
Federal Trade Commission Act
Wheeler-Lea Amendment to the FTC Act

trust
Antitrust Division of the
  Department of Justice
Federal Trade Commission
stock acquisition vs. asset
  acquisition
exclusive dealing arrangement
tying arrangement
interlocking directorates
"unfair methods of
  competition"
"unfair or deceptive acts or
  practices"
predatory price cutting
the rule of reason
"Merger Guidelines"
price fixing
illegal per se
cartel
Organization of Petroleum
  Exporting Countries (OPEC)

social regulation
monopoly regulation
regulated industries
public enterprise
public utility
"a fair return on a fairly valued
  rate base"
rate base
"normal profit on replacement
  cost of capital"
replacement cost
cost-plus-normal-profit formula
original cost
reproduction cost
regulatory lag
marginal cost pricing
average cost pricing
rate structure
peak-load user
contestable market

Completion

antitrust

Sherman Antitrust

1890

trust

competition

**monopolization,
monopolize**

are

Clayton, 1914

**price discrimination,
mergers**

**exclusive dealing
and tying arrange-
ments**

Government policy that deals with anticompetitive market practices
is referred to as _____ policy. The first major law prohibiting anticompetitive practices was the _____
Act, passed in _____ . There are two major sections to this law:
the first section prohibits "every contract, combination in the form
of a _____ or otherwise, or conspiracy" that limits
_____ ; the second section prohibits
_____ or attempts to _____ .

Penalties _____ (are/are not) specified for violations.

    The _____ Act, passed in _____ , dealt more
specifically with anticompetitive practices. It specified four types of
potentially anticompetitive business practices:
_____ , _____ ,
_____ , and

interlocking direc-
torates

_____ . One of two important

Robinson-Patman

amendments to this act, the _____ Act, is considered one of the most controversial of all U.S. antitrust laws.

price discrimination

It deals with _____ . The other amendment, the

Celler-Kefauver
Antimerger

_____ Act, broadened

mergers

the coverage of the Clayton Act with respect to _____ .

Federal Trade Com-
mission

Another act passed in 1914, the _____

Federal Trade Com-
mission

Act, established the _____ .

Antitrust

This Commission, like the _____ Division of the De-

Justice

partment of _____ , is an enforcement agency. The Federal Trade Commission Act prohibited unfair practices between

firms, Wheeler-Lea

_____ . An amendment to this act, the _____ Amendment, extended the concern to unfair practices between

firms, consumers

_____ and _____ .

Nearly all American businesses are regulated. When regulation deals with environmental protection, food and drugs, and occupa-

social

tional health and safety, it is referred to as _____ regulation.

monopoly

Regulation involving pricing and output is _____ regulation. Industries that are subject to both types of regulation are

regulated

referred to as _____ industries.

Regulatory commissions become involved in nearly all aspects of a regulated firm's business. Their most important concern, however,

pricing, level

is with _____ . They are interested in both the _____

structure

and the _____ of the firm's rates. With regard to the

fair

return on invested capital, regulators usually allow a _____

fairly valued

return on a _____ rate base or, in economic

normal, replacement

terms, a _____ profit on the _____ cost of capital. According to this approach, the value of capital or the

rate base

_____ is determined by estimating what it would cost

replace

to _____ a firm's capital. Earning a normal profit on the

continue to

replacement cost of capital means that consumers will _____

(continue to/no longer) receive the services provided by the firm

minimum

with the _____ (minimum/maximum) amount of resources being used.

Problems and Applications

Use the following graph to answer problems 1 and 2.

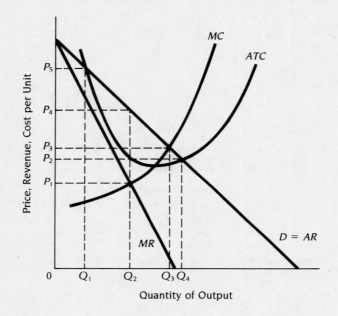

1. Consider the monopolist described by the graph above. For each of the following pricing policies, indicate the price and output levels and determine whether the monopolist earns positive, zero, or negative economic profit:
   a. monopoly pricing
   b. marginal-cost pricing
   c. average-cost pricing

2. Note that the monopolist described by the graph is able to cover its full costs of production at an output of Q_1 and a price of P_5. Why would you not expect to see a regulatory commission force the monopolist to operate at this position?

Use the following graph to answer problems 3 and 4.

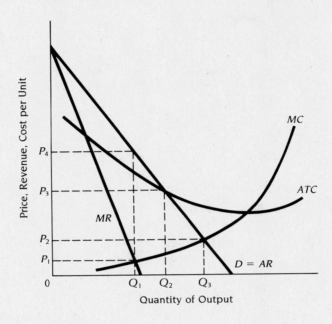

3. Consider the natural monopolist described by the graph above. For each of the following pricing policies, indicate the price and output levels and determine whether the monpolist earns positive, zero, or negative economic profit:
   a. monopoly pricing
   b. marginal-cost pricing
   c. average-cost pricing

4. What would be the problem with a policy that forces the natural monopolist described by the graph to engage in marginal pricing?

True-False

Indicate whether each of the following statements is basically true or false. If the statement is false, rewrite it so that it is true.

_____ 1. Antitrust policy basically is designed to promote anticompetitive practices.

_____ 2. A trust enables a central board of trustees to vote all of the stock of supposedly competing firms.

_____ 3. The Clayton Act, passed in 1890, was the first federal antitrust law.

_____ 4. The Sherman Antitrust Act set up the Antitrust Division of the Department of Justice to enforce the act.

_____ 5. The Sherman Antitrust Act failed to identify specific anticompetitive practices.

_____ 6. The Clayton Act prohibits all price discrimination.

_____ 7. The Robinson-Patman Act is highly controversial, believed by many to have protected inefficient companies that would have otherwise been driven out of business.

_____ 8. The Clayton Act did not cover vertical and conglomerate mergers.

_____ 9. A tying arrangement exists when a firm obtains the product of a certain supplier on the condition that it will not buy from a competing supplier.

_____ 10. Tying arrangements are more often found to be illegal than are exclusive dealing arrangements.

_____ 11. The Federal Trade Commission Act has been interpreted by the courts to refer only to relationships between firms and consumers.

_____ 12. The Federal Trade Commission Act created the Federal Trade Commission.

_____ 13. The Wheeler-Lea Amendment prohibited ''unfair or deceptive acts or practices'' aimed at consumers.

_____ 14. The Justice Department characterizes an industry as unconcentrated if it has a Herfindahl-Hirschman Index of 2000.

_____ 15. Predatory price cutting refers to price cutting aimed at forcing competitors out of business.

_____ 16. OPEC is an example of a cartel.

_____ 17. Regulated industries are typically governed by monopoly regulation rather than by social regulation.

_____ 18. A monopoly that is owned and operated by the government is called a public utility.

_____ 19. The length of time it takes a regulatory commission to bring about a rate change that reflects the regulated company's change in average cost is called the regulatory lag.

_____ 20. The rate structure refers to the variation in rates that are charged according to such variables as quantity purchased and time of delivery.

_____ 21. Price differentials may not constitute price discrimination if they result in higher prices for peak-load users.

_____ 22. A contestable market is one that is being challenged under antitrust legislation.

Multiple Choice   Choose the *one best* answer in each of the following cases:

_____   1. Which of the following major laws does *not* prohibit anticompetitive behavior?
   a. Clayton Act
   b. Robinson-Patman Act
   c. Sherman Antitrust Act
   d. Rockefeller Antitrust Act
   e. Federal Trade Commission Act

_____   2. The Sherman Antitrust Act
   a. was passed in 1890.
   b. prohibits monopolization.
   c. was poorly enforced in its early years.
   d. allows injured parties to sue for treble damages.
   e. all of the above

_____   3. The Clayton Act
   a. set up the Antitrust Division of the Department of Justice.
   b. was passed in 1903 to strengthen the Sherman Antitrust Act.
   c. deals specifically with four types of anticompetitive practices.
   d. all of the above
   e. does not specify particular anticompetitive practices.

_____   4. The Robinson-Patman Act
   a. deals specifically with price discrimination.
   b. amended section 2 of the Sherman Antitrust Act.
   c. prevents exclusive dealing and tying arrangements.
   d. is generally considered to be the most effective of our antitrust laws.
   e. none of the above

_____   5. Mergers
   a. of all types were outlawed by the Clayton Act.
   b. by stock acquisition were not covered by the Clayton Act.
   c. were specifically prohibited under the Sherman Antitrust Act.
   d. by asset acquisition were covered by the Celler-Kefauver Antimerger Act.
   e. none of the above

_____   6. The Celler-Kefauver Antimerger Act
   a. was passed in 1975.
   b. amended the Robinson-Patman Act.
   c. deals only with horizontal mergers.
   d. has been interpreted by the Supreme Court to cover vertical mergers.
   e. has been interpreted by the Supreme Court to exclude conglomerate mergers.

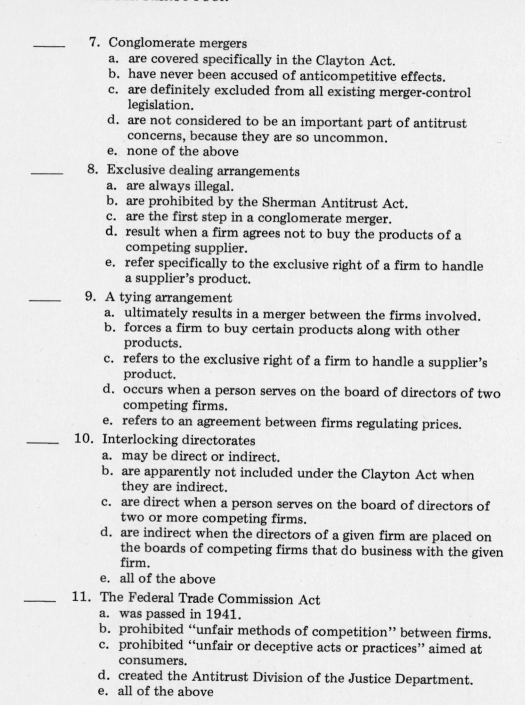

_____ 7. Conglomerate mergers
   a. are covered specifically in the Clayton Act.
   b. have never been accused of anticompetitive effects.
   c. are definitely excluded from all existing merger-control legislation.
   d. are not considered to be an important part of antitrust concerns, because they are so uncommon.
   e. none of the above

_____ 8. Exclusive dealing arrangements
   a. are always illegal.
   b. are prohibited by the Sherman Antitrust Act.
   c. are the first step in a conglomerate merger.
   d. result when a firm agrees not to buy the products of a competing supplier.
   e. refer specifically to the exclusive right of a firm to handle a supplier's product.

_____ 9. A tying arrangement
   a. ultimately results in a merger between the firms involved.
   b. forces a firm to buy certain products along with other products.
   c. refers to the exclusive right of a firm to handle a supplier's product.
   d. occurs when a person serves on the board of directors of two competing firms.
   e. refers to an agreement between firms regulating prices.

_____ 10. Interlocking directorates
   a. may be direct or indirect.
   b. are apparently not included under the Clayton Act when they are indirect.
   c. are direct when a person serves on the board of directors of two or more competing firms.
   d. are indirect when the directors of a given firm are placed on the boards of competing firms that do business with the given firm.
   e. all of the above

_____ 11. The Federal Trade Commission Act
   a. was passed in 1941.
   b. prohibited "unfair methods of competition" between firms.
   c. prohibited "unfair or deceptive acts or practices" aimed at consumers.
   d. created the Antitrust Division of the Justice Department.
   e. all of the above

_____ 12. The Wheeler-Lea Amendment prohibits
    a. false advertising claims.
    b. corporate spying.
    c. both a and b above
    d. predatory price-cutting.
    e. interlocking directorates.

_____ 13. According to the "rule of reason,"
    a. monopoly control in itself is illegal.
    b. abuse of monopoly control is illegal.
    c. both a and b above
    d. market share in excess of 50 percent is illegal.
    e. possession of power cannot be separated from the abuse of power.

_____ 14. The rule of reason was
    a. established in the 1911 Standard Oil case.
    b. overturned later in 1911 in the American Tobacco Company case.
    c. invoked in 1920 when the Supreme Court found U.S. Steel (now USX Corporation) guilty of violating the Sherman Antitrust Act.
    d. reaffirmed in the 1945 Alcoa case.
    e. all of the above

_____ 15. Horizontal and vertical mergers
    a. have been consistently challenged in the 1980s.
    b. are less likely to be denied by the courts than are conglomerate mergers.
    c. are not likely to be illegal unless there are conglomerate aspects to the merger.
    d. have been denied by the courts when companies have had as little as 5 percent of the market share.
    e. none of the above

_____ 16. With regard to price fixing, the Supreme Court
    a. has never heard a case.
    b. has consistently applied the "rule of reason."
    c. generally has found it to be illegal per se.
    d. has not been particularly consistent in its rulings.
    e. originally applied the "rule of reason," but reversed its thinking during the Great Depression.

_____ 17. Cartels are
    a. collusive arrangements among sellers.
    b. more stable the greater the number of firms involved.
    c. more successful when firms maintain independence in decision making.
    d. less successful when subject to discipline by an outside agency such as a government.
    e. all of the above

_____ 18. Monopoly regulation includes
    a. food and drug regulations.
    b. truth-in-packaging regulations.
    c. environmental protection regulations.
    d. occupational health and safety regulations.
    e. none of the above

_____ 19. A private firm that is granted a monopoly position by the government is a(n)
    a. pure monopoly.
    b. public utility.
    c. natural monopoly.
    d. public enterprise.
    e. unregulated monopoly.

_____ 20. When a regulatory commission permits "a fair return on a fairly valued rate base," it most likely means
    a. there is a regulatory lag.
    b. that "the rule of reason" is operative.
    c. "normal profit on replacement cost of capital."
    d. that original cost, reproduction cost, and replacement cost are equal.
    e. none of the above

_____ 21. Marginal-cost pricing requires that the regulated firm
    a. charge the price associated with minimum marginal cost.
    b. charge the price associated with maximum marginal cost.
    c. produce the output that equates marginal cost and demand.
    d. produce the output that equates marginal cost and average cost.
    e. produce the output that equates marginal cost and marginal revenue.

_____ 22. Average-cost pricing
    a. assures the firm a normal profit.
    b. assures the firm a positive economic profit.
    c. may result in positive, negative, or zero economic profit.
    d. will typically cause a monopolist to exit an industry in the long run.
    e. both a and d above

_____ 23. Those who favor deregulation are apt to argue that
   a. natural monopolies are likely to arise as a result of regulation.
   b. regulation prevents the introduction of new competitors and new technologies.
   c. the existence of contestable markets will prevent the development of natural monopolies.
   d. all of the above
   e. none of the above

Discussion Questions

1. Explain why oligopolists are likely to engage in collusive behavior. What effect would the level of economic concentration and the extent of entry barriers have on the tendency to collude? What effect would the number of firms in the industry have on the success of a collusive agreement?

2. Why do we have laws prohibiting the restriction of competition?

3. Discuss the impact of antitrust policy on the chief merger movements in our history.

4. Trace the history of OPEC and its changing influence on the price of oil. What other factors have influenced oil prices in the last two decades?

5. Define and explain the purpose of public enterprises and public utilities. Discuss the issues involved in determining whether these forms of business are in the public interest.

6. Define and compare monopoly pricing, marginal-cost pricing, and average-cost pricing. Which do you think would provide best for society in general? Explain.

7. Provide arguments for regulation of natural monopolies. Provide arguments for deregulation of natural monopolies.

Answers

Problems and Applications

1. a. P_4, Q_2, positive economic profit
   b. P_3, Q_3, positive economic profit
   c. P_2, Q_4, zero economic profit (or just-normal profit)

2. Though these output and price levels guarantee just-normal profit for the monopolist, they result in an even smaller output and higher price than the monopolist would choose in the abscence of regulation. The purpose of the regulation is to counteract the monopolist's tendency to restrict output in order to receive a higher price.

3. a. P_4, Q_1, positive economic profit
    b. P_2, Q_3, negative economic profit
    c. P_3, Q_2, zero economic profit (or just-normal profit)
4. If forced to engage in marginal-cost pricing, the natural monopolist incurs an economic loss and would therefore choose to exit the industry in the long run.

True-False

1. F. Antitrust policy basically is designed to fight anticompetitive practices.
2. T.
3. F. The Sherman Antitrust Act, passed in 1890, was the first federal antitrust law.
4. F. The Sherman Antitrust Act did not set up an agency to oversee enforcement of the act; the Antitrust Division of the Department of Justice was created in 1903.
5. T.
6. F. The Clayton Act prohibits price discrimination when it "substantially lessens competition or tends to create a monopoly."
7. T.
8. T.
9. F. A tying arrangement exists when a firm must buy certain products along with certain other products; an exclusive dealing arrangement exists when a firm obtains the product of a certain supplier on condition that it not buy from a competing supplier.
10. T.
11. F. The Federal Trade Commission Act has been interpreted by the courts to refer only to relationships between firms and not between firms and consumers.
12. T.
13. T.
14. F. The Justice Department characterizes an industry as unconcentrated if it has a Herfindahl-Hirschman Index of 1,000.
15. T.
16. T.
17. F. Regulated industries are typically governed by monopoly regulation as well as by social regulation.
18. F. A monopoly that is owned and operated by the government is called a public enterprise.
19. T.
20. T.

21. T.
22. F. A contestable market is one that is very easy to enter and exit.

Multiple Choice

1. d	2. e	3. c	4. a	5. d
6. d	7. e	8. d	9. b	10. e
11. b	12. a	13. b	14. a	15. d
16. c	17. a	18. e	19. b	20. c
21. c	22. a	23. b		

35 *International Microeconomics: Free Trade Versus Protection*

Summary

Free international trade results in increased total output because it enables specialization in accordance with comparative advantage. In terms of real income and output, both parties to the trade benefit, though it is not necessarily true that all individuals within an economy will benefit. In fact, consumers in the exporting country and producers in the importing country tend to lose. Producers and consumers of nontraded goods may also lose as a result of the trade if the nontraded goods are substitutes or complements in production or consumption. Trade, then, tends to have redistribution effects that may or may not be considered desirable.

The benefits of trade arise when countries specialize in accordance with comparative advantage. It is not necessary that a country have an absolute advantage in the production of the good it exports. A country has an absolute advantage in the production of a good if it is a more efficient producer of the particular good than other producers. A comparative advantage requires only that the country's pretrade relative price of the good be lower than that of its trading partner. One should recognize, however, that comparative advantage is not a static concept; it may change over time as a country grows and develops.

In the absence of transportation costs, free international trade tends to result in an equalization of product and resource prices for traded products. The tendency for factor price equalization sometimes results in protectionist arguments on the part of high-wage countries.

In addition to the high wages argument, there are other economic arguments for protection. These include infant industry, senile industry, terms of trade, home market, capital attraction, retaliation, and macroeconomic arguments. Political arguments for protection include national defense, critical minimum, predatory foreigner, and special interest arguments.

Instruments of protection may be open or disguised. Open forms of protection primarily include tariffs, quotas, and administrative protection. Disguised protection includes voluntary export restrictions, orderly marketing agreements, and the trigger-price mechanism.

International agreements dealing with economic and trade relations are likely to be specified in commercial treaties. Today, these treaties are generally reciprocal and typically are in force for a number of years. However, the legal standing of such treaties varies between countries. Commercial treaties may raise the degree of economic integration among countries. Recent economic integrations have taken the forms of free trade areas and customs unions, both of which encourage trade between member countries and divert trade from nonmember to member countries.

Major Objectives

After you have finished this chapter, you will be able to do the following:

1. Identify and explain the advantages of free trade.
2. Analyze the effects of two countries trading a single commodity, compare the equilibrium prices and quantities before and after trade between the two countries, and indicate the gains and losses to producers and consumers.
3. Explain how real income gains from trade may result in losses to some, and identify the potential losses.
4. Define and cite examples of substitutes in production and complements in production.
5. Explain why relative prices are likely to differ between nontrading countries (or between countries with restricted trade).
6. Explain and distinguish between comparative advantage and absolute advantage.
7. Explain and illustrate the principle of comparative advantage, utilizing the classical (Ricardian) approach.
8. Explain the principle of comparative advantage, utilizing the concept of differences in endowments of productive inputs.
9. Identify sources of complications and modifications in utilizing the principle of comparative advantage to determine specific patterns of trade.
10. Explain how comparative advantages are likely to change over time.
11. Explain the product cycle and its potential implications.

12. State, explain, and illustrate the factor price equalization theorem.
13. Identify factors that limit the actual equalization of factor prices.
14. Identify and define the major instruments of protection.
15. Define, distinguish between, and show the relationship between nominal protection and effective protection.
16. Identify and describe the three forms of hidden or disguised protection.
17. Define dumping, indicating its traditional and current meanings.
18. Identify and explain the economic arguments for protection and their counterarguments.
19. Identify and explain the political arguments for protection.
20. Define, provide examples of, and indicate the limitations of commercial treaties.
21. Define and distinguish between a free trade area and a free port, and a free trade area and a customs union.
22. Explain the effects on trade of free trade areas, customs unions, or other experiments in partial economic integration.
23. Briefly explain the significance of the following: European Community, European Free Trade Association, International Trade Organization, General Agreement on Tariffs and Trade, and New International Economic Order.
24. Describe the U.S. trade position, how and why it has shifted, and the consequences of these shifts.

Review Terms

productivity	consumer surplus
real income	income distribution
aggregate	utility
input	substitutes (in consumption)
output	complements (in consumption)
export	price inelastic
import	value added
market	monopoly power
demand	macroeconomics
supply	balance of payments deficit
equilibrium price	foreign exchange value
equilibrium quantity	shortage
excess demand	cartel
excess supply	

Important Terms and Concepts

free trade
specialization
per capita
internationalism
distributional effects
substitutes in production
complements in production
comparative advantage
absolute advantage
product cycle
factor price equalization theorem
protection
tariff
quota
administrative protection
bounty
subsidy
specific vs. general protection
nominal protection
effective protection
voluntary export restrictions
bilateral
orderly marketing agreements
multilateral
trigger-price mechanism
dumping
antidumping duties
"intense minorities" or "special interests"
infant industry argument
senile industry argument
high wages argument
terms of trade
terms of trade argument
monopsony
monopsony power
home market argument

risk aversion
capital attraction or tariff factory argument
European Community (EC)
retaliation or bargaining argument
macroeconomic arguments
national defense argument
critical minimum argument
basic industry
predatory foreigner argument
intense minority or special-interest pressure
commercial treaty
more-developed countries (MDCs)
less-developed countries (LDCs)
free trade area
free port
customs unions
European Free Trade Association (EFTA)
trade-creation effect vs. trade-diversion effect
International Trade Organization (ITO)
General Agreement on Tariffs and Trade (GATT)
New International Economic Order (NIEO)
balance of trade
budget deficits
anti-inflation monetary policies
aggregate supply shock
dollar glut
dollar shortage era

Completion

specialize

Free trade makes it feasible for people or regions to _____ in those tasks for which they are relatively well suited. Specialization

increased

tends to result in _____ (increased/decreased)

higher

productivity and therefore in _____ (higher/lower) standards of living.

both economies

With free international trade, _____ (both economies/only one economy) gain(s). The gains from trade

may not

_____ (must/may not) be evenly divided. Generally, the

greater

country that experiences the _____ (greater/lesser) price change for the traded commodity will gain more. Furthermore,

cannot

though a country gains from trade, we _____ (can/cannot) be certain that the majority of individuals in the country gain. Indi-

even

viduals may _____ (even/not) lose as a result of the trade. Under

lose

competitive conditions, consumers of exportable goods _____ (gain/lose) from export trade and producers of importable or import-

lose

competing goods _____ (gain/lose) from trade. In evaluating the effects of trade, one should also consider the effects of trade on producers and consumers of nontraded goods if these nontraded

complementary, substitutes

goods are _____ to or _____ for imports or exports in either production or consumption.

Though there are gains in production and real income for all countries involved in free trade and a tendency for factor prices to

equalized

be _____ as a result of free trade, real-world countries

protection

limit trade through various instruments of _____ .
These instruments include three basic types of open protection:

tariffs, quotas

_____ , which are taxes on imports; _____ ,

administrative

which are limitations on the quantity of imports; and _____ protection, which includes bans on or inspection of imports. There

subsidies

also may be open protection in the form of bounties or _____ .
In addition, there are three basic forms of disguised protection:

voluntary export

_____ restrictions, in which exporting countries agree to lower exports to a certain level or in accordance

orderly marketing

with a certain formula; _____ agreements, which attempt to prevent disorderly price cuts in importing coun-

trigger-price

tries; and the _____ mechanism, in which importing countries announce lower limits on prices and subject higher-priced

antidumping

imports to _____ duties.

Problems and Applications   Use the following graphs to answer problems 1 and 2.

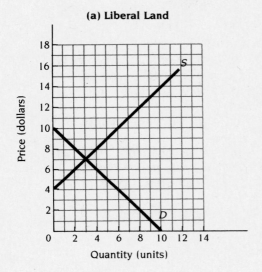

(a) Liberal Land

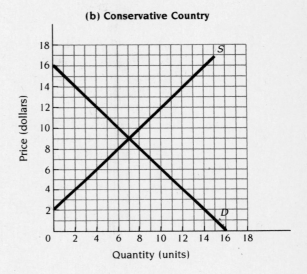

(b) Conservative Country

1. Liberal Land and Conservative Country have been advised that free trade between two countries results in net gains for both. They decide to experiment by engaging in the free trade of politikos. Pretrade demand and supply conditions for the two economies are given in the graphs above. Liberal Land is described by panel (a), and Conservative Country by panel (b). Assume that there are no costs associated with transporting politikos.

   a. Identify the pretrade equilibrium price and quantity in each country.

   b. At prices between $7 and $9, does Liberal Land experience a positive excess demand or a positive excess supply? At prices between $7 and $9, does Conservative Country experience a positive excess demand or a positive excess supply?

   c. Which country will export politikos?

   d. Draw the appropriate demand and supply curves, assuming free trade.

   e. Identify the new equilibrium price of politikos.

   f. Assuming free international trade, how many units of politikos will be purchased domestically in each country? How many units will be traded internationally?

   g. Do consumers in Liberal Land gain or lose as a result of international trade? Do producers in Liberal Land gain or lose as a result of international trade? Do consumers in Conservative

Country gain or lose as a result of international trade? Do producers in Conservative Country gain or lose as a result of international trade?

h. Graphically identify the areas representing the gains and/or losses to consumers and producers in each country.

i. Graphically show the net gain in each country.

2. Consider the situation described in problem 1 on page 671. Assume that the production of politikos is labor-intensive and that pretrade equilibrium prices reflect wage rates in the two countries.

a. Which is the relatively low-wage country? What is the relatively high-wage country?

b. What will happen to the demand for labor in Liberal Land as a result of international trade? What will happen to the demand for labor in Conservative Country as a result of international trade?

c. What is the effect on wages of these changes in the demand for labor in the two countries?

3. The following table identifies the costs of production of cloth and wine in Portugal and England. Assume that at equilibrium, in international trade, one unit of cloth trades for one unit of wine.

	Labor Cost per Unit Traded	
Country	Cloth	Wine
England	80	100
Portugal	75	50

a. Which country has the absolute advantage in the production of cloth? Which country has the absolute advantage in the production of wine?

b. What are the relative prices of cloth and wine in each country?

c. What is the opportunity cost of producing a unit of wine in England? What is the opportunity cost of producing a unit of cloth in England. What is the opportunity cost of producing a unit of cloth in Portugal? What is the opportunity cost of producing a unit of wine in Portugal?

d. Which country has the comparative advantage in the production of cloth? Which country has the comparative advantage in the production of wine?

e. Which country will produce cloth? Which country will produce wine?

f. If England produces one unit of cloth and one unit of wine, what is England's labor cost? If Portugal produces one unit of cloth and one unit of wine, what is Portugal's labor cost?

g. Assume that England and Portugal produce on the basis of comparative advantage. What will be the cost to each country if each one produces two units of the good for which it has the comparative advantage?

h. If England and Portugal engage in trade in accordance with comparative advantage, what are the gains to each (in hours of labor)?

True-False   Indicate whether each of the following statements is basically true or false. If the statement is false, rewrite it so that it is true.

_____ 1. Economic theory suggests that free international trade can raise real income in all trading countries.

_____ 2. Economic theory suggests that free international trade will benefit all individuals who are affected by that trade.

_____ 3. When two countries engage in the free trade of a single commodity, the equilibrium price of the commodity will differ in the two countries by the cost of transporting the commodity between the two countries.

_____ 4. When two countries engage in the free trade of a single commodity, they gain equally from the trade.

_____ 5. A good may not be traded internationally when the cost of transporting the good is relatively high in comparison to the price of the good.

_____ 6. Two goods are complementary in production when they are joint products of a single production process.

_____ 7. Heckscher and Ohlin explained that comparative advantage may arise because of differences between countries in their endowments of productive inputs.

_____ 8. An economy has an absolute advantage in the production of a particular good if it is more proficient in producing that good than other goods.

_____ 9. A country with an absolute advantage in the production of a good would never import that good.

_____ 10. International trade generally takes place in accordance with absolute advantage.

_____ 11. Over time, international trade may affect tastes and production techniques so much that pretrade relative prices become essentially obsolete.

_____ 12. As a country develops, its comparative advantages generally remain the same.

_____ 13. Economic development is usually associated with shifts in a country's comparative advantages away from farming to service industries to heavy industries and later to light industries.

_____ 14. According to the concept of product cycles, it is conceivable that a country would reach a point at which it ceases to export goods altogether.

_____ 15. According to the factor price equalization theorem, free trade equalizes the difference between output and input prices.

_____ 16. In the real world, the factor price equalization theorem holds exactly.

_____ 17. A tariff is a limitation on the quantity of a good that can be imported.

_____ 18. Effective protection is simply the rate of tariff imposed on imports of the product.

_____ 19. The infant industry argument for protection claims that a mature industry cannot compete effectively with a new, or infant, industry.

_____ 20. The senile industry argument maintains that a dying industry that hires workers with specialized skills should be protected in order to avoid increases in welfare expenditures.

_____ 21. A country's terms of trade are measured by the average of its export prices index minus the average of its import prices.

_____ 22. The home market argument for protection would eliminate import tariffs on foreign goods in order to promote the export of goods produced in home markets.

_____ 23. The capital attraction or tariff factory argument for protection would favor the protection of given markets in the home country in order to limit imports and encourage foreign capitalists to invest and employ labor in the home country.

_____ 24. Historically, retaliatory tariffs have apparently led to further retaliation rather than to a lessening of protective measures.

_____ 25. The national defense, critical minimum, and predatory foreigner arguments for protection are basically political arguments.

_____ 26. The European Community, a free trade area, is an important experiment in economic integration.

_____ 27. The U.S. balance of trade has been positive throughout its history.

_____ 28. The most important trading partners for the United States are Canada and Japan.

Multiple Choice   Choose the *one best* answer in each of the following cases:

Use the following graphs to answer questions 1–6.

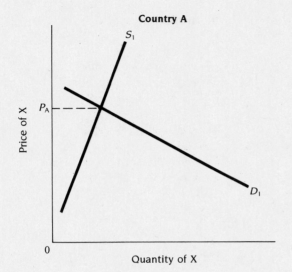

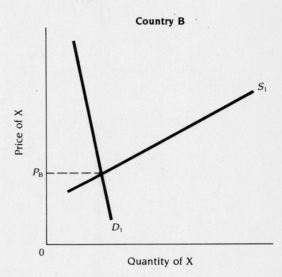

_____   1. Assume a world consisting of two countries, A and B, that trade in a single commodity, good X. Demand curves D_1 and supply curves S_1 in the graphs above indicate the domestic demand and supply conditions for good X. Assume that there are no costs associated with shipping good X from one country to another. From this information, one can conclude that, in the absence of trade,

    a. the price of X will be P_A in both countries.

    b. the price of X will be P_B in both countries.

    c. there will be a positive excess demand for good X in both countries.

    d. the equilibrium price of X will be higher in country A than in country B.

    e. there will be an excess demand for good X at prices above P_A in country A.

_____   2. Consider the economic situation described in question 1 and the graphs above. If countries A and B engage in free trade in good X, one would expect

    a. country A to export good X.

    b. country B to export good X.

    c. both countries to export good X.

    d. both countries to import good X.

    e. neither country to export good X.

_____ 3. Consider the economic situation described in question 1 and the graphs. If countries A and B engage in free trade in good X, one would expect that
  a. the equilibrium price will be the same in both countries if there are no costs associated with shipping good X.
  b. at equilibrium the quantity of X imported by country B is equal to the excess supply of X in country A.
  c. at equilibrium the quantity of X imported by country B is equal to the quantity of X exported by country A.
  d. all of the above
  e. none of the above

_____ 4. Consider the economic situation described in question 1 and the graphs. If countries A and B engage in free trade in good X, one would expect that, as a result of a trade, consumers of good X
  a. in country A gain.
  b. in country A incur a loss.
  c. in both countries gain.
  d. in both countries incur a loss.
  e. experience neither gain nor loss.

_____ 5. Consider the economic situation described in question 1 and the graphs. If countries A and B engage in free trade in good X, one would expect that, as a result of a trade, producers of good X
  a. in country A gain.
  b. in country A incur a loss.
  c. in both countries gain.
  d. in both countries incur a loss.
  e. experience neither gain nor loss.

_____ 6. Consider the economic situation described in question 1 and the graphs. If countries A and B engage in free trade in good X, one would expect that, as a result of the trade,
  a. country A experiences a net gain and country B experiences a net loss.
  b. country A experiences a net loss and country B experiences a net gain.
  c. both countries experience a net gain.
  d. both countries experience a net loss.
  e. none of the above

_____ 7. Assume a world consisting of two countries that trade in a single commodity. Assume that there are no costs associated with shipping the good from one country to another. If gains and losses are measured in terms of real income and output, one can conclude that the
  a. countries will experience equal gains from the trade.

b. country that experiences the greater price change for the traded commodity will gain more than the country that experiences the lesser price change.

c. country that experiences the greater price change for the traded commodity will gain less than the country that experiences the lesser price change.

d. country that experiences the greater price change for the traded commodity will experience a net gain, whereas the country that experiences the lesser price change will experience a net loss.

e. country that experiences the greater price change for the traded commodity will experience a net loss, whereas the country that experiences the lesser price change will experience a net gain.

_____ 8. When a trading country experiences a gain in terms of real income and output, we can conclude that

a. trade must be desirable.

b. all citizens in the country gain from the trade.

c. all citizens will experience an increase in satisfaction.

d. no citizens in the country experience a loss from the trade.

e. none of the above

_____ 9. Assume that countries A and B both produce ticks and tocks. If country A has an absolute advantage in the production of both goods, then one could accurately conclude that

a. country A should produce ticks and export them to country B.

b. country A should produce tocks and export them to country B.

c. country A should produce both goods and export them to country B.

d. there is no basis for trade between countries A and B.

e. there may be a basis for trade between countries A and B.

Use the following table to answers questions 10 and 11.

	Labor Cost per Unit (in hours)	
Country	Bread	Cheese
Alphaland	75	100
Betaland	150	125

_____ 10. Consider the table above, describing the costs for the production of bread and cheese in Alphaland and Betaland. If, at equilibrium with international trade, one unit of bread is exchanged for one unit of cheese, then
a. relative prices would be 3 : 5 in Alphaland.
b. Alphaland has an absolute advantage in the production of bread.
c. Betaland has an absolute advantage in the production of cheese.
d. in Betaland, bread would be relatively cheap by comparison to cheese.
e. all of the above

_____ 11. Consider the table above. If, at equilibrium with international trade, one unit of bread is exchanged for one unit of cheese, then
a. Alphaland has a comparative advantage in the production of bread.
b. Betaland has a comparative advantage in the production of cheese.
c. if Alphaland trades bread for cheese from Betaland, Alphaland gains the output of 25 hours of Alpha labor.
d. if Betaland trades cheese for bread from Alphaland, Betaland gains the output of 25 hours of Beta labor.
e. all of the above

_____ 12. The concept of a product cycle explains how
a. comparative advantage changes over time.
b. the demand for a product changes over time.
c. a product is produced within a given economy.
d. factor prices affect the production of a good.
e. the demand for a product changes with changes in comparative advantage.

_____ 13. In the real world, factor price equalization
   a. occurs only with the labor factor.
   b. can occur only in the absence of free trade.
   c. is less likely if markets are purely competitive.
   d. is more likely with the labor factor than with capital.
   e. tends to occur, but not to the extent of full factor price equality.

_____ 14. Nominal protection is measured by the
   a. value added by the protected industry.
   b. rate of tariff imposed on imports of the good.
   c. extent of protection of goods that are inputs in the production of the good.
   d. all of the above
   e. none of the above

_____ 15. Effective protection of a good involves the
   a. value added by the protected industry.
   b. rate of tariff imposed on imports of the good.
   c. extent of protection of goods that are inputs in the production of the good.
   d. all of the above
   e. none of the above

_____ 16. Effective protection of a good will typically be
   a. zero.
   b. equal to nominal protection.
   c. less than nominal protection.
   d. zero, unless there is no direct protection of the good.
   e. greater than nominal protection, unless the protection of inputs used in the production of the good is substantial.

_____ 17. Voluntary export restrictions are generally
   a. bilateral.
   b. multilateral.
   c. completely voluntary.
   d. considered to be a form of dumping.
   e. both a and c above

_____ 18. A trigger-price mechanism typically
   a. is multilateral.
   b. prohibits antidumping measures.
   c. involves an agreement to prevent disorderly price cuts.
   d. prevents the sale of imports at less than the trigger price.
   e. subjects imports selling at less than an announced price to special duties.

_____ 19. Dumping is
  a. an orderly-marketing agreement.
  b. currently defined to include any sale below average cost plus a "fair" markup.
  c. traditionally defined as the practice of selling a product at a higher price internationally than domestically.
  d. all of the above
  e. the difference between nominal and effective protection.

_____ 20. The high wages argument for protection would
  a. protect high wages.
  b. eliminate high wages.
  c. make wages more nearly equal.
  d. eliminate cheap foreign labor.
  e. directly implement the theory of comparative advantage.

_____ 21. Which of the following is true of an economy's terms of trade?
  a. Terms-of-trade arguments for protection require pure competition.
  b. A country's terms of trade improve when its average export price falls.
  c. A country's terms of trade improve when its average import price rises.
  d. For a given trade volume, lower terms of trade are considered beneficial.
  e. none of the above

_____ 22. Macroeconomic arguments for protection might include the recommendation of protection in order to
  a. raise revenue.
  b. fight domestic unemployment.
  c. reduce a balance of payments deficit.
  d. help alleviate macroeconomic problems.
  e. all of the above

_____ 23. Commercial treaties
  a. are always reciprocal.
  b. cannot be used to form free trade areas or customs unions.
  c. can be used to form customs unions, but not free trade areas.
  d. are always legally binding for the time period stipulated by the treaty.
  e. are agreements between countries dealing with economic and trade relations.

24. Free trade areas and customs unions differ in that in free trade areas
    a. there are no commercial treaties, whereas in customs unions members are legally bound by commercial treaties.
    b. there are no restrictions on any country (whether it is a member or not), whereas in customs unions nonmember countries may face restrictions.
    c. member countries all impose the same restrictions on non-member countries, whereas in customs unions each member country has its own set of restrictions.
    d. each member country has its own set of restrictions against nonmember countries, whereas in customs unions restrictions against nonmember countries are prohibited.
    e. each member country has its own set of restrictions against nonmember countries, whereas in customs unions member countries impose common restrictions on nonmember countries.

25. Free trade areas and customs unions tend to
    a. discourage trade.
    b. encourage free trade among both members and nonmembers.
    c. create trade between both member and nonmember countries.
    d. encourage trade between member countries and divert trade from nonmember to member countries.
    e. discourage trade between member countries and encourage trade between member and nonmember countries.

26. The General Agreement on Tariffs and Trade (GATT)
    a. seeks to reduce the level of protection among members.
    b. was started as an organization of less-developed countries.
    c. has been replaced by the International Trade Organization (ITO).
    d. is considered by the U.S. Congress to be discriminatory against the United States.
    e. all of the above

27. The change in the international trade position of the United States in recent decades can be attributed to
    a. changing factor endowments.
    b. an accelerated product cycle.
    c. the passing of the dollar-shortage era.
    d. all of the above
    e. none of the above

Discussion Questions

1. Explain how it is possible for both parties involved in trade to benefit from that trade.

2. Explain the difference between absolute advantage and comparative advantage. Which is most appropriate as the basis for exchange?

3. Demonstrate the factor price equalization theorem. Provide reasons to explain why factor prices are not equal throughout the world.

4. Would you expect the effective rate of protection to be greater or smaller than the nominal rate if inputs are not highly protected? Explain.

5. Would you expect the effective rate of protection for a particular good to be relatively large or small if the value added to the good by a particular firm is relatively small? Explain.

6. The authors comment that "Free trade wins all the arguments, but protection wins all the votes." What do they mean? Now that you have studied free trade and protection, would you vote for protection? Do you think free trade "wins all the arguments"?

7. Explain the recent shifts in the position of the United States in terms of international trade.

Answers

Problems and Applications

1. a. Liberal Land—$7, 3 units; Conservative Country—$9, 7 units
   b. positive excess supply; positive excess demand
   c. Liberal Land
   d.

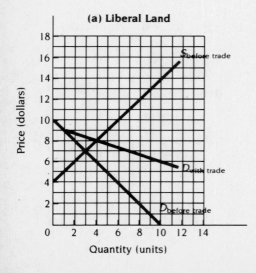

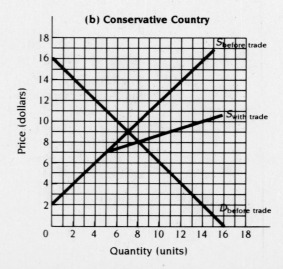

e. $8

f. Liberal Land, 2 units; Conservative Country, 6 units;
   internationally, 2 units

g. lose; gain; gain; lose

h. and i. Liberal Land: loss to consumers is area shown by vertical lines;
   gain to producers is shaded area; net gain is area shown by
   horizontal lines. Conservative Country: gain to consumers is
   shaded area; loss to producers is area shown by vertical lines;
   net gain is area shown by horizontal lines

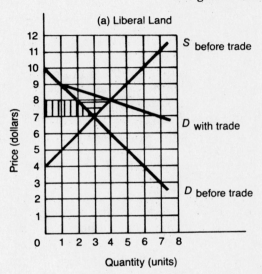

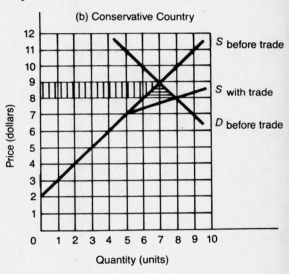

2. a. Liberal Land; Conservative Country

   b. increase; decrease

   c. Wages increase in Liberal Land and decrease in Conservative
      Country; that is, there is a tendency toward wage equalization.

3. a. Portugal; Portugal

   b. 8:10, or 4:5, in England; 75:50, or 3:2, in Portugal

   c. 1.25 units of cloth; 0.8 units of wine; 1.5 units of wine;
      0.67 units of cloth

   d. England; Portugal

   e. England; Portugal

   f. 180 hours of English labor; 125 hours of Portuguese labor

   g. 160 hours of English labor; 100 hours of Portuguese labor

   h. 20 hours of English labor; 25 hours of Portuguese labor

True-False

1. T.
2. F. Even though free international trade can be expected to raise real income in all trading countries, it is not true that all persons who are affected will gain from that trade.
3. T.
4. F. When two countries engage in the free trade of a single commodity, they both gain from the trade, but the gains are not necessarily equal.
5. T.
6. T.
7. T.
8. F. An economy has an absolute advantage in the production of a particular good if it is more proficient in producing that good than are other economies that also produce it.
9. F. A country with an absolute advantage in the production of a good might import that good, depending on comparative advantage.
10. F. International trade generally takes place in accordance with comparative advantage.
11. T.
12. F. As a country develops, its comparative advantages generally shift away from farming to light industry, then to heavy industry, and then to service industries.
13. F. Economic development is usually associated with shifts in a country's comparative advantages away from farming to light industries to heavy industries and later to service industries.
14. T.
15. F. According to the factor price equalization theorem, free trade equalizes input prices across trading countries.
16. F. In the real world, the factor price equalization theorem operates only as a general tendency.
17. F. A tariff is a tax on imports (or in some cases exports).
18. F. Nominal protection is simply the rate of tariff imposed on imports of the product.
19. F. The infant industry argument for protection claims that a new or infant industry cannot compete effectively with established or mature industries.
20. T.
21. F. A country's terms of trade are measured by the average of its export prices divided by the average of its import prices.
22. F. The home market argument for protection would impose import tariffs on foreign goods, even though it would hinder the export of goods produced in home markets.

23. T.
24. T.
25. T.
26. F. The European Community, a customs union, is an important experiment in economic integration.
27. F. The U.S. balance of trade has generally been negative since about 1970.
28. T.

Multiple Choice

1. d	2. b	3. a	4. a	5. b
6. c	7. b	8. e	9. e	10. b
11. e	12. a	13. e	14. b	15. d
16. e	17. a	18. e	19. b	20. a
21. e	22. e	23. e	24. e	25. d
26. a	27. d			

36 *Agriculture, Food, and Hunger*

Summary

Though American agriculture is envied by many countries around the world, the "farm problem" continues. Farmers' complaints center around two basic issues. Individual farmers see themselves as pure competitors or price takers who must deal with monopolistic sellers and monopsonistic buyers (one buyer in each market). In addition, the price and income elasticities of demand for farm output are generally low.

In the past, farmers have based their arguments for support on the doctrine of agricultural fundamentalism. This argument holds that, since food is a necessity, farmers should be at least as well off as any other group. Farmers also maintain that they make up a major market for manufactured goods. If farmers do not consume these goods, claim the agricultural fundamentalists, there will be overproduction and depression. As farmers have become less important an outlet for manufactured goods, agricultural fundamentalism has lost much of its popularity.

Farmers have reacted to their problems by leaving the farm, supplementing their farm income with nonfarm income, taking nonfarm jobs in rural areas, and in many cases moving to the city. Farmers also have formed farm organizations and have used political pressure to secure support from government programs.

Government agricultural policies include support and target prices. Farm prices are supported at some percentage of parity, and farmers can obtain no-recourse loans from the government at some percentage of parity. Target prices, which involve deficiency payments from the government to farmers, do not result in higher consumer prices (though they do affect taxpayers). The government system of price supports involves government purchases of buffer stocks and production controls that limit agricultural production. Production restrictions are designed to lessen the burden on taxpayers, but they may not be successful in actually limiting the supply of farm output.

The future of agriculture depends on demographic, technical, and economic factors as well as on patterns of international trade and world population growth. Many forecasts suggest that the future will see worldwide famine and malnutrition. Hopes that this can be averted center on continued technological progress in agriculture, on family planning and declining population growth, on the redistribution of world income and wealth, and on a restructuring of productive activity in the direction of food for the poor.

Major Objectives   After you have finished this chapter, you will be able to do the following:

1. Briefly describe the historical patterns and highlights of U.S. agriculture.
2. Identify and explain the basic complaints of farmers.
3. Identify the alleged exploiters of farmers.
4. Identify the complaints on both sides of the market for farm land.
5. Explain how a low price elasticity of demand may result in a lower income for farmers with a large crop as compared to a small crop.
6. State and explain the importance of Engel's law.
7. Identify and discuss the major responses of farmers to their economic plight.
8. Describe and explain agricultural fundamentalism.
9. Identify and discuss the major government agricultural policies.
10. Define and explain what is meant by a parity price, 100 percent of parity, market price, support price, target price, a no-recourse loan, buffer stocks, ever-normal granary, and deficiency payment.
11. Explain verbally and graphically the systems of support prices, target prices, and production controls, identifying the effects of each on farmers, consumers, and taxpayers.
12. Discuss the costs and benefits of the U.S. farm program.
13. Cite and discuss the conventional views about the future of U.S. agriculture.
14. Discuss the demographic, technological, and economic factors influencing the future of agriculture in the United States.
15. Discuss the importance of population growth with respect to agriculture.
16. Identify and describe ways in which world famine may be prevented.

17. Explain the meaning and consequences of the Green Revolution.
18. Describe and explain the "Food First" policy.

Review Terms

shortage	price elasticity of demand
tax	income elasticity of demand
interest rate	free market
deflation	surplus
export	cartel
import	national income
market structures	strike
inelastic	labor union
pure competition	subsidy
monopoly	surplus
price taker	monopoly control
input or factor of production or resource	collectivist
	real income
collusion	changes (or shifts) in supply
conglomerate	innovation
demand	economic growth
investment	positive vs. normative
inflation	marginal

Important Terms and Concepts

the "farm problem"	price supports
Whiskey Rebellion	farm parity
gold standard	parity price
nominal	market price
Populism	support price
People's Party	target price
Greenback Party	buffer stocks
"golden age of agriculture"	ever-normal granary
overproduction	no-recourse loans
"tractoring off"	surplus commodities
commodity exchanges	deficiency payment
capital gains	production controls
nonliquid assets	soil bank
Engel's law	demographic
agricultural fundamentalism	corporate farming
tenant farmer	urban sprawl
enclosure movements	Green Revolution
producers' co-ops	natalist religions
marketing co-ops	income redistribution
American farm program	"Food First" policy

Completion

market structures

inelasticity of
demand

pure competitors
or price takers

monopolistic,
monopsonistic

price, income

low

lower

low

falls

leave

nonfarm

organizations

political

strike

Farmers' complaints generally center around two issues: the

_____ in which they buy and sell, and the

_____ for farm products.
With regard to the first complaint, farmers argue that they are

_____ who must face

_____ sellers and _____
buyers. With regard to the second complaint, farmers are concerned

about both the _____ and the _____ elasticities of
demand for their output. The price elasticity of demand for many

individual products is _____ (low/high). Consequently, large

crops often result in _____ (lower/higher) incomes than
would smaller crops. The income elasticity of demand for individual

farm products as well as for food in general tends to be _____
(low/high). This means that as consumers' per-capita income rises,
the percentage that they spend for a given food product (or food in

general) _____ (falls/rises).
    Farmers have responded to their problems in several ways. Their

most important reaction, quantitatively, has been to _____

the farm. They have supplemented their income with _____

employment. They have formed farm _____ and

have attempted to use _____ means. They have not

been as likely to _____ or take other direct action as have
labor unions.

Problems and Applications

1. Consider the graph below, describing demand and supply conditions in an agricultural market.

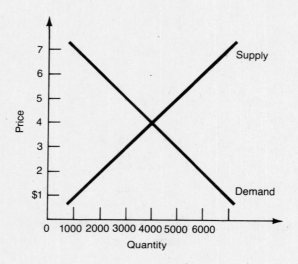

a. What is the equilibrium price and quantity in the absence of government price and production controls? How much revenue do farmers earn at equilibrium?

b. Assume that the government supports the price of $5. How many units will consumers purchase? What price will they pay? How many units will the government have to purchase? What price will the government pay? How much revenue do farmers earn? What is the total expenditure by consumers? What is the total cost of the program to taxpayers?

c. In addition to its implementing a price support at $5 per unit, assume that the government sets a target price of $6 per unit. How many units will consumers purchase? What price will consumers pay? What is the total expenditure by consumers? How many units will the government purchase? What price will the government pay? How much does the government spend on this purchase? What will be the per-unit deficiency payment to farmers? What will be the total deficiency payment to farmers? What will be the total government expenditure with the price support and target price? How much revenue do farmers receive?

2. Consider the graph below, describing demand and supply conditions in an agricultural market.

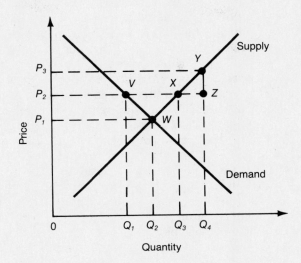

a. What is the equilibrium price and quantity in the absence of government price and production controls? How much revenue do farmers earn at equilibrium?

b. Assume that the government supports the price of P_2. How many units will consumers purchase? What price will they pay? How many units will the government have to purchase? What price will the government pay? How much revenue do farmers earn? What is the total expenditure by consumers? What is the total cost of the program to taxpayers?

c. In addition to its implementing a price support at P_2 per unit, assume that the government sets a target price of P_3 per unit. How many units will consumers purchase? What price will consumers pay? What is the total expenditure by consumers? How many units will the government purchase? What price will the government pay? How much will the government spend on this purchase? What will be the per-unit deficiency payment to farmers? What will be the total deficiency payment to farmers? What will be the total government expenditure with the price support and target price? How much revenue do farmers receive?

3. Consider the agricultural market described by the graph below. Demand curve D and supply curve S_1 describe the free market demand and supply conditions. Supply curve S_2 shows the effect of government production controls.

   a. What would be the price of the good without government production controls? What happens to the price as a result of the government production controls?

   b. Graphically identify the total revenue associated with production and sale under the conditions of a free market. Graphically identify the total revenue as a result of the production controls. Did total revenue increase or decrease as a result of the production controls? What does this suggest about the elasticity of demand for the product?

   c. In addition to the production controls, assume that the government supports the price at $2 per unit. How many units of the good will the government have to buy? What price will consumers pay for the good? What price will the government pay?

   d. Assume that the government decides to support the price at $2 per unit but eliminates the production controls. How many units of the good will the government have to buy? What price will consumers pay for the good? What price will the government pay?

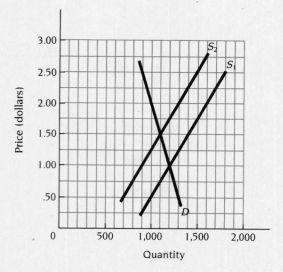

True-False

Indicate whether each of the following statements is basically true or false. If the statement is false, rewrite it so that it is true.

_____ 1. There has been virtually no farm problem in the United States until recent years, though it has been a persistent problem throughout the history of other countries.

_____ 2. The Civil War was financed by inflation.

_____ 3. The government adhered to the gold standard to control inflation during the Civil War.

_____ 4. "Tractoring off" of tenant farmers refers to the substitution of machinery for labor.

_____ 5. Agricultural problems are basically the same throughout the world.

_____ 6. Monopsony is a market structure characterized by one buyer.

_____ 7. Farmers typically have complained that they are pure competitors buying and selling in purely competitive markets, so that all prices must be taken as dictated by markets.

_____ 8. Farmland in the United States is a very liquid asset.

_____ 9. The price elasticity of demand for farm products tends to be relatively low, and the income elasticity of demand is relatively high.

_____ 10. Price inelasticity of demand for farm products means that large crops may result in relatively low income.

_____ 11. The price elasticity of demand for the output of any individual farm is almost infinite.

_____ 12. Cartel arrangements are typical for most major crops when there are many producers.

_____ 13. Nonfarm production amounted to only about a third of farm production in the United States at the turn of the century.

_____ 14. Quantitatively, the farmer's most important reaction to the farm problem has been to leave the farm.

_____ 15. Farmers have generally used voting power rather than the strike as a means of securing benefits.

_____ 16. The farm program basically refers to programs for six basic commodities and major storable commodities.

_____ 17. Farm price supports and income supplements began as a temporary program in the 1930s.

_____ 18. Deficiency payments to farmers tend to hold down food prices at taxpayer expense.

_____ 19. Farm price supports in the United States are designed to eliminate parity.

_____ 20. Surplus buffer stocks in the United States have sometimes been exported as aid to foreign countries and/or distributed domestically as surplus commodities to people on relief.

_____ 21. Production controls in the United States are typically designed to limit the production of farm products, though they probably do not limit production as much as intended.

_____ 22. Approximately two-thirds of American farmers receive aid from farm supports.

_____ 23. Agricultural productivity per worker has declined steadily since World War II.

_____ 24. More than most other kinds of work, farming is becoming a part-time or part-family business.

_____ 25. World population in 1980 has been estimated as 2.7 times greater than in 1900.

_____ 26. In his *Essay on Population*, Thomas Malthus wrote that "positive checks" such as war, famine, and pestilence would place natural limits on population growth.

_____ 27. Economic growth is usually followed by a decrease in birth rates.

Multiple Choice   Choose the *one best* answer in each of the following cases:

_____ 1. The Whiskey Rebellion
   a. occurred just after the Civil War.
   b. had nothing at all to do with whiskey.
   c. involved farmers' refusal to pay a tax.
   d. all of the above
   e. none of the above

_____ 2. The concept of populism
   a. grew out of the depression of the 1930s.
   b. opposed the election of William Jennings Bryan.
   c. grew in popularity when farm prices rose just before World War I.
   d. was the basis for the establishment of the two-party political system.
   e. none of the above

_____ 3. Which of the following is true with respect to farm production and prices in the United States?
   a. They have both tended to rise during major wars.
   b. They both decreased as a result of the New Deal.
   c. They have both tended to decline during major wars.

d. Postwar conditions and government policies have tended to increase both.

e. Underproduction during and just after World War I and II resulted in high farm prices.

_____ 4. Farmers have often felt exploited by
   a. local money lenders.
   b. speculators on the commodity exchanges.
   c. local storage companies that hold farm goods for shipment.
   d. railroad and trucking companies that transport farm goods to market.
   e. all of the above

_____ 5. Regarding the elasticity of demand for farm products,
   a. both price and income elasticities are unitary elastic.
   b. both price and income elasticities are relatively low.
   c. both price and income elasticities are relatively high.
   d. the price elasticity is relatively high and the income elasticity is relatively low.
   e. the price elasticity is relatively low and the income elasticity is relatively high.

_____ 6. The price elasticity of demand for the output of any particular farm is
   a. zero.
   b. unitary.
   c. almost infinite.
   d. relatively low, but greater than zero.
   e. approximately equal to the price elasticity of demand for the market as a whole.

_____ 7. Engel's law refers to the
   a. low price elasticity of demand for food.
   b. high price elasticity of demand for farm products.
   c. high income elasticity of demand for farm products.
   d. none of the above
   e. both b and c above

_____ 8. Farmers have reacted to unfavorable conditions by
   a. using political means.
   b. moving to urban areas.
   c. forming farm organizations.
   d. supplementing farm income with nonfarm employment.
   e. all of the above

_____ 9. Agricultural fundamentalism argues that
   a. food is necessary for life.
   b. depressions are "farm led and farm fed."
   c. overproduction in urban areas is the result of a lack of farm purchasing power.
   d. all of the above
   e. both a and b above

_____ 10. Nonfarm production in the United States
   a. is a declining percentage of total production.
   b. was over 38 times as great as farm production in 1984.
   c. amounted to about one-fourth of total production in the early 1900s.
   d. was less than farm production during the depression of the 1930s.
   e. none of the above

_____ 11. Agricultural price supports generally
   a. raise food prices.
   b. have no impact on the prices of nonfarm goods.
   c. impose minimum wages in agricultural markets.
   d. impose price ceilings in agricultural markets.
   e. are designed to lower the prices of agricultural inputs.

_____ 12. The parity price of a farm product refers to the
   a. market-clearing price.
   b. current cost of producing the product.
   c. price that would prevail in a free market.
   d. price that would guarantee the farmer a normal profit.
   e. none of the above

_____ 13. Farm prices
   a. have never been supported in the United States.
   b. are supported at exactly 100 percent of parity.
   c. are supported at less than 100 percent of parity.
   d. are not permitted to exceed 100 percent of parity.
   e. are likely to exceed 100 percent of parity when demand for farm products is low and supply is great.

_____ 14. A no-recourse loan
   a. permits a farmer to borrow from the government without repayment.
   b. permits a farmer to borrow from banks when government funds are unavailable.
   c. permits a farmer to borrow from the government when private funds are unavailable.

d. means that the government cannot require the farmer to do more than surrender the crop that serves as collateral for the loan.

e. none of the above

_____ 15. Buffer stocks

a. are called an ever-normal granary.

b. are government reserves of farm products.

c. are held in case of bad weather or natural disasters.

d. all of the above

e. both b and c above

_____ 16. Production controls

a. often reduce production more than intended.

b. are designed to encourage farmers to increase production.

c. aim, in part, to keep land fallow and reduce soil depletion.

d. were eliminated by the Agriculture and Consumer Protection Act of 1973.

e. always prevent farmers from using land for the protection of nonsupported crops.

_____ 17. Under the program of target prices,

a. the need for government purchases of farm output is eliminated.

b. farmers may receive payments up to $20,000 a year for each controlled crop.

c. farmers receive payments directly from the government when the price falls below the target.

d. farmers are required to make payments directly to the government when the price rises above the target.

e. all of the above

_____ 18. Production controls are intended to

a. result in a lower product price.

b. shift the supply curve to the left.

c. shift the supply curve to the right.

d. shift the demand curve to the left.

e. shift the demand curve to the right.

_____ 19. Historical trends suggest that the future of U.S. agriculture will be characterized by a fall in the

a. average size of farms.

b. number of farms and farmers.

c. average price of farm land per acre.

d. proportion of farm families who rent part or all of their land from others.

e. all of the above

_____ 20. Which of the following statements is true with respect to the relationship between world population growth and world famine?
   a. Economic growth generally leads to increase in birth rates, thus contributing to the likelihood of world famine.
   b. According to the "Food First" policy, neither technology nor population restriction will prevent future malnutrition for the world's poor.
   c. Julian Simon believes that the fewer people there are, the greater is the long-term likelihood of technological innovations and advances that may help prevent world famine.
   d. By benefiting relatively small farmers, the Green Revolution has done little to counteract the likelihood of world famine associated with continued world population growth.
   e. none of the above

Discussion Questions

1. Explain verbally and graphically how a low price elasticity of demand may result in lower income with a relatively large crop as compared to a small crop.

2. Explain why cartel arrangements are unlikely to be successful where most major crops are concerned.

3. What is meant by farm parity prices? Explain.

4. If we are going to support farmers, would you prefer to see the government use support prices, target prices, and/or production controls? Compare the outcomes and explain your choice.

5. Do you think the government should continue to support farmers? Explain. What do you think would be the consequences of your decision? What do you think would be the consequences of the alternative?

6. Identify and describe ways in which world famine may be prevented. Which one(s) do you find most credible? Discuss.

Answers

Problems and Applications

1. a. $4; 4,000 units; $16,000
   b. 3,000; $5; 2,000; $5; $25,000; $15,000; $10,000
   c. 3,000; $5; $15,000; 3,000; $5; $15,000; $1; $6,000; $21,000; $36,000

2. a. P_1; Q_2; $0P_1WQ_2$
   b. Q_1; P_2; $Q_3 - Q_1$; P_2; $0P_2XQ_3$; $0P_2VQ_1$; Q_1VXQ_3
   c. Q_1; P_2; $0P_2VQ_1$; $Q_4 - Q_1$; P_2; Q_1VZQ_4; $P_3 - P_2$; P_2P_3YZ; $Q_1VZQ_4 + P_2P_3YZ$; $0P_3YQ_4$

3. a. $1; the price increases to $1.50
   b. Total revenue associated with free market output and pricing
      is shown by the area with horizontal lines; total revenue asso-
      ciated with government production controls is shown by the
      shaded area. Total revenue increases as a result of the produc-
      tion controls, indicating that demand is relatively inelastic.

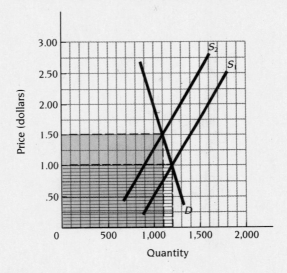

   c. 300 units; $2; $2
   d. 600 units; $2; $2

True-False

1. F. The farm problem has been a recurring one in the United
      States as well as in the rest of the world.
2. T.
3. F. The government abandoned the gold standard in order to
      print money to finance the Civil War.
4. T.
5. F. Although the problems are similar for agricultural-exporting
      countries such as the United States, Canada, Australia, and
      Argentina, agricultural problems in India, the Soviet Union, and
      the African Sahel center around malnutrition and famine.
6. T.
7. F. Farmers typically have complained that they are pure com-
      petitors who must often buy from monopolistic sellers and
      sell to monopsonistic buyers.
8. F. Farmland in the United States tends to be a very nonliquid
      asset.

9. F. Both the price and income elasticities of demand for farm products tend to be relatively low.
10. T.
11. T.
12. F. Cartel arrangements are uncommon for major crops when there are many producers.
13. F. Nonfarm production in the United States was about three times as great as farm production at the turn of the century.
14. T.
15. T.
16. T.
17. T.
18. T.
19. F. Farm price supports in the United States are based on the concept of parity for farm prices and incomes.
20. T.
21. T.
22. F. Approximately two-thirds of American farmers receive no aid from farm supports.
23. F. Since World War II, agricultural productivity per worker has grown more rapidly than American industrial productivity per worker.
24. T.
25. T.
26. T.
27. T.

Multiple Choice

1. c	2. e	3. a	4. e	5. b
6. c	7. d	8. e	9. d	10. b
11. a	12. e	13. c	14. d	15. d
16. c	17. c	18. b	19. b	20. b

37 Natural Resources and the Environment

Summary

Conservation is a major economic problem. Natural resources may be either exhaustible or renewable, depending on the ability of nature to reproduce them. In the case of exhaustible resources, our main concern is the speed with which we utilize these resources. In the case of renewable resources, our main concern is resource management. In addition to these concerns is the concern with protection of the environment from waste generated by production and consumption.

Resource extraction costs tend to rise as an exhaustible resource becomes increasingly scarce. Rising costs tend to reduce the supply of the resource and result in a higher market price. *Ceteris paribus*, the increase in market price will reduce the quantity traded, so that market forces result in a tendency toward conservation. The greater the price elasticity of demand for a particular resource, the greater the tendency toward conservation.

Interest rates also affect the amount of an exhaustible resource that will be traded and therefore the extent of conservation. Resource owners may extract and sell their stock of resources or withhold them in anticipation of a sufficiently higher future price. Assuming equal risk, relatively high interest rates on alternative investments provide an incentive for extraction and sale of the resource in order to finance the alternative investment. When the earnings on alternative investments of equivalent risk are expected to be less than the expected rate of increase in the price of the resource, resource owners will conserve the resources for extraction and sale in the future. That is, relatively low interest rates encourage conservation and high interest rates discourage it.

Interest rates also link resource conservation to other variables in the economy. To a large extent, interest rates are a reflection of the time preferences of potential lenders and the productivity of capital equipment. When a change in one of these variables results in a change in interest rates, conservation of resources is likely to be affected.

Conservation of exhaustible resources is not entirely determined by free and competitive market forces. Government and central bank policies may affect conservation indirectly by influencing interest rates. Government policy may also have a direct impact on conservation through preferential tax treatment and price controls. Price ceilings, for example, tend to encourage conservation of the controlled commodity, *ceteris paribus*. Conservation of resources may also be influenced by the existence of monopoly control. Resource owners often have monopoly control. Furthermore, firms that purchase these resources often have monopoly control. Since firms with monopoly control tend to restrict output in order to charge a higher price, they may promote conservation of natural resources.

In the case of renewable resources, the major concerns are allocating adequate amounts of living space for these resources and determining acceptable rates of harvesting for human use. There is good reason to believe that we, as humans, have made excessive claims on nature and have reduced the supply of renewable natural resources too much. The benefits from expanding the human domain (to the detriment of natural resources) tend to be recognized through the establishment of property rights. The costs of our human expansion, however, tend to be externalized and not clearly recognized.

The second basic concern in the management of renewable resources is determining acceptable harvesting rates for these resources. The annual sustainable-yield curve for a given renewable resource identifies, for each population size, the quantity of the resource that could be harvested without altering the population size. Conservation concerns would suggest that a resource should not be harvested in excess of the maximum sustainable yield.

Once determined, the appropriate harvesting rate for a renewable resource is not likely to be accomplished under a system of common property. Government regulations, such as licensing requirements and quantity restrictions, may be effective. However, there may be difficulties when natural resource habitats extend across borders of different governmental units or when no government has clear jurisdiction. An alternative means to control harvesting may lie in the extension of private property rights. Property owners are inclined to build future interests into their current supply decisions by means of a device called the reservation price.

Production and consumption not only utilize natural resources but also contribute to pollution of the environment. The existence of externalities in waste production and disposal interferes with the use of the free market to guarantee socially efficient outcomes. Consequently, government intervention may be appropriate.

Government action in the form of corrective taxation, effluent charges (waste disposal charges), and/or standards and controls may be used to encourage a more efficient allocation of resources. These regulatory instruments tend to result in higher prices for the goods involved and a corresponding decrease in the quantities demanded. Hence, to some extent at least, the externalities are internalized. Corrective taxes and effluent charges provide a source of revenue for the government. Determining the appropriate amount of tax or effluent charge is one of the limiting factors of these forms of regulation. Standards and controls have the advantage that they enable the government to deal with qualitative issues of externalities as well as quantitative issues. However, standards and controls tend to force uniformity in the production process and provide limited incentives for technological improvement.

Subsidies for waste treatment tend to be used more frequently than corrective taxes and effluent charges. Subsidies seem to be a politically popular approach to dealing with harmful externalities. However, this approach tends to increase, rather than reduce, the amount of waste produced.

Major Objectives

After you have finished this chapter, you will be able to do the following:

1. Define, provide examples of, and distinguish between exhaustible and nonexhaustible resources.
2. Define, provide examples of, and identify the economic problems associated with exhaustible resources.
3. Describe the market for exhaustible resources by indicating the meanings of supply and demand and explaining their slopes.
4. Identify and explain the determinants of the supply of exhaustible resources.
5. Explain how changes in the supply of exhaustible resources affect the equilibrium price and quantity.
6. Explain and resolve the mystery of proven reserves.
7. Explain how the market system automatically encourages the conservation of exhaustible resources.
8. Explain the importance of the price elasticity of demand in the conservation of exhaustible resources.
9. Indicate the effect on exhaustible resources of changes in the price elasticity of demand over time.

10. Explain how interest rates affect the prices of exhaustible natural resources.
11. Define and explain the reservation price and explain how it is determined.
12. Identify and explain the two major forces that determine interest rates.
13. Demonstrate how interest rates relate conservation to other economic values.
14. Explain how government tax and budget policies, central bank policies, and market failures affect conservation of exhaustible resources.
15. Identify and explain government policies that have had an important impact on the rate of extraction of resources in the United States.
16. Describe the experience with natural gas price controls in the United States and compare the actual experiences with economic theory.
17. Describe the experience with oil price controls in the United States and compare the actual experiences with economic theory.
18. Define, provide examples of, and identify the economic problem associated with renewable resources.
19. Explain the concept and discuss the importance of environmental constraints.
20. Explain how the existence of externalities may lead to excessive reduction in the supply of renewable natural resources.
21. Explain how externality problems in natural resource conservation might be resolved.
22. Discuss the difficulties associated with identifying and measuring property rights in the case of natural resources.
23. Explain the concept and discuss the importance of harvesting constraints.
24. Define and explain the concept of the annual sustainable yield.
25. Describe and explain the annual sustainable yield curve and indicate the implications of it.
26. Identify practical ways of moving the economy toward an efficient use of renewable natural resources, explain how these operate, and identify the problems associated with using them.
27. Explain why a system of common property does not move the economy toward an efficient use of renewable natural resources.
28. Discuss and explain the importance of the concept of a reservation price in conserving renewable resources and explain how this price is determined.
29. Discuss the importance of the laws of conservation of energy and matter for a study of waste treatment.

30. Explain and graphically represent the demand for waste disposal services, the supply of waste disposal services, and the marginal cost to society of waste disposal services.
31. Verbally and graphically identify the socially efficient quantity of waste disposal and the equilibrium quantity of waste disposal with and without effluent charges.
32. Discuss the importance of correctly estimating the marginal cost curve to society of waste disposal services.
33. Define effluent and effluent charge and discuss the issues associated with waste disposal.
34. Verbally and graphically explain how the imposition of an effluent charge can lead to equilibrium at the socially efficient level of waste disposal.
35. Identify and explain the advantages and problems associated with the use of effluent charges.
36. Graphically represent the total amount of money paid in effluent charges at equilibrium and the total cost to society of the waste disposal.
37. Explain the purpose of standards and controls, identify the advantages and problems associated with their use, and compare and contrast their use with the use of corrective taxes and effluent charges in dealing with harmful externalities.
38. Discuss the effect of subsidies in dealing with waste treatment, explain their appeal and the problems associated with them.

Review Terms

microeconomic
natural resources
input or factor of production or resource
market system
supply
demand
equilibrium price
equilibrium quantity
change in demand vs. change in quantity demanded
change in supply vs. change in quantity supplied
ceteris paribus
profit
shortage
price elasticity of demand
elastic
inelastic

substitutes
interest rate
discounting
present value
roundabout production
loanable funds
macroeconomic
market failure
monopoly
monopoly control
OPEC
concentration
subsidy
import
price control
inflation
natural monopoly
monopsony
average total cost

marginal cost
economic efficiency
cartel
externalities
free rider
economic growth

derived demand
marginal cost
single-tax
price discrimination
subsidy
vote-trading

Important Terms and Concepts

nonexhaustible natural
  resources
exhaustible natural resources
conservation
rate of use per unit of time
cost of extracting a resource
accessibility of deposits
proven reserves
the mystery of proven reserves
reservation price
time preference
productivity of capital
depletion allowances
Federal Power Commission or
  Federal Energy Regulatory
  Commission
entitlements
renewable resources
constraint
environmental constraint
harvesting constraint
extinction

natural population increase
sustainable annual yield
sustainable annual yield curve
natural equilibrium for a
  population
maximum sustainable annual
  yield
common property
bounty
the law of the conservation of
  matter
the law of the conservation of
  energy
waste disposal
the efficient quantity of waste
  by-products
demand for waste disposal
  services
marginal cost to society of waste
  disposal services
supply of waste disposal services
effluent charge

Completion

exhaustible

how quickly this
stock should be used

rise

conservation

also

encourage

discourage

When there is a fixed stock of a resource, the resource is said to be

_____ . In this case the economic problem is

_____ .

The relative price of an exhaustible natural resource will probably

_____ (rise/fall) as the resource becomes more scarce. This

provides an incentive for _____ of the resource. Inter-

est rates _____ (also/do not) affect conservation of exhaustible

natural resources. Low interest rates _____ (encourage/

discourage) conservation, and high interest rates _____

(encourage/discourage) conservation, *ceteris paribus.* Monopoly power may encourage conservation to the extent that firms with

restrict

monopoly power _____ output.

When nature can replace the quantity of a resource rather quickly,

renewable

the resource is _____ . From the standpoint of economics, the problem is working with nature to maintain adequate

reproduction, growth

_____ and _____ of these resources. Two key issues arise as a result of this concern: first, to determine

living space

the appropriate quantity of _____ to allocate to these resources; second, to determine how rapidly these rescources

harvested

should be _____ for human use. With regard to the first issue, resource habitats may have been reduced too much, thus

interfering with

_____ (encouraging/interfering with) conservation of these resources. This is a potential result of the

property

failure to clearly define _____ rights. With regard to determining the quantities of renewable resources to harvest for for human use, one gains important information from the

sustainable annual yield

_____ curve. This curve identifies the quantities of the resource that may be

harvested, change in the population

_____ without causing a _____ of the species. To conserve the resource, harvesting should not exceed the _____ .

maximum sustainable yield

The economics of waste treatment is greatly influenced by the

conservation, energy

laws of the _____ of _____ and

matter

_____ . The law of the conservation of matter states that the mass of waste material is approximately equal to the mass of

raw materials used in production

_____ . This

change the form

means that production and consumption simply _____ of materials. There is no change in the mass of these materials; all

waste

that is used eventually becomes _____ . Similarly, the law of

redirect

conservation of energy suggests that we can _____ (redirect/

destroy

destroy) energy but cannot _____ (redirect/destroy) it.

These laws of conservation suggest that any action that increases the mass of material taken out of the earth or the amount of energy

increases

diverted from its usual path _____ (decreases/has no necessary effect on/increases) the amount of waste that must finally be put back into the earth or its atmosphere. This lends support to the argument that economic growth should emphasize increases in

services, nonma-
terial satisfactions

_____ and _____
rather than in material goods.

The laws of conservation also suggest that the waste treatment

cannot

industry _____ (can/cannot) reduce the mass or the heat or

can only

other energy aspects of waste. Waste treatment _____
(can also/can only/cannot) move the waste to more acceptable places or process it into more acceptable forms before putting it back into the earth or the atmosphere.

Problems and Applications

1. Consider the graph below, illustrating two potential demand curves for an exhaustible natural resource.
   a. Assume that the supply of the resource is *S* when relatively accessible deposits of the resource are being utilized. What happens to supply as relatively accessible deposits of the resource are used up and resource owners must resort to extracting relatively inaccessible deposits? What happens to the equilibrium price and quantity of the resource for each of the demand curves?
   b. Assuming that resource supply decreases, will conservation of the resource be promoted more when demand is elastic or inelastic?

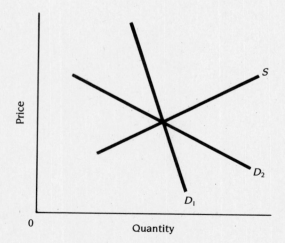

2. Assume that you own a known amount of an exhaustible natural resource. The current market price of the resource enables you to earn $150 per unit after all extraction and marketing costs have been paid. The present rate of interest on securities of equivalent risk is 15 percent.

   a. What is the resource price one year from now if you are indifferent between selling the resource this year and one year from now? Assume that you do not expect extraction and marketing prices to change over the next year.

   b. If you expect next year's resource price to enable you to earn $160 per unit after all extraction and marketing costs have been paid, will you sell the resource this year or hold it for potential sale in one year? What will happen to the current market supply of the resource if other resource owners make similar decisions? What will this do to the current resource price? What will happen to next year's market supply of the resource if other resource owners follow your decision with respect to this year's extraction? What will this do to next year's resource price?

   c. If you expect next year's resource price to enable you to earn $195 per unit after all extraction and marketing costs have been paid, will you sell the resource this year or hold it for potential sale in one year? What is your expected rate of return? What will happen to the current market supply of the resource if other resource owners make similar decisions? What will this do to the current resource price?

   d. Assuming that in the long run the rate of interest on securities of equivalent risk continues to be 15 percent, what will be the expected percentage difference between the resource price from year to year?

3. Consider the graph below, describing the demand for an exhaustible natural resource.
   a. What is the equilibrium price of the resource? How many units will be traded at equilibrium?
   b. Assume that the government imposes a price ceiling at $1 per unit. How many units of the resource will be demanded at the controlled price? How many units will be available for sale at the controlled price? How many units will actually be traded at the ceiling price? What are the implications of the ceiling price for conservation of the resource?

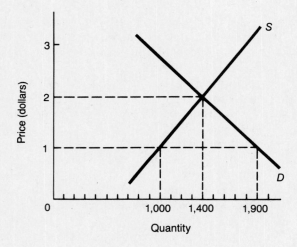

4. Consider the graph below, describing the market for waste disposal service by "Mother Nature." Curve MC_s is the marginal cost to society.

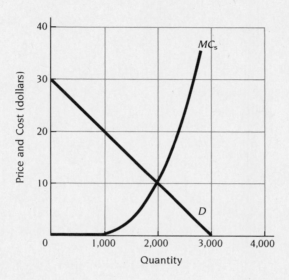

a. What effluent charge will guarantee an efficient quantity of waste disposal?

b. Draw the supply curve for waste disposal service if the effluent charge is $10.

c. Assuming a single per-unit effluent charge of $10, graphically identify the total revenue received by the government as a result of this charge. Also identify the total cost to society of the waste.

d. Assume that the government acts as a price-discriminating monopolist in the imposition of effluent charges. Graphically identify the maximum potential total revenue received by the government if the government imposes effluent charges so as to guarantee production of the efficient quantity of waste disposal services.

True-False   Indicate whether each of the following statements is basically true
or false. If the statement is false, rewrite it so that it is true.

_____   1. Resources are exhaustible if they can be destroyed by our use
or abuse of them.

_____   2. As relatively accessible deposits of a resource are exhausted so
that supply must come from less accessible deposits, the market
supply curve for the resource will shift to the right.

_____   3. A competitive market for an exhaustible natural resource will
tend to conserve the resource when supply of the resource decreases as a result of the increased costs associated with
extracting relatively inaccessible deposits of the resource.

_____   4. A decrease in the supply of a resource will have a greater conservation effect the more inelastic the demand for the resource.

_____   5. Conservation of a resource is easier and more likely better than
the substitutes for the resource.

_____   6. At equilibrium, the yearly increase in the price of an exhaustible
natural resource will equal the rate of interest paid on alternative
investments of equal risk.

_____   7. As interest rates on alternative investments of equal risk rise, the
difference between the future and current prices of exhaustible
resources decreases.

_____   8. When people's preference for future consumption rises in relation to current consumption, interest rates tend to fall.

_____   9. The budget policies of the federal government may affect the
supply of loanable funds but are not likely to affect the demand
for these funds.

_____   10. Conservation efforts are hindered by monopoly control in output markets that utilize exhaustible resources.

_____   11. As a result of depletion allowances, resource owners need not
count the entire value of extracted resources as income.

_____   12. Preferential tax treatment that allows owners of exhaustible
natural resources immediate tax deductions for the expenses of
unsuccessful searches tends to discourage conservation.

_____   13. Price controls on natural gas in the United States have typically
resulted in market prices in excess of equilibrium prices.

_____   14. Renewable resources can normally be replaced by nature rather
quickly.

_____   15. When human intrusion in nature's domain is characterized by
private benefits and external costs, we are likely to reduce the
supply of renewable natural resources too much.

_____ 16. Control over the harvesting of renewable resources refers to control over the quantities of these resources that can be taken during a period of time for human use.

_____ 17. The sustainable annual yield curve is positively sloped throughout.

_____ 18. Efficient conservation of renewable resources suggests that harvesting of resources should not exceed the maximum sustainable annual yield.

_____ 19. A system of common property gives rise to externality problems.

_____ 20. Externalities result in an efficient allocation of resources from the standpoint of society at large.

_____ 21. A corrective tax imposed on a good characterized by harmful externalities will cause the externalities to be internalized if the tax shifts the private marginal-cost curve so that it coincides with the demand curve.

_____ 22. A misallocation of resources always involves more than just one good or service.

_____ 23. The reallocation of resources that results from the corrective taxation of a good with negative externalities typically means that there will be additional jobs in the industry producing the good.

_____ 24. If we assume that a certain volume of waste can be handled without damage to nature's existing ecological system, the marginal-cost curve will be vertical at that volume.

_____ 25. If the harmful effects of waste are overestimated, the marginal cost to society would be overestimated and we would justify the production of too much waste.

_____ 26. If the marginal-cost curve for nature's waste disposal service underestimates the effects of wastes, then the marginal-cost curve should be shifted to the left, resulting in a decrease in the efficient quantity.

_____ 27. The costs of waste disposal are primarily private costs.

_____ 28. Effluent charges are effective primarily because they force consumers of waste-producing products to bear the costs of waste disposal.

_____ 29. Though it may be difficult to determine the location of the demand curve for waste disposal services, the marginal cost to society of waste disposal is easily ascertained.

_____ 30. One reason why standards and controls are used frequently for dealing with harmful externalities is that they may be politically more acceptable than corrective taxes and effluent charges.

_____ 31. Treatment facilities tend to increase the social costs of waste.

_____ 32. The major criticism of government subsidization of waste treatment facilities is that it tends to increase the quantity of waste.

_____ 33. As the price of dumping waste materials increases, prices for consuming waste-producing goods are likely to increase and thereby limit the extent of waste production.

Multiple Choice   Choose the *one best* answer in each of the following cases:

_____ 1. If upon use a natural resource cannot be regenerated by natural processes within a reasonable time span, the resource is said to be
   a. exhaustible.
   b. regenerative.
   c. degenerative.
   d. nonproductive.
   e. renewable.

Use the following graph to answer questions 2 and 3.

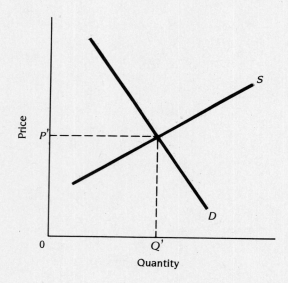

_____ 2. In the graph above, representing a market for an exhaustible natural resource, one can conclude that a movement to the right along the horizontal axis will result in a decrease in the
   a. demand for the resource.
   b. quantity of the resource demanded.
   c. quantity of the resource supplied.

    d. rate at which the resource is used.

    e. quantity of the resource that will be available for future generations.

_____ 3. In the graph, one can conclude that

    a. the equilibrium price is P'.

    b. the equilibrium quantity is Q'.

    c. there is a shortage of the resource at prices below P'.

    d. the supply curve represents the willingness of resource owners to extract the resource from its natural state.

    e. all of the above

_____ 4. An increase in the cost of extracting an exhaustible natural resource, *ceteris paribus*, will most likely result in a(n)

    a. decrease in the supply of the resource.

    b. increase in the demand for the resource.

    c. decrease in the equilibrium price of the resource.

    d. increase in the quantity of the resource demanded.

    e. all of the above

_____ 5. *Ceteris paribus*, as relatively accessible deposits of a resource are exhausted and supply must come from less accessible deposits, the

    a. price of the resource will tend to fall.

    b. quantity of the resource demanded will rise.

    c. quantity of the resource supplied will rise.

    d. all of the above

    e. quantity of the resource traded will tend to fall.

_____ 6. *Ceteris paribus*, improvements in the technology of extracting a resource will tend to result in a decrease in the

    a. supply of the resource.

    b. demand for the resource.

    c. equilibrium price of the resource.

    d. equilibrium quantity of the resource.

    e. none of the above

Use the graph below to answer question 7.

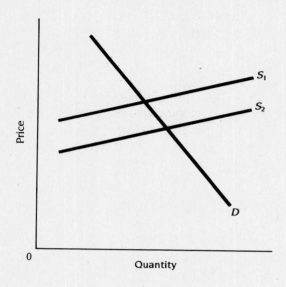

7. Consider the graph above, describing the market for an exhaustible natural resource. The shift in the supply curve from S_1 to S_2 could most likely be caused by a(n)
   a. decrease in the price of the resource.
   b. change in the quantity demanded of the resource.
   c. increase in the cost of extracting the resource.
   d. all of the above
   e. improvement in the technology of extracting the resource.

8. The price elasticity of demand for a resource increases
   a. over time.
   b. with increased availability of substitute resources.
   c. both a and b above
   d. as the resource becomes relatively cheaper.
   e. none of the above

9. Use of the market to encourage conservation of exhaustible resources is likely to be more effective
   a. the cheaper the resources.
   b. the more specialized the resources.
   c. the more inelastic the demand for resources.
   d. over time as the price elasticity of demand increases.
   e. the more limited the existence of substitute resources.

_____ 10. Proven reserves refer to
    a. resources that are renewable.
    b. resources that have been extracted.
    c. the current excess supply of resources.
    d. the known available amounts of resources.
    e. resources that have been shown to be effective inputs.

_____ 11. The mystery of proven reserves refers to the fact that
    a. proven reserves are both renewable and exhaustible.
    b. the quantity of proven reserves demanded decreases as the price of the reserves decreases.
    c. the amount of proven reserves often seems to increase even though exhaustible natural resources continue to be extracted.
    d. the reserves are especially difficult to locate, relatively costly to extract, and not particularly efficient in production.
    e. though they have been shown to be effective inputs, proven reserves are never utilized in the production process.

_____ 12. *Ceteris paribus*, the difference between the future and current prices of an exhaustible natural resource will
    a. approach zero at equilibrium.
    b. be larger the higher the interest rate on alternative investments of equivalent risk.
    c. reach its maximum value as the interest rate on alternative investments of equivalent risk approaches zero.
    d. approach the reservation price of the resource as the interest rate on alternative investments of equivalent risk increases.
    e. none of the above

_____ 13. The reservation price of an exhaustible natural resource refers to the
    a. maximum price of the resource.
    b. maximum future price of the resource.
    c. expected future price of the resource.
    d. interest rate paid on alternative investments of equal risk.
    e. none of the above

_____ 14. In the market for loanable funds, the
    a. price of funds is measured by the reservation price of capital.
    b. demand for funds will change when there is a change in the interest rate.
    c. quantity of funds demanded will change with changes in the productivity of capital.
    d. supply of funds will change when there is a change in the time preferences of lenders.
    e. all of the above

_____ 15. When interest rates fall as a result of a rise in the preference for future consumption in relation to current consumption, the
  a. future price of exhaustible resources will rise.
  b. current price of exhaustible resources will rise.
  c. future supply of exhaustible resources will fall.
  d. current supply of exhaustible resources will rise.
  e. rate of extraction of exhaustible resources will rise.

_____ 16. When interest rates rise as a result of a rise in the preference for current consumption in relation to future consumption, the
  a. rate of extraction of exhaustible resources will rise.
  b. current and future prices of exhaustible resources will rise.
  c. both a and b above
  d. rate of extraction of exhaustible resources will most likely be unaffected.
  e. difference between the future and current prices of exhaustible resources will lessen.

_____ 17. Assume that there is an improvement in technology that increases the productivity of physical capital. One could accurately conclude that the
  a. interest rate will fall.
  b. demand for loanable funds will increase.
  c. current price of exhaustible resources will rise.
  d. rate of extraction of exhaustible resources will fall.
  e. none of the above

_____ 18. Interest rates are likely to be affected by
  a. the demand for cash.
  b. government budget policies.
  c. the supply of loanable funds.
  d. the demand for loanable funds.
  e. all of the above

_____ 19. Conservation of exhaustible resources is
  a. always aided by the existence of monopoly control in output markets that utilize these resources.
  b. usually aided by the existence of monopoly control in output markets that utilize these resources.
  c. generally hindered by the existence of monopoly control in output markets that utilize these resources.
  d. generally hindered by the existence of monopoly control in the resource market.
  e. both c and d above

_____ 20. Conservation of domestic exhaustible natural resources would likely be encouraged by
    a. price ceilings.
    b. depletion allowances.
    c. tax deductions for unsuccessful searches.
    d. import quotas on foreign supplies of the resources.
    e. none of the above

_____ 21. Depletion allowances
    a. tend to encourage conservation.
    b. are applicable only when resources are extracted.
    c. require owners of exhaustible natural resources to pay a special tax as they deplete the reserves of the resources.
    d. all of the above
    e. require buyers of exhaustible natural resources to pay a special tax to discourage depletion of the resources.

Use the following graph to answer question 22.

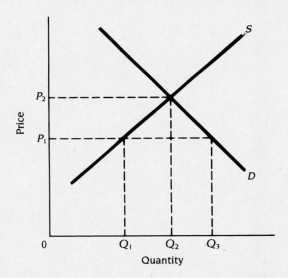

_____ 22. Consider the market for an exhaustible natural resource described by the graph above. Assuming that government price controls prevent the price from rising above P_1, one can accurately conclude that
    a. demand for the resource will increase.
    b. a shortage of the resource will develop.
    c. quantity traded at the controlled price is Q_3.
    d. quantity demanded at the controlled price is Q_1.
    e. conservation of the resource is discouraged by the artificially low price.

_____ 23. U.S. price controls on oil after the OPEC embargo in 1973
    a. brought stability to the market.
    b. encouraged U.S. extraction of oil.
    c. discouraged U.S. extraction of oil.
    d. eliminated the previous system of entitlements.
    e. resulted in a uniform price for domestic and imported oil.

Use the following graph to answer questions 24 and 25.

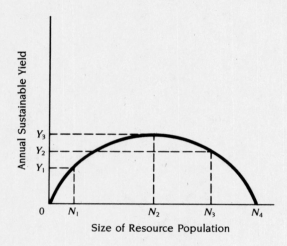

_____ 24. Consider the graph above, showing the sustainable annual yield
curve of a renewable natural resource. According to this graph,
    a. at the origin the annual natural population increase is
       maximized.
    b. at a resource population size of N_2, the birth rate equals the
       death rate.
    c. as the resource population increases in size between N_2 and
       N_4, the death rate exceeds the birth rate.
    d. at a resource population size of N_3, we could harvest Y_2 units
       of the resource without lowering the population size.
    e. none of the above

_____ 25. According to the graph,
    a. at the origin the species is extinct.
    b. at a population size of N_1, births exceed deaths.
    c. as the population size rises beyond N_2, the death rate rises.
    d. at a population size of N_4, the annual natural population
       increase is zero.
    e. all of the above

_____ 26. A reservation price for a renewable natural resource
    a. is a government-imposed price floor designed to promote conservation.
    b. identifies the price of a renewable resource under a system of common property.
    c. permits a private resource owner to consider future interests in current supply decisions.
    d. is a government-imposed price ceiling designed to encourage harvesting at the maximum sustainable annual yield.
    e. none of the above

_____ 27. An effluent charge is the
    a. cost of producing an effluent.
    b. price charged for buying an effluent.
    c. monetary cost of preventing negative externalities.
    d. price charged for using nature's waste disposal service.
    e. none of the above

_____ 28. The demand for nature's waste disposal service is
    a. a derived demand.
    b. equal to the demand for those goods that produce the waste.
    c. both a and b above
    d. a direct relationship between the quantity of service and the effluent charge.
    e. all of the above

_____ 29. The marginal cost to society of nature's waste disposal service is
    a. negatively sloped throughout.
    b. negatively sloped at high levels of waste.
    c. zero at relatively high levels of waste, since there are decreasing costs in the production of waste disposal services.
    d. zero at relatively low levels of waste, if one assumes that a limited amount of waste can be handled within the ecological system.
    e. zero at relatively low levels of waste, since all costs will be borne in the market by the private individuals and firms who buy the responsible goods.

Use the graph below to answer question 30.

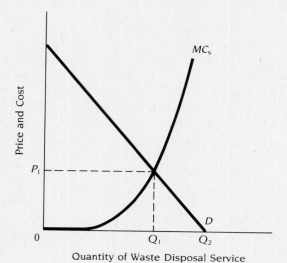

Quantity of Waste Disposal Service

_____ 30. Which of the following statements is true with respect to the graph above, describing a market for nature's waste disposal service?
   a. If waste disposal services are provided at zero price, the efficient quantity is Q_2.
   b. For waste disposal services between Q_1 and Q_2 units, the benefits exceed the costs.
   c. The benefits associated with a volume of waste disposal greater than Q_2 exceed the costs.
   d. An effluent charge of P_1 will result in an efficient quantity of waste disposal service at equilibrium.
   e. If the price of waste disposal is greater than P_1, the equilibrium quantity of waste disposal service will be greater than Q_1.

_____ 31. The use of standards and controls in dealing with waste disposal
   a. is limited to rules governing the characteristics of goods.
   b. directly utilizes the profit motive to encourage corrective action.
   c. is generally favored because of the uniformity of standards and controls.
   d. tends to provide a good incentive for firms to develop better methods of waste treatment or new production methods that generate less waste.
   e. none of the above

_____ 32. Reliance on standards and controls in the handling of waste disposal problems is criticized because
    a. it tends to result in too much uniformity in production methods.
    b. standards and controls directly utilize the profit motive to encourage corrective action.
    c. standards and controls allow the government to address qualitative as well as quantitative concerns.
    d. standards and controls are not politically acceptable.
    e. all of the above

_____ 33. Government subsidization of waste treatment
    a. tends to increase the market price of waste disposal.
    b. tends to reduce the amount of waste generated.
    c. often concentrates the benefits in local areas while spreading the tax costs over larger areas.
    d. all of the above
    e. none of the above

_____ 34. When waste materials are dumped,
    a. there are no problems with externalities.
    b. there are likely to be problems with externalities.
    c. problems with externalities arise only if property rights are clearly established.
    d. both b and c above
    e. all of the costs are internalized by the private individuals and firms that purchase the waste-producing goods.

Discussion Questions

1. Explain the importance of the price elasticity of demand for an exhaustible natural resource in terms of conservation of that resource.

2. Resolve the mystery of proven reserves.

3. Define the reservation price of a resource and explain how it is determined. What is the effect of a reservation price on conservation of the resource?

4. Explain how depletion allowances encourage the extraction of natural resources.

5. What does the economist mean by a "shortage" of a resource? Would you recommend the use of public policy to eliminate shortages? Are there situations in which shortages might be desirable? Explain.

6. Discuss the history and consequences of the use of price controls in the United States for the purpose of promoting conservation of resources.

7. What is the relationship between externalities and the supply of renewable natural resources? Would you recommend government action to promote internalization of these externalities? If so, what form of government action would you recommend? Why?

8. Explain how the imposition of an effluent charge can lead to equilibrium at the socially efficient level of waste disposal. What are the major problems associated with attempting to identify the appropriate charge?

9. Explain and distinguish between the marginal cost to society of waste disposal services and the supply of waste disposal services.

10. Explain how the government might increase its revenue by acting like a price discriminating monopolist in the imposition of effluent charges.

Answers

Problems and Applications

1. a. supply decreases; price increases and quantity decreases for each demand curve
   b. elastic

2. a. $172.50
   b. sell this year; current supply increases; this year's price decreases; next year's supply decreases; next year's price increases
   c. hold it for potential sale next year; 30 percent; current supply decreases; current price increases
   d. 15 percent

3. a. $2; 1,400 units
   b. 1,900 units; 1,000 units; 1,000 units; ceiling price promotes conservation and creates a shortage of the resource

4. a. $10 per unit

   b.

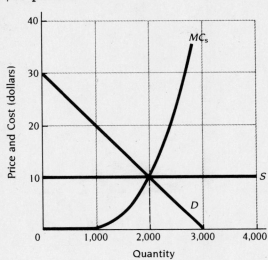

   c. In the graph below, total revenue is shown by the shaded area. Total cost is shown by the area with vertical lines.

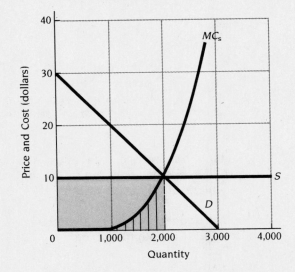

d. On the graph below, maximum potential total revenue is
shown by the shaded area.

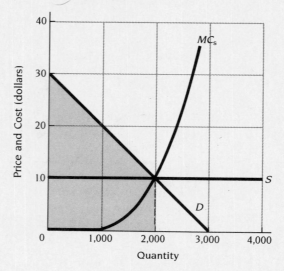

True-False

1. T.
2. F. As relatively accessible deposits of a resource are exhausted
   so that supply must come from less accessible deposits, the
   market supply curve for the resource will shift to the left.
3. T.
4. F. A decrease in the supply of a resource will have a greater
   conservation effect the more elastic the demand for the resource.
5. T.
6. T.
7. F. As interest rates on alternative investments of equal risk rise,
   the difference between the future and current prices of nonre-
   newable resources increases.
8. T.
9. F. The budget policies of the federal government are likely to
   affect both the supply of and the demand for loanable funds.
10. F. Conservation efforts are probably aided by monopoly con-
    trol in output markets that utilize nonrenewable resources, since
    monopolists typically restrict output. However, this is not a cer-
    tain consequence of monopoly control, since the ultimate effect
    on conservation may be affected by the specific situation, the

particular policies of the firms involved, and the impact of government policies.

11. T.
12. T.
13. F. Price controls on natural gas in the United States have typically resulted in market prices below equilibrium prices.
14. T.
15. T.
16. T.
17. F. The sustainable annual yield curve is positively sloped until environmental constraints cause the death rate to rise sufficiently to lower the annual natural population increase.
18. T.
19. T.
20. F. Externalities result in an inefficient allocation of resources from the standpoint of society at large.
21. F. A corrective tax imposed on a good characterized by harmful externalities will cause the externalities to be internalized if the tax shifts the private marginal cost curve so that it coincides with the social marginal cost curve.
22. T.
23. F. The reallocation of resources that results from the corrective taxation of a good with negative externalities typically means that there will be fewer jobs in the industry producing the good.
24. F. If we assume that a certain volume of waste can be handled without damage to nature's existing ecological system, the marginal-cost curve will be zero up to that volume (that is, it will coincide with the horizontal axis).
25. F. If the harmful effects of waste are underestimated, the marginal cost to society would be underestimated and we would justify the production of too much waste; if the harmful effects of waste are overestimated, the marginal cost to society would be overestimated and we would not make full and efficient use of available natural resources.
26. T.
27. F. The costs of waste disposal are primarily external costs.
28. T.
29. F. The greatest technical problem with effluent charges is determining the marginal cost to society of waste disposal; accurately determining the demand for waste disposal services may also be difficult.
30. T.
31. F. Treatment facilities tend to decrease the social costs of waste.
32. T.
33. T.

Multiple Choice

1. a	2. e	3. e	4. a	5. e
6. c	7. e	8. c	9. d	10. d
11. c	12. b	13. e	14. d	15. b
16. a	17. b	18. e	19. b	20. a
21. b	22. b	23. c	24. d	25. e
26. c	27. d	28. a	29. d	30. d
31. e	32. b	33. c	34. b	

38 Comparative Economic Systems—More Planning or Less?

Summary

Economic systems may be distinguished in accordance with ownership or mechanism bases. In terms of the ownership basis, economies may be capitalist or collectivist (including socialist and syndicalist). Capitalist systems are characterized by private ownership of land and physical capital. In collectivist systems, land and physical capital are owned by collective bodies. In the case of socialism, the government is the collective body; in the case of syndicalism, labor unions are the owners.

In terms of the mechanism basis, economies are typically planned or market systems. An economy is planned only when some individual or organization in a public position plans for others who have little to say about the plan and whose economic freedom is restricted by the planning decision. A market economy relies on the interplay of supply and demand to answer the basic economic questions.

Though most collectivist economies are planned, they can be market systems. Similarly, though most capitalist economies rely primarily on market forces, they can be planned. Our current concern is with planned economies.

There are five major types of planning. Imperative planning is the most rigorous form. It is imperative in the sense that a plan is considered to be a command. Imperative planning goes beyond the aggregate economy to include the fine structure of the economy as a whole and its regions. Indicative planning, which is usually consensual, operates basically by convincing participants that it is in their best interests to follow the plan. As the name suggests, public-sector planning covers only the public sector. However, there are important consequences for the private sector. Macroeconomic planning leaves microeconomic decisions to the market. This type of planning involves setting target quantities for standard national income measures such as gross national product. Finally, planning is said to be magic-wand planning when it is built around a collection of projects and/or an appealing slogan.

The Soviet Union provides an example of a planned collectivist economy that uses imperative planning. Planning is centralized under Gosplan. In order to coordinate the parts of a plan, the Soviets rely on materials balancing and input-output analysis. The major problems with Soviet planning are low productivity, a sacrifice of quality for quantity, and rigidity in the plans. Soviet planning has become less rigid since the death of Stalin, though the changes are less pronounced in the USSR itself than in Soviet-bloc countries of Eastern Europe and China. The principal reforms are sometimes referred to as Libermanism.

The history of the United States has not been devoid of economic planning. Businesspeople and academics led a move for increased planning during the Great Depression of the 1930s. The desire for planning seemed to revive with the stagflation of the 1970s.

Japan and Sweden both provide examples of planned capitalism, though their experiences are markedly different. Japan's long-range plans are purely indicative. They are formulated by the Economic Planning Agency with information from other government departments, business firms and organizations, agricultural organizations and their government representatives, and from the Ministry of Agriculture and Forestry. Workers and consumers are not really involved in the actual planning. As long as they operate within the plan, the government protects large Japanese companies against failure, forced cutbacks, and "excessive competition." Labor productivity in Japan is especially high, and because the typical (male) worker is hired for life, employers tend to have good reason to invest in human capital.

Sweden is noted for being a welfare state. This means that it places high priority on an equitable distribution of income and wealth and on a secure living standard. The Swedish mixed economy remains largely capitalist, with laboristic features. Most Swedish planning is short term, indicative, and consensual. The Meidner Plan would move Sweden in the direction of collectivism. It would increase corporate income taxes, giving the revenues to trade unions, which would use them to buy shares in Swedish corporations.

Yugoslavia and China provide examples of market forces operating under socialism. In Yugoslavia, though natural and physical capital resources are publicly owned, many of these resources are leased to and operated by workers' collectives. These collectives make their own hiring, pricing, and output decisions, and they elect their own managers. Central economic authorities enforce minimum income levels for participants in the cooperatives. They judge the credit-worthiness of firms and keep them from wasting resources. Macro-economic planning includes the goal of bringing Yugoslav republics closer together.

China's capitalist roaders have introduced changes in Chinese communism. Though the state still owns agricultural land, it leases plots to individual families. One is no longer required to join collec-tive farms or communes. Workers continue to be assigned in batches and receive fixed wages; full employment is still officially enforced, but one may have to wait months for a work assignment. A one-child policy has been imposed on urban families. Foreign companies have been invited to operate in special economic zones.

The Lange-Lerner model is an adaptation of the microeconomics of pure competition to a socialist system. Under this system, prices would be set by public authorities, but they would be changed when necessary to approximate the equilibrium conditions that character-ize a market economy.

The Austrian school basically is against planning, maintaining that planning becomes increasingly arbitrary and dictatorial and eventu-ally gives rise to "serfdom." This school is criticized by many who support planning. The simplest argument for planning is the claim that the benefits of planning are worth the costs.

Major Objectives   After you have finished this chapter, you will be able to do the following:

1. Identify and discuss the six social goals suggested by the authors.
2. Identify and explain the criteria for determining whether or not an economy is planned.
3. Distinguish between freedom and power.
4. Define and distinguish between collectivism, socialism, commu-nism, and capitalism.
5. Define and distinguish between planned and market economies.
6. Define, distinguish, and provide examples of planned collectiv-ism, planned capitalism, market collectivism, and market capitalism.
7. Define and explain the concept of a welfare state.
8. Identify, explain, distinguish, and provide examples of the five major types of planning.
9. Briefly describe planned collectivism as practiced in the Soviet Union.
10. Explain the purpose and functioning of Gosplan.
11. Explain and distinguish between materials balancing and input-output analysis.

12. Describe, construct, and interpret simple input-output tables.
13. Identify and discuss the problems in Soviet planning and explain the concept of a leading links system.
14. Explain and discuss Libermanism.
15. Explain the role of communes in planned collectivism.
16. Identify four conditions under which procapitalists might support planning.
17. Briefly describe planned capitalism as practiced in Japan and Sweden.
18. Identify and discuss major problems in the Japanese economy.
19. Explain what is meant by "laboristic" features in the Swedish economy.
20. Explain what is meant by codetermination in corporate decision making.
21. Explain what is meant by consensual macroeconomic planning in Sweden.
22. Identify and discuss the major problems with Swedish planning.
23. Describe, discuss, and indicate the arguments against the Meidner Plan.
24. Briefly describe market socialism as practiced in Yugoslavia.
25. Define and discuss anarchism.
26. Explain and discuss the role of workers' collectives in Yugoslavia.
27. Identify and discuss the major weaknesses of the Yugoslav system.
28. Briefly describe market socialism as practiced in China.
29. Discuss the role of "special economic zones" in China.
30. Describe and discuss the Lange-Lerner theory of markets under socialism and distinguish it from pure competition.
31. Identify and discuss the major criticisms of the Lange-Lerner theory.
32. Explain and discuss the Austrian view of planning.
33. Explain why Hayek thinks planning leads to serfdom.
34. Identify and discuss the major criticisms of the Austrian view of planning.

Review Terms	scarcity	income
	market economy	wealth
	planned economy	input or factor of production
	traditional economy	or resource
	pure economy	land
	mixed economy	physical capital
	normative	monopoly
	growth	competition
	equity	aggregate

private sector
public sector
macroeconomic
productivity
craft unions
European Community
protectionism
capital
strike
wage differential
transfer payments
trade union

syndicalism
featherbedding
subsidy
monopoly power
microeconomics
pure competition
equilibrium
marginal cost
marginal revenue product
short run
shutdown
long run

Important Terms and Concepts

"magic-wand" planning
planning
freedom
power
collectivism
socialism
capitalism
communism
planned collectivism
planned capitalism
market capitalism
market collectivism
welfare state
imperative planning
the "fine structure" of an
    economy
indicative planning
consensual
public-sector planning
macroeconomic planning
Humphrey-Hawkins bill
Gosplan
materials balancing technique
input-output analysis
input-output table
leading links system
LDCs
Libermanism

cooperatives
dual economy
communes
National Recovery
    Administration
nationalization
"Japan, Incorporated"
Ministry of International Trade
    and Industry (MITI)
"excessive competition"
"administrative guidance"
"dead wood"
laboristic
codetermination
consensual
first-best assumptions
the Meidner Plan
anarchism
"capitalist roaders"
"iron rice bowl"
"assignment problems"
"special economic zones"
the Lange-Lerner theory
social dividend
individualist
the Austrian school
"serfdom"

Completion

planned

An economy is _____ only when some individual or organization in a public position plans for another individual or organiza-

economic freedom

tion that has little say about the plan and whose _____ is restricted by the planning decision. Public planning, when carried out through laws and regulations, may be more or less restrictive of freedom than private planning, when carried out through

market forces, are not

_____ . Freedom and power _____ (are/are not) synonymous. You may be free to do something but be

powerless

_____ to exercise that freedom. Alternatively, having the power to do something does not guarantee that you have the

freedom, power

_____ to do it. Planners often do not have the _____

free

to carry out the plans that they are _____ to make.
    When economic systems are distinguished in accordance with the

market, planned

mechanism basis, they are typically _____ or _____ . Economic systems may also be distinguished in accordance with who

land, physical capital

owns the _____ and _____ . When land and machinery can be privately owned, the system is said to be

capitalist, collectivist

_____ . The system is _____ when

Socialism

land and machinery are owned by collective bodies. _____ is a particular type of collectivist system in which the government is the collective body that owns the land and physical capital. Syndi-

labor unions

calism is a particular type of collectivism in which _____ own the land and machinery.

collectivist

    Most planned economies are _____ and most of

socialist, capitalist

these are _____ . Most market economies are _____ .

is

It _____ (is/is not) possible to have planned capitalism. Further-

is

more, it _____ (is/is not) possible to have market collectivism. Just as people often confuse planning with socialism and a reliance

planning

on market forces with capitalism, they also associate _____ (planning/market forces) with the welfare state. In fact,

any type of economy

_____ can be a welfare state. A welfare state is an economy that places an especially high

equity, income and wealth

value on _____ in the distribution of _____

security

and on _____ of the standard of living.

There are a number of situations in which businesspeople and pro-capitalists might desire planning. One is when an economy is experi-

depression

encing a serious and prolonged _____ . Planning might be desirable to a businessperson when the economy is preparing for,

war

in the midst of, and readjusting after a major _____ . Planning might also be desirable to a businessperson when there is a wide-

economic growth

spread desire to speed up _____ beyond what the market provides. Finally, planning may be desirable to a business-person when there is a desire to ensure that political power will be held by moderates more dedicated to planning than to

socialization

_____ .

There are several major types of planning. The most rigorous form

imperative

is _____ planning. This type of planning goes beyond

fine structure

the aggregate economy to include the _____ of the economy as a whole and its regions. When planning operates mainly by convincing plan participants that following the plan will

indicative

help them economically, it is _____ planning. This type

consensual

of planning is also usually _____ , meaning that the planning authority includes representatives of various interest groups as well as civil servants and planning technicians. Planning that covers

public-sector

only the public sector is _____ planning. The

is also

private sector _____ (is also/is not) affected by this type of

sell to and buy from

planning, because private firms _____ public agencies and because the plan gives the public sector priority

strategic, imported

over _____ and _____ resources. A less

macroeconomic

ambitious type of planning is _____ planning. In this case, planned or target quantities generally include the standard

national income

_____ measures, but the fine structure of

market

the aggregates is left to the _____ . Macroeconomic planning

forecasting

generally includes _____ the consequences of

policies

current _____ or the results of certain changes that have been

is not

proposed. Technically, forecasting _____ (is/is not) planning. Finally, when planning is built around a collection of projects and/or

magic-wand

an appealing slogan, it is called _____ planning.

Problems and Applications

1. Consider the information in the following table, taken from an input-output table describing Eyeoh.

		Using Industry		
		X	Y	Z
Supplying Industry	X	0.1	0.2	0.0
	Y	0.2	0.3	0.4
	Z	0.1	0.0	0.0

   a. How much of the output of Industry X does Industry X use to produce a unit of output?
   b. How many units of X are needed to produce one unit of Z?
   c. How many units of Z are needed to produce one unit of X?
   d. How many units of Y are needed to produce one unit of Y?
   e. What percentage of its own output is used by Industry Z?
   f. What percentage of the output of Industry Z is used by Industry Y?

2. Assume that there are only three goods in Teetopia: tics, tacs, and toes. The production of any one of these goods requires, at most, the good itself, the other two goods, and labor. Assume that the production of a dollar's worth of tics requires 10 cents' worth of tics, 20 cents' worth of tacs, 30 cents' worth of toes, and 40 cents' worth of labor. The production of one dollar's worth of tacs requires 30 cents' worth of tacs, 20 cents' worth of toes, 30 cents' worth of labor, and an unidentified amount of tics. The production of one dollar's worth of toes requires 30 cents' worth of tics, 40 cents' worth of tacs, 10 cents' worth of labor, and an unidentified amount of toes. Complete the following input-output table for Teetopia, indicating the unidentified information.

		Using Industry			
		Tics	Tacs	Toes	Other Demand
Supplying Industry	Tics				0.4
	Tacs				0.1
	Toes				0.3
	Labor				0.2

True-False   Indicate whether each of the following statements is basically true or false. If the statement is false, rewrite it so that it is true.

_____   1. An economy is planned whenever an organization in a public position plans for others.

_____   2. Public planning carried out through laws and regulations is more restrictive of freedom than private planning carried out through market forces.

_____   3. The issue of freedom versus power arises whenever the protection of someone's freedom interferes with someone else's planning power, or vice versa.

_____   4. Most collectivist economies are socialistic.

_____   5. Imperative planning is concerned solely with the aggregate economy.

_____   6. Indicative planning typically relies on a system of penalties to assure that a plan is followed.

_____   7. Planning is technically equivalent to forecasting.

_____   8. The Humphrey-Hawkins bill is an example of magic-wand planning.

_____   9. Under Lenin, imperative planning in the USSR seemed to adhere to a belief that business administration could be reduced to the clerical routine of office management if firms had sufficient information and no competition.

_____ 10. Liberplan is the Russian agency that has responsibility for imperative planning.

_____ 11. Plans in Russia are always for five-year intervals.

_____ 12. Libermanism refers to principal reforms in Soviet-style planning.

_____ 13. The Chinese system of planning is more centralized than the Russian system.

_____ 14. When people speak of "Japan, Incorporated," they are most likely referring to the fact that big business has an important influence on Japanese planning.

_____ 15. In Sweden, most indicative plans are five-year plans.

_____ 16. In Sweden, corporations may invest special reserves tax free in parts of the economy where there is underemployment and surplus labor.

_____ 17. Anarchists propose to abolish all forms of government.

_____ 18. Labor-managed firms of the Yugoslav type tend to maximize net income per worker.

_____ 19. Labor-managed firms of the Yugoslav type are likely to use relatively large amounts of labor.

_____ 20. China now requires that everyone belong to collective farms or communes.

_____ 21. Hayek maintains that planning leads to serfdom and that "the worst get on top."

Multiple Choice   Choose the *one best* answer in each of the following cases:

_____ 1. In collectivist economies, land and physical capital are
    a. nonexistent.
    b. owned by the government.
    c. owned by collective agencies.
    d. owned privately by individuals.
    e. owned by private business firms.

_____ 2. Which of the following is a characteristic of socialism?
    a. equivalent to communism
    b. equivalent to the welfare state
    c. land and physical capital owned by labor unions
    d. all of the above
    e. land and physical capital owned by the government

_____ 3. A capitalist economy
    a. can never be planned.
    b. must be a market system.
    c. is characterized by private ownership of capital.
    d. all of the above
    e. both a and b above

_____ 4. A welfare state
    a. has no poverty.
    b. may be a market economy.
    c. must be a planned economy.
    d. requires government ownership of physical capital.
    e. requires an equal distribution of income and wealth.

_____ 5. Imperative planning is
    a. always consensual.
    b. limited to the public sector.
    c. less rigorous than macroeconomic planning.
    d. likely to treat failure to reach an important target as a criminal offense.
    e. like macroeconomic planning in that it deals only with the aggregate economy.

_____ 6. Most peacetime planning under capitalism is
   a. imperative planning.
   b. indicative planning.
   c. magic-wand planning.
   d. public-sector planning.
   e. macroeconomic planning.

_____ 7. Public-sector planning
   a. has no impact on the private sector.
   b. never takes place in mixed economies.
   c. is the most rigorous form of planning.
   d. is fairly easy to enact, because there are no conflicting interests.
   e. none of the above

_____ 8. Macroeconomic planning
   a. generally includes forecasting.
   b. is also known as magic-wand planning.
   c. can exist only in collectivist systems.
   d. is usually more rigorous than imperative planning.
   e. is exemplified by the "fourth national plan" proposed for Japan by Herman Kahn.

_____ 9. The Soviet Union is an example of
   a. pure socialism.
   b. market socialism.
   c. market capitalism.
   d. planned capitalism.
   e. planned collectivism.

_____ 10. Japan is an example of
   a. pure socialism.
   b. market socialism.
   c. market capitalism.
   d. planned capitalism.
   e. planned collectivism.

_____ 11. Of the following, market socialism is best exemplified by
   a. Japan.
   b. Sweden.
   c. Yugoslavia.
   d. the Soviet Union.
   e. the United States.

_____ 12. Imperative planning in Russia under Lenin
   a. essentially viewed the economy as a huge factory.
   b. decentralized planning under the leadership of Gosplan.
   c. relied on profit maximization to ensure the maximization of social welfare.
   d. recognized a need to provide education and training in economics and statistics for the average worker.
   e. none of the above

_____ 13. Gosplan is
   a. subdivided along regional lines.
   b. subdivided along industrial lines.
   c. the planning agency for the Russian economy.
   d. the final authority for input and output decisions of individual Russian factories.
   e. all of the above

_____ 14. Coordination in Russian planning
   a. has relied solely on materials balancing.
   b. has relied solely on input-output analysis.
   c. has relied on materials balancing and input-output analysis.
   d. is not considered to be important.
   e. is considered to be important but has never been given attention.

_____ 15. Input-output analysis
   a. was developed by Gosplan.
   b. is based on matrix algebra.
   c. is usually preferred to materials balancing because input-output is simpler.
   d. relies on an input-output table whose entries show the profits associated with particular goods.
   e. all of the above

_____ 16. Input-output analysis recognizes
   a. interdependence between the industries in an economy.
   b. that the output of Industry X may be used as an input in Industry X.
   c. that the output of Industry X may be used as an input in Industry Y.
   d. all of the above
   e. both a and c above

_____ 17. Which of the following is *not* a problem of Soviet planning?
   a. overly flexible plans
   b. relatively low productivity of labor
   c. sacrifice of quality for quantity
   d. potential volume of computer output
   e. postponements in carrying out plans in some sectors

_____ 18. Under Russia's leading links system of planning,
   a. certain leading links are completed in full.
   b. all but the leading links must be completed in full.
   c. the leading links are generally in consumption goods.
   d. certain leading links may be postponed in part until the next period.
   e. all of the above except a

_____ 19. Libermanism calls for
   a. more rigid plans.
   b. the elimination of all profit in future planning.
   c. an unplanned, private, and usually capitalistic dual economy alongside the planned socialist one.
   d. all of the above
   e. none of the above

_____ 20. In the People's Republic of China,
   a. communes strive for self-sufficiency.
   b. only a select few are allowed to live and work in communes.
   c. both a and b above
   d. cooperative farms are intentionally interdependent and rely on free trade to meet their individual needs.
   e. a central planning authority draws up production and consumption plans for each of the many cooperative farms.

_____ 21. With regard to planning in the United States, it can be accurately said that
   a. the United States has been immune from planning.
   b. large-scale capitalist planning has been very successful.
   c. the original Humphrey-Hawkins bill reflected a desire for some planning.
   d. the United States experienced imperative planning under the New Deal of the 1930s.
   e. the National Recovery Administration was a highly successful planning agency.

_____ 22. Planning in Japan
   a. is imperative planning.
   b. has resulted in relatively minor gains in GNP.
   c. protects larger companies against excessive competition.
   d. relies heavily on strict penalties to ensure adherence to administrative guidelines.
   e. is conducted in its entirety through the Ministry of International Trade and Industry.

_____ 23. Japanese business firms
   a. must contend with low labor productivity.
   b. have little incentive to invest in human capital.
   c. find most workers and their unions opposed to technological progress.
   d. cannot fire or lay off any workers unless the company goes out of business.
   e. none of the above

_____ 24. Sweden provides an example of
   a. a welfare state.
   b. planned capitalism.
   c. laboristic features.
   d. all of the above
   e. planned socialism.

_____ 25. Swedish planning
   a. is consensual.
   b. has eliminated wage differentials.
   c. is carried out by the Meidner Agency.
   d. has greatly reduced the problem of inflation.
   e. never relies on "first-best" assumptions because of the problems they create.

_____ 26. Under the Meidner Plan, Sweden would
   a. become a syndicalist system.
   b. follow the Lange-Lerner model.
   c. eliminate the corporate income tax.
   d. distribute most government revenue to individual workers.
   e. all of the above

_____ 27. In Yugoslavia,
   a. central authorities set all prices.
   b. monopoly power has been eliminated.
   c. inflation has been virtually eliminated.
   d. land and physical capital are privately owned.
   e. workers' collectives make their own pricing and output decisions.

_____ 28. Recent changes in China include
   a. elimination of communes.
   b. elimination of birth control.
   c. implementation of the "iron rice bowl" rule.
   d. the creation of special economic zones for invited foreign companies.
   e. all of the above

_____ 29. The Lange-Lerner model
  a. recommends market anarchism.
  b. is a version of market socialism.
  c. relies heavily on Stalinist imperative planning.
  d. does not recognize any advantages in the market system.
  e. calls for monopoly pricing in a basically market economy.

_____ 30. In the Lange-Lerner system, managers of firms would be
  a. entitled to any profits.
  b. allowed to set output prices.
  c. expected to keep marginal cost approximately equal to output price.
  d. expected to hire inputs such that marginal product and marginal revenue remain approximately equal.
  e. all of the above

_____ 31. The Austrian school
  a. opposes planning.
  b. expects planning to end in a servile state.
  c. is represented by Hayek, Mises, and Schumpeter.
  d. criticizes planning as highly arbitrary and dictatorial.
  e. all of the above

Discussion Questions

1. The authors maintain that "Public planning, when carried out through laws and regulations, may be either more or less restrictive of freedom than private planning, when carried out through market forces." Explain.

2. In what ways might the private sector be affected by public-sector planning?

3. Do you think further advances in computer technology will make a difference in planned economies? In what way?

4. Identify and discuss the problems in Soviet planning and explain the concept of a leading links system.

5. As long as they operate within the plan, Japan protects larger companies against failure, forced cutbacks, and "excessive competition." Do you think this is inconsistent with capitalism? Why or why not?

6. Would you support the Japanese example of lifetime employment? Identify the benefits for each group: the employee, the employer, and the economy.

7. Explain why a firm in the Japanese economy may be more inclined than an American firm to invest in human capital.

8. Explain why the authors describe Japan as "a fragile economy, dependent on the goodwill of its suppliers and its customers."

9. Explain what is meant by "laboristic" features and codetermination in corporate decision making in the Swedish economy. Do you think the U.S. economy would function better if such features were incorporated? What problems do you foresee?

10. What is the problem with using "first-best" assumptions in planning?

11. What problems arise when firms maximize net income per worker (as in the Yugoslav plan) rather than profit? Which system do you think maximizes social welfare?

12. For each of the six goals indicated in Chapter 1 of the text, identify the economic system that you think best serves the goal. Explain your choices.

Answers

Problems and Applications

1. a. 0.1 unit   b. 0.0 unit   c. 0.1 unit
   d. 0.3 unit   e. 0 percent   f. 0 percent

2.

		Using Industry			
		Tics	Tacs	Toes	Other Demand
Supplying Industry	Tics	0.1	0.2	0.3	0.4
	Tacs	0.2	0.3	0.4	0.1
	Toes	0.3	0.2	0.2	0.3
	Labor	0.4	0.3	0.1	0.2

True-False

1. F. An economy is planned only when an individual or organization in a public position plans for another individual or organization that has little say about the plan and whose economic decision is restricted by the planning decision.

2. F. Public planning carried out through laws and regulations may be more or less restrictive of freedom than private planning carried out through market forces.

3. T.

4. T.

5. F. Imperative planning is concerned with more than the aggregate economy; it includes the "fine structure" of the economy as a whole and its regions.

6. F. Indicative planning typically attempts to ensure that a plan is followed by convincing participants that following the plan will help them economically.
7. F. Planning often relies on forecasting but is not equivalent to it.
8. T.
9. T.
10. F. Gosplan is the Russian agency that has responsibility for imperative planning.
11. F. Plans in Russia are usually, but not necessarily, for five-year periods.
12. T.
13. F. The Chinese system of planning is more decentralized than the Russian system.
14. T.
15. F. In Sweden, most indicative plans are short-term, usually one-year, plans.
16. T.
17. T.
18. T.
19. F. Labor-managed firms of the Yugoslav type are likely to use relatively small amounts of labor.
20. F. China no longer requires that everyone belong to collective farms or communes, although a great majority have chosen to remain members.
21. T.

Multiple Choice

1. c	2. e	3. c	4. b	5. d
6. b	7. e	8. a	9. e	10. d
11. c	12. a	13. e	14. c	15. b
16. d	17. a	18. a	19. e	20. a
21. c	22. c	23. e	24. d	25. a
26. a	27. e	28. d	29. b	30. c
31. e				

39 *Radical Economics*

Summary

Criticisms of capitalism generally center around its alleged failure to provide an equitable distribution of income and wealth, a secure standard of living, and a system compatible with full mental health. Capitalism is blamed for poverty and insecurity, technical change that results in unemployment, pollution, and depletion of resources. Capitalism is guilty of exploitation, say the critics, and therefore it leads to alienation.

Those who advocate the overthrow of capitalism often base their arguments on Marxism. Marxists believe that surplus production has historically been appropriated by the social class that owns certain strategic factors of production (the capitalists). Furthermore, they contend that history is a record of conflict between those who exploit and their victims, or between one exploiting class and its successor. According to Marxists, capitalism will be overthrown by a revolution that involves the proletariat or exploited working class. It will be replaced by a socialist regime with no classes to be exploited. In a few years, after socialism is established in the major countries, a New Socialist Man and Woman will emerge. These men and women will not only work harder and more skillfully than anyone in the past but will take less from society in terms of wealth and consumer goods. In a few generations, abundance will overcome scarcity and the repressive political state will dissolve.

Marxian economics is about capitalism and its downfall, not about socialism. According to Marx, value is determined by labor rather than by demand and utility. There is a surplus value when the value of what workers produce is greater than the value of what they are paid. This surplus value is the Marxian concept of profit and it is appropriated by the capitalists. Marx used the phrase *organic compo-sition of capital* to express the ratio between constant capital (the labor embodied in raw materials and depreciation) and variable capital (the direct labor needed to produce goods consumed by workers). Over time, as the organic composition of capital rises, the rate of profit declines and/or the rate of exploitation (the ratio of surplus value to variable capital) rises. One or the other of these de-velopments will eventually lead to the downfall of capitalism by way of a liquidity crisis or a realization crisis.

Radicals support extreme change. They call for considerable de-parture from what is usual and/or they would use extreme methods to accomplish the desired changes. Politically, they may be on the left or the right. If we think of Marxism as the Old Left, then the New Left grew out of a desire for unity in the fight against fascism. Though not exclusively a radical movement, the leadership of the New Left has generally been radical. The entire radical element is collectivist. It can be divided into anarchists, socialists, and syndical-ists. The New Right, on the other hand, supports market capitalism. Those who see a decline of competition and fear the growth of big business are called trust busters. Otherwise, the New Right supports the laissez-faire concept. In terms of platform, the most radical branch of the New Right is the Libertarians. They would rely en-tirely on the free capitalist market. Another branch is composed of objectivists. Objectivism has been described as "rational selfishness" and is related to Social Darwinism.

Major Objectives   After you have finished this chapter, you will be able to do the following:

1. Identify the three criteria for judging economic systems that seem to have caused the greatest discontent under capitalism and explain why there is so much discontent with regard to these criteria.
2. Identify and discuss the threats to the security of the standard of living at the individual level.
3. Explain the meaning and importance of alienation.
4. Identify and explain the eight Marxian propositions that are summarized in your text.
5. Explain the meaning of exploitation.
6. Explain the meaning and importance of the Marxist statement that "history is the record of class struggles."
7. Define and explain the importance of the proletariat.
8. Describe and explain the role of the New Socialist Man and Woman.

9. Identify the Marxian components of national income evaluated in hours of labor.
10. Explain the concepts of constant capital, variable capital, surplus value, and the rate of surplus value (or exploitation rate).
11. Use Marxian economics to calculate national income and the rate of surplus value given the components of national income.
12. Explain the significance of the rate of surplus value and identify the value of this rate in the United States, according to Marxists.
13. Explain the Marxian concept of profit.
14. Define and explain the concept of the organic composition of capital.
15. Determine the formula for, and calculate, the rate of profit in terms of the components of national income and in terms of the organic composition of capital.
16. Identify and distinguish between Marxian statics and Marxian dynamics.
17. Explain what happens to the organic composition of capital over time, why it happens, and the implications of it for the profit rate and the exploitation rate, according to Marxian dynamics.
18. Explain why a falling rate of profit and/or a rising exploitation rate will ultimately be disastrous for capitalism, according to Marxian dynamics.
19. Explain what is meant in Marxian literature by a liquidity crisis.
20. Explain what is meant by a realization crisis and describe how the argument is used by Marxists.
21. Identify the basic concern of Marx's *Capital.*
22. Identify the basis for Marx's labor theory of value.
23. Identify the role of government fiscal and monetary policy in Marxian analysis.
24. Define and discuss what it means to be a radical.
25. Distinguish between the radical Left and the New Right.
26. Distinguish between the New Left and the Old Left.
27. Distinguish between liberals and social democrats.
28. Briefly describe the historical development of the New Left.
29. Identify, describe, and distinguish the five groups that make up the radical New Left.
30. Distinguish between socialism and communism.
31. Define syndicate.
32. Explain the meaning of economic *blitzkrieg.*
33. Identify and distinguish the major branches of the New Right.
34. Identify and distinguish between the branches of the market economy New Right.
35. Define and/or describe the trust busters, the Libertarian movement, objectivism, and Social Darwinism.

Review Terms	capitalism	cartels

capitalism
market economy
criteria for evaluating
  economic systems
income
wealth
standard of living
poverty
protectionism
multinational corporation
input or factor of production
  or resource
inflation
pollution
socialism
surplus
scarcity
macroeconomics
microeconomics
market capitalism
national income
interest
rent
profit
labor force
innovation
equilibrium
national output

cartels
demand
utility
fiscal policy
monetary policy
pure vs. mixed economy
planned economy
marginal
anarchism
nonrational ways of knowing
socialism
syndicalism
collectivism
barter
communism
imperative planning
monopoly
strike
gold standard
balanced budget
competition
trust
oligopoly
product cycle
invention
innovation
progressive tax

Important Terms and Concepts

radical economics
affluence
maldistribution
"cultural rape"
insecurity
"rust bowls" of obsolete
  factories
alienation
Marxism
abundance
exploitation
"history is the record of
  class struggles"
proletariat
New Socialist Man and Woman

statics
dynamics
national income evaluated in
  hours of labor (W)
constant capital (C)
variable capital (V)
direct labor
"productive" labor
"unproductive" labor
surplus value (S)
rate of surplus value or exploitation rate (S')
Marxian concept of profit (P')
organic composition of capital
stagnation

liquidity crisis	parasitism
realization crisis	Anarchism II
Marx's labor theory of value	terrorism
radical	Socialism I
conservative	neo-Stalinist
reactionary	Socialism II or Marxist
direct action	humanism
New Left	Syndicalists
anarchists	syndicate
reformists	government's "power of the
First International (International	purse"
Workingmen's Association)	economic *blitzkrieg*
liberal	New Right
social democrat	laissez-faire
fascism	trust busters
"McCarthyism"	flat tax
Students for a Democratic	libertarian
Society (SDS)	objectivism
"Port Huron Statement"	"survival of the fittest"
Anarchism I	Social Darwinism
communes	

Completion

Critics of capitalism are discontented with capitalism's response to the six criteria for evaluating economic systems, but the greatest amount and intensity of discontent is with three of the six. Critics

maldistribution

allege that capitalism is characterized by _____ of

insecurity

income and wealth within and between countries, _____

incompatibility

of the achieved standard of living, and _____ of the system with full mental health.

In terms of the distribution of income and wealth, people at the

poverty

bottom live in _____ . For the majority of people, up-

essentially blocked

ward mobility within the world economy is _____ (essentially blocked/relatively easy) except for that which is in ac-

those already at the top

cordance with rules and terms set by _____ . When, for example, protectionism prevents a low-wage country from

competitive advantage

using its cheap labor as a _____ , the country has little opportunity for upward mobility. Aid may be

giver

made available but often on terms set by the _____ . Other

restrictive

routes to upward mobility may include a more _____

more   (lenient/restrictive) population policy and/or _____ (less/more) reliance than desired on unskilled hand labor in agriculture and mining. Within a country such as the United States, upward mobility for minorities may require conformity with the standards

cultural rape   set by the dominant culture. This is referred to as _____ .

prejudice   To some extent, inequality is based on _____ . Capitalism is blamed for fostering prejudice to keep workers and farmers

disunited, reducing   _____ (united/disunited), thereby _____ (enhancing/reducing) their economic and political power.

both individual and mass   Under capitalism, _____ (individual/mass/both individual and mass) living standards are under pressure

short-term shocks   from _____ associated with declines in the

long-term shocks   business cycle. They are also threatened by _____

chronic, change   associated with _____ inflation, technological _____ ,

exhaustion   pollution, resource _____ , warfare, and so on. In all of these cases, capitalism is blamed for not preventing the catastrophes

safety nets   phes or for failing to provide adequate _____ to those who bear the costs.

alienation   The critics of capitalism blame it for causing _____ , the psychological ailment of capitalism. This occurs when one feels

hostile, indifferent   _____ or _____ to someone or something that

attractive   most people in the society consider _____ . It may appear in many different forms, from boredom to mass murder.

exploitative   Some critics of capitalism believe that an _____ society is itself responsible for the behavior of those it alienates.

Problems and Applications

1. Assume that in 1975 in Laborland the number of labor hours embodied in raw materials and the depreciation of machinery was 400, that there were 400 hours of direct labor, and that 400 hours of direct labor bought 300 hours of labor embodied in consumer goods.
   a. In 1975, how much variable capital did Laborland have? How much surplus labor was there in 1975? What was the 1975 national income of Laborland expressed in labor hours?
   b. Determine the rate of surplus value, the profit rate, and the organic composition of capital for Laborland in 1975.

2. Laborland in 1985 was characterized by 5,000 labor hours of constant capital, a national income of 12,000 labor hours, and an organic composition of capital equal to 1.
   a. In 1985, how much variable capital did Laborland have? How much surplus labor was there in 1985?
   b. Determine the rate of exploitation and the profit rate for Laborland in 1985.

True-False

Indicate whether each of the following statements is basically true or false. If the statement is false, rewrite it so that it is true.

_____ 1. "Cultural rape" occurs when members of a culture are forced or bribed to conform to the standards of another, quite different culture.

_____ 2. Alienation is synonymous with exploitation.

_____ 3. Those who believe that capitalism is guilty of exploitation may also hold it responsible for the actions of those whom it alienates.

_____ 4. Marx used the term *proletariat* to refer to the military.

_____ 5. Marxian economics deals with socialism and actually says very little about capitalism.

_____ 6. According to Marxian economics, $W = S/(C + V)$.

_____ 7. Constant capital and variable capital are terms used by Marxists to refer to fixed capital and variable capital, respectively.

_____ 8. Marxists believe that in the United States today the rate of surplus value is less than one and is tending to fall over time.

_____ 9. The exploitation rate is the rate of surplus value to variable capital.

_____ 10. The liquidity crisis in Marxism refers to the eventual stagnation that occurs when the profit rate increases so much that capitalists no longer feel a need to invest.

_____ 11. Marx predicted that capitalism would eventually fall, because of a liquidity crisis brought on by a falling rate of profit or because of a realization crisis associated with high profits, rising unemployment, and overproduction.

_____ 12. Radical economics may be of the political left or the political right.

_____ 13. Socialism I refers to a group of New Left radicals who are neo-Stalinists in support of imperative planning.

_____ 14. A syndicate is a guild or trade union.

_____ 15. The Ku Klux Klan and the Survivalists are examples of the radical New Right.

_____ 16. The American New Right deals exclusively with economic issues.

_____ 17. Objectivism has been characterized as "rational selfishness."

Multiple Choice   Choose the *one best* answer in each of the following cases:

_____ 1. Security of the standard of living may be threatened by
   a. inflation.
   b. pollution.
   c. automation.
   d. resource exhaustion.
   e. all of the above

_____ 2. Critics of capitalism are likely to claim that capitalism
   a. leads to alienation.
   b. eliminates exploitation.
   c. allocates resources efficiently.
   d. promotes an equitable distribution of income.
   e. is compatible with physical and mental health.

_____ 3. Marxian propositions include a belief that
   a. scarcity can never be abolished.
   b. capitalism exploits the proletariat.
   c. our welfare system should do more to "regulate the poor."
   d. the New Socialist Man and Woman are likely to be alienated.
   e. under socialism the military will have to control the workers.

_____ 4. According to Marxian economics, national income (evaluated in hours of labor) is equal to
   a. fixed labor plus variable labor.
   b. constant labor plus variable labor.
   c. constant capital plus variable capital plus surplus value.
   d. fixed capital plus variable capital plus valuable surplus.
   e. none of the above

_____ 5. To a Marxist, constant capital refers to
   a. the quantity of physical capital that is fixed in the short run.
   b. machinery, tools, and equipment that do not depreciate over time.
   c. labor hours embodied in raw materials and the depreciation of capital.
   d. physical and human capital inputs that do not change in the short run.
   e. none of the above

_____   6. In Marxian economics, surplus value is
            a. equivalent to normal profit.
            b. the payment to productive labor.
            c. a measure of the depreciation of constant capital.
            d. used to pay interest, rent, dividends, profits, and unproduc-
                tive labor.
            e. the excess supply of goods produced under a system of
                market capitalism.

_____   7. Assume that you work 48 hours per week but that your wages
            will buy only the equivalent of 36 hours of others' labor. Ac-
            cording to Marxian economics, your 48 hours of labor represent
            a. 48 hours of variable capital.
            b. 36 hours of constant capital and 12 hours of surplus value.
            c. 36 hours of variable capital and 12 hours of surplus value.
            d. 12 hours of constant capital and 36 hours of variable capital.
            e. 36 hours of constant capital and 12 hours of variable capital.

_____   8. The rate of surplus value is
            a. SV.
            b. S/V.
            c. V/S.
            d. S/W.
            e. $S/(C + V)$.

_____   9. In Marxian economics, the exploitation rate is equal to
            a. the rate of profit.
            b. the rate of surplus value.
            c. the organic composition of capital.
            d. constant capital divided by total capital.
            e. constant capital divided by variable capital.

_____ 10. The Marxian concept of profit
            a. includes all surplus value.
            b. includes constant but not variable capital.
            c. is equivalent to the accountant's concept of profit.
            d. includes all surplus value except payments to unproductive
                labor.
            e. all of the above except a

_____ 11. When Marxists refer to the organic composition of capital, they
            mean the ratio between
            a. depreciation and constant capital.
            b. depreciation and total labor input.
            c. constant capital and surplus value.
            d. surplus value and total labor input.
            e. constant capital and variable capital.

_____ 12. As the organic composition of capital increases, the profit rate
  a. and the exploitation rate remain constant.
  b. and the exploitation rate will fall.
  c. and the exploitation rate will rise.
  d. will fall and/or the exploitation rate will rise.
  e. will rise and/or the exploitation rate will fall.

_____ 13. According to Marx, the liquidity crisis
  a. is equivalent to the realization crisis.
  b. occurs when the organic composition of capital falls.
  c. refers to the formation of cartels to maintain high prices.
  d. would be intensified if wages were raised in relation to prices.
  e. can be solved only by the use of government fiscal and
     monetary policy.

_____ 14. Radical economists are likely to believe that
  a. society must be gradually reformed but not restructured.
  b. marginal analysis is the only way to answer the basic
     economic questions adequately.
  c. representative government results in sufficient reform so that
     revolution is not necessary.
  d. all of the above
  e. none of the above

_____ 15. The New Left
  a. is an exclusively radical movement.
  b. was unified in support of McCarthyism in the United States.
  c. has a following that includes liberals, reformists, and
     collectivists.
  d. has always supported and relied on violence to accomplish
     its objectives.
  e. both a and b above

_____ 16. Which of the following would *not* be included among the New
         Left radicals?
  a. socialists
  b. communists
  c. libertarians
  d. syndicalists
  e. collectivists

_____ 17. Anarchist groups
  a. have been accused of parasitism.
  b. fear the state as much as they fear capitalists.
  c. favor placing control of capital goods in the hands of
     voluntary associations.
  d. all of the above
  e. believe the state should own and control the means of
     production.

____ 18. The economic doctrines of Socialism II include the belief that
    a. there should be equality of income and wealth.
    b. the price system adequately allocates resources.
    c. alienation and exploitation are not important issues.
    d. "material incentives" are needed to stimulate economic activity.
    e. "moral incentives" are not likely to stimulate economic activity.

____ 19. With regard to productive facilities, syndicalists favor ownership by
    a. no one.
    b. the party.
    c. anarchists.
    d. groups of workers.
    e. the government.

____ 20. The market economy New Right does *not* support
    a. laissez-faire.
    b. increased taxation.
    c. return to the gold standard.
    d. an annually balanced budget.
    e. decreased regulation of business.

____ 21. The New Right trust busters
    a. fear control by big business.
    b. are typically radical syndicalists.
    c. would support the decline of competition.
    d. favor government ownership of the means of production.
    e. none of the above

____ 22. A libertarian is likely to support
    a. imperative planning.
    b. collectivist anarchy.
    c. private ownership of capital.
    d. increased reliance on syndicates.
    e. Students for a Democratic Society.

____ 23. Which of the following is *not* associated with objectivism?
    a. Ayn Rand
    b. the New Right
    c. Social Darwinism
    d. survival of the fittest
    e. market restrictions to assist those who are least fit

Discussion Questions

1. Do you think "cultural rape" has taken place in the United States? Explain. What is the significance of the answer to this question?
2. What do the authors mean by the "rust bowls" of obsolete factories? How do these "rust bowls" affect the security of the standard of living?
3. Do you think an exploitative society is responsible for the actions of those whom it alienates? What constitutes an exploitative society? Explain.
4. Do you think economics as a profession will ever become obsolete? Explain.
5. What do Marxists mean when they refer to history as "the record of class struggles"?
6. Explain how scarcity will be eliminated, according to Marxism.
7. Explain why increases in the organic composition of capital result in decreases in the rate of profit and/or increases in the rate of exploitation.
8. Identify and describe the five groups that make up the radical New Left.
9. Identify and describe the major branches of the New Right.
10. What is the role of government in a society run by objectivists? Explain.

Answers

Problems and Applications

1. a. 300 labor hours; 100 labor hours; 800 labor hours
   b. 1/3; 1/7; 4/3
2. a. 5,000 labor hours; 2,000 labor hours
   b. 2/5; 1/5

True-False

1. T.
2. F. Alienation is a feeling of hostility or indifference to someone or something that people in one's society generally finds attractive; exploitation occurs when some members of society are excluded from the bulk of that society's economic surplus.
3. T.
4. F. Marx used the term *proletariat* to refer to the workers.
5. F. Marxian economics is not about socialism of any kind; instead, it deals with capitalism.

6. F. According to Marxian economics, $W = C + V + S$.
7. F. Constant capital refers to labor hours embodied in raw materials and in the depreciation of physical capital; variable capital refers to hours of direct labor needed to produce the goods that workers consume.
8. F. Marxists believe that in the United States today the rate of surplus value is greater than one and, in times of prosperity at least, tending to rise over time.
9. T.
10. F. The liquidity crisis in Marxism refers to the eventual stagnation that occurs when the profit rate decreases so much that capitalists no longer find it worthwhile to invest more than enough to cover depreciation.
11. T.
12. T.
13. T.
14. T.
15. T.
16. F. The American New Right is composed of three intertwined branches, one of which is economic, one ethical, and one political.
17. T.

Multiple Choice

1. e	2. a	3. b	4. c	5. c
6. d	7. c	8. b	9. b	10. a
11. e	12. d	13. d	14. e	15. c
16. c	17. d	18. a	19. d	20. b
21. a	22. c	23. e		